SOCIOCULTURAL RESEARCH ON MATHEMATICS EDUCATION
An International Perspective

SOCIOCULTURAL RESEARCH ON MATHEMATICS EDUCATION

An International Perspective

Edited by

Bill Atweh
Queensland University of Technology, Australia

Helen Forgasz
Deakin University, Australia

Ben Nebres
Ateneo de Manila University, Philippines

2001

LAWRENCE ERLBAUM ASSOCIATES, PUBLISHERS
Mahwah, New Jersey   London

Lawrence Erlbaum Associates, Inc., Publishers
10 Industrial Avenue
Mahwah, NJ 07430

Cover design by Kathryn Houghtaling Lacey

Library of Congress Cataloging-in-Publication Data

Sociocultural research on mathematics education : An international
perspective / edited by Bill Atweh, Helen Forgasz, Ben Nebres.
p. cm.
Includes bibliographical references and index.
ISBN 0-8058-3725-6 (cloth : alk. paper)
ISBN 0-8058-3726-4 (pbk. : alk. paper)
1. Mathematics—Study and teaching—Social aspects. 2. Minorities—
Education. I. Atweh, Bill. II. Forgasz, Helen. III. Nebres, Ben.
QA11S665   2001
510'.71—dc21   00-059264
                                                        CIP

Books published by Lawrence Erlbaum Associates are printed on
acid-free paper, and their bindings are chosen for strength and durability.

Printed in the United States of America
10 9 8 7 6 5 4 3 2 1

Contents

Preface   ix

Contributors   xix

**I   PSYCHOLOGICAL, SOCIAL, AND POLITICAL
     PERSPECTIVES**

1 A Cultural/Discursive Psychology for Mathematics Teaching
       and Learning   3
       Stephen Lerman

2 Mathematics Education in Late Modernity: Beyond Myths
       and Fragmentation   19
       Paul Dowling

3 Breaking Political Neutrality: The Critical Engagement of Mathematics
       Education With Democracy   37
       Ole Skovsmose and Paola Valero

4 Mathematical Literacy and Common Sense in Mathematics Education   57
       Uwe Gellert, Eva Jablonka, and Christine Keitel

II GLOBAL, REGIONAL, AND LOCAL CONTEXTS

5 Internationalization and Globalization of Mathematics Education:
       Toward an Agenda for Research/Action   77
       Bill Atweh and Phil Clarkson

6 Globalization and the Politics of Mathematics Education   95
       Jan Thomas

7 Situated Sociocultural Mathematics Education: Vignettes From
       Southeast Asian Practices   113
       *Khoon Yoong Wong, Zaitun Binti Hj Mohd Taha,
       and Palanisamy Veloo*

8 Mathematical Ideas and Indigenous Languages   135
       Bill Barton and Roslyn Frank

9 The Sociopolitical Context of Mathematics Education in Guatemala
       Through the Words and Practices of Two Teachers   151
       Richard S. Kitchen

III   TEACHERS, STUDENTS, AND CLASSROOMS

10   Continuous In-Service Professional Development of Teachers and
         School Change: Lessons From Mexico   167
         Bill Atweh and Marcos Daniel Arias Ochoa

11   Resourcing Practice and Equity: A Dual Challenge
         for Mathematics Education   185
         Jill Adler

12   Mathematics, Social Class, and Linguistic Capital: An Analysis
         of Mathematics Classroom Interactions   201
         Robyn Zevenbergen

13   Longitudinal Evaluation of Mathematics Participation in American
         Middle and High Schools   217
         Xin Ma

14   Sociocultural Considerations and Latino Mathematics Achievement:
         A Critical Review   233
         Luis Ortiz-Franco and William V. Flores

15   The Social Constructs of the Mathematical Experiences
         of African-American Students   255
         Vivian R. Moody

IV   NUMERACY AND EVERYDAY MATHEMATICS

16   Numeracy: Negotiating the World Through Mathematics   279
         Betty Johnston and Keiko Yasukawa

17   Modeling With Purpose: Mathematics as a Critical Tool   295
         Swapna Mukhopadhyay and Brian Greer

18   Contribution of Ethnomathematics to Mainstream Mathematics
         Classroom Practice   313
         Gloria Stillman and Jo Balatti

19   Teaching and Learning School Mathematics by Building on Students'
         Out-of-School Mathematics Practice   329
         Joanna O. Masingila and Rapti de Silva

**V   RECENT DIRECTIONS IN GENDER AND MATHEMATICS
     EDUCATION**

20   "A+ for Girls, B for Boys": Changing Perspectives on Gender Equity
         and Mathematics   347
         Helen Forgasz and Gilah Leder

21   Single-Gender Schooling in the Public Sector in California: Promise
         and Practice   367
         Joanne Rossi Becker

22   Fables: The Tortoise? The Hare? The Mathematically Underachieving Male?   379
         Leone Burton

23 Girls, Mathematics, and Technology   393
        Nicola Yelland

24 Creating a Connected, Equitable Mathematics Classroom: Facilitating
        Gender Equity   411
        Joanne E. Goodell and Lesley H. Parker

Author Index   433
Subject Index   443

Preface

It is widely accepted today that as general research in mathematics education evolved during the 1960s and 1970s, psychological paradigms, methodologies, and research questions dominated the field. A few researchers then began to investigate factors related to the performance of under-represented and underachieving segments of the school population. These research foci opened the gate for the consideration of social factors as critical in understanding how they affected the outcomes of mathematics teaching. Arguably, the majority of these early studies that were undertaken from a social perspective used mainly quantitative research methodologies that were prevalent at the time. In the 1980s and 1990s, mathematics education research witnessed a diversification of research thrusts and theoretical models coming from sociology, anthropology, and linguistics. Perhaps less so in Anglo-Saxon countries than in others, qualitative researchers working from sociocultural perspectives had few battles to fight for acceptance and respectability within the general educational research community.

A special day on Mathematics Education and Society at the Sixth International Congress in Mathematical Education [ICME] 6 in Budapest in 1988 resulted in a set of conference proceedings, edited by Keitel, Damerow, and Bishop (1989) and published by UNESCO, constituting the first such international collection of research into the social factors in mathematics education. The contributions of 90 presenters from 40 countries on that day alerted the editors of that collection to the "increasing awareness" of sociocultural aspects of mathematics education. Some of the themes addressed in this book overlap with the themes discussed in 1989. The authors of at least six chapters in this book were among the authors contributing to the proceedings of that day at ICME 6. Many of the other authors writing in this collection have joined this field of research since that time. Many of the themes and topics discussed here are also new. For us, this is a healthy sign of the coming of age of this field of mathematics education research.

Perhaps it needs to be stressed here that drawing the dichotomy of psychological versus social perspectives is a convenient oversimplification of a myriad of theoretical and methodological prespectives. For example, the International Group of Psychology of Mathematics Education [PME] included social psychology under its umbrella of research strands of interest to members. Social psychology deals with some of the issues normally discussed under sociocultural perspectives. Some researchers in the field were unsatisfied with working in the shadow of an overarching psychological paradigm. As a result, in 1998, the first international conference of Mathematics Education and Society was held in the University of Nottingham in the United Kingdom. Close to 100 participants, representing many countries around the world, attended. Papers presented covered a wide range of topics and perspectives including critical theory, post-modernism, ethnomathematics, feminism, sociology, theories about democracy, and so on. Once again, a considerable number of authors in the present book contributed to the proceedings of that conference. Undoubtedly, the gathering confirmed the field's broad identity within the mathematics education international community.

Within this context, this edited collection represents the variety of mathematics education research questions raised from sociocultural perspectives and reflects the current status of knowledge in this important area of mathematics education. We aimed for a collection to be wide in its scope but do not propose that it is encyclopedic or fully comprehensive. One noted feature of research in the field of sociocultural aspects of mathematics education is the wide scope of theoretical perspectives and the range of research questions that are encompassed. Recent developments in more well-established areas of research that are still prominent in the field—gender, social class, and ethnicity—are examined in some chapters. In other chapters, authors explored topics that received considerable attention during the past decade, such as ethnomathematics and mathematics education and culture. Some authors discussed the more recently emerging issues such as postmodernism and globalization.

The Context for This Book

The publication of this book coincides with what has been widely accepted as the first year of the third millennium of the "Western" calendar. There are two observations that can be made about this occasion that might be relevant to the themes addressed in this book. First, the celebration of the commencement of the new millennium in the year 2000 is erroneous from a mathematical point of view. Perhaps this is a reminder that factors other than logic and reason can dominate some societal decisions. Second, what started out basically as a Euro-Christian calendar, has, in practice, grown to be a universal calendar. Mathematics and society and mathematics education in a global context are themes that are addressed by several authors in this book. More importantly, the publication of this book at this milestone in history is a celebration of about 30 years of research in the field and provides a futuristic overview of some issues that still need to be addressed.

The year 2000 is also the year declared by the International Mathematics Union, and supported by UNESCO, as World Mathematical Year 2000. The declaration for World Mathematical Year 2000 set three goals:

- The determination of great mathematical challenges of the 21st century.
- The promulgation of mathematics, both pure and applied, as one of the main keys for development.
- The recognition of the systematic presence of mathematics in the information society (the image of mathematics).

Perhaps it is relevant here to quote the entire UNESCO resolution in support of this declaration.

The General Conference

Considering the central importance of mathematics and its applications in today's world with regard to science, technology, communications, economics and numerous other fields,

Aware that mathematics has deep roots in many cultures and that the most outstanding thinkers over several thousand years contributed significantly to their development, and numerous other fields,

Aware that the language and the values of mathematics are universal, thus encouraging and making it ideally suited for international cooperation,

Stressing the key role of mathematics education, in particular at primary and secondary school level, both for the understanding of basic mathematical concepts and for the development of rational thinking,

Welcomes the initiative of the International Mathematical Union (IMU) to declare the year 2000 the World Mathematical Year and carry out, within this framework, activities to promote Mathematics at all levels world-wide.

(International Mathematics Union, 1999)

The resolution contains many assertions about mathematics and society, particularly in a global context, that are relevant to the themes addressed in the following chapters. As the role of mathematics and mathematics education is considered around the world, this book represents a critical gaze, by an international group of mathematics educators, on aspects of the field as social and cultural phenomena.

It is noteworthy that the "new" millennium and World Mathematical Year 2000 also coincide with the ninth International Congress in Mathematics Education [ICME 9] held in Japan in July. Previous such gatherings have proven to be one of the main venues for mathematics educators from around the globe to share understandings and learnings. Such sharing has been influential in determining the shape of many mathematics education reforms and programs in many countries. For example, contributions at past ICME conferences have been significant in popularizing theoretical constructs such as constructivism and ethnomathematics. The launching of this book during ICME 9 is an appropriate acknowledgment of the collaboration of the international community in shaping the ideas expressed in these chapters and of the importance of this international venue for sharing and developing our collective learning.

The Story of the Book

The compilation of this book is, perhaps, an educative example of international collaboration worth retelling in part.

The Mathematics Education Research Group of Australasia (MERGA) has been instrumental in sponsoring a series of publications at national and international levels. Previous publications include two publications reviewing research in mathematics education in Australasia (Atweh & Watson, 1992; Atweh, Owens, & Sullivan, 1996), an edited collection of research on children learning of number (Mulligann & Mitchelmore, 1996), and an edited collection on issues in research and supervision in mathematics and science education (Malone, Atweh, & Northfield, 1998). This is the second of MERGA's sponsored international publications.

Having initially conceptualized the book as having three foci: gender, social aspects, and mathematics and culture, a call for chapter proposals went out electronically on several different international education lists. Recipients were asked to circulate the invitation widely in their geographic regions, especially to those who may not have had access to e-mail. Many of the authors whose work is included here learned about the book in this way. Perhaps not surprisingly, certain regions of the world were still underrepresented among the proposals received. As Editors, we used personal contacts to achieve wider representation. Authors of all chapter proposals that showed promise and were relevant to the aims and focus of the book were invited to submit a first draft of their chapters. The final group of authors represents mathematics educators from every continent of the globe, although there is greater representation of authors from English speaking countries. We are proud of the high proportion of authors from non-English-speaking backgrounds represented here. However, we realize that a better representation of voices from developing countries is both possible and desirable in future collaborative projects such as this one.

Authors of chapter proposals were consulted about the reviewing process. The result was that chapters were subjected to a semi-blind peer review. Three other authors read each chapter; some externally invited mathematics educators were also invited to participate. Most authors commented on the thoroughness of the reviews and how useful the suggestions provided were in improving their chapters. The whole process was marked by a highly collegial spirit appreciated by all involved.

Throughout the process electronic telecommunication was used extensively. The editors were able to coordinate the whole process without meeting face to face. The call for chapter proposals, the submission of chapters, and the review process were conducted electronically with only minor problems due to software incompatibility. Contingency plans were made to ensure that any limitation in access to computers would not prevent participation. This problem did not eventuate.

An electronic list of all authors was also established. It served two purposes. First, it allowed for an efficient communication channel among editors, authors, and publishers on procedural and business matters. Second, and more importantly, the list allowed the authors to discuss issues of common concern and to vote on aspects of the book's evolution. E-mail allowed the process to be more democratic and accountable. The process of the compilation of this book demonstrated that we live in a world where the tyranny of geographical distance need not be a stumbling block in achieving a collaborative international community effort, as it might have been few decades ago.

The Scope and Structure of the Book

With some difficulty, and in consultation with all authors, the final contributions in this book were grouped under five parts: Psychological, Social, and Political Perspectives; Global, Regional, and Local Contexts; Teachers, Students, and Classrooms; Numeracy and Everyday Mathematics; and Recent Directions in Gender and Mathematics Education. An overview and a short synopsis of the contributions found in each part follow. Further details about each chapter are included in the part introductions.

Part I: Psychological, Social, and Political Perspectives

As indicated previously, research into the sociocultural aspects of mathematics education employs a huge variety of theoretical perspectives. Authors in this part attempted to theorize mathematics education and mathematics education research from sociocultural perspective informed by the so-called late modernity and postmodernity. Others have attempted to look critically at the role of mathematics education in society in new times using recent developments of theories and thinking about democracy and numeracy.

Stephen Lerman points out that the field of psychology has undergone considerable changes in the last decade or so, in line with developments in cultural studies, feminist research, postmodernism, and so on. In his chapter he outlines a research program for mathematics education that is firmly based in cultural, discursive psychology. The chapter by **Paul Dowling** introduces new perspective and terminology to understand some of the practices in mathematics education today. He argues that mathematics education as it is widely practiced is a mythologizing activity in that it regards other activities as themselves instances of or representable by mathematics. The author demonstrate that many current state initiatives in the United Kingdom (and elsewhere) are tending toward a narrowly instrumental and fragmented interpretation of schooling. In the chapter by **Ole Skovsmose** and **Paola Valero**, the authors observe that, although in many of the current justifications to include mathematics education as a relevant part of the national curricula the connection between mathematics education and democracy is highlighted, little systematic reflection has been given to this area in the international community of researchers in mathematics educators. Finally, the chapter by **Uwe Gellert, Eva Jablonka**, and **Christine Keitel** argues that the different conceptions of mathematical literacy are related to how the relationship among mathematics, reality, and society is conceived. They use the term "mathematical literacy" as a metaphor referring to well-educated and well-informed individuals.

Part II: Global, Regional, and Local Contexts

Most mathematics educators are directly experiencing and being affected by a world that is getting closer and smaller. Intercultural exchanges have increased in quantity and have become much easier and widespread. Further, economic considerations and cultural factors are interacting in new and powerful ways. Questions need to be asked about the shape of mathematics education within a global society in which our students will live; about how much of the mathematics education should be local to meet their needs to understand and control their immediate life and how much of it should prepare them to survive globally; and finally, what is the meaning of ethnomathematics within this new global context? Questions need to be asked about the politicohistorical development of mathematics education curriculum and practices in different countries in order to enable rational reform in their mathematics education. These questions are addressed in the following chapters.

Bill Atweh and **Phil Clarkson's** chapter discusses theoretical issues in globalization and internationalization of mathematics education. The authors present a tentative theoretical model for understanding the variety of international activities in mathematics education community. In particular they discuss issues related to cross-country collaboration in mathematics education reform and curriculum development. The chapter by **Jan Thomas** seeks to explore the complex issues that surround and influence policy decisions, especially at the government level, in mathematics education. In particular it explores possible trends toward diminishing the influence of expert opinion as governments seek rapid solutions in a global framework. The chapter by **Khoon Yoong, Zaitun Binti Hj Mohd Taha**, and **Palanisamy Veloo** proposes a "situated sociocultural" model to show how five locally situated sociocultural factors, namely, historical background, cultural mores, major political events, national education structure and aims, and language policy, together with an external global factor, can influence the nature and practice of mathematics education in a country. The model is illustrated with vignettes taken from practices of three ASEAN countries. The chapter by **Bill Barton** and **Roslyn Frank** argues that recent interest in how anthropology and linguistics relates to mathematics led to recognition that mathematical thinking is a function of language in ways not previously recognized. Ethnomathematics, cognitive linguistics, and anthropology are all pointing to a way of understanding mathematical ideas based on human experience and cultural activities. Finally, the goal of the study conducted by **Richard Kitchen** is to understand some of the complicated and dynamic issues that affect the pedagogy of secondary-level mathematics teachers in Guatemala, Central America.

Part III: Teachers, Students, and Classrooms

The classroom as a social context with different backgrounds, beliefs, agendas, and expectations of its players has been a focus of much research in mathematics education. The first two chapters in this part raise issues related to the teachers. In their chapter **Bill Atweh** and **Marcos Daniel Arias Ochoa** offer a critical assessment of common methods of in-service professional development of teachers available in many countries around the world. This critique relies on literature in the West as well some developing countries in Latin America. They describe a project called TEBES in Mexico for the professional development of teachers in compulsory education. **Jill Adler** argues that behind common and prevalent laments on the "lack of resources" across many schools is the history of inequity in provision in South Africa. She demonstrates how resourceful teachers can function is a context of schools that still do not have basic resources such as water and electricity, let alone sufficient classrooms and learning materials.

The other four chapters in this part deal with issues related to the students' background and success or failure in mathematics. **Robyn Zevenbergen**, using the theoretical tools offered by Bourdieu, explores the ways in which mathematics classrooms, and their inherent culture, position students as learners of mathematics. Drawing on qualitative data from classrooms, the chapter explores the construction of social difference, that is, social class. From a quantitative perspective, the chapter by **Xin Ma** reviews most recent longitudinal studies that examine the probability of high school students dropping out of mathematics courses. These studies attempt to determine whether there are critical transition points in student mathematics participation and if so, whether certain student or school factors have stronger effects at those points. The purpose of the chapter by **Luis Ortiz-Franco** and **William Flores** is to discuss in a historical perspective the question of income and mathematics achievement among Latino K–12 students in the United States. This chapter identifies some of the sociocultural variables that may help explain the differences in the relationship between income and mathematics achievement among this group of the population and the general U.S. society. Similarly, the chapter by **Vivian Moody** discusses complex social and cultural issues and their role in addressing the nature of equity in the mathematics education of African-American students. Based on the experiences of two African-American female college students, the chapter concludes with questioning and evaluating oppressive schooling practices that perpetuate inequities existing in the mathematics education of African-American students.

Part IV: Numeracy and Everyday Mathematics

In many countries around the world there is a great attention, often unmatched by actual resources, given to numeracy. For some mathematics education and numeracy are used interchangeably. There are a variety of ways in which the relationships between school mathematics and everyday mathematics are constructed. With the decline in student numbers studying mathematics and persistence in negative attitudes and experiences, questions as to the relevance of mathematics to students' lives are as important as ever. The different chapters in this part deal with the different meanings of term numeracy, mathematical applications, and ethnomathematics.

Betty Johnston and **Keiko Yasukawa** offer a critical reflection of the authors' own journey in developing a personal theory of numeracy. By drawing on the theories that they have considered and the continuing interrogation of their own teaching practice, they tell the tale of various milestones they have reached in their theory development and connections they have made with theories and developments in other areas, such as mathematics education, literacy education, and critical pedagogy. **Swapna Mukhopadhyay** and **Brian Greer** point out that the most common justification given for school mathematics is that mathematics has its roots in and is usefully applicable to real-world problems, yet research and documentary evidence show that most children regard mathematics as useless, uninteresting, and irrelevant to their lives. In this chapter, they examine the reasons for this state of affairs through analysis of word problems. **Gloria Stillman** and **Jo Balatti** examine some of the current suggested approaches for incorporating ethnomathematics within classroom mathematics in the context of an upper secondary school classroom. These are illustrated by examples in the literature and from student research projects. Finally, the chapter by **Joanna Masingila** and **Rapti de Silva** argues that students need mathematically meaningful contexts through which to learn mathematics. They discuss a 4-year project titled Connecting In-school and Out-of-school Mathematics Practice in which they (a) investigated how middle school students use mathematical ideas in a variety of out-of-school situations and then (b) used ideas from these situations to support the students' classroom learning and examine how they made sense of ideas mathematically.

Part V: Recent Directions in Gender and Mathematics Education

The chapters included in this part reflect contemporary concerns in the field. There is recognition of the significant contributions of earlier research and the work here builds on that solid foundation. A range of theoretical perspectives and research methods were used to explore new research questions and to re-examine old ones. **Helen Forgasz** and **Gilah Leder** explore the basis of concerns about boys' educational disadvantage. Media reports are examined and evidence of changing belief patterns from four research studies are presented that contextualize the issues raised. **Joanne Rossi Becker** reports on an evaluation of a single-gender academy in California. Situated on the same site, male and female students were separately taught by the same teachers. The findings revealed that potential equity opportunities presented by this unique setting were not fully realized. Findings from an interview-based study with an equal number of male and female practising research mathematicians are presented by **Leone Burton**. The relationships between the sex of the mathematicians and their epistemologies, the disciplinary branches of mathematics in which they work, and their career experiences are examined. Links are made to the learning of mathematics in schools. **Nicola Yelland** discusses findings of a project in which pairs of children (girls, boys, and boy/girl) interacted with computer-based LOGO learning tasks. The differences evident in the tactics deployed and the interpersonal exchanges among the various dyadic groupings are presented. Drawing on previous research and various feminist perspectives, **Joanne Goodell** and **Lesley Parker** develop a detailed operational definition of the ideal Connected Equitable Mathematics Classroom [CEMC] in which students, classroom practices, and the curriculum are the focal elements. The definition is complemented by research evidence highlighting factors within the model that can affect on the implementation of a CEMC.

External Reviewers

As noted previously, the majority of reviewers of book chapters were the authors themselves. For some chapters, we needed the assistance of other colleague. We wish to publicly acknowledge and express our most sincere thanks for the professional contributions of the following external reviewers:

Barbara Allen, Open University, United Kingdom
Glenda Anthony, Massey University, New Zealand
Andy Begg, Waikato University, New Zealand
Jo Boaler, Stanford University, United States of America
Patti Brosnan, Ohio State University, United States of America
Andrew Brown, Institute of Education, University of London, United Kingdom
Tan Kowk Chun, Open University, Hong Kong
Gail FitzSimons, Swinburne University, Australia
Sandra Frid, University of New England, Australia
Merrilyn Goos, University of Queensland, Australia
Patricio Herbst, Michigan State University, United States of America
Mary Klein, James Cook University, Australia
Colleen McMurchy-Pilkington, Auckland College of Education, New Zealand
Jim Neyland, Victoria University of Wellington, New Zealand
Thomas Popkewitz, University of Wisconsin, United States of America
Arthur Powell, Rutgers University, United States of America
Fredrick Silverman, University of Northern Colorado, United States of America
Beth Southwell, University of Western Sydney, Australia
John Truran, University of Adelaide, Australia
John Watts, Central Queensland University, Australia
Vicki Zack, McGill University, Canada

REFERENCES

Atweh, B., Owens, K., & Sullivan, P. (1996). *Research in mathematics education in Australasia 1992–1995*. Sydney, Australia: Mathematics Education Research Group of Australasia.

Atweh, B., & Watson, J. (1992). *Research in mathematics education in Australasia 1988–1991*. Brisbane, Australia: Mathematics Education Research Group of Australasia.

International Mathematics Union. (1999). World Mathematics Year 2000. http://wmy2000.math.jussieu.fr.

Malone, J., Atweh, B., & Northfield, J. (1989). *Research and supervision in mathematics and science education*. New York: Lawrence Erlbaum Associates.

Mulligann, J., & Mitchelmore, M. (Eds.). (1996). *Children's number learning*. Adelaide, Australia: Mathematics Education Research Group of Australasia & Australian Association of Mathematics Teachers.

Contributors

Editors

Bill Atweh is a senior lecturer in mathematics education at the Queensland University of Technology, Brisbane, Australia. His main research interests are in the areas of social context of mathematics education, including gender and class, the use of action research, and, more generally, social justice issues in education. He has served for 6 years as Vice President (Publications) for the Mathematics Education Research Group of Australasia. He is the co-editor of two volumes of research reviews in Australasia as well as the *Action Research in Practice: Partnerships for Social Justice in Education* (1998, Routledge) and *Research and Supervison in Mathematics and Science Education* (1998, Erlbaum). <b.atweh@qut.edu.au>

Helen Forgasz is a lecturer in mathematics education at Deakin University, Australia. Her main research interests include mathematics education, gender issues, the affective domain, classroom learning environments, and mature-age students. She has published widely in a range of scholarly journals and books, written a monograph, *Society and Gender Equity in Mathematics Education* (1994, Deakin University Press), edited a special issue of the *Mathematics Education Research Journal*, and co-authored major reviews on gender and mathematics. She is the current Vice President (Conferences) of the Mathematics Education Research Group of Australasia. <forgasz@deakin.edu.au>

Ben Nebres did his early studies in classics and philosophy in the Philippines and earned his PhD in mathematics, specializing in mathematical logic, at Stanford University. He was one of the founders of the Mathematical Society of the Philippines and the Southeast Asian Mathematical Society. Together with colleagues in these societies he has worked to improve graduate mathematics education and research as well as teacher training in a network of Philippine high schools. He is currently President of the Ateneo de Manila University, one of the leading universities in the Philippines, which also has responsibility for a grade school and a high school. He also holds leadership positions in projects to strengthen science and engineering in a network of universities and schools and to improve elementary education in the 26 poorest provinces of the country. <bnebres@pusit.admu.edu.ph>

Authors

Jill Adler is a professor of the Mathematics Education Development, University of the Witwatersrand, South Africa. Her main research areas include mathematics teacher development, mathematics teaching, and learning in multilingual classrooms. Her main teaching areas are sociocultural theory and mathematical learning, mathematics curricula—selection and transmission and assessment practices. She published journal articles in *Journal for Research in Mathematics Education, For the Learning of Mathematics, Educational Studies in Mathematics, Educational Action Research and Teaching* and *Teacher Education* as well as chapters in books such as *Situated Cognition and the Learning of Mathematics* and *the International Handbook of Mathematics Education.* <022jill@mentor.edcm.wits.ac.za>

Jo Balatti is a researcher in the School of Education, James Cook University, Cairns, Australia. Her main areas of research are adult learning and vocational education and training. She retains a strong interest in the mathematical discourses of postmodernity. <josephine.balatti@jcu.edu.au>

Bill Barton is Head of the Mathematics Education Unit at the University of Auckland, New Zealand. His research areas are ethnomathematics, particularly language issues, and he helped develop the Maori mathematics vocabulary. He is the author of a chapter on mathematics and anthropology in the *International Handbook of Mathematics Education* published by Kluwer (1996). He produced television programs and magazine columns on mathematics. Bill is currently on the Executive of the New Zealand Mathematics Society and is organizer of the Working Group on Language and Mathematics for ICME-9 in Japan. <b.barton@auckland.ac.nz>

Joanne Rossi Becker is a professor in the Department of Mathematics and Computer Science at San Jose State University, California, where her specialty is mathematics education. Joanne taught at SJSU since 1984 and regularly teaches content and methods courses for prospective teachers and supervizes secondary student teachers. She regularly contributes to *Psychology of Mathematics Education* and *Psychology of Mathematics Education-North America* and is co-editor of a forthcoming volume from National Council for Teachers of Mathematics: *Changing the Faces of Mathematics: Perspectives on Gender.* <becker@mathcs.sjsu.edu>

Leone Burton is professor of education (mathematics and science) at the University of Birmingham, United Kingdom. She is author of *Thinking Things Through* (1984, Basil Blackwell), *Children Learning Mathematics—Patterns and Relationships* (1994, Simon & Schuster), and, with John Mason and Kaye Stacey, *Thinking Mathematically* (1982, Addison Wesley) and editor of *Girls into Maths Can Go* (Cassell, 1986), *Gender and Mathematics—An International Perspective* (Cassell, 1990), *Who Counts? Assessing Mathematics in Europe* (Trentham, 1994), and, most recently, *Learning Mathematics—From Hierarchies to Networks* (1999, Falmer). Her most recent research has been in the area of mathematical epistemology. <burtonl@edusrv3.bham.ac.uk>

Philip Clarkson is an associate professor at the Australian Catholic University. Much of his research has centred on the connections between language and mathematics learning, spatial ability, and the art of teaching mathematics. At present he is directing a 5-year longitudinal project evaluating primary and secondary pre-service education programs throughout Papua New Guinea. He is also a member of a team evaluating the way computer technology is used in teaching across the curriculum at both secondary and primary level in schools funded especially to set up comprehensive networks and the co-director of a project investigating whether implicit values teachers use when teaching mathematics can be made explicit to the teachers as well as thinking through some implications of globalization for education. He has spent most of his working life in Australia with visits to a number of countries and nearly 5 years in Papua New Guinea. <p.clarkson@mercy.acu.edu.au>

Paul Dowling is a sociologist with a particular interest in mathematics education at the Institute of Education of the University of London. His principal line of research involves the development of "constructive description" through and for the sociological analysis of educational texts, sites, and action. Empirically, he has recently been focusing on information and communications technology and alternative pedagogic sites (such as castles and zoos). His recent publications include (jointly with Andrew Brown) *The Sociology of Mathematics Education: Mathematical Myths/Pedagogic Texts* (1998, Falmer) and *Doing Research/Reading Research: a Mode of Interrogation for Education* (1998, Falmer). He is currently a member of the Culture Communications and Societies group. <p.dowling@ioe.ac.uk>

William V. Flores is a professor of political science and the Dean of the College of Social and Behavioral Sciences at California State University at Northridge. He was co-director of the Center for Southern California Studies. He previously served as Associate Dean at California State University, Fresno, and held positions at Stanford, Santa Clara University, California State University Hayard. In 1993 he was a Rockefeller Fellow in the Humanities at Hunter College of City University of New York. He is co-editor of *Latino Cultural Citizenship: Claiming, Identity, Space and Rights* and published articles in such areas as community organization, empowerment, voting rights, and violence prevention. <bill.flores@csun.edu>

Roslyn Frank is a professor in the Department of Spanish and Portuguese at the University of Iowa. She is also a senior research consultant for the Institute of Basque Studies, Guildhall University, London. She has written in both Euskara and English, particularly on the ethnomathematical systems of the Basque people. Her main research areas are at the interface of science (especially astronomy) and linguistics, specifically with reference to Basque culture. She is exploring the noncommensurability of metaphors in Basque and European image schemata. She is Editor of the *Journal of the Institute of Basque Studies* and Coordinator of the Iowa Hispanic Institute, Valladolid, Spain. <roz-frank@uiowa.edu>

Uwe Gellert currently is an assistant professor at the Department of Education and Psychology at Free University of Berlin. He worked on ethnomathematics and the history of mathematics, focusing on social aspects of mathematics and mathematics education. His doctoral thesis is a sociocultural analysis of the beliefs of elementary teachers as effecting their professional conceptions. <ugellert@mail.zedat.fu-berlin.de>

Joanne Goodell is assistant professor of Mathematics Education at Cleveland State University, Ohio. She came to Cleveland State in 1999 and works with Cleveland-area school districts on professional development and research projects focused on equity and reform issues for teaching and learning in mathematics. Previously Head of the Mathematics Department and teacher of mathematics in Western Australia, she also has served as a Research Associate for Ohio's systemic initiative and as Women in Engineering coordinator at Curtin University, Western Australia. Her publications include a chapter in *Research on Effective Models for Teacher Education: Teacher Education Yearbook VIII*. <j.goodell@csuohio.edu>

Brian Greer, at the time of writing his chapter, was a half-time reader in the School of Psychology, Queen's University, Belfast, and is the Crossword Editor of the (London) *Times*. He studied mathematics as an undergraduate before switching to psychology and developing an interest in mathematics education. His current interests include the interpretation of word problems—a book on this topic with Lieven Verschaffel and Erik de Corte is in press. He is an associate editor of *Mathematical Thinking and Learning*. Ambitions for the future include a book on problem solving based entirely on the Isis problem and a project with Swapna Mukhopadhyay to interview people about their conceptions of mathematics. <b.greer@queens-belfast.ac.uk>

Eva Jablonka is an assistant professor at the Faculty of Education and Psychology at the Free University of Berlin. She is currently researching pupils' theories about mathematics teaching and learning. She received her doctoral degree in mathematics education (with a thesis on applications of school and college mathematics) at the University of Technology, Berlin, where she worked as a lecturer in mathematics teacher education for primary, secondary, and vocational schools from 1990 to 1995. <jablonka@mail.zedat.fu-berlin.de>

Betty Johnston is a senior lecturer in the Faculty of Education at the University of Technology, Sydney, Australia. Over the past few years she has been teaching in the areas of adult numeracy and school mathematics education and has been involved in research into numeracy practices and mathematics, gender, and rationality. <betty.johnston@uts.edu.au>

Christine Keitel is professor for mathematics education at the Free University of Berlin. She is a member of the BACOMET-group (Basic Components of Mathematics Education for Teachers) and President of the Commisssion Internationale pour L'Etude et l'Amélioration de l'Enseignement des Mathématiques (CIEAEM). She has been the director of the NATO Advanced Research Workshop on "Mathematics Education and Technology"; member of the Steering Committee of the OECD-project "Future Perspectives of Science, Mathematics and Technology Education"; and Convenor of the International Organization of Women and Mathematics Education (IOWME). She received a Humboldt Scholarship Award for research in South Africa and an Honorary Doctorate of Science from the University of Southampton. Her research studies focus on the relationship between mathematics and its social practice, on attitudes and belief systems of teachers and students, and on the history and current state of mathematics education in various countries, in particular in European countries, the United States, the former USSR, China, and Indonesia. <keitel@pixie.udw.ac.za>

Richard Kitchen is an assistant professor in the College of Education at the University of New Mexico in Albuquerque, United States. His interests in mathematics education include mathematical problem solving in political, social, and cultural contexts. He is fascinated by Latin American history and culture. He hopes that some day he would be able to dance the salsa. <kitchen@unm.edu>

Gilah Leder is director of the recently established Institute for Advanced Study at La Trobe University, Bundoora, Australia. She is a professor in the Graduate School of Education at the same institution. Her teaching and research interests embrace the interaction among teaching, learning and assessment of mathematics, effect, gender issues, and exceptionality. She published widely in each of these areas. Gilah serves on various editorial boards and educational and scientific committees and is a past President of the Mathematics Research Group of Australasia and the current President of PME. <g.leder@latrobe.edu.au>

Stephen Lerman is professor of mathematics education and head of Educational Research at South Bank University in London. He was president of PME and was chair of the British Society for Research into Learning Mathematics. His research interests include sociocultural theories, equity issues, learning theories, and classroom research. He was co-editor with Marilyn Nickson *of The Social Context of Mathematics Education: Theory and Practice* (1992, South Bank Press) and editor of *Cultural Perspectives on the Mathematics Classroom* (1994, Kluwer). <lermans@sbu.ac.uk>

Xin Ma is an assistant professor of educational psychology at University of Alberta. His main areas of research include mathematics education, school effects, policy analysis, human development, program evaluation, and advanced statistical methods. He is the author of the book *A National Assessment of Mathematics Participation in the United States: A Survival Analysis Model for Describing Students' Academic Careers* (1997, Edwin Mellen). He has been the program chair for the Canadian Educational Researchers' Association and the American Educational Research Association (SIG Longitudinal Studies). <xma@pop.srv.ualberta.ca>

Joanna Masingila is an associate professor of Mathematics and Mathematics Education at Syracuse University, New York. Her primary interests lie in the areas of ethnomathematics, connecting in-school and out-of-school mathematics practice, and mathematics teacher education. In 1998, she was a Fulbright Scholar in the Department of Educational Communication and Technology at Kenyatta University in Nairobi, Kenya. She has spoken widely on everyday mathematics practice, realistic problem solving, assessing mathematical understanding, and related topics and has authored or co-authored numerous chapters and journal articles on these topics. <jomasing@sued.syr.edu>

Vivian Moody has a special interest in issues of equity in mathematics education and is developing a research agenda around the mathematical experiences of African-American students. Through this research, her goal is to contribute to the understanding of African-American students' mathematical achievement by (a) providing insight into successful African-American mathematics students' perceptions of their mathematical experiences, (b) helping mathematics educators create a dialogue about influential factors that contribute to African-American students' succeeding in mathematics, and (c) helping mathematics educators embellish teaching practices that embody equity and counter oppression. <vmoody@bamaed.ua.edu>

Swapna Mukhopadhyay, at the time of writing the chapter, was an assistant professor at Antioch University Seattle. She believes that the focus of all cognitive inquiry is centered in sociocultural processes. Her primary area of interest is in the development of mathematical cognition, viewing mathematics as a mode of thinking that is a cultural expression. This philosophy reflects her intellectual background—teaching in an alternative school in Calcutta, carrying out an ethnographic study on children's intuitive understanding of geometry in rural India for her doctoral research, and later studying, in particular, children's intuitions about negative numbers. She sees mathematics as a human activity embedded in people's lives and as a tool for addressing issues of social justice. <swapna_mukhopadhyay@mist.seattleantioch.edu>

Marcos Daniel Arias Ochoa is a lecturer at the Universidad Pedagógica Nacional, Mexico, and a doctoral candidate at Universidad Nacional Autónoma de México. He is a founding member and co-ordinator of the national collaborative project between schools and universities "Transformación de la Educación Básica desde la Escuela. His main interest in research is in the area of in-service continuous professional development of teachers in compulsory education. His publications include articles and videos on the conduct of school-based research. <ibtebes@correo.ajusco.upn.mx>

Luis Ortiz-Franco is associate professor of mathematics at Chapman University in Orange, California. He has written articles in mathematics education on assessment, equity issues, culture, ethnomathematics, problem solving, and social issues. He has also published works in collaboration with other educators in the social sciences such as demographics and a multidisciplinary annotated bibliography on discrimination and prejudice. He is the co-editor of *Changing Faces of Mathematics: Perspectives on Latinos* (1999, NCTM). He is currently working on a book based on biographical and career profiles of Latino mathematicians in the United States. <ortiz@chapman.edu>

Lesley Parker is Senior Deputy Vice Chancellor at Curtin University of Technology, Australia. She has been at Curtin since 1991, initially as Assistant Director of the National Key Centre for Teaching and Research in Science and Mathematics Education and most recently as professor of higher education. Her research focuses on structural curriculum change, professional development, and policy and practice in gender equity, particularly in science and mathematics. Currently, she is a member of the Council of Questacon (Australia's National Science and Technology Centre) and chair of the Curriculum Council of Western Australia and of the Board of Directors, which administers the Education Network Australia. Recently, she was awarded the Order of Australia for services to education, especially in relation to the achievement of gender equity in science and mathematics. <iparkerl@info.curtin.edu.au>

Rapti de Silva is presently finishing up her doctoral thesis at Syracuse University, New York. The fieldwork for her dissertation *Learning and Teaching Mathematics in Sri Lanka: An Ethnographic Study of Primary Teachers in a Continuing Education Program* was partially funded by a grant from the International Federation of University Women. Her research builds on her interests in teacher education, distance learning, and the use of limited resources. <rmdesilv@syr.edu>

Ole Skovsmose is a professor at Aalborg University, Denmark. He is a member of BACOMET, an international research group in mathematics education and a member of the editorial board of *Nordic Studies in Mathematics Education* and *For the Learning of Mathematics*. He is the coordinator of the initiative Mathematics Education and Democracy (Denmark) and Director of The Centre for Research of Learning Mathematics, a cooperative project among Roskilde University, Aalborg University, and The Royal Danish School of Educational Studies. His publications include *Towards a Philosophy of Critical Mathematics Education* (1994, Kluwer) and several journal articles and chapters in books. <osk@dcn.auc.dk>

Gloria Stillman is a lecturer in mathematics and computer education in the School of Education, James Cook University, Townsville, Australia. She teaches methods in secondary pre-service teacher education as well as mathematics methods and content in primary and early childhood pre-service teacher education. Her main areas of research are metacognition and the assessment of applications in senior secondary level mathematics. She is one of the current editors of the Mathematics Education Research Group of Australasia journal *Mathematics Teacher Education and Development*. <gloria.stillman@jcu.edu.au>

Jan Thomas is a senior lecturer in mathematics education at Victoria University of Technology, Melbourne, Australia. Her main areas of research are in the politics of mathematics education and the cultural and linguistic effects on learning mathematics in a second language. She was president of the Australian Mathematical Sciences Council and is currently Vice President of the Federation of Australian Scientific and Technological Societies, the national science lobbying group. She is part-time Executive Officer for the Australian Mathematical Society. <jan.thomas@vu.edu.au>

Paola Valero is currently writing her doctoral dissertation in mathematics education at The Royal Danish School of Educational Studies, Denmark. She is from Colombia. Being a political scientist and linguist, her research work is interdisciplinary, focusing on the political dimension of mathematics education and organizational approaches to reform in mathematics teaching in secondary school. Her research work has been on alternative approaches to mathematics teachers' in-service education, the school organization as a unit of analysis in mathematics education, and theoretical considerations about mathematics education, democracy, and society. <paola@dlh1.dlh.dk>

Palanisamy Veloo is a doctorate candidate at the Department of Education, University of Canterbury, Christchurch, New Zealand. He has extensive teaching and curriculum experiences in Malaysia and Brunei Darussalam. His research areas are children's learning difficulties in mathematics and mathematics instruction. <pkveloo@xtra.co.nz>

Khoon Yoong Wong is a senior lecturer in the Department of Science and Mathematics Education, Sultan Hassanal Bolkiah Institute of Education, Universiti Brunei Darussalam. He has worked as a mathematics teacher and educator in Malaysia, Singapore, Australia, and Brunei Darussalam and participated in the revision of the national mathematics curriculum in these three Southeast Asian countries from 1980 to 1990. His research interests cover learning strategies, multimodal teaching, and computer-based mathematics instruction. He has published several mathematics textbooks and research papers on mathematics education. <wongky@ubd.edu.bn>

Keiko Yasukawa is an educational developer and lecturer in the Faculties of Engineering and Education at University of Technology, Sydney, Australia. She is involved in teaching mathematics and numeracy to engineering students and adult education students. <keiko@eng.uts.edu.au>

Nicola Yelland is a senior lecture at the Queensland University of Technology, Brisbane, Australia. She is the editor of *Gender in Early Childhood* (1998, Routledge) and the co-author of *Early Mathematical Explorations* (1999, Pearson). She is currently working with Andee Rubin on a text about research by women with technology to be published by Peter Lang. She is the founding editor of a new research journal titled *Contemporary Issues in Early Childhood* (http://www.triangle.co.uk/ciec) and an Associate Editor *of Information Technology in Childhood education.* <n.yelland@qut.edu.au>

(Hajah) Zaitun Taha is a senior lecturer and head of the Department of Science and Mathematics Education, Sultan Hassanal Bolkiah Institute of Education, Universiti Brunei Darussalam. She has held several senior administrative posts in Brunei schools and the university. She was also past president of the Mathematical Society of Brunei Darussalam. Her main research interests are beliefs and attitudes toward learning and teaching mathematics. <zaitunht@ubd.edu.bn>

Robyn Zevenbergen is a senior lecturer in mathematics education at the Griffith University, Gold Coast, Australia. Her research is primarily focused in the area of social justice and equity in mathematics from a sociocultural perspective. She is particularly interested in the areas of social class and culture. She has been the secretary of MERGA since 1994 and is currently involved in Mathematics Education and Society at the organizational level as well as coordinator of the Mathematics Education and Equity Topic Study Group for *International Congress in Mathematics Education* 9. Her publications have been in the areas of methodology (particularly in relation to ethnography and qualitative methods), equity and social justice, and situated learning in workplace contexts. <r.zevenbergen@eda.gu.edu.au>

I

PSYCHOLOGICAL, SOCIAL, AND POLITICAL PERSPECTIVES

As discussed in the Preface, research into the sociocultural aspects of mathematics education employs a huge variety of theoretical perspectives. Authors in this collection use theories previously unknown in mainstream mathematic education such as Bourdieu, Habermas, Bernstein, Vygotsky, Apple, Gilligan, and many others. Several authors here and elsewhere have attempted to theorize mathematics education and mathematics education research from sociocultural perspective informed by the so-called late modernity and postmodernity. Others have attempted to look critically about the role of mathematics education in society in new times. These are some of the themes addressed by authors in this section.

Stephen Lerman points out that the field of psychology has undergone considerable changes in the last decade or so, in line with developments in cultural studies, feminist research, postmodernism, and so on. In mathematics education research one can see the evidence of such developments, albeit as yet in a limited way. In publications over the last few years the author has argued the case for a cultural psychology and for a move away from constructivism. In this chapter he outlines a research program for mathematics education that is firmly based in cultural, discursive psychology. The author discusses theoretical issues, refers to some of the important literature, and presents some research in aspects of the program.

Paul Dowling argues that mathematics education as it is widely practiced is a mythologizing activity in that it regards other activities as themselves instances of or representable by mathematics. The myth of participation renders invisible its distinction between mathematics and nonmathematical practices. Effectively, this constitutes mathematics as a necessary component of, for example, everyday domestic practices. The myth of reference, on the other hand, privileges specialized mathematical knowledge. The nature and distribution of these and other mathematical myths reflect social and cultural divisions that relate more closely to an earlier phase of modernity than to the current global configuration. Many current state initiatives in the United Kingdom (and elsewhere) are tending toward a narrowly instrumental and

1

fragmented interpretation of schooling. The challenge for mathematics education is to move beyond both its own traditions and the bureaucratic structures that are being imposed upon it.

In the chapter by Ole Skovsmose and Paola Valero, the authors observe that, although in many of the current justifications to include mathematics education as a relevant part of the national curricula the connection between mathematics education and democracy is highlighted, little systematic reflection has been given to this area in the international community of researchers in mathematics educators. The chapter brings together different social disciplines from which the basic theoretical tenets of mathematics education for democracy can be stated. As a result, it provides an international, nonexclusively Western view of the different and more relevant theoretically and practically oriented projects that have this connection as their central theme.

Finally, the chapter by Uwe Gellert, Eva Jablonka, and Christine Keitel argues that the different conceptions of mathematical literacy are related to how the relationship among mathematics, reality, and society is conceived. They use the term "mathematical literacy" as a metaphor referring to well-educated and well-informed individuals. In surveying some of the major conceptions designed to deal with the new demands for mathematics education, they look for essential components of a conception of mathematical literacy from a general education perspective. Then they consider commonsense conceptions of mathematics. The conclusion connects the two topics by introducing the concept of reflectiveness as a necessary competence for mathematical literacy.

1

A Cultural/Discursive Psychology for Mathematics Teaching and Learning

Stephen Lerman
South Bank University

IN THE BEGINNING WAS THE WORD

Mathematics education as a theoretical field has its roots in mathematics classrooms, from nursery age to those in university. It draws on a range of theoretical resources in developing its own body of theory to account for what goes on in those settings in relation to teaching and learning. The concern of workers in the field is to find a language with which to describe the process of the acquisition of mathematics and through which to draw inferences for what teachers might do to bring about that acquisition by as many students as possible. That language has to account for a great deal, much of it tacit in teaching, such as a notion of development as being toward something, the goals and values of education in general and of mathematics education in particular, the relationship between teaching and learning, and the particularities of the nature of mathematics. That language has to be informed by empirical studies and has therefore to incorporate a process for its own continuing elaboration. At the same time it needs to take account of relations of power, of voice and of silence of any theory, of any account of teaching and learning, of any set of goals for education, and for any notion, usually implicit, of development.

Traditional psychology, for all that its field of study is human behavior, has offered little that can help to improve society. "[M]odern psychology has been incapable of making serious contributions to Third World [sic] development ... it is important to point out that mainstream psychology has also failed to make significant contributions to national development and the lives of the poorest sectors in Western societies" (Harré, 1995, p. 54).

> In the process of individualizing its view of students, it (mathematics education) has lost
> any serious sense of the social structures and the race, gender and class relations that
> form these individuals. Furthermore, it is then unable to situate areas such as mathe-
> matics education in a wider, social context that includes larger programs for democratic
> education and a more democratic society. (Apple, 1995, p. 331)

I believe they are right to say that psychology cannot provide such a language, at
least psychology as understood to be the study of learning as the individual's cognitive
reorganization, albeit caused by social, physical, or textual factors (von Glasersfeld,
1994, p. 6) through equilibration. I want to suggest, however, that psychology can be
seen as a moment in sociocultural studies, as a particular focusing of a lens, as a gaze
that is as much aware of what is not being looked at as of what is. This is an adaptation
of Rogoff's planes of analysis, into a dynamic metaphor in which one might envisage
a researcher choosing what to focus on in research through zooming in and out in a
classroom, as with a video or still camera, and selecting a place to stop. Rather than
seeing social factors as causative of learning, they can be seen as constitutive (Smith,
1993). As such, I argue that psychology from this perspective can respond to Apple's
critique. A discursive, cultural psychology locates its interpretation of the individual at
the intersection of overlapping language games in which the person has developed and
thus is necessarily rooted in the study of cultures and histories. Draw back in the zoom,
and the researcher looks at education in a particular society, at whole schools, or whole
classrooms; zoom back in and one focuses on some children or some interactions. The
point is that research must find a way to take account of the other elements that come
into focus throughout the zoom, wherever one chooses to stop.

In this chapter I address the issue of what is the terrain of such a psychology, that
is, what counts as an appropriate language, for mathematics education. I describe
the move in psychology over the last decade or so (Cole, 1996; Harré, 1995) to one
that is fully cultural and focused on the way in which consciousness is constituted
through discourse. That move can be seen as part of the reaction in sociology and
philosophy to the 19th-century challenge by Durkheim and Marx to the image of the
individual as the source of sense making and as the autonomous builder of her or his
own subjectivity. It is also a response to Wittgenstein's later work on language and
to the anti-essentialism of poststructuralism. I attempt to engage with the elements
of a theory for mathematics teaching and learning that I mentioned previously: what
might be understood as teleology/development, the connections between teaching and
learning, the process of acquisition, the particularities of mathematics, the inevitable
coercion and denial of voice of any theory, and the role of empirical study. I am
choosing to undertake an impossibly large agenda for one chapter as I wish to present
as comprehensive a map as possible. It is more of a recipe for a life's work, and, in that
it is a recounting of developments in my own learning and research and a setting out of
a program upon which I am engaged with colleagues and with some of my students, it
is self-consciously broad and overambitious. However, I endeavour to sketch the main
outlines of this program and give some illustrations of relevant research, my own or
that of others, where appropriate. These illustrations are inevitably briefly described,
due to limitations on space.

Vygotsky, whose work has become better known in the mathematics education community in recent years (e.g., Bartolini Bussi, 1991; Boero et al., 1995; Lerman, 1992) is a major figure in the development of cultural and discursive psychology (Cole, 1996; Harré & Gillett, 1994). Feminist research, in particular, has invited us, researchers and writers, to be forthcoming about our biographies and to own up to where we are located in our work. I happily confess that I became fascinated and excited by Vygotsky's ideas when I first came across them some 8 years ago and immediately found a strong resonance with the way in which I perceive myself to be culturally and socially situated (Lerman, 1999).

The theoretical resources to which I referred previously come from outside mathematics education, and I endeavour to signal from where I draw inspiration. I also attempt to do justice to those ideas despite the limitations of time and space, an essential task for researchers. Although recontextualization is inevitable (Bernstein, 1996), it is incumbent on researchers to take theories seriously. Elsewhere (Lerman, 1996), I argued that the consequences of superficial readings can result in incompatible theories being conflated.

DEVELOPMENT AND TEACHING/LEARNING

The question of what is consciousness and how it develops was the subject of Vygotsky's (1979) first major public paper. In his subsequent writing he argued for development to be seen, from the first moments, as brought about by communication. "Instruction and development do not meet for the first time at school age; rather, they are in fact connected with each other from the very first day of a child's life" (Vygotsky, 1956, cited in Wertsch, 1985, p. 71).

As Minick described it (1987), referring to the third and final stage of the development of Vygotsky's ideas in the period from 1933 to his death:

> He (Vygotsky) argued that when the infant cries or reaches for an object, the adult attributes meaning to that behaviour. Though the infant has no communicative intent, these acts nonetheless function to communicate the infant's needs to his caretaker. Here, as in the adult's attempts to interact with the infant, the infant is included in communicative social activity before he has the capacity to use or respond adequately to communicative devices. Vygotsky argued that this provides the foundation for the transformation of the infant's behaviours into intentional indicative gestures. (p. 28)

This account of how the baby becomes conscious exemplifies Leont'ev's (1981) description of how the mental plane is constituted in the process of internalization. In this sense, learning is inseparable from "teaching." That teaching may not be deliberate and intentional, as it is in school or in parental instruction. In everyday situations of the child's life, he or she learns how to be, in gendered, ethnic, class, and other historical, sociocultural identities. Learning how to be, or to become, is motivated by desire, goals, and needs to be accepted, to emulate a desired person, or to join a group. Lave and Wenger's (1991) account of learning in workplace situations presents that theory of learning as becoming, and Lave (1996) and Winbourne and Watson (1998) discussed the notion in relation to the classroom.

Concomitant with this view of learning and development is an interpretation of concepts and knowledge that is neither of the two choices rejected by Piaget, empiricism and innatism (1970/1972), nor the individualistic, constructivist world that he proposed in their place. It is one where meanings historically precede the individual, which the individual internalizes, and through which the individual perceives the world. "How do I know that this colour is red?—It would be an answer to say: 'I have learnt English" (Wittgenstein, 1958, 381). "I did not get my picture of the world by satisfying myself of its correctness; nor do I have it because I am satisfied of its correctness. No: it is the inherited background against which I distinguish between true and false" (Wittgenstein, 1969, section 94).

Those meanings are not static and singular. As they are experienced and internalized from a range of discursive situations they may well carry the meanings, integrally imbued with affect, of those situations (Evans, 1993).

Vygotsky emphasized the presentation of scientific concepts to students and opposed the idea that they need to rediscover the development of mankind for themselves (1988). This formulation is taken to be very close to a transmission style of teaching by some. However, Vygotsky was opposed to merely telling learners. He was centrally concerned with the mediation of cultural tools and of metacognitive tools. "Scientific concepts. . . just start their development, rather than finish it, at a moment when the child learns the new term or word-meaning denoting the new concept" (Vygotsky, 1988, p. 159).

Two aspects of a discursive psychological approach to development are reported here: first, that of Vygotsky's argument for teaching from the general to the particular and, second, cultural mediation in learning, through Lave's work on learning as social practice.

1.   Vygotsky drew on Marx's notion of ascent from the abstract to the concrete in his theory of the acquisition of scientific concepts, and one development of this perspective has been toward the teaching of general principles to students, with particular questions being seen as instances in which the general principles need to be identified and applied (Galperin, 1969; Talyzina, 1981). This runs contrary to the usual tendency to work inductively from a range of everyday examples to general principles. Day (in press) has been working on utilizing this approach in mathematics classrooms. In a study of students in three inner-city schools in the United Kingdom across all levels of achievement according to national tests, principles for calculations of rates of processes were taught. Students were shown a generalized model for the conception of the values involved and the relations between them in the form of a visual structure for combining given data, such as time and rate, and using it to calculate the quantity. The teaching was orientated toward success in using the model for a range of problems of increasing complexity, both set by the teacher and invented by the students. That success was measured by a dynamic assessment procedure based on the amount and type of assistance they required. Analysis of quantitative data and of videos is currently taking place. Interim results show a level of achievement and change in

attitude, across the ability range, which has surprised the classroom teachers and the researchers, and the results certainly support the argument for a "theoretical learning approach" (Karpov & Haywood, 1998).

2. The metaphor of students as passive recipients of a body of knowledge is terribly limited; so too is the metaphor of students as all-powerful constructors of their own knowledge, and indeed of their own identities. Lave's (e.g., 1996) focus on the shaping of identity in social practice, extended by an analysis that takes account of the differences between schooling and the practices that she has studied (Lerman, 1998b), emphasizes the centrality of the social relationships constituted and negotiated during classroom learning. Lave spoke of learning as "an aspect of participation in socially situated practices" (p. 150). Provided we do not expect those practices to be those of the mathematics teacher, or of the mathematician but, instead, of the practices of the classroom culture, her description of learning can be very fruitful, as is shown by Winbourne (1997), for example. In that study, he described the demonstration of creativity and expertise in the use of graphical calculators among a class of 13-year-old girls and the subsequent display of mastery and learning through participation in mathematical activities, which he and a colleague have since described in terms of local communities of practice (Winbourne & Watson, 1998).

To summarize, Vygotsky outlined a method for accounting for development that is rooted in a historical, sociocultural notion of mind. This method brings together teaching and learning. In terms of a telos, or direction for development, Wertsch (cited in Cole & Wertsch, 1996) argued that Vygotsky offered, although not explicitly, a somewhat confused account of a telos of abstract rationality, an enlightenment principle, and one of a "harmony of imagination," a kind of mythical thinking. The former is evidenced in his and Luria's studies in Uzbekistan (Luria, 1976) and the latter in Vygotsky's *The Psychology of Art*. These two teloi co-exist in dialectic with each other, much like thinking and speech. Lave offered an interpretation that is, inevitably, more recent and partial and hence more appropriate to discursive psychology than Vygotsky's, although it has clearly grown from his ideas, that of the desire of the individual to "become." Again I mean here such desires as pleasing parents, emulating a sibling, becoming a member of a desired group, fulfilling goals, and so on.

THE PROCESS OF ACQUISITION—THE zpd

For psychologists of education, as distinct from sociologists, cultural theorists, and others who also study the situations in which meanings are manifest, the concern is with the process of acquisition of meanings. Vygotsky introduced the zone of proximal development (ZPD) in a lecture given in March 1933 (van der Veer & Valsiner, 1991, p. 329), although he pointed out that the idea was not originally his own. He died only 15 months later and clearly had not been able fully to elaborate his thoughts on the ZPD. Along with Newman and Holzman (1993), I take it to be the explanatory framework for learning as a whole, both in intentional settings, such as schooling, and in informal settings—in other words, all sociocultural milieus. It recognizes the fundamental asymmetry of the teacher–student(s) relationship, an asymmetry often denied or underplayed by more individualistic approaches. It provides the framework, in the form of a symbolic space (Meira & Lerman, in press), for the realization of Vygotsky's central principle of development. "In our conception, the true direction of the development of thinking is not from the individual to the socialised, but from the social to the individual" (Vygotsky, 1988, p. 32).

Such a definition opens a space for a unit of analysis of consciousness that incorporates affect and cognition. "When we approach the problem of the interrelation between thought and language and other aspects of mind, the first question that arises is that of intellect and affect. Their separation as subjects of study is a major weakness of traditional psychology..." (Vygotsky, 1988, p. 10).

The interpretation of Vygotsky's ZPD on which we draw (Meira & Lerman, in press), is closer to that of Davydov (1988, 1990) and is less "internalist" than Vygotsky's own version might appear. Vygotsky wrote that the instruction process creates the ZPD, but he also wrote that instruction is "fruitless if it occurs outside, below, or above the ZPD" (Vygotsky, 1987, p. 213). He probably intended to emphasize jointly the roles of the learning activity and the learning potential of the child. The ZPD is often described as a kind of force field that the child carries around, whose dimensions must be determined by the teacher so that activities offered are within the child's range. According to Davydov and followers, on the contrary the ZPD is created in the learning activity, which is a product of the task, the texts, the previous networks of experiences of the participants, the power relationships in the classroom, and so on. They speak of the ideas offered by one student potentially pulling other students into their ZPD (Lerman, 1994b). The ZPD is the classroom's, not the child's. In another sense, the ZPD is the researcher's; it is the tool for analysis of the learning interactions in the classroom (and elsewhere).

Teachers use a variety of strategies to try to create a ZPD, including reminders of past lessons, events, and language (Edwards & Mercer, 1987); references to outside school objects or meanings; and so on. Much can be learned by the researcher, focusing on these strategies of the teacher. Similarly, pairs of students can create their own ZPDs if they are motivated, taught how to share ways of working, have an appropriate personal relationship, and/or other factors. Students can be, and very often are, pulled into their ZPDs by imposition. For reasons of desire to become like another person, or to please another person, to be accepted into a group, or to achieve other such goals, a student will copy or emulate another, and subsequently that behavior may become part of that person. However, it is certainly not the case that learning always takes place. In both teacher–student interactions and student–student interactions, the participants may not engage together in the activity. They may act separately or one and/or the other may not act at all. In Meira and Lerman (in press), we provide some instances of a ZPD being created in which a nursery teacher almost "grasps" a child's attention and orientates it toward what she wants the child to learn. In one scenario, the interaction is initiated by the child's questioning gesture, and as observers, we were unable to ascertain whether the child was pointing at the objects on which the teacher chose to focus. This did not matter, however; the child responded to the teacher and became involved in the activity. We also offer instances where, despite the teacher's best efforts, a ZPD is not created in the activity, the teacher missing the child's experience immediately preceding her intervention and offering something not relevant. In another study (Lerman, in press), I argued that as much may be learned from incidents where a ZPD is not created as when it is. Two 13-year-old students were engaged, ostensibly together, on a task to simplify a ratio expression, ab:ab. A close analysis revealed that they chose different methods, and, although they spoke, one might say, at each other about their methods, they did not pay attention to each other and so did not move forward. As we described elsewhere, students may not catch each other's ideas (Vile & Lerman, 1996) and hence not create a ZPD. Creating a ZPD is more about mutual orientation of goals and desires than about the intended content of the interaction. In that study, I was looking at the interactions between the subjects of the video, trying to identify when they were communicating their ideas and reasoning to each other. Acts of communication, as objects of study, are the signs of sociogenesis, the social origins of psychogenesis and internalization. I was looking for clues from all the elements of the data set, videos, transcripts, and interviews to help in drawing inferences about the nature of that communication. For instance, in that study I indicated that the behavior of the teacher and the students with regard to their mathematical activity is framed by a discourse of ability. This constituted one of the students as more able and therefore more powerful in the interactions between them. Some time after the interaction used in the study the teacher looked at and read the video and the interactions of the students as confirming her evaluation in terms of ability.

This is the relevant extract from the transcript.

1. M: What? Equals ab? [pause, D looks on M's page] Equals ab?
2. D: Yeah.
3. M: No, it equals 1.
4. D: Wait a second. . .
5. M: 'Cause 1, [punching calculator buttons] 12 times tw . . . no. One, look, look, look times 2, divide 1 times 2 . . . it shouldn't equal 4. [M appears to be substituting the d 2 for a and b]
6. D: [laughs]
7. M: Um, yeah, it's, 'cause I'm doing [punching buttons] 1 times 2, divide 1 times
8. D: So that's canceled. The two b's are canceled out.
9. M: Equals 1.
10. D: Right? The two b's are canceled out.
11. M: Hey, where'd my pen go? No come on, look, look, look, look. You've got MAS. Watch, watch, watch, watch. [punching buttons] One times 2, divide, 1 times 2. That's stuffed up. [with emphasis] One.

The outcome was that the "more able" student M ignored the ideas of the "less able" D and firmly tried to impress his method on D. D seemed to lose heart quickly and did not press his method. In order to give an account that is adequately framed in a theory, and that also offers a description of the objects about which one, as researcher, is making statements, one has to delimit one's text. A Piagetian model would argue that power, in the form of authority, inhibits equilibration. Vygotsky's ZPD, working from a sociogenetic perspective, assumes imbalances in social relations as part of being human and communicating (Brodie, 1995; Matos, 1995; Santos, 1995), and therefore these were identified as an element of my account.

Following an account of teaching and learning and development from the perspective of discursive psychology, I have argued that the ZPD offers a sociogenetic mechanism for interpreting learning particularly suited to microgenetic studies. In mathematics education research, activity theory has been used to take account of goals and needs as they change over time, by Crawford and Deer (1993), Bartolini Bussi (1996), and Lerman (1997). "Leont'ev and his fellow activity theorists explain that humans understand the world and develop knowledge about it by acting purposefully in it. In turn this activity changes the world" (Gordon, 1998, p. 41).

MATHEMATICAL MEANING MAKING

In mathematics education, we are confronted with powerful models of the process of mathematics learning, based on Piaget's constructivism. According to Steffe and Wiegel (1996), a model of mathematics learning consists, at least, of a meaning for operations and for representation. The former "are part of a system of operations that is goal directed" (p. 486), and the authors draw distinctions between Piaget's notion of actions and activity and the Soviet notion in activity theory. The latter are of greatest concern to me here. "Many accounts of knowledge representation are misleading because they are based on the assumption that concepts are things—mental objects— 'out there' to be represented . . . we regard mathematical concepts as mental acts or operations, and it is these operations that are represented" (p. 487).

Piaget's familiar ontological choices, between reality imposing itself on a person empirically or platonically and the person constructing her/his own internal individual world, are evident here. There is another option, that mathematical concepts are social acts and tools. Consciousness is constituted in historical, sociocultural settings, and cultural tools are internalized in the strong sense that the mental plane is formed in that process. Thus, cultural tools (analogous with Marx's thesis concerning physical tools) both transform the person and the world for that person, and these cultural tools precede the individual. Words and symbols are mediators of thought. "It is the world of words which creates the world of things" (Lacan, 1966, p. 155); objects, including concepts, have meanings only within relations of signification (Walkerdine, 1988).

From the teaching and learning mathematics perspective, the research program would therefore be to study empirically the semiotic mediation of those objects. The language of semiotic mediation, whereby the person and the world for that person are transformed by the acquisition or appropriation of cultural tools, is a theoretical resource that engages with the fact of signification as well as the specificity of relations of signification. It rejects the notion of decontextualized, abstract concepts. It offers a medium through which one can account for cultural specificity, such as the mathematical meanings of Aboriginal students (Klein, 1997) and of multiple subjectivities as a result of the overlapping social practices of gender, ethnicity, class, family relations, and so on, in which people develop. The richness of the social and cultural implications of a discursive approach to psychology and the range of theoretical resources (e.g., sociolinguistics, cultural theory, semiotics, and postmodernism) on which it draws are enough to support its adoption.

In Vile (1996) and Vile and Lerman (1996), students' work in linear equations and coordinates were examined as case studies for the elaboration of a developmental semiotics, taking together the science of signs and the functioning of the process of mediation in learning, which is interpreted as making meaning that allows appropriate use in relevant contexts. In the study of coordinates (Vile, 1996), students were asked a series of questions in clinical interviews concerning the distance between two points, in two, three, and four dimensions. The intention was to examine the meanings that students gave when working in the different dimensions and to try to identify which meanings corresponded with successful transfer to four dimensions:

> Students who retained a concrete, measuring meaning for the distance between two points were unable to cope with the distance between 4 dimensional co-ordinates.... Those students who did make the appropriate symbolic meaning but only as a process ... were unable to make recourse to a more iconic representation if they were unsure. ... Students who were able to make the more generalised sign-sign foregrounded meaning early in their development are able to transfer to the more generalised dimension with relative ease. (pp. 176–177)

This study pointed to the kinds of meanings that can mediate the generalizations needed in mathematical thinking and hints at the classroom activities that might encourage their appropriation. The transformation in thinking and acting, when students learn mathematics using such software as Cabri Géomètre or technological tools such as the graphics calculator, is accessible with the notion of semiotic mediation, which also opens the possibility for analyses of social transformations of the classroom (Winbourne, 1997).

In another study (Finlow-Bates, 1997), the mathematics proof activities of undergraduates were examined through an analysis of proof as a process of social negotiation of meaning rather than an "understanding" or its lack.

Wertsch (1991) argued that focusing on mediation offers a unity for analysis that neither the individual nor mathematical knowledge can offer, with their implied separation of subject and object. Drawing on meaning as the mediation of cultural tools enables the study of other aspects of the positioning brought about in learning, through the social and political associations of concepts or knowledge as power. For example, recent sociological studies (Cooper & Dunne, 1998) offer insights into how contexts mediate differently for students of different social groups. In the first stage of their research on mathematics assessment items set in realistic (everyday) settings and esoteric ("pure" mathematical) settings, Cooper and Dunne found that working-class children "failed to demonstrate competences they have" (p. 115), through misreadings of the realistic settings. Cole (1996) argued that a focus on the mediation of cultural tools does not take account of action on the world in the sense of tool use that Marx described. I suggested previously that in the ZPD, one can study the mediation of cultural tools but that activity theory is more fruitful for longer term studies, taking account of goals and needs. There is a dialectical unity in these two methodologies in that, whereas both are rooted in the cultural psychology of Vygotsky, mediation is a generalizing principle, looking for similarities, whereas activity theory is a specializing one.

I gave this section the title "Mathematical Meaning Making" rather than mathematical understanding, with the intention of writing this chapter without using the term. Indeed, I have scarcely used it, apart from in this paragraph. The term is part of the "regime of truth," which locates power in the hands of teachers who can say when a child understands or doesn't, independently of what he or she produces, verbally or in writing (Watson, 1995). Its entirely internal nature makes it a rather useless notion (Lerman, 1994a), whereas its association with closure places it in a positivist paradigm. Much of Wittgenstein's later work can be seen as a deconstruction of attempts to find essences behind social meanings. His well-known argument (e.g., Wittgenstein, 1974) that to understand a concept is to know its use is to locate meanings in grammar and in rule following.

VOICE

Confrey (1995) argued that constructivism offers a space for individuality of interpretation, or voice, that Vygotsky's emphasis on scientific concepts replacing spontaneous concepts appears to deny. This aspect of his theory has often been interpreted, wrongly in my view, to recall the possibility of learning through transmission. First, spontaneous concepts do not disappear under scientific ones, which might be seen to lead to a uniformity that denies the possibility of individual voice. In general, they co-exist with spontaneous concepts, through a splitting of subjectivities, the child having learned in which situations the differing meanings are appropriate. As a rather simplistic example, a child might know to use "my half is bigger than your half" in the playground but not in the mathematics classroom. This offers a discursive interpretation of intuitions in mathematics (Fischbein, 1987). Second, as I discuss subsequently, the notion of the ZPD requires from the teacher, (desired) peers, and texts the particular experiences of individuals.

The method that Vygotsky's work offers is also often misunderstood, in large part because of the time and forms in which it was used. Vygotsky died in 1934, at the age of 38. The theoretical discourses available at that time, and especially the particular circumstances of the Soviet revolution, limited the perspective for the theorizing and therefore for the choice of research programs of Vygotsky and his colleagues. This is inevitable and is actually an application of Vygotsky's own theory that concepts are related to their time and place. Thus, Luria's work in Uzbekistan (1976) presents a strong image of the valuing of a particular interpretation of advanced societies as against primitive ones and of progress. However, Vygotsky's method is, through his argument for the priority of the intersubjective, to enable the study of consciousness as the internalization of sociocultural meanings, the appropriation of cultural tools, and the transformation that this effects for the individual and for her or his world. The origins of individual meanings being located in sociocultural tools, root "voice" in its proper framework. It is not the individualism of private world views that has dominated the debate around subjectivity and voice in recent decades. In cultural, discursive psychology individuality is the uniqueness of each person's collection of multiple subjectivities, through the many overlapping and separate identities of gender, ethnicity, class, size, age, and so on, to say nothing of the "unknowable" elements of the unconscious.

Discourses that dominate in the classroom, and everywhere else for that matter, distribute powerlessness and powerfulness through positioning subjects (Evans, 1993). Walkerdine's (1989) report of a classroom incident in which the emergence of a sexist discourse bestows power on 5-year-old boys, over their experienced teacher, dramatically illustrates the significance of a focus on discourse, not on individuals. In some research on children's interpretations of bigger and smaller, Redmond (1992) found some similar evidence of meanings being located in practices:

> These two were happy to compare two objects put in front of them and tell me why they had chosen the one they had. However when I allocated the multilinks to them (the girl had 8 the boy had 5) to make a tower ... and I asked them who had the taller one, the girl answered correctly but the boy insisted that he did. Up to this point the boy had been putting the objects together and comparing them. He would not do so on this occasion and when I asked him how we could find out whose tower was the taller he became very angry. I asked him why he thought that his tower was taller and he just replied "Because IT IS." He would go no further than this and seemed to be almost on the verge of tears. (p. 24)

Many teachers struggle to find ways to enable individual expression in the classroom, including expressing mathematical ideas, confronting the paradox of teachers giving emancipation to students from their authoritative position. However, this can fruitfully be seen as a dialectic, whereby all participants in an activity manifest powerfulness and powerlessness at different times, including the teacher. When those articulations are given expression, and not denied as in some interpretations of critical pedagogy (Lerman, 1998a), shifts in relationships between participants, and crucially between participants and learning, can occur (Ellsworth, 1989; Walcott, 1994). Learning is predicated on one person learning from another, more knowledgeable, or desired, person.

In the classroom, Davydov's learning activity structure of a lesson encourages, and actually requires voice, the expression of individual life experience and perspective. When a teacher offers an activity in a classroom, say to share two oranges among three children, the different answers offered by the children arise from their previous experiences, what has been called the zone of actual development, and potentially pull the others, including perhaps the teacher, into their ZPDs. Similarly, powerful technologies can offer possibilities for novel ideas by children that create ZPDs for other participants and change the social relationships in the classroom.

The account of a discursive psychology for mathematics education that I have attempted to develop in this chapter incorporates action, goals, affect, and power and its lack, based on sociocultural origins. A psychology focused on the individual making her or his own sense of the world does not engage with social and cultural life; other theoretical discourses, such as approaches to sociology that merely describe, are not adequate for mathematics education either. I agree with Harré (1997) when he wrote, referring to discursive psychology, "Psychology is the study of the skills necessary to live as a human being with others" (p. 189). It should be clear that such a definition, particularly when related to education, is open to contestation concerning what is valued as development and what constitutes cultural capital. A cultural, discursive psychology places that contestation at the heart of what constitutes consciousness, meaning making, and, in this chapter, mathematics teaching and learning.

THEORETICAL AND EMPIRICAL FIELDS

Theories need to account for their ongoing development in relation to their empirical work. Brown and Dowling (1998) proposed that "the research process itself is properly conceived of as the construction of the theoretical and empirical as increasingly coherent and systematically organized and related conceptual spaces" (p. 11). Since Kuhn (1970), researchers have been forced to recognize that they create the objects of their research; they are not entities existing independently of the research discourse or the researcher. This is not to prioritize theory but to recognize the dialectic between the two fields, the empirical and the theoretical, and it distinguishes between mathematics education as a set of practices and mathematics education as a field of knowledge (Patricio Herbst, personal communication). I began this chapter by pointing out that there is an overlap because all mathematics education has its roots in the classroom whether its aim is to say something about practice or about how one might think and speak about mathematics education. In the main, however, this chapter has been about the latter. My intention has been to map out the field, from the point of view of a discursive psychology. I have also tried to indicate its implications for mathematics education as a set of practices through the examples of research and other classroom illustrations.

Steffe and Wiegel (1996) challenged researchers to provide an account of the self-reflexivity of their theories, although why this should be a sign of a good theory is not spelled out, except as a counter to naiveté. They argued that, according to radical constructivism, theories of learning can be seen as making what they call second-order models of students' understandings, which are understood as first-order models constructed by students to order their experiences. This symmetry is very appealing.

In that the objects of research, the products of research, the theories drawn on, the methodologies used, and so on, are all cultural products, texts, the theoretical program outlined here is, in its entirety, reflexive. Language precedes phenomena, which precede experience. To refer again to Kuhn, however, researchers are forced to admit their allegiances to their theories. In one direction, empirical research leads to elaboration of theory, as our work on, for example, the ZPD, on developmental semiotics, and on teaching general principles demonstrates. In the other direction, theory, as outlined in this chapter, provides the resource for interpretation and for methodology and its justification. Rarely does one's theory as a whole change (although see Lerman, 1989, in comparison with this chapter!).

The metaphor of the zoom lens is part of my theory; to sustain the metaphor a little further, it has framed my writing here and thus offered me both possibilities and limitations. It is a rhetorical tool for expressing the need to take into account all of the social and cultural life of the classroom, but it cannot quite capture the histories of the participants, or the classroom, and perhaps it is too linear. However, if it is the zoom lens of a video camera it can capture development and change. How we read the tapes remains the challenge for research.

ACKNOWLEDGMENTS

My thanks to Peter Winbourne and Ros Sutherland for comments on an earlier draft.

REFERENCES

Apple, M. (1995). Taking power seriously: New directions in equity in mathematics education and beyond. In W. G. Secada, E. Fennema, & L. B. Adajian (Eds.), *New directions for equity in mathematics education* (pp. 329–348). Cambridge, UK: Cambridge University Press.

Bartolini Bussi, M. G. (1991). Social interaction and mathematical knowledge. In F. Furinghetti (Ed.), *Proceedings of the fifteenth annual meeting of the International Group for the Psychology of Mathematics Education* (Vol. 1, pp. 1–16), Italy: Dipatimento di Mathematica dell'Università di Genova.

Bartolini Bussi, M. G. (1996). Mathematical discussion and perspective drawing in primary school. *Educational Studies in Mathematics, 31*(1–2), 11–41.

Bernstein, B. (1996). *Pedagogy, symbolic control and identity: Theory, research, critique*. London: Taylor & Francis.

Boero, P., Dapueto, C., Ferrari, P., Ferrero, E., Garuti, R., Lemut, E., Parenti, L., & Scali, E. (1995). Aspects of the mathematics—Culture relationship in mathematics teaching-learning in compulsory school. In L. Meira & D. Carraher (Eds.), *Proceedings of the nineteenth annual meeting of the International Group for the Psychology of Mathematics Education* (Vol. 1, pp. 151–166). Brazil: Universidade Federal de Pernambuco, Recife.

Brodie, K. (1995). Peer interaction and the development of mathematical knowledge. In D. Carraher & L. Meira (Eds.), *Proceedings of nineteenth international meeting of the Group for the Psychology of Mathematics Education* (Vol. 3, pp. 216–223). Brazil: Universidade Federal de Pernambuco, Recife.

Brown, A., & Dowling, P. (1998). *Doing research/reading research: A mode of interrogation for education*. London: Falmer.

Cole, M. (1996). *Cultural psychology: A once and future discipline*. Cambridge, MA: Harvard University Press.

Cole, M., & Wertsch, J. V. (1996). *Contemporary implications of Vygotsky and Luria*. Worcester, MA: Clark University Press.

Confrey, J. (1995). Student voice in examining "splitting" as an approach to ratio, proportions and fractions. In L. Meira & D. Carraher (Eds.), *Proceedings of the nineteenth annual meeting of the International Group for the Psychology of Mathematics Education* (Vol. 1, pp. 3–29). Brazil: Universidade Federal de Pernambuco, Recife.

Cooper, B., & Dunne, M. (1998). Anyone for tennis? Social class differences in children's responses to National Curriculum mathematics testing. *The Sociological Review, 46*(1), 115–148.

Crawford, K., & Deer, E. (1993). Do we practise what we preach?: putting policy into practise in teacher education. *South Pacific Journal of Teacher Education, 21*(2), 111–121.

Davydov, V. V. (1988). Problems of developmental teaching. *Soviet Education, 30,* 6–97.

Davydov, V. V. (1990). *Soviet studies in mathematics education: Vol. 2. Types of generalization in instruction* (J. Kilpatrick, Ed., & J. Teller, Trans.). Reston VA: National Council of Teachers of Mathematics.

Day, C. (in press). *Making sense of modelling with mathematical functions: A rational, reasonable and rigorous approach*.

Dowling, P. (1995). A language for the sociological description of pedagogic texts with particular reference to the secondary school mathematics scheme SMP 11–16. *Collected Original Resources in Education, 19.*

Edwards, D., & Mercer, N. (1987). *Common knowledge: The development of understanding in the classroom*. London: Methuen.

Ellsworth, E. (1989). Why doesn't this feel empowering? Working through the repressive myths of critical pedagogy. *Harvard Educational Review, 59*(3), 297–324.

Evans, J. (1993). *Adults and numeracy*. Unpublished doctoral thesis, University of London Institute of Education, London.

Finlow-Bates, K. (1997). *Investigating notions of proof: A study of students' proof activities within the context of a fallibilist and social theory*. Unpublished doctoral thesis, South Bank University, London.

Fischbein, E. (1987). *Intuition in science and mathematics. An educational approach*. Dordrecht: Kluwer.

Galperin, P. Y. (1969). Stages in the development of mental acts. In M. Cole & I. Maltzman (Eds.), *A handbook of contemporary Soviet psychology* (pp. 34–61). New York: Basic Books.

Gordon, S. E. (1998). *Understanding students' learning statistics: An activity theory approach*. Unpublished doctoral dissertation, Faculty of Education, The University of Sydney, Australia.

Harré, R. (1995). But is it science? Traditional and alternative approaches to the study of social behavior. *World Psychology, 1*(4), 47–78.

Harré, R. (1997). Forward to Aristotle: The case for a hybrid ontology. *Journal for the Theory of Social Behaviour, 27*(2/3), 173–191.

Harré, R., & Gillett, G. (1994). *The discursive mind*. London: Sage.

Karpov, Y. V., & Haywood, H. C. (1998). Two ways to elaborate Vygotsky's concept of mediation: Implications for instruction. *American Psychologist, 53*(1), 27–36.

Klein, M. (1997). Constructivist practice in preservice teacher education in mathematics: Aboriginal and Torres Strait Islander voices heard yet silenced. *Equity & Excellence in Education, 30*(1), 65–71.

Kuhn, T. S. (1970). *The structure of scientific revolutions*. Chicago: Chicago University Press.

Lacan, J. (1966). *Ecrits 1*. Paris: Seuil.

Lave, J. (1996). Teaching, as learning, in practice. *Mind, Culture & Activity, 3*(3), 149–164.

Lave, J., & Wenger, E. (1991). *Situated learning: Legitimate peripheral participation*. New York: Cambridge University Press.

Leont'ev, A. N. (1981). The problem of activity in psychology. In J. V. Wertsch (Ed.), *The concept of activity in Soviet psychology* (pp. 37–71) Armonk, NY: Sharpe.

Lerman, S. (1989). Constructivism, mathematics and mathematics education. *Educational Studies in Mathematics, 20*, 211–223.

Lerman, S. (1992). The function of language in radical constructivism: A Vygotskian perspective. In W. Geeslin & K. Graham (Eds.), *Proceedings of the sixteenth annual meeting of the International Group for the Psychology of Mathematics Education* (Vol. 2, pp. 40–47), Durham, New Hampshire.

Lerman, S. (1994a). Changing focus in the mathematics classroom. In S. Lerman (Ed.), *Cultural perspectives on the mathematics classroom* (pp. 191–213). Dordrecht: Kluwer.

Lerman, S. (1994b). Towards a unified space of theory-and-practice in mathematics teaching: A research perspective'. In L. Bazzini (Ed.), *Proceedings of the fifth International Conference on Systematic Co-operation between Theory and Practice in Mathematics Education*, (pp. 133–142), Italy: Universita degli Studi di Pavia.

Lerman, S. (1996). Intersubjectivity in mathematics learning: A challenge to the radical constructivist paradigm? *Journal for Research in Mathematics Education, 27*(2), 133–150.

Lerman, S. (1997). The psychology of mathematics teachers' learning: In search of theory. In E. Pehkonen (Ed.), *Proceedings of the twenty-first meeting of the International Group for the Psychology of Mathematics Education* (Vol. 3, pp. 200–207). Lahti, Finland.

Lerman, S. (1998a). The intension/intention of teaching mathematics. In C. Kanes, M. Goos, & E. Warren (Eds.), *Proceedings of the 21st meeting of the Mathematics Education Research Group of Australasia* (pp. 29–44). Griffith University at Gold Coast, Queensland.

Lerman, S. (1998b). Learning as social practice: an appreciative critique. In A. Watson (Ed.), *Situated cognition and the learning of mathematics* (pp. 33–42). Oxford, UK: Centre for Mathematics Education Research, University of Oxford Department of Educational Studies.

Lerman, S. (1999). Mathematics, critical pedagogy, and the Jewish question. In H. S. Shapiro (Ed.), *Strangers in the land: Modernity, pedagogy and Jewish identity*. New York: Lang.

Lerman, S. (in press). Accounting for accounts of learning mathematics: Reading the ZPD in videos and transcripts. In D. Clarke (Ed.), *Perspectives on meaning in mathematics and science classrooms*.

Luria, A. R. (1976). *Cognitive development: Its cultural and social foundations*. Cambridge, MA: Harvard University Press.

Matos, J. F. (1995). Ethnographic research methodology and mathematical activity in the classroom. In D. Carraher & L. Meira (Eds.), *Proceedings of nineteenth international meeting of the Group for the Psychology of Mathematics Education* (Vol. 1, p. 211). Recife, Brazil.

Meira, L., & Lerman, S. (in press). *The zone of proximal development as a symbolic space*.

Minick, N. (1987). The development of Vygotsky's thought: An introduction. In R. W. Rieber & A. S. Carton (Eds.), *The collected works of L. S. Vygotsky: Vol. 1: Problems of general psychology* (pp. 17–36). New York: Plenum Press.

Newman, F., & Holzman, L. (1993). *Lev Vygotsky: Revolutionary scientist.* London: Routledge.

Piaget, J. (1970/1972). *The principles of genetic epistemology* (W. Mays, Trans.). London: Routledge & Kegan Paul.

Redmond, J. (1992). Are 4–7 year-old children influenced by discursive practices when asked to make comparisons using quantities? Unpublished manuscript, South Bank University, London, UK.

Santos, M. (1995). Mathematics learning as situated learning. In D. Carraher & L. Meira (Eds.), *Proceedings of nineteenth international meeting of the Group for the Psychology of Mathematics Education* (Vol. 1, p. 222). Recife, Brazil.

Smith, L. (1993). *Necessary knowledge: Piagetian perspectives on constructivism.* Hove, UK: Lawrence Erlbaum Associates.

Steffe, L. P., & Wiegel, H. G. (1996). On the nature of a model of mathematical learning. In L. P. Steffe, P. Nesher, P. Cobb, G. A. Goldin, & B. Greer (Eds.), *Theories of mathematical learning* (pp. 477–498). Mahwah, NJ: Lawrence Erlbaum Associates.

Talyzina, N. F. (1981). *The psychology of learning.* Moscow: Progress Books.

van der Veer, R., & Valsiner, J. (1991). *Understanding Vygotsky: A quest for synthesis.* Oxford: Blackwell.

Vile, A. (1996). *Developmental semiotics: The evolution of a theoretical framework for the description of meaning-making in mathematics education and mathematics.* Unpublished doctoral dissertation, South Bank University, London.

Vile, A., & Lerman, S. (1996). Semiotics as a descriptive framework in mathematical domains. In L. Puig & A. Gutiérrez (Eds.), *Proceedings of the twentieth annual meeting of the International Group for the Psychology of Mathematics Education* (Vol. 4, pp. 395–402). Valencia, Spain.

von Glasersfeld, E. (1994). A radical constructivist view of basic mathematical concepts. In P. Ernest (Ed.), *Constructing mathematical knowledge: Epistemology and mathematics education* (pp. 5–7). London: Falmer.

Vygotsky, L. (1979). Consciousness as a problem in the psychology of behaviour *Soviet Psychology, 17,* 5–35. (Original work published 1924)

Vygotsky, L. S. (1987). *The collected works of L. S. Vygotsky: Vol. 1. Problems of general psychology.* New York: Plenum.

Vygotsky, L. S. (1988). *Thought and language.* Cambridge MA: MIT Press.

Walcott, R. (1994). Pedagogical desire and the crisis of knowledge. *Discourse, 15*(1), 64–74.

Walkerdine, V. (1988). *The mastery of reason.* London: Routledge.

Walkerdine, V., & Girls And Maths Unit. (1989). *Counting girls out.* London: Virago.

Watson, A. (1995). Evidence for pupils' mathematical achievements. *For the Learning of Mathematics, 15,* 16–21.

Wertsch, J. V. (1985). *Vygotsky and the social formation of mind.* Cambridge, MA: Harvard University Press.

Wertsch, J. V. (1991). *Voices of the mind: A sociocultural approach to mediated action.* Cambridge, MA: Harvard University Press.

Winbourne, P. (1997). Looking through the graphical calculator: An examination of beliefs concerning the teaching and learning of algebra. In E. Pehkonen (Ed.), *Proceedings of the twenty-first meeting of the International Group for the Psychology of Mathematics Education* (Vol. 1, p. 270). Lahti, Finland.

Winbourne, P., & Watson, A. (1998). Participating in learning mathematics through shared local practices. In A. Olivier & K. Newstead (Eds.), *Proceedings of the twenty-second annual meeting of the International Group for the Psychology of Mathematics Education* (Vol. 4, pp. 177–184). Stellenbosch, South Africa.

Wittgenstein, L. (1958). *Philosophical investigations.* Oxford, UK: Blackwell.

Wittgenstein, L. (1969). *On certainty.* Oxford, UK: Blackwell.

Wittgenstein, L. (1974). *Philosophical grammar.* Oxford, UK: Blackwell.

2

Mathematics Education in Late Modernity: Beyond Myths and Fragmentation

Paul Dowling

*Culture Communication & Societies,
Institute of Education, University of London*

The science of myth is entitled to describe the syntax of myth, but only so long as it is not forgotten that, when it ceases to be seen as a convenient translation, this language destroys the truth that it makes accessible. One can say that gymnastics is geometry so long as this is not taken to mean that the gymnast is a geometer.

—Bourdieu (1990, p. 93)

The artisan who imitates a known production technique is—generally—not doing mathematics. But the artisan(s) who discovered the techniques, did mathematics, developed mathematics, was (were) thinking mathematically.

—Gerdes (1985, p. 12)

These two claims clearly stand in stark contrast to each other. Gerdes' "defrosting" of Mozambican hut building is not merely an anthropological description. Rather, his concern is the emancipation of a culture subordinated by European/American cultural imperialism. He hopes to achieve this by demonstrating that mathematical reasoning is not the exclusive achievement of the dominant culture. Unfortunately, however, he can achieve this only by projecting onto Mozambican culture not one but three distinctly European/American cultural forms: first, shall we say, a Fordist model of production that denies creativity to the "artisan", second, a mode of historiography that generates historical narrative in terms of the acts and inventions of "great men," and, third, a mathematical discourse that enables the arrangement of objects in space to be described as geometry. In particular, to claim that hut building entails mathematical reasoning, Gerdes must make the move that Bourdieu warns against.

I refer to Gerdes' particular form of mathematizing as the myth of emancipation (see Dowling, 1998). This myth is the globalization of a myth that is rather more common in school mathematics, the myth of participation. I shall introduce an example from a school mathematics book. The book shows a photograph of two boxes of potatoes. One box shows "reds" at £1.00 per 5-pound bag; the other shows "whites" at 18p per pound. The accompanying text reads:

> This shop sells potatoes loose or in bags. The shop weighs things in pounds (lb). The loose potatoes cost 18p for 1 lb. A 5 lb bag of potatoes costs £1.00. You can work out which gives more for your money in two ways. [Shown adjacent to photograph of boxes of 'reds' and 'whites'.]
>
> These potatoes cost 18p for 1 lb. So 5 lb cost 5 × 18p or 90p. The 5 lb bag costs £1.00. So the loose potatoes work out cheaper. [Shown beneath a second copy of the photograph and indicating the 'whites'.]
>
> 5lb of these potatoes cost £1.00. so 1 lb cost £1.00 ÷ 5 or 20p. The loose potatoes only cost 18p a lb. So the loose potatoes work out cheaper. [Shown beneath a third copy of the photograph and indicating the 'reds'.] (School Mathematics Project, 1987, SMP Book G7, Cambridge: CUP, p. 4)

Another strategy might be to note that 10 pounds of loose potatoes cost £1.80, which is less than the cost of two bags. In practice, however, it is quite possible, indeed, even quite likely that none of these strategies would be used. In my experience, bagged and loose potatoes sold in supermarkets are rarely identical in quality. In this example, they are actually different varieties suited to quite different culinary uses. Bagged potatoes tend to vary in size (presumably in order to make the correct weight) and you can't choose them individually. These and a range of other general and contingent considerations will routinely enter into shopping decision-making processes. In the United Kingdom, supermarkets must display the unit price of such bagged products so that calculations are generally not necessary. Furthermore, even when "best-buy" calculations are performed, they seem to be achieved very successfully with very little reliance on this kind of school maths algorithm, as Jean Lave and others (1984) have famously demonstrated.

My point is not to deny the potential use-value of mathematics. Rather, it is the mythologizing of shopping that I am questioning. In this case, the myth of participation proposes that mathematics is a necessary feature of everyday practices such as shopping and other domestic labor. Shopping, of course, is not on the school curriculum (not in the United Kingdom, anyway). It is a domestic practice primarily acquired in the family site. However, schooling, it would seem, must compensate for the inadequacies of (at least) some families by providing the mathematical component that will enable optimum participation in domestic life.

Thus, what is presented on the curriculum is mythologized or recontextualized shopping that privileges mathematical rather than domestic principles. Such recontextualized practices constitute what I refer to as the public domain of school mathematics: mathematics parading as something other than itself.

Here are two more quotations:

> Just as the Romans and the Etruscans divided the sky by rigid mathematical lines, and in this way delimited space as a templum and conjured up a God, so every people has above them such a sky divided up by mathematical concepts and, under the demand for truth, it intends that from now on every conceptual God should be sought nowhere other than in this sphere. (Nietzsche, cited in Baudrillard, 1993, p. 203)

> So far as we can tell, mathematical relationships should be valid for all planets, biologies, cultures, philosophies. We can imagine a planet with uranium hexaflouride in the atmosphere or a life form that lives mostly off interstellar dust, even if these are extremely unlikely contingencies. But we cannot imagine a civilization for which one and one does not equal two or for which there is an integer interposed between eight and nine. (Sagan, cited in Cockcroft et al., 1982, p. 3)

Just as Bourdieu spotlights the myth in Gerdes, so Nietzsche does for Sagan. But now it's a different myth. Mathematics no longer stands as the cultural achievement of the object (albeit imagined) society. Rather, Sagan seemed to claim to have identified in mathematics a universal body of platonic truths. Alternatively, perhaps, he may be regarding mathematics as Kantian conditions of existence of our knowledge of the universe—we can imagine only in mathematical terms. To be revealed in all their infalibilist splendor, these truths must be stripped of all cultural and biological localizations to emerge as a pure esoteric domain of mathematics.

Julian Roberts (1995) identifies this position as "mimesis," which, he claims, is the defining characteristic of modernity:

> This is a view we would term mimesis; it rests on the assumption that knowledge reflects and, in reflecting, lifts the things that it reflects into a higher sphere of generality. [...] Its paradigm [...] is arithmetic, which represents the purest of the "ideas". Arithmetic is, in this account, absolute mimesis; it exhaustively captures the quantifiable aspects of reality, while at the same time remaining completely distinct from it. (p. 132)

I have referred to this form of mathematical myth as the *myth of certainty*. It may be construed as the universalizing of a more local myth, the myth of reference. This is another feature of school mathematics texts. Here is an example:

> When you buy a quantity of something, sometimes the cost is proportional to the quantity, and sometimes not. Suppose you buy dress material which costs £3 a metre. Every metre you buy costs the same, and the graph of (quantity, cost) is a straight line through (0, 0). (It goes through (0, 0) because if you buy 0 metres you pay £0.) In this case the cost is proportional to the quantity. [Graph shown adjacent to text.]
> Now look at these prices of bags of crisps in a supermarket.

Weight	25g	50g	75g
Cost	15p	25p	30p

If the cost were proportional to the quantity, we would expect a 50g bag to cost the same as two 25g bags, which would be 30p. But in fact the extra 25g costs only 10p. And if we buy a 75g bag, we get the next 25g for only 5p. The graph of (quantity, cost) looks like this. It goes through (0, 0) because 0g costs 0p. But it in not a straight line. The cost here in not proportional to the quantity. [Graph shown adjacent to text.] (School Mathematics Project, 1985, SMP Book Y5, Cambridge: CUP, p. 10)

Although the public domain setting again refers to shopping, this text is clearly very different from the previous one. The realism of "this shop sells potatoes . . . " and the photographs are replaced by "suppose you buy . . . " The first text never leaves the public domain, whereas the second moves quickly into esoteric modes of expression, "straight line," (0, 0), "proportional to," as well as a table and graphs that are not generally associated with shopping. Unlike the first text, this is not, of course, for shopping. Rather, the shopping setting is introduced as a public domain portal into the esoteric domain. This text is about mathematics.

Both forms of text recontextualize their public domain objects by casting a mathematical gaze onto them. In constituting the myths of participation or emancipation, however, the text conceals the esoteric domain origin of the gaze, projecting mathematics into the public domain itself. The myths of reference and of certainty operate by revealing and explicitly privileging the mathematical principles that constitute the esoteric domain. What they conceal is the cultural arbitrariness, in Bourdieu's and Passeron's (1977) terms, of this privileging; the mathematical gaze is only one of many.

In the remainder of this chapter, I shall argue, first, that school mathematics is an activity that constitutes two polarized and hierarchised categories of ideal student. I shall do this by introducing some elements of my language for the sociological analysis of texts and of social activity and by summarizing some key findings of my deployment of this language in the analysis of school mathematics texts. I shall then argue that socioeconomic developments over the past two centuries have culminated in a condition whereby both categories of ideal student constructed by school mathematics have become or are becoming obsolete. Finally, I want to draw out some implications from my social and textual analysis for the activity of mathematics education. In essence, I shall conclude that what is called for is a shift in emphasis from relations of school and pedagogy to relations of the market and exchange.

In order (I hope) to ease the reception of this argument, I want to make two brief comments on methodology. First, I am deploying a constructivist general methodology that I refer to as constructive description. This approach is outlined in more detail elsewhere (Dowling, 1998, 1999, 2000). For my purposes here, however, it is sufficient to emphasise that my constructivist method does not depend for its validity on some reality that exists independently of our means of accessing and describing it. Rather, it is measured in terms of the explicitness and internal coherence of the language or theory that is deployed and of its deployment in the analysis of empirical data. Second, I will make reference in the chapter to texts as the empirical objects of analysis. I understand a text to be a bounded instance of a social activity. Thus, a mathematics textbook and a mathematics lesson are instances of school mathematics activity; a supermarket—its organization, content, and the actions of a shopper over a specific period of time and in a particular place (between 10.56 and 11.47 in the Sainsburys in Winchmore Hill, for example)—are instances of a rather different form of activity. In the discussion that follows, I shall introduce different modes of text and different modes of social activity.

TEXTUAL VOICES AND RELATIONS

All texts may be interpreted as encoding or constructing relations between a range of voices. These voices will always include an authorial and a reader voice. Additional objectified voices may be constructed where a text makes reference to a third party—a shopper, for example. Both of the school texts that I have introduced are examples of what I refer to as *pedagogic texts*. By this I mean, first, that they construct a form of relationality between authorial and reader voices that is concerned with the transmission or regulation of a privileged content (such as school mathematical practice). Second, the text locates the principles of evaluation of potential performances with the authorial voice; the author knows, the reader doesn't, at least not yet.

The two texts are examples of, respectively, a regulatory text and a transmission text. Both texts are privileging particular forms of mathematical commentary upon shopping. This commentary is the product of the esoteric domain gaze. However, the second text, but not the first, strongly indicates a division between the esoteric and public domains—between mathematics per se and shopping—by its introduction of specifically mathematical language within a shopping setting. Such a division is a necessary condition for the transmission of the mathematical principles that generate the privileged content because these can be fully expressed only in the specialized terms of the esoteric domain.[1] The transmission of these principles is the basis of an apprenticing pedagogic action that constructs the reader as a potential subject of mathematical practice—as a potential mathematician. The first text does not facilitate this transmission. Rather, the ideal reader's practice in the domestic setting is regulated by principles that are invisible. This reader is not a potential subject so much as a regulated object.

As I have defined it, a pedagogic text constructs pedagogic relations between author and reader voices, locating the author in the dominant position. The logical opposite of a pedagogic text is a text that locates the principles of evaluation of potential performances with the reader voice. In ideal typical terms, the supermarket—as text— claims no authority with respect to the principles of selection, rejection, evaluation, or use of its merchandise. Rather, these principles are devolved to its customers.[2]

---

[1]I am interpreting mathematical knowledge as an achievement of social action in discursive and nondiscursive practice. I am, therefore, rejecting an understanding of mathematics as the conditions of existence of human rationality that essentially grounds Piagetian Kantianism and allows his liberal and a-social form of nonauthoritarian pedagogy (see Dowling, 1998).

[2]Of course, the supermarket management may attempt to create rather than respond to a market for some or all of its commodities. In such circumstances, it would be acting pedagogically. Pedagogic and market modes are ideal types in the Weberian sense (Blau & Meyer, 1971; Dowling, 1998; Weber, 1964;). This entails that empirical instances are likely to involve both but will commonly be dominated by one.

		Range	
		Limiting	Expanding
Discursive Saturation	Low	Localizing	Articulating
	High	Specializing	Generalizing

FIG. 2.1. Strategic action.

I refer to this kind of text as a *market text*. Relations between author and reader are now relations of exchange. I return to some consideration of such texts at the end of this chapter. I move, first, to an outline of a description of the modality of social action.

THE MODALITY OF SOCIAL ACTION[3]

The texts that I have introduced make reference to two social activities, school mathematics and shopping. On the face of it, these appear to be quite different kinds of activity. In this section I want to begin to put some structure on the ways in this these and other modes of activity are differentiated in and through their respective texts. The categories of strategic action that I shall introduce are shown in Fig. 2.1.

In the figure, the four categories of strategic action are differentiated vertically in terms of *discursive saturation*. This term refers to the extent to which the principles of an activity are made available linguistically or within discourse. Domestic activities such as shopping and activities that are commonly referred to as "manual" or as "skills" are differentiated from intellectual activities such as mathematics through the opposing strategies of localizing and specializing. Localizing is concerned with the acquisition and deployment of competence in relation to physically specific sites and forms. Pedagogic action may be tacit or may involve a comparatively limited argot. Specializing, on the other hand, is concerned with the acquisition and deployment of competence in relation to discourses that are, in general, not limited to specific physical sites or forms. Pedagogic action must always be explicit because the discourse entails

---

[3]In formulating my theory of social action I have engaged with the work of a range of theorists including, most notably, Jean Baudrillard, Basil Bernstein, Pierre Bourdieu, Émil Durkheim, Umberto Eco, Michel Foucault, Ernesto Laclau and Chantal Mouffe, Alexander Luria, Ignacio Matte-Blanco, Jean Piaget, Ferdinand de Saussure, Lev Vygotsky, and Max Weber. Unfortunately, it is not possible to make these links explicit here, although I have incorporated a discussion of the theoretical antecedents of my work in my book (Dowling, 1998) and have included a few illustrative references in the bibliography of this chapter. I should emphasize, however, that my recruitment of this diversity of work does not constitute my own work as a pastiche. Rather, I have attempted to construct an explicit and coherent theoretical structure. This structure is heavily indebted to but is ultimately inconsistent, to a greater or lesser degree, with each of these antecedent works.

a linguistic system. Discourses will vary in terms of their internal coherence and consistency. Nevertheless, the term refers to something that is far more systematic than the argots that may be associated with localizing strategies.

I shall introduce an anecdote from Mike Cooley (which I have used many times before) in order to illustrate the operation of these strategies. Cooley (1985) reported on an aircraft company that engaged a team of four highly qualified mathematicians to design a program that would produce a drawing of the complex shape of a jet engine afterburner. The team worked for 2 years without success. On visiting the experimental workshop, however, they found that a skilled sheet metal worker together with a draughtsman had drawn and indeed made the afterburner. One of the mathematicians reportedly observed, "They may have succeeded in making it but they didn't understand how they did it." As localized action the efforts of the manual workers were successful. The implied specializing strategy of the mathematician, however, lays claim to a higher order of discourse that, s/he claims, accesses "understanding." We might speculate that the response of the manual workers, had they overheard the mathematician, might have been such as to invert this hierarchy via a localizing strategy and making reference to "ivory towers" and the "real world."

My point is not to privilege either strategy above the other, although they are clearly constitutive of the intellectual/manual hierarchy that has characterized the earlier phases of modernity, nor do I intend to attribute essential qualities to mathematics or to sheetmetal work. Both entail discursive and nondiscursive practice. Rather, I want to illustrate how we might conceive of social differentiation as the product of ongoing localizing and specializing strategic action.

The categories in the cells of Fig. 2. 1 are differentiated horizontally according to whether they tend to limit or to extend the range of an activity. Thus, in mythologizing other activities, a high discursive saturation (DS$^+$) activity such as mathematics is generalizing its field of reference.[4] Low discursive saturation (DS$^-$) practices cannot mythologize to the extent that they do not constitute discursive systems. The nature of the relationship is therefore qualitatively different, so I employ a different term, *articulation*. An example of articulation would be the recruitment by one activity of a material resource originating in another (using a supermarket basket to contain a floral arrangement, perhaps). Mythologizing is, of course, a metaphorical recruitment.

The limiting strategies associated with domestic practices such as shopping are, in general, localizing (and I again index the work of Lave and colleagues by way of illustration), that is, they constitute shopping as a DS$^-$ practice. The limiting strategies associated with school mathematics are more commonly specializing, that is, they constitute mathematics as a DS$^+$ practice. School mathematics, then, mythologizes shopping, as I have illustrated; it generates general strategies. Shopping, however, will tend to articulate with other practices, including mathematics, by recruiting to specific

---

[4]An activity generates DS$^+$ practice via specializing strategies that function to make its principles as available as possible within discourse, which is to say, to make them explicit and systematic. Mathematics is clearly a prime example of such an activity. An activity generates DS$^-$ practice via localizing strategies that constitute its principles in the context or location or in bodily control rather than in discourse. Such practices are commonly, but not exclusively, tagged "manual."

and local contexts. The notion of transfer in the form of a *push technology*[5] from one activity to another is clearly problematized in this schema (as it is empirically, again; see Lave, 1988, and Nunes et al., 1993). It is precisely that which constitutes mathematics as a generalizing/generalized discourse that must be lost in any recruitment by a DS⁻ practice; mathematics loses (at least much of) its generalizability when used in the supermarket just as shopping loses its local specificity when incorporated into the mathematics lesson or textbook.

I shall now assemble the theoretical elements that I have introduced in order to produce a description of contemporary school mathematics in relation to key characteristics of early and late modernity.

SCHOOL MATHEMATICS AS AN ACTIVITY

My analysis (Dowling, 1998) of the prominent U.K. school mathematics scheme, SMP 11-16, has revealed the following structure[6]. First, the scheme is explicitly differentiated according to "ability." Second, the scheme incorporates both general forms of myth in the forms of the myths of participation and reference. It will be recalled that the myth of participation privileges the public domain, whereas the myth of reference privileges the esoteric domain. Third, these myths are distributed such that there is a strong correlation between high and low ability on the one hand and reference and participation on the other. Fourth, there is a dichotomizing in respect of discursive saturation. Texts targeted at high ability readers—"Y" texts—employ specializing strategies that enable the explicit elaboration of a complex discursive system, that is, they constitute mathematics as DS⁺. Texts targeted at low ability readers—"G" texts—disrupt the discursive system through the deployment of localizing strategies that render the discourse context dependent. These strategies include the reliance upon standard algorithms. In summary, then, the high-ability, Y texts are constituted as transmission texts that construct a reader that is to be apprenticed into mathematical subjectivity. The low-ability, G texts are regulatory texts that objectify their reader, presenting a spurious apprenticeship into mythical or recontextualized domestic and other, principally DS⁻ practices.

The "Teacher's Guides" accompanying the G series explicitly objectify the student by constituting them as a problem, that is, the G student has particular needs in terms of practical work and slow pacing, has difficulties in handling complex situations, and has limited concentration. They also place considerable relevance upon (mythically) localized "relevance," thus:

> We hope that much in the G materials will act as a "model" for work of your own devising. Work on timetables, map-reading, shopping and so on is far more motivating form pupils if it is seen to be "real." Blagdon can never substitute for your own town! So

---

[5] I am using this term as a metaphorical recruitment from the field of information and communication technology. A push technology is a strategy increasingly deployed by dominant Internet presences to install unsolicited information or facilities on users' local machines.

[6] I have developed some of the terminology since the publication of this book. In particular, I have substituted the term *articulating* for *fragmenting* and have tightened my use of *generalizing* and its distinction from *specializing*.

in a sense, we hope that pupils never use some chapters in the books. They are written to be replaced by work which is firmly based on the pupils' own environment. Of course, replacement may not always be possible, but work based on the pupils' own school, town or surroundings may be added to a particular chapter. Some of the later topic booklets in the fourth and fifth years particularly can be thought of as models for a booklet based on the pupils' own environment. (G1TG, p. 8[7])

The Teacher's Guides accompanying the Y make minimal reference to the student and focus almost exclusively on their mathematical content. In general terms, the Y scheme is about and for mathematics, whereas there is a real sense in which the G scheme is about the student and about their lives. This differentiation is iconized on the front covers of the first books in the respective series. Book Y1 shows an enigmatic image, a contour map of a face; Book G1 shows pictures of a clock and two wristwatches. The Y reader is to be introduced to something new; the G reader gets only what they know already.

Finally, the two series of texts show a tendency to recruit as object voices occupational groups and settings that are differentiated in terms of social class. There is a sense, then, in which the SMP 11-16 scheme constitutes a device that translates objective differences in social class into differences in terms of pedagogic relations.

Now I have limited myself here to describing some of the results of my analysis of a single school mathematics scheme—albeit by far the most popular scheme in secondary mathematics in England and Wales. I do not claim that the results of this analysis will automatically generalize to all school mathematics schemes, far less to all practices in mathematics classrooms. They do, however, reflect a dominant polarizing tendency in mathematics education that apprentices one group of students to academic mathematics and regulates another in terms of what is intended to be practically relevant mathematics. It is the former group that is destined for comparative academic success, whereas the latter is most likely to be directed toward low-level vocational courses and comparatively early exit from schooling. Furthermore, the relation between academic success and social class of origin constituted in the SMP scheme continues to be a prominent result of schooling in many if not most parts of the world. The SMP scheme, then, may constitute too small a sample to justify strong claims about school mathematics generally. Nevertheless, its analysis is certainly illustrative of strategies that are operating far more broadly. I now want to consider some of the implications of this description of school mathematics in relation to current trends and developments.

CURRENT TRENDS AND DEVELOPMENTS

On the face of it, the simple differentiation into categories of successful and unsuccessful student that I have described would seem to be an entirely satisfactory state of affairs provided that one finds oneself in the successful category, that is, the privileging of a dominant social class would seem to be okay as far as members of that class are

---

[7]Blagdon is a fictitious town used in the G series.

concerned. However, this may not necessarily be the case. As I have argued, school mathematics distributes myths to both categories, not just to the subaltern. In the latter case, the myth of participation conceals the esoteric domain. The myth of reference also entails a dissembling. In this case it concerns the cultural arbitrariness of the practice into which successful students are to be apprenticed. Again, this is perhaps acceptable to the extent that mathematical success guarantees economic success, that is, that cultural capital realized as schooling is exchangeable for economic capital, borrowing Bourdieu's term (1984). It may be, however, that the guarantee is currently becoming weaker.

This suggestion is, of course, somewhat speculative, because the kinds of data on which we might draw always entail a looking backwards. Nevertheless, some structural consideration may be informative. In relation to DS$^+$ activities, such as mathematics, the university stands as the principal institution of elite cultural production and reproduction. However, over the past two centuries, the university has become progressively articulated with mass schooling in the constitution of an ideal education. We may describe mass schooling at its inception as being concerned with the transmission of certain basic skills and comportments that would optimize participation in the industrial production of 19th-century modernity and disciplinary systems of governance (e.g., see Gordon & Lawton, 1978; Hunter, 1994). With respect to the latter, a key feature seems to have been the development of self-regulation via panopticon-like tactics (see Hunter, 1994). In these early days, the elementary school was seen, by and large, as a terminal educational institution so that apprenticeship into the skills and comportments transmitted (not necessarily acquired) by the school was constituted as relatively brief. However, successive reorganizations and official and de facto raisings of the school-leaving age have produced a far more extended sequence from primary school through secondary school to higher education, which also has its sequence of degrees. Selection within this sequence is predicated upon successful performances at various key assessment points (nominally at ages, 11—increasingly, perhaps—16, 18, and 21). This scheme constructs the ideal educational career as one that culminates in a PhD, which may be described as an apprenticeship into the highest level of discursive saturation within a given specialism.

The educational institution, described thus, provides for a range of specialisms, so that the achievement of apprenticeship entails a navigation through points of choice. The institution is, to this extent, plural or "dialogic," in Bakhtin's (1981) sense. However, this navigation must be undertaken within a regime of regulatory assessment practices that achieve pedagogic authority. Educational success in general may be dialogic, but it is only experienced/achieved by specialization, so that educational success within any given curricular specialism is always single voiced or "monologic" and generative of, say, specifically mathematical subjectivity. Lower levels of discursive saturation and, in particular, manual activities are constructed as subordinate and, at the lowest level, default routes subsequent to academic failure.

The point, then, is that the ideal education takes a very long time, and, indeed, this is the nature of apprenticeship. The more highly specialized or localized the practice, the more extended the apprenticeship. For the ideal student, investment in educational cultural capital is of necessity very heavy. Furthermore, by definition, the level of specialization and/or localization that is achieved in apprenticeship is inversely related to the range of application[8]. The privileging of extended apprenticeship is thus inhibitive of mobility. In the current system, failure also takes quite a long time.

Now in public discourse, if not quite yet in economic practice, the new form of the division of labor is characterized by mobility, flexibility, risk, and the end of the job for life. As Bauman put it:

> In this world, not only have jobs-for-life disappeared, but trades and professions which have acquired the confusing habit of appearing from nowhere and vanishing without notice can hardly be lived as Weberian "vocations"—and to rub salt into the wound, the demand for the skills needed to practise such professions seldom lasts as long as the time needed to acquire them. Jobs are no longer protected, and most certainly no better that the stability of places where they are practised; whenever the word 'rationalization' is pronounced, one knows for sure that the disappearance of further jobs and places is in the pipeline. (Bauman, 1996, pp. 24–25)

The payoff for extended apprenticeship is, it would seem, decreasing rapidly. It may take a leap of imagination to envisage a time when an airline pilot might reasonably retrain as a general practitioner, but technological developments in both of these fields are proceeding apace. These developments are concretized in what I refer to as *operational matrices*. These are defined as infrastructural or procedural settings that incorporate the principles of their use such that the level of competence required by (and, therefore, the range of options available to) the effective user is minimized. An operational matrix is therefore to be understood as a disembodied analogue of competence. Crudely, the incidence of operational matrices within any given field corresponds to a transformation and disembodiment of forms of competence that would otherwise be embodied in skilled or knowledgeable subjects. An interesting (and, here, rhetorical) question would be what level of operational matrix is required to reduce the necessary training of pilots and G.Ps to the equivalent of that received by, say, bus drivers and first-aiders? I am not auguring for a generalized deskilling within societies but rather for uncertainty regarding the stability of any specific competence over the period of a lifecycle.

Indeed, initiatives by states and within educational institutions themselves seem frequently to be geared to the destabilizing of established apprenticeship tracks. I am thinking, here of, for example, the fragmenting of schooling via schemes such as the National Curriculum for England and Wales and the National Assessment and school inspection programs.[9] In U.K. higher education, course modularization, and the managerialism of academic work (e.g., see Smith & Sachs, 1995) is similarly

---

[8]This is not equivalent to a limitation on the potential range constituted by generalizing or articulation. However, as I have illustrated earlier in the chapter, the effect of the generalization of, say, school mathematics is a mythologizing of the practices that come under its gaze rather than the simple extension of its range of application.

[9]See Dowling and Noss (1990), for some discussion of the implications of the U.K. National Curriculum for the mathematics curriculum.

fragmenting. The widespread development of many doctoral programs to include a substantial component of short-taught courses at the expense of time available on the thesis seems likely substantially to reduce the specializing and localizing potential of schooling at the very highest level.[10] A dramatic initiative currently in play is the attempt by the South African state to establish a National Qualifications Framework (see, for example, HSRC, 1995). This scheme apparently seeks to codify within a single system everything that might conceivably be thought of as education, from everyday spoken interaction to a PhD.

Elsewhere (Dowling, 1998), I have described these bureaucratizing developments as signaling an order of practice that transcends the DS^+/DS^- polarization. This is not a particularly new order. It is certainly characteristic of 19th-century European state practices in population management, one outcome of which was the field of statistics (see Hunter, 1994; MacKenzie, 1981). In the latter half of this century, however, the order has been expanding with exponential rapidity via the development of information and communications technologies and what Manuel Castells (1996) refers to as the "network society." Within this bureaucratic order, all practices must be codifiable. These forms of practice are clearly consistent with my definition of an operational matrix. To recast, then, many current state initiatives within schooling at all levels and an increasing proportion of initiatives within schooling institutions entail the construction of bureaucratic operational matrices. The result, according to my schema, must be the reduction of levels of specialization and localization and the shortening of necessary apprenticeship. The abbreviation of de facto apprenticeship may take a little longer.[11]

I have argued that the construction by the institutions of schooling of the ideal student as following an extended apprenticeship into a highly specialized practice may be outmoded. I have also argued that current developments with respect to state practices in relation to schooling seem likely to weaken these institutions as institutions of extended apprenticeship. It remains to consider the implications of this state of affairs with respect to a way forward for mathematics education.

BEYOND MYTHS AND FRAGMENTATION

With particular regard to higher education, there is no shortage of calls for an end to bureaucratic domination and fragmentation of academic work and an implicit (sometimes explicit) plea for a return to the good old days (if such there ever were, see Smith & Sachs, 1995). In relation to school mathematics, I suggest that the good old days were, indeed, often characterized by the myth distribution that I have illustrated through the SMP texts—not so good, perhaps. Luddism never did have a future,

---

[10] Although the university is most obviously associated with DS^+ practices, not all that constitutes, say, mathematics or sociology is appropriately interpreted as DS^+. Many of the practical (and invisible to the public eye) skills associated with research, problem solving, and so forth seem to be far more context dependent and more likely to be achieved via localizing strategies.

[11] Although not necessarily. In some universities in the United Kingdom it is possible to obtain a "professional" doctorate via accreditation of prior experience following only a year's registration.

though, and we would be better advised to consider our options within the dynamic configuration of late modernity.

I have defined pedagogic relations as locating the principles of evaluation of potential performances on the transmitter side. In these terms, school is certainly a pedagogic institution. As such, the school produces apprenticed subjects—the successful students—and regulated objects—the less successful. If my argument holds, neither of these categories may have much of a future. Schooling also produces another category relating to the regulated objects. Less successful students are constructed by pedagogic practices, including textbooks, as objects. However, empirical individuals thus objectified do not necessarily constitute themselves in the same way as Willis' (1977) famous study illustrates. In formulating and elaborating their identities, these individuals establish alternative relations to pedagogy that challenge pedagogic authority. In other words, they lay claim to the principles of evaluation of their own performances. Here, then the relations are to be described not as pedagogic but as relations of exchange; the principles of evaluation are located with the acquirer.

The activities of Willis' "lads" are to be understood as acts of resistance in the face of attempts to impose pedagogic authority that would regulate them. On the other side, it would seem that the "earoles" had been successfully recruited as apprentices. The identity of each group is elaborated in alternative responses to the pedagogic strategies of the school. Both are, by my reckoning, redundant. The anachronism lies not so much in the failure of pedagogic authority to maximize its recruitment of the whole of each cohort, as the rhetoric of school improvement tends to suggest. Rather, it is pedagogic authority itself that is misplaced. In order to operate in ways that are consistent with the structuration of late modernity, the school will need to move in the direction of exchange relations at the expense of pedagogy. Ironically, those very initiatives, such as the National Curriculum in England and Wales, that are currently fragmenting pedagogic practice are themselves implemented in such a way as to crystalize pedagogic authority at the heart of state schooling. They deny mathematics a voice while nevertheless insisting that it be taught. It is, of course, hardly unreasonable to expect the social democratic state to be somewhat behind socioeconomic development.

As things stand, then, the greatest scope in late modernity in the United Kingdom, anyway, for a mathematics education beyond myths and fragmentation may lie beyond the state-regulated sector. On the face of it, this space does seem to be opening up as the U.K. state progressively withdraws from educational provision by encouraging private initiatives. I shall not pursue this issue here. Rather, I want to give some brief consideration to what a mathematics education for late modernity might look like in terms of my analysis here.

The shift that is demanded is from pedagogic to exchange relations, that is, the location of the principles of evaluation of performances moves toward the acquirer— the student, perhaps more appropriately conceived as a client. Now, under pedagogic relations, the evaluative principles are constituted primarily in terms of mathematics, as is apparent from my discussion of the SMP examples earlier in this chapter. This cannot be the case under exchange relations because the acquirer has no privileged access to mathematical discourse. Conventionally, the teacher deploys a range of classroom tactics in bolstering or mollifying pedagogic authority, most obviously (and possibly least effectively) coercion. Charismatic authority is certainly, in my experience, more effective but highly localized in terms of individual teacher qualities. Attempts to hook students' engagement with qualities supposed to be intrinsic to mathematics are also likely to be localized in terms of individual student identities. Both of these latter approaches, of course, carry the danger that existing classroom structures in terms of social exclusion will be reproduced or enhanced. An example of the former is Bob Connell's (1985) charismatic teacher, Jack Ryan, whose success with Australian working class boys depended on his complicity with White working class sexism. Accounts of the gendering of mathematical identities provide innumerable illustrations of the dangers of the "intrinsic interest" approach.

Alternatively (and to recruit Marx's crude but still useful distinction), the teacher may attempt to market mathematics on the basis of its exchange value as cultural capital or on the basis of its use value in nonmathematical contexts. I have already called into question the long-term reliability of mathematics as cultural capital exchangeable for economic capital. Claims to extramathematical use-values under pedagogic relations can be made, as I have illustrated, only via the deployment of the myth of participation. The only viable option that seems to be open, then, is to reconsider the possibilities for use-value evaluation under relations of exchange.

As I have argued, the problem with the myth of participation is that it employs (tacitly) mathematical principles of realization for extramathematical settings effecting a recontextualization of these settings as a mathematical public domain. To do otherwise would entail a more genuinely user-centred approach to the design of curricular units. I shall outline a simple model of such an approach that I have drawn from practice in commercial user-centred information and communications technology systems design.

The model might consist of five phases: research, design, evaluation, modification and implementation.[12] In the first phase, the unit designer engages in research in identifying a demand that might plausibly be met by deploying mathematical resources. Essentially, this phase concerns the potential validity of the unit in terms of use-value. This validity tends to reduce to zero under the myth of participation, as I have argued and illustrated.

The second phase is the main design phase. Here, the designer must consider resource needs in terms of mathematical and other knowledges and skills. In designing the unit, the designer must consider its potential reliability across a range of users and settings. In relation to users, the learnability and re-learnability of the unit is likely to be crucial. The latter refers to the extent to which the unit facilitates retention on the part of the user. In considering setting reliability, the designer is concerned with the flexibility of the unit across as wide a range of potential settings as possible. The

---

[12]I am grateful to Dr Chris Fowler of British Telecom, Visiting Fellow at the Institute of Education in 1999, for introducing me to some of the ideas and terminology presented in this section. The model that I am introducing here is a modification and simplification of one that he presented as a guest lecturer on a master's course that I run with a colleague in the area of Information and Communications Technology in Education.

evaluation phase concerns user trials. Here, the designer measures the validity and reliability of the unit in the terms that I have described by recruiting a sample of potential users. In the next phase, the design is modified on the basis of the results. Finally, the unit is ready for implementation or, perhaps I should say, marketing. It is important to remember that the market is the potential user, which is to say, the student and not, directly anyway, the teacher or potential employers. To the extent that schools, for example, may be considered to be analogous to retailing outlets, the curricular units will need to be packaged with that in mind.

I want to make three points about this approach. First, the issue of learnability, here, is not a function of the level or nature of mathematical or other knowledge that goes into the construction of the unit. This is because the use-value of the unit is measured in terms of its applicability within a non-mathematical setting. The situation is the same as is the case for, say, an Information and Communications Technology (ICT) system. The necessary level of user access to the principles of generation of the unit or system is dictated by what the user needs in order to make use of it. The basis of the design approach is user centered and not system-centered—the system referring to mathematical knowledge.

Second, the approach clearly opens up a key space for the activity of mathematics education. Curriculum design within the exchange relations model involves skills in research methods,[13] evaluation procedures, design skills, mathematical knowledge and knowledge in fields that may legitimately be associated with design (e.g., ICT, semiotics, sociology, and theories of learning, perhaps), and marketing. Because such a range of skills is unlikely to be embodied in a single individual, we should also add management to the list.

Finally, it will be noticed that what is omitted from the scheme is any provision for the reproduction of skills and knowledges such as those that I have just attributed to mathematics educationalists. This is because the reproduction of skills and knowledges necessarily entails pedagogic relations which, as I have argued, are inappropriate in the context of schooling in late modernity. I want to qualify this last point.

Traditionally, schooling is institutionalized as two components of variable length. The first component includes primary, secondary, and higher education and constitutes the ideal education to which I have referred previously. Students are recruited into pedagogic relations and follow a track leading to progressive levels of specialization and localization, or they are objectified and expelled at some point prior to doctoral level. I will refer to this as the academic component. The second component is vocational and ideally follows on from the point of expulsion from the academic component. The vocational component may be run within an educational institution, or the workplace, or a combination of both. Now the approach that I have introduced replaces the academic component with a (presumably far shorter) component organized on the basis of exchange relations—a market component. I would suggest, then, that the vocational component logically follows on from or runs partly concurrently with the market component.

---

[13]By way of my marketing my own product in this area, readers are invited to consult Brown and Dowling (1998).

Insofar as vocational education is centrally concerned with the reproduction of knowledges and skills, it must be based on pedagogic relations. It is here, I suggest, that mathematics education per se is properly located, alongside other academic and non-academic vocations. I suspect that I have introduced enough contention for one chapter (and I am also closing in on my word limit), so I will not extend my discussion of the vocational component but will move on to give a brief summary and conclusion.

CONCLUSION

My intention in writing this chapter is fourfold. First, I have introduced some of the elements of my theoretical language. My claim is that this language is potentially powerful in developing an understanding of the operation of texts and of social activity and social action, Second, I have introduced some of the findings resulting from the deployment of this language in the analysis of school mathematics as a social activity. Specifically, I have focused on my analysis of the U.K. secondary school mathematics scheme, SMP 11-16. In particular, I have illustrated the prevalence of myths in school mathematics. These myths conceal either the esoteric domain structuring of school texts—the myth of participation—or the culturally arbitrary status of the esoteric domain—the myth of reference. School mathematics as represented by the SMP texts distributes these myths on the basis of social class via the deployment of regulatory and transmission texts, respectively.

Third, I have given a brief analysis of current trends with respect to the implications of the dynamic configuration of late modernity for the institutions of schooling and of current developments in state initiatives in schooling. I have concluded that the ideal education as extended apprenticeship as constructed in the dominant institutions of schooling fails to meet the apparent demands of the current configuration. My analysis points to a need for a shift of emphasis from pedagogic to exchange relations in schooling. Ironically, and with most direct reference to England and Wales, the bureaucratizing activities of the state with respect to the state-regulated sector seem geared toward inhibiting such a shift. To the extent that my analysis is plausible, this may signal the ultimate demise of the state sector as a dominant force in schooling. One can envisage, perhaps, the progressive shrinking of the state sector to the point at which it serves purely as a catch-all for the economically most deprived groups. Again, ironically, the result would be the reinforcement of those very patterns of social exclusion that are the declared targets of the official rhetoric of state initiatives.

Finally, I have explored some of the implications of my analysis for a form of mathematics education practice for late modernity that moves beyond the mythologizing of current school mathematics and the fragmenting effects of the bureaucratizing state. As a result I have suggested or, perhaps, predicted the replacement of the current academic–vocational system by a market–vocational system. The latter emphasizes a user-centred approach to the design of curriculum elements and locates the reproduction of mathematical knowledge as such within vocational education.

As I have suggested, my proposals–predictions open up a crucial space for the activity of mathematics education. This activity must involve what we currently understand as academic knowledges and skills but also entrepreneurial skills with respect to taking risks and marketing. The proposals–predictions also raise a very serious challenge for mathematics educationalists: to the extent that it proves impossible to generate the kinds of useable curriculum units that I have proposed, what is left of the claims of mathematics to a central or indeed any place on the school curriculum?

REFERENCES

Bakhtin, M. M. (1981). *The dialogic imagination.* Austin: University of Texas Press.

Baudrillard, J. (1993). *Symbolic exchange and death.* London: Sage.

Bauman, Z. (1996). From pilgrim to tourist—or a short history of identity. In S. Hall & P. du Gay (Eds.), *Questions of cultural identity.* London: Sage.

Bernstein, B. (1996). *Pedagogy, symbolic control and identity: Theory, research critique.* London: Taylor & Francis.

Blau, P. M., & Meyer, M. (1971). *Bureaucracy in modern society* (2nd ed.). New York: Random House.

Bourdieu, P. (1984). *Distinction: A social critique of the judgement of taste.* London: RKP.

Bourdieu, P. (1990). *The logic of practice.* Cambridge, UK: Polity.

Bourdieu, P., & Passeron, J.-C. (1977). *Reproduction in education, society and culture.* London: Sage.

Brown, A. J., & Dowling, P. C. (1998). *Doing research/reading research: A mode of interrogation for education.* London: Falmer Press.

Castells, M. (1996). *The rise of the network society.* Malden: Blackwell.

Cockcroft, W. et al. (1982). *Mathematics counts.* London: HMSO.

Connell, R. W. (1985). *Teachers' work.* Sydney: Allen & Unwin.

Cooley, M. (1985). Drawing up the corporate plan at Lucas Aerospace. In D. MacKenzie & J. Wajcman (Eds.), *The social shaping of technology.* Milton Keynes: Open University Press.

Dowling, P. C. (1998). *The sociology of mathematics education: Mathematical myths/pedagogic texts.* London: Falmer Press.

Dowling, P. C. (1999, April). *Interrogating education: Texts, social activity and constructive description.* Plenary presentation at Centro de Investigação em Educação da Faculdade de Ciências da Universidade de Lisboa. (www.ioe.ac.uk/ccs/dowling/lisbon1999).

Dowling, P. C. (2000). 'A manifesto for Design and the Charismatic Intellectual' presented at Education for Social Democracies: changing forms and sites, Institute of Education, July 2000. www.ioe.ac.uk/ccs/dowling/c2000.

Dowling, P. C., & Noss, R. (Eds.). (1990). *Mathematics versus the national curriculum.* London: Falmer Press.

Durkheim, É. (1984). *The division of labour in society.* Basingstoke: MacMillan.

Eco, U. (1979). *The role of the reader.* London: Hutchinson.

Foucault, M. (1970). *The order of things: an archaeology of the human sciences.* London: Tavistock.

Gerdes, P. (1985). Conditions and strategies for emancipatory mathematics education in undeveloped countries. *For the Learning of Mathematics, 5*(1), 15–20.

Gordon, P., & Lawnton, D. (1978). *Curriculum change in the nineteenth and twentieth centuries.* London: Hodder & Stoughton.

Human Sciences Research Council. (1995). *Ways of seeing the national qualifications framework.* Pretoria: Author.

Hunter, I. (1994). *Rethinking the school: subjectivity, bureaucracy, criticism.* St. Leonards: Allen & Unwin.

Laclau, E., & Mouffe, C. (1985). *Hegemony and socialist strategy: Towards a radical democratic politics.* London: Verso.

Lave, J. (1988). *Cognition in practice: Mind, mathematics and culture in everyday life.* Cambridge, UK: Cambridge University Press.

Lave, J., Murtaugh, M., & de Rocha, O. (1984). The dialectic of arithmetic in grocery shopping. In B. Rogoff & J. Lave (Eds.), *Everyday cognition: Its development in social context.* Cambridge, MA: Harvard University Press.

Luria, A. R. (1976). *Cognitive development: its cultural and social foundations.* Cambridge, MA: Harvard University Press.

MacKenzie, D. A. (1981). *Statistics in Britain 1865–1930.* Edinburgh: Edinburgh University Press.

Matt-Blanco, I. (1988). *Thinking, feeling, and being: Clinical reflections on the fundamental antinomy of human beings and the world*. London: Routledge.

Nunes, T., Schliemann, A. D., & Carraher, D. W. (1993). *Street mathematics and school mathematics*. Cambridge: Cambridge University Press.

Piaget, J. (1995). *Sociological studies*. London: Routledge and Kegan Paul.

Roberts, J. (1995). Melancholy meanings: Architecture, postmodernity and philosophy In N. Wheale (Ed.), *The postmodern arts*. London: Routledge.

Saussure, F. de (1983). *Course in general linguistics*. London: Duckworth.

Smith, R., & Sachs, J. (1995). Academic work intensification: Beyond postmodernism. In R. Smith & P. Wexler (Eds.), *After postmodernism: Education, politics and identity*. London: Falmer Press.

Vygotsky, L. S. (1986). *Thought and language*. Cambridge MA: MIT Press.

Weber, M. (1964). *The theory of social and economic organization*. New York: The Free Press.

Willis, P. E. (1977). *Learning to labour: How working class kids get working class jobs*. Aldershot: Gower.

3

Breaking Political Neutrality: The Critical Engagement of Mathematics Education With Democracy

Ole Skovsmose
Aalborg University

Paola Valero
National University of Education, Denmark

The connection between mathematics education and democracy is neither obvious nor clear. Nevertheless, current curricular reform documents seem to agree on the fact that mathematics education can contribute to the achievement of the democratic ideals of society. For example, Curriculum 2005 (South African Ministry of Education, 1997) declares that the reconstruction of South Africa into a "prosperous, democratic country, free of discrimination and violence, and able to compete internationally" needs a new educational system and a new curriculum. The latter will provide the conditions for students to solve problems by making responsible decisions, to work effectively with others, to handle and critically evaluate information, to communicate effectively by means of oral or written language—mathematics is a relevant language that should be mastered, and to use science and technology effectively, critically, and responsibly (Brodie, 1997, p. 29). Mathematical literacy, mathematics, and mathematical sciences constitute one of the eight proposed learning areas that will contribute to the achievement of these general outcomes.

In a similar way, the Colombian General Educational Act of 1994 (Ministerio de Educación Nacional, 1995) proclaims that the educational system should emphasize respect for all human rights and for democratic principles, empower people's participation in decisions affecting them, and develop a critical, reflective, and analytic capacity that strengthens scientific and technological advancement and the improvement of living conditions. Mathematics, as one of the curricular areas that is more directly connected to the scientific and technological understanding of the world, plays an important role in the achievement of these goals.

In the United States, the National Council of Teachers of Mathematics (NCTM) Curriculum and Evaluation Standards, concerning how mathematics helps maintaining democratic values, also state that mathematical literacy should not be restricted to an elite of the population, but that every student should possess personal, technological, and thinking skills to apply mathematics meaningfully: "These are the prerequisites for understanding the world in which we live, for realizing the potential of technology, and for maintaining our system of government" (NCTM, 1992, pp. 5–6).

Finally, the Curricular Guidelines in Mathematics of the Danish Ministry of Education (Undervisningsministeriet, 1995, our translation) state that:

> The teaching [of mathematics] should help students experiment and recognize the role of mathematics in society and culture. In order to be able to take responsibilities and to participate in a democratic community, students should be able to understand the ways in which mathematics is used. (p. 9)

Despite the clarity of these formulations, mathematics education, as carried out in classrooms, often appears to be a long way from contributing to democratic life. Mora (1996) offered an example of how the teaching and learning of mathematics in Nicaragua and Venezuela still follow a "frontal imposition methodology" (p. 86s, our translation). Teachers are the center of an autocratic teaching–learning interaction, and students are passive listeners. In these two countries, mathematics is used as an obedience tool, coercing students to observe teachers' words and to respect them on the grounds of the prestige and status of their mathematical knowledge (p. 87). These practices, contributing to the alienation of citizens, are justified by the argument that "we [teachers] are automatically giving [the students] freedom of choice by giving them [mathematical] knowledge" (p. 89). Naidoo (1999) also showed how some novice teachers in South Africa establish a culture of regimentation and threat in the classroom. These cultures generate a strong connection between the reproduction of violent, unbalanced relationships between teachers and students, on the grounds of the mathematics that has to be learned in school.

It is evident that the connection between mathematics education and democracy is not a straightforward matter. First, an investigation of this connection implies an acknowledgment of the political dimension of mathematics education (Mellin-Olsen, 1987). This recognition should lead us to question the power of mathematics and mathematics education in society and how that power is exercised. Second, we should also interrogate the very same concepts of democracy and mathematics education. What is the meaning of democracy when considered in the educational arena and when put together with mathematics education? What is the meaning of mathematics education when linked to democratic aims in education and in society? Finally, we should query the implications of that connection for mathematics education research. What are the priorities of a research agenda that considers the linkage between mathematics education and democracy?

This chapter presents some literature in mathematics education addressing the connection between mathematics education and democracy. We put forward three theses about such a link: the thesis of *intrinsic resonance*, the thesis of *dissonance*, and the thesis of the *critical relationship*. Each thesis expresses particular assumptions about mathematics, mathematics education, and their connection to democracy. Democracy and mathematics education are discussed as open concepts and activities. This allows us to highlight potential scenarios for democratic development that could be approached in research on mathematics education and democracy.

IS MATHEMATICS EDUCATION DEMOCRATIC? SUPPORTING AND CONTESTING ARGUMENTS

In the literature addressing directly or indirectly the relationship between mathematics education and democracy, we find supporting and contesting arguments and evidence about that link. In what follows, we identify three different interpretations of the relationship between democracy and mathematics education.

Intrinsic Resonance?

Different justifications to include mathematics as a relevant subject in schooling and different goals to pursue its teaching/learning have been given through time (Griffiths & Howson, 1974). Many of these justifications are associated to ideas such as: Mathematics education contributes to the technological and socioeconomic development of society. It contributes to society's political, ideological, and cultural maintenance and development, and it provides individuals with prerequisites they may need to cope with life in its various spheres (Niss, 1996).

The rise and consolidation of the Western world and its scientization, industrialization, and technologization—processes closely interconnected and strongly dependent on mathematics—gave mathematics and its applications a central role in social development. As a consequence, mathematics education was entrusted with the function of supporting technological capacities at all levels of society. Although we have witnessed different attempts to reform the teaching of mathematics that pursue different aims, this basic justification of mathematics teaching and learning by association to technological development and, therefore, social progress and well-being has not changed in essence in the last 50 years. In 1959, the mathematician M. H. Stone gave the introductory lecture to the Royaumont seminar—the starting point of the New Maths Movement in Europe—and argued in favor of a mathematical education that could be

> clearly recognized as the true foundation of the technological society which it is the destiny of our time to create. We are literally compelled by this destiny to reform our mathematical instruction so as to adapt and strengthen it for its utilitarian role carrying the ever heavier burden of the scientific and technological superstructure which rest upon it. (O.E.E.C., 1961, p. 18)

The NCTM Standards, 30 years later, argue how, in a postindustrial society, the teaching of mathematics should provide citizens with a mathematical competence that allows them to understand technology and its application in the working place, and, therefore, be competitive at international levels (NCTM, 1992). In the case of the United Kingdom, Noss (1998) advocated the need for more complex mathematical abilities in highly technological working environments. In order for people not to be simple alienated adjuncts of technology, they need to "understand [. . .] basic principles; they will need to sort out what has gone wrong, what mathematical knowledge has been buried invisibly beneath the surface of their computers, and how to dig into it" (p. 7).

Mathematics education has also been connected with politics. By reference to the development of mathematics and democracy in Ancient Greece, some people have argued (see Hannaford, 1998) that there is a straightforward connection between mathematics education and democracy. Mathematics became the base of the *techne logos*, the rational debate that substituted old rhetoric discourses and that supported the new democratic polis. Through the precise, well-sustained, irrefutable discourse based on mathematical reasoning, citizens can present their arguments in public meetings and make their voices heard in decision-making processes. Mathematics education, then, is a means of giving the opportunity to all citizens, not only the elite, of learning this powerful style of argument needed in political life. Therefore, mathematics teaching empowers people: "If children are taught mathematics well, it will teach them much of the freedom, skills, and of course the disciplines of expression, dissent and tolerance, that democracy needs to succeed" (p. 186).

These arguments, supporting the contribution of mathematics and mathematics education to democracy, suggest that there is an *intrinsic resonance* between mathematics education and democracy. This thesis is based on the assumption that, due to the nature of mathematics, democratic interests and values can safely be taken care of by mathematics education. The relationship between mathematics education and democracy is harmonious in the sense that there is a match between the basic qualities of mathematics education and democratic principles. Naturally, pathological cases of mathematics education might be observed in order to avoid disrupting the harmony. However, when eliminated, the harmony is reestablished.

If an intrinsic resonance can be assumed, it is not necessary for mathematics education research explicitly to discuss the relationship between mathematics education and democracy. The attractive political qualities of mathematics education can be assumed a priori to any research program. Certainly, if we analyze most of the current research in mathematics education, we do not find many references to its role in hindering democracy. In a search (Spring 1999) in the MATHDI database, which has registered approximately 74,000 papers and reviews since 1977, we found only 28 items that have "democracy" as a key word. This lack is not surprising given that statements such as "[m]athematics and its specificities are inherent in the research questions from the outset. One is looking at mathematics learning and one cannot ask these questions outside of mathematics [. . .]" (Sierpinska & Kilpatrick, 1998, p. 26) are frequently used to define the scope and concerns of this field of study.

Internalism in mathematics education research emerges as a characteristic of this academic endeavor. It supports the development of research programs that safeguard their research questions from the "contamination" of society and politics. For example, the conceptual framework described by Brousseau (1997) specified the nature of the didactical system in terms of the interaction among a didactical agent, a subject, and a milieu and sets an agenda for more detailed research in such specificities. Didactical engineering (Artigue, 1995) constitutes a research methodology that focuses on the didactical system and that, therefore, produces internalistic research that eliminates considerations about democracy and other topics related to the broad social context where mathematics education takes place. Another illustration of internalism in mathematics education research is found in studies adopting radical constructivism. As an illustration, Glasersfeld (1991, 1995) invited investigations focusing on the individual cognitive processes of mathematical notions. No reference to economic, cultural, political, or social aspects of mathematics education is presented, nor is it encouraged. Such programs could, as a justification of this lack, refer to the assumption of the existence of a harmonious relationship between mathematics education and democracy.

Intrinsic Dissonance?

In the literature we can also find contesting evidence depicting the negative influence of mathematics in society. In its association with technology and science, mathematics has assisted contemporary warfare, insecurity, diseases, and the decay of the environment (D' Ambrosio, 1994). Through its participation in building models that support decision making in social affairs, mathematics is associated with the creation of risk structures threatening humanity. Mathematics has a power that escapes the boundaries of rationality and argumentation, and, through its applications, it has become one of the forces of social reflexive modernization (Skovsmose, 1998a, 1998b). As a subtle and implicit force, disguised and protected by the ideology of certainty (Borba & Skovsmose, 1997), the destructive power of mathematics has escaped the suspicions of citizens, scientists, and social scientists.

Furthermore, mathematics education has also played a negative role. Despite the democratic discourses that justify its permanence in school, mathematics education fulfils social functions of differentiation and exclusion. For example, Volmink (1994) stated that mathematics is a mystery to many and has been given the role of an "objective" judge, deciding who are or are not able in society: "It has therefore served as the gatekeeper to participation in the decision-making processes of society. To deny some access to participate in mathematics is then also to determine, a priori, who will move ahead and who will stay behind" (pp. 51–52). Instead of opening opportunities for all, mathematics education generates selection, exclusion, and segregation. A demarcation is established between those who have access to the power and prestige given by mathematics and those who do not. Bourdieu's (1996) observations on the role of mathematics education in the production of an elite, the "state nobility," also illustrates how mathematics education exercises a power by maintaining social filters for social mobility and ideological filters for understanding. Nevertheless, the belief in the goodness and intrinsic resonance of mathematics in regard to democracy legitimizes the stratification that mathematics education provides. This fact is not consistent with most conceptions of democracy as a social organization where people have equal opportunities and chances to choose in their life.

These arguments allow us to give another interpretation to the relationship between mathematics education and democracy. Mathematics as actually used and applied in society and mathematics education as actually carried out in many classrooms oppose democratic values. The thesis of *dissonance* suggests that mathematics education has established a systematic access denial on the grounds of people's gender (Leder, Forgasz, & Solar, 1996; Rogers & Kaiser, 1995), race (Khuzwayo, 1998; Stanic & Hart, 1995), language (Licón-Khisty, 1995), and class or socioeconomic status (Boaler, 1997; Frankenstein, 1995; Zevenbergen, 1999).

As a harsh reminder of antidemocratic historical episodes, we can refer to Mehrtens' (1993) study of mathematics and mathematics education during the Nazi period in Germany. The Association of the Mathematics Society (MR) advanced the task of legitimating the discipline "by deeply bowing to the new powers" (p. 239):

> One of the first tasks the MR set for itself was the production of a handbook with exercises that would show the value of mathematics to the new powers. The book included military, economic, and ideological topics of all kinds, for example: "It requires six million reichsmark to built a lunatic asylum; how many new homes, each costing fifteen thousands reichsmark, could have been built for this cost?" (p. 235)

Despite the belief that "natural science and mathematics are inherently democratic" (p. 241), Mehrtens reminded us that with Nazi mathematics this was not the case. He showed how mathematics supported technological advancements that later produced the aerodynamic theory and the calculations in the development of the V2 rockets and how it offered means for social control in the form of the statistics of inheritance. Furthermore, "mathematicians did offer these services without becoming outcasts of the discipline. To the contrary, they also found a market with the victorious powers, immediately after the war" (p. 241).

We should also refer to H. Verwoerd's statement in his address to the South African Senate in 1954:

> When I have control over Native education I will reform it so that the Natives will be taught from childhood to realise that the equality with Europeans is not for them [. . . .] People who believe in equality are not desirable teachers for Natives [. . . .] What is the use of teaching the Bantu mathematics when he cannot use it in practice. (cited in Khuzwayo, 1997, p. 9)

The paramount task of Apartheid's education was to make sure that Blacks did not have any access to the social ladder. Being excluded from mathematics also meant being excluded from the possibility of "advancement" in society. This observation led Khuzwayo (1998), in his study of the history of mathematics education in South Africa, to conclude that mathematics education in fact has served an "occupation of the mind."

If we accept that the dissonance claims are relevant, research in mathematics education should, on the one hand, deconstruct internalism and, on the other hand, provide alternative conceptualizations of the discipline. Concerning the first point, Apple

(1995) pointed out that most of the discussions about mathematics education have not included "critical social, political, and economic considerations"; they have limited their scope to the individual realm and, therefore, "lost any serious sense of the social structures, race, gender, and class relations" that constitute individuals; and finally, they have not been situated "in a wider social context that includes larger programs for democratic education and a more democratic society" (p. 331). This main criticism is seen in works such as Cotton and Gates (1996), Lerman (1998), and Vithal (2000).

Critical Relationship?

Many studies supporting the thesis of dissonance do not assume that it represents the only possible relationship between mathematics education and democracy. However, they show that certain forms of mathematics education produce dissonance. Therefore, we do not rely on the thesis of intrinsic resonance nor are we ready to accept the thesis of dissonance. Instead, we maintain that the relationship between mathematics education and democracy is *critical*, that is, that the relationship can go "both ways." We do not rely on any claim identifying an intrinsic connection between mathematics thinking and democratic ideals nor do we accept an argument excluding mathematics education from a struggle for democracy. Mathematics education (including research) can take many directions. Which direction it may take is an open question—a critical issue to both society and education. There is no internal logic that guides the development of mathematics education in either one or the other. A mathematics education that is committed to democracy cannot simply rest on the intrinsic qualities of mathematics or the conceptual constructs of the discipline itself. Instead, many social, political, economic, and cultural factors have to be seen as constantly directing and redirecting its development.

Mathematics, mathematics education practices, and mathematics education research face this critical situation when meeting democracy. First, mathematics cannot be assumed any more to be the "Queen of Sciences," sleeping on the limbo of neutrality, a-sociality, a-morality, and a-politicy. It cannot be conceived independently of the people who in a historical and social process created and have used it—nor can it be separated from the values, intentions, and interests of those people (Martin, 1997), nor can it be detached from the social frameworks where it grew or from the socio-historical structures that conferred it with power. Because mathematics nowadays is very different from what it was just 50 years ago, it is constantly developing and so are its social functions; it is important that mathematics education helps to identify the different possible social roles and functions of mathematics as society advances and becomes more complex.

Mathematics education practices are also challenged. The concept of mathematics education has to be reformulated. From a narrow definition covering the interactions among teacher and students for the learning and teaching of mathematics in a classroom context, we should move toward a broader notion including other types of social practices that have an impact on the learning and teaching of mathematics. Mathematics education practices should also consider, for example, general and curricular policy-making, mathematics textbook writing, institutional activities to organize mathematics education inside the school, and preservice, in-service, and graduate teacher education (Valero, 1999). With this more inclusive definition we could hope to grasp the complexity of mathematics education practices in society.

We consider that mathematics education has the potential to contribute to the development of democratic forces in society. However, such potential is not linked intrinsically to the nature of mathematics and mathematics education. It emerges from a combination of factors such as who is engaged in mathematics education practices, whose purposes they serve, which aims they pursue, when and where they occur, and why they are executed. As much as mathematics education could serve democratic interests, it has also served antidemocratic ones. The examples of Nazi Germany and Apartheid South Africa clearly suggest that the relationship between mathematics education and democracy is critical, highly critical!

This critical situation makes it relevant to suggest general aims for mathematics education, which support the development of connections between mathematics education and democracy. However, it is important to realize that such aims are without much descriptive value. Even if they guide mathematics curricula, the actual mathematics education may not necessarily support the development of democratic values nor have such aims much prescriptive force because what in fact prescribes the practices of mathematics education is that whole range of external factors considered as a justification for the thesis of dissonance. However, such general aims can be read as recommendations for struggling with critical issues—we see the current curricular guidelines from South Africa, Colombia, Denmark, and the United States as such recommendations.

As a result of this critical situation, mathematics education research is also challenged. The recognition of the complexity of mathematics education practices leads us to reconceptualize mathematics education research. Such an endeavor, whatever explicit formulation it takes, should open a space for considering the critical relationship between mathematics education and democracy as a relevant, legitimate research question. This implies, for instance, that psychologically oriented mathematics education research should be broadened, and it should bring to the center that critical relationship. Mathematics education research should also be put under critical scrutiny. Which theoretical frameworks are frequently used? Why? Which purposes does research serve? What is its connection to social transformation?

We have considered how mathematics, mathematics education practices, and mathematics education research are challenged when conceived from the thesis of the critical relationship between mathematics education and democracy. Nevertheless, we have not yet revised the meaning of democracy within this relationship.

DEMOCRACY: AN OPEN CONCEPT, AN OPEN ACTION

Perhaps the following dictionary definition of democracy approximates the intuitive understanding that most of us have. Democracy means "government by the people; a form of government in which the supreme power is vested in the people and exercised directly by them or by their elected agents under a free electoral system; a state of society characterized by formal equality of rights and privileges" (Webster's Encyclopedic Unabridged Dictionary, 1996, p. 530). This simple definition involves the ideas of government, election, representation, and formal equality. However, the idea of democracy is much more complex. Actually, it has been extensively discussed and theorized in political science (Held, 1987, 1993, 1995; Mouffe, 1992) and sociology (Giddens, 1994). This complexity puts us in a paradox. On the one hand, we cannot leave democracy as a concept with a tacitly agreed meaning. Each one of us may have a particular interpretation of the concept—and thus of our whole chapter! On the other hand, the very richness of definitions as well as of their applications suggests that democracy has an open nature. By this we understand that the concept can be specified only by related notions that are even less clearly specified than the concept itself. This means that, in one way or another, we cannot define the concept of democracy. Our way out of this situation begins by acknowledging that democracy is an open concept and, as a result, saying that we have no intention of providing any clear-cut definition of the concept. However, we can mention different aspects of the concept in order to locate it in a space where we can give it meaning in connection with mathematics education. We can also highlight some of the characteristics of the concept as potential notions that could provide an entry into democratic mathematics education.

Let us start by challenging the idea that democracy is an achieved reality. Wherever we find a society that claims to be "democratic," we can analyze the degree to which it provides an organization that establishes political, juridical, economic, and cultural values, norms, and behaviors aiming at furnishing a better living for the whole community. This means that democracy is not an actual reality, but an ideal to reach. This distinction is relevant in any discussion of democracy because it allows discerning between theoretical or normative formulations and the real conditions of social organizations. In this sense, democracy is "what we cannot have but, still, we can not stop desiring" (Zemelman, 1992, our translation).

Let us also contest the idea that democracy is a formal procedure of election or a "method for government" (Schumpeter, 1971). Currently we can see how "formal democracies" preserve and reproduce social inequalities and promote the imposition of particular interests over social ones. Even if we enlarge participation in decision making through the use of mechanisms such as plebiscite or referenda, governments cannot assure equity in society. It is evident that democracy needs to consider how social relationships determine the attainment of the ideal as a whole.

Let us defy the idea that democracy is mainly concerned with the guarantee of individual rights. In the liberal tradition, democracy is centered on the individual. The person has to be guaranteed the conditions for expressing her or his personal preferences and to pursue her or his own interests. This conception is definitely shaken when collective or third-generation rights enter the scene of social life. Nowadays we fight for the defense of the environment from catastrophes such as nuclear pollution, war, global illnesses, and so on. Providing these rights require a collective compromise of society as a whole. This change suggests that individuality as the great democratic value is questioned and collectivity is brought into the political scene (Mouffe, 1992).

Finally, let us also challenge the idea that democracy is only connected with formal organizations. Expressions such as the "government is democratic," the "school is democratic," or the "classroom is democratic" portray the belief that democracy is "external" to people, in the sense that it resides only in formal organizations and not in the everyday relationships among the people who constitute them. An organization cannot be democratic if the people in it do not share values such as respect, equality, social responsibility, and concern and if they do not act accordingly when relating to other members of the institutional community.

These challenges allow us to refocus our lenses and stop seeing democracy exclusively as a formal political organization located in the sphere of the State and in the sphere of the relationship between rulers and voters. We could focus democracy on the sphere of social interactions, where people every day relate to each other in order to produce their cultural and material living conditions. There, democracy represents a "way of life," an *open political action* carried out by people in "the complex intermeshing of local, national, regional and global relationships and processes" (Held, 1995, p. ix). Exploring democracy in this realm has two main justifications. On the one hand, we see that one of the current obstacles for democratic progression, both in developing and developed countries, is the lack of a cultural democracy on which the other political and economic levels can be sustained. Without the entrenchment of democratic values in people's actions democracy is incomplete (Fukuyama, 1995). On the other hand, we think that it is in this realm where democracy can offer interesting, unexplored connections with mathematics education understood as practices that are also located in the same sphere of social interactions.

Now, let us think about the different characteristics of democracy understood as an open political action. Such an action is undertaken by a group of people. It has a purpose. It requires communication. It involves understanding and development. Let us propose four notions that refer to each one of these four characteristics. (These are further elaboration of earlier work by Valero, 1999, pp. 22.)

Collectivity

People act as individuals to defend private interests. This is the kind of political action expected in the liberal tradition. Nevertheless, people are not free monads but social beings whose existence is deeply entrenched in the intricate, multilateral relationships established among people to create their material conditions of living. As Lave (1996) stated: "Being human is a relational matter, generated in social living, historically, in social formations whose participants engage with each other as a condition and precondition for their existence" (p. 149). Adopting this view allows us to see that human action is social and that democracy requires people sharing an awareness of the need of cooperating to make decisions and generate appropriate living conditions for all. Collectivity refers to that consciousness and to its application in the undertaking of social actions.

Collectivity is not possible without a sense of equality in a community. This notion here refers to the shared view that all the members of a community can actually play a role in a joint action. The community should tackle issues of inclusion—or exclusion—in order to assure an active participation of its members in achieving the goals of their political action.

Transformation

Political action has the purpose of change. This notion refers to the capacity of democratic collective actions to modify and improve the living conditions of those involved and of society in general. It is associated with a perception of "life not as a static state of being but as a process of becoming" (Aronowitz, 1993, p. 11), where people can transcend themselves by realizing what they miss and engaging in the enterprise of achieving what is missing (Freire, 1990).

Justice also comes to be relevant in this political action because, first, a motivation for action can be the transformation of unfair conditions of living and, second, the actual result of transformation should benefit all members of the community.

Deliberation

In *Long Walk to Freedom*, Mandela (1994) described the tribe meetings in the old Thembuland:

> Everyone who wanted to speak did so. It was democracy in its purest form. There may have been a hierarchy of importance among the speakers, but everyone was heard [...] The foundation of self-government was that all men were free to voice their opinions and were equal in their value as citizens. (Women, I am afraid, were deemed second-class citizens.)[...] The meetings would continue until some kind of consensus was reached. They ended in unanimity or not at all. Unanimity, however, might be an agreement to disagree, to wait for a more propitious time to propose a solution. Democracy meant all men were heard, and a decision was taken together as a people. (pp. 24–25)

For us, this fragment exemplifies part of the characteristics of collective and transformative actions, which rely on the capacity of the people involved to establish a dynamic, deliberative dialogue. Deliberation refers to the communicative process through which people consider attentively and carefully three things: the reasons or lack of reasons for people's preliminary opinions and judgments before actually making a final statement, the pros and cons of possible decisions before actually making them, and the benefits and losses of possible courses of action before engaging in them. Deliberation is a particular kind of social dialogue that empowers people to engage in problem-posing, decision-making, and problem-solving processes.

Coflection

Political action also requires that people engage in epistemic processes. Because transformative collective action based on deliberation is the focus, we would like to propose a way of knowing of the people who participate in this process. There is both an individual aspect of this knowing process—which we will not consider here—and a collective aspect—to which we will give special attention.

As individuals, human beings reflect. "Reflection" comes from the Latin reflexus, which has two components: the prefix *re*, which means back or again, and the word *flexio*, which means bending. Reflection as a whole, then, means bending back

(Webster's Encyclopedic Unabridged Dictionary of the English Language, 1996, p. 1620). A connotation of the word is related to the individual thinking process by means of which a person bends back on his or her own thinking, actions, or experiences in a conscious way. It is an individual process because the center of the process is the person.

As a part of a community, people coflect. Coflection—co-flection—is the word that refers to the thinking process by means of which people, together, bend back on each other's thoughts and actions in a conscious way, that is, people together consider the thoughts, actions, and experiences they live as a part of their collective endeavor, and they also adopt a critical position toward their activity. This is an epistemic process because it generates knowledge and understanding in the participants of the situation about the situation itself.

A POTENTIAL RESEARCH AGENDA FOR MATHEMATICS EDUCATION AND DEMOCRACY

The thesis of the critical relationship between mathematics education and democracy led us to describe democracy as an open political action including collectivity, transformation, deliberation, and coflection. Mathematics education, both as social practice and as an academic activity, also has an open nature. It could be developed in many alternative forms: as humanistic mathematics education, as ethnomathematics, as critical mathematics education, or as deliberative mathematics education. It is actually possible to deal with the critical relationship between mathematics education and democracy in many ways.

We suggest possible critical scenarios where this relationship can be tackled and where concepts such as collectivity, transformation, deliberation, and coflection can be explored. We see these scenarios as overlapping spheres, each one of which has a particular focus. A first scenario has as a center the content of mathematics education. The second builds around the relationships between teachers and students in the classroom. The third opens up to the sphere of the school organization. The fourth is located in the realm of national educational systems. The fifth highlights the issues of globalization. We mention some research and developmental experiences as we explore these critical scenarios. In this way we want to present some of the issues of a research agenda for mathematics education and democracy.

Critical Scenario 1: Interdisciplinary Mathematics

That mathematics education concerns mathematics seems to be a simple truth. However, this is not the case if we think of mathematics education as part of a democratic endeavor. This education concerns much more than mathematics. We could ask: What is the meaning of mathematics in an educational environment that does not have as an aim to educate pure mathematicians but citizens? Which are the competencies, abilities, and values that such an education intends to bring to these people?

There is a need to redefine mathematics in connection with the social context in which it operates and with the educational phenomena in which it is embodied. This double definition suggests a need to go further in noninternalistic, interdisciplinary attempts to tackle questions such as what is mathematics and what is its "didactical transposition" when conceived as a complex social phenomenon from which school mathematics emerges. Moreira and Matos (1998) exemplified how sociology may offer relevant insights into what mathematics and mathematics education are when seen as social practices.

There is also a need to consider that mathematical competencies do not operate in isolation outside school but as part of integrated units assembled in schooling. This implies interdisciplinarity among the school subjects as an important research issue. Competencies in one discipline interact—or counteract—with competencies developed in other disciplines. Even more, competencies development in a school setting interact—or counteract—with competencies formed and used outside the school. In particular, mathematics-classroom routines and competencies may be counterproductive for engaging, later in life, in a critical discussion of technological initiatives. Therefore, it becomes essential that the research in mathematics education pays special attention to interdisciplinary aspects of mathematics. For example, the development of competencies connected with collectivity and transformation as indispensable citizens' capacities should be tackled. In current social organizations, mathematics provides a basis for planning and realizing technological initiatives. Therefore, mathemacy should be a prioritized competence, allowing people to engage with mathematical questions and, simultaneously, with a critique toward the impact of mathematics in society. The association of mathematics education and critical citizenship should be both a theoretical and a developmental issue to keep in focus.

Within critical mathematics education different research and developmental experiences have been carried out. For example, Christiansen (1996) studied how mathematical modeling in high school can be a means for student-citizens to develop a general democratic competence, needed in highly technological societies. Frankenstein (1995) also showed a curriculum aimed at unmasking the way mathematics is used to support a particular interpretation and organization of society that reproduces class exclusion and exploitation. Although exemplary, the experiences of critical mathematics education still lack a more systematic development in school life, as Bohl (1998) suggested in his analysis of different tendencies of critical mathematics education. There has not been sufficient textbook writing to promote stable, critical mathematics education in practice.

Ethnomathematics has also inspired several research and development programs that address the connection between mathematics as an integrated cultural practice and mathematics as an institutionalized scientific system (Powell & Frankenstein, 1997). In the frame of the Brazilian landless peasants' struggle, Knijnik (1998) described a pedagogical project involving peasants, school students, and technicians experiencing an educational interaction where local and global knowledge are confronted and incorporated both inside and outside the school, in other words, in the life of the community (p. 188). This two-way interaction was achieved by focusing the educational experience on the practical and material needs of the students, the technicians, and the whole community.

Critical Scenario 2: Classroom Interaction

If mathematics education is concerned about democracy, then mathematics classrooms should represent democratic forms of interaction. As democracy represents collectivity, transformation, deliberation, and coflection, then all the activities happening between teacher and students and among students have to be in focus. Many mathematics classrooms are permeated by communication forms that assume the existence of an omniscient authority, represented, if not by the teacher, by the textbook or by technological tools. Communication, then, gets structured around a bureaucratic absolutism, according to which no particular justification for the different learning activities presented for the students is needed (Alrø & Skovsmose, 1996). It becomes important to pay attention to the social life in the classroom, including communication for the development of democratic discussions (Nielsen, Patronis, & Skovsmose, 1999).

A key issue for research in this area is to identify deliberation and coflection as resources for mathematical learning. These notions used to characterize democracy can also be developed as epistemic concepts, being part of a theory of mathematical learning. Burton (1996) offered an example of how a "narrative approach" to mathematics learning can offer a possibility for students to engage in the creation of meaningful, contextualized mathematical narratives, by engaging in a dialogue where critique and disagreement can emerge.

In a preservice, mathematics teacher education classroom, Vithal et al. (1997) presented a possibility for teacher-students and teacher-educator relationship. As a part of their teaching practice, teacher-students developed a series of teaching/learning projects inspired by a "social, cultural and political approach" (p. 261), integrating theoretical ideas about project work, critical mathematics education, and ethnomathematics. This kind of approach allowed the teacher-educator, the teacher-students, and their school students to engage in a reflective and deliberative learning and teaching experience. In this experience, Vithal (1999) found how democracy coexists with authority in a complementary relationship.

Critical Scenario 3: The Organization of School Mathematics Education

One aspect of democracy is people's involvement in deciding on the activities that they have to perform. This also applies to mathematics education, especially to its functioning inside the school. What takes place in the mathematics classroom is, however, determined by many factors operating outside it. We can, therefore, conceive the institutional system of mathematics education (ISME) as a critical scenario for democratic development—or for a blockage of democratic endeavors in education. The notion of ISME refers to the set of actors and factors and their relationships, which determine the functioning of the teaching and learning of mathematics inside a school (Perry et al., 1998). These actors are the teachers as individuals, the group of mathematics teachers in the school, and the school administrators, especially the headmaster and the coordinator of the mathematics teachers. The factors are connected to each actor as, for example, the teacher's professional knowledge, beliefs, interest, and reflection on his or her own practice are linked to individual teachers; the professional culture is associated with the group of teachers; and the leadership with the administrators.

In this scenario, we could pose different research issues. For example, Perry et al. (1998) showed how the ISME can reach a potential equilibrium for sustained change when a professional culture is consolidated and, therefore, collective values, views, and behaviors come to support both teachers' and administrators' practices. Jess and Valero (1999) illustrated how teacher education that can help to consolidate communication fora among mathematics teachers and administrators in the school is a necessary support for teachers to qualify and improve their practices. Valero (1998) also suggested that the way educational reforms are actually implemented in schools depends on how, within the ISME structure, democratic ideologies about mathematics and its teaching and learning cohere and struggle against other existing traditional ideologies. Collectivity and transformation then come to be relevant in this scenario and can be potential sources for research questions in the complexity of the functioning of mathematics education inside the school.

Critical Scenario 4: Stratification and Examination

On a national scale, mathematics education serves different functions, one of which is to provide public stratification of students. The huge effort put into the development of mathematical examinations, nationally and internationally, illustrates this fact. However, if mathematics education is governed by democratic principles of equity and justice, what is the meaning of examination and stratification?

It is broadly assumed that it is not possible to justify difference in "treatment" with reference to race, gender, religion, class, or any other similar category. Where did the idea that "ability" might be an exception emerge from? Examinations may have a role to play in education, but examinations need not be related to passing and nonpassing, or to public stratification. We believe that, if an educational system does set up examinations with the possibility of failure, and if public stratification takes the forms of streaming (into A, B, and C levels), then the link between mathematics education and democracy is broken.

It becomes essential for research and developmental work to address how mathematics education can ensure equity and justice. How is it possible for mathematics education, as a part of a national educational system, to react against the reproduction of social inequalities? For instance, Morgan (1998) posed the question of how to develop assessment with social justice concerns. Instead of setting assessment based exclusively on curricular objectives and methods, assessment should consider and set its criteria according to the signs of mathematical understanding developed by learning communities in practice. Could we think of alternative criteria that find inspiration in notions such as collectivity, transformation, deliberation, and coflection?

Such questions also concern the particular organization of the classroom. For instance: How can a learning environment that does not presuppose an "ability grouping" of students be provided? How can equity and justice be combined with diversity? How can a computer-based mathematics education make students' streaming irrelevant? This last question should be given special attention in research since it seems that the introduction of computers in the classroom is associated to new forms of stratification: Only A-level students can have access to computers—as some inspectors in England have actually recommended!

Critical Scenario 5: Globalization and the "Fourth World"

There is no doubt that the South African concern for setting up a new curriculum is essential. To engage everybody in mathematics education has a specific significance in a country where mathematics education has been an explicit instrument of apartheid. The emergence of the "network society" raises, however, new aspects concerning discrimination. As mathematics education is part of the general educational process that propels us into a network society, questions of stratification acquire a new significance. Globalization means that people are linked in many new ways and that we come to share the same network. At least some of us.

Globalization is not based on equity and justice. Castells (1998) defined social exclusion "as the process by which certain individuals and groups are systematically barred from access to positions that would enable them to an autonomous livelihood within the social standards framed by institutions and values in a given context" (p. 73). Social exclusion is not just exemplified by racism in South Africa. Any other society can provide examples of social exclusion, although only few cases are as gruesome as apartheid. If we consider the postindustrial, information, network society, then we face new sources of exclusion and new consequences of being excluded. The rise of the Fourth World—which is not exactly linked to geographic borders—represents an exclusion at a grander scale based on people's access to technology and computer networks. Who will then become the "untouchable" in this global society?

Against this background it is important to raise questions such as: Does mathematics education, as a global enterprise, serve the function of managing inclusions and exclusions from the network society? In what ways can research in mathematics education address the possibility that mathematics education may also be engaged not only with bringing people into the network society but also dumping the rest in the Fourth World? Collectivity and transformation, now in a global interpretation, should also be on the research agenda.

We are absolutely sure that more issues must be put on the agenda of a research program that acknowledges the critical relationship between mathematics education and democracy. We are also sure that such a program must not ignore the issues that internalistic research has dealt with because they have provided an insight and understanding of mathematics education practices. Nevertheless, particular aspects of mathematics education must be analyzed in such a depth that their external aspects also become clarified. This research agenda should pay special attention to the way collectivity, transformation, deliberation, and coflection, as key notions of sociocultural democracy, operate in at least the five overlapping scenarios presented here. If these issues are ignored, mathematics education research risks assuming an intrinsic resonance and becoming blind to the necessity of combating dissonance. Breaking political neutrality demands deliberate action to commit mathematics education to democracy.

ACKNOWLEDGMENTS

We acknowledge that we, the two authors, have contributed equally to the writing of this chapter. We thank Iben Christiansen, Thomas H. Jensen, Lena Lindenskov, Marilyn Nickson, Jeppe Skott, and Bettina D. Søndergaard for their comments on previous versions of this manuscript. This chapter is part of the research initiated by the Centre for Learning Mathematics, Royal Danish School of Educational Studies, Roskilde University, and Aalborg University in Denmark.

REFERENCES

Alrø, H., & Skovsmose, O. (1996). On the right track. *For the Learning of Mathematics, 16*(1), 2–8, 22.

Apple, M. (1995). Taking power seriously: New directions in equity in mathematics education and beyond. In W. Secada, E. Fennema, & L. Adajian (Eds.), *New directions for equity in mathematics education* (pp. 329–348). Cambridge: Cambridge University Press.

Aronowitz, S. (1993). Paulo Freire's radical democratic humanism. In P. McLaren & P. Leonard (Eds.), *Paulo Freire. A critical encounter*. London: Routledge.

Artigue, M. (1995). Ingeniería didáctica. In P. Gómez (Ed.), *Ingeniería didáctica en educación matemática. Un esquema para la investigación y la innovación en la enseñanza y el aprendizaje de las matemáticas* (pp. 33–60). México, D.F.: una empresa docente—Grupo Editorial Iberoamérica.

Boaler, J. (1997). *Experiencing school mathematics*. Buckingham: Open University Press.

Bohl, J. (1998). Critical mathematics education: An exploration of existing curricular materials. Unpublished masters dissertation, University of Winsconsin at Madison.

Borba, M., & Skovsmose, O. (1997). The ideology of certainty in mathematics education. *For the Learning of Mathematics, 17*(3), 17–23.

Bourdieu, P. (1996). *The state nobility: Elite schools in the field of power*. Cambridge: Polity Press.

Brodie, K. (1997). A new mathematics curriculum: Reflecting on outcomes in process. In P. Kershall & M. de Villiers (Eds.), *Third national congress of the Association for Mathematics Education of South Africa. Proceedings 1: General & primary* (pp. 26–41). Durban: AMESA.

Brousseau, G. (1997). *Theory of didactical situations in mathematics: Didactique des mathématiques, 1970–1990* (N. Balacheff, M. Cooper, R. Sutherland, & V. Warfield, Eds. & Trans.). Dordrecht: Kluwer Academic Publishers.

Burton, L. (1996). Mathematics, and its learning, as narrative—A literacy for the twenty-first century. In D. Baker, J. Clay, & C. Fox (Eds.), *Challenging ways of knowing: In English, mathematics and science* (pp. 29–40). London: Falmer Press.

Castells, M. (1998). *End of millennium. The information age* (Vol. 3). Malden: Blackwell.

Christiansen, I. M. (1996). Mathematical modelling in high school: From idea to practice. Unpublished doctoral dissertation, Aalborg University, Denmark.

Cotton, T., & Gates, P. (1996). Why the psychological must consider the social in promoting equity and social justice in mathematics education. In L. Puig & A. Gutierrez (Eds.), *Proceedings of the 20th conference of the International Group for the PME*, (Vol. 2, pp. 249–256). Valencia: University of Valencia.

D' Ambrosio, U. (1994). Cultural framing of mathematics teaching and learning. In R. Biehler, R. W. Scholz, R. Strässer, & B. Winkelmann (Eds.), *Didactics of mathematics as a scientific discipline* (pp. 443–455). Dordrecht: Kluwer.

Frankenstein, M. (1995). Equity in mathematics education: Class in the world outside the class. In W. Secada, E. Fennema, & L. Adajian (Eds.), *New directions for equity in mathematics education* (pp. 165–190). Cambridge: Cambridge University Press.

Freire, P. (1990). *Pedagogy of the oppressed.* New York: Continuum.

Fukuyama, F. (1995). The primacy of culture. *Journal of Democracy, Special Fifth Anniversary Issue* 7–14.

Giddens, A. (1994). *Beyond left and right. The future of radical politics.* Cambridge: Polity Press.

Glasersfeld, E. von (1991). *Radical constructivism in mathematics education.* Dordrecht: Kluwer.

Glasersfeld, E. von (1995). *Radical constructivism. A way of knowing and learning.* London: Falmer Press.

Griffiths, H. B., & Howson, A. G. (1974). *Mathematics: Society and curricula.* London: Cambridge University Press.

Hannaford, C. (1998). Mathematics teaching is democratic education. *Zentralblatt für Didaktik der Mathematik, 98*(6), 181–187.

Held, D. (1987). *Models of democracy.* Cambridge: Polity Press.

Held, D. (1993). *Prospects for democracy.* Cambridge: Polity Press.

Held, D. (1995). *Democracy and the global order.* Cambridge: Polity Press.

Jess, K., & Valero, P. (1999). Faglig forum for matematiklærere. Kommunikation, kvalificering og udvikling i skolen. In K. Jess & P. Valero (Eds.), *MAPUFU I Projekt. Matematiklæreres professionelle udvikling gennem forskning i egen undervisning* (pp. 4–17). København: Center for forskning i matematiklæring.

Khuzwayo, H. (1997). *Mathematics education in South Africa: A historical perspective from 1948–1994.* Copenhagen: Royal Danish School of Educational Studies, Department of Mathematics, Physics, Chemistry and Informatics.

Khuzwayo, H. (1998). Occupation of our minds: A dominant feature in mathematics education in South Africa. In P. Gates (Ed.), *Proceedings of the first International Mathematics Education and Society Conference* (pp. 219–232). Nottigham: Centre for the Study of Mathematics Education.

Knijnik, G. (1998). Ethnomathematics and political struggles. *Zentralblatt für Didaktik der Mathematik, 98*(6), pp. 188–194.

Lave, J. (1996). Teaching, as learning, in practice. *Mind, Culture, and Activity, 3*(3), 149–164.

Leder, G, Forgasz, H., & Solar, C. (1996). Research and intervention programs in mathematics education: A gendered issue. In A. Bishop, K. Clements, C. Keitel, J. Kilpatrick, & C. Laborde (Eds.), *International handbook of mathematics education* (pp. 945–985). Dordrecht: Kluwer.

Lerman, S. (1998). A moment in the zoom of a lens: Towards discursive psychology of mathematics teaching and learning. In A. Olivier & K. Newstead (Eds.), *Proceedings of the 22nd conference of the International Group for the PME* (Vol. 1, pp. 66–81). University of Stellenbosch.

Licón-Khisty, L. (1995). Making inequality: Issues of language and meanings in mathematics teaching with Hispanic students. In W. Secada, E. Fennema, & L. Adajian (Eds.), *New directions for equity in mathematics education* (pp. 279–297). Cambridge: Cambridge University Press.

Mandela, N. (1994). *Long walk to freedom.* London: Abacus.

Martin, B. (1997). Mathematics and social interests. In A. Powell & M. Frankenstein (Eds.), *Ethnomathematics. Challenging eurocentrism in mathematics education* (pp. 155–171). Albany: State University of New York Press.

Mehrtens, H. (1993). The social system of mathematics and national socialism: A survey. In S. Restivo, J. P. Bendegem, & R. van Fisher (Eds.), *Math worlds: Philosophical and social studies of mathematics and mathematics education* (pp. 219–246). Albany: State University of New York Press.

Mellin-Olsen, S. (1987). *The politics of mathematics education.* Dordrecht: Kluwer.

Ministerio de Educación Nacional. (1995). *Ley General de Educación. El Salto Educativo. Serie Documentos Especiales.* Bogotá: Empresa Editorial Universidad Nacional.

Mora, D. (1996). *Opinión de maestros y profesores sobre la problemática de la enseñanza de la matemática en Nicaragua y Venezuela.* Unpublished manuscript, University of Hamburg, Germany.

Moreira, D., & Matos, J. M. (1998). Prospecting sociology of mathematics from mathematics education. In P. Gates (Ed.), *Mathematics education and society. Prooceedings of the first International Mathematics Education and Society Conference (MEAS 1)* (pp. 262–267). Nottingham: Nottingham University.

Morgan, C. (1998). Assessment of mathematical behaviour: A social perspective. In P. Gates (Ed.), *Mathematics education and society. Prooceedings of the first International Mathematics Education and Society Conference (MEAS 1)* (pp. 277–283). Nottingham: Nottingham University.

Mouffe, C. (Ed.). (1992). *Dimensions of radical democracy.* London: Verso.

Naidoo, A. (1999). *The impact of the experiences of novice teachers on the mathematics curriculum at a South African college of education.* Unpublished doctoral dissertation, Aalborg University Center and Royal Danish School of Educational Studies, Aalborg and Copenhagen.

NCTM. (1992). *Curriculum and evaluation standards for school mathematics. Addenda series, grades 9–12.* Reston, VA: Author.

Nielsen, L., Patronis, T., & Skovsmose, O. (1999). *Connecting corners of Europe. A Greek-Danish project in mathematics education.* Aarhus, Denmark: Systime.

Niss, M. (1996). Goals of mathematics teaching. In A. Bishop, K. Clements, C. Keitel, J. Kilpatrick, & C. Laborde (Eds.), *International handbook of mathematics education* (pp. 11–47). Dordrecht: Kluwer.

Noss, R. (1998). New numeracies for a technological culture. *For the Learning of Mathematics, 18*(2), 2–12.

O.E.E.C. (1961). *New thinking in school mathematics.* Paris: Author.

Perry, P., Valero, P., Castro, M., Gómez, P., & Agudelo, C. (1998). *La calidad de las matemáticas en secundaria. actores y procesos en la institución educativa.* Bogotá: una empresa docente.

Powell, A., & Frankenstein, M. (Eds.). (1997). *Ethnomathematics. Challenging eurocentrism in mathematics education.* Albany: State University of New York Press.

Rogers, P., & Kaiser, G. (Eds.). (1995). *Equity in mathematics education. Influences of feminism and culture.* London: Falmer Press.

Schumpeter, J. (1971). *Capitalismo, socialismo y democracia.* Madrid: Alianza Editorial.

Sierpinska, A., & Kilpatrick, J. (Eds.). (1998). *Mathematics education as a research domain: A search for identity.* Dordrecht: Kluwer.

Skovsmose, O. (1994). *Towards a philosophy of critical mathematics education.* Dordrecht: Kluwer.

Skovsmose, O. (1998a). Aporism: Uncertainty about mathematics. *Zentralblatt für Didaktik der Mathematik, 98*(3), 88–94.

Skovsmose, O. (1998b). Linking mathematics education and democracy: Citizenship, mathematical archaeology, mathemacy and deliberative interaction. *Zentralblatt für Didaktik der Mathematik, 98*(6), 195–203.

South African Ministry of Education (1997). Curriculum 2005. http://www.nwtads.co.za/2005/need_change.htm.

Stanic, G., & Hart, L. (1995). Attitudes, persistence, and mathematics achievement: Qualifying race and sex differences. In W. Secada, E. Fennema, & L. Adajian (Eds.), *New directions for equity in mathematics education* (pp. 258–276). Cambridge: Cambridge University Press.

Undervisningsministeriet. (1995). *Matematik. Faghæfte 12.* København: Forfatter.

Valero, P. (1998). Ideology and power relationships in the teaching of critical mathematics within schools. *Skolefag, læring og dannelse i det 21. århundrede. Projektbeskrivelser* (pp. 129–133). København: Danmarks Lærerhøjskole.

Valero, P. (1999). Deliberative mathematics education for social democratization in Latin America. *Zentralblatt für Didaktik der Mathematik, 98*(6), 20–26.

Vithal, R. (1999). Democracy and authority. A complementarity in mathematics education? *Zentralblatt für Didaktik der Mathematik, 98*(6), 27–36.

Vithal, R. (2000). *In search of a pedagogy of conflict and dialogue for mathematics education.* Unpublished doctoral dissertation, Aalborg University, Aalborg, Denmark.

Vithal, R., Parras, J., Zuma, Z., Desai, S., Ramdas, R., Samsukal, A., & Gcabashe, E. (1997). Student teachers doing project work in primary mathematics classrooms In P. Kershall & M. de Villiers (Eds.), *Third national congress of the Association for Mathematics Education of South Africa. Proceedings 1: General & primary* (pp. 261–276). Durban: AMESA.

Volmink, J. (1994). Mathematics by all. In S. Lerman (Ed.), *Cultural perspectives on the mathematics classroom* (pp. 51–68). Dordrecht: Kluwer.

Webster's encyclopedic unabridged dictionary of the English language (1996). New York: Gramercy Books.

Zemelman, H. (1992). La democracia limitada y los excesos teóricos. In P. González & M. Roitman (Eds.), *La democracia en América Latina: Actualidad y perspectivas* (pp. 91–102). Madrid: Universidad Complutense de Madrid, Centro de Investigaciones Interdisciplinarias en Humanidades de la U.N.A.M.

Zevenbergen, R. (1999). Boys, mathematics and classroom interactions: the construction of masculinity in working-class mathematics classrooms. In O. Zaslavsky (Ed.), *Proceedings of the 23rd conference of the International Group for the PME* (Vol. 4, pp. 353–360).

4

Mathematical Literacy and Common Sense in Mathematics Education

Uwe Gellert
Eva Jablonka
Christine Keitel
Free University Berlin

Mathematics education has recently undergone critical reappraisal. Public debates about its value and importance in general education still give cause for controversy. The low levels of performance observed and measured in the mathematics classroom and the measured differences in achievement among countries (e.g., by TIMSS) are often used both as a justification for demanding a teaching practice that can be scrutinized for successful output by means of standardized tests and for emphasizing basic skills. At the same time, the mathematics curricula are strongly criticized by some people for not providing the skills appropriate for the 21st century. Indeed, advances in technology are increasing the level of knowledge necessary for the solving of problems by means of this technology. Consequently, such abilities as using technological aids, validating results, searching for information, and representing data are gaining importance at the expense of skill development.

On the other hand, for many academic mathematicians, the most powerful aspect of mathematics is the fact that it has little to do with reality. Mathematics is appreciated for being beyond and above real constraints and restrictions and as the most formal art of pure thinking and playing. For most laypersons, therefore, it is a mystery that mathematics is an efficient and effective device for solving real problems. This contradictory message is still transmitted to our pupils in the mathematics classroom where they have to apply mathematical concepts and operations to real situations but do not understand how this application works. In the mathematics classroom, it is rarely asked why mathematics is useful, what the relationship between mathematics and reality is, and how we perceive reality.

In this chapter we first raise the issue of what *mathematical literacy* means. We argue that different conceptions of mathematical literacy are related to how the relationship among mathematics, reality, and society is conceived. As an introduction, therefore, we briefly discuss how mathematics and society are linked. In the second main section of this chapter we consider commonsense conceptions of mathematics. The conclusion connects the two topics by introducing the concept of reflectiveness.

MATHEMATICS AND SOCIETY

In highly technological societies mathematics is used within technological processes as a means for communication, extrapolation, justification, control, and organization. Mathematical structures can serve both as a representation in search for a description or even a "cause" (a mechanism accounting for it) of an observed fact or as a presentation in constructing a design for something that does not already exist or for developing a plan for an action. Mathematical modeling is not restricted to physical reality, be it natural or human. It is also directed toward social systems, psychological phenomena, procedures of distributing power or money, and other regular forms of social interactions. Within technological processes the descriptions of reality transform themselves into that reality that they have been invented to describe so that it is not possible to imagine how reality might have appeared before. A major part of what our pupils use to take as naturally given and "objective" constraints, the factual circumstances and situations in which they grow up (their "natural environment"), are artefacts resulting from this process. However, when living and dealing with them, we are rarely aware of that. The construction of all those mathematical models was originally developed for very specific purposes that might have vanished while still effective.

A cyclic process is involved here. Technical and mathematical expertise leads to large-scale economic and technological change. In turn, the increasingly technologically dominated environment increases the level of technical and mathematical expertise required to sustain and develop it. Society is thus becoming increasingly formalized and mathematized.

However, although the objective importance of mathematics in our society has increased considerably, the importance of much of the mathematics taught in schools to individual pupils has rapidly decreased. Apart from the work of a minority of specialists, the explicit mathematical operations associated with particular occupations, trades, and daily life in general are now undertaken by a variety of machines and technological devices. The mathematical skills of the so-called "basics," which constitute the common core of all mathematical education in elementary schools, have been rendered superfluous by the advent of computers and pocket calculators. An increasing mathematization of our society is complemented by an increasing demathematization of its individual members.

As a consequence of this development, it seems that the argument that more people need to learn more mathematics in a more successful way is based more on common sense than on rational reason or on justifiable evidence. This includes a plea for focusing on a new determination of what constitutes basic mathematical skills and on new and effective teaching methods including technological devices.

MATHEMATICAL LITERACY AND MATHEMATICS EDUCATION

We use the term *mathematical literacy* as a metaphor referring to well-educated and well-informed individuals. In surveying some of the major conceptions designed to deal with the new demands for mathematics education, we look for essential components of a conception of mathematical literacy from a general education perspective. In short, we want to discuss which mathematical concepts, methods, experiences, and opportunities can be seen as essential components of mathematical literacy for civic responsibility, for personal self-fulfillment, and for social change in an increasingly complex society. We regard it as crucial not being obliged to accept those assertions of experts that are based on mathematical models but rather develop a comprehensive picture of mathematics and its social role.

The following issues form the structure of our discussion:

- To what extent is mathematical literacy related to the teaching of mathematical concepts and structures?
- What is the role of mathematical applications for mathematical literacy?
- What is the value of mathematical literacy for social critique?
- To what extent do ethnomathematical practices contribute to mathematical literacy?
- How far is democratic competence based on mathematical literacy?

Mathematical Literacy: By Progressive Mathematization and Theorizing Mathematics

The failure of a curriculum based upon mathematically fundamental structures and their embodiments in providing a basis for flexible understanding and application of the concepts is to be found at all levels of mathematics education. Instead, learning mathematics in context, mathematical modeling, and applications in classroom practice have been promoted in many countries of the world (Blum, Niss, & Huntley, 1989; Burckhardt, Keitel, & Malone, 1989).

Gaining a level of mathematical understanding that goes beyond the minimal abilities of calculating, estimating, gaining some number sense, and basic geometrical understanding and that nevertheless still provides a mathematics that is useful for all does seem possible by seeing the power of mathematics in its potential of abstracting from concrete realities by generating concepts and structures for universal application. Hence, the skills necessary for using mathematics as a flexible tool are identified with the ability of behaving mathematically. This ability is to be developed by experiencing mathematical modes of thinking, such as searching for patterns, classifying, formalizing and symbolizing, seeking implications of premises, testing conjectures, arguing, thinking propositionally, and creating proofs and all at increasingly higher levels of mathematical abstraction (Mason, 1988). Curricula based on this approach, especially those for primary school level, use (not so real) world situations as a starting point for mathematization. The mathematical models of the situations in the course of learning eventually become prototypical models of mathematical concepts and structures (De Lange, 1993; Freudenthal, 1991; Gravemeijer, 1994). The content of the problems is not as important as the mathematical productiveness of the questions that can be asked. In comparison with a more traditional curriculum that focuses on mathematical structures, this approach is thought to be more promising with respect to developing the ability of applying and using mathematical concepts.

Mathematical modes of thinking are seen as matching the "natural" activities of the students. This is underpinned by results from cognitive psychology or metaphors of evolutionary biology that explain the logico-operational level of mathematical thinking as a "functional organ" that has emerged in adaptation to the environment. Consequently, fundamental mathematical modes of thinking are conceived of as an extension of commonsense and native intuitive interpretations and indeed as generally culture free and not depending much on communication and conventions. However, the tension between informal, practical mathematics and formal, academic mathematics and associated values is not easily resolved. A prerequisite for thinking and acting mathematically at a higher level is the introduction into the symbolic language of mathematics for representing and communicating abstract concepts. This goes far beyond natural language and depends highly on conventions. The application of mathematical structures to certain properties of material or social phenomena often goes against common sense or leads to obvious results that can be obtained by another (more commonsense) method. As a consequence, many students end up struggling with symbolism, lose interest, and fail to appreciate the mathematical mode of thinking. Even those who appreciate the richness and beauty of mathematical structures are often not able or willing to "see" these structures elsewhere.

Mathematical Literacy: By Teaching Modeling and Applications

Another approach to teaching useful mathematics may be characterized as treating mathematics and science mainly as possible resources, as "toolboxes" for solving (individual or social group) problems. This is facilitated by using computers for simulation, for graphical representation, and for solving equations. The problems are not contrived but they are, as far as possible, "real and direct problems in real situations" which are of direct concern to students' interests and the environment—at least it is postulated as such in the philosophy of this approach.

Giving pupils the opportunity of experiencing the process of applying mathematics is certainly an essential contribution to developing methodological insights into the process of mathematical modeling. However, are these experiences exemplary of the ways mathematics is used in our society? Do such experiences really show the difficulties of mathematical modeling processes, or is there not a risk of promoting a biased image of the usefulness and direct applicability of mathematics in the form of unjustified evaluation or exaggerated optimism? An analysis of proposed or documented school projects shows that many are based on unreliable measurements and unreasonable assumptions. Moreover, many lack validation and encourage a biased interpretation of the results (Jablonka, 1996). Are the goals of this conception of mathematical literacy merely aiming at appreciation for mathematics and its benefits or also at the ability of critically evaluating applications and models developed by experts that affect society?

Mathematical models might have different epistemological underpinnings. Modeling can hardly be described as a straightforward activity because problem specification, observation, classifying, identifying relevant factors, hypothesizing, choosing assumptions, interpreting, and other subprocesses are mutually related and driven by the aims and underlying interests and intentions of those who are the inventors of the models. Evaluation takes place throughout the whole process. The mathematical concepts and methods at hand, the technical means (measuring devices, procedures for collecting data, calculators, computers), including rules for their use, domain-specific conceptual frames, or (scientific) theories, all influence the form of the model. Thus, the model is by no means fully determined by the constraints of the situation. Depending on the aims and underlying interest, there may result qualitatively different descriptions of the same "reality," none of which are just a refinement or generalization of the other.

The theoretical justification of teaching mathematics by applications and modeling tends to be reduced to a simplistic description of the process of applying mathematical models, a description that is underpinned by a utopian view of the power of mathematics to resolve complex and global problems, such as population growth, flood, storms, epidemics, and other identifiable discomforts and constraints of life (Banu, 1991; Ormell, 1993). The problem of using mathematics as a means of solving such problems that themselves may be partly caused by the application of mathematical technology is not reflected within these conceptions. Thus, this very philosophy of developing mathematical literacy by application and modeling may also serve as justification for a higher qualified workforce and for introducing a vocational aspect into general education. The difference between these conceptions only consists of the problems to which mathematics is applied. This is shown by a similar discussion at university level, where diverse courses in mathematics as a service subject are critiqued as theory laden, difficult, and meaningless. Academics from other disciplines often do not value the esoteric research of modern academic mathematics. To differentiate between the demands of teaching mathematics as a service subject (for future scientists, engineers, biotechnologists, computer specialists, and other professional careers relying on mathematics) and the demands of mathematically literate citizens a different perspective is needed. An external view of mathematics and mathematical modeling is required to develop deeper insights into the relationship among economic and technological competitiveness, social progress, and the development, application, and educational functioning of mathematics (Bishop, 1989; De Vore, 1987).

Mathematical Literacy: By Using Mathematics as a Means for Social Critique

Sometimes, the mathematical skills of daily life are considered just as "survival mathematics." However, this view underestimates the importance and the power of the concept of abstraction. A certain type of abstraction takes place in the brain and, thus, offers an enormous flexibility. It is possible to create an image of the world and then test a possible action in this imaginary universe without having to be afraid of any consequences. The power of mathematics lies in the representation of abstract trial and error, which is conducted as a scientific enterprise. It is, therefore, a filter between the inner and outer world and, as such, a world between them.

However, mathematics presupposes abstractions when creating and using abstract or formal concepts. These presupposed abstractions are not abstractions in the brain, but in action. For instance, the abstraction of the exchangeable value of goods is performed in trading situations. This type of abstraction might be called a real abstraction. Mathematics, then, reflects on such real abstractions and constructs abstract or formal concepts, for example, calculation models, that might be called thinking abstractions. A thinking abstraction, therefore, is a reflection of a real abstraction. Basic mathematical abstractions (particularly those such as the number system) can be explained by reference to real abstractions. These real abstractions are taken for granted because they are socially established (Damerow, Elwitz, Keitel, & Zimmer, 1974; Sohn-Rethel, 1970).

In contrast to the real abstraction that is encapsulated in the actions of people, it is the thinking abstraction that offers much more flexibility. Consequently, becoming conscious about the functioning of mathematical abstractions is a means for empowering the individual user of everyday mathematics.

The process through which basic mathematical skills are acquired and the power relations between groups engaged in schooling make these skills appear to be neutral and value free. However, they are always related to prefabricated structures (real abstractions) that make it possible to use them and that are socially established, that is, created by interests and intentions.

An argument against neutrality of basic mathematical skills was made by Mellin-Olson (1989). He argued that, if the problems used in school mathematics do not reflect the interests and practices of the pupils, especially of those already marginalized, but only permit them to reproduce school knowledge, an unhealthy relationship to school learning will be developed. A similar argument was launched by Gerdes (1985). School knowledge will not be used to communicate the pupils' interests. Thus, mathematics will not be seen as a tool to transform reality by thinking abstractions. It is argued further that using basic statistical data and asking statistical questions can change people's perceptions and help them to question the assumptions of how a society is structured (Frankenstein & Powell, 1989). On the other hand, an overemphasis on numerical information is seen to obscure the reality of peoples' lives and to divert attention from ways in which those lives might be changed. In essence, the argument here is that the extensive use of quantitative methods shifts debates about the effect of system deficiencies to a technical, "scientific" debate about the appropriateness of quantitative data or about the ways in which those quantitative data are being handled.

It is therefore important to develop the ability and the confidence to analyze data about issues of importance to oneself, which are presented by others, allied with the knowledge to make decisions about the kind of numerical data needed to analyze these issues and the skills to research and use statistical information (Frankenstein, 1989).

Mathematical Literacy: By Using Ethnomathematics as Cultural Critique

The culturally alienating effect of mathematics education in school is extremely destructive in nonindustrialized countries that have imported mathematics and science curricula. It is not appropriate here to discuss whether the problem-solving capacity of mathematics and science can be linked directly with economic performance (see the argument of the "overselling" of mathematics, science and technology by Nelkin, 1987, and Chapman, 1991). However, it is obvious that the import of mathematics education, in the form of the curricula, textbooks, techniques, tests, and so on, often involves a break in cultural identity and can generate an ambiguity in an individual's sense of self. People in developing countries may adopt, uncritically, Western thinking in mathematics and science and thereby abandon some of their cultural identity, or they may come to regard themselves as lacking in mathematical ability and retain their involvement with "protomathematical" or "paramathematical" activities judged to be different from and "inferior" to the "real" mathematics or science.

A major point is that the dominating concept of number in Western school mathematics best illustrated and propagated by the National Research Council, 1989, publication Everybody Counts, which mainly correlates with Western economic concepts and practices and Western mathematics, science, and technology has to be adopted when mathematics curricula have been imported (Keitel, 1993). When this occurs, ethnomathematical practices and problem-solving strategies that have successfully been employed for a long time are labeled as outdated and in need of replacement by more advanced methods and technologies. Ethnomathematics, therefore, confronts modern mathematics. Formal school mathematics is experienced as contrary to, and a distortion of, street or rural mathematics.

Ethnomathematics, a term first defined by D'Ambrosio (1985) became a subject of scientific debate when research on difficulties with learning school mathematics in nonindustrial countries provided fascinating insight into mathematical practices outside school. Studies of "street mathematics" or "rural mathematics" as examples of ethnomathematical practices were initially concerned to identify differences or similarities between in and outside school mathematics in order to facilitate school learning (Carraher, 1988; Carraher, Carraher, & Schliemann, 1984). Striking features were identified, which have been characterized as a conflict between the manipulation of quantities and the manipulation of symbols. These symbols are bound and restricted to the context in which they are used, in contrast to the generalized, abstract, and decontextualized symbols that are the focus and goal of school mathematics. Ethnomathematics proposes to give a basis to the teaching of school mathematics in problems and contexts that are familiar and meaningful in the cultural environment of the pupils. Researchers are anxious to avoid the impression that mathematics is a rigidly defined field of human activity. Instead, they are seeking to emphasize the different mathematical approaches of different cultures and the diversity of mathematics found within and throughout those cultures.

Mathematical practices within classrooms obviously differ considerably from the mathematical activities described as ethnomathematics. Although the former exists mainly to promote the learning of mathematics, the latter is intimately bound to its setting as well as to the content of the activity. Although some (formal or symbolical) mathematics can be identified in ethnomathematical practices—by analyzing and considering them from a distance (Gerdes, 1996)—those engaged in these practices do not necessarily recognize this. Mathematical signs within these practices have references to a mathematics that is inseparable from the specific context and purposes (e.g., interest rates or prices of certain goods) and its associated goals (buying and selling, quantifying objects, measuring products, etc.).

Ethnomathematics does not amount to a set of general thinking tools because the mathematical activity is "locked" into the practice, of which it is part, and it cannot function as a tool or basis to act as a critique of that practice itself. Being critical toward the use of mathematics in the context of practice requires viewing that practice from an external perspective in a way that allows the mathematics to be distinguished in some way from the remaining aspects. It is this complete integration of mathematical activity with practice that marks it as distinct from the mathematics of the classroom.

However, ethnomathematics can serve well as a means for critically confronting the formal mathematics because it can be described as a technology and, as such, be regarded as a culturally determined version of implicit mathematics (cf. next section). Ethnomathematics does not, of course, automatically lead toward formal mathematics—on the contrary, it rather excludes such mathematics. However, studying and analyzing ethnomathematical practices and comparing them as culturally different "technologies" make it possible to identify "frozen" (Gerdes 1985) or "crystallized" (Chevallard 1985) mathematics.

Mathematical Literacy: By Analyzing and Evaluating the Social Use of Mathematics

In an already highly mathematized society the definition of democratic competence has to be extended. If democratic competence involves an ability to judge and act competently, then it cannot rely on common sense alone. It must also involve the competence of reflective thinking to analyze and evaluate technological developments and to reconstruct the use of mathematics and to explicate the interests and intentions that brought them into existence (Skovsmose, 1992).

Democratic competence has to compensate for the increasing shift in society from democracy to "expertocracy." The mechanisms of social control in a democracy are increasingly replaced by those of an expertocracy within which lay people are unable to contribute to the expert discourse. Experts are, for the most part, defined by their strict specialization. However, do these specialized experts understand the full range of social uses of mathematics and are they aware of the processes involved in the development of implicit mathematics? For whom and for whose benefit is mathematics created and used?

The concept of implicit mathematics refers to the process of incorporating thinking abstractions into material and social technologies that provide substitutes for abstraction processes used to determine and sustain social processes. The process of mathematizing society via thinking abstractions on the basis of real abstractions—which began as intentions and interests—eventually acquires a somewhat self-contained and automatic character that by its nature can become undemocratic. The interaction of technology and the organization of labor, of daily life, and of social processes produces patterns that are best described as implicit mathematics. At checkout counters the bill is automatically recorded. Income tax systems, examination grades, IQ tests, life insurance, switching systems, credit cards, zip codes, proportional representation or point systems (for mortgages, for civil service appointments, for driving offences, for military demobilization), and index systems for documents, for measurement of living standards as well as rating systems all involve implicit mathematics (Davis 1989), as do the modern technologies (e.g., telecommunication, biotechnology, robotics, and microelectronics).

There are many other more obvious relationships between technology and mathematics. Mathematics is a language and a methodology for scientists and engineers. Such a language may be seen as a prerequisite of technology. For educational purposes, therefore, one could explore a particular technology or a technological artefact and try to trace back the mathematical theories and methods that underpin its construction and use. An analysis of this kind is sometimes undertaken to identify the "new basics" upon which to construct various courses at school or university level. This approach presents the relationship between mathematics and technology as an instrumental one and as such is seemingly one-sided: if the big "mathematical toolbox" does not provide enough assistance, then the mathematician is asked to devise a suitable tool to address the special problem in hand. However, it is also the case that technology presents mathematicians with new problems, which themselves constitute a foundation for further mathematical research, and mathematical research itself is dependent on technology.

Technology can be seen as the theory underlying technological artefacts such as tools and machines and, consequently, is independent of social and individual needs, goals, applications, and consequences. On the other hand, technology can also be regarded as an essential social undertaking, providing the material means for the exchange process between human beings and the natural world, offering new possibilities to society for dealing with organizational issues and reproducing social patterns and routines—so-called "petrified social structures"—which can be formalized and simulated by machines. Consequently, technology can be interpreted as a prerequisite and driving force for social development. Moreover, social structures and organizations can be viewed as manifestations of possibilities made available by technology. Embedded in this interpretation is the idea that mathematics is seen as the driving force behind both technological and social development and change. However, technology and mathematics are human activities executed in a social environment and are influenced by social structures. As a result, mathematics itself is shaped and determined by forces external to the "pure" discipline itself, and neither mathematics education nor technology can be discussed independently of the relevant social contexts and conditions.

The growing influence of technology on society will increasingly require educational aims to be rethought. However, before being in a position to argue for specific educational strategies, we need to understand what might be involved in critiquing the formalized techniques integrated in the powerful information technologies available to us. What does it mean to critique the use of technology as materialized mathematics? If mathematics is deemed an essential—although not the only—precondition of technology, then mathematics teaching and learning are equally prerequisite for understanding, reconstructing, or developing technology and for making judgments about its use or abuse. However, what kind of mathematics education is required to promote and sustain this approach?

One can only partly develop an understanding of mathematical technology by referring to mathematics itself because the means-and-ends-relation stringently requires knowledge about both the objective and subjective contexts of this relation. Hence, an introduction to the understanding and evaluation of technology within mathematics education cannot be restricted to mathematical techniques or theorems but must constantly encompass a broader understanding of the social context. This presupposes an analysis of the social practice of mathematics and of the function of implicit mathematics and its consequences for school mathematics (Keitel 1989).

To sum up, mathematical literacy requires the mathematical competence to understand the mathematical methods involved and the analytical competence to demystify the justifications for specific mathematical applications as well as to assess their consequences. However, this competence has to be based on a willingness to use it and to become engaged and to become involved in a democratic society. The reconstruction of implicit mathematics, the tracing back of various forms of mathematization by analyzing their context, their social purpose and function in school mathematics, and the debate about far-reaching applications of mathematics are all among the concepts of so-called "critical mathematics" (Christiansen, 1996; Frankenstein, 1989; Mellin-Olsen, 1989; Skovsmose, 1992). It is these concepts that might be the closest to a new understanding of mathematical literacy linked with scientific and technological literacy.

COMMON SENSE
AND MATHEMATICS EDUCATION

Mathematics still is a subject that evokes strong emotions such as aversion, anxiety, and feelings of incompetence. Why is mathematics perceived as so difficult and so complicated that pupils rate themselves "mathematically handicapped," that they feel incapable of experiencing anything of value for their personal development in learning or practicing mathematics?

Teachers, pupils, and parents talking about mathematics and success in mathematics education often use the concept of talent and of an inborn capability of mathematical thinking. They perpetuate the image of a "natural interest" in mathematics: some people are naturally interested in mathematics, some are not. Theories of talent or giftedness release us of the need to analyze pupils' difficulties, demands, or aversions. They function as the basis for more or less explicit intentions to teach mathematics in a way that the few mathematically gifted can display their potential without being disturbed by the majority low-achievers. Although learning difficulty is an issue in mathematics education research that has traditionally received much attention, the integration of pupils aiming to become mathematicians and those labeled "not gifted" remains a seemingly unsolvable dilemma.

The separation of pupils along these lines results on the one hand in a majority of young citizens being neither prepared nor willing to critically value the use of mathematics in social life, on the other hand in a minority of mathematical "experts" for whom critically evaluating mathematics would counteract their career aspiration. In short, there is a strong need to change the public image of giftedness as the chief cause for interest in mathematics and its use. It is necessary to leave essentially individualistic and competitive perspectives on mathematics learning and to develop a collective awareness—an "extended" common sense—of the relationship among mathematics, technology, and society.

The notion of implicit mathematics, the mathematics already installed in our social life, questions the design of school mathematics courses and challenges the idea that mathematics as a discipline is the unique source of reference for their construction. It no longer makes sense to require pupils to learn techniques that can be executed much more quickly and reliably by machines or to withhold from them the insight into the structures by which society is shaped via social and material technologies, that is, to restrict them to the "grammar" of mathematics at the expense of the "literature." Implicit mathematics can be discovered, reconstructed, and analyzed. However, this does not necessarily affect wider attitudes toward, and beliefs about, mathematics. The social image of mathematics, which paradoxically accommodates a general belief in the social necessity of mathematics alongside a sense of cultural isolation, mystery, and aversion, is often prompted by pupils' experiences of mathematics at school and subsequently promoted by public opinion and the various media.

A New Common Sense: By Changing Attitudes and Belief Systems Among Pupils

Even those pupils who experience no great difficulty with mathematics at school often avoid the subject as much as possible outside school. Hostile feelings and negative attitudes toward mathematics (and science), therefore, are much more influential on general behavior and values than epistemological issues. These feelings and attitudes that sustain a dislike of mathematics—or hinder any interest in mathematics—are much more significant obstacles to the development of mathematical literacy than any lack of particular concepts, skills, or thinking abilities.

Belief systems and attitudes toward mathematics, science, and technology are the focus of much research attention from those interested in issues related to gender, class, and ethnicity and mathematical and scientific activities. A wide range of research studies and publications at all levels of public and scientific debate emphasize that the discussion about mathematical literacy must address (and change) the aversion that girls and women are said to have toward these subjects. However, a seemingly contradictory feature characterizes the discussion. Comparisons of achievement tests all over the world reveal girls and women outperforming their male counterparts in arithmetical skills, whereas the reverse is the case when the comparisons are based upon "text problems" or "problem-solving" exercises (First International Mathematics Achievement Study, Second International Mathematics Achievement Study). Girls' success in school mathematics is mainly due to their success in arithmetic where their dealing with numbers and algorithms is more accurate and careful and their number sense more appropriate than is the case with boys. However, their application of these arithmetical skills to so-called "word" problems and to the (often seen as unrealistic and meaningless) contexts offered at school is either avoided entirely or not successful in its outcome. The encounters of girls and women with school mathematics, therefore, seem to be a good indication that mathematical literacy cannot be described adequately in terms of skills but must also address mathematical and scientific problems in contexts that respect and carefully develop such attributes as self-confidence, awareness, and independence.

School activities, therefore, should be directed at creating a willingness on the part of pupils to approach problems by mathematical and scientific means as well as fostering the ability to critique mathematical applications and the use to which mathematics and science are put in society. Many of published reports on project work indicate possible ways in which active involvement, positive attitudes, and critical awareness can be promoted.

The production of context knowledge alongside more generalized mathematical knowledge can be complemented by a direct involvement of pupils and teachers in understanding and improving their environment. This involvement can take many forms of expressions as exemplified in reported projects:

- Asking and informing other pupils (and other people!) about relevant findings. Research activities to gather and critically analyze evidence are a necessary prerequisite for these activities, but to "wrap" them up for the information and understanding of others by presenting them to the public needs another kind of involvement.
- Convincing others of the usefulness and feasibility of certain changes by means of personal example, by petitions, public hearings, letters, by involving the local media; in short, exerting public pressure goes further than just producing insights for themselves.
- Developing hands-on descriptions of alternative environments; for example, Writing reports published in newspapers, buying land for ecological initiatives, developing the ambience at school, reducing waste at school, and so on may give support and acceptance from outside the school to continue such kinds of learning experiences.

Activities designed to study and possibly change the local environment (be it the school or the neighborhood or aspects of the community life) confront pupils with open-ended situations that necessarily entail contentious perceptions of reality, interests, and values. Such situations challenge pupils to use their intellectual, emotional, creative, and organizational capacities; they also provide first-hand experience and understanding of the fact that humans create their social life and they, as pupils, can play a real part in this. The justification of activities of this kind derives not from their assumed learning potential but from the determination to realize values in the pupils' lives and their future. In this context, mathematical literacy means understanding that, first, by creating, interpreting, reflecting upon, and controlling numbers, it is possible to address some social problems and that, second, numbers are determined by interests and intentions and are not the only means of interpreting and understanding a situation in which change is being considered.

A New Common Sense: By Changing Attitudes and Belief Systems in Mathematics Teacher Education

There are several investigations into teacher's professional knowledge focusing on the underlying beliefs of what mathematics consists of and how it should be taught. The outcomes of these studies differ substantially with respect to the status of teachers observed. Elementary teachers, in general, use only mathematically weak conceptions that often do not help them to realize their educational ambitions. Relying on mathematical literacy as "survival mathematics" they tend to perpetuate the image of secondary and tertiary mathematics as complicated and useless for the average person. Higher secondary teachers, in contrast, value mathematics as important, useful, indisputable, and beautiful, but they generally lack any critical attitude to mathematics itself. Both sets of beliefs, when transmitted to pupils, provide a restricted conception of mathematics and its possible use and value. Mathematics instruction, then, perpetuates the concept of mathematical literacy as "survival mathematics for all." In order to break this circle, it may be advisable to modify the beliefs and attitudes of teachers at the moment when they begin to conceptualize their mathematics teaching. However, this seems to be a complex task. It is widely accepted that it is a difficult and lengthy process to change beliefs (Ernest, 1989; Gellert, 1999; McLeod, 1988).

However, there are reasonable assumptions that educators of mathematics teachers themselves play a prominent role in the perpetuation of a certain image of mathematics (Mura, 1995). We want to question

- whether what passes as mathematics teacher education is justified methodologically in relation to the issues of the field. For instance, mathematics teacher education in Germany is partly institutionalized in universities where introductory courses are often given to hundreds of students in the form of lectures. How is this method grounded in a conception of learning?
- whether the scholarship of mathematics teacher education exhibits a preparedness to critique the basis of its approach as well as questioning its technicalities. For instance, what is the meaning of "to prepare" student teachers for their future profession? Does this imply to give them "tools" to engineer the classroom?

- whether the theory and practice of mathematics teacher education are clear about limitations and are able to demonstrate critical understanding of the outstanding problems. It is easier to teach students courses on issues where solutions and answers exist, but does this foster critical thinking?

These points question common metaphors about teachers' work such as teachers as technicians, as artisans, as evaluators, or as intellectuals (Giroux, 1985). The concept of teachers as minor technicians within an industrial process or as human manpower in terms of national needs equipped with prepackaged materials does not credit them with being critical. On the one hand, teacher education based on this view is effective in the sense of preparing them against the possible shock effects of practice; on the other hand, this view trivializes the work of teachers and, thus, denies its complexity. Smyth (1998) called this phenomenon "proletarianization of teachers' work" (p. 1250), alluding to what happened to factory workers in the 19th century. Although denying the complexity of teaching, this "proletarianization" also tries to produce a nonscientific, noncritical habit in the teacher's mind. Alluding to the phenomenological distinction between the cognitive styles of scientific enquiry and everyday life (Goffman, 1974), the noncritical habit is characterized by a mere looking for normality and certainty. It tries to interpret actions as well known so that it is then easy to react. Given the fact that the teacher's capability to react on the spot is helpful in most classroom situations, the looking for certainty is essential when under pressure to act. In addition, the critical mind is looking for doubts and uncertainties after the situation under pressure. Then, it is the time to analyze systematically the performed actions. Thus, "proletarianization" means a shift toward nonreflection.

THE IMPORTANCE OF REFLECTIVENESS

In the section on mathematical literacy, we analyzed what mathematical and analytical competence is needed to understand and demystify the role of mathematics in society. In the section on an "extended" common sense, we described the perpetuation of attitudes and belief systems that work conservatively against the necessary extension. These two sections may become strongly connected by the notion of reflectiveness. Reflection, which is a well-known principle in education, has a high value in various fields of teaching and learning.

In this conclusion, we introduce reflectiveness as a necessary competence for mathematical literacy. Therefore, different levels of reflective thinking have been analytically separated (cf. Jablonka, 1997; Keitel, Kotzmann & Skovsmose, 1993). These levels may provide a basis on which it is possible to build an extended mathematical common sense.

At a first level, pupils and teachers could reflect on their mathematical work in the classroom by asking: Have we done the calculation correctly? Have we used the algorithm accurately? What different ways to check the calculation do we know? Questions of this type are concerned with the mathematical aspects of the problem-solving process involved, and, although they might sometimes be raised within the classroom, they are still rare and often the only kind of reflection provided in mathematics education. These questions also presuppose the true–false dichotomy incorporated in school mathematics, so that reaching only this level of reflective understanding merely reinforces the belief that tasks or problems always have a single correct answer.

A second level of reflection, therefore, is needed: Was the right method of calculation used? Are different algorithms available to address the same problem? Has an appropriate algorithm been used? Is the algorithm fit for the purpose in hand and is it sound, valid, and reliable for the range needed?

At a third level, it is necessary to address the notions of appropriateness and reliability in a specific context in a way that explicitly accommodates the nonmathematical constituents. Even when calculations are done correctly and the techniques have been checked for consistency, the result may not be useful for the purpose in hand. Reflection at this level, therefore, goes beyond the true–false dichotomy and examines more seriously the use of mathematics in relation to the means and ends. The focus of attention is not the mathematical tool per se but the technological aspect of contextualizing mathematics.

At a fourth level, more general questions can be raised about the appropriateness of the formulation of the problem prior to solution. Is it possible to think of a way of solving the problem without using mathematics at all? Is a formal method needed and, if so, for what in particular? Is the result obtained by mathematical means more reasonable and reliable than a solution derived intuitively or derived on the basis of more global considerations? The contrasting of formal and intuitive techniques of problem solving can offer the experience that formalization is simply one way of dealing with problems and can illustrate that mathematical tools per se are not always necessary or even useful.

A fifth level of reflectiveness directs pupils' attention to wider perspectives on the use of special techniques of problem solving: What are the general implications of trying to solve a problem by formal means? How does the use of algorithms influence our perception of (a part of) reality? What do we think of mathematical tools when using them universally? What is the general role of mathematics in our society? How is problem-solving work to be evaluated?

At Levels 1 and 2 the focus is the mathematical tool, at Levels 3 and 4 the relationship is between means and ends, and at, Level 5, the object of reflection is the global impact of using formal techniques and the evaluation process itself.

REFERENCES

Banu, H. (1991). The importance of mathematical modelling in Bangladesh. In M. Niss, W. Blum, & I. Huntley (Eds.), *Teaching of mathematical modelling and applications* (pp. 117–120). Chichester: Ellis Horwood.

Bishop, A. (1989). *Mathematical enculturation. A cultural perspective on mathematical education.* Dordrecht: Kluwer.

Blum, W., Niss, M., & Huntley, I. (Eds.). (1989). *Modelling, applications and applied problem solving.* Chichester: Ellis Horwood.

Burckhardt, H., Keitel, C., & Malone, J. (Eds.). (1989). *Curriculum for the year 2000. Reports and papers of the theme group 7 at ICME VI.* Perth: Curtin University.

Carraher, T. N. (1988). Street mathematics and school mathematics. In A. Borbas (Ed.), *Proceedings of Psychology of Mathematics Education XII* (pp. 1–23). Veszprem: OOK.

Carraher, D. W., Carraher, T. N., & Schliemann, A. D. (1984). Having a feel for calculations. In P. Damerow, M. E. Dunkley, B. F. Nebres, & B. Werry (Eds.), *Mathematics for all* (pp. 87–89). Paris: UNESCO.

Chapman, B. (1991). The overselling of science education in the eighties. *School Science Review, 260*(72), 47–64.

Chevallard, Y. (1985). *La transposition didactique.* Grenoble: La Pensée Sauvage.

Christiansen, J. M. (1996). *Classroom interactions in applied mathematics courses.* Aalborg, Denmark: Aalborg University, Department of Mathematics and Computer Science.

D'Ambrosio, U. (1985). Ethnomathematics and its place in the history and pedagogy of mathematics. *For the Learning of Mathematics, 5*(1), 44–48.

Damerow, P., Elwitz, U., Keitel, C., & Zimmer, J. (1974). *Elementarmathematik: Lernen für die Praxis?* Stuttgart: Klett.

Davis, P. (1989). Applied mathematics as social contract. In C. Keitel, P. Damerow, A. Bishop, & P. Gerdes (Eds.), *Mathematics, education, and society* (pp. 24–28). Paris: UNESCO.

De Lange, J. (1993). Innovation in mathematics education using applications: Progress and problems. In J. de Lange, C. Keitel, I. Huntley, & M. Niss (Eds.), *Innovation in maths education by modelling and applications* (pp. 3–17). Chichester: Ellis Horwood.

De Vore, P. W. (1987). Cultural paradigms and technological literacy. *Bulletin of Science, Technology and Society, 7*(5 and 6), 711–719.

Ernest, P. (1989). The impact of beliefs on the teaching of mathematics In C. Keitel, P. Damerow, A. Bishop, & P. Gerdes (Eds.), *Mathematics, education, and society* (pp. 99–101). Paris: UNESCO.

Frankenstein, M. (1989). *Relearning mathematics. A different third R—Radical maths.* London: Free Association Books.

Frankenstein, M., & Powell, A. (1989). Empowering non-traditional college students. *Science and Nature, 9*(10), 100–112.

Freudenthal, H. (1991). *Revisiting mathematics education.* Dordrecht: Kluwer.

Gellert, U. (1999). Prospective elementary teachers' comprehension of mathematics instruction. *Educational Studies of Mathematics, 37*(1), 23–43.

Gerdes, P. (1985). Conditions and strategies for emancipatory mathematics education in underdeveloped countries. *For the Learning of Mathematics, 5*(1), 39–44.

Gerdes, P. (1996). Culture and mathematics education in (southern) Africa. In C. Alsina, J. M. Alvarez, B. Hodgson, C. Laborde, & A. Pérez (Eds.), *8th international congress on Mathematical Education. Selected lectures* (pp. 221–232). Sevilla: S.A.E.M. Thales.

Giroux, H. (1985). Intellectual labour and pedagogical work: Re-thinking the role of the teacher as intellectual. *Phenomenology and Pedagogy, 3*(1), 20–32.

Goffman, E. (1974). *Frame analysis. An essay on the organization of experience.* New York: Harper & Row.

Gravemeijer, K. (1994). *Developing realistic mathematics education.* Utrecht: CD-β Press.

Jablonka, E. (1996). *Meta-Analyse von Zugängen zur mathematischen Modellbildung und Konsequenzen für den Unterricht.* Berlin: transparent verlag.

Jablonka, E. (1997). What makes a model effective and useful (or not)? In S. K. Houston, W. Blum, I. Huntley, & N. T. Neill (Eds.), *Teaching and learning mathematical modelling: Innovation, investigation and applications* (pp. 39–50). Chichester: Albion.

Keitel, C. (1989). Mathematics education and technology. *For the Learning of Mathematics, 9*(1), 7–13.

Keitel, C. (1993). Implicit mathematical models in social practice and explicit mathematics teaching by application. In: J. de Lange, C. Keitel, I. Huntley, & M. Niss (Eds.), *Innovation in maths education by modelling and applications* (pp. 19–30). Chichester: Ellis Horwood.

Keitel, C., Kotzmann, E., & Skovsmose, O. (1993). Beyond the tunnel vision: Analysing the relationship of mathematics, technology and society. In C. Keitel & K. Ruthven (Eds.), *Learning from computers. Mathematics education and technology* (pp. 243–279). Berlin: Springer.

Mason, J. (1988). modelling: what do we really want pupils to learn? In D. Pimm (Ed.), *Mathematics, teachers and children* (pp. 201–215). London: Hodder & Stoughton.

McLeod, D. B. (1988). Affective issues in mathematical problem solving: some theoretical considerations. *Journal for Research in Mathematics Education, 19*(2), 134–142.

Mellin-Olsen, S.(1989). *The politics of mathematics education.* Dordrecht: Reidel.

Mura, R. (1995). Images of mathematics held by university teachers of mathematics education. *Educational Studies of Mathematics, 28*(4), 385–399.

National Research Council. (Ed.). (1989). *Everybody counts. A report to the nation on the future of mathematics education.* Washington, DC: National Academy Press.

Nelkin, D. (1987). *Selling science. How the press covers science and technology*. New York: Freeman.

Ormell, C. (1993). A pedagogy based on projective modelling In: J. de Lange, C. Keitel, I. Huntley, & M. Niss (Eds.), *Innovation in math education by modeling and applications* (pp. 53–62). Chichester: Ellis Horwood.

Skovsmose, O. (1992). Democratic competence and reflective knowing in mathematics. *For the Learning of Mathematics, 2*(2), 2–11.

Smyth, J. (1998). Three rival versions and a critique of teacher staff development. A. Hargreaves, A. Lieberman, M. Fullan, & D. Hopkins (Eds.), *International handbook of educational change* (pp. 1242–1256). Dordrecht: Kluwer.

Sohn-Rethel, A. (1970). *Geistige und körperliche Arbeit*. Frankfurt: Suhrkamp.

II

GLOBAL, REGIONAL, AND
LOCAL CONTEXTS

Most mathematics educators are directly experiencing and being affected by a world that is getting closer and smaller. Intercultural exchanges have increased in quantity and have become much easier and widespread. Further, economic considerations and cultural factors are interacting in new and powerful ways. Questions need to be asked concerning what is the shape of mathematics education within a global society in which our students will live their adult lives. How much of the mathematics education should be local to meet their needs to understand and control their immediate life, and how much of it should prepare them to survive globally? What is the meaning of ethnomathematics within this new global context? Questions need to be asked about the politicohistorical development of mathematics education curriculum and practices in different countries in order to enable rational reform in their mathematics education. These questions are addressed in the following chapters.

Bill Atweh and Phil Clarkson claim that mathematics education is one of the most internationalized areas of higher education. This is evidenced in similarity of the curriculum reforms happening around the world and the number of international conferences and research activities that have propagated during the past few decades. Yet, very few research studies have problematized the processes and outcomes of such internationalization. This chapter discusses theoretical issues in globalization and internationalization of mathematics education with particular emphasis on cross-country collaboration in professional development.

The chapter by Jan Thomas seeks to explore the complex issues that surround and influence policy decisions, especially at the government level, in mathematics education. In particular it explores possible trends toward diminishing the influence of expert opinion as governments seek rapid solutions in a global framework. The framework for discussion is that universal education is dependent on public funding and therefore on government. Most nations now consider themselves to be democracies but, because education is so dependent on government funding, it is often difficult for individuals to actively participate in debate critical of government policies without being penalized in some way. The role of professional societies becomes critical and, for research-based groups, this is often at odds with their perceived role and purpose.

Khoon Yoong Wong, Zaitun Binti Hj Mohd Taha, and Palanisamy Veloo, look at three ASEAN countries, Brunei Darussalam, Malaysia, and Singapore, which have much in common in mathematics education, in particular, a common British colonial heritage and national examinations dominantly influenced by the Cambridge 0-level examination. Still, mathematics education has developed in a different way in each country, under the influence of situated sociocultural factors, namely, historical background, cultural mores, major political events, national education structure and aims, and language policy. The differences in these sociocultural factors in each national situation led to distinct school systems and different experiences of student achievement. The "Situated Sociocultural Model," which is presented seeks to show the dynamic interplay between the different factors and their impact on school mathematics.

The chapter by Bill Barton and Roslyn Frank argues that recent interest in how anthropology and linguistics relate to mathematics led to recognition that mathematical thinking is a function of language in ways not previously recognized. Ethnomathematics, cognitive linguistics, and anthropology are all pointing to a way of understanding mathematical ideas based on human experience and cultural activities. Formal mathematics can be seen to have developed from metaphors deeply embedded in our languages. This raises the question of relativity in mathematics. Do different languages embody different types of mathematics? This chapter examines some emerging evidence in the grammar and syntax of indigenous languages, that is, languages structurally very different from the Indo-European linguistic tradition. The educational consequences of the possibility of different mathematical thinking are briefly discussed.

The goal of the study conducted by Richard Kitchen is to understand some of the complicated and dynamic issues that affect the pedagogy of secondary-level mathematics teachers in Guatemala, Central America. Several authors have argued that national school systems are situated within the context of unequal power relations among nations. The historical roots of this unequal relationship date back to when colonialized countries adopted transplanted educational models that usually did not fit the countries' actual needs, circumstances, and resources. The goal of this study is to disrupt power by actively listening to two mathematics teachers laboring in inner-city public schools in Guatemala describe the political and social contexts of their work. Poverty and lack of resources create a context where the students do not have textbooks. The teacher teaches from a 30-year-old textbook and photocopies exercises for homework. Political unrest leads to many missed classes and limited teaching time. The study should help experts from developed countries understand the world of teachers in poorer countries. Before any new interventions are made, we should ask whether these can prosper in the desperate classroom situations in many developing countries.

5

Internationalization and Globalization of Mathematics Education: Toward an Agenda for Research/Action

Bill Atweh
Queensland University of Technology

Phil Clarkson
Australian Catholic University

Consider the following anecdotes based on real experiences:

- A group of students from a state school in Brisbane uses the Internet to study mathematics within a "community of learners" with other students from Canada.
- A developing country in Latin America thinking about education reform in particular with regard to assessment invites researchers from the United Kingdom to give advice about what they need to do. To keep the advice more comprehensive, they make it a point to invite people from both sides of the debate about national testing and national curriculum.
- At the induction ceremony of a group of PhD students in Colombia, a professor is giving a lecture on the major developments of educational thought during this century. He cites Ausubel, Piaget, Von Glaserfeld, Kuhn, and many other very familiar theorists. He did not make a reference to Orlando Fals Borda of Colombia or Paulo Freire of Brazil.
- A group of 30 educators from Spain, the United States, and Canada volunteered their holiday time to assist students from Universidad Nacional de El Salvador to obtain master's degrees in mathematics education.

Perhaps similar experiences are quite familiar to many mathematics educators around the world. Numerous other examples could be also given about the divergence of general culture and values. There is little doubt that the world that some have prophesized in terms of a "global village" (McLuhan & Bruce, 1992) is well and truly here. For many, it is an exciting world. Yet, at the same time, it is a worrying world.

It is a world with great potential for many—if they can afford the privilege to actively participate in it.

The UNESCO (1998) World Declaration on Higher Education for the Twenty-first Century claims that "[t]he second half of this century will go down in the history of higher education as the period of its most spectacular expansion. . . . But it is also the period which has seen the gap between industrially developed, the developing countries and in particular the least developed countries with regard to access and resources for higher learning and research, already enormous, becoming even wider" (p. 1–2). The document goes on further to point out that without adequate higher education such a gap can not be bridged.

In particular, mathematics education is becoming a truly international activity. Robitaille and Travers (1992) argued that mathematics education is perhaps the most international subject of higher education. This is reflected in the number of international conferences and journals in the field as well as the divergence of views in curriculum development and research. This chapter examines some emerging issues that are facing mathematics education at the outset of the third millennium. Some of these issues stem from the literature within the mathematics education community itself. However, because these processes have been undertheorized in mathematics education, we have made extensive use of literature from outside the field as well. We have dual aims in this chapter: first, to develop an initial tentative theoretical model to investigate the conglomerate activities and issues related to internationalization and globalization of mathematics education and, second, using this model we hope to identify some needed action and/or research within the mathematics education community toward dealing with the rapidly changing global context.

Perhaps at the outset we need to stress two limitations of the chapter. Because of the limited research base investigating the processes of globalization and internationalization of mathematics education, the ideas here are rather developmental. Second, we are well aware that the views reported here are in the main the product of thinking embedded in developed English-speaking countries. Both chapter authors have experience in developing countries—the first author by birth and initial education and the second by work as educator. We have attempted to reflect some voices from developing countries, but we do not claim to speak from their perspective. One thing that troubled us in reviewing the literature in this area is the scarcity of voices from developing countries about their experiences, aspirations, and wishes.

CONCEPTUALIZATION OF INTERNATIONALIZATION AND GLOBALIZATION

Although the terms *internationalization* and *globalization* are relatively recent in academic discourse (Waters, 1995), they are playing an increasingly significant role in higher education policy and practice. Waters claimed that, whereas postmodernism was the concept for the 1980s, globalization and internationalization may well be the key concepts "to understand the transition of human society into the third millennium" (p. 1). Moreover, because the terms at times are given different meanings by different authors and at other times are used interchangeably, we need to conceptualize their usage in this chapter. Taylor, Rizvi, Lingard, and Henry (1997) understood internationalization as "relationships and transactions between nations rather than those which transcend national boundaries" (p. 57). According to this understanding, any activity that involves a cross-country collaboration contributes to the internationalization of the activities of the partners. In this context, we will interpret such transactions in a rather inclusive sense. They can be either official at state-to-state level or less formal interaction at a professional or even personal level, they may involve two or more countries, and they may be at a regional level (e.g., Latin America or South East Asia) or more extensive international level.

In this chapter, we are particularly interested in internationalization of mathematics education. Perhaps it is useful to provide some examples of internationalization activities and processes involving mathematics education. Internationalization of teaching might include international students in undergraduate or postgraduate courses, internationalization of the curriculum, and comparative curricula studies. Internationalization of research might include international research conferences, international publications, and collaborative and/or comparative cross-country research projects. Finally, internationalization of service may be activities such as curriculum development, less formal professional development programs, and international consultancies.

Robertson (1992, cited in Henry & Taylor, 1997) defined *globalization* as "a concept which refers both to the compression of the world and the intensification of consciousness of the world as a whole" (p. 46). This is in line with Giddens' (1994, cited in Henry & Taylor, 1997) concept of compression of time-space. Waters (1995) used the term *globalization* as "a social process in which the constraints of geography on social and cultural arrangements recede and in which people become increasingly aware that they are receding" (p. 3). This is in line with Giddens' assertion that globalization is not simply the formation of large-scale organizations and systems that determine what happens in each place, but also refers to the day-to-day awareness of global issues. Some examples of processes that may reflect globalization trends in mathematics education are the convergence of school mathematics and mathematics education curricula around the world, similarity in research questions and methodologies as well as standards of reporting research, and widespread acceptance of some epistemological positions such as constructivism.

Perhaps it is worthwhile making some comments on these two constructs and their definitions.

• First, even though two distinct constructs have been identified, this does not mean that the two are disjoint or unrelated. Obviously, globalization, in some sense, may be an outcome or result of intense internationalization. However, the relationship is not necessary or deterministic. Hence, even though we cannot necessarily discuss one construct without reference to the other, it is useful to make this differentiation because of the nonsymmetric relationship between them as well as the distinct value criteria that may be applied to each.

• Second, the two constructs can be differentiated on the dimension of autonomy of the partners. McGinn (1995) argued that "efforts at internationalization . . . [are]

seen by... authors as activities that improve higher education institutions without diminishing their autonomy. . . . There is some evidence, however, that the processes of globalisation are compelling rather than invitational, and therefore require careful scrutiny" (p. 78). Similarly, Waters asserted that globalization is often associated with "forces [that] are impersonal and beyond the control and intentions of any individual or groups of individuals" (p. 2).

• Third, internationalization and globalization are not the same as homogenization (Henry & Taylor, 1997). For these authors, globalization consists of "contradictory impulses of integration, fragmentation and differentiation" (p. 47). For example, although intense internationalization may lead to globalization, these same processes may lead to fragmentation at local level. For example, even though issues such as feminisms, indigenous land rights, gay rights, and human rights have gained global status, issues related to local context cannot be overlooked. For instance, the globalization of concerns about status of women raised issues about voices and the right of middle class, heterosexual Anglo-Saxon women to speak on behalf of black women, lesbians, or women from developing countries. This resulted in the impossibility of talking about "a feminist perspective" and gave rise to a multiplicity of feminisms (Gunew, 1990).

• Fourth, surely, as social processes, the two activities are open to value judgments that are open to contestation (e.g., see the debate between McGinn, 1996, and Ilon, 1997). However, in this context, we do not understand the two constructs as necessarily related to a particular moral judgment (Robertson, 1992, cited in Taylor et al., 1997). In other words, aspects of internationalization and globalization processes may be good, whereas others may be less desirable and should be contested. Further, what is considered good aspect of internationalization and globalization for a particular group of people may very well be at the expense of other groups.

• Finally, Falk (1993, cited in Taylor et al., 1997) distinguished two forms of globalization processes. He called them globalization "from above and from below." Globalization from above was understood as "[t]he collaboration between leading states and the main agents of capital formation. This type of globalisation disseminates a consumerist ethos and draws into its domain transnational business and political elites" (p. 75). On the other hand, globalization from below "[c]onsists of an array of transnational social forces animated by environmental concerns, human rights, hostility to patriarchy and a vision of human community based on the unity of diverse cultures seeking an end to poverty, oppression, humiliation and collective violence" (p. 75).

INTERNATIONALIZATION PROCESSES IN MATHEMATICS EDUCATION

Internationalization of mathematics is not a recent phenomenon. The movement of the earliest mathematical knowledge between east and west dates back to early recorded history. However, here we are more interested in mathematics education and, in particular, mathematics education research and curriculum reform. Perhaps the first models of internationalization activities that can be noted are informal and erratic.

Countries such as the United States, United Kingdom, France, and the former Soviet Union have had a significant number of overseas, or international students, mainly at postgraduate levels. More recently, countries such as Spain and Australia are receiving increasing numbers of postgraduate students from Latin America and the Asian Pacific region, respectively. Many of those studying overseas return to their home countries to occupy prominent positions in curriculum development and teacher development. Undoubtedly, the priorities and curriculum and research principles influence their views, and hence the underlying values embedded in these, of the host country where they have received their education. Furthermore, the "brain drain" caused by the non-return of many of these academics to their home countries is a serious loss for many developing countries (UNESCO, 1998).

Other processes of internationalization are more systematic and perhaps more far reaching. The pattern of overseas studies discussed previously is closely related to wider patterns of colonialization of developing countries. At the conclusion of both world wars, many developing countries came under the mandate of the "winning" countries, which were given the responsibility of preparing these dependent countries for independence and statehood. A number of the colonialism countries have modeled their education systems, including their teacher education programs, on that of the mandate country. Nebres (1995) discussed some of the initial difficulties encountered by Southeast Asian educators in developing regional collaboration until they "realised how deeply imbedded [their] mathematics education systems [were] in the cultural and colonial histories of [their] countries. . . . [R]epresentatives from Singapore, Malaysia and Hong Kong were describing variations within the British system, the Philippines of the American system; the Vietnamese of the French and so on" (p. 32).

In the post-world war era, other processes evolved in the form of international organizations such as the United Nations, UNESCO, and the World Bank—or its regional equivalents. Jacobson (1996) discussed the role of the different projects of these organizations during the "decade of decolonisation in the 1960s" (p. 1239) initially for the implementation of policies of universal primary education and later for the elimination of illiteracy. These organizations have been highly influential in the developing of the mathematics education programs in many developing countries (Souviney, 1983). The work of these organizations was tied to assisting developing countries to make use of the benefit of the experience of the more developed countries for improving their educational systems. Not surprisingly, these projects were supported mainly by Anglo-European monies and conducted with expertise predominantly from these countries.

Perhaps, the more direct effect of these organizations on mathematics education was through the formation of the International Commission of Mathematics Instruction (ICMI) in 1908. Since 1952, the commission has been affiliated with the International Mathematics Union, which in turn is a member of the International Council for Scientific Unions. ICMI has been very active during the second half of the 20th century. Perhaps the most widely familiar ICMI activity is the International Congress of Mathematics Education (ICME), held every four years. Thousands of educators from all over the world attend these congresses. Occasionally, the proceedings of some of the working groups of ICME are translated into languages other than English and are made available through UNESCO.

Also widely familiar are the ICMI Studies. Since 1986, there have been about 10 of these studies in areas such as school mathematics in the 1990s, the popularization of mathematics, mathematics and cognition, and research on gender and mathematics. Each study is conducted by a Program Committee, which calls for submissions from the mathematics education community on the topic of the study, collates the information, organizes an international conference by invitation, and produces the final publication. Another ICMI activity is the holding of regional meetings of mathematics educators. Such meetings have been held in East Asia, Australia, Latin America, and Africa. Likewise, ICMI also has four affiliated permanent study groups: the International Study Group for the Relationship Between the History and Pedagogy of Mathematics, the International Organization of Women and Mathematics Education, the International Group for the Psychology of Mathematics Education (PME), and the World Federations of National Mathematics Competitions. Many of these organizations hold their own annual conferences. Perhaps a less-known activity of ICMI is the Solidarity Program in Mathematics Education. The overall aim of the program is to foster commitment and involvement of mathematics educators around the world for the advancement of mathematics education in "less affluent and less free countries" ICMI (undated).

Within the international community of mathematics educators there are other professionally based organizations that provide for international contacts. The Inter-American Committee on Mathematics Education, The South East Asian Mathematics Society, and African Mathematics Union, CLAME, and the Mathematics Education Research Group of Australasia hold regular, if not annual, conferences. With great difficulty in obtaining funds for overseas travel, attendance at these conferences varies depending on the location of the conference and the official language of communication. It is a common practice for many of these gatherings to invite keynote speakers from United States and United Kingdom.

Another important process of internationalization of mathematics education research is the emerging international publications. The most widely distributed research journals are in English. Perhaps the most known in the English-speaking countries are *Journal for Research in Mathematics Education (JRME)*, *Educational Studies in Mathematics (ESM)*, *and For the Learning of Mathematics (FLM)*. These vary in the type of articles and or research paradigms that they specialize in as well as in their research criteria for publication. Some are published by professional organizations, whereas others are published commercially. With the increasing availability of the Internet, some of these journals are already being published electronically, whereas new on-line publications, such as *Chreods* and the *Philosophy of Mathematics Education*, are emerging. Also worth mentioning are some journals that publish articles in more than one language such as *Didactique des Mathmatiques* and the *International Newsletter on Proof*.

Issues in Internationalization

Arguably the increasing ease in travel and communication as well as the increase in numbers of venues for international contacts have increased the chances for educators from around the world to meet, share their findings; discuss their mutual interests;

challenge each others learning and practices, and generally to increase their knowledge about problems of mathematics around the world and about solutions that have worked in other places. Undoubtedly, the benefits of such means of international dialogues are varied and significant. However, there are some inherent limitations that need to be addressed.

A major concern often raised about the currently available international channels of communication is their dominance by views and voices of educators from the Anglo-European[1] educators (Bishop, 1992; Clements & Ellerton, 1996). Discussing the role of international ICME conferences, Jacobson (1996) noted that the number of people from developing countries attending such conferences "is still depressingly low, accurately reflecting today's economic realities" (p. 1241). Educational funding, hence funding for international travel, continues to decline in many countries—arguably more so in the developing countries. Further, all major international forums use English as their first official language, with occasionally a second language of the host country. Translation facilities are either nonexistent or at best limited. There are rarely separate strands on the conference program for presentations in other languages. Naturally these limitations reduce the accessibility of conferences for educators from many non-English-speaking and developing countries.

The dominance of Anglo-European views and voices is also reflected in areas of research reporting. We have noted that the most widely circulated journals in mathematics education are exclusively in English. Silver and Kilpatrick (1994) showed that only 22% of the articles published in the *JRME* during the period 1984 to 1993 are from educators affiliated with universities from outside North America. Many of these articles are co-authored with North American researchers. Further, the acceptance rate of manuscripts submitted to that journal from non-North American researchers is half that of their North American counterparts. Naturally one has to keep in mind that the *JRME* is, in the first place, the official research journal of a North American professional body, the National Council for Teachers of Mathematics. However, considering the avowed international status of that publication, concerns about the dominance of certain views and paradigms is a valid concern. Silver and Kilpatrick demonstrated that the patterns of contribution to *ESM* are less dominated by North American researchers. Perhaps it is not necessary to stress the great contribution of researchers from North America to mathematics education research and knowledge; however, it is necessary to raise concerns about wider representation of views, theories, and paradigms of research.

Obviously, the multiplicity of natural languages that mathematics educators represent is an ever-present hindrance to communication and sharing of ideas through conferences and publications. There are no simple solutions to these difficulties. However, with awareness of these limitations and collective dedication to tackling them, it is possible to make international collaborations more accessible to non-English-speaking educators and hence more equitable and just. There are recent technological developments—such as the emergence of the first generation of computer programs that are capable of translation between languages—which may be used toward this purpose. Naturally, there is often a gap in time between when these new resources become

---

[1] We are aware that the use of the term *Anglo-European* is somewhat problematic in that it hides the at times substantial differences between the many countries that it covers.

first available and the time in which they become powerful enough to satisfy the needs of the educational community and/or become widely accessible to educators from less-developed countries. Similarly, the increase in multilingual publications would make international dialogue more accessible and representative than it is at present.

Similarly, there is an imbalance in the number of conferences that are held in North America and Europe. Naturally, this is partly justifiable by the fact that there are higher concentration of people interested in these conferences in North America and Europe and that these countries have the necessary infrastructure to mount successful large congresses. However, the expenses necessary to participate at these conferences are a burden for all researchers, yet more so for those from developing countries.

There are other economical aspects behind international collaboration that need to be raised in this regard. Perhaps this can best be illustrated through the case study of changes in international students' policy in Australia between 1950 and modern times (Back, Davis, & Olsen, 1996). At the conclusion of World War II, Australia played a key role in the implementation of the Colombo Plan for cooperative development in South and Southeast Asia. This role included the sponsorship by the Australian Government of international students to study at Australian universities. With the increase of international students, both sponsored and private, studying in Australia, the government introduced certain charges for international private students—commencing at a rate of 10% of the cost of the tuition escalating to about 55% by the late 1980s. However, in the mid-1980s there was an increasing emphasis on the role of higher education as an income generator for Australia. Back et al. described this as a shift from "educational aid" to "educational trade" (p. 7). By 1990 the educational subsidies had all but ceased. It was also notable that the benefits of international students to the Australian culture and the role and status of the country internationally have been rarely identified in government reports and academic research. Hence, there was a second shift in policy from "education as an export" to "internationalisation of higher education" (p. 7). This is not to say that economic interests and discourses in international collaboration were abandoned, but there was, and still is, several, often conflicting, discourses of quality, flexibility, equity, economic, humanism, and so on, informing internationalization practice and structures within many universities. In the mid-to late 1990s, Australian funding to universities changed toward increasing the ability of and expectation for public universities to raise parts of their funding from external sources. International students, as discussed previously, constitute a significant part of sources of funds for some universities. Needless to say, such considerations can be in conflict with the quality of education and fairness of access.

Jacobson (1996) discussed the increasing gap between the rich and poor countries and the curtailing of funds from these international agencies make it "more difficult to look for governments for improved international cooperation in mathematics education" (p. 1253). He joined Miguel de Guzman, past president of ICMI, in calling for an increasing role of cooperation between professional mathematics educators and their associations to work to improve mathematics education worldwide. Activities such as the Solidarity Program in Mathematics Education, mentioned previously, is a step in the right direction. Of course, there is room for many other such projects at all levels, including personal, professional, and official. For example, many

Anglo-European universities have study leave or sabbatical programs that allow educators to conduct research in overseas countries. The staff destination on the majority of such programs is other Anglo-European countries.

A further limitation to communication available within the existing forums is the limited possibility of deep dialogue due to their format. Conference and journal articles are restricted in space and/or time. Concern has been raised as to their ability to provide for deep analysis of the context behind the research (Silver & Kilpatrick, 1994). Some participants find international conferences too busy, large, and hectic to establish meaningful contacts (Johnston, 1992) or keeping sight of big picture on problems of mathematics education (Usiskin, 1992). Last, we raise the question of whether there are cultural differences and norms in forms of establishing contacts and collaboration. Admittedly, empirical research findings are almost nonexistent in this area. However, experience in travels by both authors to a number of different developing countries shows there are differences in patterns of working and communication. For example, in many cultures personal contacts, established over long periods of time and developed in less formal association, are essential conditions of collaboration. Conferences may not be the best venue to develop such associations for some people.

GLOBALIZATION PROCESSES
IN MATHEMATICS EDUCATION

Two areas in which questions have been raised about the effects of the processes of globalization of mathematics education are curriculum development and types of research conducted. A striking feature of the different curriculum documents and textbooks in mathematics education around the world is their similarities rather than their variety (Oldham, 1989, cited in Clements & Ellerton, 1996). Such similarities are quite obvious in the areas of content and sequencing of topics and, to a certain extent, in the focus and aims of mathematics. Moreover, these similarities have proven to be rather stable across the years; changes in curriculum in one country or certain region (mainly Anglo-European) are often reflected in other countries within few years. Note, for example, the wide acceptance of the New Maths movement in the 1960s and the more recent widespread "assessment-driven reforms" (Hargreaves, 1989) based on standards and profiles. In both sets of reforms, the impetus arose from similar reforms in the United States and United Kingdom and spread to many other countries. Further, the emphasis on mathematics education is similar in many countries. Mathematics as a school subject is given special importance second only, if nor equal, to language education in most countries around the world. In many countries mathematics is tied to scientific, technological, and hence to economic development. Perhaps, this widespread importance put on mathematics learning is reflected in the international declaration of the year 2000 as the International Year of Mathematics. Undoubtedly, these similarities have added ammunition to the often expressed view that mathematics is a "universal language" (Robitaille & Travers, 1992). Such similarities in curriculum reform and emphasis on the role of mathematics are often reflected and perpetuated in higher mathematics education courses and academic writing.

Because of these similarities in the curriculum, two types of research flourished in the second half of the 20th century: international comparative studies on the curriculum and international studies on mathematics achievement. Silver and Kilpatrick (1994) claimed that the first type of research has escalated because of the relative ease in which such comparisons can be made in isolation to the very specific sociopolitical contexts of the countries involved. Robitaille and Travers (1992) argued the case for international studies on achievement, whereas others identified concerns about their validity, usefulness, misuses, and abuses (see special issues of *Prospects*, Volume 22, Number 3; *Comparative Education*, Volume 31 Number 1; and Keitel & Kilpatrick, 1999).

In the area of research in mathematics education, Bishop (1992) argued that similarity is a feature of many research traditions evolving in different countries around the globe. Although research in mathematics education is a relatively recent phenomena in many countries, research questions, methods, practices, and publications are becoming more standardized. Bishop concluded that these similarities led to difficulties in identifying a "national perspective" of mathematics education research in any country. He rightly added that these similarities should not be taken to mean that there is a universal acceptance of particular research methods or paradigms. Researchers around the world have a greater variety of research paradigms that they can employ in the conduct of their investigations. However, the variety and tensions between different paradigms in research are similar in many countries (Silver & Kilpatrick, 1994). Perhaps this illustrates the tension between globalization and fragmentation referred to by Henry and Taylor (1997).

Issues in Globalization of Mathematics Education

There is a great unease expressed by many English-speaking researchers about the dominance of Anglo-European thinking about mathematics education for countries around the world. Commenting on the 7th ICME conference in Canada, Usiskin (1992), perhaps summarizing the feeling of many participants, noted "the extent to which countries have become close in how they think about their problems and, as a consequence, what they are doing in mathematics education" (p. 19). Yet, he goes on to express his hope "that the new world order does not result in a common worldwide curriculum; our differences provide the best situation for curriculum development and implementation" (p. 20). This concern about uncritical globalization of issues is shared by Rogers (1992) who, commenting on the same conference, lamented that "all our theories about learning are founded in a model of the European Rational Man, and that this starting point might well be inappropriate when applied to other cultures" (p. 22). He went further to assert that "the assumptions that mathematics is a universal language, and is therefore universally the same in all cultures cannot be justified. Likewise, the assumptions that our solutions to local problems ... will have universal applications is even further from the truth" (p. 23). This unease about the dominance of Western mathematics is quite strongly expressed in a keynote address to the ICME Regional Collaboration conference held in Melbourne, Australia, where Clements (1995), a leading Australian mathematics educator with extensive international experience, outlined his concerns in the following manner. "Over the past 20 years I have often had cause to reflect that it is Western educators who were responsible not only for getting their own mathematics teacher education equation wrong, but also for passing on their errors to education systems around the world" (p. 3).

However, often these concerns do not match voices from the developing countries. At the same ICME regional conference, the president of the African Mathematical Union (Kuku, 1995) warned against the overemphasis on culturally oriented curricula for developing countries that act against their ability to progress and compete in an increasingly globalized world. He calls for "a global minimum curriculum below which no continent should be allowed to drift, however under-developed" (p. 407). Some of the reasons he presented are very relevant to the discussion here. The phenomenon of dropping out of mathematics is not restricted to developing countries. Hence, he argues, cultural relevance of the mathematics content to the culture of the student is not the only consideration in determining participation and success. Kuku expressed concern that the overemphasis on ethnomathematics may be at the expense of "actual progress in the mathematics education of the students" (p. 406). Presumably this mathematics education is the mathematics education that is needed for economic and technological progress within their countries. Furthermore, within each Third World country there are many different cultural groups. There are no resources for implementing an appropriate ethnomathematics program for every student group. He concluded by citing examples of Asian countries that were able to achieve huge leaps in economic development through their use of "imported curricula" (p. 408).

Also at the same conference, a similar call was given by Sawiran (1995), a mathematics educator from Malaysia. Sawiran based his comments on the belief that "our experience shows that mathematics is an important ingredient of technology and therefore is a key element to 'progress'" (p. 603). He concluded his address by saying that "[t]he main thrust in enhancing better quality of education is through 'globalization' of education. In this respect, it is proper to consider globalization in mathematics education" (p. 608, quotes in original). He added that the most important step in globalization is through "collaborative efforts" (p. 608).

The phenomenon of, and arguments for, globalization of mathematics education curriculum in schools around the world is often attributed to the (mistaken) belief about mathematics objectivity and culturally independent truth (Bishop, 1988; Clements & Ellerton, 1996). However, at least according to the voices from the developing countries reported previously, the calls for globalized mathematics curricula stem from other considerations. Mathematics education is often associated with claims of relevance to employment, economic, and scientific development (Harris, 1991). These views are shared by mathematics educators both in developed and developing countries. Kuku's (1995) concern about the emphasis on ethnomathematics does not stem from his concern that it is not "real mathematics." He raised doubt as to whether this mathematics is appropriate to economic development of African countries in a globalized world. Naturally, it would be very presumptuous to say that, because Western mathematics, or what Bishop (1988) called Mathematics with capital "M," has a proven track record in technological development, it should be used as a model for curriculum development worldwide. What this does imply is that investigations on local versions of curricula and ethnomathematics should take into consideration not only the historical context of the culture, a factor of utmost importance we might add, but also the country's aspirations and its role in a globalized context. Perhaps this area requires further theorization in the ethnomathematics literature (for a critique of ethnomathematics, see Vithal & Skovsmose, 1997).

For many mathematics educators in the West, the very term *global curriculum* as it is often understood in Western experience, is an abomination. Rightly so, we may hasten to add. The experience of the National Curriculum in the United Kingdom has raised ample concerns about the lack of sensitivity of attempts for standardization to differences due to cultural and social background of students and their effect on demoralization and deprofessionalization of teachers (chap. 10, this volume). Yet the call of these and perhaps other mathematics educators from developing counties cannot and should not be dismissed. Let us examine issues related to globalized curriculum reform a little further. Naturally, the aim of such examination is not to argue for an international standardization of mathematics curriculum; rather, we aim to widen the debate about international collaborations to include issues arising from a globalized context of our new times.

GLOBAL APPROACHES TO REFORM

The first possible concern about globalized approach to reform in mathematics education is that the imposition of curricula from outside the profession, that is, by governments and bureaucrats, cannot be sensitive to real problems that schools and teachers face. Furthermore, many national approaches to reform are often not built on the principles derived from research and thinking within the profession. Such external imposition of curricula is also deprofessionalizing to teachers in schools. If we examine the reform experience of three English-speaking countries with which the authors of this chapter are familiar, we note different approaches to national reform agendas. The reform model of the National Curriculum in the United Kingdom was based on the assumed right, some would say duty, of the central government to legislate for education welfare in the nation. It is a reform that is accompanied by legislation guaranteeing adherence by all local authorities, schools, and teachers. Arguably due to the nature of the Australian nation as a federation of separate states with their individual authority over school education, rather than perhaps due to different philosophical considerations, reform in Australia proceeded in a different way. By mutual agreement between the different state ministers of education and their federal counterpart, a National Statement for School Mathematics was produced, with the assistance of mathematics educators, consisting of principles for mathematics content and teaching approaches. The statement was never intended to be a national curriculum.[2] Individual state education systems could implement the statement as they saw fit. Different still was the experience of reforms in the United States. At the

---

[2]It is worthwhile to point out that the extent of professional involvement and the denial of the developers of the Statement that it forms a national curriculum has been contested by some mathematics educators (see Ellerton & Clements, 1994).

initiation of a professional body, the National Council for Teachers of Mathematics, mathematics educators at all levels collaborated to produce the well-known Standards Documents for Curriculum and Assessment. The statement had no legally binding status. However, it was used as the basis of several reforms at local school and school district levels.[3]

In noting these three different processes for mathematics education reform followed by the three countries, we do not intend to make judgments on the soundness or otherwise of their content or principles; in reality they have many similarities in their mathematical content and approaches to teaching. What we would like to note, however, is that not all efforts for establishing curriculum guidelines need to bypass the profession itself. Perhaps the U.S. experience has shown that, if the profession takes initiative in developing guidelines for reform, they may steal the agenda from governments and bureaucrats. Reviewing the curricula reforms around many English-speaking countries, Davis and Guppy (1997) demonstrated how these reforms are transforming education by "squeezing power from the middle" (p. 459). They point to the paradoxical pressures faced by professional educators stemming from power sharing and claims on curriculum between state officials on one hand and the well-organized community associations on the other hand. In other words, the opposing trends of decentralization and devolution on one hand and centralization and standardization of curriculum design and testing on the other have challenged the role of the professional educator. Arguably, the challenge of globalization could be taken as an opportunity by professional mathematics educators around the world for drawing up their new roles and establishing new coalitions for reclaiming their role in the curriculum debate.

The second type of concern against globalized approach to reform is that it challenges the right of the individual nation-states to determine the curricula for their young people in their schools. There are two considerations here. First, many developing nation states do not have the resources to develop their own educational reforms based on their own educational problems and priorities (Jacobson, 1996). There is a real danger in such situations that their attempts to reform mathematics education in schools would be based on copying overseas reforms. This concern about the importation of curriculum reform implies that "local educators have been denied the experience of developing the material themselves" (Clements & Ellerton, 1996, p. 161). Clements and Ellerton called for increased adoption of action research where curriculum developers work collaboratively with local educators to develop culturally sensitive curriculum that is empowering both for the educators and their students. Second, as Taylor, Rizvi, Lingard, and Henry (1997) argued, the function of the nation-state is changing in the face of globalization. They note that the emergence of the nation-state is a relatively recent phenomenon that dates to the 19th and 20th centuries. Such institutions have taken responsibility for welfare, defense, and foreign trade. They also had the role of developing a cohesive sense of identity between the different ethnic groups that constituted the population within their boundaries.

---

[3] According to some educators, these efforts have also lead to a "backlash" such as the "maths wars" in some educational districts (see Kilpatrick, 1999).

The patterns of globalization have shown that the nation-state is an "unstable entity" (p. 61). Undoubtedly, with increased immigration, the population constitution of almost all nation-states has changed significantly this century. Further demands for diversity of needs stem from the increasing awareness of the needs of the local ethnic and cultural groups for local control over the curriculum and recognition of their cultural values. Hence, a global approach to curriculum reform should be based on variety and difference rather than standardization. As we argued previously, these reforms should best be developed from within the profession. Also, we argue that such reforms would be based on genuine collaboration (Hargreaves & Evans, 1997) between the educators from different countries. This is an example of globalization "from below" discussed by Falk (1993, cited in Taylor, Rizvi, Lingard, & Henry, 1997).

The third type of concern is the argument that globalized approaches to reform are a blueprint for standardization and homogeneity and, hence, fail to take into consideration diversity, equity, and cultural and local concerns.[4] This is a valid concern that can be also raised about many national curricula in existence (Ellerton & Clements, 1994). There are examples of national reform movements that acknowledge issues of diversity and equity. For example, the National Statement on Mathematics in Australian Schools recognizes the importance of mathematics for citizens' daily life, their civic life, work, and culture (Australian Education Council, 1990, p. 7). It also posits the belief that "all but few exceptional students are capable of achieving the mathematical confidence and competence needed for personal and civic activities, the skills needed for vocational purposes, and some appreciation of the social and cultural significance of mathematics. For some students this will take longer than for others" (p. 8). "Understanding ourselves requires that we understand how mathematics is integral to our ways of thinking about the world" (p. 7). Finally, we argue that acknowledgment of these curricula of local and cultural differences is a necessary but not sufficient condition to achieve curricula localization and equity and social justice. Following the ideals and principles of the critical mathematics movement (Frankenstein, 1998; Skovsmose, 1994), educators, including teachers, may ensure that the mathematics curriculum is experienced as an empowering activity for all students depending on their background, immediate needs, and future aspirations. Perhaps this is how we may meet the challenge raised by Nebres (1995). He provided an axiom (paradox?) for globalizations, as: "The more global and multicultural we seek to become, the deeper must be our local and personal cultural roots" (p. 39).

The debate of what is culturally bound and what is culture free in mathematics is an ongoing debate in mathematics education literature. One area that has received considerable debate in this literature is the relationship of mathematics learning to its cultural, language, and social context (Bishop, 1988; D'Ambrosio, 1985; Ellerton & Clarkson, 1996; Lave, 1988). In reviewing the literature on ethnomathematics, Nunes (1992) referred to the debate in the literature between those who assert that different contexts give rise to different types of mathematics and those who argue for some

---

[4]Brown and Dowling (1989) argued that internationalism does not automatically guarantee the move away from a monocultural view of the mathematics curriculum.

invariant features underneath surface differences. The work of Bishop (1988) also points to aspects of mathematical thinking that are universal. Further theorizing and research is perhaps needed in this area.

CONCLUSION

In this chapter, we surveyed some of the processes of internationalization and globalization in mathematics education and raised some of the issues that face the profession as a result of these processes. It is obvious that aspects of mathematics education are already being globalized and standardized, and the infrastructure for increased cross-fertilization of ideas is in place. Hence, ignoring these processes by the profession is not possible and even less desirable to do so. We conclude this discussion by identifying some areas of needed action by mathematics educators worldwide for dealing with these processes. It would be far too ambitious for us to attempt to outline a comprehensive agenda for action for the international mathematics education community. Much more debate is needed in the international community before such a plan crystallizes—if indeed such an agenda is possible or desirable. At best what we can do is to identify some possible items for needed action and research by individual educators, professional organizations, official organizations, and the international community as a whole.

We have identified some potentially conflicting discourses behind the processes of internationalization and globalization: for example, economic gain versus concern about equity, local concerns versus global concerns, standardization versus plurality. Perhaps the modernist binary logic of good versus bad is not useful to deal with the complexity of such constructs. For us, such constructs should be used to evaluate particular actions in which mathematics educators are engaged in all their international contacts. We argue that every cross-country activity should be subjected to careful scrutiny as to the motivation behind it, the principles and processes it employs, and the outcomes and benefits it provides to for all participants.

Such careful scrutiny commences at the level of the individual professional. Mathematics educators involved in international activities should examine their motivation behind international collaboration and its effects not only for them personally and for mathematics education in their community but also globally. Such questions should be raised when educators are planing overseas travel to conferences, spending their sabbatical leave, engaging in staff exchange programs, or planning international joint research projects.

Similarly, international programs such as those that cater to international students, professional development, and/or curriculum development, should subject themselves to critical self-reflection as to the roles of the different parties. We suspect that many such activities uncritically make the claim of being collaborative (see chap. 10, this volume). Such programs should be very open about the roles of each of the partners and their contribution to and gains from the project. They should also examine their assumptions about what are global and what are local concerns and values and how they are reflected in the processes and outcomes of the program.

Likewise, professional organizations planning international gatherings as well as editors of international journals should develop policies to encourage more equitable representations of views from developing countries. These may include multiple language presentations, differential fee structure and subsidies, and encouraging alternative research methodologies and styles of reports. It seems to us that as mathematics educators we are more concerned about standardization and uncontested acceptance of what constitutes good research at the expense of whose voices are represented.

At the level of international organization, ICMI has the infrastructure to play a leading role in getting mathematics educators to form international collaborations and communities. Efforts are in place to deal with issues of representations of views. We argue that more effort should be made in this regard. In particular, the ICMI studies could be used to investigate issues related to globalization of mathematics education, with intensive effort to represent the voices of educators from developing countries. Such a study could examine many of the issues raised in this chapter that need a much more solid research base and debate. Also, more awareness and collaboration are needed in the mathematics education community about the functions of international organizations such as the UNESCO and the World Bank.[5]

Particularly, in research the following are some possible areas that may benefit from more systematic research. Needless to say, we encourage programs of research that involve genuine collaboration between researchers from developing countries and developed countries.

Little is known about the perceptions about and problems encountered by developing countries' educators from international contacts such as international conferences, publications, and joint research and development projects.

There is very limited information about the different forms of international collaborative projects and their principles and effects on academics from developing countries in contrast to benefits to developing countries.

Little is known about the processes of curriculum reform in developing countries and the roles of economic considerations in those processes. In particular, more careful scrutiny is needed about processes and outcomes of projects supported by international organizations.

More information is needed about the social and cultural values embedded in learning theories such as constructivism, and the associated pedagogies that they might imply, that have been widely adopted in the developed countries.

Further theorizing may be necessary about the processes of integration and fragmentation of curricula not only between nations but also within every nation.

Finally, the questions of similarities and differences between different "ethnomathematics" should be carried out with specific reference to values, including those about the aspirations of developing countries and economic realities of a globalized world.

---

[5]The involvement of the World Bank in educational funding to developing countries has been problematized by a variety of researchers. Due to space limitations these concerns are not discussed here. For a comprehensive analysis see Jones (1992).

REFERENCES

Australian Education Council. (1990). *A national statement on mathematics for Australian Schools*. Canberra: Curriculum Corporation and Australian Education Council.

Back, K. Davis, D., & Olsen, A. (1996). *Internationalisation of higher education: Goals and Strategies*. Canberra, Australian Government Publication Service.

Bishop, A. (1988). *Mathematical enculturation: A cultural perspective on mathematics education*. Dordrecht: Kluwar.

Bishop, A. J. (1992). International perspectives on research in mathematics education. In D. Grouws (Ed.), *Handbook of research on mathematics teaching and learning* (pp. 710–723). New York: Macmillan.

Brown, A., & Dowling, P. (1989). *Towards a critical alternative to internationalism and monoculturalism in mathematics education* (Working Paper No. 10). London: Centre for Multicultural Education, Institute of Education, University of London.

Clements, K. (1995). Restructuring mathematics teacher education: Overcoming the barriers of elitism and separatism. In R. Hunting, G. Fitzsimons, P. Clarkson, & A. Bishop (Eds.), *Regional collaboration in mathematics education* (pp. 1–10). Melbourne: Monash University.

Clements, M. A., & Ellerton, N. (1996). *Mathematics education research: Past, present and future*. Bangkok: UNESCO.

D'Ambrosio, U. (1995). Ethnomathematics and its place in the history and pedagogy of mathematics. *For the learning of mathematics, 5*(1), 44–48.

Davis, S., & Guppy, N. (1997). Globalisation and education reform in Anglo-American democracies. *Comparative Education Review, 41*(4), 435–459.

Gunew, S. (1990). *Feminist knowledge: Critique and construct*. London: Routledge.

Ellerton, N., & Clarkson, P. C. (1996). Language factors in mathematics. In A. Bishop et al. (Eds.), *International handbook of mathematics education* (pp. 991–1038). Dordrecht: Kluwer.

Ellerton, N., & Clements, K. (1994). *The national curriculum debacle*: Perth: Meridian Press.

Frankenstein, M. (1998). Reading the world with maths: Goals for a critical mathematical literacy curriculum. In P. Gates (Ed.), *Mathematics education and society. Conference proceedings*. Nottingham: Centre for the Study of Mathematics Education.

Hargreaves, A. (1989). *Curriculum and assessment reform*. Milton Keynes: Open University Press.

Hargreaves, A., & Evans, R. (Eds.). (1997). *Beyond educational reform*. Buckingham, UK: Open University Press.

Harris, M. (Ed.). (1991). *School, mathematics and work*. London: Falmer Press.

Henry, M., & Taylor, S. (1997). Globalisation and national schooling policy in Australia. In B. Lingard & P. Porter (Eds.), *A national approach to schooling in Australia: Essays on the development of national policies in school education* (pp. 46–59). Canberra: Australian College of Education.

Ilon, L. (1997). Education, Honesty and Globalisation: A response to the presidential address of Noel F. McGinn. *Comparative-Education-Review, 41*(3), 351–359.

The International Commission of Mathematical Instruction (ICMI). (undated). (ICMI). [http://elib.zib.de/IMU/ICMI]. (20/4/1999).

Jacobsen, E. (1996). International Co-operation in mathematics education. In A. Bishop et al. (Eds.), *International handbook of mathematics education* (pp. 1235–1256). Dordrecht: Kluwer.

Johnston, B. (1992). Walled city. *For the Learning of Mathematics, 12*(3), 23–24.

Jones, P. (1992). *World Bank financing of education: Lending, learning and development*. London: Routledge.

Keitel, C., & Kilpatrick, J. (1999). The rationality and irrationality of international comparative studies. In G. Kaiser, E. Luna, & I. Huntley (Eds.), *International comparisons in mathematics education* (pp. 241–256), London: Falmer Press.

Kilpatrick, J. (1999). Ich bin Euproäisch. In K. Krainer & F. Goffree (Eds.), *On research in mathematics teacher education* (pp. 49–68). Osnabräck, Germany: Forschungsinsitut fär Mathematikdidaktik.

Knight, J. & de Wit, H. (1995). Strategies for internationalisation of higher education: Historical and conceptual perspectives. In H. de Wit (Ed.), *Strategies for internationalisation of higher education* (pp. 5–32). Amsterdam: EAIE.

Kress, G. (1996). Internationalisation and globalisation: Rethinking a curriculum of communication. *Comparative Education, 32*(2), 185–196.

Kuku, A. (1995). Mathematics education in Africa in relation to other countries. In R. Hunting, G. Fitzsimons, P. Clarkson, & A. Bishop (Eds.), *Regional collaboration in mathematics education* (pp. 403–423). Melbourne: Monash University.

Lave, J. (1988). *Cognition in practice: Mind, mathematics & culture in everyday life*. New York: Cambridge University Press.

McGinn, N. (1995) The implication of globalisation for higher education. In L. Buchert, & K. King (Eds.), *Learning from experience: Policy and practice in aid to higher education* (pp. 77–92). Hague: CSEDC.

McGinn, N. (1996). Education, democratization, and globalization: A challenge for comparative education. *Comparative Education Review, 40*(4), 341–357.

McLuhan, M., & Bruce, R. (1992). *The global village: Transformations in world life and media in the 21st century*. Oxford: Oxford University Press.

Nebres, S. J. (1995). Mathematics education in an era of globalisation: Linking education, society an culture in our region. In R. Hunting, G. Fitzsimons, P. Clarkson, & A. Bishop (Eds.), *Regional collaboration in mathematics education* (pp. 31–41). Melbourne: Monash University.

Nunes, T. (1992). Ethnomathematics and everyday cognition. In D. Grouws (Ed.), *Handbook of research on mathematics education* (pp. 557–574). New York: Macmillan.

Print, M. (1987). *Curriculum development and design*. Australia: Allen & Unwin.

Robitaille, D. F., & Travers, K. J. (1992). International studies of achievement in mathematics. In D. Grouws (Ed.), *Handbook of research on mathematics education* (pp. 687–709). New York: Macmillan.

Rogers, L. (1992). *Then and now. For the learning of mathematics, 12*(3), 22–23.

Sawiran, M. (1995). Collaborative efforts in enhancing globalisation in mathematics education. In R. Hunting, G. Fitzsimons, P. Clarkson, & A. Bishop (Eds.), *Regional collaboration in mathematics education* (pp. 603–609). Melbourne: Monash University.

Sierpinska, A., & Kilpatrick, J. (Eds.). (1998). *Mathematics education as a research domain: A search for identity (Book 1 & 2)*. Dordrecht: Kluwer.

Silver, E., & Kilpatrick (1994). E Pluribus unum: Challenges of diversity in the future of mathematics education research. *Journal for Research in Mathematics Education, 25*, 734–754.

Skovsmose, O. (1994). Towards a critical mathematics education. *Educational Studies in Mathematics, 27*(1), 35–57.

Souviney, R. (1983). Mathematics achievement, language and cognitive development: Classroom practices in Papua New Guinea. *Educational Studies in Mathematics, 14*, 183–212.

Taylor, S., Rizvi, R., Lingard, B., & Henry, M. (1997). *Educational policy and the politics of change*. London: Routledge.

UNESCO. (1998). World declaration on Higher education for the twenty-first century: Vision and action. [www.unesco.org/education/educprog/wche/index.html] (20/4/1999).

Usiskin, Z. (1992). Thoughts of an ICME regular. *For the Learning of Mathematics, 12*(3), 19–20.

Vithal, R., & Skovsmose, O. (1997). The end of innocence: A critique of "ethnomathematics." *Educational Studies in Mathematics, 34*, 131–157.

Waters, M. (1995) *Globalisation*. London: Routledge.

6

Globalization and the Politics of Mathematics Education

Jan Thomas
Victoria University of Technology

Mellin-Olsen (1987) viewed mathematics as important as a structure for young people to understand, build, or change a society. He saw mathematics, along with language education, as giving young people a way of compensating for difficult life situations by being constructive, inventive, and forceful rather than turning to drugs or hooliganism. The kind of mathematics curriculum he envisaged to give students the thinking tools needed was based on the relationship between theoretical mathematics and the solving of realistic problems. It exemplified the importance of social context in the teaching of mathematics.

This chapter explores these notions of social contexts in the mathematical sciences—where "mathematical sciences" is as an inclusive term for teaching and research in both the disciplines and mathematics education—in the context of changing world political structures and economic patterns. Specifically, it explores the politics that currently surround mathematics educators, whether they be engaged in teaching or research, and the implications for the mathematical sciences more generally.

Traditionally, a nation's wealth has predominantly been dependent on either its industrial capabilities or its natural resources. It is now accepted that the wealth of nations in the future will be dependent on knowledge and the ability to turn good ideas into commercial activity in a global economy. This is exemplified by, for example, changes to Japanese law to promote technology transfer from the universities (Saegusa, 1999) and a group of key industry and university personnel in Australia who recently listed the actions being taken in many OECD and Asian countries in the "realisation that knowledge and its application is now the major driving force of economic performance" (Business/Higher Education Round Table, 1999).

The role of mathematics in underpinning the science and technology, which is the heart of a knowledge-based economy, offers opportunities, but there are also inherent dangers. A recent piece in *Nature* was headed "Promises and Threats of the Knowledge-Based Economy" and suggested that: "The key lies in combining commitment to two concepts that are far easier to define that to achieve: scientific excellence and social equity" ("Promises and Threats," 1999, p. 1). This notion would have strong resonance with many in the mathematical sciences. However, any discipline that assumes economic importance is likely to attract much more government interest. This can have positive effects, but it can also lead to more outside control and interference by people who may not share the values of many of those involved as teachers or researchers.

Since the 1980s, a major issue for mathematics educators has been social context and its important in the teaching and learning of mathematics. The Fifth International Congress on Mathematical Education (ICME 5) in Australia devoted a theme group to mathematics for all, and the papers were subsequently published by UNESCO (Jacobsen, 1986). In a plenary at ICME 5 D'Ambrosio noted the notion of mathematics for all made it urgent to question ". . . the place of mathematics education in societies as a whole" (p. 1) and mathematics and society became a dominant theme at the Sixth International Congress on Mathematical Education (ICME 6) in Hungary. Culture, language, politics, ethnomathematics, and social and economic contexts were some of the topics discussed on what was known at the "5th Day Special" devoted to the political dimension of mathematics education (Keitel, 1989).

Considerable literature concerned with social context has developed since the mid-1980s, and the issues are still current as, for example, this book and the National Council of Teachers of Mathematics 1997 Yearbook (Trentacosta, 1997) and others (e.g., Lerman, 1994; Secada, Fennema, & Adajian, 1995) clearly identify. They continue to be issues of immense concern to many mathematics educators, and the focus is still very much on equity, access, and excellence. The political climate has, however, changed dramatically.

In discussing the politics of mathematics education after ICME 6, it was noted that D'Ambrosio's address at ICME 5 had been greeted by responses that varied from enthusiastic endorsement to total rejection and that many ICME 6 participants had accepted a naïve view of social context (Thomas, 1989). It became important to distinguish between the "politics of mathematics education," which were concerned with very broad definitions of social context and a much narrower definition concerned with government policy and practices. It is this narrower definition that is used here.

The issues being discussed are complex and, because they are political, subject to personal interpretation. It will be taken as accepted that mathematics education is political, and it will be argued that to ignore the effects of this in an economically globalized and changing world has the potential to constrain or render ineffectual much mathematics education research. In spite of the attention given to social context, the politics of mathematics education research is given very little attention, and many mathematics educators tend to ignore the political milieu in which their work is situated.

Clements (1996) argued that one of the greatest achievements of mathematics educators over the past two decades was to bring to center stage that all forms of mathematics education are surrounded by cultural constraints and forces. This is true of many mathematics educators in Australia where Clements has worked extensively but it is not what shaped government policy. Mathematics at all levels has become more centralized and at the same time it became less well funded. As a result it is now less able to cater to the needs of individuals by taking account of cultural constraints and forces (Clements & Thomas, 1996; Thomas, 1992, 1997a; Zevenbergen, 1997).

The following attempts to identify the political forces that can affect the mathematical sciences as a whole rather than mathematics education research specifically. In part this is in recognition of the interdependence of the components of the mathematical sciences where a strong discipline base in the tertiary sector tends to provide good teachers and teaching in schools and vice versa. Such a climate also supports mathematics education research. Australia is used as a specific case study in the politics of mathematics education as it is a wealthy nation with a reputation for egalitarianism and open government but with a complex multicultural population. This includes a minority indigenous population that also has great diversity in language and cultural traditions. However, there is a growing literature that indicates that factors affecting mathematics education in Australia are global requiring responses from the international community of mathematical scientists.

It will be argued that what the mathematics education community in Australia and elsewhere has been trying to achieve over the last two decades is at odds with the way political systems have developed. The politics of mathematics education as pursued by governments in the 1980s and 1990s have often conflicted with what mathematics educators have tried to achieve especially in regard to equity and social context.

A constant theme throughout the following sections will be that mathematics education exists in a world where the gap between rich and poor is widening. Access to quality mathematics education is now much more resource intensive, and it is often assumed students will have access to computers, especially at the tertiary level. The mathematical scientists—teachers, mathematics educators, and discipline specialists—are more remote from decision making that is increasingly influenced by bureaucrats and global economic considerations rather than educational and equity considerations. There is a need to find a political voice for mathematics education to counter this.

GLOBALIZATION AND MATHEMATICS EDUCATION

The profound change in the dynamics of the world's political framework is exemplified by considering that, when mathematics educators went to ICME 6 in 1988, the Berlin Wall was still intact. A little more than 10 years later, the map of Europe has been rewritten. At the same time there has been a development of huge multinational companies controlling budgets and assets far in excess of those of many smaller nations. Many of us now work in universities and other educational settings where words such as "globalization" and "internationalization" are part of the daily lexicon, especially at the administrative level.

Levin (1999) noted that the term *globalization* is multidimensional and sometimes used as a negative term. In the discussion here it is used to refer to trends in the world's economic and political structures and the way these can impact on aspects of education at the local or national level. Clearly, globalization can have positive effects, but the potential for negative effects needs to be understood and countered. Porter (1999) argued:

> Pedagogy is deeply influenced by the economic and political environment, particularly at a time of massive change. . . the school is under threat and there is an attempt to neutralise it as an independent institution. Pursuing a deeply flawed free market ideology, leading governments and major international agencies have severely limited the capacity of the school to fulfil the varied functions that are required in a democratic state. This is happening at a time of unprecedented challenge from forces of globalisation. (p. 50)

In 2000s, these new political realities need to be part of the discussion of the social context of mathematics education. There is a need to examine whether the voices of mathematics educators are heard in the search for global solutions by governments and a world economy increasingly dependent on, and manipulated by, huge multinationals. Porter (1999) also identified bodies such as the World Bank, the International Monetary Fund, and U.N. agencies as increasingly insisting that aid and loan packages be tied to the use of education for competitiveness in the global economy. Developing economies and Third World countries seem to have been all too aware of the influence of these agencies for some years. For obvious reasons this is seldom documented but mentioned at international conferences and in private conversations. It can be argued that many in the "Western democracies" have been ill prepared for the kind of economically based influence that can now occur in any nation, whereas educators in many other nations have found some ways to deal with this phenomenon.

The emerging question is how relevant can discussion of social context in mathematics education be in a globalized economy that may lead to a globalized curriculum? In his analysis of the justification and goals of mathematics education Niss (1996) concluded that during the 1990s these have "not been given a terribly great amount of explicit attention by researchers in mathematics education" (p. 43). One of the reasons he suggested for this is an increased interest in the needs of individuals by mathematics educators. It may also be that mathematics educators have not thought it was necessary to justify what they did on the assumption that mathematics education would continue to be seen as important and that they would control it. However, without clearly defined justification and goals, and where mathematics begins to be valued by government for its economic importance rather than any intrinsic value, this may be a dangerous assumption.

Australia is one example where economic rationalism and internationalization have seen the development of a kind of government where the needs of individuals are becoming subservient to economic goals. It is also a country where mathematical scientists now have a greatly reduced role in influencing many aspects of their professional lives.

THE VULNERABILITY OF MATHEMATICS CURRICULUM: AN AUSTRALIAN PERSPECTIVE

Kemmis (1989) noted that the almost universal acceptance of the link between a nation's school mathematics and its economic well-being meant that the dangers of theory being replaced by policy were particularly acute in mathematics education. He argued:

> If curriculum and assessment decisions are left to the policy makers and system managers, school communities and professional organisations can expect to be marginalised. If they are, education theory and the justification of policy and practice will become the preserve of policy makers and administrators; education practice will be directed by the system, with teachers and school communities acting as the education technicians supporting education delivery systems designed by curriculum developers at a distance from schools and communities; the autonomy and responsibility of school communities and the teaching profession will be eroded, with teachers becoming, to a new and unprecedented degree, functionaries of the state. (p. 135)

Kemmis was writing about the situation in Australia and in the decade since most of this has come to pass. In 1989, state and federal education ministers met and formulated what became known as the Hobart Declaration on Schooling. This joint statement marked a new stage of educational development in Australia as prior to this each state had jealously guarded its right to determine its own curriculum even though they were dependent on centrally collected taxes to do so. Clearly, such a system in a country with a population the size of Australia's was not very efficient in many ways. However, Australia is geographically very large, and it did allow diversity and local control by state governments rather than being centrally controlled. The national government had a key role in providing additional funding for equity programs, professional development for teachers, and the development of exemplary curriculum materials. The Mathematics Curriculum and Teaching Program (Lovitt & Clarke, 1988/1989) was one such initiative in mathematics but other areas, especially curriculum and materials for the teaching of English as a second language, thrived under this system. Research in both of these areas also prospered.

At the meeting that formulated the Declaration, notions of national collaboration were strengthened, and it was decided that the first area for action would be in the development of a statement of common principles in mathematics (Ellerton & Clements, 1994). There were a number of reasons why national collaboration in curriculum matters was attractive to ministers at this time, but the overwhelming one was almost certainly driven by budgetary concerns rather than educational theory. As the political orthodoxy moved to low tax and small government, they were finding it increasingly difficult to maintain their own curriculum and support services. In a very real sense state ministers probably believed that they would have considerable discretion in how any national documents would be used as they had always done in the past.

The statement of common principles in mathematics rapidly grew into a major project to produce national statements and profiles that divided the curriculum into eight learning areas, of which mathematics was one. Ellerton and Clements (1994) gave a detailed description of their development and the concerns with the process and products. When the mathematical sciences community succeeded in having them temporarily slowed, the federal government retaliated by directing professional development money only to those who were prepared to implement them. This had the effect of tempering any opposition as mathematics educators in the universities and the teacher professional associations knew they had little chance of getting grants for teacher professional development if they were not seen as being fully supportive of the approaches being taken.

It is important to realize that at no time was there any real objection to the idea of a national statement or framework for mathematics and that many in the mathematical sciences saw this as highly desirable. The major concerns were with the quality of the documents produced, the outcomes-based approach, and especially the lack of consultative processes. In a very short period of time Australia went from a locally controlled, consensus model of curriculum development, which was assisted by generous central funding to support equity issues, to a model that largely excluded expert opinion. Importantly, reduced funding was specifically directed to an outcomes-based approach supported by documents that were seen as seriously flawed.

Australia still does not have an official national curriculum, but by 1995 Wilkins and Doyle were able to report on the possibility of collecting nationally comparable information on students and stated that: "This is made possible because of the large degree of consistency that appears to be emerging in the implementation of profiles across Australia, and by the efforts being made by jurisdictions to link their State-wide tests to profiles" (p. 30).

A move to whole cohort national testing was always a major concern for a number of reasons. It was considered it was unlikely that it could be done well and take account of social context. Davies (1990), for example, showed that non-English-speaking background children's results on mathematics tests used in New South Wales were influenced by their proficiency in English. There was also concern that this kind of accountability mechanism would be seen as the principal means of school improvement without commensurate resources for teaching and research.

The most articulate public speakers on issues to do with access to quality mathematics education in Australia are now mathematicians who are immediately dismissed as elitist academics only concerned with the best and brightest. Nothing could be further from the truth, but it sounds credible when teachers and mathematics educators remain largely silent and do not support what the mathematicians say. Each year Australia moves closer to a national mathematics curriculum reminiscent of the 1950s and 1960s except that there is some use of the newer technologies grafted onto it. From a global perspective it is important to realize where the locus of control now appears to be and why there are so many silenced voices.

MATHEMATICS CURRICULUM
AND THE BUREAUCRACY

At a superficial level there appears to be little in common between the Australian and English experiences. In England, a national curriculum with associated national testing was mandated in the late 1980s and has been through several iterations since. There was none of the tortuous process that has led to a de facto national curriculum in Australia. At another level there are remarkable similarities. In particular, the similarity of the dismissive responses given to a report prepared by the London Mathematical Society and to the criticisms made by Australian mathematicians to both projects were remarkably similar (Ellerton & Clements, 1994).[1]

Gardiner (1998), one of the people involved in the London Mathematical Society report, recently noted that the situation in regard to the mathematics curriculum has been complicated by two rival philosophies of mathematics facing a third force that he described as more powerful and less principled than either, which he called "burgeoning bureaucracy." He cautioned about the use of labels and suggested that these forces be seen as three opposing tendencies—traditionalist, revisionist, and bureaucratic—which may coexist within individuals. In his view traditionalists may struggle to find new ways of doing things but are determined not to reject key elements, revisionists believe more strongly that the old ways have failed, and bureaucrats come from either or both camps but they, or their superiors, believe that educational effectiveness comes from central control and formal accountability.

The result of this third force in both England and Australia seems to have been very similar. A recent study by Horwood (1999) on the influences on secondary mathematics curriculum in Victoria, Australia, in recent years concluded:

> One outcome of this whole process was the strengthening of the role of the professional administrator in the control of the curriculum. Thereafter, the role of mathematicians and mathematics educators would seem to be one of expert adviser to bureaucracy, within the framework of terms of reference decided by the bureaucracy. The decision as to who constitutes the expert, and whether advice is accepted, now appears to rest with the bureaucracy. (p. 273)

Ball (1999), commenting in the *Mathematics Teacher*, noted the mismatch between what many contributors were saying and the message of government and others who are trying to influence the teaching of mathematics. She quoted the rejection of results of commissioned research when it did not achieve the expected result. In Australia, it is more likely that such documents will not become public unless they achieve the expected result. Part of a recent tender document in Victoria read: "The report remains the property of the DoE, the CECV and the AISV through the Successful Interventions Steering Committee and cannot be distributed in any format without the express permission of the DoE, the CECV and the AISV" (Department of Education, 1999, p. 7).[2]

---

[1]It is not being suggested that the mathematicians should dominate curriculum debates. However, they have a legitimate role and their input should be given serious consideration especially as many are also parents and teachers.

[2]The section was emphasized in bold.

There is anecdotal evidence that the results of such studies are becoming increasingly difficult to present publicly.[3] For example, it was recently reported that the DoE (Department of Education) was refusing permission for a presentation on the results of an investigation into support for students with difficulties in mathematics in the early years of secondary schooling. It illustrates the changes that have occurred as 10 years ago it would have been more likely for DoE personnel to be actively involved in such reports and to present jointly with others, including teachers, who were involved. Importantly, many mathematics educators are only just beginning to realize the impact of the changes and that they may not be able to publish or publicly present some of the work that they are involved in.

The implications for research in mathematics education in Australia, and any other nation where this is occurring, are profound. At the same time there is a weakening discipline base emerging in many parts of the world. Without a strong discipline base, mathematics in schools and mathematics education research must also be diminished.

THE DISCIPLINE OF MATHEMATICS

Kline (1953) wrote that "Mathematics is, itself, a living, flourishing branch of our culture . . . whose essential characteristics should be familiar to every educated person" (p. 453). A review of advanced mathematical sciences in Australia claimed " . . . modern mathematical science, is in its own right a supreme creation of the human intellect; it is also critical for economic competitiveness and a basis for investigations in many fields . . . " (National Committee for Mathematics, 1996, p. ix). The basis of this description is the power and beauty of mathematics linked to its economic value.

Brinkworth and Truran (1998) reported that students " . . . have a distorted view of mathematicians and users of mathematics, whom they see as somewhat cloistered individuals . . . not very concerned with social issues" (p. 56). This view is probably shared by many in the community and in government. There is also a community perception that advances in technology, especially calculators and computers, have reduced the need for people with mathematical skills. The mathematical skills needed to use the newer technologies well are not understood. As a result Australia, for example, has an oversupply of doctors and lawyers but is short of doctors with a good statistical education for research and lawyers who can handle some of the more complex mathematical modeling underpinning much business and commerce.

In the foreword to the Australian review of advanced mathematical sciences, the Chair of the Australian Research Council at the time wrote:

> The report demonstrates with clarity the extraordinary way in which this most fundamental of disciplines is intertwined with other disciplines, and with the life of the nation.

---

[3]One of the reasons this remains anecdotal is that interaction with the DoE and other bureaucracies is usually by telephone or meeting and there is seldom anything in writing. On one occasion the Catholic Education Commission of Victoria (CECV) wanted to republish an article of mine relating to the teaching of mathematics to students whose first language was not English (Thomas, 1997b). It was part of a joint project with the DoE, and the DoE would not publish without editing, preferable by them. Nothing was ever put in writing about this except by me. It should be noted that these kinds of issues become even more complex when multiple bureaucracies are involved.

It makes a persuasive case that the mathematical sciences at an advanced level play a crucial role in the nation's economic competitiveness and social justice issues. (Brennan, 1996, pp. iii–iv)

The review also showed that the mathematical base in Australia was fragile. Since then the economy in Australia has remained strong, but funding for universities has been reduced. Data collected by the Heads of Mathematical Sciences Departments showed an alarming decline in staff of about 20% over three years, although student numbers had remained about the same.[4] A review of the state of mathematical sciences in New Zealand found similar results to those for Australia (Ministry of Research, Science & Technology, 1998).

The global indications are that the mathematical sciences are in decline in many parts of the world. Australia's and New Zealand's difficulties are small compared with those that our colleagues in the mathematical sciences appear to confront in Russia (Arnol'd, 1998). The Indonesian university system has been seriously affected by economic factors (Nicholls, 1999), and Japanese mathematicians are concerned about a reduction in the time spent on mathematics in schools. Those of us in Western societies see Asian nations as valuing mathematics, but some of the newer universities in Malaysia have been set up with no mathematics department and mathematicians employed in isolation to teach service courses.[5]

This devaluing of mathematics in the tertiary sector has very serious implications for mathematics education in schools and mathematics in the community. Tertiary mathematics provides the base for well-qualified and enthusiastic teachers. Moreover, Steen (1998) argued that mathematical competence is now as important for self-fulfillment as literacy has been in the past. He suggested that not all of the learning required can be accomplished in secondary education, suggesting a view that access to postsecondary mathematics is also important. The multiplicity of career options he identified requiring mathematics needs, in many cases, different approaches to teaching tertiary mathematics. This is proving difficult in countries such as Australia where fewer staff have to teach more students from more diverse backgrounds.

The need for young people and the community in general to have a greater appreciation of mathematics in society is important. Mathematics educators are crucial to this, but they must have the freedom to use local contexts to make it meaningful, and this could be undermined by a global curriculum.

What Might a Globalized Mathematics Curriculum Look Like?

In the narrowest definition of curriculum that considers only content, mathematics has been "globalized" as content taught worldwide is very similar. It was this content-based globalized curriculum that took little account of students' interests, social context,

---

[4]A copy of data that has been used extensively in the media is held by author. Over two thirds of departments participated.

[5]Personal communication following comments made about the state of mathematics in Australia in the Melbourne Age were printed by the Borneo Post.

or values that mathematics educators have challenged in the search for the kind of curriculum that breaks down the barriers of gender, class, and ethnicity.

A 1998 issue of the *Australian Universities Review* was devoted to the theme of higher education and the politics of difference. A commentary by Lewis (1998) was not included in the feature section but would have been a fitting introduction. Lewis dealt with the commodified curricula, which he described as "essentially course materials packaged as coursebooks . . . to ensure that course delivery is standardised" (p. 3). He notes that these depart from a descriptive or framework for teaching in that they specify each step of a teacher's interaction with students. He concluded:

> The issue of contextual appropriacy is one of many problems resulting from the commodification of curricula. What is perhaps most disconcerting is that the market forces which have so instrumental in driving the development of theses curricula, also mitigate against their critique. The intensified exploitation of teachers which has been exacted through the operationalization of sourcebook-curricula has pre-empted debate over the pedagogical impasse they present for educators. Indeed the worse excesses of commodified curricula have seen teachers' roles completely redefined and their professional autonomy undermined. (p. 4)

Lewis discussed intensive English courses for overseas students, but the difficulties and dangers he identified are just as real in mathematics. For example, considerable commodification of English language teaching in Australian schools has taken place in the last few years under the banner of "literacy education." The most recent casualty of this has been funding for aboriginal bilingual programs (Lo Bianco, 1999; Tomlinson, 1999), but considerable other funding from other equity and English as a second language programs have also be subsumed under "literacy" and the development of various packages for school use.

The emphasis on literacy, especially in the early years of schooling, in Australia has much to recommend it. It appears to be underpinned by a genuine desire for all students to learn to appreciate the richness and power of language. The key concerns of educators are with narrow prescribed approaches, lack of appreciation of the role of first language for students from a non-English speaking background—in both learning of English and in cultural identify- and whether it is possible to develop appropriate assessment regimes in a multicultural society that satisfy the federal government's requirements that there be whole-year level reporting and accountability.

Similar concerns are being raised in regard to "numeracy." There is, however, a fundamental difference in the way numeracy is being defined in that there appears to be no underpinning of a desire for all students to appreciate the richness and power of mathematics. Documents emanating from the federal bureaucracy, and more disturbingly from the Australian Association of Mathematics Teachers (1998), are attempting to define numeracy in a way that distances it from mathematics. As a result no clear definition of what is meant by numeracy has emerged. At the same time "numeracy benchmarks" have been developed, which are not benchmarks in the usual sense but are low-level goals defined as something the majority of students should achieve easily.

There are many contradictions in the Australian numeracy work. These arise from a number of sources but especially the exclusion of the discipline societies from any of the discussion about what is meant by numeracy. However, it also seems to have disregarded the work of people such as Johnston (1995) in the adult education sector on critical numeracy and the writing on critical mathematics (e.g., see, Lerman, 1994; Skovsmose & Nielsen, 1996). As a result both the mathematics and social context have not be adequately addressed in deciding what it is the numeracy benchmarks will assess and how it will be done.

The issue of numeracy is emerging in other nations. It is now in common usage in England where it also seems to be more attached to the national curriculum, and therefore bureaucratic control, rather than a real appreciation of mathematics. There is some work being done in the United States, but hopefully the greater involvement of the discipline societies in a more open debate in that country will alleviate some of the problems that have emerged in countries such as Australia.

There are clear messages in this that need to be heeded. When the bureaucrats have undue influence on mathematics curriculum in the current political climate, the curriculum that emerges may pay scant attention to social context and even less to the discipline of mathematics. Apple (1995) cautioned on curriculum that concentrates on the "practical" for poor and working class and leaves access to the skills of critical reasoning to those who already have power. If a global bureaucracy produces a global curriculum, there is a very real danger that this curriculum would do precisely that.

In the working group on policy at the ICMI study conference on the teaching and learning of mathematics at the university level, it was suggested that mathematicians and mathematics educators need to work together to maintain the integrity of the mathematical sciences in the same way that minority cultures have had to work to preserve their languages, cultures, and values. The membership of this group had representatives from Western, Asian, and developing nations.

GLOBALIZATION AND RESEARCH IN MATHEMATICS EDUCATION

Central to research in mathematics education are researchers in the university sector and the funding for research. However, they also need access to schools, teachers, and students who are fundamental in the conduct of research. A number of problematic issues are emerging relating to the conduct of mathematics education research.

Levin (1999) identified a number of consequences global forces of change have had on Canadian higher education and they would be recognizable to many in other nations. He noted:

> There is increasing evidence that colleges have less ability than in the past to act independently of either government or the private sector, both strongly tied to a global economy. Already in some of their behaviors, colleges are lessening their focus on the community, giving way to the global at the expense of the local, yet rationalizing their

embraces of new structures such as international education and distance education by connecting these to local needs. (p. 397)

Mathematics education research now operates in a world where it is theoretically much easier to access global knowledge. At the same time many researchers are located in situations where they have less ability to act independently.

As universities find it increasingly difficult to maintain their funding base for both teaching and research, gaining government contracts and tenders becomes a means of survival. Not only does this restrict and control what can be reported but it engages researchers in these tasks at the expense of other research that could be public.

Government control of research through such mechanisms is seldom openly debated. When it is raised it can provoke division within the research community between those who have had government contracts and those who try to raise questions about this kind of research. Ellerton (1995) argued:

> We can allow our research priorities to be dictated by funding agencies and political considerations even though our research may do little more than ratify the status quo. Such compromises made to achieve funding or recognition can, in fact, keep researchers away from doing the very investigations that are needed to clarify our thinking in the realm of mathematics education and thereby improve the teaching and learning of mathematics. (p. 93)

A subsequent letter in response by Willis (1996) indicated that further debate on this issue was likely to provoke divisions within the mathematics education research community in Australia, and the discussion stopped.

Some years later, examples of bureaucratic interference in educational research are beginning to be documented. Kamler, Reid, and Santoro (1999) documented their experiences with the Department of Education, resulting in nine months of delays in a research project that required access to teachers and already had university ethics approval. They ask a rhetorical question as to whether they should have taken the DoE advice and given up on the project and suggest their analysis says not. They note that controversial questions "may be silenced and less likely to gain approval than those that bolster the status quo" (p. 64).

There is a need to learn how to deal with these issues. Peoples' careers and higher degree scholarships are often dependent on being able to get on with their research within ethical but not externally controlled environments. There have always been issues about particular kinds of research being preferred by funding agencies. Bureaucratic interference in the actual research to the extent documented by Kamler et al. is new in Australia, and the debate that Ellerton tried to start is now urgent.

In a further development in Australia, ways in which the key funding arrangements for supporting research are currently the subject of a discussion paper (Department of Education, Training and Youth Affairs, 1999), with the federal education minister due to announce his final decision in 2000. If the current proposals are adopted, it is possible that money generated from consultancies will be given equal weighting to that generated by peer-reviewed research funding. Serious scholarship may be given the same weighting as a report someone wants and may be suppressed if it fails to produce the "right" answers.

These kinds of developments have serious implications for the credibility of mathematics education research. "Research" publications commissioned by government to support a particular policy will do little to support the credibility of educational research in general if it is subsequently revealed that selected reporting was done. Dressman (1999) recently described what he perceived as the using and misusing of research evidence in Texas and California as producing little more than predetermined political rather than educational ends. Apple (1986) identified these two states as having the largest guaranteed market for textbooks and that they could therefore influence education across America. The implications for the credibility of educational research in America if the literacy programs supposedly based on research fail are enormous.

If educational research, including mathematics education research, is to be taken seriously then the potential uses and abuses of such research must be debated and it must be public. Keeping abreast of the ramifications of political decisions affecting mathematics education is becoming increasingly difficult. The speed with which government decisions are now sometimes implemented means that there is often little opportunity to write carefully researched analyses of proposed changes. However, there is nothing wrong with, and much to commend on, the "quick and dirty" research analysis that may occasionally be called for to start the debate.

In Australia there is a publication called *Directions in Education*. It provides comment on issues that have appeared in the media, and contributors are limited to about 300 words that usually have to be written on a very tight deadline. It goes to many of Australia's educational administrators. In a recent interview with the chair of a faculty's research committee it was made clear he considered this kind of comment had little to do with research and that anything of such short length was not important. However, are not short summary pieces that busy administrators have time to read more likely to make a difference than the carefully worded full-length paper read by the tiny minority?

In the globalized world of rapid political change, research findings may need to be used in ways that risk them being misquoted and misused in, for example, daily newspapers. To remain silent while a bureaucracy decides what is research risks the integrity of mathematics education research.

IMPLICATIONS AND DISCUSSION

In the introduction it was noted that discussions of political issues by their nature tend to be personal. The interpretation of the issues discussed must be to some extent personal, and they are deeply influenced by what has happened in Australia. However, I think there are some salutary messages for those outside of Australia.

The third force identified by Gardiner (1998), the bureaucracy, now controls education in Australia. However, what Apple (1995, p. 333) described as the "rapid growth in the adoption of reductive procedures of standardization and rationalization" is not confined to Australia. It is now possible to discern the movement of bureaucrats between nations and agencies. Hence, a central figure involved in the Australian national curriculum moved to a key role in the OECD. Another is involved in a major project in America. Within Australia there is a greater tendency to see senior bureaucrats take senior administrative, not academic, positions in universities. The growth of this third force helps explain why there can be a change of government and, like in England, very little changes in education. An English colleague described education under Blair as a more efficient form of Thatcher's educational policies. Similarly, little has changed in Australia at either a national or state level during recent changes of government.

In mathematics education there is a need to be attentive to, and constantly challenge, what is becoming a global network of powerful bureaucrats and their advisers, many in universities, who are pushing a common line about education. Their views of mathematics and mathematics education are at odds with most mathematics educators and the majority of mathematicians. There is little in their rhetoric that allows a view of mathematics as part of culture and worthy of study in its own right for its power and beauty.

Those engaged in mathematics education research are seeking clearer understanding of the teaching and learning of mathematics. It can be assumed they see this as an important part of education, and it suggests that they value mathematics as a discipline. It is something they share with teachers of mathematics and others engaged in the mathematical sciences. There may be disagreement as to what to teach and how to teach it but there is a shared commitment to the idea that mathematics is useful. For many there is also a deeper appreciation of mathematics in cultures and the discipline itself.

Research in the sociocultural aspects of mathematics education has revealed a complex mixture of factors that affect the learning of mathematics. There are many that are still not fully understood, but it is clear that an appreciation of the discipline itself and its development is important. There is a need to demystify mathematics and to recognize that, like the appreciation music or art, it is possible to appreciate the power and beauty of a discipline without having the personal talents to participate at the highest levels. There is a need to ensure that a globalized numeracy curriculum based on what is perceived as useful and relevant skills does not emerge while a small elite has access to a much richer curriculum.

The dangers are especially real in school mathematics teaching when the continuing shortfalls in the supply of adequately qualified mathematics teachers in many countries are taken into consideration. Unfortunately, good mathematics education is becoming very expensive. Good teachers are much more difficult to get without better pay than some other disciplines and access to computers at senior levels is usually assumed. So, mathematics may be headed for the gatekeeper role, which is very different to any in the past.

Universal education is dependent on public funding and therefore on governments. At the end of the 1990s, access to mathematics education in Third World countries remains problematic. In many developed countries such as Australia there is now a greater divide between rich and poor that there was 10 years ago. Many countries such as Russia have lost considerable ground. There will never be an equitable education system until the nations of the world collectively take on the multinationals and ensure that they pay their fair share of tax so that education for all can be considered a possibility. The root causes of the problems in mathematics education are economic, and the economic problems are global.

Mathematics educators can quietly go on doing useful research into the teaching and learning of mathematics where children have those opportunities. We can pretend we still live in thriving democracies and turn a blind eye to the kind of curriculum being thrust on children and ignore the control of teachers and what they do. The alternative is to be much more articulate about why all children need access to an excellent mathematics education.

During the last election in Australia I was asked to take part in a forum on the state of science. I concluded with a plea to the media:

> The media needs to get behind the glossy brochures and have a look at what some of our schools, in particular, are like. Walk into any Victorian government school and you will be met by a gleaming, modern reception area. But it often hides a ghetto of cold and horrible rooms, the most dismal of which are often the science laboratories.
>
> Analogies exist in all our universities and in every sector of society dependent on public funding. To the Treasury bureaucrats who frame budgets this is another world they know nothing about. They, and the public, all need to know the misery that lies behind the glossy brochures, manipulated statistics and silenced voices. (Thomas, 1998)

The media is itself constrained, but the stories they portray are also only as good as the information they are given. The role of professional societies becomes critical because they can speak when individuals may be constrained.

Globalization poses many threats to a quality mathematics education. These threats are of a political nature and will require political responses. The profession can only deal with this if it attempts to come to terms with this and become political also. Jacobsen (1996) noted the growing political conservatism, the rich becoming richer and the poor becoming poorer, and that it is becoming more difficult to look to governments for improved international cooperation in education. All of this is true but it ignores the kind of globalized curriculum that governments might support, and it is difficult to envisage that this is what mathematics educators would want.

There is a current International Commission on Mathematical Instruction (ICMI) study on the teaching of tertiary mathematics (ICMI, 1997). I have argued in that discussion that, like many professional groups, the role of ICMI needs to change. International bodies and emerging international bureaucracies are influencing mathematics education in ways that serve a particular form of global economy. ICMI itself needs to become much more articulate in describing what is equitable and democratic mathematics education. This is an international challenge—it needs to be addressed by the international body in close and constructive collaboration with all its members.

In many Western societies we have taken democracy and freedom of speech for granted. There is a tendency to forget that a strong democracy depends on vigorous and open debate on all aspects of society. The repression of individuals in modern Western economies is not overt as it has been in many other societies but much more subtle and manipulative. It makes it easy to ignore the underlying equalities by giving people the basics—a job provided you do what you are told, a vote but limited opportunity for real involvement in political debate or decision making, and a mathematics education provided it meets certain government-imposed criteria.

In 1988, we recognized cultural imperialism in mathematics education. As the new century begins the concern should be with the economic imperialism that is creating a greater divide between rich and poor both within and between nations. It is also effectively removing mathematics curriculum from collaborative and cooperative models to manipulated and controlled ones where dissenting voices are silenced. The mathematics education community can either join those silenced voices and accept the growing inequalities, or it can find a way to continue articulating mathematics for all. This is the courageous path because it will not be risk-free. However, if mathematics for all is an equity and social justice issue, is it not worth a few risks?

REFERENCES

Apple, M. W. (1986). *Teachers and texts: A political economy of class and gender relations in education*. New York: Routledge & Kegan Paul.

Apple, M. W. (1995). Taking power seriously: New directions in equity in mathematics education and beyond. In W. G. Secada, E. Fennema, & L. B. Adajian (Eds.), *New directions for equity in mathematics education* (pp. 329–348). New York: Cambridge University Press.

Arnol'd, V. I. (1998). Mathematical illiteracy is more pernicious than the fires of the inquisition. *London Mathematical Society Newsletter, 259*, 18–20.

Australian Association of Mathematics Teachers (1998). *Policy on numeracy education in schools*. Author: Adelaide, Australia.

Ball, B. (1999). Editorial. *Mathematics Teacher, 168*, 2.

Brennan, M. (1996). Foreword. *Mathematical sciences: Adding to Australia* (pp. iii–iv). Canberra: Australian Government Publishing Services

Brinkworth, P., & Truran, J. (1998). *Research report of a study of the influences on students' reasons for studying or not studying mathematics*. Adelaide: The Flinders University of South Australia.

Business/Higher Education Round Table. (1999). *BHERT News, 5*, 9–10.

Clements, K. (1996). Introduction to section 3. In A. J. Bishop, K. Clements, C. Keitel, J. Kilpatrick, & C. Laborde (Eds.), *International handbook of mathematics education* (pp. 821–825). Dordrecht: Kluwer.

Clements, M. A., & Thomas, J. (1996). Politics of mathematics education: Australasian perspectives. In P. Sullivan, K. Owens, & B. Atweh (Eds.), *Research in mathematics education in Australasia 1992–1995* (pp. 89-117). University of Western Sydney: Mathematics Education Research Group of Australasia.

D'Ambrosio, U. (1986). Socio-cultural bases for mathematical education. In M. Carss (Ed.), *Proceedings of the fifth international Congress on Mathematical Education*. Boston: Birkhauser.

Davies, A. (1990). *Evaluation of the New South Wales 1989 basic skills testing program*. Sydney: Ethnic Affairs Commission of New South Wales.

Department of Education. (1999). *Project brief: Middle Years Numeracy Research Project: 5–8+ (Stage 2)*. Author: Melbourne, Australia.

Department of Education, Training and Youth Affairs. (1999). *New knowledge: New opportunities*. Author: Canberra.

Dressman, M. (1999). On the use and misuse of research evidence: Decoding two states' reading initiatives. *Reading Research Quarterly, 34*(3), 258–285.

Ellerton, N. F. (1995). Moral dilemmas for mathematics education research. *Mathematics Education Research Journal, 7*(2), 91–93.

Ellerton, N. F., & Clements, M. A. (1994). *The national curriculum debacle*. Perth: Meridian Press.

Gardiner, T. (1998) The art of knowing. *Mathematical Gazette, 82*, 353–372.

Horwood, J. (1999). Influences on secondary mathematics curriculum in Victoria. In J. Truran & K. Truran (Eds.), *Making the difference* (pp. 269–274). The University of Adelaide: Mathematics Education Research Group of Australasia.

ICMI (December 1997). Bulletin, http://www.icfes.gov.co/EMIS/mirror/IMU/ICMI/bulletin/

Jacobsen, E. (Ed.). (1986). *Mathematics for all*. Paris: UNESCO

Jacobsen, E. (1996). International co-operation in mathematics education. In A. J. Bishop, K. Clements, C. Keitel, J. Kilpatrick, & C. Laborde (Eds.), *International handbook of mathematics education* (pp. 1235–1256). Dordrecht: Kluwer.

Johnson, B. (1995). Which map shall I use? *Numeracy in Focus, 5*(3), 33–37.[6]

Kamler, B., Reid, J-A., & Santoro, N. (1999). Who's asking the questions? Researching race, ethnicity and teachers. *Australian Educational Researcher, 26*(1), 55–74.

Keitel, C. (1989). *Mathematics, education, and society*. Paris: UNESCO.

Kemmis, S. (1989). From curriculum innovation to educational reform: Changing schools. In M. A. Clements & N. F. Ellerton (Eds.), *School mathematics: The challenge to change* (pp. 120–138). Geelong: Deakin University Press.

Kline, M. (1953). *Mathematics in western culture*. New York: Oxford University Press.

Lerman, S. (Ed.). (1994). *Cultural perspectives on the mathematics classroom*. Dordrecht: Kluwer.

Levin, S. L. (1999). Missions and structures: Bringing clarity to perceptions about globalization and higher education in Canada. *Higher Education, 37*, 377–399.

Lewis, R. (1998). Commodified curricula: the coursebook. *Australian Universities Review, 11*(2), 3–4.

Lo Bianco, J. (1999). Struggle to speak: Taking funding away from Aboriginal bi-lingual education. *Australian Language Matters, 7*(1), 1, 6.

Lovitt, C. J., & Clarke, D. M. (1988/1989). *Mathematics Curriculum and Teaching Program Activity Bank* (Vols. 1 and 2). Curriculum Corporation, Carlton, Victoria, Australia.

Mellin-Olsen, S. (1987). *The politics of mathematics education*. Dordrecht: D. Reidel.

Ministry of Research, Science & Technology. (1998). *Mathematics in New Zealand: Past, present and future*. Wellington: Author.

National Committee for Mathematics. (1996). *Mathematical sciences: Adding to Australia*. Canberra: Australian Government Publishing Services.

Nicholls, J. (1999). Hysteria, history and hope: Higher education policy reform set against the Indonesian political and economic crisis. *Australian Universities Review, 42*(1), 40–46.

Niss, M. (1996). Goals of mathematics teaching. In A. J. Bishop, K. Clements, C. Keitel, J. Kilpatrick, & C. Laborde (Eds.), *International handbook of mathematics education* (pp. 11–47). Dordrecht: Kluwer.

Porter, J. (1999). Education and the global future. *New Era in Education, 80*(2), 50–51.

Promises and threats of the knowledge-based economy. (1999). *Nature, 397*(6714).

Saegusa, A. (1999). Japan acts to speed technology transfer from universities. *Nature, 401*(6748), 3.

Secada, W. G., Fennema, E., & Adajian, L. B. (Eds.). (1995). *New directions for equity in mathematics education*. New York: Cambridge University Press.

Skovsmose, O., & Nielsen, L. (1996). Critical mathematics education. In A. J. Bishop, K. Clements, C. Keitel, J. Kilpatrick, & C. Laborde (Eds.), *International handbook of mathematics education* (pp. 1257–1288). Dordrecht: Kluwer.

Steen, L. A. (1998). Refining university mathematics: The stealth campaign. In *Pre-proceeding of the ICMI Study Conference on the teaching and learning of mathematics at university level* (pp. 1–6). Singapore: National Institute of Education.

Thomas, J. (1989). The politics of mathematics education: A personal construction. In M. A. Clements & N. F. Ellerton (Eds.), *School mathematics: The challenge to change* (pp. 139–154). Geelong: Deakin University Press.

Thomas, J. (1992). Politics of mathematics education in Australia. In B. Atweh & J. Watson (Eds.), *Research in mathematics education in Australasia 1988–1991* (pp. 26–42). Queensland University of Technology: Mathematics Education Research Group of Australasia.

Thomas, J. (1997a). The politics of mathematics education 1997. In F. Biddulph & K. Carr (Eds.), *People in mathematics* (pp. 505–512). Proceedings of 20th Conference of the Mathematics Education Research Group of Australasia. Rotorua, New Zealand: Mathematics Education Research Group of Australasia.

Thomas, J. (1997b). Mathematics, numeracy and language: Issues of equity and social justice. *Learning Matters, 2*(3), 15–19.

Thomas, J. (1998, September). *Thriving, surviving or diving? Science in 1998*. Australian and New Zealand Association for the Advancement of Science Forum, University of New South Wales.

Thomas, J. (2000). Policy issues in the teaching and learning of the mathematical sciences at the university level. *International Journal of Mathematical Education in Sciences and Technology, 31*(1), 133–142.

---

[6]Replaced regular edition of *ARIS Bulletin*, 5(3).

Tomlinson, J. (1999). NT bilingual policy should be reinstated. *Campus Review, 9*(2), 8.

Trentacosta, J. (Ed.). (1997). *Multicultural and gender equity in the mathematics classroom: The gift if diversity.* Reston, VA: National Council of Teachers of Mathematics.

Wilkins, R., & Doyle, K. (1995). Benchmarking school education. *Unicorn, 21*(2), 24–32.

Willis, S. (1996). Letter to the editor. *Mathematics Education Research Journal, 8*(1), 95–96.

Zevenbergen, R. (1997). Do disadvantaged students fail mathematics or does mathematics fail disadvantaged students? In F. Biddulph & K. Carr (Eds.), *People in mathematics* (pp. 23–38). Proceedings of 20th Conference of the Mathematics Education Research Group of Australasia. Rotorua, New Zealand: Mathematics Education Research Group of Australasia.

7

Situated Sociocultural Mathematics Education: Vignettes From Southeast Asian Practices

Khoon Yoong Wong
Zaitun Binti Hj Mohd Taha
Universiti Brunei Darussalam

Palanisamy Veloo
Universiti Brunei Darussalam

Sociocultural context encompasses many interrelated factors: history, politics, ethnic composition, languages, cultural values and ways of life, customs, different gender roles, and others. These factors have different impacts on the nature and practice of mathematics education of a country. One way to study them is to focus on a specific factor in depth, for example, the politics of mathematics education (chap. 6, this volume), the development of a mathematics reform (Ellerton & Clements, 1994; Horwood, 1999), the nature and development of ethnomathematics (Ascher, 1991; Gerdes, 1996; Nelson, Joseph, & Williams, 1993; Nunes, 1993; Nunes & Bryant, 1996; Stillman & Balatti, chap. 18 this volume), gender differences (Rogers & Kaiser, 1995), philosophies of mathematics (Hersh, 1997), or sociological histories of Western and non-Western mathematics (Restivo, 1992). These analyses have produced interesting and useful insights into how various sociocultural factors have affected mathematics education, but there is a need to examine some of these factors at a more systemic level.

In this chapter, we adopt a broader perspective by examining how several factors can work together to affect mathematics education. To do this, we first propose a Situated SocioCultural (SSC) model to delineate the influences of and interrelationships among selected factors. We then explore how this model applies to mathematics education in three ASEAN countries, namely Brunei Darussalam, Malaysia, and Singapore. We have chosen to focus on these three countries because we have spent most of our working lives there, and many practices found here are not widely known outside the ASEAN region. Another reason is the interesting fact that these three countries share a common British colonial heritage but have diverged considerably after gaining independence. This divergence is particularly illuminating because it shows how some of the sociocultural factors have worked at a systemic level.

Given the limited space, we cannot hope to describe all that has happened in mathematics education in these countries, hence the term *vignettes* in the subtitle. We draw on examples based on our personal experiences, anecdotal observations, and local research to illustrate how the SSC model works. We do not claim this model to be all encompassing, which is quite impossible given the complexity of education matters, so we have included only those factors that we have something meaningful to say, leaving more knowledgeable others to modify the model as they see fit. However, we do hope that our discussion, consistent with a phenomenological perspective, will better inform mathematics educators around the world about the mathematics education in these three countries and hence generate further discussion about the relevance of theoretical frameworks, such as this SSC model, to explain what happen in mathematics education in a particular country.

THE SITUATED SOCIOCULTURAL MODEL

The proposed SSC model is shown schematically in Fig. 7.1.

The historical background and cultural mores of a country determine the milieu in which the present mathematics education has evolved and now functions. Major historical events often continue to exert their influences on current practices. Cultural mores, defined in terms of shared values, beliefs, customs, and ways of life of a

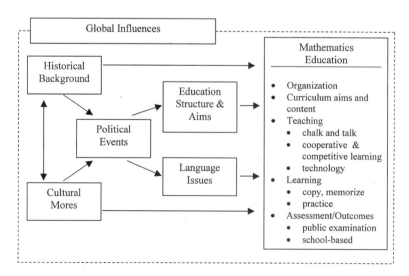

FIG. 7.1. Situated sociocultural model of mathematics education.

particular group, are important determinants of educational practices. In each of these three countries, there is a major, dominant culture (Malay in Brunei and Malaysia and Chinese in Singapore) with several influential minority cultures based on a combination of ethnic and religious differences. In the tortuous process to develop a national identity since independence, each of the three governments has successfully handled in its own ways the tensions that arise from the conflicting demands and aspirations of different ethnic groups to build a harmonious, multicultural nation. A national education system has been designed to propagate shared aspirations, and mathematics education is an important component of the national system.

Major political events, especially those after independence, have given rise to two other important factors, namely, a national education vision to serve a country no longer under a colonial master and a national language policy that is more relevant to local political needs than one served by an outside power. These five factors are localized within the specific context of the country involved, hence they are said to be situated factors, borrowing an idea from Lave (1988). These factors, collectively as well as individually, define and continue to affect the nature and practice of mathematics education in the country. However, in this modern world dominated by high-speed information and communications technologies, no country can be insulated from global influences. In mathematics education, the Cockcroft Report and the various NCTM Standards documents have exerted considerable influences on the thinking of mathematics educators in these three countries, although these influences are not very noticeable at classroom levels. Local educators are also keen to promote the use of computer and the Internet to teach school mathematics, and we will mention some of these efforts later on. Thus, in the SSC model, these global influences form an umbrella under which are found the situated factors. This arrangement also highlights the issue of whether current Anglo-American education values (e.g., democracy and individualism) and pedagogy (e.g., self-discovery, constructivist approaches, and investigation) can be adapted to meet local needs and yet are not in serious conflicts with local sociocultural traditions.

With this brief sketch of the SSC model in mind, we shall now examine these factors in greater details. Before that, some background information about the three countries is given to make the subsequent discussion and comparison more concrete.

GENERAL INFORMATION

Some general information is given in Table 7.1. The three countries differ vastly in area, population, ethnic composition, pupil enrolments, and teaching staff. However, in each country, the education system is managed by a highly centralized ministry of education.

Before turning to education matters, it is important to give a brief sketch of the three national ideologies because they are the bedrock of the educational aims and are rigorously promoted through the education system. In Brunei, it is the Malay Islamic Monarchy (MIB) concept. It was included in Brunei's first written constitution in 1959 and is widely promoted after independence in 1984. MIB is now a compulsory subject in schools and university. The inclusion of the MIB concept in the national education

TABLE 7.1
General Information About Brunei Darussalam, Malaysia, and Singapore

	Brunei Darussalam	Malaysia	Singapore
Independence	1984	1957 Malaya 1963 Malaysia	1963 part of Malaysia 1965 Singapore
Area	5,765 sq km	330,000 sq km	647 sq km
Population (main ethnic groups)	300,000 (70% Malays, 18% Chinese, 5% Indigenous)	20.5 million (62% Malays, 28% Chinese, 8% Indians)	3 million (77% Chinese, 14% Malays, 7% Indian)
National ideology	Malay Islamic Monarchy (MIB)	Rukunegara	Singapore Pledge
Main structure	6 + 3 + 2	6 + 3 + 2	6 + 4, 6 + 4 + 1
Primary pupils	55,170	2,872,000	288,300
Primary teachers	3,540	154,800	11,400
Secondary pupils	26,030	1,889,000	178,800
Secondary teachers	2,180	102,000	9,140
Primary mathematics education	P1–P3: in Malay P4–P6: in English PCE examination	P1–P6: in Malay (mainstream), in Chinese or Tamil (vernacular schools) UPSR examination	English is used throughout Foundation: P1–P4: no streaming Orientation: P5–P6: EM1, EM2, EM3 PSLE examination
Secondary mathematics education	English is used throughout F1–F3: Levels 1 & 2 PMB examination Cambridge O-Level: F4–F5 N-Level: F4N–F5N; N-Level examination; F6N for O-Level examination	Malay is used throughout Remove classes: for pupils from Chinese or Tamil primary schools F1–F3 PMR examination F4–F5 SPM examination	English is used throughout S1–S4: Special, express streams; Cambridge O-Level Examination S1–S4: Normal Academic, Normal Technical streams; N-Level Examination; S5N for O-Level Examination
Education vision	Thoughtful schools	Smart schools	Thinking schools

curriculum is to attain the following aims:

1. To inculcate in our children a mental outlook and attitude of life and such positive qualities of character as will enable the realization of a society that is consistent with traditional Brunei virtues, such as strong religious faith, loyalty to the Monarch, and a desire for balanced progress and development.

2. To transmit teachings that are consistent with national aspirations whereby the Nation is seen as a Malay Islamic Monarchy in which responsibilities are to be

shouldered by all people at all levels of society, without regard to descent, beliefs, religious faith, or traditional customs. (Brunei Ministry of Education, 1992, p. 59)

Malaysia introduced the Rukunegara after the racial riot in 1969 as one way to promote national unity. One can find this Rukunegara painted on the walls of many school buildings as well as in exercise books. It contains the following five principles:

- Kepercayaan kepada Tuhan (Belief in God)
- Kesetiaan kepada Raja dan Negara (Loyalty to King and Country)
- Keluhuran Perlembagaan (The Supremacy of the Constitution)
- Kedaulatan Undang-undang (The Rule of Law)
- Kesopanan dan Kesusilaan (Mutual Respect and Good Social Behaviour)

In Singapore, all pupils begin each school day by reciting the Singapore Pledge: "We, the citizens of Singapore, pledge ourselves as one united people regardless of race, language or religion to build a democratic society based on justice and equality so as to achieve happiness, prosperity and progress for our nation."

It is difficult to assess the impacts of these ideological pronouncements on pupils' behaviors; nevertheless, they are part and parcel of the national consciousness in each country and, as such, should be taken into account when one tries to understand the impacts of culture on education.

EDUCATION STRUCTURE

In 1980, Singapore implemented a distinctive streaming policy for its 6 + 4 or 6 + 4 + 1 school structure that is very different from what was left from the colonial time. It was later modified in 1994. The six years of primary education are divided into two stages, Foundation and Orientation. The Foundation stage is from Primary 1 to 4, when all pupils follow a common curriculum with English as the medium of instruction. At the beginning of the Orientation stage (Primary 5 and 6), the pupils are streamed into EM1, EM2, or EM3 according to abilities. Pupils take the public examination (PSLE) at the end of Primary 6, and their results will determine which of the four streams they will enter in secondary schools: Special, Express, Normal (Academic), or Normal (Technical). Those in the Special or Express stream follow a 4-year program and take the Cambridge O-Level examination at the end of Secondary 4. Pupils in the two Normal streams take a less intensive 4-year program and sit for the Singapore-Cambridge N-Level at the end of Secondary 4N. Those who perform well in the N-Level examination will go on for a fifth year and sit for the O-Level examination at the end of Secondary 5N. This elaborate streaming system is a unique Singapore innovation designed to cater "to every child's abilities, interests and aptitudes so as to help each develop to his fullest potential" (Singapore Ministry of Education, 1999).

Malaysia continues to use the 6 + 3 + 2 school structure inherited from the colonial period. At each transition, the pupils sit for a public examination: at the end of primary schools (UPSR), at Form 3 (PMR), and at Form 5 (SPM). There is no streaming in

Malaysia as in Singapore, except that pupils when entering Form 4 may opt for the Science, Arts, Commerce, or Technical streams, based on results in PMR and personal choice. It is worth mentioning that, in Malaysia, the primary schools are divided into National and National-type (vernacular) schools. About 76% of primary pupils are enrolled in the National schools, where Malay is the medium of instruction; 21% in National-type Chinese schools, where Chinese is the medium of instruction; and 3% in National-type Tamil schools. This distinction is interesting because pupils who attend Chinese primary schools are often perceived to have higher mathematical performance than pupils attending the other schools. The reasons for this have not been studied systematically, but plausible factors are the emphasis in Chinese schools on hard work, discipline, memorization with understanding, and the "advantages" of the Chinese language in mathematics learning (discussed later).

Until recently Brunei also has a $6 + 3 + 2$ system. In 1996, the N-Level stream (modeled after the Singapore system) was introduced for the weaker pupils. In the following year, the results for the first batch of N-Level were found to be unsatisfactory. The ministry of education is closely monitoring the N-level program. At the lower secondary level, pupils are now divided into Level I for the average and above-average pupils and Level II for the weaker pupils. These changes are initiated to help the weaker pupils better cope with schooling. In addition to the general education, all Muslim pupils in the primary to lower secondary years attend Islamic religious classes outside school hours. Thus, they spend about 8 hours per school day in classes: 5 hours in schools and 3 hours in religious classes. This general-cum-religious education in Brunei Darussalam is quite unique in the world.

This brief survey shows how the three governments have designed their education structure to suit local needs. Different mathematics curricula are also developed to fit into the overall education structure. This is taken up in the next section.

EXTENDING THE COLONIAL MATHEMATICS CURRICULUM

According to Schmidt, McKnight, Valverde, Houang, and Wiley (1997), there are two hypotheses about the development of mathematical thinking: it either follows a well-defined sequence independent of cultures or depends on how mathematical knowledge is socially constructed in a particular culture. On the other hand, mathematics education will vary across countries. As Ascher (1991) put it, educators "are interested in modifying mathematics education so that it can effectively build upon and reinforce diverse cultural traditions" (p. 195). These changes are becoming more evident as mathematics educators explore the mathematics curricula and practices of different countries. In all the three countries, mathematics is a core subject from Primary 1 to the final year of secondary schooling, and we examine its implementation subsequently.

Despite decades of efforts to develop indigenous education systems since gaining independence, these three countries are still under considerable British influences. The most entrenched influence is the Cambridge O-Level Examination, which is the public examination taken by most pupils in Brunei and Singapore at the end of their secondary schooling. Parents, teachers, ministry officials, and employers continue to recognize the Cambridge results as the "standard" of academic performance to be used for employment or admission to further studies at local or overseas institutes. Malaysia has devised its own SPM examination to replace the Cambridge examination, but the administration, contents, and assessment procedures of the SPM are strongly reminiscent of the Cambridge system.

In the past 50 years, the Cambridge O-Level mathematics syllabus has undergone several revisions: Syllabus A in the 1950s, Syllabus B in the 1960s, Syllabus C (Modern Mathematics) in the 1970s, and Syllabus D (since 1980s). The three countries have followed these syllabus changes over the years, but they did not accept the Cambridge GCSE when it was introduced in the late 1980s because of concerns about the GCSE's coursework component, in particular, copying and subjectivity in assessment. Thus, the O-Level syllabus defines the contents of secondary mathematics in these countries. Primary mathematics, however, is not directly related to this O-Level syllabus, and, as shown in Table 7.2, its contents are fairly universal.

The theoretical framework underlying a curriculum can provide an encapsulated picture of its intended goals and structure. Of the three countries, the Singapore mathematics curriculum has the most well defined framework, which was developed

TABLE 7.2
Topics in Primary Mathematics Curriculum of Brunei Darussalam, Singapore, and Malaysia

Topics	Brunei Darussalam	Singapore	Malaysia
Whole numbers and operations	Up to 7 digits	Up to 8 digits	Up to 7 digits
Factors, multiples	+ prime numbers	✓	
Fractions	✓	✓	✓
Decimals up to 3 decimal places	✓	✓	✓
Percentages	✓	✓	✓
Direct Proportion	✓	✓	
Rate, Ratio		✓	
Integers	✓		
Money, time, and measures	✓	✓	✓
Mensuration: perimeter, area of quadrilaterals, volume	+ circles	+ circles	✓
Geometry: triangles, quadrilaterals, circles, angles, bearings, solids, nets, symmetry	✓	+ tessellation	Only naming of triangles, quadrilaterals, and solids
Statistics: average, charts	✓	✓	✓
Algebra	Equation in one unknown	Evaluate, solve, up to 3 variables	
Set	Sets and subsets		
Coordinates and graph	First quadrant, line		

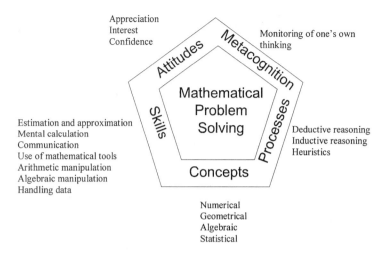

Appreciation
Interest
Confidence

Monitoring of one's own
thinking

Estimation and approximation
Mental calculation
Communication
Use of mathematical tools
Arithmetic manipulation
Algebraic manipulation
Handling data

Deductive reasoning
Inductive reasoning
Heuristics

Numerical
Geometrical
Algebraic
Statistical

FIG. 7.2.   Framework of Singapore mathematics curriculum.

in 1990 (see Wong, 1991, for a personal reflection of this curriculum change). This framework, as shown in Fig. 7.2, is applicable to both primary and secondary levels (Singapore Ministry of Education, 1990). It places mathematical problem solving at the center, reflecting the aim emphasized by the minister of education at that time and the influences of the NCTM Agenda for the 1990s. Teaching and learning include not only traditional skills but also understanding of concepts, development of thinking processes and metacognitive strategies, and inculcation of positive attitudes toward mathematics and its learning. The Singapore N-Level syllabus contains about 70% of the O-Level syllabus. The Normal pupils have one mathematics lesson per week more than the Express or Special stream pupils. It is hoped that less contents and more teaching time will help the weaker pupils learn mathematics better. Teachers are urged to use more hands-on activities when teaching mathematics to the weaker pupils.

From the 1950s to early 1980s, the Malaysian secondary mathematics curriculum also followed the changes in the Cambridge O-Level syllabus. However, in 1989, the KBSM (New Secondary School Curriculum) was introduced. Its mathematics curriculum is based on an Input–Process–Output model, as shown in Fig. 7.3 (Malaysia Ministry of Education, 1988; translated by K. Y. Wong). The contents are similar to the Cambridge O-Level Syllabus C, with two additional items: the fostering of moral values in mathematics lessons and the language of logic (see Wong, 1993, for further details). The moral values to be promoted include kindness, self-reliance, honesty, cooperation, and public spiritedness. However, we have not come across any report about how effectively these values have been taught in mathematics lessons.

The primary mathematics curricula in the three countries are shown in Table 7.2. The Brunei and Singapore curricula have very similar contents. The Malaysian primary mathematics curriculum is the lightest of the three. It has very little geometry content and no algebra. Besides mathematics, the Malaysian primary curriculum also includes a subject called Commercial Practices, which intends to acquaint pupils with the elements of commercial and business practices. The topics shown in Table 7.2 are

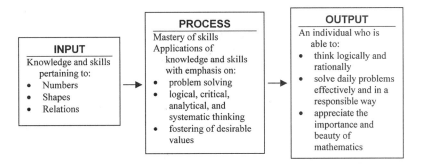

FIG. 7.3. Structure of the Malaysian secondary mathematics curriculum.

also found in the mathematics curricula of many other countries, thus demonstrating a degree of universality of primary school mathematics.

It is interesting to note that ethnomathematics is not specifically mentioned in the extensive analyses of the mathematics curricula of 45 countries (Schmidt et al., 1997). In some Western countries, ethnomathematics seems to be one way to make mathematics more "culturally relevant" to the nonwhite pupils who come from different cultures, under the name of multicultural education (see also chap. 18, this volume). In these three countries, however, ethnomathematics has received scan attention from mathematics educators and mathematicians. A plausible reason is that ethnomathematics, such as different numeration systems, out-of-school ways of computations, and Islamic patterns, is perceived to lack the rigor of Western mathematics, which is an essential prerequisite for further studies, especially in science, technology, and commerce. Thus, for example, even though the Brunei curriculum includes Islamic calendar, it refers only to the names of the Islamic months; the mathematics underlying Islamic calendar and its relationship to the common calendar are not dealt with. Local contexts, such as prayer times, takaful plan, payment of zakat, and the school environment (Teh, 1998), have been used in word problems and activities. This is an important step toward linking mathematics to the daily lives of the pupils. Other examples of ethnomathematics may be included to enrich the learning of mathematics, but they will not replace the current (Western) contents.

One important difference in the mathematics curricula between these three countries and the West is that a calculator is not allowed in mathematics lessons in primary schools in these three countries. We say more about calculators in a subsequent section.

LANGUAGE FACTORS

During colonial times, English was the main official language in these three countries, and competence in English was a prerequisite to gain admission to higher education and the civil service. After independence, each country developed its own language policy that reflects the political aspirations and practical needs of its people.

In 1985, Brunei Darussalam implemented a bilingualism policy. Under this system, all subjects, except English, which is a compulsory subject, are taught in Malay from

Primary 1 to Primary 3. From Primary 4 onward, English becomes the medium of instruction for many subjects including mathematics. Thus, Bruneian pupils learn mathematics in Malay during the first three years of primary schooling and then switch over to English from Primary 4 onward. This switchover is often used to explain why there is a sharp drop in mathematics performance from Primary 3 to Primary 4. More significantly, the generally poor command of English is widely recognized as a crucial factor why many Bruneian pupils are weak in mathematics, especially in solving word problems given in English (Koay, 1990; Veloo et al., 1993; Yong, 1997). However, the role of language in mathematics learning is quite complex. In a recent small-scale investigation (Rasidah & Wong, 1998), 51 Form 1 pupils (12+) were asked to solve word problems in English and in Malay. Their performance in both tests was weak and did not differ significantly by the language used. Girls performed slightly better than boys in both tests. These pupils did not understand the key mathematical terms used and what the questions asked, and they failed to identify specific items in the given diagrams. These difficulties seem to be about mathematical concepts and go beyond comprehension of everyday language in Malay or English.

In Malaysia, Bahasa Malaysia (the Malay language) has been the main medium of instruction from primary to university levels since 1983. This is based on the government's political agenda to use Bahasa Malaysia as the language to unify people of different ethnic backgrounds and as a tool to reduce British influences in the postcolonial period. English, however, remains a compulsory second language. Thus, mathematics is taught in Bahasa Malaysia at all levels, except in vernacular primary schools, where it is taught in Chinese (Mandarin) or in Tamil.

Singapore has a bilingual policy in which English is the medium of instruction and the pupil's mother tongue (Malay, Chinese, or Tamil) a compulsory subject. This policy serves two purposes. First, English is the international language for commerce and high technology, which provide the main sources of national income for the island state. Thus, mastery of English has important economic values. Second, the study of mother tongue is used to promote traditional values and moral education. This is seen as one way to counteract some undesirable Western influences. Because mathematics is taught in English right from Primary 1, Singapore pupils do not face the switchover problems experienced by the Bruneian pupils. Nevertheless, some primary teachers still feel that lower primary pupils may have difficulty solving lengthy word problems due to poor knowledge of English (Foong, Yap, & Koay, 1996).

The study of language on mathematics education has attracted considerable international attention (e.g., Clements & Leong, 1999; Ellerton & Clarkson, 1996). Here we wish to extend the work done on the number language of English and Chinese (Bell, 1993; Fuson & Fraivillig, 1993; Geary, 1994; Hoosain, 1997; Miura, 1993) to the Malay language.

First, consider the number of syllables of number words. Chinese words are monosyllabic; for example, the number 9 is read as jiu (one syllable) in Chinese and sembilan (3 syllables) in Malay. The mean number of syllables for the number words from 0 to 10 in Malay is 2.1 compared to 1 in Chinese. Hoosain (1997) cited studies showing that adults speaking Chinese have a digit span of 9.2, whereas that for English is 7.21. The more the number of syllables the longer it takes to recite the number and more difficult to keep it in short-term memory. This becomes even more striking when pupils learn the multiplication tables. For example, $9 \times 9 = 81$ is read as jiu jiu ba shi yi (5 syllables) in Chinese, nine times nine equals eighty one (8 syllables) in English, and sembilan kali sembilan sama lapan puluh satu (16 syllables) in Malay. In addition to this syllabic characteristic, Chinese is an ideograph language, and learning it requires much memorization, hard work, and discipline. Thus, pupils learning Chinese have much practice in memorization. This practice and the monosyllabic property of the Chinese language may partly explain why pupils in Chinese schools seem to master the multiplication tables faster than pupils from other schools. Mastery of the multiplication tables is obviously essential for efficient mental work. It also boosts pupils' self-confidence and may enhance acquisition of skills in more complex mathematical tasks because the working memory is not burdened by having to work out these basic facts from scratch when they are needed. If this memory load hypothesis is valid, then it should apply to other mathematical words as well, although this has not been researched (see Bell and Woo, 1998, for a comparative study of geometry terms in English and Korea). For example, equilateral triangle (8 syllables) is deng bian san giao xing (5 syllables) in Chinese and segitiga sisisama (8 syllables) in Malay. Square grids (2 syllables) becomes petak-petak segi empat sama yang sama besar (15 syllables) in Malay, further illustrating this memory load issue. Further research is required to determine the relationships between memory load of linguistic artifacts and mathematical performance.

Another issue relates to the ten-structure of the Chinese language (Fuson & Fraivillig, 1993; Geary, 1994). For example, 12 is shi er (meaning 10 2) in Chinese, showing a clear one-to-one correspondence between the sound and the base-10 symbol, whereas twelve in English is not directly linked to 10 and 2, requiring the pupils to learn a new word for this number. In Malay, this is dua belas, which has the two (dua) in the reversed position, similar to fifteen for 15 in English. It is not clear whether this juxtaposition has any adverse effect on counting and doing sums in Malay. The extent to which these linguistic factors might affect mathematics learning beyond counting, basic number concepts, and solving arithmetic problems is largely unknown.

CULTURAL MORES AND TEACHING PRACTICES

Teaching practices in the classroom constitute a major facet of the implemented curriculum. The researchers of the Survey of Mathematics and Science Opportunities (SMSO) coined the term characteristic pedagogical flow (CPF) to describe the complex interplay among content representation, content presentation, and the classroom discourse. They believe that "lessons within a country tend to exhibit a consistent CPF" (Schmidt et al., 1996, p. 74). An underlying factor of a consistent CPF is the local cultural mores.

The two major cultures (Malay and Chinese) in these three countries stress strong hierarchical social structure based on age and social status. Respect for authority and elders is recognized as a virtue for social cohesion. Traditionally teachers are held in high esteem even though they are less well paid than other professionals. In Malaysia in particular, many teachers in the pre-independent days were also political and community leaders, thus exerting considerable influences and enjoying wide respect by the populace. Although the status of the teaching profession has been eroded drastically in recent years, the traditional function of the teachers to transmit knowledge, as from a master to a disciple, has never been seriously questioned. This transmission model is seen to fit well in these cultures, described by Buzan and Buzan (1995) as, "master teachers traditionally gave new pupils only three basic instructions: 'obey', 'cooperate' and 'diverge'" (p. 92). The Malay term for teacher is guru or cikgu, which means an influential or revered teacher. The teachers have "superior knowledge" to pass on to the pupils, who must be willing to receive this knowledge. In return, the pupils must show respect and gratitude to the teachers. In Brunei, this relationship is captured by the following comments from some primary school teachers: "Especially in front of our pupils, we have to be able to do those exercises ourselves, otherwise the pupils say that we are not fit to be teachers. I think the teacher is a very strong influence on the pupils' learning. If the children respect the teacher, they will learn more from them" (Zaitun, 1995, p. 233).

In these countries, a lesson always begins with the pupils standing neatly and greeting the teacher "good morning/afternoon sir/teacher" and ends with them standing and reciting "thank you, teacher." Such practice is unheard of in most Western classrooms! Another practice in these three countries is to celebrate an annual Teacher Day, when pupils give small gifts to their teachers as tokens of gratitude. Thus, in general, there are less serious disruptive pupil behaviors in the classrooms in these countries compared to Western ones.

This cultural mode supports the "chalk and talk" method used predominantly to teach mathematics in these three countries. It also partly explains why this transmission method is resistant to change. In most classes, the pupils sit in neat rows and pay careful attention to the teachers' explanations. In a 1994 study, some Singapore secondary pupils ($N = 246$) were asked to draw pictures of "good" and "bad" mathematics lessons. Of the "good" lessons, 65% of the drawings showed the teacher in front of the class and 24% showed a blackboard, giving a total of 89% on whole-class setting. Only three "good" lessons depicted group work (Wong, 1996). Of the drawings of "bad" lessons, 87% also depicted whole-class setting. An example of each type of drawing is given in Fig. 7.4. Whole-class instruction was also reported to be most commonly used in a later longitudinal study involving 64 lower secondary classes in Singapore (Kaur, 1999).

Under this mode of learning, pupils are given many exercises to practice on. Some pupils asked for more, as shown by the following observation:

> The teacher wrote just 6 questions based on the word problems on the blackboard, the pupils answering these questions within 15 minutes. There was about 10 minutes left of the lesson before break time. The pupils were asking the teacher to give them more classwork. The teacher wrote another 4 questions on the blackboard. (Zaitun, 1995, p. 233)

What goes on in whole-class instruction requires further study. It can be used to develop mathematical concepts and procedures (the how and why) through demonstrations and discussions or just used to state the procedure without conceptual development. The recent TIMSS video study of American, German, and Japanese classrooms has

FIG. 7.4. Drawings of (a) "good" and (b) "bad" mathematics lessons.

provided clear evidence of these differences (Stigler, 1997). In these three countries, both scripts are used. Besides these, pupils are often asked to show their workings on the board for the whole class to comment on. In general, these whole-class lessons are carried out in an atmosphere of enthusiasm and interest.

In recent years, mathematics teachers in these countries have been urged to use less direct teaching and more cooperative learning techniques or group activities. Using the TIMSS data, Soh (1998) found that Singapore primary school teachers reported using whole-class teaching to group-pair work in the ratio 2.7:1 when they teach mathematics. This is comparable to the American result. Mathematics educators in the ASEAN region are also conducting research into cooperative learning (see Arañador, Valencia, & Vui, 1997). A relevant example is a small-scale experimental study using STAD (Student-Teams Achievement Divisions) to teach topics of everyday mathematics in Brunei lower secondary classes (Rose & Wong, 1999). Pupils in the STAD group and the control group gained significantly in mathematics test scores after the treatment but there were no statistically significant differences in achievement or attitude between the two groups. More local research is required to examine the effects of other cooperative learning techniques on mathematics achievement and attitude.

Teaching involves using many different activities and asking pupils what they think of these activities may promote metacognition. In a recent study, Tan (1998) asked a group of Singapore Primary 4 and 5 pupils ($N = 109$) what activities they liked in mathematics lessons. On the whole, they favored the use of technology (computer and video), games, and nonroutine activities such as outdoor work and riddles. She pointed out that "not all pupils of the same class possess a unitary interest" (p. 35), so teachers should find various ways to cater to these interests and needs.

Parents rarely voice their opinions about what happen in mathematics lessons, although there are some exceptions. When Modern Mathematics was first introduced in Malaysia in late 1960s, some parents wrote to the press expressing concerns about "all play and no work" in these lessons. These concerns made little impacts. In Singapore, parents' reactions to the "challenging problems" used in the PSLE examination in the 1980s led to in- service courses to prepare teachers on how to teach thinking methods to solve these problems. Many Singapore parents are prepared to pay to attend training courses so that they can coach their children on how to solve these problems. More recently in Brunei, a project to introduce the Multi-Modal Teaching Strategy in lower secondary mathematics lessons met with some opposition from a few vocal parents who wrote to the local press (Wong, Lim-Foo, & Veloo, 1998). Given this adverse publicity, as well as the tendency of teachers to stay with well-established classroom behaviors, especially in teacher-dominated instruction (Marlowe & Page, 1998), all but one of the teachers had dropped out of the project. This experience suggests that more studies are needed to understand parents' perceptions about mathematics instruction, which have received scant attention among mathematics educators worldwide.

To summarize, the characteristic pedagogical flow found in these three countries is compatible with a cultural mode that places the teachers in an authoritative (not in a negative sense) position. This method has several advantages, especially for teaching in developing countries (Guthrie, 1990), and it is also used in developed countries such as France and Switzerland (Schmidt et al., 1996). We have explained the cultural basis of this teaching method. Any attempt to tinker with this CPF must be analyzed critically so that it does not conflict seriously with cultural mores; otherwise, it will be resisted. Educational technologies have recently made major changes to teaching and learning of mathematics in many Western countries. Are these technologies likely to challenge the CPF in these countries?

EDUCATIONAL TECHNOLOGIES

As indicated earlier, an electronic calculator of any kind is not allowed in primary schools in these three countries. It is allowed in secondary schools when big numbers and values of standard functions are required in problem solving. Even then, the public examinations include one paper where calculator is not allowed. This requirement is to check that pupils can solve problems using paper-and-pencil techniques.

The common perception among teachers in these countries is that a calculator in primary schools will make pupils "mentally lazy" and dependent on its use. This is illustrated by the following comment from a Bruneian primary school teacher: "I am afraid they will depend on the calculators every time. With calculator also they can get the answer straight away. How? They cannot show the working, isn't it? It is not really them who are doing the work. It is the calculators. I am afraid they will not use their brains" (Zaitun, 1995, p. 74).

This also suggests that pupils who use calculators tend to focus on getting answers rather than trying to master the methods. This is supported by Gardiner's observation after grading thousands of competition papers in the United Kingdom that pupils in the post-Cockcroftian period had switched from methods to caring only about the answers displayed on the calculator screen (cited in Mackey, 1999). The negative effects of the calculator receive some local publicity, for instance, the Singapore's *Straits Times* carried a report with the heading "Without the aid of a calculator, young British workers cannot count" (1st October, 1996, p. 4). Graphics calculators have not yet caught on locally. There is no major local research about calculator use, although local educators are aware of the controversy surrounding this issue in other countries.

In contrast to "pushing buttons on a calculator," the use of an abacus as a tool to develop facility in mental arithmetic is gaining wide acceptance in Malaysia. In the 1950s, many Chinese primary schools in Malaysia taught abacus techniques in mathematics lessons, and many still do today. In 1996, the abacus was included as a teaching aid for national primary schools in Malaysia. The abacus, as a pedagogic tool, has several advantages over the calculator. First, using the abacus at the initial stage requires pupils to understand how the numeration system works symbolically and in concrete. For example, consider the addition of 8. The procedure depends on what number already exists on the abacus, giving rise to three sets of rules, as shown in Table 7.3. The table also shows how the rules are recited in Chinese and Malay. In

TABLE 7.3
Rules for Adding 8 on the Chinese Abacus

Existing Number	Rule	Chinese	Malay
0 or 1	$+8$ Move down 1 upper bead and move up 3 lower beads	ba, shang ba	lapan, naik lapan
2, 3, 4, 7, 8, or 9	$10 - 2$ Move down 2 lower beads and move up 1 lower left bead	ba, qu er jin yi	lapan, buang dua mengumpul satu
5 or 6	$+3 - 5 + 10$ Move up 3 lower beads, move up 1 upper bead, and move up 1 lower left bead	ba, shang san qu wu jin yi	lapan, naik tiga buang lima mengumpul satu

the Chinese abacus, each upper bead represents 5 and each lower bead represents 1. A bead in the left column indicates multiplication by 10.

Initially the pupils are made to understand why adding 8 is equivalent to $10 - 2$ or $+ 3 - 5 + 10$. These steps are reflected in the action of moving the beads. Once the thinking is understood, the pupils recite the rules that describe the action. With practice, the recitation takes over the thinking, the action becomes automatized (kinesthetic learning), a mental abacus is formed, and the fingers move as if handling the real thing (Dehaene, 1997; Geary, 1994, citing the work of Stigler and co-workers). This mental action provides the speed and accuracy so that a proficient abacus user can easily beat the calculator. Thus, using the abacus does not make the brain "lazy" as is claimed for the calculator. By comparison, pushing buttons on the calculator bears no intrinsic relationships to the number or the operation involved, the algorithms used in calculators are "blind" to the users, and, hence, the action does not reinforce the thinking. It will be fascinating to compare the acquisition of concepts and skills of pupils who are schooled in the use of abacus or calculators.

The monosyllabic property of Chinese words makes the recitation of abacus rules rhythmic and efficient. In contrast, as shown in Table 7.3, the rules recited in Malay have many more syllables, which takes much longer to recite and remember. This brings us back to the linguistic memory load hypothesis, which may partly explain why the abacus is still not popular among Malay pupils in Malaysia.

A fast-emerging educational technology that has attracted enormous interest here and elsewhere is the computer. All the three countries have introduced computer studies as a formal or informal subject in the school curriculum. They also have plans to use computers as an instructional tool. In Malaysia and Singapore, private companies have marketed courseware used to teach mathematics according to the official syllabuses. These courseware programs make use of multimedia features, drill and practice with hints and solutions, and sophisticated systems of keeping records of pupils' performance. Teachers, parents, and pupils are very enthusiastic about such courseware because of their visual appeal and obvious links to examination requirements.

Some efforts have been made to use application software to develop creativity and problem solving in mathematics. Ilango and Lim (1997) conducted a study on a class of 23 Secondary 2 (13+) Singapore pupils who were in the Gifted Educational Program. These pupils were taught to use Mathematica and QBASIC to learn about functions and to solve real-life problems. After seven sessions, the pupils were able to think up original projects (such as predict the chances of getting a book in the school library, how long a pop song will stay in the local charts) and applied critical thinking skills to complete them. They "enjoyed discovery learning but would prefer to be guided by teachers" (p. 71). The last part of this comment once again reflects the authoritative role expected of the teachers.

A large-scale study of the effects of computer-assisted learning on creativity in mathematics was conducted in Malaysia in 1996, involving 1,212 Primary 5 pupils from six primary schools. Pupils who used KBSR courseware to learn fractions and ge-ometry made significant gains in teacher-made mathematics tests and several measures of mathematical creativity, whereas the control group did not make significant gains in these measures (See, 1998).

The use of computers to teach mathematics in Brunei Darussalam is still in the developmental stage. A Computers for Mathematics Instruction (CMI) project was recently implemented to train secondary school teachers to teach mathematics using Excel and Graphmatica (Wong, 1998b). Pupils enjoyed these computer lessons, but there was limited evidence about higher order thinking. For example, given the open-ended task, "Write down as many different quadratic equations as you can whose roots are 2 and 5," none of the 14 Form 5 Arts pupils (generally quite weak in mathematics) could give more than one solution.

To conclude this section on the influence of technology on mathematics education, it is clear that teachers and pupils are very enthusiastic about high technology but less so for calculators. When the technology contains intrinsic features that can promote mathematical thinking, say the abacus, it holds potentials that should be further studied.

MATHEMATICS OUTCOMES

Pupils' learning outcomes, both cognitive and affective, are the yardsticks used to measure the effectiveness of the implemented curriculum. Of the various outcome measures, the one that is of the greatest interest in these three countries is the results of public examinations. Indeed, to many pupils, parents, teachers, and education authorities in these countries, the percentages of various grades in public examinations provide the most acceptable measure of effective teaching. This is stressed by a mathematics inspector from the Brunei Ministry of Education: "[G]iving a lot of exercises to the students will make the students skilful in answering the questions in the examination. The focus is, at the end of the day, on the examination" (Zaitun, 1995, p. 269).

Some teachers believe that public examinations are good because they keep them on their guard, but others feel that the pressure of public examinations, together with factors such as an overprescribed scheme of work, hinders innovation in teaching methods.

As mentioned earlier, Bruneian and Malaysian pupils take three and Singapore pupils take two public examinations in the course of their schooling. As mathematics is a compulsory subject, many parents in these countries send their children to tuition classes that specialize in helping pupils pass these public examinations, hopefully with flying colors! This shows that many parents value their children's mathematics achievement and are prepared to provide the necessary financial support.

Another powerful effect of public examinations is the proliferation of books that give complete solutions and detailed analysis of the patterns of past examination papers. These so-called "Ten-Year Series" books are used extensively by teachers to plan daily lessons and to drill pupils on typical examination questions. It is not exaggerating to say that these Ten-Year Series books are more widely used than textbooks. Unfortunately, these books were not studied in the extensive analysis of curriculum materials undertaken by TIMSS (Schmidt et al., 1997).

In Brunei Darussalam, pupils' mathematics performance at public examinations is not very satisfactory (Veloo et al., 1993). This has been attributed to weak foundation, poor attitude toward mathematics, lack of parental concern about their children's schoolwork, lack of incentive to complete homework, poor command of English, and poor study habit. On the other hand, a study (Lua & Koay, 1990) found that primary and secondary Bruneian pupils tended "to attribute effort (an internal factor) as a cause for success in mathematics performance, and task difficulty (an external factor) as a reason for failure in mathematics performance" (p. 212).

Of the three countries, only Singapore took part in TIMSS. Its eighth grade pupils (13+) ranked first among the 41participating countries, scoring an average of 643, compared to the international average of 513. The Singapore Ministry of Education attributed this impressive achievement to the streaming system that allows teachers to be more focused in their teaching, Singapore pupils doing the most homework, teachers spending the longest time marking and planning work, and good home support (Straits Times, 21st November, 1996, p. 50). In Singapore, the secondary schools are ranked (since 1992) according to their absolute as well as value-added performance in the O-Level examination, and these rankings are published so that parents can make informed choices when selecting secondary schools for their children. The value-added performance is computed using pupils' performance based on their PSLE scores. The top 10 schools with high value-added performance are given financial awards of S$20,000 each and the next 10 schools given S$10,000 each. The message is abundantly clear that getting good grades in public examinations is of top priority.

In addition to these public examinations, pupils in these countries also take monthly tests, midyear examinations, and final year examinations. These examinations usually take several days and are invigilated by the teachers during school hours. They serve several important functions: to assess pupils' understanding of the content, to motivate them to study harder, to prepare them for the public examinations, to report to parents about their children progress in schools, and, in the case of Brunei, to decide whether the pupils have to repeat a particular grade level due to poor performance. These periodic examinations are very much an accepted part of the local school life.

THE VISIONS: SMART SCHOOLS, THINKING SCHOOLS, AND THOUGHTFUL SCHOOLS

The education systems described earlier are being modified from time to time through various initiatives to meet the changing demands of society and policymakers. These initiatives are often couched as visions for the future. They are particularly relevant in order to keep pace with, if not to anticipate, changes brought about by globalization and advances in information and communications technologies.

In Malaysia, a major initiative is the Smart Schools concept first proposed in 1996. It is one of the seven flagship applications of the ambitious Multimedia Super Corridor

(MSC) project. The main thrust is to use IT in all aspects of education, by

changing the culture and practices of Malaysia's primary and secondary schools, moving away from memory-based learning designed for the average student to an education that stimulates thinking, creativity, and caring in all students, caters to individual abilities and learning styles, and is based on more equitable access. (Malaysia Ministry of Education, 1998)

The pilot project involving 90 schools will begin in 1999, and, by 2010, all primary and secondary schools are expected to be Smart schools.

In Singapore, recent education reform centers on three initiatives: critical and creative thinking skills, IT skills, and National Education (to develop the feeling of commitment and confidence in the future as Singaporean). The first initiative on thinking skills is an extension of earlier work done using de Bono's thinking program, CoRT, and is now captured succinctly by the vision, Thinking Schools, Learning Nation. The purpose of stressing thinking is that young Singaporeans in the next century will need to think for themselves to solve unexpected problems. They cannot rely on strategies that have worked in the past. The second initiative is being realized through the Masterplan for IT in Education, which provides an IT-enriched curriculum and an environment that links schools to the world to encourage creative thinking and life-long learning. This plan will be completed for all schools in 2002. In terms of school curriculum, the contents of various subjects will be reduced by 30% to allow more time to teach thinking and IT skills. The contents will draw on examples and issues related to the Singapore context, as part of the strategy for National Education. As an example, a mathematics exercise may ask pupils to calculate the monthly water bill of their family (typical mathematics application). A spreadsheet is then used to compute the mean consumption for the whole class (use of IT). Finally, this is followed by a discussion about how water can be used wisely to preserve water in Singapore (creative thinking and national context). This curriculum change for Secondary 1 and 3 will be implemented in 2001. Local Web sites, such as Derrand Education (http://come.to/derrand), are contributing toward the use of IT in education by offering online educational resources and tuition.

In Brunei Darussalam the vision of Thoughtful Schools was announced by the minister of education in 1997 to "produce thoughtful students, who are not only capable of thinking critically and creatively but will always be reflecting on how they can contribute to the development of a peace-loving and progressive nation" (Abdul Aziz, 1997, p. v). Sim (1998) proposed that thoughtful teaching and learning encompasses the four dimensions of creativity, reflectivity, responsibility, and reciprocity. Several projects have been developed to explore various aspects of thoughtful teaching and learning in primary schools (see Wong, 1998a).

As these visions are translated into practices, there are obstacles to overcome. For instance, the implementation of Smart Schools in Malaysia has slowed down because of the financial crisis in 1997–1999. It is also not yet clear how mathematics education will be changed by the visions in Malaysia and Brunei. Building a visionary mathematics education for the next millennium is a momentous task for survival. It will take years before we know how successful these reforms will help the pupils in these countries to become better literate mathematically to face challenges in the future.

CONCLUDING REMARKS

There are other sociocultural factors peculiar to each of these three countries that have influenced the development of mathematics education that we have not covered in this chapter. However, this brief sketch has demonstrated the ways in which these countries have attempted to incorporate Western mathematics contents, as exemplified by the Cambridge O-Level syllabus, within a national education structure and vision and instructional practices that suit local cultural mores, subject to increasingly pervasive global influences. It is our hope that the SSC model has clarified some of these interlocking relationships that deserve further reflection and discussion.

REFERENCES

Abdul Aziz Umar (1997). Opening address. In R. B. Burns (Ed.), *Preparing children and adolescents for the next millennium* (pp. v–vii). Bandar Seri Begawan: Universiti Brunei Darussalam.

Arañador, L. C., Valencia, I. N., & Vui, T. (Eds.). (1997). *Proceedings of 1997 International Conference on Cooperative Learning and Constructivism in Science and Mathematics Education*. Penang: SEAMEO RECSAM.

Ascher, M. (1991). *Ethnomathematics: A multicultural view of mathematical ideas*. Pacific Grove, CA: Brooks/Cole.

Bell, G. (1993). Setting the theme: Researching Asian mathematics education. In G. Bell (Ed.), *Asian perspectives on mathematics education* (pp. 1–20). Lismore: Northern Rivers Mathematical Association.

Bell, G., & Woo, J. H. (1998). Probing the links between language and mathematical conceptualisation. *Mathematics Education Research Journal, 10*(1), 51–74.

Brunei Ministry of Education. (1992). *Education in Brunei*. Bandar Seri Begawan: Author.

Buzan, T., & Buzan, B. (1995). *The mind map book*. London: BBC Books.

Clements, M. A., & Leong, Y. P. (Eds.). (1999). *Cultural and language aspects of science, mathematics, and technical education*. Bandar Seri Begawan: Universiti Brunei Darussalam.

Dehaene, S. (1997). *The number sense: How the mind creates mathematics*. Oxford: Oxford University Press.

Ellerton, N. F., & Clarkson, P. C. (1996). Language factors in mathematics teaching and learning. In A. Bishop, K. Clements, C. Keitel, J. Kilpatrick, & C. Laborde (Eds.), *International handbook of mathematics education* (pp. 987–1033). Dordrecht: Kluwer.

Ellerton, N. F., & Clements, M. A. (1994). *The national curriculum debacle*. Perth: Meridian Press.

Foong, P. Y., Yap, S. F., & Koay, P. L. (1996). Teachers' concerns about the revised mathematics curriculum. *Mathematics Educator, 1*(1), 99–110.

Fuson, K., & Fraivillig, J. (1993). Supporting children's ten-structured thinking in the classroom. In G. Bell (Ed.), *Asian perspectives on mathematics education* (pp. 42–55). Lismore: Northern Rivers Mathematical Association.

Geary, D. C. (1994). *Children's mathematical development: Research and practical applications*. Washington, DC: American Psychological Association.

Gerdes, P. (1996). Ethnomathematics and mathematics education. In A. J. Bishop, K. Clements, C. Keitel, J. Kilpatrick, & C. Laborde (Eds.), *International handbook of mathematics education* (pp. 909–943). Dordrecht: Kluwer.

Guthrie, G. (1990). To the defence of traditional teaching in lesser-developed countries. In W. D. Rust & P. Dalin (Eds.), *Teachers and teaching in the developing world* (pp. 219–232). New York: Garland.

Hersh, R. (1997). *What is mathematics, really?* London: Jonathan Cape.

Horwood, J. (1999). Cultural aspects of the definition of secondary mathematics curriculum. In M. A. Clements & Y. P. Leong (Eds.), *Cultural and language aspects of science, mathematics, and technical education* (pp. 326–334). Bandar Seri Begawan: Universiti Brunei Darussalam.

Hoosain, R. (1997). Language and thought. In H. S. R. Rao & D. Sinha (Eds.), *Asian perspectives on psychology* (pp. 113–126). New Delhi: Sage.

Ilango, R., & Lim T. K. (1997). Encouraging the investigation and solution of real life problems with Mathematica and QBASIC. In T. K. Lim (Ed.), *Maximizing academic potential: The Chinese High School Gifted Education Program in Singapore* (pp. 71–81). Singapore: Times Academic Press.

Kaur, B. (1999). Mathematics classrooms of Singapore schools: Implications for fostering thinking and creativity. In E. B. Ogena & E. F. Golia (Eds.), *8th Southeast Asian Conference on Mathematics Education, technical papers: Mathematics for the 21st century* (pp. 193–198). Manila: Ateneo de Manila University.

Koay, P. L. (1990). Performance of Bruneian school children in addition and subtraction word problems. Unpublished report. Universiti Brunei Darussalam, Bandar Seri Begawan.

Lave, J. (1988). *Cognition in practice: Mind, mathematics and culture in everyday life*. Cambridge: Cambridge University Press.

Lua, S., & Koay, P. L. (1990). Bruneian pupils' perspectives on their mathematics performance: An attributional analysis. In P. K. Veloo, F. Lopez-Real, & S. Terlochan (Eds.), *Proceedings of the fifth South East Asian Conference on Mathematical Education* (pp. 209–213). Bandar Seri Begawan: Universiti Brunei Darussalam.

Mackey, K. (1999, May/June). Do we need calculators? *Mathematics Education Dialogues*, p. 3.

Malaysia Ministry of Education. (1988). *Sukatan pelajaran sekolah menengah: Matematik*. Kuala Lumpur: Author.

Malaysia Ministry of Education. (1998). A vision of the Malaysian Smart School. [on-line]. Available: http://eprd.kpm.my/smartsc.html

Marlowe, B. A., & Page, M. L. (1998). *Creating and sustaining the constructivist classroom*. Thousand Oaks, CA: Corwin Press.

Miura, I. (1993). Exploring Asian numerical cognition. In G. Bell (Ed.), *Asian perspectives on mathematics education* (pp. 36–41). Lismore: Northern Rivers Mathematical Association.

Nelson, D., Joseph, G. G., & Williams, J. (1993). *Multicultural mathematics: Teaching mathematics from a global perspective*. Oxford: Oxford University Press.

Nunes, T. (1993). The socio-cultural context of mathematical thinking: Research findings and educational implications. In A. J. Bishop, K. Hart, S. Lerman, & T. Nunes (Eds.), *Significant influences on children's learning of mathematics* (pp. 27–42). Paris: UNESCO.

Nunes, T., & Bryant, P. (1996). *Children doing mathematics*. Oxford: Blackwell.

Rasidah Junaidi & Wong, K. Y. (1998). Pupils' performance in solving mathematical word problems in English and in Bahasa Melayu. In Y. P. Leong, L. M. Ferrer, & M. Quigley (Eds.), *Science, mathematics and technical education for national development* (pp. 154–163). Bandar Seri Begawan: Universiti Brunei Darussalam.

Restivo, S. (1992). *Mathematics in society and history: Sociological inquiries*. Dordrecht: Kluwer.

Rogers, P., & Kaiser, G. (Eds.). (1995). *Equity in mathematics education: Influences of feminism and culture*. London: Falmer Press.

Rose, Dalilah Ramlee & Wong, K. Y. (1999). Effects of Student-Teams Achievement Divisions (STAD) on mathematics achievement and attitude among lower secondary students. In M. A. Clements & Y. P. Leong (Eds.), *Cultural and language aspects of science, mathematics, and technical education* (pp. 289–298). Bandar Seri Begawan: Universiti Brunei Darussalam.

Schmidt, W. H., Jorde, D., Cogan, L. S., Barrier, E., Gonzalo, I., Moser, U., Shimizu, K., Sawada, T., Valverde, G. A., McKnight, C., Prawat, R. S., Wiley, D. E., Raizen, S. A., Britton, E. D., & Wolfe, R. G. (1996). *Characterizing pedagogical flow: An investigation of mathematics and science teaching in six countries*. Dordrecht: Kluwer.

Schmidt, W. H., McKnight, C. C., Valverde, G. A., Houang, R. T., & Wiley, D. E. (1997). *Many visions, many aims: Vol. 1. A cross-national investigation of curricular intentions in school mathematics*. Dordrecht: Kluwer.

See, K. H. (1998). Effects of computer assisted learning on creative performance in mathematics. In Y. P. Leong, L. M. Ferrer, & M. Quigley (Eds.), *Science, mathematics and technical education for national development* (pp. 266–274). Bandar Seri Begawan: Universiti Brunei Darussalam.

Sim, W. K. (1998). Project SOLD: An Overview. In K. Y. Wong (Ed.), *CARE Review 1998* (pp. 146–156). Bandar Seri Begawan: Universiti Brunei Darussalam.

Singapore Ministry of Education. (1990). *Mathematics syllabus (Lower secondary)*. Singapore: Author.

Singapore Ministry of Education. (1999). Education in Singapore. [on-line]. Available: http://www1.moe.edu.sg/educatio.htm

Soh, K. C. (1998). How do Japanese, American, and Singaporean primary school mathematics teachers teach. *Mathematics Educator, 3*(2), 88–99.

Stigler, J. W. (1997). Classroom mathematics instruction in three cultures: An overview of the TIMSS video study. In L. K. Chan & K. A. Toh (Eds.), *Research across the disciplines: Proceedings of the 1997 annual conference of Educational Research Association* (pp. 1–9). Singapore: Educational Research Association.

Straits Times, Singapore (1st October, 1996). Without the aid of a calculator, young British workers cannot count. p. 4.

Straits Times, Singapore (21st November, 1996). Singapore tops survey of 45 countries. p. 50 (by-line: M. Nirmala)

Tan, A. G. (1998). Exploring primary pupils' desirable activities in mathematics lessons. *Mathematics Educator, 3*(2), 26–37.

Teh, K. C. (1998). The gradient tour. *Science and Mathematics Education, 13*, 19–21.

Veloo, P. K., Leong, Y. P., Lopez-Real, F., Lim, H. B. G., Lee, K. P., Sakdiah Ladi, & Mastan (1993). *Report of the Jawatankuasa Mata Pelajaran Matematik bagi Peperiksaan Brunei-Cambridge GCE 'O' Level*. Unpublished report. Ministry of Education, Bandar Seri Begawan.

Wong, K. Y. (1991). Curriculum development in Singapore. In C. Marsh & P. Morris (Eds.), *Curriculum development in East Asia* (pp. 129–160). London: Falmer Press.

Wong, K. Y. (1993). Overview of mathematics education in Malaysia. In G. Bell (Ed.), *Asian perspectives on mathematics education* (pp. 90–110). Lismore: Northern Rivers Mathematical Association.

Wong, K. Y. (1996). Assessing perceptions using student drawings. In M. Quigley, P. K. Veloo, & K. Y. Wong (Eds.), *Assessment and evaluation in science and mathematics education: Innovative approaches* (pp. 370–379). Bandar Seri Begawan: Universiti Brunei Darussalam.

Wong, K. Y. (Ed.). (1998a). *CARE Review 1998*. Bandar Seri Begawan: Universiti Brunei Darussalam.

Wong, K. Y. (1998b, October). *A cyclic model to train teachers to use computers to teach mathematics in Brunei secondary schools*. Paper presented at the ICCE 98 International Conference on Computers in Education, Beijing.

Wong, K. Y., Lim-Foo, V., & Veloo, P. (1998). Multi-modal teaching strategy (MMTS): Some lessons from a pilot study. In K. Y. Wong (Ed.), *CARE Review 1998* (pp. 135–144). Bandar Seri Begawan: Universiti Brunei Darussalam.

Yong, B. C. S. (1997). Causes of educational failure among elementary school students in Brunei Darussalam as perceived by mathematics and science teachers. *Asia Pacific Journal of Education, 17*(2), 31–40.

Zaitun Taha. (1995). *Teaching primary mathematics in Brunei Darussalam: The interplay between teachers' beliefs and practices*. Unpublished doctoral thesis. King's College, University of London.

8

Mathematical Ideas and Indigenous Languages[1]

Bill Barton
University of Auckland

Roslyn Frank
University of Iowa

The rise of interest in several quite diverse fields has led to a recent recognition that mathematical thinking is a function of language in ways not previously recognized. Concepts as basic as numbers or geometric objects seem to be conceived in ways that are different from those of conventional mathematics.

The cultural renaissance of indigenous peoples has resulted in a call for schooling in indigenous languages, which, in turn, has resulted in a broadening of the ways in which it is possible to talk about mathematics. A case in point is the Maori of New Zealand. A political renaissance and push for self-determination in the mid-1970s had education as a major initiative, which led to immersion preschools, then primary education, and, by the 1990s, there was a demand for Maori language secondary education in all subjects. Interestingly, mathematics was one of the first subject areas to develop a specific register and curriculum in Maori (Barton, Fairhall, & Trinick, 1998).

There have been the continuing linguistic and anthropological investigations into languages and the "world views" they represent. Part of this has been renewed recognition of the work of Benjamin Whorf (Lee, 1996; Whorf, 1956) and the principle of linguistic relativity. This principle states that speakers of languages that are different structurally and grammatically are led to different ways of construing the world. Whorf, and his supervisor Sapir, used evidence from studies of Hopi and English to

---

[1]This project has been supported, in part, by the Institute of Basque Studies, Guildhall University, London, a nonprofit research trust dedicated to the promotion and dissemination of investigations related to Euskal Herria, the Basque Country, its people, language, and culture.

show how these languages resulted in different interpretations of events, although they believed that all humans had the same basic cognitive processes. Recent extensions of this work can be found in Lucy (1992a, 1992b). Another strand is the work of Lakoff and others in the area of language and cognition. Lakoff (1987) produced a convincing argument against the idea that thoughts correspond to objects in the real world and for the deep influence of metaphorical thinking in all aspects of human cognition, including mathematics and logic. More recent work (Lakoff & Núñez, 1997) details the way our environment acts to embed cognitive structure.

Within the field of mathematics there has been a long history of attempts to view mathematics as a cultural activity (Mac Lane, 1981; Struik, 1942; Thom, 1992; Wilder, 1981), but these have received renewed impetus with the emergence of ethnomathematics (Ascher, 1991; D'Ambrosio, 1985, 1990; Gerdes, 1986, 1994). The idea that mathematics manifests itself differently in different social or cultural contexts has been embraced by an educational world looking for answers to differences in mathematical achievement. Another educational theme has been a developing literature on bilingual education, including the possibility of cognitive advantage for speakers of more than one language.

It is no surprise, therefore, that questions are being asked about the way in which mathematical ideas are conceived and are exploring the conventional assumptions about mathematical objects and operations. If mathematics is more relative than has been assumed, where is this relativity? Is there a different mathematics? Why does mathematics have an aura of universality? Why does mathematics seem to correspond with the real world? The thesis of this chapter is that the answers to such questions lie well below the level of usual mathematical activity, they lie within the language used in mathematical talk, and, what is more, they lie embedded within the very grammar of that language.

WHAT ARE WE LOOKING FOR?

Fifty years ago, the linguist Benjamin Whorf (1956) suggested that different mathematical systems might be sought and would more likely be found in languages fundamentally different from our own, those that he referred to collectively as Standard Average European. Such languages might be geographically remote, spoken by indigenous peoples, that is, linguistic systems that have evolved separately and that have a relatively recent history of interaction with languages such as English, French, or Spanish. The Asian languages, such as Mandarin and Japanese, are different again because their symbols are pictorial rather than phonological. The different ways this might affect mathematical thinking are not part of this chapter.

What does "different mathematical systems might be sought in other languages" mean? We are not looking for anything resembling mathematics as it appears in a school textbook. Our view must be widened to embrace mathematical thinking generally. We are looking for what we might call "QRS systems," that is, systems by which we make meaning of quantity, relationships, or space. Even this is to presume too much. A language does not contain a system like a measurement system of metres, grams, and litres. We are looking for something more fundamental than that.

Lakoff, Núñez, Johnson, and others, in a series of works over the last 20 years (Lakoff, 1987; Lakoff & Johnson, 1980; Lakoff & Núñez, 1997; and books in preparation) presented compelling linguistic evidence for the deep use of metaphor and metonymy in the way humans structure their concepts, including the concepts of mathematics. Their work begins by examining the way we classify concepts and then discusses examples of concepts in linguistics and mathematics. It shows clearly that mathematical concepts cannot be attached to ideal mathematical objects that exist independently and objectively in some world; rather the concepts are developed, through language, from human experiences. In addition, the shape of that development itself derives from fundamental experiences. Experience is embodied in the form of metaphors within the language we use. Some of the fundamental ones in English (Lakoff & Núñez claim that they are universal) include the "container" metaphor (the idea for sets in mathematics), the "things in piles" and "points on line" metaphors (the ideas for numbers), the "arrow" metaphor (the idea for functions), and the "turning around" metaphor (used in geometry).

At present there is a lack of theoretical tools and approaches that would cope adequately with the idea that there are no language universals at all. Thus, it is difficult to find ways to even talk about, for example, "another mathematics" that make sense. Such a concept requires that the development of QRS systems, and other cognitive structures, start very early. The idea that the way in which very young children "see" their world—precognitive perceptual activity—may be language based is only recently being discussed (Levinson, 1996).

A leading algebraist, Saunders Mac Lane (1981, p. 465) once described mathematics in these terms: "Mathematics starts from a variety of human activities, disentangles from them a number of notions which are generic and not arbitrary, then formalises these notions.... Thus ... mathematics studies formal structures by deductive methods ..."

He goes on to say that it would be possible to construct mathematics using, say, the notion of arrows (something linked directionally to something else) rather than containers (sets) and that if this was done then mathematics would look quite different. We are suggesting that Mac Lane's "notions" are embedded grammatically and metaphorically in our language of human activities and, furthermore, that the deductive methods used in mathematics are also prescribed by the metaphors and grammar of our communication. What we are interested in is whether other languages have different metaphors—or, possibly, a greater propensity for one metaphor over another—embedded in their grammar of quantity, relationship, or space.

There are various levels on which we might conduct our search. At the most superficial level we can examine the words that make up the language. Then we might look more deeply at the way in which the words are used, that is, the syntax and morphology of the language. Finally we might look at a still deeper level at the ethos of the language, at the metaphors it uses and propensities it encourages, in other words, its repertoire of image schemata (Frank & Susperregi, 1999).

FOCUS ON VOCABULARY, SYNTAX, AND GRAMMAR

Most work on mathematical ideas in language has focused on the different number words used around the world, examining them for the implied base used in counting and for relationships between languages. (Lean, 1995; Menniger, 1969). More recent work has had a semiotic focus, examining mathematical ideas and their symbols as communicative acts (e.g., Rotman, 1987). A feature of all of these works is an implied universality in the way numbers, shapes, or operations are thought about and used. Even Crump's Anthropology of Number (1989) made assumptions about what "number" might be, although it does focus on the role of number in different societies.

Such assumptions are challenged by a closer examination of the way vocabulary is used. Even at a surface level, attention to vocabulary can alert us to different conceptual systems. As part of other work one of the authors asked a Maori weaver about some basket-weaving patterns and was surprised to discover that several patterns that appeared to bear no relationship to each other were given the same name. To a conventional mathematician these patterns have different symmetry. To the weaver's eyes they are the same because they require the same initial setup of black and white strands in order to create each pattern. What might be called "strand symmetry" is so important that it is reflected in the naming system. This classification of pattern cannot be subsumed by the usual classification by line and rotational symmetries. It may be context specific, but the example at least shows that the usual forms of symmetry are not universally applicable.

As another example, Lipka (1994) noted a pattern system based on what mathematicians might call polar coordinates in the basket making of the Yup'ik in Alaska. It would be interesting to know whether this was confirmed by the presence and manipulation of related conceptual categories from their lexical repertoire. Indeed such an analysis might be the best way discover to what extent this pattern is generalized by the Yup'ik themselves, for example, whether there is evidence that they tend to organize other aspects of space in terms of a polar-like symmetry.

Another source for finding QRS systems is among those words that do not have equivalents when translated into English. These concepts have referential domains that only partially overlap, or that are noncommensurate, with those of English. In Fiji there are several words that are names for cultural practices that have to do with transferring goods. These practices are not trading in any generally accepted sense of that word but represent specific practices that have no equivalent. For example, solevu is a public, ceremonial exchange of goods between groups; kerekere is a form of gifting in response to a request (Bakalevu, 1998). Both of these concepts involve a quantification but not an accounting as it is understood in European trade terms. For example, it is important that the size of the presentation is known, recognized, and returned in excess and that a public sharing takes place. Neither of these practices is formalized mathematics; however, they are systems that deal with quantity and cannot be adequately represented by the measuring and numerical operations taught as part of a formal mathematics lesson.

There is a suggestion that the dominant position held by the world view of European languages has affected the way vocabulary items map meaning. In Maori tonga means south. It has its equivalent in Hawaiian: kona meaning leeward. In Hawaii this happens to be a southwesterly direction. It seems likely that this word at some point got fixed to a north–south grid reference instead of its wind-direction referent (which would be more practical in a Pacific Island context with prevailing winds and local sea travel). The Maori word muri means north, and also means behind (being associated with mua meaning in front). Trinick (1999) suggested that, as the initial migration to New Zealand came from the northeast, behind would be associated with that direction (it is also used to refer to the stern of a canoe). Again the referent was, at some later time, fixed onto a north–south grid referent, as the orienting direction of "home" lost its relevance for local travel. Did this refixing of the referent occur at the time of European contact—contact with sailors and others who would only think about directions in terms of compass points?

It is likely that specialized navigational vocabulary will hold the key to identifying more systematic differences in the way location is represented. Pacific navigation seems to have been conceived as "pathways" rather than "position"; thus navigating from one place to another is understood as a journey and described by what might be seen or experienced along the way and how to tell whether one is on the correct track rather than as a series of positions at any particular time. Sea travel for Pacific navigators was more like a car journey for a modern traveler than like a chart-plotted sea journey for a yachtsman.

Harris (1991) also used linguistic evidence to suggest that the Australian Aborigines use a north/south/east/west location system even in very local situations such as describing where in a room a piece of furniture is located. The implication is that Aboriginal children are disadvantaged in schools because the curriculum assumes easy familiarity with right/left/front/back orientation systems in such contexts, and their superior ability to use the north/south/east/west directional system is not utilized.

However, much more fundamental differences can be found by examining the syntax and grammar of languages. An early work that explicitly addressed the mathematics in the syntax of a language was Gay and Cole's (1967) work concerning Kpelle mathematical concepts. Empirical evidence is presented for the conclusions that Kpelle find disjunction and negation considerably easier than American English speakers, and, further, "[the Kpelle] find disjunction easiest; in order of increasing difficulty are conjunction, negation, and implication. Equivalence they find very difficult. This pattern contrasts significantly with American behaviour, and many of the differences seem to reflect differences in linguistic structure between Kpelle and English" (Gay & Cole, 1967, p. 83).

Gay and Cole note differences in the way the Kpelle discuss and argue. However, they analyze the logic of the language in classical terms. Perhaps the differences in logical understanding reflect a more fundamental difference in the way relationships are expressed?

Many indigenous languages are being seriously affected by the dominant world language in the region: Maori in New Zealand by English, Yup'ik in Alaska by Russian and English, Euskara of Basque country by Spanish and French, and so on. As a result some of the grammatical constructions that indicate other ways of conceptualizing quantity, relationships, or space are being lost. For example, in modern Maori, number words are treated as they are in English: "three bottles" has the number acting like an adjective in the same way as "red bottles" or "tall bottles." However, recent work with older speakers of Maori produced evidence of a different role for number words in traditional speech (Trinick, 1999). It was first noticed that number words in Maori are often used with verbal time markers. Many Maori sentences start with e, kia, ka, kua, or i. These indicate tense. That the first three of these are often used with the number words indicates a verbal origin. Further evidence comes from the grammar of negation. Consider the three sentences:

E wha nga kina	= There are four sea-eggs (Four the sea-eggs)
Kei te haere tatou ki Te Kaha	= We are going to Te Kaha (Going we to Te Kaha)
He pouaka nui tenei	= This is a big box (Box big this)

And now look at how each sentence is negated:

Kaore e wha nga kina, (e toru ke)	= There are not four sea-eggs (there are three)
Kaore tatou i te haere ki Te Kaha	= We are not going to Te Kaha
Ehara tenei i te pouaka nui	= This is not a big box

The form of sentence negating the number is the same as the form of the sentence negating the action and different from the sentence negating an adjective.

Thus, numbers were expressed as actions. In English this would be like saying, "the bottles are three-ing on the table." A similar use of number is found in Haida, a language spoken among First Nations people on the coast in northwest British Columbia. Here the verbal form is explicit: "Dii daghalang stingaagang = My brothers two. This is a sentence, in which "two" ["sting" in Haida] is the verb. In English, of course, we would say, "I have two brothers." In Haida, one cannot "have" brothers; brothers "are." They exist—and being discreet and countable entities, they exist numerically" (Bringhurst, 1999).

Denny (1986) noted a verbal use of number words for Ojibway:

nis-iwag	= they (animate) are three
nis-inoon	= they (inanimate) are three
nis-ing	= multiply by three (three times)

In mathematical talk we use numbers as objects, that is, as nouns. Denny (1986) also reported numbers having a noun morphology in the Inuktitut language of Aivilingmiut.

This is indicated by the use of noun suffixes:

one	atausiq	(none)	(singular noun)
two	marruuk	-uk	dual noun ending
three	pingasut	-t	plural noun ending

Thus, pingasut means a group of three. In order to say three caribou, you would say pingasut tuktuit, that is, a three-group of caribou or a caribou group-of-three.

These alternative ways of talking about quantity do not constitute a mathematics. However, it is interesting to speculate on what sort of mathematics might have arisen had an extensive formalization of quantity taken place in a linguistic environment where numbers were actions not objects. An experienced mathematician noted that scalar quantity can be regarded as the first in a sequence of operators in analysis: function value, first derivative, second derivative, and so on (Butcher, 1998). In such a conceptualization it might be more natural to think of scalar quantity as an action. Alternatively, what concept of the continuum might we have if we spoke of quantity as "becoming one, becoming two, and so on"?

Another aspect of the conventional way of making sense of quantity is the number line. Rulers are obvious examples, but also the base ten system is often represented to small children as bundles of marks (sticks, tallies) lined up together. Lipka (1994), however, gave an example where the number words of the Yup'ik seem to suggest a cyclic image rather than a linear one. Derived from body counting of fingers and toes, Yup'ik teachers used a cycle based on 20, which is used to represent numbers symbolically—a representation approved by Yup'ik elders as in tune with their understanding.

A further example of linguistic difference in the idea of number is illustrated in the Indonesian language of Kedang. In that language the words udeq, sue, tèlu, apaq, leme are one, two, three, four, and five, respectively. However, there are also the nouns munaq (one unit), suen (two units), . . . , lemen (five units), and so on (Barnes, 1982). Hence, multiplication is expressed abstractly as lemen sue (two lots of five units), which is different from suen leme (five lots of two units). In English, multiplication can be expressed as, say: "five times two" or "two times five" where the five and two can be interchanged without altering the word forms, the grammar, or the sense. In other words, commutativity is part of the language of multiplication in English; noncommutativity is the privileged form in Kedang. (Note that this is not to say that Kédang speakers cannot understand or express commutativity if they wish to do so.)

The point being made is that, within each language, there are particular ways of expressing ideas of quantity, relationships, or space. Although it is possible to describe all these linguistic expressions in each language, there remains a question mark over whether the full complexity of the expression can be rendered in another language. So we are concerned not just with individual features of, say, whether a number is an action or a description or a thing in itself but with the whole way in which quantity is approached in its myriad of instantiations and its relationship to, say, measurement, comparisons, or time. Then there is the further question as to whether such culture-specific concepts are formalized or, if they were, what the result would be.

FOCUS ON ETHOS

Such questions cannot be answered simply by examining the lexicon (conceptual repertoire), syntax, or grammar of a particular language. Rather we need to focus on the interaction between these linguistic characteristics and the overall metaphysics expressed by what we might call the ethos, or world view, of a given speech community. In order to illustrate this idea, we turn to another indigenous language that, although embedded in an Indo-European linguistic environment, is very different in its ethos. Euskara is the language of the Basque people of northern Spain/southern France. It is an important example because virtually all of the speakers of Euskara are bilingual, either in French or Spanish. Consequently, their schooling is done through recourse to Indo-European language models of number construction even though the language of schooling is often Euskara. These Indo-European cognitive models are taking over and affecting the indigenous structures in profound ways. The two models struggling with each other inside one linguistic system provide us with an interesting vantage point from which two radically different systems can be examined.

In Euskara (and in certain other non-Western languages, e.g., Yucatec Maya) the ontology of "being" is differently positioned. In describing it we are hampered by the "spatiotemporal particulars" (Watson, 1990) imposed by English, which enculturate us to perceive "a universe consisting of (a) void or 'holes,' and (b) substance or matter which has 'properties' and forms island-like 'bodies,' [and] an absolute unbridgeable difference between the matter and the 'holes'..." (Whorf, 1938). Thus, in English the "matter" is set against a backdrop of "nothingness"; that is, the "void" sets off the object itself. The void is passive in terms of its meaning making.

However, in Euskara what is the void (from the point of view of English) is completely "full." Thus "matter" becomes the "ground" and forms are cut out from it, as cookies from undifferentiated dough. Thus, what's inside the figure and what is outside of it are the same "stuff." This cutout operation is accomplished linguistically by manipulating suffixes indicating particular qualities, shapes, and modes of being and extension. In this sense it could be argued that the ontology intrinsic to Euskara concentrates far more attention on constructing the boundaries, borders, or edges of the "matter-stuff," that is, on shaping it. It could be argued that the ontology intrinsic to Euskara is one that concentrates its attention far more on what would be understood, in English, as "negative space" or, perhaps, as the space between the outlines of objects hence, the need for a mind-set that recognizes these spaces as real—as real as the "positive" forms of English. It is interesting to compare this with Watson (1990, p. 297) of an African language: "The objects which Yoruba speakers are committed to saying there are in the world are sortal particulars—material objects defined through their particular nature. Certain sets of characteristics form definitive boundaries of the material objects that Yoruba speakers talk about as being infinitely scattered through space and time."

Some of the flavor of this way of viewing the world can be understood with respect to an atomic scientist's view of, say, a table. The table is understood to be made up from atoms and molecules that are not different from those in the air around it, the floor on which it stands, or the person viewing it. Indeed, on our present understanding of atoms, there is much more "empty space" within the table than there is matter. The table, therefore, is simply a particular collection of molecules—what we observe is these molecules "table-ing."

However, even this different way of conceiving is still affected by our English perception and its emphasis on spacial form. In Euskara, the form of an object is also defined by the "mode" of its being, that is, by its qualities. Thus, physical shape and whether it exists now or existed in the past are not as relevant as they are in English. A way to illustrate this point is to explain, for example, that an Euskara–English Dictionary would give su for fire. However, su corresponds to the inner intrinsic nature of fire. If we wish to talk about this fire-stuff as a entity extended in time and space as an event, as in the English " There was a fire on Oak Street," then the suffix -te must be added to indicate this: sute. As another example, in English the sentence "he saw four dogs" speaks of four objects in space with the size, shape, and characteristics of a dog that were observed; in contrast, in Euskara "Lau txakuer ikusi zuen" speaks of matter with the characteristics of dogness and fourness that was seen. Note that in this example number is realized as a possible mode of being, (cf. the Haida examples previously and similar ones in Yoruba discussed by Watson, 1990).

Levinson referred to similar linguistic implications in his discussion of Lucy's (1992a, p. 73ff) work on Yucatec (Levinson, 1996):

> Like Tzeltal, Yucatec has a developed set of numeral classifiers. The motivation, Lucy claims, is that nominals in Yucatec fail, by themselves, to individuate entities. It is only by collocation with a numeral classifier or some other shape-discriminating phrase that such nouns can come to designate countable entities. This thesis, carried to its logical extreme, would amount to the claim that all nominals in Yucatec are essentially "mass" nouns and that the language makes no ontological commitment to "entities" as opposed to materials, essence or "stuff" at all. In order to individuate entities, a numeral classifier or some predicate is required to impose individuation on the material, metaphorically in much the same way that a cookie-cutter cuts up undifferentiated dough! (p. 185)

The idea that objects only come into being when the word for their essence has some kind of classifier attached to it would help to explain the Tzeltal insistence on specifying the geometrical nature of the figure. Thus, it is not only numbers that are conceived as qualities but also geometric figures. Other works dealing with geometric conceptualizations are Pinxten, van Dooren and Harvey (1983), and Pinxten, van Dooren, and Soberon (1987).

The suggestion contained in these paragraphs that indigenous languages such as Euskara, Yoruba, Yucatec Maya, and Haida embody a metaphysical view of the world with common elements is probably a reflection of the lack of understanding we have of the subtle differences between the world view of each of these languages. To us as English speakers they are so different from our understanding that they just seem the same. From a typological point of view, it is unlikely that these linguistic systems, drawn from four continents, would appear so similar if additional aspects of them were subjected to analysis.

Sapir and Whorf, American linguists of the first half of this century, wrote explicitly of the way languages codify a particular dissection of nature. To quote Lee (1996):

> Thus both Sapir and Whorf made it clear that the possibility of comparing geometries is based on an implicit assumption that what they systematize in the first instance is a common reality—space as it may be experienced by human beings—and that this is differently described and mentally organized according to principles embodied in each geometrical method. [...] It may be useful to give a little more attention to the way different geometries (which are effectively different mathematical perspectives brought about by different ways of talking) articulate different conceptions of space. (p. 113)

Most writers who have attempted to examine spatial questions in non-Western languages, have started from the unexamined premise that the objects themselves are in need of no further elaboration and can be equated safely with those found in English. As Levinson (1996) noted, Lyons (1977) as well as other writers pointed out that we only identify nouns, verbs, and so on in another language on the basis of a mix of syntactic and ontological criteria. Consider again Lucy's conjecture about Yucatec nouns as denoting material or essence, not objects as is the case in English: that would make the ontological prototypes for nouns in Yucatec a property and not an entity. We need to keep in mind that the conceptual frames initially brought into play in linguistics (and mathematics) were those readily available to Standard Average European (SAE) speakers. In summary, it is not just the way in which the universe is understood but also the way in which we talk about language, the very terminology we use, that may not be appropriate when we are discussing linguistic systems fundamentally different from English and other Indo-European languages.

There is the additional problem that on occasion the referential object produced in, say, Euskara or Yoruba, appears to coincide with that of a spatiotemporal particular in English. That apparent translatability is particularly deceptive because such a case makes the language learner or linguist assume that this similarity can be extended to the system as a whole (Watson, 1990). Furthermore, the impact of the ontology of a dominant SAE language on that of minority one like Euskara or Yoruba can result in the introduction of subtle cognitive shifts that, in turn, encourage additional copying of the QRS system of the prestige language into the minority one.

IMPLICATIONS FOR MATHEMATICS EDUCATION

What does all this mean for mathematics education? First, it should be said clearly that these ideas do not mean that different peoples are limited by their language to the concepts expressed in that language or to the ethos it embodies. This chapter is an example of the way that it is possible to consider ideas that have arisen in other language structures. Thus, the mathematical, or QRS, ideas that might emerge from a study of indigenous (or any) language add to the potential concepts from which formal mathematics may draw or act as a creative source for speakers of other languages. This applies as easily, for example, to ideas moving from English to Haida as it does for those moving from Haida to English.

The next point is that the use of culturally specific resources to achieve the conventional aims of mathematics education is still a very open question. One the one hand, the existence of fundamentally different networks of image schemata (sometimes referred to as world views), including those aspects regarded as mathematical, calls into serious question the use of isolated materials from other cultures in the promotion of educational objectives from, say, an English or European culture. For example, the use of weaving patterns or number words from other cultures in the service of geometry or numeracy is likely to devalue those materials by stripping them of the linguistic and practical contexts in which they are meaningful. There may be other educational reasons for their use, (e.g., motivation or creating links with particular students), but such practices are likely to need constant re-evaluation of their effectiveness and an awareness of hidden consequences. For example, if practices that can be evaluated as elementary in conventional mathematics terms are presented as the "mathematics" of a particular culture, then there is a danger of that culture being labeled "primitive." On the other hand, without presenting ideas from fundamentally different image schemata, it is not possible to illustrate the way in which conventional mathematics developed in a particular way that could have been different. Bishop promoted this idea with his concept of using cultural conflict within the enculturation of mathematics (Bishop, 1994).

A further implication for classroom mathematics is that the evidence presented previously indicates a fundamental relationship between mathematical thinking and language—and this means any language, including the specialized language of a mathematics classroom. There is increasing research into how mathematical discussion affects the concepts that are formed. However, there is a need to open this up to consider the image schemas embedded in the ontology of the language, not just the differences between, say, informal and formal language. For example, do new learners of mathematics have some fundamental concepts that get suppressed in the environment of a conventional mathematics classroom? Will increased classroom talk allow unconventional schemas to be valued, and will this increase mathematical ability? Will increased talk just increase the distance (measured in academic achievement) between those who quickly adopt conventional schemata and those who do so only slowly?

As far as teaching is concerned, there is a challenge to educate mathematics teachers, particularly monolingual ones, to review their conceptions of mathematics as a more contingent subject than that which was taught to them. It will make it more difficult to present the content of mathematics as "how the world is": teachers will need to develop ways of talking about their subject that bring out the conventional nature of its concepts, not just its symbolism and methods.

The main implication for mathematics education, however, is with respect to learners from indigenous or minority cultures who are often disadvantaged with respect to mathematical achievement in conventional terms. It has long been known (e.g., D'Ambrosio, 1990) that the basis for this lies in the cultural estrangement of studying a field of knowledge that has been developed through another world view. D'Ambrosio referred to the way this manifests in the classroom and the community as the "social terrorism" of mathematics. Overcoming this estrangement is no easy task, but acknowledging the problem must be an essential feature.

Such acknowledgment must come not just in the minds of the educators but also in the curriculum as it is received by students. One attempt at this was described by Lipka (1994, p. 25):

The pressure behind developing a Yup'ik mathematics is threefold:

1. To show students that mathematics is socially constructed.
2. To engage students in a process of constructing a system of mathematics based on their cultural knowledge.
3. To connect students' knowledge of "their mathematics" through comparisons and bridges to other aboriginal and Western systems.

In other words, access to the conventional, widespread field known as mathematics must come through the world view in which it has been developed and is mostly expressed: that of Indo-European languages. If your network of image schemata is different from the dominant one, then the first step is to understand the role of your own world view in making sense of quantity, relationships, and space so you can appreciate another one. It should be noted, in addition, that a facility with non-Indo-European ontologies and QRS systems may shed a new light on concepts that exist in the dominant culture of mathematics.

Such an educational task seems to place an added burden on anyone who is starting from a world view different from that of the knowledge he or she is seeking. In a sense this is true, but there are two important points to be made. There is evidence (Cummins, 1986) that bilingual learners, provided they have a "threshold fluency" in both languages, have a cognitive advantage in any educational task. Knowing a language implies an intuitive understanding of a whole network of image schemata. Perhaps knowing a language well enough to internalize its world view is the criterion of the "threshold fluency" below which the cognitive advantage does not occur? Thus cognitive advantage might be interpreted to mean that the sort of knowing that results from having two or more world views is a deeper, more-aware sort of knowing than that which results from having only one. If this is right, then it is probable that the more dissimilar are the representations of reality that the learners have access to, then the greater will be their potential for perceiving differences between the two linguistic systems and gaining from that experience. Hence, the added burden mentioned previously does not mean that people from a different world view have to do more to reach the same place but that they are going to a different, deeper place.

The second point is that, if someone already inhabiting the world view of, say, conventional mathematical knowledge wishes to reach this deeper level of understanding, then he or she also has an added task. It is a feature of many education systems, especially monolingual English-speaking ones, that such an alternate kind of understanding is not even recognized. To quote Whorf (1956):

> ...but to restrict thinking to the patterns merely of English...is to lose a power of thought which, once lost, can never be regained. ...I believe that those who envision a future world speaking only one tongue...hold a misguided ideal and would do the evolution of the human mind the greatest disservice. Western culture has made, through language, a provisional analysis of reality and, without correctives, holds resolutely to that analysis as final. The only correctives lie in all those other tongues which by aeons of independent evolution have arrived at different, but equally logical, provisional analyses. (p. 244)

CONCLUSIONS

There is an exciting, unexplored challenge for the linguistic suggestions mentioned in this chapter to be further researched. Specific questions for mathematics educators include the following:

- Are there children for whom the (conventionally) "basic" mathematical concepts (e.g., number, shape, sets, symmetry, logical relations) are not readily available because of conflicting (or incommensurable) concepts powerfully present in their own cultural–linguistic heritage?
- If (as the writers believe) such children exist, how can their mathematical thinking best be acknowledged, and can it be maintained at the same time as learning conventional mathematical ways of thinking?
- What are the conditions under which such children have a cognitive advantage in mathematics, and what is the nature of this advantage?
- What is the contribution of teaching mathematics as a universal subject with respect to the phenomenon variously known as math phobia or the social terrorism of mathematics?
- If (as the writers believe) it is substantial, what needs to happen in teacher education, in classroom practice, and in social attitudes to the subject in order that significant changes occur?

Another question, which is outside the scope of this chapter but which is critical if change is to take place, is whether sufficiently strong evidence can be provided to convince mathematicians that their subject can be seen as relative at a fundamental level. Searching for this material within mathematics itself and presenting it appropriately are important next tasks.

All the previous ideas have been approached from different directions by ethnomathematicians, anthropological and cognitive linguists, educationalists, and cultural psychologists. The ideas are particularly important because of the fundamental nature of conceptions of quantity, relationships, and space. To quote Whorf (1956) once more, and this time with more insight into what he meant: "... an important field for the working out of new order systems, akin to, yet not identical with, present mathematics, lies in more penetrating investigation than has yet been made of languages remote in type from our own" (p. 255).

REFERENCES

Ascher, M. (1991). *Ethnomathematics: A multicultural view of mathematical ideas*. New York: Brooks/Cole.

Bakalevu, S. (1998). *Fijian perspectives in mathematics education*, Unpublished doctoral thesis, The University of Waikato, New Zealand.

Barnes, R. H. (1982). Number and number use in Kédang, Indonesia. *Man, 17*(1).

Barton, B., Fairhall, U., & Trinick, T. (1998). Tikanga Reo Tatai: Issues in the development of a Maori mathematics register. *For The Learning of Mathematics, 18*(1), 3–9.

Bishop, A. J. (1994). Cultural conflicts in mathematics education: Developing a research agenda. *For the Learning of Mathematics, 14*(2), 15–18.

Crump, T. (1989). *The anthropology of number*. Cambridge: Cambridge University Press.

Cummins, J. (1986). *Bilingualism in education: Aspects of theory, research and practice*. London: Longman.

D'Ambrosio, U. (1985). Socio-cultural bases for mathematics education, In M. Carss (Ed.), *Proceedings of the fifth international Congress on Mathematics Education* (pp. 1–6). Boston, MA: Birkhäuser.

D'Ambrosio, U. (1990). The role of mathematics education in building a democratic and just society. *For the Learning of Mathematics, 10*(3), 20–23.

Denny, P. (1986). Cultural ecology of mathematics: Ojibway and Inuit hunters. In M. P. Closs (Ed.), *Native American mathematics* (pp. 129–180). Austin: University of Texas Press.

Frank, R., & Susperregi, M. (1999, July) Conflicting identities: A comparative study of non-commensurate root metaphors. *Basque and European image schemata. Sixth international Cognitive Linguistics Conference*. Stockholm, Sweden, 1999.

Gay, J., & Cole, M. (1967). *The new mathematics and an old culture: A study of learning among the Kpelle of Nigeria*. New York: Holt, Rinehart & Winston.

Gerdes, P. (1986). How to recognise hidden geometrical thinking? A contribution to the development of anthropological mathematics. *For the Learning of Mathematics, 6*(2), 10–12, 17.

Gerdes, P. (1994). Reflections on ethnomathematics. *For the Learning of Mathematics, 14*(2), 19–22.

Harris, P. (1991). *Mathematics in a cultural context*. Geelong: Deakin University.

Lakoff, G. (1987). *Women, fire and dangerous things: What categories reveal about the mind*. Chicago: Chicago University Press.

Lakoff, G., & Johnson, M. (1980). *Metaphors we live by*. Chicago: University of Chicago Press.

Lakoff, G., & Núñez, R. (1997). The metaphorical nature of mathematics. In L. English (Ed.), *Mathematical reasoning: Analogies, metaphors and images* (pp. 21–89). Mahwah, NJ: Lawrence Erlbaum Associates.

Lean, G. A. (1995). *Counting systems of Papua New Guinea and Oceania*. Unpublished doctoral thesis, Papua New Guinea University of Technology, Lae.

Lee, P. (1996). *The Whorf theory complex: A critical reconstruction, Vol. 81. Studies in the History of Language Series*, Amsterdam: John Benjamins.

Levinson, S. (1996). Relativity in spatial conception and description. In J. Gumperz & S. Levinson (Eds.), *Rethinking linguistic relativity, Studies in the social and cultural foundations of language 17* (pp. 177–202). Cambridge: Cambridge University Press.

Lipka, J. (1994). Culturally negotiated schooling: Toward a Yup'ik mathematics. *Journal of American Indian Education, 33*(3), 14–30.

Lyons, J. (1977). *Semantics*. Cambridge: Cambridge University Press.

Lucy, J. (1992a). *Grammatical categories and cognition: A case study of the linguistic relativity hypothesis*. Cambridge: Cambridge University Press.

Lucy, J. (1992b). *Language, diversity and thought: A reformulation of the linguistic relativity hypothesis*. Cambridge: Cambridge University Press.

Mac Lane, S. (1981). Mathematical models: A sketch for the philosophy of mathematics. *American Mathematical Monthly, 88*(7), 462–472.

Menninger, K. (1969). *Number words and number symbols: A cultural history of numbers* (P. Broneer, Trans.). Cambridge, MA: MIT Press.

Pinxten, R., van Dooren, I., & Harvey, F. (1983). *Anthropology of space: Explorations into the natural philosophy and semantics of the navajo*. Philadelphia: University of Philadelphia Press.

Pinxten, R., van Dooren, I., & Soberon, E. (1987). *Towards a Navajo Indian geometry*. Gent: K.K.I. Books.

Rotman, B. (1987). *Signifying nothing: The semiotics of zero*. London: Routledge.

Struik, D. J. (1942). On the sociology of mathematics. *Science and Society, 6*(1), 58–70.

Thom, R. (1992). Leaving mathematics for philosophy. In C. Casacuberta & M. Castellet (Eds.), *Mathematical research today and tomorrow: Viewpoints of seven Fields medalists. Lecture notes in mathematics 1525* (pp. 1–12). Berlin: Springer-Verlag.

Trinick, T. (1999). *Te Reo Tatai: The relationship between Maori culture and mathematical language*. Unpublished master's thesis, The University of Auckland.

Watson, H. (1988). Mathematics education from a bicultural point of view. In C. Keitel, P. Damerow, A. Bishop, & P Gerdes (Eds.), *Mathematics, education and society: Science and technology education document series no. 35*. Paris: UNESCO.

Watson, H. (1990). Investigating the social foundations of mathematics. *Social Studies of Science, 20*, 283–312.

Whorf, B (1938). Yale report. In P. Lee (Ed.), *The Whorf Theory Complex* (p. 264). John Benjamins.

Whorf, B. (1956). Languages and logic. In J. Carroll (Ed.), *Language, thought and reality: Selected writings by Benjamin Lee Whorf* (pp. 233–245). Cambridge, MA: MIT Press.

Wilder, R. L. (1981). *Mathematics as a cultural system*. Oxford: Pergamon.

9

The Sociopolitical Context of Mathematics Education in Guatemala Through the Words and Practices of Two Teachers

Richard S. Kitchen
University of New Mexico

Altbach, Arnove, and Kelly (1982), Carnoy (1974), and Zachariah and Silva (1980) all argued that national school systems are situated within the context of unequal power relations among nations. The historical roots of this unequal relationship date back to when colonialized countries adopted transplanted educational models that usually "grotesquely misfit the countries' actual needs, circumstances, and resources" (Coombs, 1985, p. 33). D'Ambrosio (1991) discussed how approaches to mathematics education promoted in First World nations may not be appropriate for the needs of the borrower nations. For example, the "new math" movement begun in the United States in the early 1960s influenced mathematics pedagogy differently in the Third World, depending on the context. The reforms were ignored by the military government in Brazil when they were undertaken in that country in the late 1960s "since the high level of rigor and symbolism proposed was obviously not promoting creative or critical thinking in school children and young adults" (D'Ambrosio, 1991, p. 75). Although the "new math" reform movement was heavily influenced by mathematicians, present reforms in mathematics education in the United States (NCTM, 1989) and other First World nations articulate the importance of alternative learning formats such as student-centered classrooms, emphasize mathematical problem solving, and incorporate the use of learning technologies. Jurdak (1992) wrote that Third World countries are unlikely to be able to afford the material and human resources needed to implement such reforms.

For the majority of children living in developing countries, formal school mathematics has little relevance to their lives (Gerdes, 1988). Palestinian mathematician Munir Fasheh (1988) argued that this is not a coincidence because the abstract mathematics

151

curricula that are encountered by Third World students are imported from First World countries. A traditional function of this highly symbolic, imported mathematics curriculum is to serve as an educational filter that facilitates the selection of elites (Gerdes, 1988). D'Ambrosio (1983) agreed, writing: "Mathematics has been used as a barrier to social access, reinforcing the power structure that prevails in the societies [of the Third World]. No other subject in school serves so well this purpose of reinforcement of the power structure, as does mathematics. And the main tool for this negative aspect of mathematics education is evaluation" (p. 363).

Through selecting, sorting, and certifying students, schools serve to legitimate people (Apple, 1985). In developing nations, academic success is frequently defined relative to the knowledge and skills valued in academic institutions in the First World. Reflecting upon his training as a mathematician, Fasheh (1988) wrote "the training of colonial intellectuals directs them to derive their sense of worth and status from this vicarious participation, alienating them from their own culture, history, and people" (p. 85). Ultimately, Fasheh's education led him to lose a sense of belonging to his own culture and society. To counteract mathematical imperialism, Gerdes (1985) believed that mathematics education in the Third World should nurture cultural affirmation. Such an approach to mathematics education places the mathematics of the local culture at the forefront of instruction. This perspective, called ethnomathematics, fosters the idea that mathematics is a product of culture and is affected by cultural forces (Bishop, 1988; D'Ambrosio, 1983).

Scholars who advance ethnomathematics argue that all peoples have invented mathematical ideas about counting, measuring, locating, designing, and even playing, with corresponding symbols and vocabulary to communicate mathematically to others (Bishop, 1988; Gilmer, 1990). The study of ethnomathematics also legitimates local peoples' ways of mathematizing the world. Others have argued that mathematical problems be selected for study specifically because the problems motivate critical reflection among students (Abraham & Bibby, 1988; Mellin-Olsen, 1987). For example, Kitchen and Lear (1999) found that the study of the measurements of Barbie dolls inspired a group of Latinas to reconsider their views on body image.

In this chapter, my goal is to investigate sociopolitical aspects of mathematics education in a developing country. My examination is informed by a research project carried out during the summers of 1994 and 1995 in Guatemala, Central America. The study addressed the question: What sense do two Guatemalan mathematics teachers make of the social and political contexts in which they work? My review of the literature revealed that no research exists in which mathematics teachers from developing nations depict their work in their own words. Lincoln (1993) asserted that without literature from people who have traditionally been silenced: "We will probably not have a full critique of the social order from their perspective" (p. 44).

An overview of Guatemalan history is initially presented to understand the larger sociopolitical context in which the teachers worked. The research methodology and the two participants in the study are then introduced. The proceeding section elucidates aspects of the sociopolitical context of mathematics education in the research participants' country; the teachers characterize education in Guatemala and at their schools, profile their students, discuss student activism, and afford insight into their pedagogical goals and practices. Finally, I reflect on what can be learned from the two teachers' narratives regarding the social and political context of mathematics education in Guatemala.

INTRODUCTION TO THE HISTORY
OF GUATEMALA

Guatemala is a society divided between the ruling Latino population and the sub-jugated indigenous peoples. Any analysis of the country's educational system must take account of how Latinos have used their power in Guatemala to run the national government,[1] to maintain control, and to influence schooling. Simon (1987) charac-terized, in poignant terms, the present situation in Guatemala:

> Guatemala is a place where the political, economic, and social panorama is unfairly skewed in every possible way. In Guatemala, no one outside the charmed circle of the army and the very rich is safe, almost everyone is a victim in one way or another and cowardice or greed conditions even those privileged few that remain immune from repression. Guatemala is a place where coups are plotted after minimal attempts at land reform, and where even talk of land redistribution is deemed "subversive" or communist. Guatemala is a place where those who have nothing offer the only chair in the house, while those who have everything will often not pay minimum wage. In Guatemala, life gets better for a minority, at the expense of millions of others. (pp. 16–17)

Efforts at land reform have been attempted in Guatemala. In 1944, after the forced resignation of the dictator Jorge Ubico, attempts were made to establish a more mod-erate democratic government (Parkyn, 1989). Two succeeding presidents, Juan José Arevalo and Jacobo Arbenz initiated a 9-year experiment of popular reforms. Arbenz' government was especially noteworthy for its efforts to halt economic dependency, converting Guatemala's feudalistic economy to capitalism, and elevating the living standards of the masses (Liss, 1991). Arbenz also instituted agrarian reforms in 1952 that included expropriating more than 400,000 acres of United Stated-based United Fruit land holdings. This was the first time that Guatemala's indigenous peoples re-ceived benefits from the government; as many as 100,000 peasant families were given plots of land to farm (Liss, 1991).

The reforms initiated by Arevalo and Arbenz, particularly their land redistribution programs for the Indians, met with disfavor from the country's powerful private sector and economic and international political interests. The United Fruit Company reacted by recruiting the United States' Central Intelligence Agency to coordinate a successful coup d'etat against the Arbenz administration in 1954. This led to the establishment of a pro-American dictator, General Carlos Castillo Armas. The Guatemalan government has ruled with an iron fist ever since.

Lack of access to land and subsequently to power led to the exclusion of indigenous peoples from positions of influence in Guatemala. The power differential fueled a war that lasted more than 30 years that only recently ceased with the signing of peace accord in 1996. According to the Inter-American Commission on Human Rights of

---

[1]The terms *government* and *state* are used interchangeably to denote the Guatemalan federal government.

the Organization of American States, private groups, and church sources, by 1991 more than 200,000 unarmed civilians, in a country of less than 10 million people, had been killed as a result of the conflict (Jonas, 1991). Despite the cessation of the war, abduction and murder continue today. According to the Mutual Support Group for Relatives of the Disappeared (GAM), 200 people were kidnapped in Guatemala in 1997, the fourth highest in absolute terms in the world (Alecio & Taylor, 1998).

INTRODUCTION TO THE PARTICIPANTS AND RESEARCH METHODOLOGY

I was introduced to "Señor Chavez" in the summer of 1993. Sr. Chavez indicated his willingness to participate in this study at that time. He worked at the "Gymnasium," a public, all-boys secondary-level school in Guatemala City that was notorious for its political activism among its students. "Señora Alvarez," a part-time mathematics teacher in Guatemala and a friend of a colleague of mine introduced me to "Señora Rodriguez" in the summer of 1995. Sra. Rodriguez' school, the "Institute," was a public, all-girls secondary institution also located in Guatemala's capital city. I became interested in working with Sra. Rodriguez because she was an experienced mathematics teacher who worked at a school that was also well known for its student activism. Both teachers had more than 20 years of experience teaching mathematics.

Sra. Alvarez accompanied me to observe Sr. Chavez teach on four different days during the summer of 1994. On each of these days we watched him teach a wide variety of mathematics classes, from Pre-Algebra through Calculus. When I returned to visit the Gymnasium in the summer of 1995, the environment at the school was tense and we chose not to do any further observations in his classrooms. I observed Sra. Rodriguez teach on five separate occasions during the summer of 1995. On each occasion, I saw her teach two or three different mathematics courses.

Structured and unstructured interviews were conducted in Spanish with the mathematics teachers during nonschool hours at their homes or other sites. These were the primary data for the study. The approach to voice scholarship chosen was narrative inquiry. In narrative inquiry, the themes that emerge as the results of a study are derived directly from the teachers' words (Riessman, 1993). I also conducted interviews with students and others at the research participants' schools to learn more about the broad context of Sr. Chavez' and Sra. Rodriguez' work environment. Both Sra. Rodriguez and Sr. Chavez had opportunities to react to the how their words were represented in this study.

THE TEACHERS DESCRIBE THE CONTEXT OF THEIR WORK

Education in Guatemala

The Guatemalan constitution states that all children in the country must be "educated." Sr. Chavez believed that the state did the absolute minimum to fulfill this promise.

The government frequently took out loans to meet its financial obligations to state workers. Occasionally, parents were asked to pay for services. At the Gymnasium, the government paid the salaries of the teachers, director, and one secretary and the costs of electricity, water, and the telephone and had purchased two typewriters for the school.

Teachers' salaries in Guatemala were not adequate, and most teachers held other jobs to supplement their income. Sr. Chavez earned approximately $280 per month as a teacher at the Gymnasium. Even though his wife worked full time, Sr. Chavez held two other jobs: working afternoons, some evenings, and Saturdays as a locksmith and part-time mathematics instructor at a university. Sra. Rodriguez complemented her income by working afternoons as a seamstress at home. Because teachers worked other jobs, they had little time to collaborate. Guatemalan teachers' vital role in street protests during the turbulent 1970s and early 1980s had diminished due to the financial necessity of working multiple jobs, not to mention violent state repression.

In the past, only the children of the elite attended public schools. During the 1970s, Guatemalan schools were transformed as the children of the rich moved to private schools and the children of the poor populated the secondary public schools. Sr. Chavez discussed why the rich began sending their children to private schools:

> It's because in this era (the 1970s and earlier), there weren't many private schools in Guatemala. There were some private schools, but the best teachers were at the public schools. Since then the population has grown; there are more people. In past times, to enroll at the Gymnasium, you [the students] needed to get a ticket to have a chance to get in. You had to go one day early to enroll, some people slept in the streets to get [a good spot] in line to enroll. This didn't necessarily guarantee enrollment. It's because there were too many people. Thus, the rich started to think about another approach and not to have to deal with all these people.

Basically, anyone who could afford even a modicum of tuition sent their child to a private institution in Guatemala. Thus, the Institute and the Gymnasium were schools that served students who, as Sr. Chavez put it, "are the richest [of the Guatemalan poor] and they can study." Sr. Chavez emphasized several times that the students at the Gymnasium were relatively privileged because they could afford to attend classes, at least part time. In a country in which 79% of the population lives in poverty and less than 50% of the population is literate (Simon, 1987), few people, especially few indigenous people, have the opportunity to pursue schooling beyond the primary school level.

The lack of funding for public schooling in Guatemala had obvious consequences for the Ministry of Education. Sra. Rodriguez explained that Ministry of Education officials did not directly supervise her. Personnel from the Ministry of Education also never visited Sr. Chavez. According to Sr. Chavez, because of the lack of supervision by the state, mathematics curricula varied greatly among schools: "In Guatemala, it's totally disorganized . . . everyone teaches how they want, there's no order." Sr. Chavez also discussed how the poor funding of public schools in Guatemala had adversely affected the preparedness of new mathematics teachers.

The Teachers' Schools

Both the Institute and the Gymnasium were public, inner-city institutions located in the center of Guatemala City. Besides being attended exclusively by the poor, inner-city schools in Guatemala were characterized by their ethnic mix; students of indigenous ancestry traveled from rural regions to continue their studies beyond the primary level. In addition, because of the schools' proximity to important government buildings in Guatemala City, both schools were infamous for their political activities.

The most obvious difference between the two schools was that the Institute served only girls, whereas the Gymnasium was all-boy. Moreover, the Gymnasium offered courses for the Básico (3-year program, roughly equivalent to a U.S. middle school degree) and Bachillerato (2-year program, most comprehensive, university preparation) degree programs, whereas the Institute only offered classes leading to the Magisterio (3-year program, leads to elementary school teaching certification). Thus, the curriculum at the Gymnasium was more rigorous than the curriculum offered at the Institute, preparing students to attend the university.

Profile of the Teachers' Students

Students came from remote rural regions to study at the Institute and Gymnasium because most public, secondary schools were located in Guatemala's urban centers. Many of the students were of indigenous descent who actively concealed their ethnic origins. According to Sr. Chavez, it was not uncommon for students at the Gymnasium to have surnames such as "coyote" and "hen," although Latinos rarely have such surnames. Sr. Chavez estimated that approximately 30% of his students were exclusively of Indian ancestry. He estimated that 5% of his students had lost a parent during the counterinsurgency fighting, some students lived in orphanages, and approximately 10% of his students lived with relatives other than their parents. Many of the boys worked while attending the Gymnasium to supplement their family's income. They worked as vendors on the city's streets, did restaurant work, labored in shoe factories, and sold shoes.

The majority of the girls from the Institute found jobs in private schools after graduation. Many could then finance their university degrees as elementary school teachers. Ironically, the girls who graduated from the Institute were qualified to seek employment, whereas graduates of the more advanced degree program at the Gymnasium had few marketable job skills.

Student Activism at the Schools

Guatemala's public schools have played an historic role in the social and political transformation of the country. Teacher- and student-incited street protests have led to many changes in the struggle for social and political justice in Guatemala. Because of the many lost school days caused by the conflicts, each academic day took on added importance. Sra. Rodriguez described how the strikes impacted her teaching:

> They shorten the communication [between her and her students] and the classes. The students go home to rest, they're not going to study. Thus, these protests interrupt school very dramatically. When I get them again, they don't know anything. This is bad for the students, and also for the teachers it's bad because you can't continue [to teach a topic] and if you do they won't understand what you're talking about.

Sr. Chavez discussed how the protests had affected his pedagogy:

> The only way is perhaps that at some moments there are problems with initiative for the students to prepare themselves better. Let me give you an example [about why the students riot]. The cheapest buses cost 65 centavos (approximately 13 U.S. cents). They want to raise their fares to one quetzal. This is 35 centavos more for each student each way. Possibly, some of their parents who make 70 quetzales per day (approximately $14) can't afford the [additional] 70 centavos. This example represents the situation in which we are living. . . . This is of use for two reasons (why students need to protest); one is to become conscious of their reality and to motivate them to study a little bit more.

Sr. Chavez frequently stated his instructional goals in terms of the number of school days canceled by strikes. Clearly, the majority of the students at the Gymnasium did very little academic work during these periods of strife. Although his peers were in the process of taking control of the Gymnasium during a student protest in the summer of 1995, one student standing outside the school told me that he planned to spend the day playing electronic games and "just hanging out."

During the student strikes in the summer of 1995, Sr. Chavez had a prominent role in resolving the conflict (the principal had literally been banished from the school by the students a year earlier). Sr. Chavez was able to resolve the conflict, although some of the student leaders were permanently expelled from the Gymnasium for their part in the strikes. The Gymnasium reopened after being shut down for almost 2 weeks. The school had endured yet another crisis.

Sra. Rodriguez' Pedagogical Goals and Practices

Sra. Rodriguez perceived herself as willing to work with all incoming students despite their academic weaknesses. She also expected them to adapt and learn at the instructional pace that she established in class:

> The beginning premise of my teaching is that I assume the student knows nothing . . . So, I start from scratch assuming that no one knows a thing, then I'll start with the simplest topic so they can understand from the beginning until things start to get more difficult. Then if they lose the flow of the teaching and they make math difficult, then that's their problem. This is no longer the instructor's responsibility.

Sra. Rodriguez explained that to start from scratch meant that she began by teaching "basic arithmetic." She began all of her classes in this manner without concern for students' grade level because she could not assume that students could "add, subtract, multiply, divide, find square roots and decimal numbers . . . since they don't know it and if they do I have to refresh it for them." Sra. Rodriguez emphasized the importance of teaching basic arithmetic because "everything else is rather simple once they have the basics. If they don't have the basic arithmetic, that's where the problem lies."

Sra. Rodriguez frequently discussed how she had been successful in the male-dominated discipline of mathematics. Her students could also succeed in mathematics and she accepted no excuses for failure. Sra. Rodriguez made no accommodations for students based on their previous backgrounds in mathematics. Students who were unsuccessful in her mathematics classes were responsible for their own failure.

Sra. Rodriguez did not permit calculator use in her classes because she believed that their usage impeded her students' learning of the basics. She also did not want her students to become too dependent on calculators: "They should be capable of manually getting the square root of a number, because if they aren't, they would already be dependent on their calculator. In the market, people cannot use calculators." Sra. Rodriguez also acknowledged that in rural Guatemala, where most of her students went to teach, calculators were not available.

During one visit to the Institute during the summer of 1995, Sra. Alvarez and I observed Sra. Rodriguez teach three different, third-year básico classes. Sra. Rodriguez had the identical objective in each class, to teach her students how to calculate whole numbers raised to varying integer exponents. The lessons consisted of Sra. Rodriguez demonstrating how to find solutions algorithmically. A distinctive feature of each lesson was that Sra. Rodriguez interjected jokes, stories, and emphasized the importance of discipline as part of her lecture. Sra. Rodriguez told me that "jokes have two functions. One is to relax the students a little bit so that they don't feel so pressured. Secondly, (so that the students) learn how to laugh!"

Sr. Chavez' Pedagogical Goals and Practices

Sr. Chavez' students did not have textbooks and he had limited access to supplementary mathematics materials. He photocopied exercises from his textbook to sell to his students for a small fee when he assigned homework. The textbook in use was more than 30 years old and was one of the few mathematics textbooks available in Guatemala. In effect, the book was the de facto secondary mathematics curriculum. Written by both U.S. and Cuban authors prior to the Cuban revolution, the textbook presents mathematics as a compilation of formulas and equations to be memorized. Classes lasted only 35 minutes and Sr. Chavez taught in poorly lit, graffitiridden classrooms. So, not only did he have few resources available to aid instruction, Sr. Chavez also had little time to teach in a poorly maintained facility.

Sr. Chavez identified strongly with his students. He believed that the most powerful way to understand and relate to his students was by speaking their language. He also believed that, for his pedagogy to be effective, he had to find real-world examples related to his students' social situations. Sr. Chavez explained how important it was to him to have good relations with his students:

> To begin with, when I enter the classroom the first day, I don't present myself as a teacher. I present myself as a friend who is there to help them. And the second thing that they understand is that I'm there everyday to teach them. Actually, for them this is a surprise. [Also], I must learn their language [idiom]. I must learn it, they have a language that's very particular. If a person goes to their classroom and speaks formal Spanish, they can't expect to achieve anything. For example, for bus they say "burra," bike—"biula," police— "tirra." You must understand these words of the street [to effectively teach these students].

Sr. Chavez spoke a language that was familiar to his students and did not abuse his authority to obtain his students' attention. His use of language exemplified his strong identification with his students. He told me, "I have more than 20 years at the school. I'm part of them now!" Students' ethnic background was unimportant to Sr. Chavez; he did not treat his indigenous and Latino students differently. He stated, on many occasions, that economic class, not ethnicity, was the great equalizer in Guatemalan society: "Basically, my students are the same—poor!" Nevertheless, Sr. Chavez acknowledged that he made accommodations in the classroom for his students from rural areas—often the indigenous students—because they did not have as strong a background in mathematics as his students from the city.

Sra. Alvarez and I observed several of Sr. Chavez' básico classes. In one class, there were 32 boys sitting in straight rows facing the front of the classroom. Sr. Chavez began each class by reviewing how to factor a quadratic equation that had been assigned for homework. He was very careful to explain the factorization in a systematic, step-by-step manner. Sr. Chavez proceeded by asking his students to factor a similar equation alone at their desks. Generally, the students were attentive during the lectures and on task while working problems. Sr. Chavez actively involved students in class, primarily by asking them questions to assess their understanding of the lesson. He moved easily around the classroom engaging students with questions.

SOCIOPOLITICAL CONTEXT OF MATHEMATICS EDUCATION IN GUATEMALA

The teachers' beliefs and practices provide some insight into the general characteristics of schooling and mathematics education in Guatemala. It appears that the sociopolitical context of working in Guatemala greatly affected the two teachers' pedagogy. For example, the lack of financial support for education in general, and mathematics education in particular, sustained conventional curricula and instruction. Furthermore, the social and political violence in Guatemala directly limited the number of contact hours that the teachers had with students and affected much of how the teachers interacted with colleagues while shaping many of the teachers' behaviors. Sra. Rodriguez, for instance, felt that she had to penalize her students when they returned to the classroom after rioting. Finally, precisely because he was a mathematics teacher and was subsequently perceived by his colleagues as politically neutral, Sr. Chavez became a leader at the Gymnasium. In this case, Sr. Chavez took advantage of his position as a mathematics teacher in a brutally oppressive environment to be an advocate for his students and school.

The general lack of support for education in Guatemala perpetuated traditional mathematics curricula and pedagogy. Both teachers used antiquated curricular materials, and neither had access to resources to supplement their mathematics instruction. Purchasing instructional technology was simply beyond the financial capabilities of both teachers' schools. Furthermore, the teachers had minimal access to professional development opportunities because teacher in-service activities were nonexistent and there were many difficulties associated with collaborating with colleagues. Besides, the teachers were too busy working additional jobs to have time to work with others. In addition, the state provided little classroom support. The Ministry of Education had few resources to mandate a mathematics curriculum and to enforce its directives. According to Sr. Chavez, the weak status of the Ministry meant that the quality of mathematics curricula in Guatemala deviated greatly among public schools.

Given the teachers' lack of access to varied curricular materials and their limited opportunities to learn from and collaborate with other mathematics educators about curricular and pedagogical innovations, it is not surprising that they were quite conventional mathematics teachers. Clearly, the underdevelopment of Guatemala granted Sra. Rodriguez and Sr. Chavez limited professional development opportunities. These findings support Jurdak's assertion (1992) that Third World countries are unlikely to be able to afford the material and human resources needed to implement the types of reforms in mathematics education being implemented in the First World. It is important to state, though, that the authoritarian and violent context in which the teachers worked also greatly affected their pedagogy.

The most obvious consequence that the political turmoil and violence in Guatemala had on the two teachers' pedagogy was that it limited the number of contact hours that they had with their students. Sr. Chavez talked about how little time he had to teach because the school year was consistently interrupted, both by outsiders who instigated problems at the schools and by student leaders protesting state and school policies.

The Gymnasium was often targeted by key politicians interested in manipulating protests for their own political gain. Student protests gave credence to the notion that the state needed a stronger army and police force while simultaneously eroding public support for the Gymnasium, a school well known for fostering subversive activities that directly threatened the state's authority. When the disturbances occurred, students often took control of the school, expelling teachers and staff from the school grounds. Police came to the school and engaged the students in violent confrontations. These battles led to the murder of more than a few students from the Gymnasium.

Sr. Chavez discussed how the staff at the Gymnasium had worked for 2 years to halt efforts by politicians to manipulate students. Faculty members who had been paid off by politicians to aid them hampered these efforts. The political activities at the Gymnasium had increased tensions between teachers who were generally suspicious of one another. The lack of trust between staff members reflected the larger societal strains symptomatic of a brutally violent, authoritarian state.

Perhaps the most profound impact that the violence had in Guatemala was to instill fear into people. Sr. Chavez frequently cited examples of the weapons, both psychological and physical, that the state regularly used against protesters. For example, he discussed instances when "stink bombs" were thrown by state police to break up protests at the university and schools. "There's lots of gas. The police throw them. Terrible! (makes a disgusted sound) And your respiratory system—the affect is totally ideological. This is exactly what they want to happen to the people." These bombs did not kill, as an "ideological" weapon; they ingrained fear in the protesters. Certainly, this fear discouraged the teachers to be risk takers in the classroom. The study of mathematics was certainly not viewed by Sr. Chavez or Sra. Rodriguez as a means to challenge students to reflect upon their world views (Mellin-Olsen, 1987). Neither teacher discussed the value of incorporating the study of ethnomathematics in the mathematics curriculum such as Bishop (1988), D'Ambrosio (1983), and Gerdes (1985). Clearly, the teachers' traditional practices reflected the context in which they worked.

The compromises the two teachers made provide additional insight into the sociopolitical context of their lives. Sra. Rodriguez frequently stressed the importance of taking personal responsibility to succeed in mathematics. She had succeeded in a male-dominated profession and so could her students. She had little tolerance for students who did poorly in her classes. Her treatment of students after they had been rioting on the streets, she punished them by "starting at scratch," is an example of how her actions reflected the state's authoritarian doctrine. The irony is that, on a daily basis, she tried to help her students be successful in mathematics and science.

Sr. Chavez understood the political confines of teaching at the Gymnasium and worked to ensure the survival of the institution through crises. Similar to D'Ambrosio's findings in Brazil (1991), traditional mathematics curricula were not viewed in Guatemala as a threat to the state. Sr. Chavez took advantage of this perception to gain his colleagues' trust. His charisma, combined with his survival at the Gymnasium through many turbulent events, solidified his leadership status. As the undisputed leader of a reactionary faculty, Sr. Chavez was more than willing to take harsh measures with student leaders of a riot that ensued during one of my visits. This incident highlights the difficult choices that teachers in Guatemala were forced to make. Sr. Chavez chose to use his position to punish a few to secure future opportunities for the majority of his students.

In closing, Sra. Rodriguez' and Sr. Chavez' narratives and practices provided insight into the general characteristics of schooling and mathematics education in Guatemala. The major finding of this study was that the two teachers' conventional pedagogy was grounded in the political and social context within which they worked. More research needs to be done in developing nations to understand how divergent political, social, as well as cultural contexts influence mathematics education. Such knowledge is necessary to inform teachers, decision makers, scholars, and nongovernmental organizations about the real needs of mathematics teachers and schools in Third World countries. Research on the context of mathematics education from the perspective of teachers working in developing countries is also important simply to support teachers working in difficult conditions. This study may serve to demonstrate to other teachers working in similar conditions that they are not alone. Finally, a reason for pursuing research projects such as this one is to build a foundation for future collaborative efforts between First World teachers/scholars and our colleagues in the developing world. Such studies inform us about how to establish cooperative, productive, and respectful relationships to improve mathematics education in developing countries.

REFERENCES

Abraham, J., & Bibby, N. (1988). Mathematics and society: Ethnomathematics and the public educator curriculum. *For the Learning of Mathematics, 8*(2), 2–11.

Alecio, R., & Taylor, R. (1998). From state sponsorship to private initiative: The persistence of terror. *Report on Guatemala, 19*(3), 2–5.

Altbach, P. G., Arnove, R. F., & Kelly, G. P. (1982). *Comparative education.* New York: Macmillian.

Apple, M. W. (1985). *Education and power.* New York: Routledge, ARK Edition.

Bishop, A. (1988). Mathematics education in its cultural context. *Educational Studies in Mathematics, 19*, 179–191.

Carnoy, M. (1974). *Education as cultural imperialism.* New York: McKay.

Coombs, P. H. (1985). *The world crisis in education: The view from the eighties.* New York/Oxford: Oxford University Press.

D'Ambrosio, B. S. (1991). The modern mathematics reform movement in Brazil and its consequences for Brazilian mathematics education. *Educational Studies in Mathematics, 22*, 69–85.

D'Ambrosio, U. (1983). Successes and failures of mathematics curricula in the past two decades: A developing society viewpoint in a holistic framework. In *Proceedings of the fourth international Congress of Mathematical Education* (pp. 362–364). Boston.

Fasheh, M. (1988). *Mathematics in a social context: Man within education as praxis versus within education as hegemony.* Mathematics, education, and society: Reports and papers presented in the fifth day special program on Mathematics, education, and society at the 6th International Congress on Mathematics Education. Paris: UNESCO.

Gerdes, P. (1985). Conditions and strategies for emancipatory mathematics education in undeveloped countries. *For the Learning of Mathematics, 5*(1), 15–20.

Gerdes, P. (1988). Culture and geometrical thinking. In *Educational Studies in Mathematics, 19*, 137–162.

Gilmer, G. (1990). An ethnomathematical approach to curriculum development. *Newsletter of the International Study Group on Ethnomathematics (ISGEm), 5*, 4–6.

Jonas, S. (1991). *The battle for Guatemala.* Boulder/San Francisco/Oxford: Westview Press.

Jurdak, M. (1992). Mathematics education in the global village: The wedge and the filter. In D. F. Robitaille, D. H. Wheeler, & C. Kieran (Eds.), *Selected lectures from the 7th international Congress on Mathematical Education.* Sainte-Foy: Les Presses De L'Universite Laval.

Kitchen, R. S., & Lear, J. M. (1999). Mathematizing Barbie: Using measurement as a means for girls to analyze their sense of body image. In W. G. Secada (Ed.), *Changing the faces of mathematics.* Reston, VA: National Council of Teachers of Mathematics.

Lincoln, Y. S. (1993). I and thou: Method, voice, and roles in research with the silenced. In D. McLaughlin & W. G. Tierney (Eds.), *Naming silenced lives* (pp. 29–47). New York: Routledge.

Liss, S. (1991). *Radical thought in Central America.* Boulder/Oxford: Westview Press.

Mellin-Olsen, S. (1987). *The politics of mathematics education.* Dordrecht: Reidel.

National Council of Teachers of Mathematics. (1989). *Curriculum and evaluation standards for school mathematics.* Reston, VA: Author.

Parkyn, L. K. (1989). *The ladinoization of the Guatemalan urban indigena: An ethnographic study of the processes of sociocultural change in Santa Cruz del Quiche.* Unpublished doctoral dissertation, Temple University, Philadelphia.

Riessman, C. K. (1993). *Narrative analysis. Newbury Park,* CA: Sage.

Simon, J. M. (1987). *Guatemala, eternal spring: Eternal tyranny.* New York/London: Norton.

Zachariah, M., & Silva, E. T. (1980). Cultural autonomy and ideas in transit: Notes from the Canadian case. *Comparative education review,* 24, 63–72.

III

TEACHERS, STUDENTS, AND CLASSROOMS

Over the past few decades, mathematics education literature has begun to focus more on what is called the implemented curriculum: teachers, students, and classrooms. There has been a sense that past reform efforts focused on curricular reform (the intended curriculum) and assessment of student achievement (the achieved curriculum) and that the limited success of these earlier efforts may be due to insufficient understanding of what actually happens in the classroom. There is a sense today that the heart of the problem, and also of the solution, lies in the interaction among teacher, students, and classroom. The chapters in this section invite us to look into the way we do research on teachers, students, and classrooms, into the relationship between home and classroom culture, into the factors that determine whether students continue in or drop out of mathematics, and into the way we should look at the relationship between teaching effectiveness and classroom resources.

Although research on these questions is perhaps well established in general, there are several new trends illustrated here. First, although early research was mainly quantitative, more recent research relied heavily on qualitative case studies and ethnographic tools. Three of the four chapters in this section use these methodologies. Second, earlier research on the teachers, students, and classroom concentrated on psychological or cognitive teaching and learning theories. All the chapters in this section examine sociological aspects of research questions.

Bill Atweh and Marcos Daniel Arias Ochoa argue that one major reason research in this area has not had more impact is that the research paradigm assumes distinct roles between investigator and the subjects of research. Educational researchers, usually from university education departments, take most or all of the initiative, and classroom teachers are generally passive subjects. The chapter argues that research and professional development programs that are empowering to the teachers are much more likely to sustain effective and continuous change in school mathematics. A case study is presented, TEBES or "Transformacion de la Education Basica desde la Escuela" ("Transforming Basic Education from/ within the School"). Here the teachers are active and leading actors in the research. The research process operates under certain underlying beliefs: that teachers are professionals, who can best promote their own professional development, and that effective knowledge for school change should develop in and from the school. A theoretical basis is given, using Habermas' theory of knowledge-constitutive interests.

Jill Adler argues that behind common and prevalent laments on the "lack of resources" across many schools is the history of inequity in provision in South Africa. There are numerous schools that still do not have basic resources such as water and electricity, let alone sufficient classrooms and learning materials. More generally, is the assumption that the quality of learning and teaching in school is related to availability and use of learning resources? In this chapter she argues that there is a tension between "we need more resources" and an uncritical application of this call through simple quantitative distribution or provisioning. Elsewhere, the author argued that a critical application entails a reconceptualization of resources as a verb so as to shift the focus of attention in mathematics teacher education, for example, away from resources themselves and an image of the good teacher as one surrounded by resources, and onto the teacher using resources in context. The image here is of the resourceful teacher. Furthermore, such a reconceptualization extends the notion of resources to include social and cultural resources such as language and languaging.

Robyn Zevenbergen notes that the typical mathematics classroom has a specific culture and proposes that the consonance or dissonance between this culture and the home cultures of the students have an important impact on learning. In a comparison of a middle-class and a working-class classroom, one sees from the transcripts that there is an ease of interaction in the middle-class classroom, whereas there is less success (interruptions and misunderstanding) in the working-class classroom. It seems clear that the typical language register of the mathematics classroom is familiar to middle-class students because it is similar to the linguistic patterns of their home environment. This is not so for working-class students and puts them at a disadvantage. Making these linguistic patterns more explicit can assist in helping students learn these cultural codes so they can participate more effectively. It may also lead to a reconstruction of classroom practice to make it more effective for a particular group of students. The theoretical framework uses the notions of habitus and field of Pierre Bourdieu.

The chapter by Xin Ma looks into the question of what internal and external factors are dominant in determining whether students in high school continue to take or drop out of mathematics courses. It looks at demographic factors, cognitive and affective factors such as prior attitude toward mathematics and influence of significant others at home, and effects of school climate and culture. Among the factors that emerge as most influential in determining whether students continue to take higher level mathematics courses are their prior attitude toward mathematics, support from the home and involvement of parents in the school, and schools "protecting the academic core," that is, minimizing the extraneous and disruptive effects that keep teachers from teaching and students from learning. The study is based on recent longitudinal studies and can help schools focus on the factors that are most likely to strengthen students' participation and performance in mathematics.

Many countries have become aware of the importance of their students' achievement in mathematics and of the situation of disadvantaged groups in their societies. This led to looking more deeply into the factors that determine success in school mathematics and, in particular, the influence of sociocultural factors. Early research in that area considered ethnic background of students as a critical factor associated with opportunity to learn mathematics and subsequent achievement in it. Perhaps the two ethnic and racial groups studied in depth are the Hispanic and Afro-American populations in the United States. The last two chapters in this section deal with recent findings from research conducted in that context.

Luis Ortiz-Franco and William V. Flores begin by reviewing studies that show that over the past decades the general family income levels of Latino students decreased but their level of mathematics achievement has actually increased. This result seems to contradict the usual hypothesis that mathematics achievement and socioeconomic status rise together. However, the gap between mathematics achievement between Latino and White students remains large, particularly in complex problem-solving skills. Some factors are presented that may help understand these results. One is the parental factor, namely, studies have shown that the involvement of Latino parents in the education of their children was equal to, or greater than, that of White parents. Also, the educational level of Latino parents has gone up considerably over the past decades. On the other hand, the fact that the achievement of Latino students in higher level mathematics skills has not improved may be due to the fact that they tend to go to poorer schools and they may not be exposed to the teaching of such skills.

Vivian R. Moody looks at the American setting and the different ways that African-American students cope with the dissonance between their indigenous world and that of school mathematics. Critical Theory, African-American cultural orientations, and their application to the mathematics education of African-American students are presented to provide a critical perspective for the understanding of the situation facing African-American students in mathematics. Two case studies, both of successful students, are presented and analyzed within this critical perspective. In one case, the student's experience can be aptly described as succeeding in situations of struggle against racial prejudices and peer criticism. The struggle is also that of moving back and forth between remaining within indigenous African-American culture and succeeding within what is perceived to be the White culture of the mathematics world. The other student's experience is more one of facing challenges, in particular, the challenge of mathematics itself. Through these cases one comes to a deeper understanding of the personal and cultural obstacles facing African-American students and their ways of overcoming them.

10

Continuous In-Service Professional Development of Teachers and School Change: Lessons From Mexico

Bill Atweh
Queensland University of Technology

Marcos Daniel Arias Ochoa
Universidad Pedagogica Nacional

Since the 1980s, there has been a major (re) focusing of attention in the mathematics education literature, both in policy and research, on the role of the teacher in understanding and implementing educational change. In the area of policy, many new curriculum reforms around the world acknowledge the need for professional development (PD) of teachers as an integral part of school change process. For example, in the United States, the National Council for Teachers of Mathematics (NCTM) published a set of standards for teacher education programs (NCTM, 1989b) and for the PD of teachers (NCTM, 1990) to parallel its earlier standards for curriculum and evaluation (NCTM, 1989a). Although concerns have been raised about the view that these documents "provide the direction, but not the mechanism, for reform in school mathematics" (Brown & Borko, 1992, p. 235), they have been used as the basis for several PD innovations (Aichele & Coxford, 1994). In Australia, the federal government has undertaken a discipline review of teacher education in mathematics and science (Department of Employment, Education and Training, 1986), raising several issues related to initial and continuing education of teachers. In Mexico, the Development of Education Program (Poder Ejectivo Federal, 1996) clearly identifies the concern of the government to strengthen basic, or compulsory, education by focusing attention on schools as places for developing effective teaching and as special places for the PD of teachers. The Program asserts that educational change is only effective if it starts from the agents of education—that is, the teachers—themselves. According to the document, teachers are seen as "essential agents in the dynamics of quality, for whom special attention should be given to their social, cultural and material conditions" (p. 13). Hence, the Program establishes teacher training and development as

167

areas of priority and calls for a re-assessment of the social role of the teacher in the whole educational system.

How effective these policy statements and reform programs are for changing actual school practice is still open to question. Sprinthall, Reiman, and Thies-Sprinthall (1996) argued that research on the gap between policy and practice has shown that often many innovations are seen by many teachers are external demands that "force" teachers to change and hence are resisted by teachers. The experience of teachers under the National Curriculum reform in the United Kingdom illustrates the effect that sudden changes imposed from outside the classroom can have on demoralizing and disempowering of teachers (Hargreaves & Evans, 1997). Similarly, Kilpatrick (1999) argued how the U.S. reforms initiated by the NCTM have lead to a "backlash" in some school districts in what has become to be known as "maths wars." Further, many of the planned provisions for professional development of teachers to deal with the suggested changes are not implemented in practice. In a book with the provocative title of "The Predictable Failure of Educational Reform" (Seymore 1990, cited in Hargreaves, 1994), the author identifies the piecemeal approach that many of these reforms take as responsible for their failure to change actual school practices. There are separate agendas of reforms. For example, there are reforms for the curriculum, for teacher professional development, for school structures and organizations, and so on. Hargreaves argued that "significant change in curriculum, assessment or any other domain is unlikely to be successful unless serious attention is also paid to teacher development and the principles of professional judgement and discretion contained within it" (p. 242). Sprinthall, Reiman, and Thies-Sprinthall argued that these "massive failures of the [many] national curriculum projects of the 1960s" (p. 666) raised interest in investigating and theorizing the teachers' role in educational change.

In the area of research, this focusing of attention on the teacher is demonstrated by the new research questions that have evolved around teachers' characteristics, beliefs (Thompson, 1992), and knowledge (Fennema & Franke, 1992). Several handbooks of research both in mathematics and general education contain chapters with extensive reviews of the literature on teachers and their PD. For example, the Mathematics Education Research Group of Australasia publishes a four-yearly review of research in mathematics education conducted in that region. Both the 1992 and 1996 reviews contain chapters on teachers' research (Mousley, 1992) and the PD of teachers (Kanes & Nisbet, 1996). Likewise, the *1992 Handbook of Research on Mathematics Teaching and Learning* (Grouws, 1992) contains two chapters on teachers beliefs and knowledge and two further chapters on the PD of teachers, whereas the more recent *International Handbook of Mathematics Education* (Bishop, Clements, Keitel, Kilpatrick, & Laborde, 1996) contains a whole section entitled "Social conditions and perspectives on professional development" consisting of eight chapters. The 1994 yearbook of the NCTM, an influential publication in English-speaking countries, was dedicated to the *Professional Development for Teachers of Mathematics* (Aichele & Coxford, 1994).

Concerns have also been raised about types of research that study the teachers' knowledge and beliefs in coming to terms with the complexity of the decision-making process in the classroom and in informing practice (Brown & Borko, 1992; Sprinthall, Reiman, & Thies-Sprinthall, 1996). Research has often identified a gap between teachers' beliefs and their practice in the classroom, the latter being influenced by the teachers' perceptions of children as young learners and the set goals of school mathematics. This research has failed to identify a relationship between teachers' characteristics and beliefs and effective teaching. Also, in general it has failed to take in to account the role of the social context issues such as gender and socioeconomic background of both teachers and students as mediating factors between beliefs and practice.

Arguably, the gap between research knowledge and classroom practice also exists in other research areas as well. Several authors raised the likelihood that the traditional processes of conducting educational research impose limits on the research's ability to inform practice (Carr, 1995; Carr & Kemmis, 1986; Clements & Ellerton, 1996; Crawford & Adler, 1996; Sprinthall, Reiman, & Thies-Sprinthall, 1996). Atweh and Martinez (in preparation) argued that one reason research often fails to be effective in changing practice is the separation of roles in the research process. In most common research paradigms, the investigator and the subjects of research play distinct roles. The investigators usually select the questions for study and the methodology used. They collect the data from the "subjects" of the research, analyze the data, and develop theories from it. They are also responsible for publishing the results, generally in academic journals that are often read by other researchers. Almost always the subjects are passive in this process—they play the role of information provider. If they benefit from the research, such benefit is indirect. In general they do not gain knowledge about their life or practice. Such a role increases their dependence on other "experts" for understanding their condition and improving their practice. Certain alternative paradigms of research, such as action research—to be discussed further, are based on different roles and, arguably, are designed to bridge the gap between theory and practice.

This chapter does not attempt to provide a review of the literature or a summary of the major findings of research on teachers. To a certain extent, this has been accomplished in the reviews mentioned previously. Rather, we aim to argue for forms of PD programs that are empowering to the teachers and are more likely to sustain effective and continuous change in school mathematics. We first present a theoretical model to analyze and compare the different types of PD activities available for teachers. Second, we present a case study of one collaborative project for PD and school change from Mexico. The chapter concludes with a discussion of effective PD activities that are based on the integration of theory and practice and more sensitive to the immediate and long-term needs and interests of teachers and are able to provide long-lasting and continual school change.

A MODEL FOR TEACHERS' PROFESSIONAL DEVELOPMENT

Theoretical Underpinnings

In their review of Australian research on teacher development, Kanes and Nisbet (1996) identified three types of PD activities based on Habermas' theory of knowledge-constitutive interests (see Carr & Kemmis, 1986; Grundy, 1987). Carr and Kemmis pointed out that the designation of this theory reflects its basic epistemological assertion that knowledge "is always constituted on the basis of interests that have developed out of the natural needs of the human species and that have been shaped by historical and social conditions" (p. 134). Habermas discussed three types of knowledge-constitutive interests: *technical, practical,* and *emancipatory.*

In general, *technical interests* are grounded in the need of the species to survive and reproduce certain valued aspects in the social and biological spheres. This type of knowledge is developed by systematic observations and hypothetical–deductive processes and, in turn, informs action according to derived rules and generalizations (Grundy, 1987, p. 11). Grundy argued that the main motivation behind this knowledge is the need to control the environment. Arguably, teachers in the conduct of their work have several interests and needs that can be classified as technical. For example, they need a huge repertoire of teaching and classroom management methods, knowledge of content, use of materials, resources and technologies, evaluation and assessment techniques, and so on. Carr and Kemmis pointed out that the concern about this type of knowledge is not about it usefulness or validity but in the mistaken assumption that "it is the only type of legitimate [or useful] knowledge" (p. 135).

Although the main motivation for technical knowledge is control, the *practical interests* are about understanding. Practical interest is "an interest in understanding the environment so that one is able to interact with it" (Grundy, 1987, p. 13). The motivating questions behind such interest are not "What can I do?" or "How to do it?" but "What ought I do?" Hence, Grundy argued that moral questions are more explicit in this knowledge-constitutive interest. It is a question of making the right action within a particular environment. Such knowledge is developed by understanding the meaning(s) associated with a phenomenon, not merely its observation. Undoubtedly, teachers also have several needs that may be classified as practical. They need to understand students' motivations, beliefs, expectations as well as their previous knowledge to be able to assist them to develop their mathematical knowledge. Likewise, the teachers themselves have interests, beliefs, and knowledge that undoubtedly influence how change is enabled in the classroom (Fennema & Franke, 1992; Thomspon, 1992). Likewise, teachers need to understand the social context of the school and of their students in order to be effective professionals.

Last, Habermas identified the *emancipatory interest,* which is intrinsically tied to autonomy and freedom from dogmatic dependence. Because technical knowledge is open to "the tyranny of regulations," and practical knowledge is open to "deceit and false consciousness,"(p. 17) a different type of knowledge is required for autonomy. Grundy argued that "the emancipatory interest gives rise to autonomous, responsible action based upon prudent decisions informed by a certain kind of knowledge" (p. 18). Although control and understanding are the motivation factors of the previous knowledge-constituted interests, empowerment, that is, "the ability of individuals and groups to take control of their own lives in autonomous and responsible ways (p. 19)" is the motivation for emancipatory knowledge. For example, teachers need to make decisions not only on "What to do?" or "What ought they to do?" but also on "Why do they ought to?" and "What are the implications of their decisions?"—in other words, what is the hidden curriculum behind what they do in the classroom. Because autonomy of one individual cannot be isolated from those of others in a social group and any practice is a social process that involves many others, there is more emphasis in this type of knowledge on the role of the social dimension of the practice. The development of such knowledge is enhanced by collaborating with other people inside and outside the practice. Also, this knowledge cannot arise simply from experiential processes, or be based on understanding, but develops through critical reflection.

Using this theoretical framework we can now attempt to categorize various types of PD activities available to teachers in many countries around the world.

Examples of Professional Development Activities

There are many examples in the profession of PD programs that cater for the technical interests of teachers. For many people, PD brings to mind a single or a series of seminar session(s) normally after school hours or during a weekend. These seminars are usually presented by a person with some experience, expertise, or formal training in the area. Such expertise is often gained from research knowledge, direct experience, or by undergoing previous training in the area. Often with limited resources, one teacher in the school is given support to undergo the training with the expectation that they become resource persons to their schools. This last model is often called "train the trainers" model. Such programs are often refereed to as in-service programs or process-product models in which specific teacher behaviors/skills are identified as desirable and attempts are made to develop them in teachers for increasing their effectiveness in teaching. Reviewing a selection of these programs in mathematics education, Brown and Borko (1992) identified some benefits to the participants yet call for further research on their long-term benefits. Likewise, Mousley (1992), reviewing research in Australasia conducted by teachers, raises some doubt that "traditionally passive roles in in-service courses do little to develop teachers' interpersonal skills and attitudes appropriate to the complex and shifting relationships within schools" (p. 97).

Other PD projects are designed to cater to the practical knowledge of the teachers. Brown and Borko (1992) identified several programs designed to develop teachers' knowledge and understanding. Similarly, Kanes and Nisbet (1996) argued that programs designed to develop teachers' confidence and attitudes and examination of their practices based on their implicit theories about mathematics and about teaching and learning are programs that attempt to develop teachers' practical knowledge. Also, programs that are based on analysis of teaching based on students' understanding, those that are based on improving practice by becoming reflective practitioners, and those that use metaphors for changing practice may fit in this category. In general, these programs are longer than in-service seminars, and hence are more demanding than those for developing technical knowledge, and demand a greater active participation from the teachers themselves.

Although Kanes and Nisbet have not found any mathematics education PD programs in Australasia during the period of their review (1992–1995) that are designed to cater to the emancipatory interests of teachers, Brown and Borko (1992) identified a few studies conducted within the critical perspective dealing with teacher socialization. PD programs under this category have similar characteristics. They are based on needs and problems identified by the teachers themselves, designed around active involvement of teachers in development of their knowledge and theories around their practice, are collaborative between the university and school, and involve teachers in writing about their projects. Perhaps widely known in the English-speaking world are projects such as the PEEL project (Baird & Northfield, 1992), the Innovative Links Projects in Australia (Yeatman & Sachs, 1995), and Low Attainers in Mathematics Project in the United Kingdom (Better Mathematics, 1987) and, in Colombia, the work of the Una Empresa Docente at the Universidad de Los Andes (Valero, Gómez, & Perry, 1997). In the educational literature, action research is often associated with these approaches to developing teachers' knowledge and changing practice (Carr & Kemmis, 1986; Kemmis & Wilkinson, 1998). The following section discusses one such project from Mexico.

A CASE STUDY FROM MEXICO: THE TEBES[1] PROJECT

The Project's Principles

In Mexico, much of the official PD of teachers is in the form of courses based on textbooks developed centrally and distributed to teachers for individual study followed by assessment. The use of these courses by teachers is optional; however, the results of these tests are used for promotion of teachers into higher pay brackets. Such material often consists of theoretical professional articles on aspects of teaching mathematics and of training in mathematical content. Such provisions are often seen as good sources of encyclopedic knowledge but as irrelevant to the needs, concerns, and problems encountered by the teachers in their classrooms (Arias Ochoa, 1998). Another form of professional development available is in terms of limited number of scholarships for full-time study at universities and other teacher training institutions, such as Normal Schools. The disadvantage of such programs is that teachers receive their professional development away from their classroom practice; hence, there is a separation between theory and practice.

TEBES is an innovative[2] program for school transformation and continuous in-service professional development of teachers in compulsory education. The name is a Spanish acronym for "Transformación de la Educación Básica desde la Escuela," which translates into English as "Transforming Compulsory[3] Education from/within the School." TEBES arose from the dissatisfaction that teachers often express with

---

[1]The second author of this chapter is the coordinator of the project and provided the information about the project in Spanish. The first author encountered the project while visiting the country on a study leave from his university. The information about the project has been translated into English by the first author and back translated into Spanish for checking its accuracy and validity.

[2]TEBES is also based on the traditions of earlier Mexican reforms such as Escuela Modelo de Orizaba (1983–1903) and Escuela Rural Mexicana (1922–1944). It follows a long-lasting traditions of collaboration, cooperation, and mutual help. Such culture commenced with the indiginous population and remains stong in the country today.

[3]In Mexico, basic education covers 9 years of schooling, including primary and secondary. It is government policy that these years are compulsory for all children in the country; however, this is not the case in practice.

many of their school practices and conditions—the indifference, apathy, and ineffective teaching practices in their schools—and from their dissatisfaction with the available provisions for professional development that is imposed on them year after year.

One underlying belief behind the activities of TEBES is the view of teachers as professionals and, as such, with proper assistance they can develop projects on significant problems that they face, projects that can have direct effects on students' learning and at the same time promote their own professional development. Several authors demonstrated that proposals for school change and PD often do not achieve the desired outcomes in the school and are often met with resistance from teachers because they are perceived as being imposed from outside the school and the classroom (Bolam, 1985; Hopkins, 1987). Hence, the challenge is to create a new culture within the school that regards the teacher as a professional who is able and willing to take control of his or her role in change and self-development.

Another main principle adhered to by TEBES is the effective knowledge for school change should develop *in* and *from* the school. It is knowledge *from* practice not knowledge *on* practice, in other words, knowledge from *within* not from *without*. This understanding is in line with the South American critical theories of education according to Freire (Freire & Shore, 1987) and principles of participatory action research of Fals Borda (Fals Borda & Rahman, 1991). It is also in line with several international educators such as Carr and Kemmis (1986), Elliott (1993), Huberman (1973), and Havelock and Huberman (1980), who assert that permanent and continuous change in education is best achieved through the initiative and efforts of the participants in the practice of teaching.

Hence, TEBES has two main and interrelated focuses: to change the practices of teaching in the schools and at the same time to provide mechanisms for continuous PD of teachers. TEBES realizes that school change does not happen overnight. It attempts to have short-, medium-, and long-term aims. In the short term, TEBES organizes collectives of teachers for commencing sharing of ideas toward simple projects in which teachers and supporting staff from the university make guesses, try, and times fail. In the medium term, TEBES assists the teachers to generate significant projects in which the collectives grow in quality and sophistication toward implementing real and deep change in their schools. In the long term, TEBES aims at the development of teachers with deep knowledge of their practice and control over its continual change and improvement.

More specifically, TEBES aims to:

- Assist in school change and transformation in compulsory education that stems from and is carried out by the teachers working collaboratively in their schools.
- Provide a space for teachers to take control over initiating and directing change in their schools, recognizing the crucial role that they have in implementing educational change.
- Implement school change in the short and long term by establishing the right conditions and atmosphere for the development of teachers' imagination, creativity, and teaching ability, which in turn helps them facilitate the development of their students' potential and creativity.

- Organize a network of "collectives" of teachers to investigate change in their schools, thus allowing exchange of ideas and collaboration between teachers in different contexts, and, at the same time.
- Change the nature of research developed at university and make it more relevant and responsive to the needs of teachers toward change and improvement in school.

Workings of the Collectives

In 1998, there were 30 collectives around the country working on some 35 different projects over a variety of school subjects and professional aspects of teachers' work. Some projects are in the area of mathematics; others are in language or other school subjects. For ease of communication, the projects can be grouped into three main categories: those dealing with curriculum development (in which lie the majority of projects), those that deal with professional development, and those that deal with aspects of school management.

The collectives vary on many dimensions. Some are small and some are large. They consist of 2 to 20 school teachers. The collectives usually are teachers from a single primary or secondary school, working together with a university lecturer as a supervisor.[4] At times, the members of the collectives are teachers from different schools working on similar problems. Some collectives are formed in response to an invitation by university staff, at other times on the request of the teachers themselves.

In general, the collectives follow cycles for their activities. A cycle commences by the cooperating teachers identifying problems that they face in their daily teaching and/or in their professional life, and through reflection and negotiation they narrow the problems into a single significant problem. Then they design a simple plan to deal with the problem and implement it. In later stages, the teachers observe the results of the trials and document both the process followed and their resulting learning. In the following cycles of action and reflection the teachers develop deeper and better plans for dealing with the identified problems. At the same time as improving their practice, the teachers develop their knowledge of the practice and their ability to critically analyze and understand the problem. Naturally, the exact procedures vary from one collective to another depending on the problems identified and the available resources. This approach to research is in line with many of the principles of critical education (Giroux, 1983), action research (Carr & Kemmis, 1986), and critical ethnography (Robinson, 1994).

Strategies Used in TEBES

1. *Regular research seminars/workshops in the school*: Initially these workshops assist in the identification of the problem, its analysis and reconceptualization, and in the development of the project arising from such analysis. Such activities are assisted

---

[4]The name used for these people in Spanish is "Asesor," which can also be translated as advisor, assessor, mentor, or consultant and is also used for thesis supervisors.

by a collection of articles and other literature on the problem, at times provided by the university supervisor, for the consideration of the teachers and their analysis and reflection. All teachers read this material before their workshops. Such reflection attempts to relate the theory presented in the literature and the experiences and practices of the teachers in their classrooms. Later workshops are used to reflect on the results and learnings from the project.

2. *Academic supervision*: Each collective is assisted by a university lecturer who acts as supervisor to the collectives. Supervision sessions may be on an individual or a collective basis or with a group of collectives working on similar problems. Such supervisors form a useful source of theoretical knowledge for the collaborating teachers as well as assist in the processes used by the collective.

3. *Academic consultancies*[5]: From time to time, the collectives call upon other lecturers from the university for consultancies. Such consultants usually have some experience in the content area relevant to the project. They offer critical advice and assistance over the project that the teachers have planned and are implementing.

4. *Rotating research seminars/workshops*: From time to time, the collectives face specific procedural needs in the planning and the conduct of their projects (e.g., problem identification, data collection and analysis, writing up results, and so on). The collectives in conjunction with their supervisors identify the needs of the participating teachers and organize a seminar of at least 8 hours with a university staff with ample experience in the area of need. At the end of the session, the teachers develop a short video on the problem identified and on their learning. This video is distributed to other collectives for their assistance.

5. *Seminars for the supervisors*: All supervisors in the project in one geographical area have regular meetings for reflection upon their experiences in the different forms of consultancies and upon the different strategies used with the various collectives. Such seminars provide opportunities for the PD of the supervisors themselves.

6. *Presentations and conferences*[6]: Collective conferences are held from time to time for the different participating collectives. These are attended by the participating teachers, the supervisors, and the consultant lecturers from the university. Such gatherings can be at local, state, national, or even international levels. These provide opportunities for the teachers to present their projects and share their understandings and learnings, for academic interchange between the different collectives, and for acting as critical friends for the others.

7. *Publications*: All collectives generate reports on their projects. As far as possible the project assists the teachers in the collectives to also publish their stories and experiences in professional journals or as chapters in books.

8. *Network of collectives*: A national bulletin or newsletter that carries news and contributions from the different collectives around the country is published from time to time. There are facilities to integrate the work of the different collectives and for sharing of experiences. Communication between collectives also is encouraged at local or regional levels.

---

[5]The Spanish term used for such people is *Lector*, which can also be translated as assistant.
[6]The Spanish term used for these events is *Encounters*.

9. *Accreditation*: Following completion of one cycle in the project, if the members of the collective wish, they can document their projects and the material can be developed toward the accreditation of their work in the form of diplomas from the university. It is worthwhile to mention that up to the present time the education authorities do not recognize the teachers' learnings from their involvement in this program as official PD activity.

The following section discusses in some detail the experiences of one of the collectives that identified problems in the assessment and teaching of mathematics as their area of interest and action.

Case Study: Collective at Huejutla State of Hidalgo

In 1993, teachers from two primary schools in two rural communities located about 7 hours by road from the capital, Mexico City, assisted by a lecturer from the National Pedagogical University formed a collective for transforming mathematics teaching in their schools. The deliberations of teachers commenced with their concerns about assessment practices in mathematics classes, in particular Grades 3 and 4. After several trials of changing their assessment practices, they realized that most of their practices in assessment centered around memorization of facts and content knowledge, which they identified as the lowest level of students' learning, and often failed to evaluate higher order learning such as analysis, synthesis, understanding, reasoning, and so on. For them, assessment was a social justice issue in their classrooms. Without comprehensive assessment of student learning, it was not possible to be fair and equitable in their teaching. They realized that the achievement of this project required analysis of the higher order thinking skills, not only from psychological but also from epistemological and philosophical aspects as well as theories of measurement.

However, their reflection on their assessment practices soon led the teachers to examine their teaching practices in the classroom as they related to the achievement of these higher order goals. The problem became how can the teachers change their teaching to best achieve these higher order aims of mathematics teaching. To achieve this, the teachers spent a considerable amount of time analyzing and reflecting on their daily practice in mathematics classes. This analysis of their assessment and teaching practices was assisted by a collection of articles that the cooperating lecturer from the university provided.

The task that the teachers embarked on was how to make mathematics teaching different in their classrooms in order to achieve these higher order aims and at the same time make mathematics classes more interesting and varied for the needs of the students. The mathematical topic under consideration was numbers, relations, and operations on numbers. The classroom activities sought were to be interesting, challenging, and have real-world contexts. The belief was that such activities would make learning more involved and lasting. Through these games-problems it was hoped also the students' perception of what is mathematics might change.

At the conclusion of their first stage of the project, the teachers collaborated to write a 50-page proposal and analysis of their situation (Sanchez et al., 1996). The proposal identified aspects of the geographical and other contextual situation at their schools, including the physical, historical, economical, cultural, and educational aspects. As the proposal demonstrates, the teachers gained a significant amount in compiling this information about their school. In addition, the proposal contained a very careful and detailed critique of the current problems encountered in their daily practices in teaching mathematics. It is interesting that the teachers did not identify the students' learning problems as environmental, or as lying in the students themselves, but in the very practices that they themselves follow. Similarly, this proposal contained an extensive review of literature on various aspects of students' learning and teachers' teaching in mathematics. Such literature covered topics such as the cognitive abilities that they aspire to develop theories of cognitive development in children, problem solving, and the role of games in education. The last section of the proposal contains a detailed proposal for changing teaching toward the achievement of the desired goals. Similarly, the proposal contained a selection of about 30 specific and general types of games that teachers may use in their classes. In addition, the proposal contained a consideration of a detailed evaluation criteria for these activities. The evaluation identified several dimensions of evaluation, levels at each dimension, and indicators for the achievement of the levels—thus achieving their original aim to make their assessment more comprehensive.

Currently, the collective is at their third application of their proposal for change. They have been able to identify needed modifications of the games and their application to the classroom. They have been able to narrow the initial list of activities to about six very general games that can be applied to many situations and that refer to contexts familiar to the students. The teachers evaluated their learning from the project as a very steep curve indeed. For them, such activity taught them about teaching, mathematics, students' knowledge, school systems, environment, methods of research, and most of all the complexity and interrelatedness of educational problems. They describe their task in the classroom as student training rather than teaching. Their task as teachers was seen as assisting students' development in mathematical knowledge as well as in their ability to think.

However, the teachers were very candid about their failures and shortcomings in their projects. They realized that the problems of teaching mathematics are not always simple. Nevertheless, they are convinced, however, that they are on the right track in their endeavors and in their learning of how to become more effective mathematics teachers. The introduction of the proposal identified the history of the group and how it operated. It also outlined the procedures that they followed and the problems that they encountered working on the project. For example, differences in opinions between the participants and the lack of ability of some to listen to other points of view, other demands on teachers' time, and a lack of system support were identified as the main problems.

The use of games and problem solving in mathematics classrooms are not new as areas of research and teaching in mathematics education. What is different in this case is that these activities were chosen and implemented in an action research context, that is, the teachers first identified a practical concern in their classrooms. Then based on reading of the literature they developed a proposal for changing current practices toward solution of this problem. Then they trialed this solution and reflected on the results critically. They learned from their experience how they can best achieve their aims in the specific context of their classrooms. Similarly, they worked collaboratively to multiply their learning. In the mind of the authors of this chapter the quality and sophistication of the work generated by the teachers would qualify for a master's degree at many universities in the many countries. Unfortunately, within the educational system and hierarchies of the country, the teachers have received no official credit for their work. Finally, it is worth stressing that, by performing this action research on their practice, the teachers aim to improve their own practice as well as be able to share their findings with other schools in compulsory education both near and far. As with all collectives in TEBES, this group of teachers presented the results of their findings and learning at various seminars for teachers organized by the network.

DISCUSSION

In this concluding section we highlight three characteristics of emancipatory PD. Based on the theoretical model presented previously, we argue that TEBES is a PD program designed to cater to the emancipatory interests of teachers. Also, we assert that the experience of teachers in collaboratively researching and changing their practice in the classroom and school is an empowering PD experience. We are also cognizant that both constructs of emancipation and empowerment are often—and we argue that they should be—contested from a critical and postmodern perspectives (a more detailed problematization of these constructs is found in Carr, 1995; Kemmis, 1995; Lankshear, 1994; Troyna, 1994; Zuker-Zkerrit, 1996).

The first characteristic of PD activities designed for emancipatory interests of teachers is that they are based on the recognition of the teacher as a professional. In two investigations Romberg (1988) and Noddings (1992) studied the status of mathematics teachers in United States and concluded that they do not reach a professional status. Arguably, this situation applies to mathematics teachers in many countries around the world. However, Noddings noted that "[t]here are bright spots, however in this bleak picture. Reform movements are pressing for changes designed to professionalize teaching" (p. 206). Noddings identified several components of a profession, three of which are relevant for the discussion in this chapter.

- Professionals are acknowledged as having special knowledge in their field of expertise. This knowledge is essential for professionals to be effective in the provision of service and in improving their practice. In the area of mathematics education there are many studies of teachers' content and pedagogical knowledge. However, very few studies have addressed how teachers develop their knowledge, and there are even fewer on how it is possible to change it. A constuctivist theory of learning (Davis, Maher, & Noddings, 1990) asserts that learners develop their knowledge based on previous knowledge and experience, and that this process is assisted by reflection and negotiation with others and not simply transmitted from expert to apprentice.

- Professionals work within an atmosphere of collegiality. Professionals worked with others to produce professional knowledge and to improve their practice and the conditions of their practice. Noddings discusses the results of research on characteristics of teachers who received national awards for excellence in teaching. These teachers have shown a greater tendency than others for collaboration with other teachers in the same or other schools and to be active in professional national associations. There is much evidence of research on school change in Australia that shows that the more effective changes result when all the teachers in a school cooperate to change their practice in their individual classes (Baird & Northfield, 1992).

- Professionals enjoy a degree of autonomy. There is some evidence that teachers' sense of autonomy is correlated with their enthusiasm about their work and even their performance (Noddings, 1992). Furthermore, changes can be more permanent and effective if initiated and controlled by the teachers themselves. The teachers do not resist reform that they chose and whose direction they control. However, it is necessary to say that total autonomy is not possible or desirable. There are other people who have an interest and a right to be involved in educational decisions. They too must be involved in educational change.

The second characteristic of PD programs that cater to emancipatory knowledge of teachers is that they involve knowledge generation and knowledge application within the same program. Traditionally, research is seen as means of knowledge/theory production and reform as knowledge application for the improvement of practice. We argue that effective professional development programs for developing emancipatory interest of teachers are possible if the activities of research and action are intermixed within the same program. Research has a negative connotation in the mind of many teachers—justifiably so in many situations. Often research questions are not relevant to the needs and concerns of the teachers. Further, research findings are often written in a language not accessible to teachers. Research questions and findings often portray images of and activity from an "ivory tower" that is at a distance from the "reality" of the classroom. We argue that emacipatory interests of teaches are served by teachers becoming active in the research process as well as in the application of the knowledge generated. Such fusion of knowledge generation and application, of action and reflection, of theory and practice, lies at the heart of participatory action research paradigm.

Kemmis and Wilkinson (1998) identified six characteristics of participatory action research (PAR). First, it is a *social* activity in that "it deliberately explores the relationship between the realms of the individual and the social". It recognizes that "no individuation is possible without socialisation, and no socialisation is possible without individuation" (Habermas, 1992, in Kemmis & Wilkinson, 1998, p. 23) and that "the processes of individuation and socialisation continue to shape individuals and social relationships in all the settings in which we find ourselves" (p. 23). PAR is also *participatory* in that "it engages people in examining their knowledge (understandings, skills and values) and interpretative categories (the ways they interpret themselves and their action in the social and material world)" (p. 23). It is also participatory in the sense that people can only do action research "on" themselves—individually or collectively. It is *not* research done "on" others. PAR is also *collaborative* in that "[a]ction researchers aim to work together in reconstructing their social interactions by reconstructing the acts that constitute them. It is a research done 'with' others" (p. 23). By collaboration, here we mean both collaboration between all people involved in the practice and between them and outsiders from universities who may have developed some experience with the processes of action research and/or wider knowledge of research in some problem area. PAR is *emancipatory* in that "it aims to help people recover, and unshackle themselves from, the constraints of irrational, unproductive, unjust, and unsatisfying social *structures* which limit their self-development and self-determination. It is a process in which people explore the ways in which their practices are shaped and constrained by wider social (cultural, economic, and political) structures, and consider whether they can intervene to release themselves from these constraints—or, if they can't release themselves from these constraints, how best to work within and around them to minimize the extent to which they contribute to irrationality, unproductivity (inefficiency), injustice, and dissatisfactions (alienation) as people whose work and lives contribute to the structuring of a shared social life" (p. 24). Likewise, PAR is also *critical* in that "[i]t is a process in which people deliberately set out to contest and to reconstitute irrational, unproductive (or inefficient), unjust, and/or unsatisfying (alienating) ways of interpreting and describing their world (language/discourses), ways of working (work), and ways of relating to others (power)" (p. 24). Finally PAR is *recursive (reflexive, dialectical)* in that "it aims to help people to investigate reality in order to change it (Fals Borda, 1979, in Kemmis & Wilkinson, 1998, p. 24), and to change reality in order to investigate it—in particular by changing their practices through a spiral of cycles of critical and self-critical action and reflection, as a deliberate social process designed to help them learn more about (and theorise) their practices, their knowledge of their practices, the social structures which constrain their practices, and the social media in which their practices are expressed and realised. It is a process of learning by doing—and learning with others by changing the ways they interact in a shared social world" (Kemmis & Wilkinson, 1998, p. 24).

The third characteristic of emancipatory PD, probably implied by the previous two, is that it is collaborative. Hargreaves (1994) argued that there is a danger that the concept of collaboration has become overused and often ill defined and vague and warns about the uncritical use of the term. Forced or contrived collaboration may be used to impose special interest agendas on participants and may be used to prohibit originality and diversity. In his book, he outlined principles of collaboration, including moral support, improved effectiveness, reduced loads, and political assertiveness. Grundy (1998) used the word "partnerships" to describe collaboration between university and schools in the area of PD. Embedding her model for research partnerships between university and schools in the traditions of teachers as researchers of Stenhouse and on the participatory action research of Kemmis and colleagues, she called for the formation of "communities" of researchers, not on one of research projects but on an ongoing basis. Grundy does not present the concept of partnership unproblematically. She discussed the need to account for the different agendas of the partners, their different backgrounds and expertise, and the different demands of their distinct context of doing research. These are not necessarily limitations to partnerships but indicate the need for open and continuing negotiation between the partners. One issue discussed by Grundy that required special attention was that of parity of esteem. She stated:

> The elimination of hierarchy does not mean the elimination of different forms or sources of knowledge. However, the differences need to be delineated, indeed, they need to become the subject of research themselves. Of course "parity of esteem" for expertise will be strongly dependent upon the other principles of partnership—trust, comparable rewards, recognition of distinctive interests. It should not be assumed, however, that these will lead to "parity of esteem" for the expertise of the various partners. The question of expertise needs to be addressed explicitly. (p. 44)

We argue that, as with any social process, partnerships in PD should be open to critical reflection by all participants so that they become PD for all participants including those at universities.

CONCLUSIONS

Undoubtedly, the failure of many reform programs in mathematics education during the past 50 years has been a source of great concern for many educators around the world. The crucial role of the teacher in success or otherwise of reform attempts is an important lesson learned from research in this area. Here, we have argued that effective and long-lasting school change should start from the needs and interests of teachers in the classroom. Not only would involvement of teachers in the design and implementation of reform acknowledge and promote the teachers' professional status but it also assures that the reform directly addresses the real problems that they face and empowers them to take control over the change process so that it becomes continuous after special projects cease. Teachers in the classroom are in a unique position to understand the real context of their students and classroom and thus can adapt the reforms to their students needs. Furthermore, reform in mathematics education is a time-consuming and complex activity. It cannot be fragmented into separate reforms in curriculum, assessment, pedagogy, teachers beliefs, and so on. This can only be achieved in real contexts of the classroom with the direct involvement of the teachers themselves. The promotion of teachers' involvement in reform processes necessitates the integration of agenda of reform and PD as attempted in this chapter.

Likewise, experience has shown that one of the problems leading to failure of reform is the lack of nexus between theory and practice. Research knowledge in mathematics education has undergone an exponential growth during the past 30 years. The application of this knowledge to classroom change had been much slower. This separation between knowledge generation and knowledge application is not appropriate in a profession such as teaching. This chapter argued that the involvement of teachers in research can lead to bridging this gap and enhance classroom reform. As such, action research can be seen as an effective form of professional development of teachers.

REFERENCES

Aichele, D. B., & Coxford, A. F. (Eds.). (1994). *Professional development for teachers of mathematics*. Reston, VA: National Council for Teachers of Mathematics.

Arias Ochoa, M. (January, 1988). *Una Programa innovador para la formación permanente del profesorados de educación primaria en servicio*. Paper presented at first international congress of primary education, University of Costa Rica, San Jose.

Atweh, B., & Martinez, A. (in preparation). *Hacer Investigación Acción Colaborativamente en el Contexto de Educación Superior: Aprendizajes de una Red de Investigadores*.

Bolam, R. (1985). *La formación de profesores en ejercicio. Condiciones de cambio en la escuela*. Madrid: Narcea.

Baird, J., & Northfield, J. (Eds.). (1992). *Learning from the PEEL experience*. Melbourne: Monash University Press.

Better Mathematics. (1987). London: Her Majesty's Stationery Office.

Brown, C. A., & Borko, H. (1992). Becoming a mathematics teacher. In D. A. Grouws (Ed.), *Handbook of research on mathematics teaching and learning* (pp. 209–239). New York: Macmillan and National Council for Teachers of Mathematics.

Bishop, A. J., Clements, K., Keitel, C., Kilpatrick, J., & Laborde, C. (1996). *International handbook of mathematics education*. Dordrecht: Kluwer.

Carr, W. (1995). *For education: Towards critical educational inquiry*. Buckingham: Open University Press.

Carr, W., & Kemmis, S. (1986). *Becoming critical: Education, knowledge and action research*. London: Falmer Press.

Clements, K., & Ellerton, N. (1996). *Mathematics education research: Past, present and future*. Bangkok: UNESCO.

Crawford, K., & Adler, J. (1996). Teachers as researchers in mathematics education. In A. J. Bishop, K. Clements, C. Keitel, J. Kilpatrick, & C. Laborde, (Eds.), *International handbook of mathematics education* (pp. 1187–1206). Dordrecht: Kluwer.

Davis, R. B., Maher, C. A., & Noddings, N. (1990). Constructivist views on the teaching and learning of mathematics. *Journal for Research in Mathematics Education*, Monograph number 4.

Department of Employment, Education and Training. (1986). *Discipline review of teacher education in mathematics and science*. Canberra: Australian Government printing Service.

Elliott, E. (1993). *Reconstructing teacher education: Teacher development*. London: Falmer Press

Fals-Borda, O., & Rahman, M. A. (1991). *Action and knowledge: Breaking the monopoly with participatory action research*. London: Intermediate Technology Publications.

Fennema, E., & Franke, M. L. (1992). Teachers' knowledge and its impact. In D. A. Grouws (Ed.), *Handbook of Research on mathematics teaching and learning* (pp. 147–164). New York: Macmillan and National Council for Teachers of Mathematics.

Freire, P., & Shor, I. (1987). *A pedagogy for liberation: Dialogues on transforming education*. Basingstoke: Macmillan.

Giroux, H. (1983). *Critical theory and educational practice*. Melbourne: Deakin University Press.

Grouws, D. A. (Ed.). (1992). *Handbook of research on mathematics teaching and learning*. New York: Macmillan and National Council for Teachers of Mathematics.

Grundy, S. (1987). Curriculum: *Product or praxis?* London: Falmer Press.

Grundy, S. (1998). Research partnerships: Principles and possibilities. In B. Atweh, S. Kemmis, & P. Weeks (Eds.), *Action research in practice: Partnerships for social justice in education* (pp. 37–46). London: Routledge.

Hargreaves, A. (1994). *Changing teachers, changing times: Teachers' work and culture in the postmodern age*. London: Cassell.

Hargreaves, A., & Evans, R. (Eds.). (1997). *Beyond educational reform*. Buckingham, UK: Open University Press.

Havelock, R., & Huberman, A. (1980). *Innovación y problemas de la educación: teoría y realidad en los países en desarrollo*. Paris: UNESCO.

Hopkins, D. (1987). *Improving the quality of schooling: Lessons from the OECD international school improvement project*. London: Falmer Press.

Huberman, A. L. (1973). *Como se realizan los cambios en educación: Una contribución al estudio de la innovación*. Paris: UNESCO.

Kanes, C. & Nisbet, S. (1996). Research into the professional development of mathematics teachers. In B. Atweh, K. Owens, & P. Sullivan (Eds.), *Research in mathematics education in Australasia 1992–1995* (pp. 237–250). Brisbane: Mathematics Education Research Group of Australia.

Kemmis, S. (1995). Emancipatory aspirations in a post modern era. *Curriculum Studies, 3*(2), 133–167.

Kemmis, S., & Wilkinson, M. (1998). Participatory action research and the study of practice. In B. Atweh, S. Kemmis, & P. Weeks (Eds.), *Action research in practice: Partnerships for social justice in education* (pp. 21–36). London: Routledge.

Kilpatrick, J. (1999). Ich bin Euproäisch. In K. Krainer & F. Goffree (Eds), *On research in mathematics teacher education* (pp. 49–68), Osnabräck, Germany: Forschungsinsitut fär Mathematikdidaktik.

Lankshear, C. (1994). Literacy and empowerment: Discourse, power , critique. *New Zealand Journal of Educational Studies, 29*(1), 59–72.

Mousely, J. (1992). Research in practice: Teachers as researchers. In B. Atweh & J. Watson (Eds.), *Research in mathematics education in Australasia 1988–1991* (pp. 96–114). Brisbane: Mathematics Education Research Group of Australia.

National Council for Teachers of Mathematics. (1989a). *Curriculum and evaluation standards for school mathematics.* Reston, VA: Author.

National Council for Teachers of Mathematics. (1989b). *Guidelines for the post-baccalaureate education of teachers of mathematics.* Reston, VA: Author.

National Council for Teachers of Mathematics. (1990). *Professional standards for teaching mathematics.* Reston, VA: Author.

Noddings, N. (1992). Professionalization and mathematics teaching. In D. A. Grouws (Ed.), *Handbook of research on mathematics teaching and learning* (pp. 197–208). New York: Macmillan and National Council for Teachers of Mathematics.

Poder Ejecutivo Federal. (1996). *Programa de desarrollo educativo 1995–2000.* México D.F.: Gobierno Federal.

Robinson, H. A. (1994). *The ethnography of empowerment: The transformative power of classroom interaction.* Washington, DC: Falmer Press.

Romberg, T. A. (1988). Can teachers be professionals. In D. A. Grouws, T. A. Cooney, & D. Jones (Eds.), *Perspectives on research of effective mathematics teaching* (vol. 1, pp. 224–244). Reston, VA: National Council for Teachers of Mathematics.

Sánchez, F. L. et al. (1996). *Juguemos a penar y resolver problemas matemáticos.* México: Universidad Pedagógica Nacional.

Sprinthall, N. A., Reiman, A. J., & Thies-Sprinthall, L. (1996). Teacher professional development. In J. Sikula (Ed.), *Handbook of research on teacher education* (pp.666–703). New York: Macmillan.

Thompson, A. (1992). Teachers' beliefs and conceptions: A synthesis of the research. In D. A. Grouws (Ed.), *Handbook of research on mathematics teaching and learning* (pp. 127–145). New York: Macmillan and National Council for Teachers of Mathematics.

Troyna, B. (1994). Blind faith? Empowerment and educational research. *International Studies in Sociology of Education, 4*(1), 3–21.

Valero, P., Gómez, P., & Perry, P. (1997). School mathematics improvement: Administrators and teachers as researchers. In V. Zacks, J. Mousley, & C. Breen (Eds.), *Developing practice: teachers' inquiry and educational change* (pp. 113–121). Geelong, Australia: CSMEE; Deakin University.

Yeatman, A., & Sachs, J. (1995). *Making the links: A formative evaluation of the first year of the innovative Links project between universities and schools for teacher professional development.* Perth, West Australia: Murdoch University.

Zuber-Zkerrit, O. (Ed.). (1996). *New directions in action research.* London: Falmer Press.

11

Resourcing Practice and Equity: A Dual Challenge for Mathematics Education

Jill Adler

University of the Witwatersrand

This chapter focuses on the issue of resource availability and use in mathematics education and possible consequences for equity. In the juxtaposition of resources and equity lies an acknowledgment that there is always and everywhere a tension between development—moving ahead with new ideas and practices in school mathematics, and democracy—access to and participation and success *for all* in mathematical learning in school.

Across quite diverse "movements" in current mathematics education practice it is feasible to read in a shared goal: to move the learning and teaching of mathematics in school beyond "mathematics as procedures" and "pedagogy as teacher dominated." Motivations behind the shared goal, however, differ in significant ways: from the learning of deep mathematical ideas and development of flexible problem solvers to social justice goals realized by all citizens who are able to engage critically and collectively with the mathematical formatting of our world and its social and political consequences and to the emancipation of colonized minds through ethnomathematical activity. Related programs emphasize different kinds of mathematical activity ranging from an emphasis on mathematical processes and apprenticeship into the activity of the mathematician to a focus on mathematical problem solving as a tool for critical action in and on the world.

In all these diverse programs, dominant functional resources in school teaching and learning, like the chalkboard, pupil exercise books, prescribed (legitimated) textbooks, and six or seven half-hour math lessons per week, come into question. In and of themselves, they no longer suffice. Teachers, as reflective or critical practitioners, draw in a range of additional resources (material and sociocultural) to create a rich mathematical and social environment for their learners. Shifting practices, as advocated, for example, by general curriculum reform in the United States and United Kingdom, by critical mathematics education (e.g., Skovsmose, 1994), ethnomathematics (e.g., Gerdes, 1996), and realistic mathematics education (e.g., De Lange, 1996), inevitably entail resources for, and a resourcing of, the practice. This is at the level of teachers themselves, and those materials and ideas to which they have access to construct problems, tasks, and activity, and at the level of their learners and learners' access to ranging resources for engaging with such tasks. It is my contention that, ironically, even those movements with an explicit social justice agenda have not paid sufficient *explicit* attention to the assumptions they make about resource availability and resourcing possibilities across contexts.

The subtext of these provocative and somewhat sweeping introductory statements is to throw into sharp relief how, in South Africa, as would be the case in other countries where poverty circumscribes the lives of the majority, the availability and use of educational resources can never be taken for granted: educational resources are not only seriously limited but also unequally distributed. Differential distribution of material and human resources in school education is highly visible across South African schools. I will not rehearse here apartheid's legacy of gross disparities across class, race, and region. The relative wealth of schools in historically white middle-class suburbs in contrast with impoverished schools in black townships, in rural areas, and in the increasing spread of informal settlements is well known. The recent Schools Register of Needs (Bot, 1997) reveals that a staggering 17% of all schools in South Africa lack basic physical infrastructure. There is serious overcrowding in some of these schools, with classes of up to 100 pupils, and in 23% of all schools there is no running water nor any toilet facilities in or close by the school. In short, not only is there little to draw on for learning and teaching in such schools but conditions actively detract from possibilities for focused attention on learning and teaching. A central educational challenge in South Africa, alongside the implementation of a new curriculum, is thus the provisioning and (re)distribution of human and material resources for learning and teaching in schools.

Any attempts to change practices, be they in the wider mathematics education field or the more politically charged South African context, will bring with them or entail new and different resources and/or new uses for existing resources—and perhaps more substantively, a resourcing of the practice. This explains why, even in educational contexts that are relatively well resourced, difficulties with change in educational practices are attributed to "lack of resources." A large-scale research project on the implementation of the National Mathematics Curriculum in the United Kingdom, for example, reported that lack of availability of resources was given by teachers as a reason for their difficulties, that at "all key stages teachers felt that they lacked suitable activities in probability, and that they had inadequate teaching materials in handling data" (Johnson & Millett, 1996, p. 62). The challenge of resourcing new practices is not exclusive to contexts of limited resources.

My interest in resourcing practice emerges from experiences in a teacher development research project in South Africa,[1] where the issue of resource availability and

---

[1] For detailed reports on the study see Adler et al. (1997, 1998, 1999).

use was examined. The research project was linked to a specific teacher development program that advocated learner-centered pedagogy on the one hand and mathematical practice that moves beyond "mathematics as procedures" on the other. The program needs to be understood as located within a highly charged context of social and political change in South Africa, one aspect of which is a new curriculum for Grades 1 through 9. The new curriculum has transformatory intentions: school education through this new curriculum is to play a significant role in the development of a vibrant and thriving post-Apartheid democracy. Within a wider outcomes-based approach to learning, learner-centered practice is advocated across the curriculum. The intended mathematics curriculum identifies 10 key outcomes that resonate with the more widely shared goals mentioned previously to move mathematics beyond procedural knowledge and include, for example, the appreciation of math as cultural tool.

The research project was carried out over 3 years with a sample of teachers from the program and included classroom observation in contexts that ranged from relatively resourced urban secondary schools to seriously impoverished rural primary schools. Over time, the research team has come to understand that, as teachers bring in additional resources or as they use existing resources to meet new and different educational goals, their emergent practices are simultaneously shaped by their histories (mathematical and professional) and by the contexts in which they work. In some cases we observed teachers harnessing additional resources to provide their learners with greater opportunities to engage and grow mathematically. In others, and particularly so in the more impoverished schools, we saw teachers unintentionally shut down opportunities for learning as they attempted to integrate new goals and resources into their practice.

In this chapter, I draw on episodes and examples from this teacher education research project in South Africa and relate them to resourcing issues that extend beyond the borders of South Africa. In so doing, I build a general argument that, whereas new practices entail "more" resources (new resources and/or different uses for existing resources), more resources do not relate in an unproblematic and linear way to better practice. There is a tension between an uncritical (re)distribution of resources to meet equity goals and how such resources are and can be used to support mathematical purposes across contexts. I develop two interrelated strands to this argument. First, it is essential that any program related to shifting mathematics classroom practices needs to interrogate its assumptions about resource availability and use. Second, resource use is always a recontextualization and appropriation—a dialectical relation between the personal and the contextual. Teachers' changing resourcefulness is partial and uneven. As we strive for greater equity in mathematical access and for mathematics education in school to play its role in building democratic practice, we need to embrace the dual challenge of resource (re)distribution and equity across contexts.

SOME CONCEPTUAL AND THEORETICAL BACKGROUND AND ELABORATION

First, what do I mean by "equity" and "resources"?

Like others (e.g., Apple, 1995; Secada, 1995) I use the term *equity* to engage diversity and difference not through sameness but through fairness. At a quantitative level, one obvious and necessary application of fairness in the current South African context is that poor schools should be receiving more resources. The disparity of resources across schools is untenable, and this needs to be addressed. However, my concern goes beyond provisioning to an interrogation of diverse conditions and contexts and what these mean for appropriate resourcing across situations.

A dictionary definition of *resource* is a noun: "stock that can be drawn on; a country's collective means for support and defense; an expedient device or practical ingenuity, quick wit." It is also possible to think about resource as the verb "resource," to source again or differently, where "source" implies origin, that place from which a thing comes or is acquired. In this chapter resource is both noun and verb; resources refers to *those objects and actions that we draw on in our various practices*.

Second, I argued elsewhere (Adler, 1998) for a reconceptualization of resources as a verb, as a doing word, thus shifting attention off resources per se and onto resources in use in context. I argued that access to any social practice, and so too to school mathematics practice, entails access to the resources in that practice. Such access hinges on the concept of *transparency* with its dual functions of visibility and invisibility (Lave & Wenger, 1991). Access to the resources in a practice requires that the resource be both visible (seen so that it can be used) and invisible (seen through so that the practice is illuminated). Effective use of the geoboard, for example, means seeing the nails, and seeing through the nails to the spatial relationships between them.

We also need to understand school mathematics practice as a hybrid of content selections on the one hand and ranging pedagogical strategies on the other. It is a practice that draws from outside of itself—resources in the practice are delocated from, say, everyday practice and relocated in the mathematics classroom. Their mathematical meanings do not shine through them but need to be mediated. Moreover, in more learner-centered strategies, resources are handed over to the learner, and mathematical meanings are then meant to be extracted through activity. In both cases the challenge of transparency arises—of how to render the resource sufficiently invisible so that school mathematics practice, and not the resource itself, becomes a focus of attention.

Brodie (1995) offered a fascinating account of a group of Grade 9 students working with a geoboard on a sequence of activities designed to enable learners to engage with the concept of area and to work across different shapes with the same area. When the teacher introduced the activities, she did not draw attention to the construction of the geoboard, leaving learners the space to bring a range of meanings to the tasks. One group of learners set off with a creative focus on the number of nails within the various shapes they had made with elastic bands on the geoboard. They then tried to capture a general rule between the number of internal nails and the areas of the shapes. Pick's theorem notwithstanding, they were not able to resolve conflicting results between the rule they developed and the actual areas of some shapes. Moreover, as the teacher attempted to work from their construction, and with limited time, she struggled to shift their attention off the nails and onto the spaces between them. The nails per se were too visible. In this case, the teacher's mathematical intentions of enabling learners to deepen their concept of area could not be realized. In the framework of resource transparency developed previously, and contrary to commonsense notions, more resources in school mathematics make more rather than less demands on mathematics teachers.

A reconceptualization of resources needs to go further. I also argued that we need to extend our understanding of the notion of resources in use beyond those "basic" human and physical resources that are typically quantified in educational studies such as buildings, water and electricity, teacher qualifications, and class size. I call these basic in that they are necessary to the enterprise of schooling, premised as it is on learning within very specific boundaries of time and space. I argue instead for a broader notion of *resources in use* that includes additional human resources such as teachers' knowledge base (as opposed to their mere formal qualifications), additional material resources such as geoboards that have been specifically made for school mathematics, everyday resources such as money, as well as social and cultural resources such as language, collegiality, and time. The table in the appendix provides a way of categorizing the range of resources in use in school mathematics and points to the numerous issues they raise.

In this chapter, I extend the conceptual frame developed so far to include two notions—recontextualization and appropriation—as explanatory tools for understanding and interrogating mathematics teachers' use of resources in context and over time. I focus on the use of two key material resources for schooling, chalkboards and textbooks, as these are usually available across wide-ranging contexts, as well as on the perceived need, availability, and use of additional material resources.

RESOURCES IN MATH CLASSROOM PRACTICE: NEED, AVAILABILITY, AND USE

Chalkboards

The chalkboard is a central resource in school mathematics teaching. In the TIMSS video study, for example, teachers made extensive and ranging use of the chalkboard (Kawanaka, Stigler, & Hiebert, 1999; U.S. DoE, 1997). This was across the six classroom lessons captured as typical of Japanese, German, and American mathematics teaching in Grade 8. There were other physical resources that teachers could and did draw on for displaying knowledge in those classrooms, for example, overhead projectors, a computer for a dynamic display of a range of different triangles with the same base and the same height. Despite its widespread use as a teaching and learning resource in mathematical classrooms, the chalkboard is often taken for granted. It does not seem to come into focus as a valued resource in mathematics in-service professional development programs. Instead, it is inserted negatively into a professional discourse that connects "chalk" and "talk" to problematize "transmission" teaching. In the rhetoric of the new curriculum and the transformation of educational practice in South Africa, chalk and talk has come to signify "old" practice that needs to be replaced with learner-centered, resource-based activity.

In most South African classrooms, the chalkboard is the only resource available for ongoing and changing displays of knowledge. Over the 3 years of the research project mentioned earlier, all the secondary teachers and most of the primary teachers in the study made continuous use of their chalkboards. What is interesting for the discussion in this chapter is the ways in which chalkboard use shifted over time and the possible consequences of such shifts. In the first year of the observations, the chalkboard (and textbook, discussed later) was the dominant available and used resource, at least for the teacher. All teachers had chalkboards (although of varying sizes), and most used them for going over homework or classwork and writing up full solutions for and with whole class.

In the second and third years of the study, there were three interesting and inter-related shifts in the use of this physical resource. First, some of the teachers harnessed the chalkboard as a shared public resource. Learners came up to the board to record a solution to a homework or classwork problem. In other words, the chalkboard was no longer *teacher owned* but *shared with learners*. Second, in most classrooms, the chalkboard was also used to publicly display diverse pupil responses to tasks or prob-lems. This was mostly by pupils presenting either an individual response or a report from group work. In some cases, the teacher wrote on the board what pupils offered. The shift in use of the board here is from *demonstration of single set procedures* to *display of diverse solutions*. Finally, instead of the *learners copying examples and procedures written by the teacher*, they were invited instead *to scrutinize procedures and solutions written by other learners*.

Black and Atkin (1996) illuminated how new practices are often incorporated into existing routinized practices, explaining that routine practices are important in teach-ing. Effective teaching appears to depend on routines. Stress levels would be enormous if in each interaction with pupils in school teachers could not draw on routinized skills. What can thus be interpreted in this extended use of the chalkboard is that values and aspects of learner-centered practice in the teacher development program such as in-creasing pupil activity and encouraging diversity were *appropriated* by some of the mathematics teachers. The form this appropriation took was to incorporate these prac-tices into existing dominant and routine uses of the chalkboard.

It is important to add here that extended chalkboard use was not evident across all teachers, and individual teachers did not use their boards in this way all of the time. In addition, the extended use was not necessarily optimal. In one primary class, for example, the teacher was restricted to a portion of the chalkboard and erased pupil responses immediately after they had been written. She thus simultaneously produced and then diminished the potential effectiveness of pupil-generated public displays. Significantly, this occurred in the poorest school in the study. Some secondary teach-ers who purposefully elicited different pupil responses did not use the opportunity for exploration provided by the public display of different solutions. Instead of prob-ing pupils' mathematical thinking by contrasting solutions, they closed down these learning opportunities by focusing only on identifying right answers.

Finally, what also emerged in the second and third year of the study was that chalkboard use disappeared in those few primary lessons where the teacher attempted more open mathematical tasks. Public display shifted from the chalkboard as a central focal point, to displays within and across groups of learners. In this setting, there is less public pointing to, or explicit marking of, those displays that are valued in terms of mathematical outcomes.

This illumination of chalkboard availability and its shifting use over time reflects teachers changing resourcefulness and how this is uneven, partial, and contextual. It also poses an interesting question for mathematics teacher development programs, specifically in-service programs that draw in teachers from schools with limited resources. Should in-service programs for mathematics teachers explicitly address optimizing the use of functional and often taken for granted resources like the chalkboard? What do teachers themselves come to value as means for resourcing their practice? Both these question take on a particular pertinence in the context of curriculum reform where professional discourse includes a general derision of "chalk and talk."

Textbooks

Two problems are frequently raised with the form and function of textbooks in school mathematics teaching. The first problem is that dominant textbooks in use for school mathematics present a narrow view of, and approach to, mathematics. They follow a well-oiled and familiar script: a concept and/or procedure is introduced, with some related worked examples; this is then followed by an exercise for pupils to practice, consolidate, and possibly extend their understanding of the concept and/or procedure. This steady diet is well known for its rather deadening effects on learner motivation and interest in mathematics on the one hand and on possibilities for learners' mathematical development on the other. The second problem raised is less on the mathematical forms in the textbook and more on how teachers are dispempowered and deprofessionalized by prescribed texts that structure all teaching and produce in teachers a reliance on single prescribed texts. Both these problems are well documented,[2] and both have been identified as problems to be addressed in a new educational dispensation in South Africa.

Between the first and second years of the research project discussed previously, the new curriculum was launched for Grades 1 through 9, with its explicit advocacy of a shift from a content-driven curriculum to an outcomes based curriculum, and to new questions about the form and function of resources such as prescribed textbooks in schools. In fact, one of the goals of the new curriculum for Grades 1 through 9 is actually for teachers to be able to design (select and generate) learning resources to support a range of contextualized teaching purposes. Through the 3 years of the research project, textbooks remained a structuring resource for math teachers, particularly at the senior secondary level. Here content remains the organizer and decider of curriculum, and key texts are indispensable for teachers' planning on the one hand and for providing a range of problems and exercises for pupils on the other. This situation might well change if and when a new curriculum takes root in senior secondary education in South Africa. However, in this context, and particularly at a secondary level, that the prescribed textbooks remain key for mathematics teachers is not surprising. Black and Atkin argued the point quite clearly: in math (and science), because content is easily defined, prescribed textbooks serve to legitimate and sequence school mathematics curricula in a number of countries, particularly at a secondary level. Teachers' reliance on such textbooks is then more appropriately interpreted as responsibly meeting the needs of their learners to succeed in secondary school mathematics.

---

[2]Love and Pimm (1996) provided an extensive interrogation of textual materials in mathematics education. Textbooks are but one part of their wide analysis. They point to the problems I have raised and refer to earlier research (or absences) in aspects of this important field.

In contrast to the secondary teachers, the primary math teachers in the research project used textbooks for some lesson preparation. Despite consistent use for this purpose, the primary teachers did not use their textbooks to assist with sequential learning. There appeared instead to be a rather fragmented selection from textbooks for individual lessons.

As with the use of the chalkboard, this discussion on textbook use by teachers raises the question as to whether in-service mathematics teacher development programs engage teachers in critical analysis of the forms and functions of a textbook in school mathematics learning. As any textbook is a selection and particular reading of mathematics for school, it is imbued with an approach to mathematical knowledge on the one hand and a set of values attached to mathematical learning on the other. A critical and reflexive use of the text entails being able to "see" this reading. However, a reflexive stance also entails "seeing" the text's attention to selection and grading of mathematical tasks, to progression and sequence and how these support (or undermine) possibilities for particular mathematical learnings. Again, as with the chalkboard, optimal use of a textbook as a teaching and learning resource is often taken for granted in in-service programs. Emphasis, particularly in reform programs, is placed instead on new and additional resources. Optimizing the use of existing textbooks is perhaps most important in impoverished areas in South Africa, where possibilities for state-provided additional resources beyond the chalkboard and textbook are unlikely in the short term, despite the government's new differential funding formula to assist the poorest schools. As Love and Pimm argued: "Text materials—even textbooks—are resources, not the curriculum. The curriculum is also how a teacher interprets or uses such texts" (1996, p. 398).

One of the rural secondary teachers in the research project, for example, explained how her experience in the program enabled her to see aspects in her textbook that she had not appreciated or even noticed before. There is a danger that, in aspiring too rapidly to the ideal situation where teachers have and can select from a range of texts to plan their curricula, the benefits and functionality of a good text that models appropriate tasks and their sequencing might well be undermined.

So far I have discussed widely available resources such as chalkboards and textbooks in the teaching and learning of mathematics and the questions that arise for in-service professional development when these dominant and key functional resources are taken for granted. The underlying argument is that the development–democracy tension might be better served through optimizing the use of such resources across contexts. Our challenge then as mathematics teacher educators is to open up possibilities for critical reflections on the forms and functions of chalkboards and textbooks in school mathematics practice, without undermining their use.

The issue of resource distribution and use is highlighted further and in a different way when we look at what happens as teachers bring in and use additional materials in the math classroom.

Additional Materials

As summarized in the appendix, material resources that are used across contexts to support mathematical learning range from technologies such as chalkboards and calculators to school mathematical materials such as textbooks and geoboards and to everyday objects such as money. In the second and third year of the research project, a range of additional material resources were brought into class by all the primary teachers observed. These ranged from school mathematics materials such as hand-written or copied worksheets, tangrams, unifix cubes, and cuisenaire rods to everyday materials such as round sweets for "seeing" nontessellations, rulers for measuring, and paper for paper folding and fractions. In all three mathematics courses in the teacher development program, there are examples and activities that draw on such material. In this section, I draw on two illustrations from the research project to illuminate a relationship between the observed widespread use of additional material resources in primary classrooms and the kinds of mathematical tasks that accompanied the recruitment of these resources.

I start with an example from one of the primary teachers in the research project who works in a semi-urban, well-functioning, and supportive school. Over the 3 years of the study, she provided her learners the most "task-based" lessons. In one set of observed lessons on tessellations, she brought in spherical sweets, homemade tangrams, and a worksheet with the intention of having a creative lesson so pupils could see some of the mathematics they were doing. Within the hour lesson, she organized the class into groups and presented pupils in their groups with three different kinds of tasks, each at an appropriate level of demand. Her pupils were provided a creative, hands-on learning experience across three different tasks. They were made to think about whether "round" objects can cover a surface, about manipulating puzzle pieces to fit a square, and about how to draw tessellating shapes so that they did cover a surface. The pupils' enjoyment was evidenced in their not rushing out the class as soon as the period ended.

There were more than 40 pupils in the class, arranged in groups of at least 6 pupils. The teacher had made the tangrams herself—enough for one per group. She used her own time and material resources to do so. However, with only one per group and six pupils in a group, there were a number of pupils who at no stage in the activity touched or moved one of the pieces. At best they watched others. More seriously, there were a number of potentially confusing "seeings" in her tasks, diminishing possibilities for optimal use of the resources she brought in. Three-dimensional sweets were used to illustrate "gaps" in covering a surface. The tangram activity was used to convey a meaning of tessellation as shapes that "fit together" and have "straight edges." Moreover, the tangram was homemade and had numerous pieces that most pupils did not manage to put together into a square. Finally, the tessellation worksheet only included shapes that did tessellate. Although there was a structure to the lessons, and the designed tasks were sequenced, the independent and relational mathematical foci of the tasks and their mathematical purposes were not clear. In discussion, the teacher shared her concern that some pupils were not participating and her recognition that this was probably because they did not understand what was required of them.

This teacher took a double risk: (a) teaching a new mathematical topic (tessellations) and (b) doing this in a new way (through a resource-based, hands on approach in which she the does not have direct pedagogical experience to draw on). Difficulties in this are widely recognized: Black and Atkin's (1996) study of teachers and change across countries points out that:

> ...changes generate more complex tasks which require new classroom routines. It is often left to the teachers to invent those routines. To do this they are, effectively, being asked to accept the responsibility for re-defining both their roles and relationships with their students and to reformulate for both the aims and image of their subject. (p. 134)

A tall order indeed, and the context in which this particular teacher's teaching and use of resources need to be understood.

To bring home the notion of resource use in context, I turn to examples from those who work in more impoverished rural school settings. One of the teachers was in a Grade 3 class, working on measurement. She brought in some rulers for a measurement task and had groups of pupils come up to "measure the desk" (her desk) one at a time. These pupils were provided closer and more practical observation of measuring. However, she only managed to have two groups accomplish the task at her desk during this lesson, and so most of the class was left with nothing to do for most of the lesson. In addition, by measure the desk she meant the perimeter and assumed that pupils could read their rulers, distinguish centimetres and millimetres, and that they could see that they only needed to measure two adjacent sides to measure the whole table. Later in the week with the same class, the lesson purpose was the consolidation of the four operations. Again, with the desire for interaction and participation, the class was organized into groups, and each was given a small piece of paper with some calculations written on for the group to complete. Each group focused on a different operation. These small "worksheets" were taken in at the end of the lesson, leaving group members with no record of their tasks. Although responses were publicly shared, the teacher was restricted to a small section of the chalkboard and kept erasing each group's work for the next group to write up its answers. As a result, each group had limited opportunity to consolidate all four operations.

The second teacher, working in similar conditions but in Grade 7, used a paper-folding task with the intention of pupils being able to name fractional parts up to sixteenths and seeing equivalence relations (such as 1/4 and 2/8). She thus set up possibilities for each pupil to actively generate fractional parts in relation to wholes that they could see. However, she did not specify that folds needed to generate equal parts, with the result that some pupils did not generate 8, let alone 16 pieces, and the lesson simply reinforced naming basic fractions (such as one eighth). This reduced the task to rather low demands for a Grade 7 class.

The other primary teachers in the research project also recruited additional material resources into the teaching and faced similar new challenges. Collectively these teachers showed interesting *improvization*. They used readily available resources in the environment. However, particularly in areas where paper is a scarcity, teachers struggled with *sufficiency*. For example, in a number of classes there were not enough worksheets for all pupils. Most pupils left lessons without a record of the day's activity. Moreover, in a number of cases (e.g., the use of a homemade tangram), the teachers had generated these additional materials at their own expense, raising the issue of *sustainability*. It is unlikely that such additions could and would be sustained over time.

In addition to questions of sufficiency and sustainability, teachers struggled to use the recruited resources to support mathematical learning. Either the tasks set were at an inappropriate level or they were poorly graded, structured, and sequenced. Alternatively, and more seriously, the possibilities for pulling through the mathematics embedded in these materials were not fully exploited and in some cases created confusion. In short, lesson purposes were often unclear.

In sharp contrast, additional materials were scarcely visible across secondary schools and classrooms in the study. As can then be expected tasks were largely textbook exercises and were largely appropriate (in terms of level and structure). In the words of one of the secondary teachers, "I still have the same textbook" and no other materials, and so she still relies on it for her teaching at grade 12 metric level. Again, this limited use of additional resources at a secondary level is understandable given the content pressures on secondary teachers and the legitimacy of the current prescribed textbooks in relation to the high-stakes matriculation examination.

The primary math teachers undoubtedly took risks in their observed lessons, with some problematic mathematical consequences. They recruited additional materials into their classroom practices, although in uneven ways and with a range of possible effects. The difficulties that emerge as teachers use these additional resources is a function of their own biography, the specificity of the mathematics they are attempting to teach, the relative transparency of the resource for mathematics learning, and the context of its use. Here, the resource (e.g., a sheet of paper to fold into fractional parts) has to be visible (so that it can be seen to be used) and invisible (so that it can be seen through to the mathematics, here as standing for a whole). The ability to render a resource both visible and invisible in class and to draw connections between mathematics and real-world objects and situations in interactions with pupils demands flexible and rich mathematical understanding of the teacher.

My intention in this discussion about recruitment and use of additional resources is to foreground the dynamic relationship between new resources and their use in context. First, there is the issue of sufficiency and sustainability over time. Implied here is the need for financial support from the state. The demands to enact new curriculum practices have resource implications that, in the current South African context, are being left to individual teachers, schools, and in-service programs. As teachers take up these responsibilities, they become open to carrying the blame for the difficulties they encounter, and these difficulties extend beyond provision.

Second, the impact of additional resources lies in their *use in context*. As additional material resources are recruited by teachers, they make more rather than fewer demands on teaching preparation and activity. It is not a new idea that the presence of a learning aid does not automatically translate into effective use and into benefits for all learners. I am suggesting rather that in-service teacher education needs to work with teachers on the use of all kinds of resources to support a range of mathematical and pedagogical purposes. This is in addition to in-service programs supporting optimal use of key functional resources such as chalkboards and textbooks. The emphasis needs to produce a shift in focus from the resources per se onto their use for supporting mathematics learning in context and hence for the support and development of the resourceful teacher.

Hence our dual challenge in teacher education: advocacy of and contribution to the distribution and provision of resources to support curriculum practice in the mathematics class on the one hand and clearly focused attention on resource use *in context* on the other, including the chalkboard and textbook. This requires careful and reflexive work with teachers on what counts, and how, in their specific contexts.

DEVELOPING A THEORETICAL DISCUSSION

Through the chapter and its discussion of resource availability and use, I described, explored, and hinted at explanation of some mathematics teachers' use of what I termed "key functional" and "additional material" resources. Adding to the categorization of resources in the appendix, I have begun a categorization of uses (mainly of the chalkboard) and a categorization of issues in use of additional resources. To shift to explanation I have drawn on the notions of transparency (which was briefly elaborated) and the notions of recontexualization and appropriation (which have not been elaborated) and used these to interrogate classroom practice and teacher education practice.

Transparency and recontextualization are explanatory tools that illuminate challenges presented by resources in classroom mathematics. They reveal how the meaning of a resource does not lie in the resource itself but in its use for mathematical learning. As we draw on resources from outside of the classroom (e.g., a sheet of paper), it needs to be rendered transparent, made simultaneously visible and invisible. The difficulty with resources such as a sheet of paper is that, as it is drawn into the classroom, it is recontextualized. It is no longer a sheet of paper but a whole. Resources that are brought into the classroom do not necessarily have educational meanings built into them nor do educational meanings shine through them. The meanings of the resources emerge in their use in the context of classroom practices and the subject knowledge being learned. There is a dialectical interaction between the bringing in of a new resource (such as a sheet of paper, greater pupil–pupil discussion) or using an existing resource in a new way (such as the chalkboard) and the shaping of classroom practices. Using the chalkboard in a new way changes classroom practices (such as participation), and, at the same time, existing classroom practices (well-established routines such as focusing on correct answers in mathematics) shape possibilities for new uses of the resource. Simply, resources shape and are shaped by their contexts of use. At the same time as the school mathematics context produces a new meaning for the resource so too the resource acts on classroom processes. This dialectical recontextualization emerges interactively from an empirical field and from growing interrogation and understanding of pedagogical practice in the theoretical field of education. Transparency and recontextualization thus provide a theoretical language with which to think and talk about resources and their use in school mathematics.

Neither, however, help to explain the heterogeneity and the uneven ways in which individual teachers take up and use additional resources or existing resources in new ways: why some teachers displayed more innovation and what could be regarded as more innovative or more successful use of resources. One explanation lies in viewing the teachers in this study as learners—they are learning more about their teaching. Interrogations of learning, particularly from a sociocultural perspective, have helped explain unevenness and heterogeneity by shifting away from cognitive science notions of internalization (a simple taking in of the external) to appropriation—where tools in the learner's environment are understood as being used adaptively (Kirshner & Whitson, 1997). There is an ongoing inter-relation between the learners' biographies, their learning in the program, and the context in which they work. In relation specifically to changing chalkboard uses, I talked of teachers' appropriation of aspects of the teacher education program (greater pupil activity and participation) through new uses of the chalkboard. In relation to recruitment of additional resources, I illuminated how appropriations of resource-based tasks were a function of biography and context, a simultaneous product of the teachers' mathematical past, their experiences in the program, and the availability and levels of resource sufficiency in their contexts.

CONCLUSION

As I reflect on what we, as teacher educators and researchers, are learning through our involvement in teacher development research, I am reminded of Jonathen Clark's ethnographic study of the trial of a package of innovative science materials in an urban black township school in South Africa. In an article "Challenges to practice, constraints to change" Clark (1998) spoke of his "sobering experience," one that "reinforces Fuller and Snyder's (1992) comment that the more we learn about what teachers should be doing, the more we realise just how constrained their social roles actually are within schools. . . ."

I am also aware that this interrogation of resources in use in mathematical learning is in my voice—the voice of researcher and teacher educator. It inevitably provides a partial reading, a reading framed by the particular shape and context of the research project. The focus of the research was to come to understand teachers' take-up from a teacher development program, and the major goal was to feedback into the program and its ongoing curriculum development. The design involved a baseline study in 1996 followed by a 1-week visit to each school and teacher in 1997 and 1998. The numerous methodological issues confronted in the research process are detailed in Adler et al. (1997, 1998). It is important, however, to note here that the design (inevitably constrained by finances and time) did not include possibilities for following up and working with teachers on issues that emerged in process—including resource availability and use. There remains a great deal of work to be done with teachers across a range of contexts and how they see their specific resource needs and use. We need to grow our understanding about resources and equity. A different project, perhaps with a more collaborative methodology, could provide for interaction and dialogue with teachers around resource availability and use. Through such activity we can confront and work on the unsettling understanding that emerged through the research project: that *in contexts of greatest need* the effects of teachers' appropriation from their in-service experiences and of the recontextualization of new or existing resources perhaps exacerbated inequality. There were teachers whose context and/or personal disposition appeared to mitigate against pedagogic innovations and where an unintended consequence of innovation appeared to be both an undermining of the teacher's resourcefulness and reduced learning opportunities for her learners.

In all contexts and particularly contexts of inequality, resource availability and use in the teaching and learning of mathematics are substantive issues. Research methodological issues aside, the reflection on mathematics teacher education practice through an interrogation of resource availability and use in this chapter provokes several questions: As mathematics teacher educators is it not our political and educational responsibility to build on existing functional resources while advocating and contributing to the provision and distribution of additional resources? How else are we to support curriculum renewal envisaged for enhancing development and democracy in and through post-Apartheid South African education? At the same time is it not also our political and educational responsibility to recognize and build critical awareness that more resources are not a decontextualized panacea for improvement in mathematics education? Hence our dual challenge?

APPENDIX: CATEGORIZATION OF RESOURCES RECRUITED IN SCHOOL MATHEMATICS

BASIC RESOURCES—MAINTENANCE OF SCHOOLING		
Resources	*Exemplars*	*Issues*
Material	School buildings, water, electricity, fence, desks, chairs, paper, pens	Absence makes demand for more resources obvious and necessary
Human	Teacher–pupil ratios, class size, teacher qualifications	Agreed as basic, but scope and content of qualification and what constitutes optimal class size are contested
OTHER RESOURCES AND THEIR TRANSPARENCY		
Human resources		Teacher's knowledge-base - Mathematics - Pedagogical content knowledge - Knowledge of world	Scope, content, weightings, orientations all contested
		Collegiality	For maintenance of the practice as well as change
Additional material resources	Technologies	Chalkboard, calculators, computers, photocopier	Need for invisibility to see through technology to mathematics
	School math materials	Textbooks, other texts, cuisenaire rods, geoboards, computer software	Mathematical meaning not obvious; mathematical meaning and pedagogical possibility is built into them; when inserted in "learner-centered" pedagogy can become too visible
	Everyday objects	Money, newspapers, stories, calculators, rulers	Uses outside of math, so need to be visible and invisible
Cultural resources	Math artifacts	Math text (e.g., proof), number lines, magic squares	Specifically mathematical
	Language	L1, L2, code-switching (CS), verbalisation, communication	Assumptions: CS, talk are enabling; need to be visible and invisible
	Time	Time table Length of periods Homework	Structuring of time needs to be visible and invisible; with new pedagogies or when schooling breaks down, can become too visible

REFERENCES

Adler, J. (1998). Resources as a verb: recontextualizing resources in and for school mathematics practice. In A. Olivier & K. Newstead (Eds.), *Proceedings of the 22nd Conference of the International Group of the Psychology of Mathematics Education* (vol 1, pp. 1–18). Stellenbosch: University of Stellenbosch.

Adler, J., Lelliott, T., & Slonimsky, L., et al. (1997) *A baseline study: teaching and learning practices of primary and secondary mathematics, science and English language teachers enrolled in the Wits Further Diploma in Education.* Report. Johannesburg: University of the Witwatersrand.

Adler, J., Lelliott, T., & Reed, Y., et al. (1998) *Mixed-mode FDEs and their effects: an interim report on the teaching teaching and learning practices of primary and secondary mathematics, science and English language teachers enrolled in the Wits Further Diploma in Education.* Report. Johannesburg: University of Witwatersrand.

Adler, J., Bapoo, A., Brodie, K., Davis, H., Dikgomo, P., Lelliott, T., Nyabanyaba, T., Reed, Y., Setati, M., & Slonimsky, L. (1999) *Mixed-mode further diplomas and the effects: Summary report on major findings of a three year research project.* Johannesburg, South Africa: University of the Witwatersrand.

Apple, M. (1995). Taking power seriously: new directions in equity in mathematics education and beyond. In W. G. Secada, E. Fennema, & L. B. Adajian (Eds.), *New directions for equity in mathematics education.* Cambridge. Cambridge University Press.

Black, P., & Atkin, J. M. (Eds.). (1996). *Changing the subject: Innovations in science, mathematics and technology education.* London: Routledge.

Bot, M. (1997). School register of needs: a provincial comparison of school facilities, 1996. *Edusource Data News,* 17.

Brodie, K. (1995). Peer interaction and the development of mathematical knowledge. In L. Meira & D. Carraher (Eds.), *Proceedings of the 19th international Conference for the Psychology of Mathematics Education* (vol 1, pp. 16–223). Recife: Universidade Federal de Pernambuco.

Clark, J. (1998). Challenges to practice, constraints to change: exploring school-based factors inhibiting a science teacher's implementation of curriculum innovation. In J. Kuiper (Ed.), *Proceedings of the 7th annual SAARMSE Conference, Harare* (pp. 100–109). Grahamstown: Rhodes University.

De Lange, J. (1996). Using and applying mathematics in education. In A. Bishop et al. (Eds.), *International handbook of mathematics education* (pp. 49–98). Dordrecht: Kluwer.

Gerdes, P. (1996). Ethnomathematics and mathematics education. In A. Bishop et al. (Eds.), *International handbook of mathematics education* (pp. 1207–1234). Dordrecht: Kluwer.

Johnson, D. C., & Millet, A. (Eds.). (1996). *Implementing the mathematics national curriculum: Policy, politics and practice.* New Bera Dialogues. London: Paul Chapman.

Kawanaka, T., Stigler, J., & Hiebert, J. (1999). Studying mathematics classrooms in Germany, Japan and the United States: Lessons from TIMSS videotape study. In G. Kaiser, E. Luna, & I. Huntley. (Eds.), *International comparisons in mathematics education* (pp. 86–103). London: Falmer Press.

Kirshner, D., & Whitson. J. A. (Eds.). (1997). *Situated cognition: Social, semiotic and psychological perspectives.* Mahwah, NJ: Lawrence Erlbaum Associates.

Lave, J., & Wenger, E. (1991). *Situated learning: Legitimate peripheral participation.* Cambridge: Cambridge University Press.

Love, E., & Pimm, D. (1996). "This is so": a text on texts. In A. Bishop et al. (Eds.), *International handbook of mathematics education* (pp. 371–410). Dordrecht: Kluwer.

Secada, W. G. (1995). Social and critical dimensions for equity in mathematics education. In W. G. Secada, E. Fennema, & L. B. Adajian (Eds.), *New directions for equity in mathematics education.* Cambridge: Cambridge University Press.

Skovsmose, O. (1994). *Towards a philosophy of critical mathematics education.* Dordrecht: Kluwer.

U.S. Department of Education (DoE). (1997). *Attaining Excellence.* Washington, DC: Office of Education Research and Improvement, United States Department of Education.

12

Mathematics, Social Class, and Linguistic Capital: An Analysis of Mathematics Classroom Interactions

Robyn Zevenbergen
Griffith University

The role of classroom interactions in the construction of mathematical meaning has been well documented, particularly by those working in the area of constructivism. This body of literature has been powerful in illuminating the role and importance of interaction in the negotiation and development of mathematical meaning. What is less researched is the political dimension of such interactions whereby the competencies needed to participate effectively, as determined by the hegemonic culture embedded with such interactional practices, are closely aligned to the social background of the students. This chapter seeks to explore one aspect of interactional patterns in mathematics classrooms in terms of the social milieu within which such interactions occur and the subsequent potential for students to participate effectively within such contexts. In so doing, my purpose is to raise awareness of how some pedagogical practices can be socially biased in order that they may be identified as contributing to the successful (or failed) participation in classroom dialogue. As a consequence of this analysis, some of the apolitical assumptions that have been built into the constructivist writings may also be challenged.

Using the theoretical constructs offered by Pierre Bourdieu, this chapter critically analyzes the three-phase interactional practices offered by ethnomethodologists in order to understand how the social context of mathematics is implicated in the construction of social disadvantage. In so doing, the purpose of the chapter seeks to raise awareness of how some students are (further) disadvantaged through the practices of classroom interactions that are often taken as normal within the everyday life of the classroom. The focus of this chapter is on practices within the primary school setting and draws on the theoretical constructs of habitus, cultural capital, and field.

It is argued that students enter the school context with a linguistic habitus that predisposes students to interact and talk in ways that will be recognized or marginalized in and through the pedagogic practices of the classroom. Where students enter the classroom with a linguistic habitus congruous with the legitimate linguistic practices of the classroom, such habitus becomes a form of capital that can be exchanged for academic success.

THEORETICAL CONSTRUCTS

The notions of habitus and field are integral to this analysis of classroom talk. For Bourdieu, habitus is the embodiment of culture and provides the lens through which the world is interpreted. Habitus predisposes (but not determines) thoughts, actions, and behaviors. Harker (1984) argued persuasively that habitus can alter over time, thereby challenging those (such as Jenkins, 1982) who suggest that habitus is deterministic. In some contexts, such as the classroom, some habitus may have the effect of conveying more power and status than in other contexts. For example, where a child has been socialized within the familial context to have particular attributes, likes, dislikes, and language forms, she or he may be able to exchange such dispositions for power within that context. The student whose language is that of the middle-class register may be positioned as a more authoritative voice within that community and hence may be positioned as having more power and status than her or his peers whose linguistic register is that of the working class. The embodiment of such characteristics of tastes, dispositions, and language can be seen to be the constitution of habitus, that is, more simplistically, the embodiment of culture.

A range of studies of home–school differences has shown that the patterns of interactions are substantially different for many students. In her comprehensive study, Brice- Heath (Heath, 1982, 1983) has shown that students from socially disadvantaged backgrounds are more likely to be exposed to declarative statements when they are expected to undertake tasks. In contrast, middle-class parents are more likely to pose a pseudoquestion when requesting their children to undertake tasks. Such practices come to be embodied in the habitus so that the student perceives task requesting within this framework. When entering the formal school context, their habitus predisposes them to frame tasks within their pre-existing habitus so that when a teacher poses the task as "Could you get out your maths books?" it is interpreted quite differently depending on the previous experiences. For the purposes of this chapter, it is important to note that the patterns of interactions within middle-class families are most similar to those of the formal school setting, whereas the converse is the case for working-class students. In this way, it can be argued that middle-class students are more likely to have a habitus that has embodied such patterns of interactions than their working-class peers. However, as Harker (1984) suggested, the habitus can be reconstituted so that, for students whose habitus is different from that of the formal school context, there is potential for it to be brought closer to that which is legitimated through school practices, thus suggesting a transformative component of pedagogy rather than a deterministic reading. However, such reconstitution must be undertaken with considerable effort.

In concert with habitus is the construct of field. Habitus can be seen to be the subjective component of analysis, whereas field can be thought to be the more objective aspect of analysis. For aspects of habitus to have more power than others—such as the familiarity with pseudoquestions over declarative statements—there must be some external, or objective, factors that determine the importance of some things over others. Such power and status are conveyed through the structuring practices of the field. Within the context of the schools and classrooms, certain practices are seen to be more legitimate than others, and those students who are able to display or assimilate those practices within their own repertoire of behaviors are positioned more favorably. For example, students who are able to display effective use of the mathematics register, test-taking skills, and the like are more likely to be positioned as effective learners of mathematics than their peers who do not demonstrate such characteristics. The skills that are seen to hold status and power within the field of mathematics may be very different from another context. This is borne out in the ethnomathematics studies where students who display the street talk and skills within street selling may be positioned as marginal within the field of education. For these students, the dispositions that have become embodied within their habitus and predispose them to be effective in bartering due to the structuring practices of the market place are positioned less favorably within mathematics education where the structuring practices do not legitimate the practices of the market place. The practices within these two divergent fields differentially convey power on the participants. Mathematics education, as a field, values and conveys power and status on those who display the characteristics, attributes, and dispositions seen as desirable within the field at any given point in time. As a field, the characteristics seen as desirable are transitory and change over time as can be readily observed through changes in what is seen as valuable knowledge within mathematics education research and publications. An example of such changes is the emergence, and later dominance, of constructivist writings.

When considering the objective structuring practices of the field in concert with the subjective components of the habitus, it can be seen that some forms of habitus are more empowering than others depending on the field within which one is operating. Within the field of mathematics education, there are particular forms of habitus that are more likely to be recognized as legitimate and valued. In terms of this chapter, it is argued that the patterns of interaction with which the student has familiarity due to familial contexts are more likely to facilitate the construction of a habitus that has greater or lesser synergy with the interactional patterns of the classroom depending on the types of interactions within a family. The structuring practices of the field of mathematics value particular practices over others so that those students for whom there is a greater synergy between the home practices and the school practices, and hence habitus, the greater the chance of being constructed as an effective participant and learner of mathematics. To this end, various characteristics embodied within the habitus have the potential to be of greater or lesser worth depending on the field. As such, such cultural characteristics can be seen to have greater or lesser value and subsequently can be exchanged for differing positions within the field. For example, the students whose habitus are more congruent with those aspects valued within the field of mathematics are more likely to be positioned as effective learners of mathematics and as a consequence reap the rewards associated with such positioning. In this way, aspects of culture can be seen to be forms of capital that, when embodied in the habitus and legitimated through the field, can be exchanged for other gains, including success in mathematics.

Language as a Form of Capital

In considering aspects of culture that can be exchanged for other rewards, the importance of language needs to be considered, particularly in relation to mathematics education. In appropriating Bourdieu's constructs, his premise that language is not just words for the expression of ideas, but rather is generated through and within social hierarchies, is central to the chapter. Linguistic exchanges are not simple exchanges of language but bring into play complex relationships of power between the student(s) and teachers.

Linguistic competence—or incompetence—reveals itself through daily interactions. Within the mathematics classrooms, legitimate participation is acquired and achieved through a competence in the classroom dialogic interactions. Students must be able to display a discursive competence that incorporates a linguistic competence, an interactional competence along with a discursive competence if they are to be seen as competent learners of mathematics. Classroom interactions are imbued with cultural components that facilitate or inhibit access to the mathematical content. To gain access to this knowledge, students must be able to render visible the cultural and political aspects of the interactions. Bourdieu, in response to questions posed by Wacquant (Bourdieu & Wacquant, 1992) argued that:

> Linguistic competence is not a simple technical ability, but a statutory ability. . . . what goes in verbal communication, even the content of the message itself, remains unintelligible as long as one does not take into account the totality of the structure of the power positions that is present, yet invisible, in the exchange. (p. 146)

As noted earlier, from their early years, students are located within familial structures and practices that will facilitate the development and embodiment of particular cultural features, the least of which is language. For these students, the embodiment of their cultural background into what Bourdieu referred to as the habitus predisposes them to think and act in particular ways. This embodiment of culture includes a linguistic component. Students whose linguistic habitus is congruent with that of the discursive practices represented in mathematics classrooms are more likely to have greater access to the knowledge represented in and through such practices.

From this perspective, language must be understood as the linguistic component of a universe of practices that are composited within a class habitus. Hence, language should be seen to be considered as another cultural product—in much the same ways as patterns of consumption, housing, marriage, and so forth (Bourdieu, 1979). When considered in this way, language is the expression of the class habitus that is realized through the linguistic habitus and is evidenced in the following comment:

> Of all the cultural obstacles, those which arise from the language spoken within the family setting are unquestionably the most serious and insidious. For, especially during

the first years of school, comprehension and manipulation of language are the first points of teacher judgement. But the influence of a child's original language setting never ceases to operate. Richness and style of expression are continually taken into account, whether implicitly or explicitly and to different degrees. (Bourdieu, Passeron, & de saint Martin, 1994a, p. 40)

To this end, the linguistic habitus of the student will have substantial impact on his or her capacity to make sense of the discursive practices of the mathematics classroom and hence their subsequent capacity to gain access to legitimate mathematical knowledge along with the power and status associated with that knowledge. The processes through which the schooling procedures are able to value one language and devalue others must be systematically understood. Through this process, we can better understand how mathematical pedagogy both inculcates mathematical knowledge and imposes domination.

Pedagogic Discourse

The study of language within the pedagogic situation can be identified within two quite distinct areas—quantitative linguistics, which is seen to embrace the objectivity associated with sociolinguistics, and the subjectivist position identifiable through interactional linguistics (Collins, 1993). Greenfell (1998) suggested that to this coupling social psychology also should be added to include those writings that address feelings, attitudes, and motivations. Bourdieu's work seeks to unite this objective–subjective dualism.

In considering the more specific language of classrooms, three principle approaches have been identified by Edwards and Mercer (1987)—linguistic, social, and anthropological. It is the linguistic approach that is of particular importance to this chapter. Within the linguistic approach, the ethnomethodological approaches of Sinclair and Couthourd (1975), Lemke (1990), and Mehan (1982a, 1982b) identified particular ritualized practices within the classroom interactions through which classroom knowledge is structured and built. The interactions occurring within the classroom have been found to have highly ritualized components with clearly identifiable discursive practices (Lemke, 1990; Mehan, 1982a). They argue that these components are not explicitly taught but are embedded within the culture of the classroom. The highly ritualized practices of classroom interactions can be seen in the types of interactions that occur across the various phases of the lesson. For example, the most common form of interaction consists of a practice in that the teacher asks a question, the students respond, and the teacher evaluates that response that Lemke (1990) referred to as "triadic dialogue." This interactional practice can be observed in the following:

T: What does area mean?
S: The outside of the square
T: Not quite, someone else? Tom?
S: When you cover the whole surface, that's area.
T: That's good

Lemke (1990) argued that this practice allows teachers to keep control of the content and flow of this phase of the lesson. Although Lemke focused on the science classroom, the style and purpose of this interaction can be just as readily applied to the mathematics classroom and are aptly summed up as follows:

> Triadic dialogue is an activity structure whose greatest virtue is that it gives the teachers almost total control of the classroom dialogue and social interactions. It leads to brief answers from students and lack of student initiative in using scientific language. It is a form that is overused in most classrooms because of a mistaken belief that it encourages maximum student participation. The level of participation it achieves is illusory, high in quantity, low in quality. (Lemke, 1990, p.168)

This practice is not made explicit to students; rather it must be learned through implicit means. To participate in the classroom interactions effectively, students must have knowledge—either intuitive or explicit—of these unspoken rules of interaction. Mehan (1982) identified three key phases of a lesson—the introduction, the work phase, and the concluding/revision phase. In each of these phases there is a shift in the power relations between the students and teacher. Such shifts permit different forms of interactions to occur (Mehan, 1982; Schultz, Florio, & Erickson, 1982). For the purposes of this chapter, I discuss the introductory phase only for this is the phase where triadic dialogue is most common. Mehan (1982) argued that, during the introductory phase of the lesson, the teacher maintains tight control over the students, initially to ensure that the students are ready for the content of the lesson. Once control has been established and attention gained, the lesson can then proceed. Triadic dialogue is commonly observed in this phase in order to keep control of the academic content of the lesson and the control of the students. Dialogue between students and between teacher and students is not generally part of this phase. If the teacher initiates a question but the student is not able to respond, it is not appropriate for students to express their lack of understanding because this will interrupt the flow of the phase. If there is a misunderstanding or lack of understanding, it is more appropriate for this to be voiced in the work phase of the lesson (Lemke, 1990).

What is not apparent from the above corpus of knowledge of classroom interaction is the recognition that these interactions recognize a particular linguistic form that will be more accessible to some students than others. Social and anthropological studies (such as Bernstein, 1986; Heath, 1983; Willis, 1977) focused on how social background is implicated in academic achievement. Heath's (1983) and Walkerdine's work with parents and children have found the forms of interactions very class oriented. Using Bernsteinian notions of register and relay, it is understood that the content of the mathematics lessons is embedded within discursive practices that, at the level of register, are more likely to be those of the middle class. For example, the common practice of asking pseudoquestions such as "Would you like to get the LEGO blocks?" is typically a middle-class register. For working-class students to then enter the classroom, there needs to be some reconstruction of the linguistic habitus if the students are to be able to participate effectively in classroom interactions. In this sense, the interactions within the classroom can be considered another cultural product that is more familiar and hence accessible to some students and not others. The linguistic habitus of the students will facilitate or hinder a student's capacity to render visible the mathematical content embedded in the pedagogic action. As Collins (1993) argued, "such cues [triadic dialogue] are not necessarily "understood" by all participants, but they are certainly part of the "functional conflict" between dominant and dominated languages in (and out of) educational settings" (p. 131).

In the preceding sections, I have drawn on the work from a number of traditions— theoretical and methodological—and have proposed that the social background of the student will facilitate the construction of a particular linguistic habitus. The field of mathematics, having its own regulatory discourses and discursive practices, will recognize and value some linguistic practices and not others.

THE STUDY

A year-long ethnographic study of two classrooms was undertaken. The two class-rooms were located in socially divergent sites—one an independent school that serves a middle to upper class clientele (Angahook). Parents typically were high-income pro-fessionals. The other classroom was in a state school serving a predominantly working-class clientele (Connewarre) where parents were typically low income, engaged either in manual occupations or in receipt of government welfare. The classrooms were in the second last year of primary school and most students were approximately 10 to 11 years old. Mathematics lessons were videotaped and later transcribed noting the language used and annotated with student actions. The videotapes and transcriptions were supported with classroom observations, field notes, and interviews. The tran-scripts were then analyzed using a variety of discursive analyses. For the purposes of this chapter, the analysis was on the use of triadic dialogue in the introductory phase of the lesson and how the students responded to the practice.

As an ethnographic study, the data used in this chapter seek to demonstrate a commonality that becomes apparent over a sustained period in the field. Over the year, aspects of the lessons would vary, but a consistency in interactional patterns was apparent, and it is these patterns that are the focus of this chapter. The data used for the following analysis could be analyzed from a number of perspectives, but this would deny the repetitiveness that could be observed across the sustained period of observation and videotape data. For example, the teacher at Angahook may be seen to be using a technique in which students are asked to define the term *degrees of difficulty*, whereas the extract from Connewarre is more of a funneling technique in which the students are required to guess the word (prism). These forms of analysis are substantively different in intent from that of this chapter. Rather, what is clear across the sustained research period is that both teachers engage in the patterns of Triadic dialogue, and the transcripts used in this chapter are representing this aspect of teaching rather than other forms of analysis. Although such alternative analyses would be valid, they would represent the immediacy of the two transcripts, rather than seeing the transcripts more holisitically within the context of the prolonged study. As such, the transcripts included in this chapter should be seen to be representative of the year-long study in terms of the means through which teachers introduced concepts rather than isolated events.

Angahook

In the lesson extract presented here, the students were undertaking an activity in the calculation of diving scores at the Olympic Games. Prior to the extract shown, the teacher (Helen) used a number of short mental arithmetic tasks. The following is the introduction to the lesson.

1. T: You are asked to judge the diving for the Olympics, you will need to know the degree of difficulty because what if someone did just a plain dive and did it perfectly and got full marks for it and what if someone else did a triple somersault, back flip, side swinger double pike and knocker banger and only got half marks for it because they entered the water and made a bit of a splash. Is that fair?
2. C: No
3. T: So we have to talk about degrees of difficulty. What do you think that means? What does that actually mean? Robert?
4. Robert: You have to add a bit more to the score because of the degrees of difficulty.
5. T: Good boy. Yes, good. Daniel?
6. Daniel: Well the performance of their dive, how they dive, and well like they might have a very good dive and make a very big splash and may even get off.
7. T: Right, good. OK you are on the right track. What do you want to say about degree of difficulty Cate?
8. Cate: How hard it is?
9. T: How hard it is. Tom what would you like to say about degree of difficulty? That's not a word we use much in our everyday language . . . degree of difficulty.
10. Tom: The percentage of how hard it is.
11. T: Good. Because you're focusing on the word degree though, aren't you? So, a really hard dive. Now you can see on this sheet they're talking about DD, which is short for degree of difficulty and a really hard dive. What would be a really hard dive? What would be the highest number for a degree of difficulty be? Have a look at your sheet. Try and work out the degree of difficulty. Vicky?
12. Vicky: 8.

From this extract it can be seen that the teacher follows the triadic dialogue identified by Lemke and others. The teacher retains control of the content and interactions through the use of the three phases of interactions. Using this approach she is able to control the flow of the lesson as can be seen in the last interaction where Tom has mentioned "percentages," which she then takes as a cue for linking percentage and degree in a way that suits her purposes. She is very focused in what she is seeking from the students and, through the use of the triadic dialogue, is able to control the content of the lesson in a manner congruent to these goals. In this extract from the introductory phase, she is seeking from the students some definition as to the meaning of "degree of difficulty." In the subsequent transcript, she then applies this definition to an example, again using the triadic dialogue to elicit responses as to how the students would use the construct in the worked example. The work phase consisted of the students working through a number of examples on a worksheet. The conclusion employed the triadic dialogue to elicit "correct" responses to the worked examples.

Examining the flow of the interactions indicates that there is a complicit agreement between the teacher and students to participate in the interactions. There are no transgressions or challenges to the teacher's authority. This allows for the content to be covered as the teacher desires.

The teacher is able to maintain control over both the form and content of the lesson and over the students through a mutual compliance with the implicit rules by both the students and the teacher. She has used triadic dialogue to structure the interactions and students infrequently transgress the rules. This allows her to retain the focus of the lesson and, in so doing, the students are exposed to a significant amount of mathematical knowledge that is embedded in that dialogue. In this extract, the students are exposed to the mathematical signifier degrees of difficulty. Similar examples are found in the other mathematics lessons. In this way, the use of the triadic dialogue acts as conduit for the relay of mathematical language and concepts. The complicity of the students in this linguistic exchange enables the teacher to expose the students to this language thereby creating an environment that is potentially rich in mathematical language.

The work of Heath (1982), for example, has shown that middle-class students are more likely to be familiar with these forms of school interactions due to their similarity with the linguistic patterns of the home environment. Similarly, Bernstein's notion of elaborated codes suggests that the linguistic patterns of middle-class families prepare the children for the language used in the schools. The complicity evident here suggests a familiarity with the discursive practice of triadic dialogue.

The methodological approach derived from Bourdieu's work has as its central focus the notion of habitus and field. The field of mathematics education has as one of its central features the specificity of the mathematical discourses so that it is expected that students will be conversant with the language of the field. From this extract, the teacher has an important role in the induction of the students into this discourse. One of her roles is supporting and extending student learning such that they are able to learn or assimilate the appropriate modes of expression. Her leading of students as they come to express what they understand to be degrees of difficulty indicates a process through which students come to learn the accepted forms of language within the field of mathematics education. The way in which she achieves this is through the pedagogical relay, which in this case was triadic dialogue. Students' familiarity and complicity with the implicit rules of interaction allow them to gain access to the concept of degrees of difficulty.

The capacity of the students to participate in this form of interaction is due, in part, to their prior experiences at home and earlier years of schooling. The patterns of interaction they have come to see as part of typical school procedures have become embodied into a habitus—this may be seen to be a middle-class habitus as well as a school habitus. This embodiment of legitimate school interactions offers greater access to legitimate school knowledge such that this habitus can be seen to be an empowering aspect of the repertoire of potential behaviors. To this end, such familiarity can be quite useful in gaining access to knowledge but equally in teachers' interpretations of performance and subsequent positioning within the classroom hierarchy.

Connewarre

Connewarre is a large government school that is located within a large housing commission estate. The clientele of the school is predominantly working class with many of the parents receiving government support. The classrooms are smaller than Angahook with approximately 25 to 30 students in each class. The mathematics curriculum is generally more open and hands-on at this school. The teacher introduces mathematics lessons with problem-solving activities undertaken in small groups. Students are physically involved in the activities, and it is not uncommon for the students to draw on the carpet with chalk to represent the task or physically construct the problem. The following transcript extract is the introduction to a lesson in which the teacher has drawn a net on the board that the students have to draw onto a card and then construct. Students are then required to develop a number of nets for nominated prisms.

1. T: So if I put those together we start talking more about a shape I am talking about. It's sort of a rectangle on the sides, all the way round but you don't call it is a rectangle, because a rectangle is just the flat surface. What do you call the whole thing if that was one whole solid shape. What do you call that?
2. C: A cube.
3. [calling out]
4. T: He said a cube. Don't call out please.
5. C: A rectangular rectangle.
6. T: You're on the right track.
7. C: A 3D rectangle.
8. T: Three dimensions, technically I suppose you're right.
9. C: A rectangular.
10. T: It's a rectangular something. Does anyone know what it is called?
11. C: A parallelogram.
12. T: Put your hand up please.
13. C: [unclear]
14. T: No.
15. [More calling out]
16. T: I guess you could have a rectangular parallelogram, but no. A rectangle is a special parallelogram.
17. C: A rectangular oblong.
18. T: The word we are looking for is prism.
19. C: Yeah that's what I said.
20. T: Say the word, please.

21.   C: Prism.

22.   T: Not like you go to jail "prison;" that's prison. Excuse me, could you return those, please.

23.   [calling out]

24.   T: So one thing that we think about with rectangular prisms and that this shape on here is, excuse me... Now you can leave them down, please. You need a little bit of practice at lunch because you can't stop fiddling. This shape here is drawn out on the graph, this grid here [net for a rectangular prism]. We're going to try and do the same thing. Draw the shape and then cut it out. If you look at the shape, it's made up of rectangles and squares.

In this extract, the triadic dialogue does not function effectively for the teacher to control the class or the content. The challenges to the teacher's authority can be observed throughout the extract, thereby distracting from the flow of content. In Lines 10 and 11 of the extract, it is apparent that a student has violated the more explicit interactional rule of indicating willingness to answer by putting up a hand. In this line the student has violated this rule by calling out, and his response is ignored and his violation of the rule acknowledged. A similar violation occurs in Line 18 where the student calls out that he has said this, but this response is ignored by the teacher. In both cases, the responses made by the students are rendered silent by the teacher's actions.

In this extract, it is apparent that the teacher had as his purpose the need to introduce students to the term "prism." He attempted this through a guided approach after the students did not recall the correct response (Line 1). Using the responses offered by students, he evaluated and extended on their responses, attempting to lead them to the response he desired. Throughout the text, his reliance on triadic dialogue can be observed, although often fragmented by the challenges made by the students. Some of the challenges are at the level of explicit challenges, whereas others are transgressions of the triadic dialogue.

In Line 10 he asks a question as to the name of the solid, yet in spite of earlier responses leading to the name, and with evaluations of responses suggesting that the term *rectangular* is a component of the name, a student suggests (improperly and incorrectly) that the solid is a parallelogram.

By Line 18, it becomes necessary for him to introduce the term himself whereupon he asks the students to repeat the name. This is not an uncommon strategy. In this case, a number of the students say the word "prison" rather than prism. In line with notions of linguistic registers, it is likely that many working-class students would not be exposed to this mathematically signifier in their nonschool contexts so that they misread the word to be prison—a far more common word. The teacher attempts to correct this misreading of the word and reiterates the word with emphasis on the ending of the word so that the students can hear the subtle difference. This example indicates the difference in linguistic registers that may be apparent in working-class schools and the need for teachers to be aware of such differences.

Unlike the interactions at Angahook, the students here are not as complicit in the patterns of triadic dialogue being attempted by the teacher. The reasons for this non-complicity cannot be ascertained from the existing data. The transgressions made by the students could be seen to be resistance to the imposition of a dominant culture as has been noted in the studies of Willis (1977). Alternatively, the noncompliance with the triadic dialogue of classroom interactions may be a result of the students' lack of familiarity with such practices due to the differences in the home-school discursive practices. These differences have been noted by Heath (1982, 1983) and Bernstein (1986). The discursive practice of triadic dialogue is not found within the home practices of working-class families so that the students have not had the opportunity to incorporate this practice into their repertoire of interactional skills. As such, the interactional practices of the home environment have facilitated the construction of a primary habitus that is incongruent with that of the school. In order for students to be complicit in this practice within the school context, they must reconstruct their primary habitus. However, as Lemke (1990) is at pains to recognize, these practices are not explicitly taught, so that working-class students are potentially excluded from this practice unless they can "crack the code" of classroom interactions. In order to be an effective participant in these interactions, working-class students must be able to identify and assimilate such practices into their school habitus.

Where the students have been able to reconstitute their primary habitus and have recognized the implicit rules of classroom interactions but continue to challenge the teacher's authority—as may be the case in this classroom—the outcome is still the same. Effectively such action excludes them from the mathematical content and their positionings are marginal within the dominant practices of school mathematics. However, in this case, there is a suggestion of agency on behalf of the student.

The linguistic habitus of the student implies a propensity to speak in particular ways that, as can be observed in the case of the interactions in this extract, work to exclude students from the mathematical content. The students are not as competent in the linguistic exchanges of the mathematical interactions as their middle-class peers, thereby marginalizing them in the process of learning. The teaching of mathematics in this way tacitly presupposes that the students will have the discursive knowledge and dispositions of particular social groups, namely, the middle class. The students are not as complicit in the classroom practices and in so doing are being excluded from active and full participation in the mathematics of the interactions. In this way, students have been exposed to the symbolic violence of formal education.

CONCLUSION

The data support Voigt's (1985, p. 81) claim that "the hidden regularities, the interaction patterns and routines allow the participants to behave in an orderly fashion without having to keep up visible order." The data, of which the transcripts used here are representative samples, confirmed the use of triadic dialogue in the mathematics classroom. The transcripts from both classrooms confirm a low level of questioning aimed at the students guessing the outcome desired by the teacher. In the instances cited here, these were both focused on guessing a particular word—degree of difficulty and prism. These do not constitute high levels of mathematical reasoning. The use of triadic dialogue in these classrooms confirms Lemke's concerns that the participation encouraged through this strategy appears to involve many students, but it is low in quality. This, in itself, raises questions about the usefulness of this practice in mathematics teaching and learning but is outside the realm of this chapter.

What appears to occur across the classrooms in this study, as represented in these two transcripts, is that the middle-class students comply with and participate in the triadic dialogue. In contrast, the working-class students appear to either resist or fail to recognize the structure of the interactions. In identifying the sociocultural norms of the classrooms, in this case, triadic dialogue, I have sought to identify a way in which some students are able to gain access to mathematical content and processes more readily than others. The compliance of the middle-class students allowed the teacher to progress through the introductory phase more easily and in so doing is able to expose the students to more mathematical content. Compliance with such practices also positions the students more favorably with the patterns of interaction most likely to occur in the secondary school context. Conversely, the noncompliance of the working-class students positions them as marginal and excludes them content while simultaneously failing to prepare them for the interactional patterns most common in the secondary school context. As such, I propose that one subtle and coercive way that some students are advantaged and others excluded in and through the practices of mathematics is through the dis/continuities between the linguistic habitus of the students and the practices of classroom interactions. Some students enter the formal mathematics classrooms with a habitus that is akin to that which is valorized within that context. These students will be able to participate more effectively and efficiently than their peers for whom the patterns of interaction are foreign to their habitus. The practice of triadic dialogue becomes a form of symbolic violence for those students whose linguistic habitus is different from that valorized within the school context. It is symbolic in that most educators are not aware of the subtle differences in patterns of language use between the home and school contexts for working-class students.

The modes of expression within classrooms are rarely explicitly taught, yet it is expected that students should participate and comply within such practices. As I have shown in this chapter, triadic dialogue is one such mode of interaction. Mathematics is embedded within these interactions, and students need to be able to crack the code of the unspoken rules of classroom interaction in order that they gain access to the mathematics. In contrast to models that suggest that violations of cultural norms within a classroom may be due to a deficit in understanding how language works as a medium for conversation, there is a need to recognize that such patterns of interaction are an integral component of school and classroom cultures. Accordingly, classroom interactional styles may be socially biased and as a consequence exclude or embrace students, depending on the interactional styles that they may bring to the classroom. "Pedagogies that tacitly select the privileged and exclude the underprepared are not regrettable lapses; they are systemic aspects of schooling systems serving class-divided societies" (Collins, 1993, p. 121).

Triadic dialogue may be implicated in the stratification of student outcomes. As a component of the culture of mathematics classrooms, and for that matter most classrooms, triadic dialogue as a practice facilitates or hinders effective participation in classroom interactions.

Quite clearly, the patterns of interaction that have been the focus of this chapter are dominant in mathematics classrooms. What is less well known are other patterns of interactions that may be found in classrooms and are influential in hindering or supporting learning of mathematics. Further studies are needed to identify and document patterns of interactions within homes and schools. These will be useful in developing a greater understanding and awareness of how schools and mathematics are implicated in the construction of advantage and disadvantage in mathematics education.

For students whose habitus is dissimilar to that valorized within the context of the classroom, in this case the working-class students, changes need to be made in order that such students can gain access to the mathematical content more readily. In most cases, such changes would be seen to be the reconstitution of the habitus whereby the students would need to learn the new codes of the classroom interactions in order to be able to participate effectively. However, it could be argued that, as educators become aware of the cultural norms of classroom practice that effectively exclude some students, it could well be the classroom practice that needs to be reconstituted. Such change may involve a radical reconstruction of classroom practice, or more simply, the making explicit of such cultural norms—in this case, triadic dialogue.

Habitus becomes a form of capital that can be exchanged for academic success within this context. The linguistic habitus of the middle-class students predisposes them to act in ways congruous with the goals of the teacher so that their possession of knowledge of what constitutes "appropriate" classroom linguistic exchanges is similar to that which the system values. This allows them to participate in effective classroom practice. Alternatively, the linguistic habitus facilitates the appropriation of what the system offers. The dispositions, as per the linguistic habitus, of each of the classes has facilitated or hindered their acquisition of mathematics. The linguistic habitus is differentially valued within the mathematics classroom. The linguistic code with which students are familiar and use within the classroom becomes a form of capital that can be exchanged for other culturally recognized goods—in this case, grades and the subsequent academic success conveyed to the individual. "The more distant the social group from scholastic language, the higher the rate of scholastic mortality" (Bourdieu, Passeron, & de saint Martin, 1994b, p. 41).

REFERENCES

Bernstein, B. (1986). On pedagogic discourse. In J. Richardson (Ed). *Handbook of theory and research in sociology of education*. Weston, CT: Greenwood Press.

Bourdieu, P. (1979). *Distinction: A social critique of the judgement of taste*. Cambridge, MA: Harvard University Press.

Bourdieu, P., Passeron, J. C., & de saint Martin, M. (1994a). *Academic discourse: Linguistic misunderstanding and professorial power* (R. Teese, trans.). Stanford: Stanford University Press.

Bourdieu, P., Passeron, J. C., & de saint Martin, M. (1994b). Students and the language of teaching. In P. Bourdieu, J. C. Passeron, & M. de saint Martin (Eds.), *Academic discourse: Linguistic misunderstanding and professorial power* (pp. 35–79). Stanford: Stanford University Press.

Bourdieu, P., & Wacquant, L. (1992). *Responses*. Paris: Seuil.

Bourdieu, P., & Wacquant, L. J. D. (1992). *An invitation to reflexive sociology*. Cambridge: Polity.

Collins, J. (1993). Determination and contradiction: An appreciation and critique of the work of Pierre Bourdieu on language and education. In C. Calhoun, E. LiPuma, & M. Postone (Eds.), Bourdieu: *Critical perspectives* (pp. 116–138). Cambridge, UK: Polity Press.

Edwards, D., & Mercer, N. (1987). *Common knowledge*. London: Routledge.

Greenfell, M. (1998). Language and the classroom. In M. Greenfell & D. James (Eds.), *Bourdieu and education: Acts of practical theory* (pp. 72–88). London: Falmer Press.

Harker, R. K. (1984). On reproduction, habitus and education. *British Journal of Sociology of Education, 5*(2), 117–127.

Heath, S. B. (1982). Questioning at home and at school: A comparative study. In G. D. Spindler (Ed.), *Doing the ethnography of schooling*. New York: Holt, Rinehart & Winston.

Heath, S., Brice. (1983). *Ways with words: Language, life and work in communities and classrooms*. Cambridge: University of Cambridge.

Jenkins, R. (1982). Pierre Bourdieu and the reproduction of determinism. *Sociology, 16*(2), 270–281.

Lemke, J. L. (1990). *Talking science: Language, learning and values*. Norwood: Ablex.

Mehan, H. (1982). The structure of classroom events and their consequences for student performance. In P. Gilmore & A. A. Glatthorn (Eds.), *Children in and out of school: Ethnography and education* (pp. 59–87). Washington, DC: Center for Applied Linguistics.

Schultz, J. J., Florio, S., & Erickson, F. (1982). Where's the floor? Aspects of the cultural organisation of social relationships in communication at home and in school. In P. Gilmore & A. A. Glatthorn (Eds.), *Children in and out of school: Ethnography and education* (pp. 88–123). Washington, DC: Center for Applied Linguistics.

Sinclair, J., & Couthourd, M. (1975) *Towards an analysis of discourse*. Oxford: Blackwell.

Voigt, J. (1985). Patterns and routines in classroom interaction. *Researches en Didactique de Mathematiques, 6*(1), 69–118.

Wacquant, L. D. (1989). Towards a reflexive sociology: A workshop with Pierre Bourdieu. *Sociological Theory, 7*.

Willis, P. (1977). *Learning to labour*. London: Kogan Paul.

13

Longitudinal Evaluation of Mathematics Participation in American Middle and High Schools

Xin Ma

University of Alberta

Mathematics is often called the "critical filter" (Sells, 1973). Participation in mathematics courses has been an educational concern for several decades in the United States. In the 1970s, Sells (1973) reported that 9 out of 10 first-year female students entering the University of California at Berkeley had such inadequate mathematics preparation that they would eventually be ineligible for 70% of the career choices available to them. In the 1980s, concerns were expressed in the national report, *A Nation at Risk*, about the large number of students who dropped out of mathematics courses, especially elective courses (National Commission on Excellence in Education, 1983). In the 1990s, concerns about mathematics preparation continued (Betz, 1992). For example, student underrepresentation in advanced mathematics courses such as trigonometry, analytic geometry, and calculus has been particularly worrisome (National Center for Education Statistics, 1993).

Participation in mathematics courses is now a serious public concern in the United States because it bears social and individual consequences. Socially, a technologically advanced society demands a mathematically literate workforce (National Council of Teachers of Mathematics [NCTM], 1989), yet a large number of high school students drop out of the study of mathematics (National Commission on Excellence in Education, 1983). Some warning signs have already emerged. The Third International Mathematics and Science Study (TIMSS) found that American eighth graders achieved below the international average in mathematics (Beaton et al., 1996). Many educators think that the poor performance of American students is due mainly to a lack of exposure to mathematics. The Second International Mathematics and Science Study (SIMSS) did find that the coverage of the tested topics in American schools was at or below the international average in most content areas (McKnight et al., 1987).

Individually, inadequate preparation in mathematics seriously limits future educational and occupational opportunities of individuals. Careers that were comfortably free of mathematics in the past now heavily depend on mathematics (NCTM, 1991). In the 1970s and 1980s, there was a decrease in employment in low-technology, low-wage industries across all countries in the Organization for Economic Co-operation and Development (OECD, 1994). The occupational projections are clearly for a weaker demand for low-skilled workers and an increased demand for moderately skilled technical and administrative workers and highly skilled professionals (OECD, 1995). The new jobs, many of which will be in the high-technology sector, will require an understanding of computerized data analyses, sophisticated mathematical models, or elaborate accounting systems (NCTM, 1991).

Traditionally, researchers have focused on demographic, psychological, and sociological factors that explain the performance of students in mathematics (see Leder, 1992; McLeod, 1992; Secada, 1992). In contrast, student participation in mathematics has not been extensively studied. Lee and Bryk (1988) pointed out that "there was little empirical scrutiny of even basic questions, such as who takes what kinds of courses and the subsequent consequences of students' course of study on their academic achievement and future educational and work opportunities" (p. 78). Until recently, longitudinal data and appropriate statistical methods have not been available to estimate comprehensive models of mathematics participation. With cross-sectional data, it is not possible to ask questions about when and why students cease taking mathematics courses (see Willett & Singer, 1991). Consequently, most previous research has been limited to descriptive analyses that portray the demographic characteristics of students who drop out of mathematics at a particular time.

THEORIES RELEVANT
TO MATHEMATICS PARTICIPATION

The issue of mathematics participation has been discussed from three different perspectives: sociological, psychological, and gender. Although each perspective has its different theoretical emphases, these perspectives are related to one another; and they interact to affect students' decision on mathematics participation.

Sociological Perspective

Sociologists have placed a great emphasis on the effects of family background on educational attainment. Several sociological theories, for example, "economic deprivation" and "status attainment," indicate that the effects come directly through the types of environments and experiences provided for children during their formative years. The Wisconsin model of social stratification shows that the effects also come indirectly through selection into different types of schools and school programs (Gamoran, 1992; Kerckhoff, 1993). All these theories suggest a useful indicator of achievement and participation: socioeconomic status (SES). Specifically, students from disadvantaged socioeconomic background are more likely to drop out of academic programs, particularly mathematics and science (Hoffer, 1997; Hoffer, Rasinski, & Moore, 1995; Teese, 1994).

Psychological Perspective

Bandura's (1977) social cognitive theory states that people evaluate whether they are able to perform certain behaviors that will bring about a desired outcome. The belief that they can perform certain behaviors is a powerful predictor of a person's course of action, in many cases more powerful than a person's knowledge, skills, or prior attainment (Pajares, 1996). The theory of "learned helplessness" (Seligman, 1975) is consistent with social learning theory. With respect to student participation in mathematics, it would maintain that repeated frustration in the learning of mathematics creates and strengthens a perception of being helpless when working with numbers and shapes. This learned perception causes students to drop out of mathematics as a way to avoid further unpleasant experiences (Blum-Anderson, 1992). Atkinson's (1964) expectancy value theory emphasizes not only the expectation of success on a task but also the subjective value that an individual ascribes to the task. Under this theory, students will persist on a "task" such as solving a mathematical problem or, in the longer term, continuing to take mathematics courses, if they expect they will be successful and if they value the endeavor (Eccles, 1994; Meyer & Koehler, 1990). All of these theories are consistent with the notion that some students develop "mathematics anxiety" associated with a fear of failure.

Other theorists, in attempting to explain why the mathematics achievement of many females is inconsistent with their overall ability, suggest that some students, particularly females, fear success rather than failure (Horner, 1968). The argument is that many females feel that if they achieve good grades they will be less popular with their peers and that this is particularly true for mathematics and science, which have been stereotyped as a masculine domain. Females who fear success resolve their conflict by opting out of intensive study in mathematics or by lowering their performance in mathematics and thus are not conspicuously successful (Leder, 1992). Therefore, peer influence, as a type of external motivation, can be an important factor when students make their decisions on academic work. Overall, both failure- and success-oriented theories call attention to one principal factor: students' attitude toward mathematics. Research on attitudes has emphasized three constructs: whether students like mathematics, whether they perceive it to be useful in their future and everyday life, and whether they are confident in their ability to learn mathematics.

Gender Perspective

Research is relatively consistent that male students participate more in mathematics than their female counterparts. Researchers offered various theoretical reasons to explain gender differences in mathematics participation (see Leder, 1992). These reasons can be summarized as (a) psychological problems of female students related to mathematics such as negative attitude, low confidence, and high anxiety; (b) educational practices in school and at home such as the differential treatment of male and female students by teachers in mathematics classrooms and the differential emphasis of parents on mathematics education between male and female children; and (c) social inequalities between men and women such as social image, social stereotypes, and career discrimination. The emphasis is on various social and cultural influences that students are subject to when they make decision about their mathematics participation, as stated in the national report in the United States, *Everybody Counts* (National Research Council, 1989), that gender differences in mathematics achievement and participation are predominantly a result of accumulated effects of gender-role stereotypes at home, in school, and in society.

All of the previous theories from the three perspectives are important and informative in the examination of mathematics participation. These theories, however, are usually disconnected, being "area specific." They do not offer an overall understanding of mathematics participation. New theoretical frameworks need to be developed to accommodate the complex, interactive process of students' decision making on mathematics participation. Nevertheless, theories discussed previously provided some useful hints and directions for the recent effort in modeling mathematics participation.

CONCEPTUAL FRAMEWORK OF MATHEMATICS PARTICIPATION

Recent studies modeling mathematics participation have two distinct characteristics. First, these studies have taken the advantage of nationally representative, longitudinal data from such important databases as the High School and Beyond (HS&B; National Center for Education Statistics, 1995), the Longitudinal Study of American Youth (LSAY; Miller & Hoffer, 1994), and the National Education Longitudinal Study (NELS; National Center for Education Statistics, 1996). Recent studies have also taken the advantage of the latest statistical techniques such as survival analysis (Yamaguchi, 1991) and multilevel analysis (Bryk & Raudenbush, 1992). Survival analysis refers to a comprehensive set of statistical models often used in medical research to describe the mortality experience of a population and to determine when and why people acquire or die from a certain disease. In the last 10 years, researchers have developed multilevel statistical models that can simultaneously estimate the effects of individual and school-level variables.

These models see individual students' decision making about mathematics participation in a dialectical relationship within a sociocultural environment as they make their decision in light of interactions with others (peers, teachers, and parents) and as they act upon their social context in ways that can reinforce their decision about mathematics participation. Departing from this theoretical framework, most models show how students' decision about participation is influenced by their sociopsychological characteristics and how students' decision is modified through sociocultural characteristics of their families and schools. Simply put, these models view mathematics participation as a "reasoned decision-making" (see Crawley & Coe, 1990) in a social environment.

At the student level, recent models estimate the likelihood that students drop out of mathematics and identify salient determinants that influence the likelihood. These models attempt to capture the influence of families as one source of adjustment over likelihood estimates. These models also hold that students examine themselves to evaluate whether their further effort in mathematics can bring them favorable results. In this regard, these student-level models overlap with Bandura's (1977) social cognitive theory. These models essentially assume that student decision in mathematics participation is made based on four categories of individual characteristics: demographic, cognitive, affective, and motivative characteristics. These categories are consistent with those theories discussed in the previous section.

At the school level, the models portray the social environment of a school in which students make decision about mathematics participation from two perspectives: the contextual characteristics of a school and the climate characteristics of the school. School context describes the physical and material characteristics of a school, such as school size and student–teacher ratio, as well as the characteristics of students and staff, such as school intake of students (often measured through school average SES) and the proportion of minority students. School climate portrays the culture and internal workings of school life, such as how students are organized for instructional purposes, the rules that govern the operation of a school, the nature of interaction among administrators, teachers, students, and parents, as well as the values, attitudes, and expectations they hold for various aspects of school life. In general, characteristics depicting school climate are categorized into several major constructs: principle leadership, disciplinary climate, academic press (academic expectation on students held by teachers and administrators), teacher autonomy, teacher moral and commitment, and parental involvement (see Willms, 1992). From a longitudinal perspective, the school-level models show the changing effects of those school contextual variables and school climate variables on mathematics participation and illustrate how school characteristics interact with student characteristics in a complex way that channels students into different course-taking patterns in mathematics.

In sum, the advantage of these recent models is that they have created a sociocultural environment in which various theories (as discussed in the previous section) show how they interact to influence student decision on mathematics participation (and how the sociocultural environment constrains or facilitates these interactive effects). Such a theoretical approach is appropriate if one considers mathematics participation as a complex decision-making subject to many factors (e.g., sociological and psychological factors) that tangle together in an interactive way. Therefore, the recent models do not intend to nullify previous theories but to connect them and explore how they interactively affect student decision on mathematics participation.

INDIVIDUAL AND SCHOOL EFFECTS ON MATHEMATICS PARTICIPATION

A brief description of educational data used in the recent models assessing mathematics participation is presented in Ma (1997). The information includes characteristics of samples, measures of variables, and definitions of specific terms (e.g., prior mathematics achievement). Using data from the LSAY, Ma (1997) developed a comprehensive,

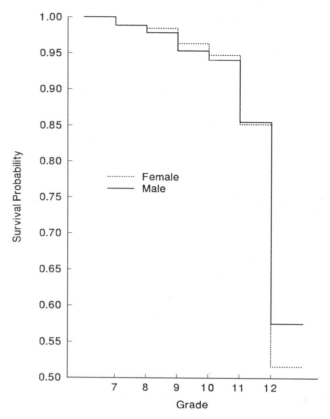

FIG. 13.1. The survival function of participation in advanced mathematics (sample survival probability vs. grade level), by gender. Adapted from *A National Assessment of Mathematics Participation in the United States: A Survival Analysis Model for Describing Students' Academic Careers*, by X. Ma, 1997, Lewiston, NY: Edwin Mellen.

longitudinal survival model of mathematics participation (across Grades 7–12). He reported that students were most likely to drop out of mathematics in the last two grades of high school (see Fig. 13.1). Models have been developed to explain the participation figures. The following section summarizes some of the most important findings from those models. Subsections are used to help connect various factors.

Individual Effects on Mathematics Participation

Effects of Demographic Factors. Gender, SES, and race-ethnicity are the commonly used demographic factors in the examination of mathematics participation. Using participation rates as the measure of mathematics participation, Ma (1997) reported that gender differences in mathematics participation appeared mainly in Grade 12 in favor of male students, and gender differences were similar across different levels of SES. This finding, to some extent, is positive news in that the gender gap, although it is undesirable, was not worse among, for example, low SES students. Ma (1997) also showed that SES played a role in the early grades of high school, and socioeconomic differences were similar across different levels of mathematics achievement or attitude toward mathematics. This is an important indication of the widespread socioeconomic influence that has penetrated various levels of achievement and attitude. Socioeconomic inequality as reflected in mathematics participation is a concern in the early grades of high school.

Davenport et al. (1998) investigated ethnic differences in mathematics participation. Using Carnegie units as the measure of mathematics participation, they found that Asians participated more in mathematics than other ethnic groups (Blacks, Hispanics, and Whites) that were not significantly different in mathematics participation. More important, Davenport et al. (1998) showed that Blacks and Hispanics participated more in the Functional Sequence (major components are Resource General, Vocational, and Consumer Mathematics) and the Preformal Sequence (major components are General and Consumer Mathematics, Pre-Algebra, and Informal Geometry), whereas Whites and Asians participated more in the Standard Sequence (major components are Algebra 1 and 2, and Geometry) and the Advanced Sequence (major components are Algebra 3, Trigonometry, Analytic Geometry, Solid Geometry, Analysis, and Calculus). At the level of Advanced Sequence, Asians participated twice as much as Whites in mathematics. This widespread of ethnic differences in mathematics participation has been large and consistent over time (see Davenport et al., 1998).

Effects of Cognitive and Affective Factors.   Ma (1997) examined the effects of prior measures of mathematics achievement, attitude toward mathematics, mathematics anxiety, and self-concept on mathematics participation in the following year. A prior measure refers to the measure obtained one grade level before the time of interest. For example, when examining mathematics participation in Grade 10, mathematics achievement in Grade 9 is considered prior mathematics achievement. He found that prior mathematics achievement was the only variable significant across all grade levels, but the influence of prior mathematics achievement decreased consistently over time. This suggests that, although it was consistently an important part of students' decision on mathematics participation, students based less and less on their mathematics achievement to make their decision.

Ma (1997) also reported that prior attitude toward mathematics became important in the later grades of high school, and the influence of prior attitude increased over time. This answers the question one may be wondering—what then is more important in the later grades of high school if prior mathematics achievement had less and less influence on mathematics participation? Therefore, students stopped taking mathematics courses in the later grades of high school not due to a lack of ability but due to their negative attitude toward mathematics. Finally, prior mathematics anxiety and prior self-concept did not show notable influences on mathematics participation across grade levels. This suggests that attitude was the most important determinant of mathematics participation among affective characteristics of students.

Effects of Motivative Factors.   In another survival analysis, Ma (1998) included motivative factors in addition to prior mathematics achievement, prior attitude toward mathematics, and student background characteristics. With participation rates as the measure of mathematics participation, he found that students with stronger prior internal motivation participated more in mathematics. Prior external motivation as measured through peer motivation and teacher motivation did not have remarkable influences on student decision. More important, the influence of internal motivation was largely independent of peer and teacher motivation. These findings imply that students' decision on mathematics participation was based on their own motivation or aspiration, and their decision was not influenced by significant others (peers and teachers) in school.

Students' decision on mathematics participation was substantially influenced by significant others at home, however. The influence of parent-related motivation (another type of external motivation) turned out to be the strongest external motivation, and parent-related motivation partly replaced the influence of internal motivation. This illustrates the important role of parents in mathematics participation. Still, prior mathematics achievement and prior attitude toward mathematics were the most important factors. The influence of internal motivation declined after achievement and attitude were controlled. Achievement and attitude also replaced substantially the influence of parent-related motivation. These findings together demonstrate a complex process of decision making—students' internal motivation on mathematics participation was modified by their parents at home, and, in the process, this "modified" motivation was also checked by students against their mathematics achievement and judged by them against their attitude toward mathematics. Students' final action was a result of this complex process of decision making.

School Effects on Mathematics Participation

Education systems are highly hierarchical—students are nested within classes; classes are nested within schools; schools are nested within districts. Any decision or action at one level is affected by schooling processes at other levels. The student-level results make more sense when they are situated into the education system. In the case of mathematics participation, school differences in policies and practices have to be considered. In other words, that students are nested within schools has to be taken into account in any data analysis of mathematics participation (see Bryk & Raudenbush, 1992). This is where the multilevel perspective of data analysis comes into play.

Ma and Willms (in press) developed a multilevel survival model to examine how the likelihood that students drop out of mathematics is influenced simultaneously and longitudinally by both student-level and school-level characteristics. A multilevel survival model enabled them to examine the characteristics that affect participation rates from one grade to another, to determine the extent to which participation rates vary from school to school, and discover whether any variation in participation rates among schools is attributable to school contextual and climate characteristics. The student-level model is essentially the same as in Ma (1997). At the school level, they included seven variables describing school climate: principal leadership, academic press, disciplinary climate, teacher autonomy, teacher commitment, material resources for mathematics, and general support for mathematics. They also used four school contextual variables: percentage of Black students, percentage of Hispanic students, percentage of parents visiting the school, and school average SES.

Effects of Contextual Factors. Ma and Willms (in press) reported that schools varied significantly in participation rates at each grade level from 8 to 12, but the variation was relatively small at both the beginning and the end of high school. In most schools, the participation rates of female students were equal to, or higher than, those of male students before Grade 12. It was only in the final grade of high school when a disproportionate number of female students dropped out of advanced mathematics. School participation rates did not vary substantially with the percentage of minority students in a school. Neither were they related with the percentage of parents visiting a school. There was a positive contextual effect associated with school mean SES that was substantial in Grade 9, smaller in Grades 10 and 11, and negligible in Grade 12. Students, therefore, were more likely to participate in advanced mathematics if they attended a high SES school than a low SES school, particularly in the early grades of high school.

Effects of Climate Factors. Generally, the results in Ma and Willms (in press) did not show strong effects associated with school climate. Most of the seven climate variables were not influential at any grade level. In Grade 11, however, just before the sharp drop in participation rates in Grade 12, there were important effects associated with teacher commitment and general support for mathematics. These effects diminished the influence associated with school average SES, indicating that the influence of school average SES was just a reflection of the differences among schools in teacher commitment and general support for mathematics. Ma and Willms (in press) concluded that schools with stronger teacher commitment and more general support for mathematics were better prepared for the critical transition from Grade 11 to Grade 12, having maintained more students in mathematics than other schools. Note that other school effects are not as strong as researchers may expect. Ma and Willms (in press) partially attributed this to the inadequate measures of school climate variables in the LSAY on which they based their analysis.

In another multilevel survival analysis, Ma (in press) examined the effects of different types of parental involvement on participation in advanced mathematics from Grade 8 to Grade 12. He used longitudinal data on four components of parental involvement at the school level: home discussion (on children's social and academic life), home expectation or supervision (on time to be home, how late to stay up, household duties, TV time, and TV shows), home–school communication (on students' school work), and volunteer work for school (or school participation). Similar to Ma and Willms (in press), results of multilevel survival analysis showed that schools varied significantly in participation rates at each grade level from 8 to 12.

As to parental involvement, Ma (in press) found that volunteer work for school was the most important school-level variable in the early grades of high school (Grades 8 to 10). The influence of parents' volunteer work for school was strong, and it remained similar in strength across the three grades. Home discussion was critical in the middle grades of high school (Grades 10 and 11). The influence of home discussion was strong, and it remained almost constant in the two grades. Home-school communication had a temporary, though strong, effect in Grade 9. The influence of home expectation was unimportant across all grades. Among the four components of parental involvement, parents' volunteer work for school turned out to have the strongest effects on mathematics participation. Ma (in press) argued that children perceive education as important and are more motivated to do well in school when they see their parents actively get involved in their education.

If considering the previous results with those from Ma (1998) together, one concludes that parents play an important role in their children's mathematics participation. Parents' role is significant not only at the student level but also at the school level. At the student level, parents encourage children's mathematics participation through external motivation (see Ma, 1998); at the school level, parents promote children's mathematics participation through active involvement with schools (see Ma, in press).

MORE ON SCHOOL EFFECTS

Given the societal emphasis on educational accountability and the shift of politicians and parents toward being more prescriptive of educational goals, the issue of school effects deserves some further discussion, particularly in terms of mathematics participation because school policies and practices, such as curricular tracking and instructional grouping, directly shape the path of student experience in mathematics. Similar to the previous section, school effects are discussed in terms of climate and context.

The early research in school effectiveness by Coleman et al. (1966) and Jencks et al. (1972) suggested that variables that could be manipulated by school policies, such as per-student expenditures and the nature of the curriculum, had very small effects when compared with the effects of family background. It led to the pessimistic conclusion that "schools don't make a difference" and provoked three decades of research on "school effects" based on the input–process–output approach (Willms & Raudenbush, 1994). Researchers developed more sophisticated models (Raudenbush & Willms, 1995), used more sensitive outcome measures (e.g., Raudenbush & Willms, 1991), and examined detailed aspects of classroom practice and school climate (e.g., Bryk, Lee, & Smith, 1990).

There is now widespread agreement that schools provide some "added value." For example, students show better schooling outcomes (e.g., achievement, attitude, participation) in schools where principals effectively "buffer the technical core" (minimize the extraneous and disruptive effects that keep teachers from teaching and students from learning; Blase & Roberts, 1994), where staff have high expectations for student performance (Rosenholtz, 1989), where teachers structure their lessons to minimize classroom disruptions and maximize time spent in teaching (Ma & Willms, 1995), where there is a high level of parental involvement (Ho & Willms, 1996), where reforms give teachers greater autonomy (Darlinghammond, 1996), where teachers actively commit themselves to their work (Rosenholtz, 1989), where liberal policies of curriculum access are practiced (Lamb, 1996), where a narrow curriculum composed mostly of academic courses (a constraint curriculum) is offered (Lee, Croninger, & Smith, 1997), where early access to advanced mathematics courses is encouraged (Smith, 1996), and where parents place importance on mathematics for their children's future (Olszewski-Kubilius & Yasumoto, 1995). Certain structural features of a school, for example, the levels of material resources, also affect student outcomes (Bryk, Lee, & Holland, 1993; Lee & Smith, 1993).

Another important aspect of the research on school effectiveness is the contextual effects: the average ability or social-class background of a school has an effect on students' academic outcomes over and above the effects of students' individual abilities or social class backgrounds. A related issue that has generated considerable concerns is the enlarged contextual effects under the condition of segregation, that is, when students are segregated, those from advantaged backgrounds do better, whereas those from disadvantaged backgrounds do worse, no matter if the segregation is between ability groups within classes (Slavin, 1987; Willms & Chen, 1989), between classes or curriculum tracks within schools (Gamoran, 1991, 1992; Kerckhoff, 1993), or between schools within communities (Rumberger & Willms, 1992; Willms & Echols, 1992). There may be some informal selection mechanisms that contribute to the contextual effects. For example, mathematics teachers often love and encourage students whom they perceive to have strong abilities in mathematics (Gill & Gaffney, 1996; Jones & Smart, 1995). If these students gather together because of segregation, this practice of teachers contributes substantially to the contextual effects of school.

Recent longitudinal studies modeling mathematics participation support the value-added theory of school effects from the perspective of mathematics participation (as the outcome of schooling). Ma (in press) and Ma and Willms (in press) did find that schools varied considerably in mathematics participation at every grade level from 8 to 12. Some schools were better prepared to maintain more students in the "mathematics pipeline" than other schools (Ma & Willms, in press). Among school climate factors, Ma (in press) emphasized that students in schools with stronger parental involvement were more likely to participate in mathematics than students in schools with weaker parental involvement. Recent longitudinal studies modeling mathematics participation also support, from the perspective of mathematics participation, the contextual effects associated with segregation—a student was more likely to drop out of mathematics if he or she attended a school with low average SES than a school with high average SES (Ma & Willms, in press).

However, recent longitudinal studies on mathematics participation have not shown a "harvest" of school effects as substantial as many researchers may expect. Ma and Willms (in press) argue that the longitudinal models of mathematics participation are sensitive to school effects but the measures of school climate may not be. The recent longitudinal models utilize data from large-scale (national) longitudinal assessments. These national surveys measure a comprehensive set of student and school characteristics using questionnaires and interviews with limited space and limited time. Therefore, scales used to measure school climate are sometimes too simple to be sensitive to school effects. There is a need to conduct longitudinal survey studies, particularly on mathematics participation, that measure various aspects of school life in detail.

IMPLICATIONS TO EDUCATIONAL PRACTICE
AND FURTHER RESEARCH

Policy Implications

It is commonly recommended that all students take 3 years of mathematics in high school regardless of ability levels (National Commission on Excellence in Education, 1983; NCTM, 1989; National Science Board, 1983), with an additional year of mathematics for college-bound students (NCTM, 1989). Ma (1997) demonstrated that the vast majority of students in the United States may have already met these recommended standards in mathematics because the sharp drop in participation rates happened in Grade 12.

Considering (a) completion of 4 years of high school mathematics is commonly regarded as a prerequisite for many college mathematics, science, and statistics courses and (b) performance and participation in mathematics at the college level are directly related to mathematics performance and participation at the high school level (Deboer, 1984; Marion & Coladarci, 1993; Payne, 1992), Ma (1997) suggested that "there should be different levels of compulsory mathematics courses until, at least, the 11th grade" (p. 134). He argued that "raising the mathematics requirement for graduation may not necessarily create cognitive difficulties for the majority of students" (p. 134) because he found, as discussed earlier, that affective, rather than cognitive, problems of students contribute to mathematics dropout in the later grades—students do not drop out of mathematics because they lack the cognitive abilities required for further mathematics courses but because they do not desire to take further mathematics courses.

The findings from recent longitudinal studies modeling mathematics participation have an especially important message for female students. Some researchers on gender differences in mathematics suggest that female students "leak" out of mathematics, which implies that it is a gradual process that occurs during the entire high school career. This is not the case in, for example, Ma and Willms (in press). As a matter of fact, achievement scores and participation rates in advanced mathematics for female students were at least equal to if not better than those of male students up to the end of Grade 11. It is only in the last grade of high school that a disproportionate number of female students did not participate in advanced mathematics.

The previous finding has implications for undergraduate education. First-year calculus is a required course for many majors such as business, science, and computing programs, and many universities are developing programs to help students overcome this hurdle. Ma and Willms (in press) suggested, however, that much of the filtering occurs before students reach first-year calculus. Schools, colleges, universities, and society at large may have to work together to educate high school students, especially female students, about the ramifications of their decision on mathematics participation so that they do not prematurely close doors on too many post-secondary programs.

Regarding the motivative factors in mathematics participation, Ma (1998) recommended four measures to improve mathematics participation: (a) promoting stronger internal motivation, (b) having programs that aim to improve mathematics achievement and attitude toward mathematics, (c) combining peer and teacher motivation with programs improving achievement and attitude, and (d) setting a higher level of parental involvement. Ma (1998) argued that schools should encourage students to appreciate personal efforts in making a prosperous future and help students set higher future expectations. Schools should also monitor the cognitive and affective progress of students regularly and intervene effectively at the early signs of problems in achievement and attitude.

One of the most important implications in Ma (1998) is that peer and teacher motivation have to be combined with cognitive and affective efforts that improve students' mathematics achievement and attitude toward mathematics. It is far from enough for teachers to motivate students academically. More important, teachers need to make ways for students to achieve the academic expectations they hold for them. That requires teachers' attention to and assistance for the cognitive and affective problems of students. It is undeniable that academic press is important (e.g., Oakes, 1989; Rosenholtz, 1989). To be more effective, schools must also have programs that help students with their cognitive and affective difficulties.

Ma (1998, in press) emphasized the significant role of parents in mathematics participation. This adds to so much evidence that effective parental involvement improves students' academic and affective outcomes (e.g., Astone & McLanahan, 1991; Ho & Willms, 1996; Muller, 1993). Schools must help parents realize the importance of mathematics in students' academic careers and the importance of internal and external motivation in promoting mathematics participation. Educators should encourage parents to set higher educational and occupational expectations for their children and give parents opportunities to interact with students in various school and home programs.

Furthermore, as discussed earlier, Ma (in press) argued that children perceive education as important when they see their parents actively get involved in their education. Children who internalize this importance of education are motivated to do more and better in school. Therefore, schools must promote parents' involvement in various school activities, particularly in the early grades of high school. Home discussion affects mathematics participation in the later grades of high school. Schools must encourage parents to spend more time with their children discussing various important matters such as future educational and occupational plans and current academic efforts that facilitate those plans. Society at large must also educate parents that schools alone are not enough to create a prosperous future for their children.

Further Research

Recent longitudinal studies on mathematics participation are influenced by the input-process-output model widely used in the research on school effectiveness (see Willms, 1992). So far, these studies did unfold some of the important effects associated with students and schools. A successful model based on the conceptual framework of mathematics participation (as discussed earlier) calls for comprehensive, detailed measures of schooling inputs (e.g., student intake), processes (e.g., school climate), and outputs (e.g., mathematics participation). Recent national education surveys have not met this requirement due mainly to the space limitation in survey questionnaires. It is certainly understandable because these national education surveys are not designed exclusively for an investigation of mathematics participation.

A consequence is the failure of the recent longitudinal studies modeling mathematics participation to include curricular variables at the school level, such as characteristics of mathematics curriculum and mathematics requirements for further studies. For example, one may consider school requirements on mathematics an important part of student decision on mathematics participation. The failure to include curricular variables is a direct result of the inadequate measure of those variables in national education surveys. There is a need for survey studies aimed at mathematics participation that measure schooling inputs, processes, and outputs in efficient details.

One of the major weaknesses of the recent longitudinal models is that they tend to focus solely on whether students continue or drop out of mathematics. In doing so, another important aspect of mathematics participation has been ignored—the coursework patterns in mathematics. Recent longitudinal models detect that some students stay longer than others in the mathematics pipeline but reveal little on the different behaviors or patterns of students in mathematics participation. Coursework patterns are important because different coursework patterns lead to different educational and occupational destinies. Further research may need a shift from "whether participate" to "participate in what." The conceptual framework of mathematics participation presented in this chapter still fits well into this new effort because students make all their decisions on mathematics participation (either it is whether to continue mathematics or what courses to enroll) in a social environment of their homes and schools.

REFERENCES

Astone, N. M., & McLanahan, S. S. (1991). Family structure, parental practices and high school completion. *American Sociological Review, 56*, 309–320.

Atkinson, J. W. (1964). *An introduction to motivation*. Princeton, NJ: Van Nostrand.

Bandura, A. (1977). Self-efficacy: Toward a unifying theory of behavioral change. *Psychological Review, 84*, 191–215.

Beaton, A. E., Mullis, I. V. S., Martin, M. O., Gonzalez, E. J., Kelly, D. L., & Smith, T. A. (1996). *Mathematics achievement in the middle school years: IEA's third international Mathematics and Science Study (TIMSS)*. Chestnut Hill, MA: Boston College.

Betz, N. E. (1992). Career assessment: A review of critical issues. In S. D. Brown & R. W. Lent (Eds.), *Handbook of counseling psychology* (2nd ed., pp. 453–484). New York: John Wiley & Sons.

Blase, J., & Roberts, J. (1994). The micropolitics of teacher work involvement: Effective principals' impact on teachers. *Alberta Journal of Educational Research, 40*, 67–94.

Blum-Anderson, J. (1992). Increasing enrollment in higher-level mathematics classes through the affective domain. *School Science and Mathematics, 92*, 433–436.

Bryk, A. S., & Raudenbush, S. W. (1992). *Hierarchical linear models*. Newbury Park, CA: Sage.

Bryk, A. S., Lee, V. E., & Holland, P. B. (1993). *Catholic schools and the common good*. Cambridge, MA: Harvard University Press.

Bryk, A. S., Lee, V. E., & Smith, J. B. (1990). High school organization and its effects on teachers and students: An interpretative summary of the research. In W. H. Clune & J. F. Witte (Eds.), *Choice and control in American education. Vol. 1: The theory of choice and control in education*. London: Falmer.

Coleman, J. S., Campbell, E. Q., Hobson, C. J., McPartland, J., Mood, A. M., Wienfield, F. D., & York, R. L. (1966). *Equality of educational opportunity*. Washington, DC: U.S. Government Printing Office.

Crawley, F. E., III, & Coe, A. S. (1990). Determinants of middle school students' intention to enroll in a high school science course: An application of the theory of reasoned action. *Journal of Research in Science Teaching, 27*, 461–476.

Darlinghammond, L. (1996). The quiet revolution: Rethinking teacher development. *Educational Leadership, 53*(6), 4–10.

Davenport, E. C., Jr., Davison, M. L., Kuang, H., Ding, S., Kim, S., & Kwak, N. (1998). High school mathematics course-taking by gender and ethnicity. *American Educational Research Journal, 35*, 497–514.

Deboer, G. E. (1984). A study of gender effects in the science and mathematics course-taking behavior of a group of students who graduated from college in the late 1970s. *Journal of Research in Science Teaching, 21*, 95–103.

Eccles, J. S. (1994). Understanding women's educational and occupational choices: Applying the Eccles et al. model of achievement-related choices. *Psychology of Women Quarterly, 18*, 585–609.

Gamoran, A. (1991). Schooling and achievement: Additive versus interactive models. In S. W. Raudenbush & J. D. Willms (Eds.), *Schools, classrooms, and pupils: International studies of schooling from a multilevel perspective* (pp. 37–52). San Diego: Academic.

Gamoran, A. (1992). The variable effects of high school tracking. *Sociology of Education, 57*, 812–828.

Gill, J., & Gaffney, J. (1996). Mathematics education in Australian school. In G. Hanna (Ed.), *Towards gender equity in mathematics education*. New York: Kluwer.

Ho Sui-Chu, E., & Willms, J. D. (1996). The effects of parental involvement on eighth grade achievement. *Sociology of Education, 69*, 126–141.

Hoffer, T. (1997). High school graduation requirements: Effects on dropping out and achievement. *Teachers College Record, 98*, 608–628.

Hoffer, T., Rasinski, K., & Moore, W. (1995). *Social background differences in high school mathematics and science coursetaking and achievement*. Washington, DC: National Center for Educational Statistics.

Horner, M. (1968). Sex differences in achievement motivation and performance in competitive and non-competitive situations (doctoral dissertation, University of Michigan, 1968). *Dissertation Abstracts International, 30*, 407A.

Jencks, C. S., Smith, M., Acland, H., Bane, M. J., Cohen, D., Ginitis, H., Heyns, B., & Michelson, S. (1972). *Inequality: A reassessment of the effect of family and schooling in America*. New York: Basic Books.

Jones, L., & Smart, T. (1995). Confidence and mathematics: A gender issue? *Gender and Education, 7*, 157–166.

Kerckhoff, A. C. (1993). *Diverging pathways: Social structure and career deflections*. New York: Cambridge University Press.

Lamb, S. (1996). Gender differences in mathematics participation in Australian schools: Some relationships with social class and school policy. *British Educational Research Journal, 22*, 223–240.

Leder, G. C. (1992). Mathematics and gender: Changing perspectives. In D. A. Grouws (Ed.), *Handbook of research on mathematics teaching and learning* (pp. 597–622). New York: Macmillan.

Lee, V. E., & Bryk, A. S. (1988). Curriculum tracking as mediating the social distribution of high school achievement. *Sociology of Education, 61*, 78–94.

Lee, V. E., & Smith, J. B. (1993). Effects of school restructuring on the achievement engagement of middle-grade students. *Sociology of Education, 66*, 164–187.

Lee, V. E., Croninger, R. G., & Smith, J. B. (1997). Course-taking, equity, and mathematics learning: Testing the constrained curriculum hypothesis in US secondary schools. *Educational Evaluation and Policy Analysis, 19*, 99–121.

Ma, X. (1997). *A national assessment of mathematics participation in the United States: A survival analysis model for describing students' academic careers*. Lewiston, NY: Edwin Mellen.

Ma, X. (1998, April). *Students, peers, teachers, and parents: The effects of internal and external academic push on participation in advanced mathematics*. Paper presented at the annual meeting of the American Educational Research Association. San Diego.

Ma, X. (in press). Dropping out of advanced mathematics: The effects of parental involvement. *Teachers College Record*.

Ma, X., & Willms, J. D. (1995, April). *The effects of school disciplinary climate on eighth grade achievement*. Paper presented at the annual meeting of the American Educational Research Association. San Francisco.

Ma, X., & Willms, J. D. (in press). Dropping out of mathematics: How much do students and schools contribute to the problem? *Educational Evaluation and Policy Analysis*.

Marion, S. F., & Coladarci, T. (1993, April). *Gender differences in science course-taking patterns among college undergraduates*. Paper presented at the annual meeting of the American Education Research Association. Atlanta.

McKnight, C. C., Crosswhite, F. J., Dossey, J. A., Kifer, E., Swafford, J. O., Travers, K. J., & Cooney, T. J. (1987). *The underachieving curriculum: Assessing US school mathematics from an international perspective*. Champaign, IL: Stipes.

McLeod, D. B. (1992). Research on affect in mathematics education: A reconceptualization. In D. A. Grouws (Ed.), *Handbook of research on mathematics teaching and learning* (pp. 575–596). New York: Macmillan.

Meyer, M. R., & Koehler, M. S. (1990). Internal influences on gender differences in mathematics. In E. Fennema & G. C. Leder (Eds.), *Mathematics and gender* (pp. 60–95). New York: Teachers College Press.

Miller, J., & Hoffer, T. B. (1994). *Longitudinal Study of American Youth: Overview of study design and data resources.* DeKalb, IL: Social Science Research Institute, Northern Illinois University.

Muller, C. (1993, February). *Parent ties to the school and community and student academic performance.* Paper presented at the conference on Sociology of Education, Asilomar, CA.

National Center for Education Statistics. (1993). *The pocket condition of education, 1993.* Washington, DC: Author.

National Center for Education Statistics. (1995). *High School & Beyond fourth follow-up (sophomore cohort) HS&B: 1992.* Washington, DC: Author.

National Center for Education Statistics. (1996). *National Education Longitudinal Study: 1988–94 data files and electronic codebook system.* Washington, DC: Author.

National Commission on Excellence in Education. (1983). *A nation at risk: The imperative for educational reform.* Washington, DC: U.S. Government Printing Office.

National Council of Teachers of Mathematics. (1989). *Curriculum and evaluation standards for school mathematics.* Reston, VA: Author.

National Council of Teachers of Mathematics. (1991). *Professional standards for teaching mathematics.* Reston, VA: Author.

National Research Council. (1989). *Everybody counts: A report to the nation on the future of mathematics education.* Washington, DC: National Academy.

National Science Board. (1983). *Educating Americans for the 21th century: A plan of action for improving mathematics, science and technology education for all.* Washington, DC: Commission on Precollege Education in Mathematics, Science and Technology.

Oakes, J. (1989). What educational indicators? The case for assessing school context. *Educational Evaluation and Policy Analysis, 11,* 181–199.

Olszewski-Kubilius, P., & Yasumoto, J. (1995). Factors affecting the academic choices of academically talented middle school students. *Journal of the Education of the Gifted, 18,* 298–318.

Organization for Economic Co-Operation and Development. (1994). *The jobs study, Vols. I–II.* Paris: Author.

Organization for Economic Co-Operation and Development. (1995). *Employment outlook.* Paris: Author.

Pajares, F. (1996). Self-efficacy beliefs in academic settings. *Review of Educational Research, 66,* 543–578.

Payne, J. T. (1992). Effects of a statewide high school math testing program on college math course entry level (Doctoral dissertation, Arizona State University, 1992). *Dissertation Abstract International, 53,* 734A.

Raudenbush, S. W., & Willms, J. D. (Eds.). (1991). *Schools, classrooms, and pupils: International studies of schooling from a multilevel perspective.* San Diego: Academic.

Raudenbush, S. W., & Willms, J. D. (1995). The estimation of school effects. *Journal of Educational and Behavioral Statistics, 20,* 307–335.

Rosenholtz, S. (1989). *Teachers' workplace.* White Plains, NY: Longman.

Rumberger, R. G., & Willms, J. D. (1992). The impact of racial and ethnic segregation on the achievement gap in California high schools. *Educational Evaluation and Policy Analysis, 14,* 377–396.

Secada, W. G. (1992). Race, ethnicity, social class, language, and achievement in mathematics. In D. A. Grouws (Ed.), *Handbook of research on mathematics teaching and learning* (pp. 623–660). New York: Macmillan.

Seligman, M. E. D. (1975). *Helplessness.* San Francisco: W. H. Freeman.

Sells, L. W. (1973). High school mathematics as the critical filter in the job market. *Proceedings of the Conference on Minority Graduate Education.* Berkeley: University of California.

Slavin, R. E. (1987). Ability grouping and student achievement in elementary schools: A best-evidence synthesis. *Review of Educational Research, 57,* 293–336.

Smith, J. B. (1996). Does an extra year make any difference? The impact of early access to algebra on long-term gains in mathematics attainment. *Educational Evaluation and Policy Analysis, 18,* 141–153.

Teese, R. (1994). Mass secondary education and curriculum access: A forty year perspective of mathematics outcomes in Victoria. *Oxford Review of Education, 20,* 93–110.

Willett, J. B., & Singer, J. D. (1991). From whether to when: New methods for studying student dropout and teacher attrition. *Review of Educational Research, 61,* 407–450.

Willms, J. D. (1992). *Monitoring school performance: A guide for educators.* Washington, DC: Falmer.

Willms, J. D., & Chen, M. (1989). The effects of ability grouping on the ethnic achievement gap in Israeli elementary schools. *American Journal of Education, 97,* 237–257.

Willms, J. D., & Echols, F. H. (1992, October). *The Scottish experience of parental choice of schools.* Paper presented at the Economic Policy Institute Symposium, Washington, DC.

Willms, J. D., & Raudenbush, S. W. (1994). Effective schools research: Methodological issues. *International Encyclopaedia of Education* (2nd ed.).

Yamaguchi, K. (1991). *Event history analysis.* Newbury Park, CA: Sage.

14

Sociocultural Considerations and Latino Mathematics Achievement: A Critical Review

Luis Ortiz-Franco
Chapman University

William V. Flores
California State University

This chapter reviews research over the past 30 years focusing on the influence of cultural and socioeconomic factors on the mathematics achievement of Latinos in the United States. Special attention is given to data provided by the National Center for Education Statistics for a 20-year period from 1972 to 1992, comparing that data with other studies addressing similar concerns. Although the article examines the experiences of Latinos in the United States, other countries are facing similar pressures to absorb new immigrants, as well as indigenous populations, into their society and their educational systems.

The world has changed rapidly, dispersing whole populations. Such factors as globalization, ethnic and religious persecution, wars and revolutions, and natural disasters have affected some countries with an influx of immigrants. Countries as diverse as Sweden, Australia, France, England, and Papua New Guinea are now addressing the special educational and linguistic needs of the new immigrant populations. In addition, many countries have large indigenous populations or encompass several different nationalities and, as a consequence, are either officially or unofficially multilingual with a variety of languages spoken in the country and within the school systems (Clarkson, 1991). The experience of Latinos in the U.S. educational system and the factors influencing their mathematics achievement may provide parallels for consideration in other countries.

Latinos, often referred to as "Hispanics," are really an amalgam of racial and ethnic groups, many of whom are indigenous to the North American continent. Racially, Latinos vary from light-skinned to Black to indigenous to Asian and all types of mixtures resulting from the colonial fusion throughout Latin America. Diverse in

233

terms of racial composition, immigration status, and language preference, Latinos in the United States are nonetheless emerging as a new social force and are developing their own distinct cultural and social practices (Flores & Benmayor, 1997).

The historical experience of Latinos is very complex and varies by nationality. Some of these groups, such as Mexicans and Puerto Ricans, were first amalgamated into the United States through colonial wars, with large-scale immigration to the United States ever since that time. The largest group is of Mexican origin, many of whom refer to themselves as Chicanos or Mexican Americans. From 1846 through 1848, the United States fought a war with Mexico and annexed over half of Mexico's territory (including California, Texas, Arizona, New Mexico, Colorado, and Nevada). The Mexican presence in some of these annexed territories dates back to prior to the arrival of the English Pilgrims in what is now the continental United States. Because the United States shares a border of more than 2,000 miles with Mexico, large numbers of Mexican immigrants come to the United States annually.

The next largest Latino group is of Puerto Rican ancestry. Located primarily on the East Coast of the United States and in Chicago, Puerto Ricans formally became U.S. citizens when the Island of Puerto Rico was claimed by the United States as a result of the Spanish-American War in the 1890s. Like Mexicans, Puerto Ricans migrate and immigrate in large numbers to the U.S. mainland, particularly to New York, Chicago, and the East Coast of the United States.

The third largest Latino group is of Cuban descent, most of whom came to the United States after the Cuban Revolution of 1959. Unlike any other immigrant group, immigrants from Cuba who enter the United States illegally have been welcomed as refugees fleeing a "communist" country and have been generally granted legal resident status as soon as they reach U.S. soil. The rest of the Latino population in the United States is of either Central American origin (Guatemala, El Salvador, Honduras, etc.), of South American origin (Colombia, Peru, Chile, Argentina, Bolivia, etc.), or from the Caribbean, particularly the Dominican Republic. Many of the immigrants from Central America and the Dominican Republic came to the United States as a result of wars and revolution in their country of origin and came fleeing death squads and torture, as did many immigrants from Argentina, Brazil, and Peru.

Despite the diversity of experience, Latinos in the United States are emerging as a significant social and political force (Flores & Benmayor, 1997). Latino voters have shifted the outcome of statewide elections and gained statewide offices in California, Texas, New Mexico, Arizona, Florida, New York, and Illinois. However, Latinos still lag behind Whites in educational achievement. For instance, in 1997, only one third of Latino 25- to 34-year-olds had attended a college or a university compared to nearly 60% of non-Latinos. Moreover, at the other extreme, only 2% of Latinos, compared to 7% of non-Latinos, had advanced university degrees (Larmer, 1999).

The low educational achievement of Latinos not only results in lower income but can have profound impact on the economic health of the country. A recent study by the State of California found that, whereas Latinos are the fastest growing demographic group in that state (accounting for 28% of the state's labor force), Latinos earn significantly less and have lower educational achievement levels than non-Latinos. Latinos account for 19% of the $461 billion in wages earned in California. According to the study, "if the educational level was raised among even 5% of the Latino labor force, these workers would earn an additional $1.4 billion" (Isackson, 1999).

However, it is doubtful that improvements in educational achievement alone can significantly improve the economic condition of Latinos. Fogel (1965, p. 16) found in his analysis of census data from 1950 and 1960 that: "Increases in the educational attainment of Spanish-surname males relative to Anglos was greater than increases in their relative incomes between 1950 and 1960." He concluded, "If this experience were to continue, the Spanish-surname group would attain Anglo educational attainment levels well before they achieved income equality." As we see, the findings in this chapter lend support to Fogel's conclusion.

We found many of the studies to be "intergenerational" or "cross-generational," as their population sample includes subjects from two or more immigrant "generations." Although many studies do not distinguish between U.S.-born and immigrant Latinos, this segmentation, along with English-language proficiency, can have profound implications for the socio-economic and educational differences of Latinos and should be taken into account in studying the educational achievement of this group. In this chapter, we distinguish among various types of Latinos. A first-generation Latino immigrant is a person who is born in a Latin American country and who immigrates to the United States. A second-generation Latino immigrant is a person who is born in the United States and whose parents, one or both, are first-generation immigrants. A third- or subsequent-generation Latino immigrant is a person who is born in the United States and whose parents are second- or subsequent-generation immigrants.

The segmentation of Latinos along these generational lines has implications for the levels of proficiency in the English language by the different demographic groups. The dominant language of a first-generation Latino is Spanish, and the student may not be proficient in English, whereas the dominant language of a second- or subsequent-generation Latino is likely to be English with varying degree of proficiency in Spanish. Spanish-language proficiency usually depends mainly on how much that language is spoken in the student's home. Generally speaking, however, the Latino population is bilingual, with dominance in either one language or the other.

SES AND MATHEMATICS ACHIEVEMENT

It is important that mathematics educators, teachers, and researchers be informed about the relationship between mathematics achievement and economic indicators among the various ethnic and racial student populations in order to gain a better understanding of those populations as well as to develop appropriate educational policy reform. Groups learn differently and have distinct cultural and linguistic needs. What works for one group may not work for another. Although much research has been conducted on the relationship between income level and mathematics achievement among the majority White student population, there is very little comparable research available concerning Latino students. This chapter reviews that research and discusses its implications for further research and for mathematics education.

The mathematics achievement level of Latino K–12 students significantly trails that of White students, and there are also wide disparities in their familial economic conditions. A general review of the relevant literature on the relationship between these variables serves as backdrop to our discussion. The correlation between socioeconomic status (SES) and mathematics performance is fairly well established. White (1982) reviewed more than 100 studies addressing the non-Latino student population and found that the correlation between mathematics achievement and SES was 0.20 when students were the unit of analysis, and the correlation was 0.70 when the school was the unit of analysis. More recently, Secada (1992), in a review of the literature on mathematics achievement and race, social class, ethnicity, and language, concluded that, in general, there should be a steady increase in achievement based on increasing SES.

These findings are consistent with earlier research findings. According to Mullis, Dossey, Owen, and Phillips (1993), countless studies found that variations in mathematics achievement between the various racial populations (African American, American Indian, Asian, Latino, and White) are related to socioeconomic background. For example, Zaslavsky (1994), who examined data from the nationally administered 1992 Scholastic Achievement Test (SAT), a test required of most U.S. high school seniors entering a university, found that students from families with higher income levels attained higher mathematics scores than students from families with lower income levels.

Taking a somewhat different approach, Anderson (1969) conducted an intergenerational study and reported that there was a positive correlation between SES and performance on mathematics achievement among three generations of Mexican-American students in El Paso, Texas. In his review of the empirical literature in mathematics education, Begle (1979) found that there was slight evidence showing that, as Mexican Americans increasingly adopted the middle-class culture of the United States, their achievement in mathematics improved. In sharp contrast to Anderson, Begle, and others, Buriel and Cardoza (1988) conducted a study of three generations of Chicano students, reporting that SES was completely unrelated to mathematics achievement.

Other recent studies have found a positive relationship between SES and mathematics achievement. For example, Bradby (1992) examined the relationship between certain demographic and language characteristics of Asian and Latino eighth graders and their scores on a mathematics test. One of his findings was that a positive relationship between SES and mathematics achievement for Latino students persisted even when some language variables were held constant (see the section on Recommendations for Future Research for further comments about this study). Green, Dugoni, Ingels, and Camburn (1995) compared the demonstrated proficiency of high school seniors at various levels of mathematics grouped along demographic characteristics, including race, ethnicity, SES, and educational level of parents. They found that in the lowest SES group, 51.4% of the Latinos scored below basic or at Level 1, whereas only 12.5% scored at Level 4 or 5 (the highest mathematics skill level). By contrast, in the highest SES group, 43.8% scored at levels 4 or 5 (1995), whereas only 16.6% of Latinos scored at below basic or Level 1. Thus, as SES rose, so did math achievement.

One might extrapolate from Begle's observations and from Green and others that if math achievement is correlated with SES, then math achievement for Latinos in the lower SES groups should remain static or decrease. These patterns outlined in the literature provide the foundation on which most educators base their expectations about mathematics achievement and income. In particular, many educators expect that the mathematics achievement of students from lower income levels is likely to improve only as their socioeconomic condition improves. However, empirical studies investigating the question of mathematics achievement and income among Latinos or specific subgroups of Latinos are inconclusive at best and sometimes indicate the opposite result: that mathematics achievement by Latino students improves even as their economic condition worsens. As we examine in the next section, many factors appear to affect math achievement.

POVERTY, INCOME, AND LATINO MATH ACHIEVEMENT

Examining U.S. Census Bureau economic data related to the distribution of income in the United States over a 20-year period, from 1972 to 1992, Tienda (1995) found persistent gaps between Latino and White family income. As shown in Table 14.1, in 1972, the median family income for Latinos was 30% that of Whites ($25,858 compared to $36,952). Two decades later, that gap increased to 41% ($40,421 for Whites families compared to $23,901 for Latino families). Significantly, between 1972 and 1992, the median family income of Latinos actually declined in absolute dollars, with more Latino families living in poverty.

Tienda (1995) found that the poverty rate among Latinos under 18 years of age, precisely the age group most likely to be in school, increased from 28.8% in 1977 to 39.9% in 1992. By contrast, poverty among Whites increased from 11.6% to 16.9% during the same period. As the National Center for Educational Statistics (NCES) observed, relative to Whites, Latino children have a greater, and increasing, likelihood of living in poverty (NCES, 1995a).

TABLE 14.1
Family Income Levels for Latinos and for Non-Latino Whites, 1972, 1992

	1972	1992	Change
Non-Latino Whites	$36,952	$40,421	+$3,469
Latinos	$25,858	$23,901	−$1,950
% Gap (L/N-L W)	69.95%	59.13%	−10.82%

Note. From "Latinos and the American pie: Can Latinos achieve economic parity?," by M. Tienda, 1995, *Hispanic Journal of Behavioral Sciences, 17(4),* p. 408. Copyright 1995 by Sage Publication, Inc.

TABLE 14.2
NCES Math Proficiency Scores for Latinos and Non-Latinos, 1973, 1992

	Whites	Latinos	Difference	% Gap
1973				
9-year-olds	225	202	23 points	0.897
13-year-olds	274	239	35 points	0.872
17-year-olds	310	277	33 points	0.894
1992				
9-year-olds	235	212	23 points	0.902
13-year-olds	279	259	20 points	0.928
17-year-olds	312	292	20 points	0.936

Note. From *The Condition of Education 1995*, by U.S. Govt. National Center for Educational Statistics, 1995, Washington, DC: U.S. Department of Education, OERI.

Given the data on Latino family income and the pattern of positive correlation between SES and mathematics achievement, the logical conclusion is that mathematics achievement of Latinos should have remained static or should have declined in comparison to that of Whites during the period 1972 to 1992. However, the actual data concerning Latino family income, as presented previously, and mathematics achievement do not support this conclusion (NCES 1995a). Quite the contrary, in the 20-year period from 1972 to 1992, despite the fact that Latino family income declined, math achievement scores remained constant or improved for each age group examined.

For example, as illustrated in Table 14.2, in national examinations of math performance of 9-year-olds in 1973, the average mathematics proficiency score for Whites was 225 and for Latinos 202, a 23-point difference. In 1992, the respective proficiency levels were 235 for Whites and 212 for Latinos, still a 23-point difference, yet Latinos in that age group improved their scores by 10 points. Similar improvements were found for 13-year-olds.

In 1973, the corresponding proficiency scores for 13-year-olds were 274 for Whites and 239 for Latinos, a 35-point difference. In 1992, the gap declined to only 20 points, 279 for Whites and 259 for Latinos, with Latinos in that age group increasing math achievement scores by 20 points over earlier exams. The same trend held true in the high school-aged population. In the 17-year-old population, the mathematics proficiency score for Whites in 1973 was 310 and for Latinos 277, a gap of 33 points. In 1992, that gap decreased to 20 points; the respective scores were 312 for Whites and 292 for Latinos, an increase of 22 points from the 1973 scores. As in the case of the 9-year-old and 13-year-old age groups, the mathematics achievement of Latinos in the 17-year-old group improved relative to that of Whites, even though the income for Latinos dropped further below the national median.

Although the math performance gap between Latinos and Whites is closing, it remains unacceptably large. Moreover, there seems to be considerable differences between Whites and Latinos in the type of math skills that they are mastering, with Whites having greater access to college preparatory math courses and more likely

TABLE 14.3

Percentage of 17-Year-Old Latinos Scoring at or Above Proficiency Levels on the National
Assessment of Educational Progress Exams: 1978, 1992

	1978	1992	Difference
Beginning problem solving	78%	94%	+16%
Moderate complex procedures	23	39	+16
Multistep/complex	1	1	0

Note. From *Mini-Digest of Education Statistics 1995*, by U.S. Govt. National Center for
Educational Statistics, 1995, Washington, DC: U.S. Department of Education, OERI.

to master higher level math skills. Several studies indicate that Latinos have made
more progress at the computational level, the lowest level of mathematical skills,
and not at the higher, multistep complex problem-solving level (e.g., see Johnson,
1989; Secada, 1992; and Silver, Smith, & Nelson, 1995). For instance, as shown in
Table 14.3, for 17-year-old Latino students, 78% performed at or above proficiency
level in numerical operations and beginning problem solving in 1978; by 1992, that
figure increased to 94% (NCES, 1995b). Similarly, in the area of moderate complex
procedures and reasoning skills, only 23% of 17-year-old Latinos performed at or
above proficiency level in 1978, whereas 39% did so in 1992. However, in the area
of multistep complex problem-solving skills in both 1978 and 1992 only 1% of the
Latino students performed at or above proficiency level (NCES, 1995b).

Stated another way, 99% of Latino students failed to demonstrate proficiency in
multistep complex problem-solving skills. This is an alarming statistic, particularly
when one considers the vast changes in technology that have occurred in our society
and in the workforce since the early 1970s. Thus, as the world has shifted to an information, global society with dependence on high technology and the rapid acquisition,
interpretation, and application of information, a shocking percentage of Latino youth
are ill prepared for the demands of this new economy.

DISCUSSION

To recapitulate, in this study we observed that between 1972 and 1992, Latino students
improved their level of mathematics achievement relative to Whites even as their
general family income level decreased and the percentage of school-aged youth in
poverty in this population group increased. These findings are at variance from the
expected pattern of improvement in mathematics achievement given the corresponding
improvement in income. Still, Latinos continue to significantly trail Whites in math
performance, particularly in the acquisition of complex problem-solving skills.

The next section addresses research and practice issues related to the previous data.
Concerning research, we identify differences in methodology and data sources that
may explain the inconsistencies in the results of several earlier studies and this

analysis. Regarding practice, we examine educational policy, curriculum, instruction, and Latino parental involvement as factors that might influence performance in mathematics.

Research

Although the family income and mathematics achievement data analyzed in this chapter were derived from published sources based on survey and census information, the NCES database referred to previously could be considered longitudinal, in one sense, as it covered a 20-year period. Moreover, because the surveys involved national population samples, we can safely assume that Latinos from different immigrant generations responded to the surveys. Thus, the data analyzed in this chapter can be considered both longitudinal and cross-generational.

Let us now examine two studies cited in our introduction: Anderson (1969) and Buriel and Cardoza (1988), comparing and contrasting their data sources and findings to our own. Both of these studies used empirical data in their analysis of the relationship between mathematics achievement and both studies derived a socioeconomic index specific to Latino students. On the other hand, although Anderson and Buriel and Cardoza utilized cross-generational data, these studies did not include longitudinal data in their analyses. In addition, there are differences in the Anderson and in the Buriel and Cardoza studies and our analysis with regard to the economic indices used. In this study, we used actual income information provided by the U.S. Census Bureau, whereas Anderson as well as Buriel and Cardoza used a combination of parents' educational attainment level, parents' occupation, and family income to determine the SES of the students.

Because the database used in this chapter was not segregated by income levels, correlational or other statistical analyses between levels of income and mathematics achievement could not be performed. Had we been able to analyze the data by income levels, it is plausible that we might have found a positive relationship between the two variables for the within levels of family income and a negative correlation for the general family income level. Another difference between those two studies and this study is that the data used here pertained to the general U.S. Latino population, whereas the data analyzed by Anderson, and Buriel and Cardoza focused only on Chicanos. It would be interesting to find out if we would get parallel results in the different subgroups of the Latino population.

An additional difference between this study and the other two investigations involves the method used to measure mathematics achievement. In the other two studies, the investigators utilized commercially available standardized mathematics achievement tests, whereas in this study we used mathematics data as reported by the NCES. The NCES data are based on information generated through the National Assessment of Educational Progress (NAEP) trends set, which is largely a basic skills examination. Moreover, subsets of the same items have been included in successive examinations to measure performance trends so that over time some items have been part of the same examination. Tests are administered to a sample of students at ages 9, 13, and 17 from across the United States. However, students with a first language other than

English who are not proficient in English are not included in the sampling. There is no indication that Anderson and Buriel and Cardoza followed this same practice. Thus, the NCES data may be skewed toward Latinos proficient in English, in possible contrast to the other two studies.

In summary, we find four methodological differences between this study and some studies cited earlier: (a) longitudinal approach, (b) within population levels of economic indices, (c) diversity of the population sample, and (d) mathematics achievement assessment instrument. Such methodological differences may account for the discrepancies in our findings. Similarly, it is possible that factors such as parental involvement in the education of their children, parents' educational attainment, the conditions of the schools students attend, and some teachers' variables might have had an influence on the mathematics achievement of Latino students. These and other variables are discussed subsequently as possible explanations of the findings in this chapter.

Practice

In this section, we discuss some aspects of parents, schools, and teachers that provide a context in which to judge the gains made by Latinos in mathematics achievement between 1972 and 1992.

Parents. In 1995, the NCES reported that the involvement of Latino parents in their children's education was equal to, and better in some respects, than that of White parents despite the enormous differences in educational attainment level and family income between the two groups of parents. For instance, in 1994, 60% of Latino adults 25 to 29 years old had the equivalent of a high school education compared to 86% of their White counterparts. Despite the differences, similar percentages of Latino and White students had parents who regularly reviewed their homework (NCES, 1995a). Moreover, Latino eighth graders were more likely than their White counterparts to report that their parents had limited their television viewing and that their parents had visited their classes (NCES, 1995a). Thus, Latino parents appear to be important partners in the education of Latino youth. It is possible that increased Latino parental involvement practices contributed to improving the achievement of their children in mathematics.

There is a body of literature in education supporting the claim that parental involvement in the education of their children has a positive impact in mathematics performance. For example, Yolanda De La Cruz (1999) described the experiences of the Children's Math World (CMW) program and reported that by stimulating parental involvement the mathematics achievement of Latino students dramatically improved. Significantly, De La Cruz found that, "Although more than 90 percent of urban CMW children met federal guidelines for the free-lunch program, they considerably outperformed heterogeneous and middle-class samples of United States children who received traditional mathematics instruction" (p. 297). In fact, on some tasks, these Latino children exceeded the performance of Japanese children and children from Taiwan and the United States using the reform curriculum Everyday Mathematics.

Thus, despite their low family household income levels, increased parental involvement dramatically improved mathematics achievement of these Latino children.

It is often assumed that Latino parents are uneducated and are unable to assist children with math lessons. However, in considering parental involvement, it should be noted that the educational level of Latino parents has dramatically increased since the early 1970s. In 1972, for example, less than half (47.6%) of 25- to 29-year-old Latinos had completed high school. By 1992, 60.9% had graduated from high school. Moreover, the percentage of Latinos completing college has also increased. For the same age bracket, in 1972, only 7.8% had completed four or more years of college in 1972, but by 1992 that percentage had doubled to 15.6 (NCES, 1995a). Thus, the segment of the Latino population most likely to be involved in raising young children is becoming more educated and, as a consequence, is better able to provide assistance to their children's learning.

Additional data that questions the effect of economic factors on mathematics achievement come from a study conducted at the RAND Corporation in 1994. In that investigation, the authors utilized the National Longitudinal Survey of data for youth ages 15 to 18 years of age for 1970, 1975, and 1990 (Grissmer et al., 1994, p. xxx) to investigate changes in student mathematics test scores that could be attributed to family characteristics such as family income and found that ". . . changing family characteristics alone cannot explain the large gains made by these [Latino and Black] students. In fact, changing family characteristics account for only about a third of the total gain."

Condition of Schools.   A great deal has been written about the gap between rich and poor schools and the growing inequality between majority White and majority Latino schools. Predominantly Latino schools are often in poor neighborhoods. Such schools tend to be older and more deteriorated or dilapidated, are more likely to be overcrowded, and are more likely to be classified as unsafe than are predominantly white schools. The issue of safety is particularly important. It is very difficult for students who perceive their school as a dangerous or threatening environment to concentrate on scholastic achievement. There are dramatic differences between Latinos and Whites in their perception of school safety. In 1992, for example, Latino seniors were more likely than White counterparts to report physical disruptions by other students, reported a greater number of interethnic fights, more often cited the presence of gangs within their school, and were more likely to state that they did not feel safe at school (NCES, 1995a). These social conditions very likely have created a stressful learning environment for Latinos in the schools and can negatively affect learning outcomes.

The conditions within the schools contextualize low levels of educational achievement among Latinos. The poor conditions within Latino schools compounds the effects of poverty and stress related to declining family income. Even so, many Latino students overcome unfavorable school environments and the effects of poverty. The number of Latino students going on to complete college has dramatically increased in the past 30 years, with most of these students coming from working-class families and many from low-income neighborhoods and predominantly Latino schools. According to Gonzalez and Padilla (1997), such achievements reflect the academic resilience of Latino high school students and their families.

Latinos also tend be concentrated in low-performing schools. Categorizing schools on the basis of students' average academic performance, in 1992, the following percentage of Latino students were concentrated in the bottom one third of schools: 57% of 4th graders, 58% of 8th graders, and 52% of 12th graders (Mullis, Dossey, Owen, & Phillips, 1993). Moreover, tracking continues to plague Latino students.

Tracking is a process by which students are placed into college-preparatory courses versus vocational training programs and noncollege preparatory courses. Racial prejudice and stereotypes often result in teachers or counselors discouraging minority students from considering college preparatory courses, tracking them instead into vocational courses. Unfortunately, tracking continues, as a disproportionate number of Latino students in secondary schools are assigned to nonacademic tracks. According to Oakes (1990), tracking means that minority students who might otherwise have qualified for college preparatory courses are forced to study unchallenging mathematics curricula that fail to prepare them for college. Such educational practices mean that Latino students have less access to mathematics courses, are less likely to take math courses, and are less likely to take math courses that prepare them for college and for the demands of a changing economy.

Reviewing the literature on mathematics achievement and race, ethnicity, SES, gender, and language, Tate (1997) found math course taking to be a powerful explanatory variable. Tate noted that there were substantial differences in mathematics achievement among secondary students of all racial/ethnic and SES groups. Even so, he found that, despite the difference in SES, all racial/ethnic groups benefited from additional mathematics coursework. In fact, the various racial/ethnic and SES groups posted similar gains in achievement gains when they completed the same number of mathematics courses.

Furthermore, Hoffer, Rasinski, and Moore (1995) examined the relationship between the number of mathematics courses and mathematics achievement among high school students of four SES levels and found that much of the differences in mathematics achievement was due to the number of mathematics courses completed and not to SES. These studies challenge the relationship between SES and math achievement.

It would appear, then, that one way to increase Latino math achievement would be to increase the number of math courses taken by Latino students. Although tracking continues to be a major obstacle for Latino students, the absolute number of Latino students taking math courses, particularly college preparatory courses, is increasing. This may partially explain the rise in Latino math student achievement, despite the continued deterioration of predominantly Latino schools and the continuation of tracking.

The substantial differences between predominantly White schools and predominantly Latino schools help explain the continuing math achievement gap between Latino students and White students. As Frankenstein (1995) and other (e.g., see Oakes, 1990, and Tate, 1995) documented, school districts have allocated more and better resources to schools attended by White middle-class and upper-class students than to schools attended by low income and non-White students. Teachers and students alike suffer from these policies, which contribute to unequal educational and learning opportunities for the students and poor working conditions for teachers. This continuing inequality worsens the achievement gap by limiting resources to those schools and students most in need of such resources.

Some scholars have argued that the inequalities in U.S. education, particularly with respect to minorities, are rooted in the racial and class nature of the society. Schools, under such perspectives, reproduce inequality and serve to perpetuate the class structure (e.g., see Apple, 1992; Bowels, 1972; Bowels & Gintis, 1976; and Reich, 1972). Under this paradigm, the disproportionate assignment of Latinos to nonacademic tracks and the unequal allocation of resources to the schools that they attend are due to racism and class elitism, which is inherent to capitalist America. However, such analyses tend to ignore efforts to improve Latino scholastic achievement, such as the alliances of teachers, parents, community members, and the business community.

Such broad-based alliances are an important source of educational reform and should be encouraged. Well-organized home–school–community alliances among mathematics educators (researchers, teachers, and administrators), Latino parents, and Latino community leaders can result in dramatic political shifts, transforming school boards, and teaching. They can also alter how resources are allocated to schools, how such resources are used, and the access of Latino students to quality mathematics instruction.

By contrast, the mathematics education reform movement has tended to ignore Latino communities by emphasizing curricular changes and neglecting to address the social aspects of mathematics education. Reform leaders usually advocate for increased emphasis on applications, mathematical reasoning, problem solving, and the use of technology in the teaching of mathematics. However, if the mathematics reform movement is to succeed, it cannot ignore the social reality of Latino students, nor can it exclude Latino parents. To be successful, education reform movement must address structural inequalities, not only seeking to improve curriculum but also striving to insure a more equitable distribution of resources to poor and predominantly Latino schools and to insure that Latino students have increased access to high-quality mathematics courses.

If we fail to accomplish such reallocation of resources, we are likely to see only very small improvement in the mathematics achievement index of Latinos, which the country can ill afford. To illustrate this point, NAEP data indicate that between 1992 and 1996 Latino students improved their average index in mathematics achievement by only four points at the 4th-grade and 8th-grade levels and by only three points at the 12th-grade level (Reese, Miller, Mazzo, & Dossey, 1997). This slight increase underscores the need for considerable change within the entire math education system.

Teachers.   The pattern of Latino students achieving higher levels of improvement in lower level mathematical skills, such as computation, than in higher level skills, such as multistep complex problem solving, reflects the nature of mathematics instruction that Latinos have received in the schools. Cole and Griffin (1987) and Frankenstein (1995) and Oakes (1990) assert that schools serving minority children tend to put more emphasis on drilling the basics than on teaching higher level skills that are needed to excel in mathematics. Although there is a dearth of empirical literature on mathematical problem solving and Latinos, the few studies that exist on this topic show that Latino students learn these high-level mathematical skills when it is taught to them. Hence, it is probably that Latinos would learn the higher order skills of mathematical reasoning and multistep problem solving *if* teachers and school districts emphasized those skills in their classroom teaching.

One study at the elementary school level demonstrated that minority students were capable of learning multistep word problems, once they were exposed to such instruction. Villaseñor and Kepner (1993) conducted a study involving 24 first-grade classrooms in a large urban school district. Twelve classrooms were in the experimental group, and 12 classrooms were in the control group. Ninety percent of the children who participated in the study were African American or Latino. The students in the experimental group received instruction based on the principles and practices of cognitive guided instruction (CGI), whereas the children in the control group did not receive such instruction. Subjects in the experimental and control groups were administered pre- and post-tests consisting of 14 arithmetic word problems. Significantly, the experimental group demonstrated superior achievement in problem-solving questions, including multistep word problems. The study is important as it challenges the prejudices of many teachers and administrators who believe that Latino and other minority students are incapable of learning such difficult mathematics subject matter.

Moreover, evidence that Latino students attending middle schools in economically disadvantaged communities can learn reasoning and problem-solving skills is provided by the findings of the Quantitative Understanding: Amplifying Student Achievement and Reasoning (QUASAR) project. Silver and Lane (1995) reported that students who received instruction through the QUASAR project, which fostered the acquisition of mathematical thinking and reasoning skills, performed better in mathematical problem solving than a comparable sample of middle-school students who did not receive instruction based on QUASAR principles.

The ability of Latino students to learn multistep problem solving, as required in calculus at the high school level, was vividly illustrated by the experiences and results of teachers Jaime Escalante and Ben Jimenez at Garfield High School in East Los Angeles. Escalante's success in preparing Garfield High School students for the advanced placement (AP) test in calculus made history in American education and was documented in the award-winning film *Stand and Deliver* (Matthews, 1988). As Escalante and Jimenez demonstrated, caring, highly motivated teachers are critical to improving the quality of mathematics education that students receive.

There are many teachers who over the years have consistently tried to provide a quality mathematics education to their Latino students without adequate support from their school bureaucracies. Latino students have been able to improve their achievement in mathematics due in large part to the encouragement and support of such teachers. On the other hand, many teachers of Latino students still have biased views and low expectations for their Latino students that negatively influence their teaching and consequently negatively affect student learning (Apple, 1992; Heide & Jump, 1993; Oakes, 1990; Silver, Smith, & Nelson, 1995; Thompson & Jakucyn, 1993; Zaslavsky, 1996).

In some instances, teachers and counselors have purposefully adopted practices that make it difficult, if not impossible, for Latino students to excel. For example, in a mathematics education conference held in California, in December 1996, a White teacher related a shocking incident that occurred in the school where she taught.

According to her, several White teachers in the school, on learning that their Latino students performed well in the teacher-generated mathematics tests, suggested increasing the difficulty level of the tests, without improving the quality of mathematics education. Their explicit intention was to make it impossible for the Latino students to pass the tests. Similar incidents have been reported in agricultural areas of California where White teachers feared that, if the Latino students scored well, those students and their parents would leave the agricultural fields, choosing to go to college or seek employment in some other area. Such practices not only restrict the ability of Latino students to succeed in mathematics but also contribute to perpetuating racial and class segmentation.

To address deep-seated racial stereotypes and prejudice, some successful programs have been established that help teachers confront issues of class, gender, race, and discrimination in mathematics education. Two such programs are the Mathematics Renaissance project in California (Acquarelli & Mumme, 1996) and the Mathematics Education Equity Leadership (MEEL) project in New York (Peterson & Barnes, 1996). These and other projects demonstrate that, whereas participating teachers are initially uncomfortable with confronting issues of equity, a series of emotionally intense sessions about the attitudes, beliefs, and classroom practices of teachers can change, with resultant improvement in their students' mathematics achievement as well. Once their views are changed, these teachers can effectively contribute to improving the mathematics education of their Latino and other minority students.

Given the inadequate educational resources, poor school learning environments, and negative social attitudes on the part of some teachers, we need to devote more energy and professional attention to teaching Latino students mathematical applications, reasoning, and multistep and complex problem solving. They are eager and ready to learn, and their parents are ready to assist us in this task.

RECOMMENDATIONS FOR FUTURE RESEARCH

As we can see from the preceding review of the literature, it is quite possible that family characteristics and course taking have a stronger influence than income on the mathematics achievement of Latino students. Based on the previous observations, we advance six hypotheses, each of which would require further research. We also suggest that more in-depth research be undertaken, including longitudinal studies, ethnographic studies, and studies that segregate data and that examine the influence of class, parents' educational level, language at home, immigration status, and so on. Following these possible hypotheses are several questions that emerge from our review our literature. Addressing these questions would greatly advance our understanding of some of the factors influencing Latino math performance. The following hypotheses are posed as possible areas of further research:

1. There is a negative correlation between mathematics achievement and declining income for the general Latino student population.

2. There is a positive correlation between parents' educational attainment level and student achievement in mathematics for the general Latino student population.

3. There is a stronger correlation between parents' educational attainment level and mathematics achievement than between family income and mathematics achievement for the general Latino population.

4. There is a positive correlation between parents' involvement in their children's education and the mathematics achievement of the general Latino student population.

5. There is a stronger correlation between parents' involvement in their children's education and mathematics achievement than between family income and mathematics achievement for the general Latino student population.

6. There is a stronger correlation between the number of mathematics college preparatory courses taken and mathematics achievement than between family income and mathematics achievement for the general Latino student population.

To test these hypotheses would require studies that consider the relative complexity of the Latino population, including segmenting the data by immigration status, language spoken in the household, and psycholinguistics factors associated with the learning of mathematics. One aspect of language in the learning of mathematics by immigrant and second-generation Latinos is related to proficiency in English. There is paucity of research on the relationship between language ability and mathematics achievement among Latino students.

In the introduction of this article, we mentioned that Bradby (1992) examined the relationship between language characteristics and mathematics achievement among Asian and Latino eighth graders. He found that among Latino students proficiency in English was strongly related to mathematics achievement. Specifically, he reported that among this student population as proficiency in English increased so did their level of mathematics achievement. Unfortunately, we cannot address this important issue with the data discussed in this chapter, and we recommend that this factor be included in future intergenerational investigations in mathematics education involving Latinos.

Studies of immigrant populations conducted elsewhere may be of use in understanding the experience of Latinos. Some studies among immigrant or bilingual populations find that fluency in the native language (L1) and fluency in the second (L2) language are important in the learning of mathematics. For instance, Dawe (1982, 1983) found that among immigrant groups in England competence in the their native language was important for their success in mathematical reasoning. Clarkson (1989) found that among bilingual students in Papua New Guinea competence in the student's native language (L1) and competence in the language of learning (L2) are both important for success on mathematics achievement tests. A comparative approach to the problem may provide insights into the experience of Latinos and may help us consider the problem from very different perspectives.

Concerning psycholinguistics and the learning of mathematics, although some investigators in other countries have begun to address these topics, to our knowledge, there are no similar studies involving Latino students. Clarkson (1983) reported that among students in Papua New Guinea logical connectives are important in mathematical competence. MacGregor and Price (1999) addressed the aspect of language competence related to the cognitive level at which symbol processing takes place in the learning of algebra by Australian students. They found that very few students with low scores on metalinguistic awareness of symbol, syntax, and ambiguity achieved high scores on an algebra test. It seems that there is an opportunity for a potentially fruitful collaboration in the United States among linguists, psychologists, anthropologists, and mathematics educators to address those and other variables with Latino students.

Moschkovich (1999) discussed some of the educational policy issues, such as placement, involved in the United States in the assessment of the mathematical knowledge of Latino immigrant students. An important question in assessment is the reliability of the instruments used. Ortiz-Franco (1990) showed that assessment instruments in mathematics that are reliable for Whites and that, when translated into Spanish, are reliable instruments for Spanish-dominant Mexican immigrant students may not be reliable for English-dominant Chicano students. Clearly, there are many research topics that need to be addressed to inform the policy concerns argued by Moschkovich. Taking a different approach, Tate and D'Ambrosio (1997) argued that whether or not language ability matters in mathematics teaching and learning is essentially a political one.

The broad conflict over bilingual education that has become very polarized in the United States is an example of the political nature of such discourse. Can mathematics education research change the sociopolitical realities in which Latinos learn mathematics in the schools? Generally, mathematics education research has not entered the realm of political debate nor altered the sociopolitical reality of power relations in the schools or in the society.

Language is embedded in culture and Begle (1973), from his attempts in finding learning correlates in mathematics for Chicano students, reminded us that cultural differences should not be ignored in mathematics education. Since then some scholars have been promoting the inclusion of the non-Western cultural dimensions of mathematics in the classroom as a way of improving mathematics instruction and the mathematics achievement of underachieving groups (e.g., see Bishop, 1991; D'Ambrosio, 1991; Fasheh, 1991; and Joseph, 1991, to name a few, for an international perspective on this theme). D'Ambrosio (1985) referred to this aspect of mathematics as ethnomathematics, whereas other people use the term multiculturalism in mathematics.

The argument is that, by including ethnomathematics topics—such as the mathematical contributions of civilizations that have been excluded heretofore from the history of mathematics—in the classroom, students from those cultural groups will feel mathematically empowered, resulting in an increase in math achievement. This theoretical orientation, when empirically tested, has the potential to address the dialectics of affect and cognition in mathematics learning in a cultural context. Unfortunately, as yet there is no research, either basic or applied, on culture and mathematics among Latino students addressing the claims raised in ethnomathematics.

On another social dimension, many of the studies cited in this chapter draw their conclusions based on data from the Latino population as a whole, without regard to the very important distinctions among immigration status, class, parental education level, or other important social economic indicators that can affect mathematics performance. In the past two decades, the Latino population in the United States has become extremely heterogeneous. Latinos immigrants are also more diverse, entering the United States from countries throughout Latin America and the Caribbean. They arrive possessing very different class and educational backgrounds as well as lived experiences. In short, Latino populations are increasingly class diverse. What impact have these changes had on the mathematics performance students?

For example, although the percentage of Latino households in poverty has increased, as has mathematics performance among Latino students, Latino households earning more than the median income have also increased. Is it possible that higher income households are disproportionately represented in the data examined in this chapter? We need to carefully tease out these variables in future studies.

Gender should also be considered as a possible explanation of changes in mathematics performance. For example, several universities have noted increased enrollments of Latinas as a proportion of all Latinos who are college ready. Math achievement is a critical requirement for admission to public colleges and universities. Is it possible that mathematics achievement has increased disproportionately for Latinas relative to Latino males? Further studies should segment the data by gender with specific studies examining the mathematics achievement of Latinas.

Structural and employment considerations might also affect mathematics performance. For example, if children are expected to leave school to follow their parents as agricultural migrant workers, it is doubtful that math performance would increase, even if the parents were very involved with the school during the time the student is enrolled. Another factor, which may influence achievement in some public schools, is the rapidly changing socioeconomic conditions and ethnic profiles of the neighborhoods surrounding those schools. Economic restructuring in many urban centers resulted in dramatic populations shifts as White and middle-class Latino families left neighborhoods to find new jobs after the demise of basic industries such as auto, aerospace, petroleum, and steel. As a result, many of these neighborhoods became more Latino and more working class in composition.

As neighborhoods change and become increasingly Latino, or increasingly Latino immigrant, or increasingly low income, what changes do we see in mathematics performance? If, for example, performance declines as Latino concentrations increase, are there other factors that might explain the decline, such as decreasing resources given to the school district or decreasing quality of teachers or principals? Similarly, if sudden improvements occur, what could explain such improvement? Perhaps reduced class size policies, adoption of year-round scheduling, budget increases, greater participation of parents in after-school programs, implementation of curricular changes, better training programs and recruitment of teachers, or other factors might be at work. However, which factors have most dramatically affected math achievement? In other words, we must look past test scores and economics to understand those mechanisms that explain changes in mathematics achievement.

Most of the studies cited in this chapter do not distinguish between U.S.-born parents and children and foreign-born parents and children, nor do they distinguish among monolingual Spanish households, monolingual English households, and bilingual households. Do these apparent correlations remain when we consider immigration status or household language? Several cities with large Latino populations have changed dramatically over the 20-year period covered in this chapter. For example, the Latino population in Los Angeles was once 90% Mexican American but today includes very large Central and South American populations. Moreover, the character of immigration has also changed, with increases in middle classes and educated populations from Mexico and all of Latin America. To what extent has this change in the character of immigration and as a result the changing character of Latino communities also affected mathematics performance? Has the changing class character of immigrant communities affected mathematics performance? Some South American immigrant populations have higher levels of educational attainment than do Mexican immigrants, perhaps because of different class backgrounds in their homeland. How do the class background and educational levels of these immigrant parents affect the mathematics achievement of their children?

Additionally, what is the impact of parental involvement in student learning or in parental attitudes toward mathematics achievement? Ethnographic studies would be useful to help us understand the relationship between these parental characteristics and the mathematics achievement of their children. Also, does past parental experience with mathematics achievement and subsequent job and career opportunities correlate with parental expectations and support for their children's mathematics achievement? Do parental expectations affect the intrinsic or extrinsic motivations of their children related to math performance (cf. Middleton & Spania, 1999).

Similarly, some studies examining cooperative behavior in the classroom indicate that Latinos exhibit preferences for cooperative behaviors, which in turn are related to intrinsic motivation, cultural factors, and academic achievement (Knight et al., 1993). Do children base their performance on their parents' expectations more than they do on their social status and income level of their parents? Do they feel that they are likely to end up in low-income, low-status occupations despite math performance? If so, how does this affect their motivation as well as performance? Are there differences in the impact of parent involvement and mathematics performance based on income, language, or immigration status of the parents?

CONCLUSIONS

The data discussed previously concerning U.S. Latino family income and mathematics achievement from 1972 to 1992 reveal the following salient facts: (a) the mathematics achievement level of Latino students increased, (b) Latino family median income level decreased significantly when compared to the national median of Whites, and (c) the poverty rate among the school-age population increased dramatically over the same period of time. These three factors provide compelling evidence that, for the general U.S. Latino population, there is a negative correlation between declining income and mathematics achievement. However, because there are no similar data for specific subpopulation of Latino groups (Chicanos, Puerto Ricans, Cubans, Salvadorans, Guatemalans, etc.), we are unable to say whether the same pattern applies to each of those groups.

In studies cited in this chapter, it was also observed that the educational attainment level of Latinos between 25 and 29 years of age increased significantly during the same period, 1972 to 1992, and that Latino parents were very involved in their children's education. It is quite possible that these family characteristics had a stronger influence than income on the mathematics achievement of Latino students. It was also noted that the gains that Latinos made were at the computational level and that their performance in applications, reasoning, and problem solving need to be improved. Teachers of Latino students are urged to put increased emphasis on the latter skills in their classroom teaching. Moreover, with respect to the unequal distribution of educational resources to schools that Latino students attend, it is recommended that a coalition of mathematics educators, parents, and community leaders be formed to bring about a more equitable distribution of resources to those schools.

Finally, we suggest that further studies be conducted to examine the relative influences of parental involvement in the schools, educational attainment of parents, parental expectations, and income separated out by income, immigration status, parental educational level, language spoken in the home, and other variables. Latinos in the United States are rapidly becoming the largest single ethnic group in many U.S. cities and have already become the largest single ethnic group in many school districts. As the Latino population increases, its importance for the economy will also increase. The United States cannot afford to have a Latino population that is math illiterate. For the United States to continue as an economic power, Latinos must improve educational attainment in all areas, particularly mathematics. We hope this chapter helps us to identify critical areas where further research is needed so that these goals can be achieved.

REFERENCES

Acquarelli, K., & Mumme, J. (1996, March). A Renaissance in mathematics education reform. *Phi Delta Kappan*, 478–484.

Anderson, J. G. (1969). *Factors affecting achievement among Mexican-Americans in a metropolitan context* (Final Report, Mathematics Education Program, Southwest Educational Development Laboratory). Las Cruces: New Mexico State University.

Apple, M. W. (1992). Do the Standards go far enough? Power, policy, and practice in mathematics education. *Journal for Research in Mathematics Education, 23*(5), 412–431.

Begle, E. G. (1973). Some lessons learned by SMSG. *The Mathematics Teacher, 66*, 207–214.

Begle, E. G. (1979). *Critical variables in mathematics education: Findings from a survey of the empirical literature.* Washington, DC: MAA and NCTM.

Bishop, A. (1991). Mathematics Education in its cultural context. In M. Harris (Ed.), *Schools, mathematics and work* (pp. 29–41). London: Falmer Press.

Bowels, S. (1972). Unequal education and the social reproduction of labor. In M. Carnoy (Ed.), *Schooling in a corporate society: The political economy of education in America* (pp. 36–66). New York: David McKay.

Bowels, S., & Gintis, H. (1976). *Schooling in capitalist America: Educational reform and the contradictions of economic life.* New York: Basic Books.

Bradby, D. (1992). *Language characteristics and academic achievement: A look at Asian and Hispanic eighth graders in NELS: 88.* Washington, DC: U.S. Department of Education.

Buriel, R., & Cardoza, D. (1988). Sociocultural correlates of achievement among three generations of Mexican American high school seniors. *American Educational Research Journal, 25,* 177–192.

Clarkson, P. C. (1983). Types of errors made by Papua New Guinea students. *Educational Studies in Mathematics, 14,* 355–367.

Clarkson, P. C. (1989). *Language and mathematics learning.* Unpublished doctoral thesis, Queensland University, Australia.

Clarkson, P. C. (1991). *Bilingualism and mathematics learning.* Geelong, Victoria, Australia: Deaking University.

Cole, M., & Griffin, P. (1987). *Contextual factors in education.* Madison: Wisconsin Center for Educational Research, University of Wisconsin.

D'Ambrosio, U. (1985). Ethnomathematics: What might it be? In *International Study Group on Ethnomathematics (ISGEm) Newsletter, 1*(1), 2.

D'Ambrosio, U. (1991). Ethnomathemtics and its place in the history and pedagogy of mathematics. In M. Harris (Ed.), *Schools, mathematics and work* (pp. 15–26). London: Falmer Press.

Dawe, L. (1982). *The influence of a bilingual child's first language competence on reasoning in mathematics.* Unpublished doctoral thesis, University of Cambridge, England.

Dawe, L. (1983). Bilingualism and mathematical reasoning in English as a second language. *Educational Studies in Mathematics, 14,* 325–353.

De La Cruz, Y. (1999). Reversing the trend. *Teaching Children Mathematics, 5*(6), 296–300.

Fasheh, M. (1991). Mathematics in a social context: Math within education as praxis versus math within education as hegemony. In M. Harris (Ed.), *Schools, Mathematics, and work* (pp. 57–61). London, England: The Falmer Press.

Flores, W., & Benmayor, R. (Eds.). (1997). *Latino cultural citizenship: claiming identity, space and rights.* Boston: Beacon.

Fogel, W. (1965). *Education and income of Mexican-Americans in the southwest* (Mexican-American Study Project, Advance Report 1. Division of Research, Graduate School of Business Administration). Los Angeles: University of California Los Angeles.

Frankenstein, M. (1995). Equity in mathematics education: Class in the world outside of class. In W. Secada, E. Fennema, & L.B. Adajian (Eds.), *New directions for equity in mathematics education* (pp. 165–190). New York: Cambridge University Press.

Gonzalez, R., & Padilla, A. (1997). The academic resilience of Mexican American high school students. *Hispanic Journal of Behavioral Sciences, 19*(3), 301–317.

Green, P. J., Dugoni, B. C., Ingels, S. J., & Canburn, E. (1995). *A profile of high school seniors in 1992.* Washington, DC: U.S. Department of Education.

Grissmer, D. W., Kirby, S. N., Berends, M., & Williamson, S. (1994). *Student achievement and the changing American family.* Santa Monica, CA: RAND.

Heide, C. A., & Jump, T. L. (1993). Females, minorities, and physically handicapped in mathematics and science: A model program. In G. Cuevas & M. Driscoll (Eds.), *Reaching all students with mathematics* (pp. 159–174). Reston, VA: NCTM.

Hoffer, T. B., Rasinski, K. A., & Moore, W. (1995). *Social background differences in high school mathematics and science coursetaking and achievement (NCES 95–206).* Washington, DC: U.S. Department of Education.

Isackson, N. (1999). Latino wage gap worries officials. *Daily News* (San Fernando Valley Edition), August 19, B1.

Johnson, M. L. (1989). Minority differences in mathematics. In M. M. Lindquist (Ed.), *Results from the fourth mathematics assessment of the NAEP* (pp. 135–148). Reston, VA: NCTM.

Joseph, G. (1991). Foundations of eurocentrism in mathematics. In M. Harris (Ed.), *Schools, mathematics and work* (pp. 42–57). London: Falmer Press.

Knight, G. P., Cota, M. K., & Bernal, M. E. (1993). The socialization of cooperative, competitive, and individualistic preferences among Mexican American children: the mediating role of ethnic identity. *Hispanic Journal of Behavioral Sciences, 15*(3), 291–309.

Larmer, B. (1999). Latino America. *Newsweek, 134*(2), 48–58.

MacGregor, M., & Price, E. (1999). An exploration of aspects of language proficiency and algebra learning. *Journal for Research in Mathematics Education, 30*(4), 449–467.

Matthews, J. (1988). *The best teacher in America.* New York: Henry Holt.

Middleton, J. A., & Spania, P. (1999). Motivation for achievement in mathematics: Findings, generalizations, and criticisms of the research. *Journal for Research in Mathematics Education, 30*(1), 65–88.

Moschkovich, J. N. (1999). Understanding the needs of Latino students in reform-oriented mathematics classrooms. In Ortiz-Franco, L., Hernandez, N., & De La Cruz, Y. (Eds.), *Changing the faces of mathematics: Perspectives on Latinos* (pp. 5–12). Reston, VA: NCTM.

Mullis, I. V.S., Dossey, J. A., Owen, E. H., & Phillips, G. W. (1993). *NAEP 1992: Mathematics report card for the nation and the states*. Washington, DC: National Center for Educational Statistics, U.S. Department of Education.

National Center for Educational Statistics (1995a). *The condition of education 1995*. Washington, DC: U.S. Department of Education, OERI.

National Center for Educational Statistics (1995b). *Mini-digest of education statistics 1995*. Washington, DC: U.S. Department of Education, OERI.

Oakes, J. (1990). *Multiplying inequalities: The effects of race, social class, and tracking on opportunities to learn mathematics and science*. Santa Monica, CA: Rand.

Ortiz-Franco, L. (1990). Interrrelationships of seven mathematical abilities across languages. *Hispanic Journal of Behavioral Sciences, 12*(3), 299–312.

Peterson, P., & Barnes, C. (1996). Learning together: The challenge of mathematics, equity, and leadership. *Phi Delta Kappan*, March, 485–491.

Reese, C. M., Miller, K. E., Mazzo, J., & Dossey, J. A. (1997). *NAEP 1996 mathematics report card for the nation and the states*. Washington, DC: National Center for Educational Statistics, 1997.

Reich, M. (1972). Economic theories of racism. In M. Carnoy (Ed.), *Schooling in a corporate society: The political economy of education in America* (pp. 67–79). New York: David McKay.

Secada, W. G. (1992). Race, ethnicity, social class, language, and achievement in mathematics. In D. A. Grows (Ed.), *Handbook of research on mathematics teaching and learning* (pp. 623–660). New York: Macmillan.

Silver, E. A., & Lane, S. (1995). Can instructional reform in urban middle schools help students narrow the mathematical performance gap? Some evidence from the QUASAR project. *Research in Middle Level Education 18*(2), 49–70.

Silver, E. A., Smith, M. S., & Nelson, B. S. (1995). The QUASAR project: Equity concerns meet mathematics education reform in the middle school. In W. G. Secada, E. Fennema, & L. B. Adajian (Eds.), *New directions for equity in mathematics education* (pp. 9–56). New York: Cambridge University Press.

Tate, W. (1995). Economics, equity, and the national, mathematics assessment: Are we creating a national tool road?" In W. G. Secada, E. Fennema, & L. B. Adajian (Eds.), *New Directions for equity in mathematics education* (pp. 191–208). New York: Cambridge University Press.

Tate, W. (1997). Race, ethnicity, SES, gender and language proficiency trends in mathematics achievement: An update. *Journal for Research in Mathematics Education, 28*(6), 652–680.

Tate, W., & D'Ambrosio, B. (1997). Equity, mathematics reform, and research. *Journal for Research in Mathematics Education, 28*(6), 650–651.

Thompson, D. R., & Jacucyn, N. (1993). Helping inner city girls succeed: The METRO achievement program. In G. Cuevas & M. Driscoll (Eds.), *Reaching all students with mathematics* (pp. 175–196). Reston, VA: NCTM.

Tienda, M. (1995). Latinos and the American pie: Can Latinos achieve economic parity. *Hispanic Journal of Behavioral Sciences, 17*(4), 403–429.

Villaseñor, A., Jr., & Kepner, H. S., Jr. (1993). Arithmetic from a problem-solving perspective: An urban implementation. *Journal for Research in Mathematics Education 24*(1), 62–69.

White, K. R. (1982). The relation between socioeconomic status and academic achievement. *Psychological Bulletin, 91*, 461–481.

Zaslavsky, C. (1994). *Fear of math: How to get over it and get on with your life*. New Brunswick, NJ: Rutgers University Press.

Zaslavsky, C. (1996). *The multicultural math classroom: Bringing in the world*. Portsmouth, NH: Heinemann.

15

The Social Constructs of the Mathematical Experiences of African-American Students

Vivian R. Moody
The University of Alabama

With complex ethnic and social ramifications apparent in schooling, it is important to conceptualize the impact of the existing social order on the mathematical experiences of culturally diverse students. As mathematics educators embrace the charge of reform documents (NCTM, 1989, 1991, 1995) that accentuate "opportunity for all" and "mathematical literacy for all," it seems that a fundamental responsibility for mathematics educators is to question those schooling practices that undermine the charge and work to maintain those aspects of social structure that are oppressive. "Education does not simply reproduce the inequality existing outside itself; it plays an active part in reinforcing the differences and inequalities that already exist" (Campbell, 1995, p. 238).

Conceptualizing African-American students' cultural orientations, the role of their ethnicity in their experiences in mathematics classrooms, and the social effects of schooling on their succeeding in mathematics are essential in circumventing schools' active roles in perpetuating inequalities and inequities that exist in society as a whole. The purpose of this chapter is to examine the mathematical experiences of African-American students within a social context. The chapter is divided into three major sections and particularly discusses the role of social and cultural factors in African-American students succeeding in mathematics. The first section presents a theoretical framework for conceptualizing the mathematical experiences of African-American students. To make sense of the literature connecting sociocultural aspects of mathematics education and African-American students' mathematical experiences, I abstracted three themes for framing the theoretical perspectives in the literature: critical theory, African-American cultural orientations, and the application of both of these to the mathematics education of African-American students.

The second section of this chapter provides the results of a research study[1] that examined the role of social and cultural factors in the mathematical experiences and success of two female African-American mathematics students. The objectives of the study were to (a) identify the African-American students' perceptions of their mathematics classroom experiences, (b) identify the students' perceptions of how their ethnicity affected their mathematical experiences and their succeeding in mathematics, and (c) determine how the students dealt with barriers, stereotypes, and/or obstacles in their mathematical experiences.

The third and final section of the chapter draws conclusions from and make inferences about the results of the research study and attempts to make links between the results and the theoretical perspectives presented. The goal of this section is to help create a dialogue among mathematics educators about the impact of social forces on the mathematical experiences of African-American students and their succeeding in mathematics.

THEORETICAL FRAMEWORK

Critical Theory

Social forces in schooling as described by critical theorists are potential barriers that African-American students contend with in their schooling and mathematical experiences. Critical theory generally "rests on a critical view of the existing society, arguing that the society is both exploitative and oppressive, but also capable of being changed" (Weiler, 1988, p. 5). Critical theory is concerned with the role of schools in maintaining the existing social structure. Thus, critical theorists have asked "why, despite the meritocratic ideology of schooling, for certain groups—[African-American] students, female students, and students of low social class—fundamental inequalities in school performance and societal position persist" (Reyes & Stanic, 1988, p. 27). Particularly, critical theorists bring into question social inequities and inequalities that exist in schooling based on race, class, and gender and "share the underlying view that students are shaped by their experiences in schools to internalize or accept a subjectivity and a class position that leads to the reproduction of existing power relationships and social economic structures" (Weiler, 1988, p. 6).

Bowles and Gintis (1976) argued that schooling is a way of preparing students to take their place in a socioeconomic system. Central to their notion of reproduction is the idea that "the educational system helps integrate youth into the economic system . . . through a structural correspondence between its social relations and those of production" (p. 131). Bowles and Gintis argued that middle- and working-class students are socialized differently in school. Working-class students' relationship with the schooling process is marked by a high degree of certainty, control, and student subordinacy to authority, whereas middle-class students' relationship with the schooling

---

[1]The research reported in this chapter is part of a dissertation study conducted at the University of Georgia under the direction of Dr. Patricia S. Wilson.

process involves students' independence and students' participation in the decision-making process. The schooling structures reproduce the existing class structures by preparing students to be workers at various levels. Bowles and Gintis (1976) elaborated on this notion as follows:

> Different levels of education feed workers into different levels within the occupational structure and correspondingly, tend toward an internal organization comparable to levels in the hierarchal division of labor. . . . Thus [African Americans] and other minorities are concentrated in schools whose repressive, arbitrary, generally chaotic internal order, coercive authority structures, and minimal possibilities for advancement mirror the characteristics of inferior job situations. Similarly, predominantly working-class schools tend to emphasize behavioral control and rule-following, while schools in well-to-do suburbs employ relatively open systems that favor greater student participation, less direct supervision, more student electives, and, in general, a value system stressing internalized standards of control. (p. 132)

Several research studies (see Anyon, 1981; Solomon, 1992; Willis, 1977) document this notion of schooling structures perpetuating social stratification. For example, Anyon (1981) found in her study of five elementary schools in a particular school district that, although the curriculum objectives were the same for all students and students had access to the same materials, they had quite different schooling experiences. Mathematics in the lower social class schools was taught by giving distinct rules and procedures. However, mathematics in the higher social class schools was taught by engaging students in reasoning, interpreting, and problem solving. Students received different mathematics instruction even though their schools had the same mathematics textbooks and materials. When teachers in the working-class schools were asked about their mathematics teaching practices, they alluded to their practices as being appropriate for the students they were teaching. One teacher referred to certain pages in the mathematics textbook and called these pages the *thinking* pages and commented that these pages were too hard for working-class students.

Bourdieu and Passeron (1977) argued that different social classes and groups are characterized by their knowledge and modes of thought (i.e., their cultural capital), and valued school knowledge is actually the cultural knowledge of the dominant classes. Thus, students whose cultural knowledge is most related to the cultural knowledge of the dominant classes will tend to be successful in school. Bourdieu and Passeron believed that students of the dominant classes appear to be naturally intelligent when, in fact, they already know what is valued. This notion is closely aligned with what Gramsci (1971) referred to as hegemony. Hegemony can be defined as the dominant classes' control of ideology through various institutional structures and cultural values and attitudes. It seems reasonable to assume that Gramsci's notion of hegemony is inherent in schools. For instance, what should be taught in schools, what is appropriate and valued knowledge, and what is important mathematics can all be considered imposed ideologies that are controlled by dominant culture (Apple, 1992). Consequently, some students contest hegemonic control by resisting school (see Anyon, 1981; Ogbu, 1991; Solomon, 1992; Willis, 1977).

African-American Culture

Because race and ethnicity are categories laden with cultural beliefs and biases that are often unconscious, it is essential to consider cultural orientations when examining the mathematical experiences of African-American students. Some scholars (Boykin 1986; Ogbu, 1986) believe there are characteristics inherent in African-American culture explaining race-related differences existing in school performance and explaining the academic success or failure of African-American students.

Ogbu (1986) argued that several minority groups co-exist, some of whom succeed in school and some of whom do not. Ogbu suggested that there are three types of minority groups—autonomous, immigrant, and castelike minorities, and the classification of these groups distinguishes those who succeed in school from those who do not. Autonomous minority groups include such ethnic groups as the Amish, the Jews, and the Mormons in the United States. Autonomous minorities are not totally subordinated politically and economically by the dominant group (Whites) and are not forced to play denigrated roles.

Immigrant minorities such as the Chinese, Filipinos, Japanese, and Koreans in the United States have come to America voluntarily to improve their economic, political, or social status. They may be subordinated politically and economically initially, but they view their conditions as much better than the conditions they left behind in their native country.

African Americans, Native Americans, and Mexican Americans are castelike minorities because they were incorporated into the country involuntarily and permanently through slavery or conquest. Specifically, Africans, now African Americans, were brought to America as slaves and were relegated to menial positions and status after emancipation.

Castelike minorities lack political power, and this is reinforced by economic subordination. Moreover, castelike minorities' structural subordination is reinforced by the ideology of the dominant group that rationalizes the menial status of the castelike minorities. As being members of a subordinate group in a stratified racial caste, African Americans face a job ceiling:

> A job ceiling is the result of the consistent pressures and obstacles that selectively assign [African Americans] and similar minorities to jobs at the low level of status, power, dignity, and income, while allowing Whites to compete more easily and freely, on the basis of individual training and ability or educational credentials, for desirable jobs above that ceiling. (Ogbu, 1986, p. 30)

According to Ogbu (1986), African Americans usually resist the dominant group's ideology by resisting school and the ideology of school because they view schooling as characteristic of the dominant group (see also Ogbu, 1991). Those African Americans who take this particular stance believe their economic, political, and social problems are due to *the system*. They believe their problems are enduring and see little chance of achieving middle-class positions (Ogbu, 1986). Therefore, schooling and behaving like the dominant culture are not viewed as avenues for self-betterment. Rather, these African Americans believe that manipulating or changing the system gives them a better chance of advancement (Ogbu, 1986). Consequently, African Americans tend to act in various ways (e.g., resistance to school) that are in opposition to dominant culture. Ogbu (1986) termed this resistance, *cultural inversion*, which may be defined as "a tendency to regard a cultural behavior, event, entity of meanings as *not* [African American] because it is characteristic of Whites or vice-versa" (p. 48). Cultural inversion is manifested in education in the sense that academic success is perceived by some African-American students as characteristic of White culture. Thus, those African-American students who are successful in school are condemned as "acting White." Ogbu stated that cultural inversion is a coping mechanism that some African-American students use to co-exist with dominant culture.

Boykin (1986) argued that the co-existence of African Americans and White Americans is framed in a *triple quandary* in which African Americans participate. In this triple quandary—the mainstream experience, the minority experience, and the African-American cultural experience—there is constant interplay among these three realms of experiential negotiation. African Americans participate in the mainstream realm through work systems, judicial systems, and bureaucratic systems. However, their participation is "tempered by concomitant negotiation through the minority and [African-American] cultural realms" (Boykin, 1986, p. 66).

"The minority experience is based on exposure to social, economic, and political oppression" (Boykin, 1986, p. 66). Consequently, the minority experience produces adaptive responses, usually defensive postures, that help African Americans cope with the predicament created by oppressive forces. From Ogbu's (1991) perspective, these defensive postures are usually manifested in education by resistance to schooling.

Boykin (1986) explained the African-American cultural experience as having a culturally indigenous basis from which African Americans interpret and negotiate social reality. The African-American cultural experience is rooted in traditional African ethos, and interrelated dimensions of African-American culture include spirituality, harmony, movement, verve, affect, communalism, expressive individualism, oral tradition, and social time perspective. These dimensions are prominent in the way African Americans interpret and view the world (Boykin, 1986).

Several scholars (Boykin, 1986; Prager, 1982) indicated that African Americans struggle with two cultural systems: what is deemed in mainstream society as ideal—the ideology, values, and beliefs of dominant culture—and traditional African propensities, that is, the African-American experience is fundamentally bicultural. Prager (1982) referred to the biculturality of African Americans as trying to fuse two cultural traditions or cultural frames of reference that are incommensurable:

It is not the mere fact that [African Americans] hold a dual identity which has constrained achievement; to one degree or another, every ethnic and racial group has faced a similar challenge. The [African American] experience in America is distinguished by the fact that the qualities attributed to [being African American] are in opposition to the qualities rewarded by society. The specific features of [being African American], as cultural imagery, are almost by definition those qualities which the dominant society has attempted to deny in itself, and it is the difference between [being African American] and [being White] that defines, in many respects, American cultural self-understanding. For [African Americans], then, the effort to reconcile into one personality images which are diametrically opposed poses an extraordinarily difficult challenge. To succeed in America raises the risk of being told—either by Whites or by [African Americans]—that one is not "really [African American]." No other group in America has been so acutely confronted with this dilemma, for no other group has been simultaneously so systematically ostracized while remaining so culturally significant. (p. 111)

What is important about Prager's remarks is whether African-American students perceive their culture as in opposition to White culture; then how these perceptions come into play in schooling may be rooted in how African-American students view their culture. For instance, if African-American students perceive mathematics as a discipline for Whites, then whether or not they perceive their culture as a counterculture to White culture becomes an important construct in African-American students becoming successful with school mathematics.

Fordham (1988) found the anthropological concept *fictive-kinship* useful in studying the social identity and cultural frame of reference among African Americans. Fictive-kinship refers to a "kinship-like connection between and among persons in a society, not related by blood or marriage, who have maintained essential reciprocal social or economic relationship" (Fordham, 1988, p. 56). The fictive-kinship extends beyond skin color and incorporates a particular mind-set or world view of those persons who are considered to be African American. Further, the fictive-kinship symbolizes a particular "people-hood" in opposition to the prevailing White society.

The collective ethos of the fictive-kinship (or indigenous African-American culture) is challenged when African-American children enter school and are faced with the individual ethos and competitiveness of dominant culture. This causes some African-American students to experience ambivalence in their schooling. There is a struggle between the two systems (fictive-kinship and dominant culture ethos), and African-American students' conformity to one of the systems challenges their loyalty to the other. Thus, some African-American students remain affiliates of the fictive-kinship, and to legitimate their membership in the indigenous African-American culture they ensure their failure in school. Conversely, those African-American students who assimilate into the school culture and minimize their connection to the indigenous African-American culture are more likely to succeed in school. These African-American students minimize their relationship to the African-American community and the stigma attached to being African American to improve their chances of succeeding in school. They take on a persona of "racelessness," which is "the desired and eventual outcome of developing a raceless persona, and is either a conscious or unconscious effort on the part of such students to disaffiliate themselves from the fictive-kinship system" (Fordham, 1988, pp. 57–58).

Fordham's (1988) notion of the fictive-kinship and Ogbu's (1986) notion of cultural inversion elicit some very compelling questions about the mathematics education of African-American students. What *should* African-American students give up in the context of mathematics education? Do some African Americans define themselves as successful although they have little commitment to the African-American community? Do some African Americans sublimate their academic goals to legitimate their commitment to the African-American community? Taking on the persona of racelessness may lead to a no-win situation. As Fordham puts it: Is racelessness a pragmatic strategy or a Pyrrhic victory? If African-American students do not succeed in school and with school mathematics, then they possibly pay a high price socially, economically, and politically. If they do succeed in school and with school mathematics, then they possibly pay a high price culturally as defined by Fordham's fictive-kinship. To fully understand the mathematical experiences of African-American students, it is important to conceptualize how African-American students view their *success* with school mathematics, namely, whether they perceive their becoming successful with school mathematics as having particular consequences.

The Nature of African-American Students Succeeding in Mathematics

Ogbu (1990) defined "secondary educational strategies" as strategies African Americans use to achieve some measure of school success. He surveyed ethnographic literature and related works and found that academically successful African-American students can be categorized according to the types of secondary strategies they use. These categories include: assimilators, emissaries, alternators, regulars, and ambivalents. *Assimilators* are academically successful students who have chosen to disassociate themselves from African-American cultural frame of reference in favor of White culture. They believe they must give up their membership in African-American peer groups or the African-American community, which usually results in peer criticism and isolation. *Emissaries* are African-American students who play down African-American identity and cultural frame of reference to succeed in school and in mainstream institutions by mainstream criteria. However, they do not reject African-American culture and identity. *Alternators* are African-American students who more or less adopt the immigrant minority students' strategy of "accommodation without assimilation." These students do not reject African-American cultural frame of reference, but they elect to play by the rules of school culture to achieve academic success. *Regulars* are accepted as members of the street culture but do not subscribe to all of its norms. At school, regulars are deemed by school authority as good students who abide by school rules. Outside of school, regulars are deemed by African-American peer groups as regular members of the group. Consequently, regulars' academic success usually lies in their ability to camouflage their academic striving. *Ambivalents* are African-American students who are caught between the desire to be with their African-American peers and the desire to achieve school success. Often they do not resolve this conflict, and their academic success is achieved at a relatively high cost and can be erratic.

Experiences in Traditional Mathematics Classrooms.   Stiff (1990) and Stiff and Harvey (1988) argued that African-American students' cultural frame of reference is opposed to the culture of the traditional mathematics classroom. They asserted that the attributes of students who are successful with school mathematics are at odds with the attributes associated with African-American cultural frame of reference. The attributes of successful students include working independently, being direct and concise, valuing direct and efficient methods of obtaining information, using accepted (elaborate) syntactical discourse, and responding in an orderly and structured matter in classroom situations (Stiff, 1990). By contrast, the African-American cultural frame of reference entails attributes that include working in support groups, telling tangential stories that may or may not relate to the problem, valuing the personal relationship that can be nurtured, using a "conversational style" discourse, and perhaps leaving one's seat to answer a question (Stiff, 1990). These attributes associated with African-American cultural frame of reference are usually condemned in traditional mathematics classrooms (Stiff, 1990; Stiff & Harvey, 1988), sending a message to African-American students: "You are not the type of mathematics student we want" (Stiff, 1990, p. 156).

Stiff (1990) and Stiff and Harvey (1988) call into question inequities in traditional mathematics classrooms due to the lack of affirming differences in students' social and cultural orientations. Hence, the classroom environment should not accentuate color blindness, meaning that teachers should accept and affirm learning style differences based on cultural orientations (Grant, 1989). What becomes tricky is whether this implies that teachers should treat all students the same (equally) or differently based on their culture. Perhaps it is essential to speak in terms of attending to the needs of all students rather than in terms of equal treatment. As such, equity becomes less confusing. Attending to the needs of all students means that teachers must take into account the cultural, socioeconomic, and political realities that students of color face (Gay, 1983). "Without some understanding of ethnic heritages, values, priorities, and perspectives it is impossible for teachers to interact most constructively with ethnic students, or relate subject matter content and schooling processes to their experiential and cultural frames of reference" (Gay, 1983, p. 81).

Mathematical Experiences Within a Social Context.   It is important to consider the ways in which the nature of the mathematical experiences of African-American students is framed in the structure of society as a whole. Schools are not immune to the stress, prejudices, inequalities, and inequities that exist in the larger society (Apple, 1985, 1992, 1995). In fact, schools may participate in maintaining or perpetuating differential economic, political, and cultural power (Apple, 1985, 1992, 1995). With social structures such as desegregation and equal opportunity laws in place, it seems all students, regardless of race, should receive the same mathematics education. In other words, these social structures should ensure equality as well as equity. However, although schools have opened their doors to an increasingly diverse student population, schools differentiate among these students internally (Banks, 1988).

To fully understand schools' active involvement in treating or socializing diverse students differently than White students, it is important to understand how diverse students view their membership in particular cultures and the relationship between this membership and their experiences in school. Specifically, we must conceptualize what diverse students find in their schooling experiences that is congruent or in conflict with their own cultural orientations. Note that "culture refers to the deep structures of knowing, understanding, acting, and being in the world" (Ladson-Billings, 1997, p. 700). Thus, cultural orientations inform students' thought and activity and play a significant role in how they perceive and respond to schooling. The study reported subsequently particularly examined the mathematical experiences of African-American students in the context of their social and cultural realities.

METHOD

This study employed a phenomenological research strategy. Phenomenological research describes subjective experiences of individuals (Tesch, 1987). It is aimed at interpretive understanding and describes individual experiences from the viewpoint of the individual (Tesch, 1987). Phenomenological research explores the personal construction of a person's world through in-depth, unstructured interviews and other data sources (Tesch, 1987). Data were collected in the form of initial surveys, autobiographies, and interviews (including a final interview that consisted of a member check by the participants) to explore life histories of the participants in the context of their mathematical experiences.

Phenomenological research involves a back-and-forth movement between a phase of thinking and analyzing and a phase of data gathering, which is analogous to constant comparative analysis (Strauss, 1987). Surveys and autobiographies were used as data sources, were analyzed, and were then used as stimuli to gather more data during interviews. The first stage of the analysis occurred parallel with and informed subsequent data collection. During this first stage of analysis, particular themes were sought that were preeminent in the data sources.

The second stage of analysis received most attention at the end of data collection. The objectives of the study guided the search for invariant themes and patterns that emerged from the data. Particularly in this second stage, the author sought to explicate, interpret, and make sense of the invariant themes in terms of theoretical perspectives.

The selection of participants in this study was a criterion-based selection. "Criterion-based selection requires that the *researcher* establishes in advance a set of criteria or a list of attributes that the units for study must possess" (LeCompte & Preissle, 1993, p. 69). The researcher "then searches for exemplars that match the specified array of characteristics" (LeCompte & Preissle, 1993, p. 69). The criteria for this study were college African-American students who were near completion of a mathematics or mathematics education degree. Four (three females and one male) African-American students were chosen to participate in the study. Two, Ashley and Sheilah, completed the study. Ashley was a junior in college pursuing a bachelor's degree in mathematics, and Sheilah was a graduate student in her final quarter of completing a master's degree in mathematics education.

RESULTS

Ashley's Mathematical Experiences

Ashley was a junior attending a predominantly Black university, was majoring in mathematics and political science, and had maintained a 4.0 grade point average (on a 4.0 grading scale). She had attended a predominantly White middle and high school.

In high school Ashley was a member of the mathematics and science magnet program. She made As in all of her high school mathematics courses and graduated from high school with honors. Ashley's plan was to serve as a role model for other African-American youths. She believed that her mathematics degree would begin the path of her finding her special place in mathematics history, a place that would contribute to the success of other African-American youths.

Elementary Experience (Grades 1–5).   Ashley did not comment on exactly what mathematics learning was like for her during elementary school, but she did contend that she was afraid of mathematics in the context of taking tests, especially placement tests. When Ashley moved from Colorado to the southeast in third grade, she was placed in a higher level class. Ashley believed that students were placed in particular classes based on their ability and that their ability was determined by standardized tests. After about a week of being in the higher level class, Ashley was given a placement test to determine if her class placement was on target. Ashley did poorly on the placement test and was then placed in a lower level class. She stated, "I know I was just a scary little girl. I am not good at taking standardized tests at all. I cannot take them. I don't know why. . .. I have to learn how to take them, I think. . . . I froze up" (Interview 2, 7/17/96). Ashley further stated, "I guess they [school administrators] thought I was kind of retarded. I felt bad because I knew it was the lowest class. Everybody used to say, that's the lowest class and Ms. [Carter] teaches the lowest class" (Interview 2, 7/17/96). It is evident that Ashley perceived her placement as resulting from the placement test and believed that her academic abilities were determined by this placement test.

Ashley commented that being removed from a higher level class to a lower level class had adverse effects on her confidence in doing mathematics. She said that she became afraid of mathematics and made an F in the subject at the end of the first grading period. Fortunately, for Ashley, Ms. Carter, who taught the lower level third grade class, began to give Ashley extra attention and help in mathematics. Ashley said, "She noticed something in me and she began to talk to me" (Interview 2, 7/17/96). Ashley stated that because of Ms. Carter's help she began to like mathematics and, consequently, made all As in mathematics the remainder of the year.

Middle School Experience (Grades 6–8).   Ashley attended a predominantly White middle school. She took sixth and seventh grade mathematics and Algebra I in eighth grade.

Ashley's seventh grade mathematics teacher encouraged her to take an algebra placement test. The results of this particular test determined whether or not students would take general mathematics or Algebra I in eighth grade. From Ashley's perspective, this placement test "would determine if I knew enough to get into algebra early" (Autobiography, 7/11/96). This test was not required for all students, but it was mandatory for those students who wanted to take Algebra I in eighth grade. Ashley did not want to take this test because of her fear of standardized tests (perhaps stemming from her third grade experience) but did so because her seventh grade mathematics teacher believed in her ability to do mathematics. Ashley's seventh grade teacher told her that she needed to get an early start in higher mathematics. At the time Ashley did not know what her teacher meant by that or what a difference getting an early start in higher mathematics would make in her mathematical experiences. Ashley did take the test and stated, "I am awful at taking placement tests, but I succeeded" (Autobiography, 7/11/96).

Although Ashley was going to get a *jump* on mathematics by being in Algebra I in eighth grade, this probably was one of the most traumatic experiences she had in her schooling. Note how Ashley described her Algebra I teacher and her experience in this class.

> In 8th grade, I took Algebra I. My teacher was Mr. [Miller]. Mr. Miller was the complete opposite of Mrs. [Stewart, her sixth grade mathematics teacher] and Mrs. [Jenkins, her seventh grade mathematics teacher]. He was a short chubby old man that always had a red neck. Mr. Miller gave tests with only four problems and no partial credit. Of course, the grading system that he was using was difficult but Mr. Miller's attitudes toward his Black students were even more difficult. My best friend [Amber] and I were the only Black students in his class. We could tell that Mr. Miller was burning with anger because we were smart enough to be in his class. When Amber asked him for help, he would just say, "Go figure it out; you have a book." On the other hand, I refused to ask him for anything because I was determined to be successful without his help. His racist jokes, ugly glares, and superior feelings only gave me the power I needed to defeat him. What I mean by "defeating" him was proving that I could make good grades and learn algebra despite his feelings. In the end, Mr. Miller had to give me credit for my work which came in the form of a "B." Ironically, I did not see getting a "B" in Mr. Miller's class as an academic achievement. I saw it as one of the many battles I would win in life. (Autobiography, 7/11/96)

Ashley only briefly mentioned what it was like to learn algebra in eighth grade, and she did not talk much about the mathematics itself. She asserted that the class was difficult because it was "a different kind of math. I was used to general math and then when I did algebra and I saw a variable for the first time, I was like, what's that?" (Interview 1, 6/27/96). Ashley's brief comments about the mathematics during the interview may have been because the experience of racism in the class was more significant for her.

High School Experience (Grades 9–12).   Ashley also attended a predominantly White high school. She had to apply to get into the school's mathematics and science magnet program. Succeeding in Algebra I in eighth grade was a prerequisite for entering the magnet program. Ashley commented that, because she was very successful in the middle school she attended, it was easy for her to get into the program. The mathematics and science magnet program was designed to prepare students for college-level mathematics and science courses. All students in this program took the same mathematics courses. These courses included Algebra II, Geometry, Statistics, and Advanced Placement Calculus I and II. Ashley received all A's in these courses.

Ashley stated that about 23 African-American students entered the mathematics and science magnet program when she did, but that number became smaller and smaller as she progressed through her high school career. During Ashley's senior year, she was the only African-American student in most of her classes. Ashley believed that the African-American students became discouraged because they were supposed to "think a certain way" (Interview 1, 6/27/96) and "they felt they did not belong" (Autobiography, 7/11/96). She said that the majority of African-American students were put in low academic tracks because they were labeled as "underachievers, low. [School administrators believed] we didn't have any kind of education. We were all on welfare. . . . I just think that" (Interview 1, 6/27/96). Ashley also stated that she did not believe that many African-American students got credit for their work in this particular high school. Note Ashley's perception of how African-American students were in some sense cheated.

> Because I think, when we were, when we were looking for colleges to go to, you know you are supposed to have a counsellor, and our counsellors, they didn't try to push us. They didn't give us any information. We had to go search ourselves. . . . We just didn't get credit. I mean, if we would do good in class or something we wouldn't get recognized as much, if we had honors program and everything. So they would try to push a certain type of people [Whites] up and make sure they got the scholarships, the good schools and everything. (Interview 1, 6/27/96)

Ashley stated that to succeed in school and with school mathematics one had to acquiesce to the ideologies of school culture that were in conflict with African Americans' ways of thinking. She said, "I think we, I think Black people look at a lot of things different. It depends on how you were raised or where you grew up. So if you don't think of it a certain way, it is wrong" (Interview 1, 6/27/96). Ashley commented that she felt as though she played a dual role in her schooling. In this sense, in schooling or a classroom context, Ashley adapted her thinking and activity in a way that was consistent with White culture. However, internally, she tried to maintain her own sense of identity as an African American. Consequently, Ashley experienced ambivalence in her schooling because of the desire to become successful while remaining a member of the indigenous African-American culture. Ashley stated, "I guess I just did what I had to do to achieve my goals. That means that sometimes I would be someone else. I mean not really change, but sometimes you wear a mask. . . . I had to do that in order to be successful and I don't even know if I should have done that, but that was my main goal then" (Interview 1, 6/27/96).

Ashley's behaving as an "alternator" (see Ogbu, 1990) or accommodating her thinking and activity to reflect that of school culture resulted in peer criticism. Her African-American peers accused her of acting White and selling out when she endeavored to become successful with school mathematics. When asked how she dealt with peer criticism, Ashley stated that she remained focused and kept studying. Ashley elaborated on this notion:

> I knew that learning was the important thing. What I knew in the end would determine my path in life. Graduating from high school with honors and being ranked as the first

Black in my class was a great accomplishment. I made up for all the times that my friends thought that I was "crazy" for staying in the program [mathematics and science magnet program]. I also made up for wearing a "mask" in my classes. The "mask" symbolized my hidden feelings about being in a class where no one had my face, my thoughts, or my beliefs. Consequently, after high school I was determined not to wear that "mask" again. (Autobiography 7/11/96)

Collegiate Experience.   At the time of the study, Ashley was attending a predominantly Black university in the same southeastern city where she grew up. Ashley stated, "I chose [this university] because I wanted to experience learning in a different environment opposed to my middle and high school, which means a predominantly Black school" (Initial survey, 6/19/96). She further stated, "I felt like it was time to be around people who [*thought*] and looked liked me" (Autobiography, 7/11/96). She believed that attending this university would allow her to remove her mask and "let her face breathe."

Ashley believed that several of her mathematics courses in her undergraduate studies were too easy for her because she had attended a strong academic high school and was a member of the high school's mathematics and science magnet program. Ashley commented in reference to her college algebra class, "Everyone in my class thought that I was so smart but I already knew what they were learning" (Autobiography, 7/11/96). It is worth noting here that Ashley's notion of already knowing what was being learned in some sense parallels what critical theorists call cultural capital (Bourdieu & Passeron, 1977). Bourdieu and Passeron (1977) believed that students whose knowledge is consistent with that of dominant culture are more apt to become successful in school because the ideology of school culture reflects that of dominant culture. Ashley believed that the ideologies of her middle and high school experience reflected that of dominant culture.

Sheilah's Mathematical Experiences

Sheilah was a graduate student pursuing a master's degree in mathematics education at a predominantly White university. Sheilah had attended a fundamental magnet middle school and a predominantly Black high school where she graduated as valedictorian (student who ranks number one academically in his or her senior class) with a 4.0 grade point average. She had obtained a bachelor's degree in mathematics from a predominantly Black university and completed her undergraduate studies with honors with a 3.97 cumulative grade point average. Sheilah's plan was to serve as a role model for other African-American youths by teaching high school mathematics. She believed that teaching mathematics would allow her to make a difference in the lives of African-American students.

Middle School Experience (Grades 6–8).   Sheilah described her middle school as a magnet school that was very strong academically and that enforced strict discipline. She referred to the school as a "melting pot," meaning that the student population was balanced racially and economically. There was no school zone for the magnet school and any students could attend, but the school always had a long waiting list of students who wanted to attend the school.

Sheilah took Algebra I in eighth grade. Although Sheilah commented that tracking was not practiced in this middle school, she stated that taking Algebra I in eighth grade was determined by a pretest. Sheilah stated, "I don't remember exactly, but I remember having to take a test to test what you know from I guess previous math courses we took and how much you would be able to learn or whatever, and only a certain group got in" (Interview 1, 7/3/96).

Sheilah did not describe the certain group of students that got into the class in terms of race, gender, and socioeconomic status. This may be the case because these characteristics in this particular instance were not significant for her. However, she did comment further on the implications for being in this class.

> We had a lot of people whose parents pressured the school to let them into the algebra class, because it was seen as a prestigious thing to be in the algebra class. So we had parents who would go and try, just have a knock-down-drag-out fight with the faculty and administration about trying to get their kids into this algebra class, because their kids should be with the other kids. And they [the students] got there and they couldn't perform and then they had to, you know, either fail the course, or had to drop back to a regular eighth grade math course and so there was a problem there. It was seen as, some people saw it as the more elite kids were in the eighth grade algebra class. And if you weren't in that class, you weren't as bright. (Interview 1, 7/3/96)

Sheilah's description of this class being characterized as a class for "elite kids" in some sense parallels what Anderson (1990) called the elitist view of mathematics, meaning that only a select few can learn and do mathematics. In Sheilah's experience, it is evident that this class seemed to have served those students who possessed some requisite knowledge denied the vast majority as determined by a pretest. Joseph (1987) believed that this often-held elitist view of mathematics extends further than the classroom and is connected to intellectual racism. Joseph (1987) stated,

> This elitism is translated at a classroom level into a view, often implicit and not spoken, that real mathematics... is an activity suited for a select few—which when extended provides the broader argument that mathematics is a unique product of European culture. Thus, elitism in the classroom is ultimately linked to the form of intellectual racism which ... [is] described as Eurocentrism. (Joseph, 1987, pp. 25–26)

High School Experience (Grades 9–12).   Sheilah attended a predominately Black high school and described her high school experience as one of the best in her life. However, she commented that, although she had had "a really good experience as far as being nurtured in math" (Interview 1, 7/3/96) in high school, she was faced with a "racial experience" that had to do with her schooling in general that really discouraged her. She said:

> I did have an experience in high school where I got discouraged as far as I was doing well, but they [White administrators] were trying to keep me down. . . . I was the number one ranked student in my freshman, sophomore, junior year, and then my senior year a

[White] student came from this private school. . . . He just counted on being valedictorian because I guess he wasn't really in the running at the private school. We had a [White] counsellor who was really nasty and she tried to see to it that he would be valedictorian. . . . I had a higher GPA and he got a B in calculus and a B in physics [Sheilah received A's in calculus and physics.]. . . . When it came time for the graduation and everything they [White administrators] didn't want to say I was valedictorian, that he was salutatorian, they just wanted to call it honor graduates, you know, first and second honor graduates. (Interview 1, 7/3/96)

From Sheilah's perception, it seemed as though her becoming valedictorian of her high school was deemed inappropriate by some of the White administrators of the school. Sheilah perceived this experience as an act by White administrators to "keep her down," and she believed that this experience was "totally racial," meaning that the only reason it took place was because she was African American. Hence, certain aspects of the social milieu of the school stemmed from the society as a whole, indicating that schools are perhaps products of the society (Bowles & Gintis, 1976).

Collegiate Experience.   Sheilah stated that she was fortunate to have had the experience of attending a predominantly Black university during her undergraduate studies because

I really think it was an advantage for me to go to a predominantly Black college because I have friends who are in the math program or math education program at [a White university] and they are struggling. I mean really struggling and they don't have that support that I had, you know. I could always go back to my teacher and say, this is what's going on, and they would call me by my first name. They knew me and some of them knew my parents. . . . I had that support and a lot of the support I had there, they [my friends] don't have [at the White university]. (Interview 2, 7/17/96)

It appears that this university provided a nurturing environment that was influential in Sheilah's success with school mathematics. By contrast, Sheilah attended a predominantly White university for her graduate studies and stated that she was very "apprehensive" when she first began her graduate degree. She said,

When I first got [there], I was like, oh my gosh, you know, I don't know what I'm in for because I mean, my high school was predominantly Black, my [undergraduate] college was predominantly Black. And I mean, I have gone to school with Whites, especially in middle school and undergraduate [school]. I mean middle school and elementary school was equally mixed, but from high school on, all I have ever known is predominantly Black, and then to be on the other side of the coin. I just didn't know what to expect. And I just thought that I wasn't going to fit in. And what I learned at [the Black university I attended], I did question was it enough, was my education enough to be [at this White university]. (Interview 1, 7/3/96)

Sheilah stated that she especially questioned her education and her ability to do mathematics during her Real Analysis class. She said in reference to this course,

When I get to a point where I just don't see, you know, where to begin or where to start and I just, I mean if I have five questions and I know they are due in two days and I don't know where to start and how to do it or you know, it's really discouraging, and I don't know who to go to, who can help me. And it just made me realize, do I really, am I in the right field, is this really for me, you know, I should be able to do some of this.... It's insulting when you have gone through all of these years of learning math and here comes something and you just can't do it and it makes you feel, you know, am I really a math major? (Interview 2, 7/17/96)

Although Sheilah stated that her White peers in this course were reluctant to study with her and work with her on homework problems (behavior she was accustomed to during her undergraduate studies), she said her difficulty in this course mainly had to do with her grasping abstract concepts.

When asked how she felt about sometimes being the only African-American student in some of her mathematics courses, Sheilah replied,

Sometimes I feel good and sometimes I feel bad. I feel good because I know I can hang with the best of them, you know, and that I'm in this top math course and I can do this. Sometimes I feel angry because there are not more of us [African Americans] in there and I feel like we have been cheated and that we have been filtered out and that I am the only one that has survived at this point. (Interview 1, 7/3/96)

It appears that Sheilah experienced some ambivalence in her mathematical experiences during her graduate studies as indicated by her feeling both good and bad about being the only African American in some of her mathematics classes. Although Sheilah in some sense felt proud to have been in higher level mathematics courses, she also felt concerned that more African Americans were not in those courses.

Sheilah stated that, during her high school experience, she was surrounded by African-American students who were in higher level mathematics courses. She said that this was not the case during her student teaching experience that took place during the final quarter of her graduate studies. Sheilah asserted that she noticed that most of the African-American students were in general mathematics or pre-algebra courses (lower-level mathematics courses). She said that she did not realize until her student teaching experience that tracking, serving as a filter, played a significant role in African-American students' mathematical experiences. Sheilah stated,

I don't know what it is, but if you have one Black student out of 1,500 students taking calculus, something is wrong, and only five out of 1,500, or maybe 10 out of 1,500 taking trig, [in] two classes [combined]. Then the pre-algebra, just full of us [African Americans], you know, and the general math, just full of us, and maybe one or two Whites there [in general math or pre-algebra]. (Interview 2, 7/17/96)

Sheilah asserted that one reason she wants to teach mathematics is that she wants to help eradicate the problem of African-American students being filtered into lower level mathematics classes. She stated,

That's probably the reason I want to go into mathematics education, you know, so it won't happen.... I mean somebody has got to look out for them [African-American students], you know, somebody has, I mean, there are so many roles I want to play. I want to play the person who even if you [African-American students] are not in my class, I can tell you, you can do this math, you are going to [do well] in that class, you know, you can do this and not let them just fall by the way-side. (Interview 1, 7/3/96)

Sheilah wanting to play these particular teaching roles parallels the underlying premise of critical theory that society is exploitative and oppressive but capable of being changed. Sheilah questioned certain aspects of schooling such as tracking that may be oppressive for African-American students and that may contribute to African-American students being filtered into lower level mathematics classes. Sheilah believed that the educational practices she plans to use in her own teaching can play a significant role in countering this oppression and consequently help change the current status of African-American students' mathematical experiences. Sheilah stated, "What disturb[s] me is that many Blacks [are] in lower level classes and their instructors [do] not qualify as good teachers to me. I decided I want to make a difference" (Autobiography, 7/9/96).

IMPLICATIONS FOR MATHEMATICS EDUCATION

Ashley's and Sheilah's stories suggest that particular schooling practices were important constituents in their schooling and mathematical experiences. Their stories raise concerns about practices such as tracking and suggest that their perceptions of and responses to their experiences in school influenced their succeeding in mathematics.

To Track or Not to Track

Examining tracking in the context of Ashley's and Sheilah's experiences indicates that at the very least there is a need to question its value or its role in contributing to their success with school mathematics. Neither Ashley nor Sheilah acknowledged tracking as a schooling practice that propelled them in mathematics. Neither of them made contentions such as "I was successful because I was in the college preparatory track." Hence, what does tracking mean in the context of these two students' success and in their mathematical experiences? For Ashley, tracking acted as a barrier she struggled with and tried to overcome. In Ashley's third-grade experience, tracking reinforced labeling and stereotyping students and reinforced the notion that particular tracks are associated with intelligence and academic ability. In Ashley's high school experience, tracking served as a *separatist agent* in which Ashley was isolated from her African-American peers who were in low tracks. Moreover, Ashley's peers associated being in high tracks with acting White, selling out, or giving up being African American. Perhaps the disproportionate number of African-Americans in higher-level mathematics courses was a significant factor in shaping Ashley's peers' belief systems about who should be doing mathematics. If the norm is lower-level mathematics courses predominated by African-American students, then it is conceivable, quite probable, that African-American students would buy into the notion that mathematics is a discipline suited for Whites. This notion seems cyclic in nature and feeds on itself, that is, African-American students' believing mathematics is suited for Whites is reinforced by lower-level mathematics courses mainly serving African-Americans students and lower-level mathematics courses mainly serving African-American students is reinforced by African-American students' believing mathematics is suited for Whites. Tracking seems to reinforce this notion rather than counteract it.

As Sheilah recognized during her graduate studies, there is a need to question schooling practices that filter a vast majority of African-American students in lower level mathematics courses. Thus, it is essential to question the role of tracking in working to undermine the notion that all students should have the opportunity to learn "important mathematics." Scholars (Oakes, 1986, 1990; Slavin, 1987) established that students in low tracks do not acquire the mathematical experiences or learn important mathematics needed to allow them to become critical thinkers and problem solvers.

Also, there is a need to question schooling practices that cause African-American students to feel "badly" about being the only African American in advanced mathematics courses (e.g., Sheilah's graduate school experiences and Ashley's high school experiences). In this sense, excelling in mathematics for these African-American students mimics a game of survival, and their perceptions of the ecology of mathematics education tend to reflect that of a struggle among students for "limited" mathematical knowledge and understanding. To eradicate such perceptions, schooling practices must ensure that African-American students understand that they are "welcomed" and expected to partake of "unlimited" mathematical knowledge and understanding.

Ashley's and Sheilah's experiences exemplify the attributes of tracking that maintain and perpetuate inequalities and inequities in society. We easily seem to buy into the rhetoric of "equality for all" and "mathematics literacy for all," while holding in place schooling practices such as tracking that ensure "equality for some" and "mathematics literacy for a few." As a consequence, tracking seems to *resegregate* our mathematics classrooms, our schools, and our society.

Perception and Response: Indicators of Mathematical Success?

According to Ogbu (1986),

> What makes children succeed in learning and demonstrating what schools teach them is not merely the type of genes they bring to school, the type of homes or environment they come from, or their cultural language, interactional or cognitive styles. It is, instead, a combination of two factors: the diligence with which schools teach the children; and how the students perceive and respond to schooling. (p. 40)

However, it is important to consider that how students perceive and respond to schooling is influenced by their cultures, orientations, and social realities.

Ashley's perception of her mathematical experiences can be characterized as *the struggle*. The struggle implies being in the trenches and is associated with fighting battles and dealing with conflict. When Ashley talked about her mathematical experiences, she accentuated the negative aspects of her experiences. Ashley's struggle with mathematics was socially imposed, meaning her struggle stemmed from the social milieu of schooling rather than from the mathematics itself. When Ashley expounded on her mathematical experiences, she specifically referred to experiencing racism from students, teachers, and school administrators (i.e., fighting battles) and to contending with peer criticism (i.e., dealing with conflict) rather than referring to any difficulty of the mathematics.

Ashley believed that the ideologies of school culture were imposed upon her and were in conflict with her own ideologies. However, instead of resisting these imposed ideologies, Ashley accepted them. Ashley's response was indeed different from what has been posited in the literature (see Ogbu, 1986, 1990; Solomon, 1992; Willis, 1977).

Ashley struggled with wanting to achieve school success and remaining a member of the indigenous African-American culture. Consider the two systems, the fictive-kinship or indigenous African-American culture and dominant culture ethos or White culture, and their role in Ashley's schooling. In Ashley's experience, there appeared to have been a struggle between the two systems, and Ashley's conformity to one of the systems (White culture) challenged her loyalty to the other. As noted earlier, Ashley was accused of acting White when she endeavored to become successful with school mathematics. Hence, her loyalty to the fictive-kinship was questioned by her peers. Further, Ashley questioned her own loyalty to the fictive-kinship. This is evidenced by Ashley stating that wearing the mask helped her become successful, but "I don't even know if I should have done that," learning a certain way helped her become successful, but "I know that is not really right," and accepting the ideologies of school culture or acting as though she accepted them helped her become successful, but "It's just an awful thing to say." Although Ashley's acceptance of imposed ideologies led to her success, she undoubtedly believed her acceptance challenged her membership in African-American culture.

By contrast, Sheilah's perception of her mathematical experiences can be characterized as *the challenge*. The challenge implies demanding but inviting. Sheilah's challenge seemed to have been couched in the mathematics itself. Although prejudices and stresses that exist in the larger society were evident in her schooling and mathematical experiences (e.g., her "racial experience" in high school and the apprehension of White students to study with her during her graduate studies), Sheilah did not refer to her challenge as having to do with the social interactions with her peers or teachers. Rather, her challenge had to do with her grasping the mathematical content of her higher level abstract mathematics courses (e.g., her difficulty in her Real Analysis course).

Sheilah's response was to work hard and persevere to reach an achievable goal. The key for Sheilah was that her goal was always achievable. Her perception was that African Americans could become successful in mathematics because her mother, who had received a master's degree in mathematics, African American-mathematics teachers, and her high school African-American peers, who were in advanced mathematics courses, were all evidence of that success. Sheilah's response (to work hard and persevere) in her experiences seemed to have been automatic. For example, Sheilah indicated that quitting was never an option for her. This implies that either Sheilah had no choice between persevering and giving up or the choice had been made in the very early stages (i.e., early childhood) of her mathematical experiences. Unlike Ashley, who clearly had the choice of accepting or resisting school, Sheilah seemed to have accepted the ideologies of school culture without questioning that acceptance. However, keep in mind that Sheilah believed the ideologies of school culture were not imposed on her; they were congruous with her own. Why would she want to resist them?

It is important to note here that the differences in Ashley's and Sheilah's perceptions may have been influenced by their social realities. It seems that Ashley belonged to an African-American social circle that tended to equate what is to be learned in school (i.e., the curriculum), the language of instruction, and the attitudes and behaviors that enhance academic success with the attitudes, language, and behavior of White culture (Ogbu, 1990). In this regard, Ashley's social circle seems to take the cultural and language differences encountered in school as symbols of identity to be maintained rather than as barriers to overcome (Ogbu, 1990). For Ashley, adopting the ideologies of school culture was detrimental to her own culture (meaning that she had to in some sense give up her own culture) because she equated the school culture with the culture of her White oppressors. Sheilah, on the other hand, seemed to have made a distinction *between* what is learned or done in school to enhance academic success *and* linear acculturation or assimilation into White culture (Ogbu, 1990).

Ashley's and Sheilah's stories suggest that perception and response are intertwined and can be powerful in influencing African-American students success in mathematics. Students' orientations toward the world can be key in how they view mathematics and the mathematics classroom culture. If African-American students perceive mathematics as irrelevant to their lives, see no benefits of learning mathematics that extend beyond the classroom, lack role models who have done well in or benefited from mathematics, or view mathematics as a discipline suited for Whites, then their response may be to *not* learn mathematics because of its "uselessness." On the other hand, those African-American students who perceive mathematics as an avenue for a variety of educational and occupational opportunities and have role models for doing mathematics may respond to mathematics by embracing it. Schools and the mathematics classroom culture play an important role in how African-American students *see* mathematics.

A CONCLUDING REMARK

The call of reform efforts (NCTM, 1989, 1991) to engage students in "worthwhile mathematical tasks" or "important mathematics" that will allow them to become mathematical problem solvers, communicate mathematically, and reason mathematically is undermined by schooling practices that reduce African-American students' access to *mathematical power*. In this respect, mathematics education takes on a political or social agenda—who has mathematical power and who does not. Clearly, those who do not have mathematical power will have limited opportunities for further mathematics education and limited occupational opportunities (Secada, 1989). As a consequence, schooling practices that lead to ethnic and socioeconomic separation reinforce the stereotypic view that African Americans are inherently intellectually inferior (Williams, 1983). Schooling practices that are reflective of the social and economic groupings in society and that provide differential access to school opportunities are likely to maintain or increase, rather than erase, the inequities that exist in the larger social structure (Oakes, 1986). Clearly, at the center of forging a new social order that embodies equity and counters oppression is the structure of schools. Ultimately, the structure of schools affects the culture of the mathematics classroom, which affects the mathematical experiences of African-American students.

REFERENCES

Anderson, S. E. (1990). Worldmath curriculum: Fighting eurocentrism in mathematics. *The Journal of Negro Education, 59*, 348–359.

Anyon, J. (1981). Social class and school knowledge. *Curriculum Inquiry, 11*, 3–42.

Apple, M. W. (1985). *Education and power*. Boston: Routledge, Kegan, Paul.

Apple, M. W. (1992). Do the *Standards* go far enough? Power, policy, and practice in mathematics education. *Journal for Research in Mathematics Education, 23*, 412–431.

Apple, M. W. (1995). Taking power seriously: New directions in equity in mathematics education and beyond. In W. G. Secada, E. Fennema, & L. B. Adajian (Eds.), *New directions for equity in mathematics education* (pp. 329–348). New York: Cambridge University Press.

Banks, J. A. (1988). Ethnicity, class, cognitive, and motivational styles: Research and teaching implications. *Journal of Negro Education, 57*, 452–466.

Bourdieu, P., & Passeron, J. (1977). *Reproduction in education, society, and culture*. London, Sage.

Bowles, S., & Gintis, H. (1976). *Schooling in capitalist America*. New York: Basic Books.

Boykin, A. W. (1986). The triple quandary and the schooling of Afro-American children. In U. Neisser (Ed.), *The school achievement of minority children*: New perspectives (pp. 57–92). Hillsdale, NJ: Lawrence Erlbaum Associates.

Campbell, P. B. (1995). Redefining the "girl problem in mathematics." In W. G. Secada, E. Fennema, & L. B. Adajian (Eds.), *New directions for equity in mathematics education* (pp. 225–241). New York: Cambridge University Press.

Fordham, S. (1988). Racelessness a factor in students success: Pragmatic strategy or Pyrrhic victory? *Harvard Educational Review, 58*, 54–95.

Gay, G. (1983). Why multicultural education in teacher preparation programs. *Contemporary Education, 54*(2), 79–85.

Grant, C. A. (1989). Equity, equality, teachers, and classroom life. In W. G. Secada (Ed.), *Equity in education* (pp. 89–102). London: Falmer.

Gramsci, A. (1971). *Selections from the prison notebooks of Antonio Gramsci*. London: Lawrence & Wishart.

Joseph, G. (1987). Foundations of Eurocentrism in mathematics. *Race and Class, 28*, 13–28.

Ladson-Billings, G. (1997). It doesn't add up: African American students' mathematics achievement. *Journal for Research in Mathematics Education, 28*(6), 697–708.

LeCompte, M. D., & Preissle, J. (1993). *Ethnography and qualitative design in education research*. San Diego: Academic.

National Council of Teachers of Mathematics. (1989). *Curriculum and evaluation standards for school mathematics*. Reston, VA: Author.

National Council of Teachers of Mathematics. (1991). *Professional standards for teaching mathematics*. Reston, VA: Author.

National Council of Teachers of Mathematics. (1995). *Assessment standards for school mathematics*. Reston, VA: Author.

Oakes, J. (1986). Tracking, inequality, and the rhetoric of reform: Why schools don't change. *Journal of Education, 168*, 61–80.

Oakes, J. (1990). Opportunities, achievement, and choice: Women and minority students in science and mathematics. *Review of Research in Education, 16*, 153–222.

Ogbu, J. U. (1986). The consequences of the American caste system. In U. Neisser (Ed.), *The school achievement of minority children: New perspectives* (pp. 19–56). Hillsdale, NJ: Lawrence Erlbaum Associates.

Ogbu, J. U. (1990). Overcoming racial barriers to equal access. In J. J. Goodlad & P. Keating (Eds.), *Access to knowledge: An agenda for our nation's schools*. New York: College Entrance Examination Board.

Ogbu, J. U. (1991). Low school performance as an adaptation: The case of Blacks in Stockton, California. In M. A. Gibson & J. U. Ogbu (Eds.), *Minority status and schooling: A comparative study of immigrant and involuntary minorities* (pp. 249–283). New York: Garland Publishing.

Prager, J. (1982). America racial ideology as collective representation. *Ethnic and Racial Studies, 5*, 99–119.

Reyes, L. H., & Stanic, G. M. A. (1988). Race, sex, socioeconomic status and mathematics. *Journal for Research in Mathematics Education, 19*, 26–43.

Secada, W. G. (1989). Educational equity versus equality of education: An alternative conception. In W. G. Secada (Ed.), *Equity in education* (pp. 68–88). London: Falmer.

Slavin, R. E. (1987). Ability grouping and its alternatives: Must we track? *American Educator*, 32–48.

Solomon, R. P. (1992). *Black resistance in high school: Forging a separatist culture*. Albany: State University of New York Press.

Stiff, L. V. (1990). African-American students and the promise of the *Curriculum and Evaluation Standards*. In T. J. Cooney & C. R. Hirsch (Eds.), *Teaching and learning mathematics in the 1990s* (pp. 152–158). Reston, VA: NCTM.

Stiff, L. V., & Harvey, W. B. (1988). On the education of black children in mathematics. *Journal of Black Studies, 19*, 190–203.

Strauss, A. L. (1987). *Qualitative analysis for social scientists*. New York: Cambridge University Press.

Tesch, R. (1987). Emerging themes: The researcher's experience. *Phenomenology and Pedagogy, 5*, 230–241.

Weiler, K. (1988). *Women teaching for change*. Massachusetts: Bergin & Garvey.

Williams, T. S. (1983). Some issues in the standardized testing of minority students. *Journal of Education, 165*, 192–208.

Willis, P. E. (1977). *Learning to labour: How working class kids get working class jobs*. Farnborough, England: Saxon House.

IV

NUMERACY AND EVERYDAY MATHEMATICS

Numeracy is attracting increasing attention in many countries around the world. However, what exactly is numeracy? For some, mathematics education and numeracy are used interchangeably. Among those who distinguish numeracy from mathematics, a variety of definitions abound. Common to these various conceptions of numeracy is the notion of mathematical knowledge that is relevant and applicable to everyday life. It is widely acknowledged that the pertinent knowledge varies across contexts (e.g., workplaces, industries, the marketplace, and home applications). Ethnomathematics is a field of research endeavor through which there has been growing recognition of diversity in the development of mathematics and in its applications across cultures and environments. From ethnomathematical and numeracy perspectives, the traditional mathematics taught in schools is often perceived to be irrelevant. The consequences can be far reaching for those who do not succeed at it. In different ways, the authors of chapters in this section have explored conceptions of school mathematics and its relationship to the lives of learners in a range of different contexts.

Betty Johnston and Keiko Yasukawa offer a critical reflection of the authors' journey—both intellectual and geographical—in developing a theory of numeracy. It is a story of a number of convergences: of theory and practice of teaching, of mathematics education and mathematics, of "basic" and "high-powered mathematics, and of Australasian and Japanese cultures. It is also a story of how we are at a point of amicable divergence. Their aim in writing this story is as much for themselves as part of their own critical reflection—or in Dave Baker's phrase, interrogative practice—as it is for mathematics and numeracy teacher educators, researchers, and teaching practioners. By drawing on the theories that they have considered and the continuing interrogation of their own teaching practice, they tell the tale of various milestones they have reached in their theory development and connections they have made with theories and developments in other areas such as mathematics education, literacy education, and critical pedagogy. They also identify the current absence of some theories with which they hope to make connections in the future.

Swapna Mukhopadhyay and Brian Greer point out that the most common justification given for school mathematics is that mathematics has its roots in, and is usefully applicable to, real-world problems, yet research and documentary evidence show that most children regard mathematics as useless, uninteresting, and irrelevant to their lives. In this chapter, they propose to examine the reasons for this state of affairs through analysis of word problems. They study examples of word problems in different cultures such as India, China, Europe, and across many centuries in the light of their sociocultural context and the explicit and implicit purposes for which they were designed. They also propose an alternative framework within which word problems are characterized as exercises in modeling aspects of the real world. Starting from this perspective, they go on to argue that, when the focus is on the modeling of social phenomena, mathematics can become a tool for justice in the tradition of Moses, Freire, Frankenstein, and D'Ambrosio.

Gloria Stillman and Jo Balatti examine some of the current suggested approaches for incorporating ethnomathematics within classroom mathematics in the context of an upper secondary school classroom. These are illustrated by examples in the literature and from student research projects. Further, the ethnomathematics of the financial planning industry is examined. This ethnomathematics is produced by an industry that in many ways displays the key characteristics of modern Western societies and as such exhibits many of the salient features of other ethnomathematics of advanced capitalist societies that are directly experienced by the consumer. School mathematics is shown to be an ethnomathematics in its own right. This allows the opportunity for comparison of two ethnomathematics coexisting in, and produced by, the same capitalist culture.

In the chapter by Joanna O. Masingila and Rapti de Silva, the authors argue that students need mathematically meaningful contexts through which to learn mathematics. They discuss some historical examples from social and cultural situations in which people sought to make sense of things from within contexts and developed mathematical ideas out of these contexts. They then tie this in with school mathematics and discuss a 4-year, National Science Foundation-funded project entitled Connecting In-school and Out-of-school Mathematics Practice, in which they (a) investigated how middle school students use mathematical ideas in a variety of out-of-school situations and then (b) used ideas from these situations to support the students' classroom learning and examine how they made sense of ideas mathematically. They end the chapter by proposing how a learning theory (Saxe's Emergent Goals Framework) and an instructional theory (Realistic Mathematics Education) might be merged with a team approach to teaching and learning to address the issues they raise in this chapter.

16

Numeracy: Negotiating the World Through Mathematics

Betty Johnston
Keiko Yasukawa
University of Technology, Sydney

This chapter is a critical reflection of the authors' journey—both intellectual and geographical—in developing a theory of numeracy. It focuses on the absences and silences in theories about mathematics and mathematics education that have led us to explore and refashion concepts of numeracy and numeracy education in a search for what was missing. It is a story of a number of convergences—of theory and practice of teaching, of mathematics education and mathematics, of "basic" mathematics and "high-powered" mathematics, and of Australasian and Japanese cultures. Our aim in writing this story is as much for our own processes of critical reflection—or as Baker calls it, interrogative practice (Baker, 1998)—as it is for sharing our process of theory generation with mathematics and numeracy teacher educators, researchers, and teaching practitioners. By drawing on the theories we considered and the action research of our own teaching practice, we tell the tale of various milestones we reached and connections we made with theories and developments in other areas such as mathematics education, literacy, critical pedagogy, and, of course, numeracy.

Our focus is on how we arrived at and then had to question, a grand vision of numeracy as "the ability to situate, interpret, critique, use, and perhaps even create mathematics in context, taking into account all the mathematical as well as social and human complexities which come with that process .. [and how, as such, it is not numeracy] unless it is political .. [and how it] cannot pretend to be objective and value free" (Yasukawa, Johnston, & Yates, 1995, p. 816). The vision was grand

---

"Maths" is used here interchangeably with the term "math" preferred in North America.

in its claim that numeracy was not less than or even just a part of mathematics but something more than mathematics. Our vision also led us to posit a new theoretical framework—critical constructivism—which encompassed what we felt was absent in the varieties of constructivisms that are commonly drawn upon by mathematics educators.

Although a degree of critical reflection has moderated the grandeur of the vision, we feel we achieved in our endeavor to define numeracy the beginning of a bridge-building process between some of the seemingly isolated studies that may help to address the social dimensions of mathematics education. This endeavor led us to, among other things, introducing a new postgraduate subject "Mathematics in Social Contexts," which challenges students to examine the nature and presence of mathematics in society in ways that, before our journey, neither of us would have contemplated. We describe this subject briefly in this chapter. Our reflections on the journey so far raise some new questions, and also point to the current absences and silences of theories with which we or others may make connections in the future.

How did it happen that we were working together, in a somewhat unusual arrangement across Faculties (Engineering and Education) in a university? To locate ourselves, we say a little about what we were doing before we started on our excursions together and why each of us was in a position to engage in theorizing numeracy at the time and in the way that we did.

Keiko is a deviant from what might have led to an academic mathematics career. She finished an undergraduate honors degree in pure mathematics, commenced a PhD in mathematics straight after that, and while briefly engaged in some potentially "useful" mathematics research became discouraged by her inability to handle the messiness of extramathematical complications and completed her thesis in a purely theoretical area. She was never convinced she was really doing mathematics until fairly late in her thesis when she suddenly formulated a problem that she recognized as a "legitimately" mathematical problem. When she met Betty, Keiko was just coming back to academia after a semiretirement from doing her thesis, teaching university mathematics and computing to students, setting up a "remedial" mathematics learning center at her previous university, and generally wondering what life was all about. Somewhat ironically, but perhaps because she was just trying to realize her own unrealized dream of doing something useful, she was at a point of designing a hands-on mathematical modeling subject for engineering students (Yasukawa, 1995).

Betty completed a graduate honors degree in mathematics and a teaching qualification before teaching mathematics in a variety of different countries and at a variety of educational institutions, including primary and secondary schools, university, and teacher education colleges. At university the higher status mathematics had been "pure" mathematics, applied mathematics being less elegant and somehow less intellectual. She had always been "good at" mathematics and had particularly enjoyed her teacher training year in England where she had been lucky to have a mathematics education lecturer who challenged the formal traditional approach. She envied, however, the social, historical elements that were intrinsic to other disciplines, such as sociology, history, and language. She had fairly recently returned to full-time work, this time in Adult Basic Education (ABE), working closely with colleagues from the fields of adult literacy and community education.

Over the years covered by the scenes that follow, Keiko and Betty came to work closely together within the Faculty of Education, with Keiko's position straddling both Faculties—Engineering and Education—a fact that kept our feet on ground that is emphatically both mathematical and practical. We both became involved in teaching something that was named "numeracy" on the timetable, a subject that grew from being a token single lecture in a literacy subject, to a whole subject in its own right, and then to its present status as the focus of a four-subject Graduate Certificate. As we began teaching numeracy, we found a variety of definitions of what it might be: a common perception of it as a functional conglomerate of "basic skills," the British Open University's "informed numeracy" (when to use mathematics, what mathematics to use, how to do it, and how to use the results; 1980), the Cockcroft Report's vision of an "at-homeness" with mathematics (1982), the Australian Council for Adult Literacy's embracing of numeracy in a policy that explicitly stated that "literacy . . . incorporates numeracy"(1989). Viewed from such a range of perspectives, numeracy seemed ripe for renovation and expansion.

THE JOURNEY

Scene 1. A Cultural Alliance: Corner of Bay St. and Broadway, 1992

We have been to a discussion of the mathematics "profiles" for schools and are walking back to work. At this point we had never worked together, although our paths crossed several times.

Betty: What irritates me is all this emphasis on "outcomes," this listing of characteristics just waiting to be ticked off.

Keiko: Yes, we talk about teachers, subject matter, and then simply outcomes.

Betty: It's so linear, so controlling, but it leaves out students, and all the mess between input and output. It's this overweening reverence for the rational—or at least the apparently rational.

Keiko: I find that curious.

Betty: What? I'm being irrational?

Keiko: No—well, maybe, but that's the very thing that I find curious—the way that one of the worst things you can say to discredit someone is to label them as irrational.

Betty: And it's especially powerful used against women.

Keiko: But, you see, in Japan it's quite different. Not that it's exactly a virtue, but it's certainly not the most disparaging thing you can say.

Betty: What would be more disparaging?

Keiko: I'm not sure, something to do with harmony, being disruptive or disturbing the harmony, perhaps not respecting the conventions.

Betty: That's quite amazing. I find it quite difficult to visualize—a society where an accusation of disrespecting the conventions discredits you more than an accusation of irrationality. I mean, just think of a husband arguing with his wife, and saying to her "But aren't you aware of social conventions?!" instead of "But you're so irrational!"

Keiko: And it means rationality isn't the dominant virtue either—in Japan.

Betty: So if our, Western, way of looking at maths is inextricably tied to our valuing of rationality, then what does this mean for the Japanese way of looking at maths?

Keiko: In general, it must mean that maths is culturally framed. I'm not sure what it means in particular . . .

Betty: It's interesting . . . for me there's been a single "rational" dimension, and this adds dimensions; it means that maths is embedded differently in different cultures.

Keiko: Yes, and it also must mean that ways of critiquing it are culturally framed.

Through the growing literature on ethnomathematics and multicultural mathematics, we had been becoming aware of how cultural issues impinged on mathematics, but this was a particular moment when we realized that *our* different cultures had shaped *us*, and our mathematical values and attitudes, differently. It was not just a matter of the interesting way that Mayans or Babylonians counted or the variety of ways in which Navajo or Inuit people classified shapes. It was not just us looking out from a mainstream "truth": our relationship to it was already shaped by our locations in different cultures.

In the ABE field, and at an individual level, this concept of cultural embeddedness is not at all strange. In fact, the traditions of adult education that inform adult numeracy teaching emphasize the importance of negotiating with the students to begin from where they are, of acknowledging what they bring, including both their experience and their goals. Thus, the work done by writers such as Ascher (1991), with her focus on the mathematics of what she calls preliterate societies, and Joseph (1987), with his challenge to what he sees as the Eurocentrism of mathematics, can be incorporated into approaches for the ABE classroom. Zaslavsky (1992) and Shan and Bailey (1991) explored some of the implications for schools, and Frankenstein and Powell (1989/1992) have taken up some of these ideas in the context of teaching mathematics to adult students who have not been successful at school. The perception that maths is embedded differently in different cultures can be used as a tool for helping students to appreciate the different individual paths they have taken to their current understandings.

The concept of the cultural embeddedness of mathematics also raises questions about power, about democratic politics, and about how mathematics can be mobilized to support collective action. D'Ambrosio (1997), Fasheh (1990), Bishop (1988), Knijnik (1996), and Freire (as cited in Frankestien, 1987), are some of those who challenged the perception of mathematics as value-free and politically neutral and developed a range of approaches to mathematics and mathematics teaching at this more collective level. Thus, from early in our journey, we found that it was important to remake connections to power and culture that had been absent in the maths that we had learned and, until then, taught.

Scene 2. Forms of Violence:
Keiko's Home, Chuter Street, McMahons Point, 1993

We are working on teaching materials for Betty's students, teachers of numeracy to adult learners. The adult learners are usually people who failed maths at school, for a variety of reasons. They often see maths as meaningless, inaccessible, not for them.

Betty: There's this book I've been reading, that's relevant to all this. *The Violence of Literacy*, by Elizabeth Stuckey[1].

Keiko: You mean, making a parallel argument about the "violence of numeracy"?

Betty: Yes, there are really strong echoes in her argument—I kept reading "numeracy" instead of "literacy" . . . .

Keiko: That's what I did with Steve Black's report on literacy and the unemployed[1], and it made a lot of sense. It's true that if the jobs aren't there, then it's a smokescreen to say that providing people with numeracy skills will be a solution.

Betty: And there's an article, too, by Lévi-Strauss[1], again about literacy, that argues that literacy isn't necessarily the wonderful progressive force that we assume it to be. In fact, he argues, if you look at the times in history when literacy has flourished, you'll find that these are also the times when slavery and oppression have flourished. Literacy has allowed control. And maybe this is true for numeracy, too? Do you think we could argue that numeracy works to control, as well as to "empower"?

Keiko: It would be interesting to try it, see what evidence you could gather. After all there's all that stuff that people have written on how statistics lie.[2] And it also happens the other way around. It's not just wicked maths exploiting the poor and oppressed. It's also people using maths badly, violating maths, if you like.

A number of writers were making explicit different ways in which the words mathematics and numeracy were used in theory and practice. Ernest (1991) was teasing out the assumptions behind different philosophies of mathematics, and therefore of mathematics education. Baker, working with Street (1994), was making an important distinction between what he and Street were calling the "autonomous" and the "ideological" models of numeracy (and literacy), tracing a paradigm shift from numeracy (or literacy) as a set of static, decontextualized skills to a more sociocultural approach.

The ideological or sociocultural model allowed us to see how more links could be made between the apparently context-free "content" of maths and the purposes for which it was learned and used. A familiar concern was the issue of gender equity: although this was beginning to change, girls had often not achieved as well as boys in mathematics, and this was mirrored, for us, in the low participation of women in the engineering courses and their high participation rate in teaching. Somehow they were failing maths, or, as it was beginning to be argued (e.g., Willis, 1995), maths was failing them. Less familiar, but still pervasive, was the concern that maths was failing other groups: that class, race, and ethnicity were pertinent factors in "success" (Apple, 1995; Secada, 1995). What was maths teaching these groups? As Volmink (1992)

---

[1]Black, 1992, expanded in 1995; Lévi-Strauss, 1974; Stuckey, 1991.
[2]Dewdney, 1993; Huff, 1954; Paulos, 1988.

argued: mathematics for many students "partakes more of the nature of obedience than of understanding." Lévi-Strauss and Stuckey provoked us into seeing that the practices of mathematics were involved in "the dynamics of gender [and other identity] construction" (Johnston and Dunne 1995) and that they generated structural inequities that we could not ignore.

Because of its insistence on contextualization, however, Baker's model also allows for Keiko's emphasis: if mathematics is "ideological," then the ideology that informs it, or appropriates it, can do so well or badly and can ask more of it than it can reasonably give. Is it useful to appropriate mathematics as a tool for analysis in all areas? Davis and Hersh (1986) gave examples of how our world is being increasingly "mathematized," not only in the traditional scientific and technological areas but also in the social sciences and policy areas. Is this increasing mathematization anything more than a gatekeeping device, or a badge of status? We started to think at this point about developing a course for our students—"The Violence and Violation of Mathematics." We began to see numeracy as mathematics with an explicit moral imperative toward social justice.

Scene 3. The Invasion:
Corner of Harris and Thomas Streets, Late 1993

Betty is planning for a "Mathematics workshop" for her students in the Graduate Diploma of Adult Basic Education, starting the following week. Chatting at the bus stop, waiting for a bus to arrive, Betty suggests that maybe Keiko would like to come and help in her workshop.

Keiko: Sure, but tell me more about who your students are, and what sort of maths we'll be teaching.

Betty: Oh, really basic stuff. You know, numeracy.

Keiko: What do you mean, "basic" stuff and "numeracy"?

Betty: Well, the maths these people, and their students would use in everyday sorts of situations—nothing high powered.

Keiko: But wait a minute. If you're saying numeracy is the maths that people need in their everyday lives, then we can talk about numeracy for engineers, numeracy for architects, numeracy for toddlers . . . what makes you want to colonize numeracy just into ABE? Seems to me numeracy should be defined a bit more broadly than the everyday needs of ABE students . . . even assuming that's identifiable in some way. And for some people, numeracy would involve very "high-powered" maths.

Betty: Well, that's the first time I've ever thought of ABE as having imperialistic intentions and power!

At the time of this dialogue, many people would have regarded numeracy as some competence in arithmetic and other "basic" maths; in fact this has not changed much as far as general perception goes. There had already been, however, much literature published on the importance of teaching mathematics in context, and many ABE teachers started to adopt a contextualized approach in their own practice. So, the idea that numeracy was somehow related to the competent use of mathematics in the learners' own context already established some roots in the ABE sector.

The emphasis away from the notion of a generic competence in "basic maths" dates back at least to the Cockcroft report in 1982 that equated numeracy with "an ability to cope confidently with the mathematical demands of adult life" (quoted in O'Donoghue, 1995, p. 393). In Australia in the late 1980s, and early 1990s we began to see ABE teaching and learning resources such as *Strength in Numbers* (Goddard, et al., 1991), and *Maths: A New Beginning* (Marr & Helme, 1987), which were based strongly on the view that numeracy involved an individual's ability to use mathematics in contexts relevant to him or her. These ABE resources were characterized by their focus on contextualizing mathematical topics in common "everyday" contexts such as household budgeting, reading timetables, and estimating discounted prices.

What we started to realize was that we could challenge the notion of "everyday" as limited to common social survival activities. Althogh it is true that relating mathematical concepts to these activities could be meaningful for some groups, there were other equally everyday mathematical activities specific to other cultural (including professional) groups within the community. The calculation of drug doses by nurses, cost-benefit analyses for engineering project managers, and time series analysis and forecasting for economists are all, for some in these groups, just as everyday as reading the timetable or household budgeting. It seemed to us that the process of learning among people in these groups could be theorized in the same way that people theorize the effective learning of mathematics in ABE classes. We began to see connections emerging between Vygotsky's notion of conceptual understanding as a process of making connections between "spontaneous knowledge" and new abstract concepts (Vygotsky, 1986) and some broader notion of numeracy as mathematical meaning making within specific cultural contexts.

It is true that the type of mathematics (some would like to use the notion of "level") and the contexts differ in, say, engineering, compared to that of ABE classrooms. However, engineers also have specific contexts in which their mathematical knowledge acquires meaning, and that meaning is constructed in relation to the work that engineers do. This became strongly evident to Keiko in teaching her engineering students mathematical modeling. Although she had a "respectable" mathematical background, she found that the engineers could more readily visualize and relate mathematical models to engineering processes and phenomena than she could. The students had a much richer understanding of the problems that were to be solved by mathematical models than Keiko had, and, although she had a more rigorous appreciation of the mathematics, she found it difficult to "activate" her mathematics productively in the context of the students' engineering concerns.

That "context" can be seen as a form of "scaffold" (an idea also from Vygotsky) for learning mathematical concepts is supported by studies such as the mathematical activities of weight watchers (Lave, 1988), street children in Brazil (Nunes et al., 1993), and packaging workers in a factory (Scribner, 1984). Such writers extended into a theory of social practice their findings that people understood their mathematical tasks in relation to (and sometimes only in relation to) the context in which they were conducted. Depending on the context, the approaches for solving the "same" mathematical problem could differ; this difference is most dramatically encapsulated in the expression "street mathematics and school mathematics" (Nunes et al., 1993).

Scene 4. A New Imperialism:
Haymarket Campus, University of Technology,
Sydney, 1994

A group of 12 or so numeracy teachers met for a Saturday workshop to develop guidelines for the writing of a substantial professional development course in adult numeracy, later called *Adult Numeracy Teaching* (ANT; Johnston & Tout, 1995).

We have been operating with a constructivist approach to knowledge, in this case mathematics, and what we have seen as the implications of such an approach for the learning, and thus the teaching, of mathematics. There is also an enthusiastic acceptance that we should incorporate relevant elements of the well-established critical literacy approach familiar to the literacy teachers among us.

Laurie: And we've already said that the content should be useful; it should be the maths that the students need in their everyday life.

Mary: So, our vision of good numeracy teaching includes a demand that students should understand the maths they are using. . .

Peter: . . . as far as possible. . .

Sally: . . . yes, I guess we need some compromise there.

Chris: And that they should be able to be critical about how they use it.

Keiko: This vision of numeracy seems to be adding things to the maths at the core of it. It should be the maths, yes, you should be able to *do* it, and we're saying you should be able to understand what you do. But it should also include the context(s) in which it is done, and an element of critique about what's being done.

Betty: And what about an appreciation of the cultural or historical origins of the maths involved?

Jill: There's a sort of accretion, adding things to maths—to teach numeracy is teach the skills, together with conceptual understanding, context, critique. . . and now culture.

Sally: So we could claim that this numeracy is not a subset of maths at all. In fact, we could say that numeracy is not less than maths but more! How about that for a new imperialism?

The realization that we could fill the gaps, that we could name the absences in our varied but nevertheless flawed experiences of mathematics, was an irresistible and liberating challenge. For too long we had remained stuck in a critique that focused on what had been wrong. The construction of this new thing, numeracy, gave us a chance to be creative, to claim for it the essentials we had for so long foregone. Numeracy involved mathematics of course—how could it not?—but it was to be a mathematics in conversation with the world, where matters of life and death, survival and destruction, were not irrelevant matters but core concerns. It was to be a mathematics used by people, meaningfully, appropriately, purposefully, justly—and enjoyably.

About the same time that our discussion was occurring in Australia, as we were envisioning a numeracy that included "skills, together with conceptual understanding, context, critique. . . and now culture!" (Johnston, 1994; Yasukawa, & Johnston, 1994; Yasukawa, Johnston, & Yates, 1995), Baker was developing his idea of numeracy as social practice. In this approach he argued that it was productive to see numeracy as a situated social practice that includes four elements—content, context, culture, and ideology (1995), an approach not so very different from our own, and possibly motivated by similar dissatisfactions.

Scene 5. V-Day: Betty's Home, Hillcrest Avenue, Gladesville, 1995

One winter afternoon, Betty and Keiko discuss the section on "theory" in *Adult Numeracy Teaching*. They are looking at a chart Betty adapted [from a discussion group led by Jayne Johnston at the conference of the Mathematics Education Research Group of Australasia (MERGA), 1990] to show how different assumptions about knowledge, learning, and teaching can be located under each of the two headings "Transmission theory" and "Constructivist theory."

Betty: So, under transmission, would be the idea of knowledge as absolute facts, learning as passive reception and regurgitation, teaching as transmission.

Keiko: And, under constructivism, we would have learning as meaning making, and teaching as facilitation ... I guess learning and teaching as a negotiated process, and knowledge as socially constructed. Do we need to tease out what we mean by "meaning making"?

Betty: Yeah ... I guess we need to spell out that we mean critical understanding.

Keiko: Because not everyone will assume that, under constructivism, will they?

Betty: But, hang on, does constructivism necessarily imply a critical understanding in the sense that we use the term ... you know, socially critical?

Keiko: No ... in fact, a lot of mathematicians would claim that they demand critical understanding in their class, meaning a good conceptual understanding ...

Betty: Which I guess is being socially critical within the tiny community of academic mathematicians, but it doesn't even begin to address the wider social uses and abuses of mathematics.

Keiko: That's right. They are interested in avoiding the *violation* of mathematics—contaminating the truth value of mathematics through incorrect, nonrigorous use, but they're not interested in the social violence of certain types of applications of mathematics ... the wider political power of mathematics.

Betty: Which means ... we need something more than constructivism ... although constructivism is part of it because we are still saying that the meaning that is made of the mathematics is very much socially constructed.

Keiko: So maybe we need a new variety of constructivism ... *critical constructivism?*

Constructivism was a powerful tool in explaining the limitations of the transmission approach to teaching and learning, not only in the school mathematics sector but also in the adult numeracy sector. Constructivism helped to differentiate between rote learning of algorithms and formulae and conceptual understanding of mathematical structures, systems, and patterns. Constructivism as it had been appropriated in the mathematics education sector added a new dimension to meaning making in adult numeracy teaching by giving recognition to the role of mathematical structures in making meaning. It did not, however, help to develop an understanding of what it means to think in a socially critical way about mathematics.

Working among language and literacy educators, we were exposed to their interest in critical literacy, and the notion of literacy not simply as a way of facilitating communication between people but also as a way of asking and acting upon critical, sociopolitical questions about the world. Critical literacy, we learned, was involved in uncovering values and assumptions held by the writer. Was there a parallel meaning for critical numeracy?

In thinking about the meaning of critique in relation to numeracy, we were influenced by works in the literacy area. In particular, Freebody and Luke (1990) categorized four reader roles that are involved in critical literacy, namely, *text decoder*, *text participant*, *text user*, and *critical analyst*. Lee, Chapman, and Roe (1993) interpreted this literacy framework into a numeracy framework that can be expressed in the following way:

> *text decoder* recognizes/uses appropriate mathematical codes (symbols) and conventions
>
> *text participant* comprehends/gains a conceptual understanding of the underlying mathematical principles and structures
>
> *text user* appreciates/translates the mathematics to appropriate and relevant purposes
>
> *text analyst* critiques/resists the use of mathematics for establishing social power

It should be noted that here we can think of "text" as any expression of mathematical reasoning, such as equations, formulae, graphs, and figures embedded in verbal text. In relation to the theories that have informed mathematics educators' understanding of learning and teaching, the transmission or instrumental model of teaching helps to explain how students may not develop as learners beyond text decoders, whereas constructivism helps to make explicit the dimension of conceptual understanding in mathematical thinking.

The teaching and learning of mathematics in context had links, as mentioned earlier, to constructivism through its idea that knowledge is not given but constructed by the learners. We can also find links with Vygotsky's activity theory—later picked up by Mellin-Olsen (1987)—through its idea of learning as a purposeful activity. These theories of mathematics learning allow for the added meaning that learners make of mathematics through putting mathematics into use.

The role of the text analyst, however, is not obviously connected to constructivism. Although it can be argued that critique involves a negotiation between the reader's own values and assumptions and those expressed in the mathematics, and therefore, a "construction" of meaning on the part of the reader, this type of meaning making is not explicitly addressed in the mathematics education literature on constructivism. Where we see attention to critique is in works such as Skovsmose's (1994), where he takes us back to problems in the philosophy of mathematics and mathematics education; in Frankenstein's (1989) and others' work in "criticalmathematics," informed by Freire and critical pedagogy; and in D'Ambrosio's (1997) and Fasheh's (1989) work on ethnomathematics as a way of challenging cultural roots of mathematics and mathematics education. This role of text analyst is an extension to constructivism.

Scene 6. Liberation or Domestication: Adult Literacy Information Office, Holden St, Ashfield, 1996

By late 1996, the professional development course ANT had been running for some time. The thinking that had gone into the development of the ANT curriculum also influenced our teaching in the Graduate Diploma in ABE. It seemed natural to share with our students the idea of "critical constructivism" as a way of theorizing numeracy. What was beginning to happen, however, was that the participants in the course were *uncritically* endorsing that framework. This led to an intriguing dilemma: were we effectively enacting a transmission approach to teaching when we were teaching about critical constructivism?

This espousal of critical constructivism as "the answer" to numeracy seemed contrary to our aims of getting our students to think critically about mathematics and mathematics education. We believe there are several related explanations of this phenomenon.

One reason for students' attraction to the framework is the inclusion of the critical dimension. Many of the students we are referring to here did not have a strong academic mathematics background; many of them identified themselves as "language, humanities types," which in their minds, were a different species to the "numbers and figures types." Many of them came with school mathematics experiences that could easily form part of a collection of mathematics anxiety case studies. The framework of critique helped these students to find an explanation for and expression of the anger and frustrations that they had felt with mathematics, especially school mathematics, throughout their lives. It allowed them to attribute the problems they had in learning mathematics to some external cause rather than to some internal fault. Other theories such as transmission theory and constructivism help to explain how people learn but do not offer much to those who don't.

The second reason our students might have felt so strongly attracted to the critical constructivist framework was that they saw strong parallels with what they were simultaneously learning in their studies of critical literacy and its focus on the dimension of social power (e.g., see Gee, 1990; Kress, 1988; Wallace, 1992). The idea that the ideology of quantitative thinking and the use of mathematical language to assert expert power could be challenged was appealing and had resonance with the idea that ideology and assumptions about power were also embedded in language.

The third reason, we suspect, that our students were attracted to critical constructivism was that, by focusing on the critical aspects of mathematics, they could mask their lack of focus on the mathematics itself. As already mentioned, only a few of these students had a high level of confidence in their mathematical knowledge or in their "ability" to learn it. Although some of their self-perceptions in relation to mathematics were challenged and overcome during their study of the subject, many of them still felt ill-equipped as teachers of numeracy. Although it is regrettable that they felt critical constructivism to be a "way out," it is also understandable given the students' circumstances and the structure of the course in which they were studying numeracy education (typically, as part of a qualification in language and literacy education).

Finally, upon reflection, we also realized that our pedagogy may have set the students up to parrot the critical constructivist view. By guiding our students through our own (reconstructed) logic of reaching this framework, we had constrained our students' vision to essentially filling in a table such as the one following:

	Transmission Model	Constructivist Model	Critical Constructivist Model
View of mathematics	Absolute truth, God-given	Knowledge as socially constructed	Knowledge as political
View of teaching	Transmission of objective truth	Facilitation of learning	As in constructivist model
View of learning	Absorption and reproduction	Active construction of meaning	As in constructivist model but with the addition of critique

This realization is leading us to interrogate our own assumptions about "critique" in mathematics education. What do we mean when we say that numeracy encompasses the critique that is lacking in mathematics education? What is the object of our critique? Is it mathematics? Mathematics pedagogy? Or is it education more generally?

CURRENT DIRECTIONS

In retrospect, we can see that the unease provoked by instances of uncritical acceptance of our framework such as we have described led us over the last 2 or 3 years to explore some of our own assertions and theories more carefully. One of us, Keiko, has taken up the question of what we mean by the "power" of mathematics (Yasukawa, 1997, 1998) and the other, Betty, has gone in a different direction, exploring ways in which mathematical practices work to shape our lives (Johnston, 1998a, 1998b, 1998c).

Both these interests weave together to form the basis of the subject that we have recently developed—*Mathematics in Social Contexts*. In this subject, students read widely around a selection of topics—the world according to mathematics, cultures of risk, the "probabilization" of the Western world, mathematics as social practice, for example, and prepare an essay and case study on one of them. The core aim of the subject is to help students appreciate that mathematics is a socially located activity or practice whose power and appropriation cannot be truly understood without also examining the contexts in which it arises. Notes from the learning guide for the subject argue:

> Even school mathematics, which for many of us has been taught as if it were the one absolute and objective truth, is a socially located activity. Consider for the moment what privileges and power are derived from being "good" in such a subject at school, and how

"goodness" in the subject is often assessed. Schools and the social functions schools serve (for stratification, gatekeeping—as well as many other more positive things) give school mathematics a particular social context which would be quite different to the learning of mathematics outside the formal classroom setting. . .

The function that school mathematics serves for individuals and society at large, cannot be assumed to be the same as the function that mathematical knowledge and thinking more generally can serve for these same individuals and society. Many people are failed by the school system; yet in many ways we find these same people surviving (sometimes thriving) in society as adults, and performing many tasks which require working with numbers, measurements, geometric thinking, and so on. . .

As teachers of numeracy, we need to understand and be able to negotiate the politics of school mathematics. . . But if we argue that mathematics is socially located, then there is not a single, monolithic numeracy, but many numeracies, depending on the social contexts to which we are referring. We need to appreciate the implications of the existence of these multiple numeracies in order to teach students from a variety of backgrounds and with different aspirations. This subject is one way of gaining some preliminary insights into this challenge.

The development of this subject reflects, for us, several shifts in our thinking about numeracy and mathematics over the past few years. We could have developed a subject with this name some years ago, but it would have been very different: its focus would have been more on the mathematics of other people and other times and on uncovering the way in which, for instance, mathematics "lies." In the current subject, the "real world" is the starting place, and it is our real world, in all its complexity and mess, and the mathematics is teased out, examined, learned, and its use is critiqued. The subject focuses on the understanding and doing of mathematics as well as what *can* become a "mere" critique: the way out of mathematics that we referred to earlier. In so doing, students have an opportunity to generate an appreciation of the power of mathematics, in both its positive and negative guises. Our exercise in theory generation enabled us to construct a subject that guides students through a rich exploration of the seemingly mundane, rather than a virtual tour of exotic terrain.

CONCLUSION

Frustrated with a mathematics whose history kept it within strong disciplinary boundaries, allowing certain questions and forbidding others, we fled to an arena whose boundaries were less defined. We colonized numeracy, permitting, indeed requiring, it to be a bridge between mathematics and society. To be numerate was to negotiate the world—including its values—through mathematics; it was also to negotiate the mathematics that constructs the social realities we live in. Both sides of the bridge were core to this concept of numeracy, both the socially critical and the mathematical. In this sense, numeracy was larger than mathematics and unable to be confined within it or within any single level of it. In traditional teaching of mathematics, the historical, the social, the cultural, and the political have a place, but as appendages, as afterthoughts, as garnishes. Mathematics is the single and explicit focus. In our teaching of numeracy, however, it is *the relationship, the negotiation*, between mathematics and the world that has become the core concern.

We have described a process of theory construction, resulting in an approach to numeracy that has been meaningful for us. There are other links we could have made; there are other directions that other people have in fact taken. Our journey is thus one account of how the concept, and practice, of numeracy itself is socially constructed, of how the generation of theory is personally contextualized and historically specific.

REFERENCES

Apple, M. W. (1995). Taking power seriously: new directions in equity in mathematics education and beyond. In W. G. Secada, E. Fennema, & L. B. Adajian (Eds.), *New directions for equity in mathematics education*. Cambridge: Cambridge University Press.

Ascher, M. (1991). *Ethnomathematics: A multicultural view of mathematical ideas*. California: Brooks/Cole.

Australian Council for Adult Literacy (ACAL). 1989. Literacy policy statement. ACAL. Melbourne.

Baker, D. A. (1995). Numeracy as a social practice: Implications for concerns about numeracy in schools. In *The third international conference on the Political Dimensions of Mathematics Education*. Bergen, Norway: Caspar Forlag A/S.

Baker, D.A. (1998). Mathematics as social practice: implications for mathematics in primary education. In P. Gates (Ed.), *Mathematics education and society—An international conference* (pp. 66–72). Centre for the Study of Mathematics Education, University of Nottingham, 6–11 September.

Baker, D.A., & Street, B. (1994). Literacy and numeracy concepts and definitions. In *International encyclopedia of education*. London: Pergamon.

Bishop, A. (1988). *Mathematical enculturation: A cultural perspective on mathematics education*. Dordrecht: Kluwer.

Black, S. (1992). *ABE provision for jobseekers: Interim report*, November (unpublished).

Black, S. (1995). *Literacy and the unemployed*. Sydney: Centre for Language and Literacy, University of Technology, Sydney.

Cockcroft, W. H. (1982). *Mathematics counts: Report of the Committee of Inquiry into the Teaching of Mathematics in Schools*. London: H.M.S.O.

D'Ambrosio, U. (1997). Where does ethnomathematics stand nowadays? *For the learning of mathematics, 17*(2), 13–17.

Davis, P. J., & Hersh, R. (1986). *Descartes' dream: The world according to mathematics*. London: Penguin.

Dewdney, A. K. (1993). *200% of nothing*. New York: John Wiley & Sons.

Ernest, P. (1991).*The philosophy of mathematics education*. London: Falmer.

Fasheh, M. (1989). Mathematics in a social context: Math within education as praxis versus within education as hegemony. In C. Keitel, P. Damerow, A. Bishop, & P. Gerdes (Eds.), *Mathematics, education and society*. UNESCO.

Fasheh, M. (1990). Community education: to reclaim and transform what has been made invisible. *Harvard Educational Review, 60*(19–35), 2–8.

Frankenstein, M. (1987). Critical mathematics education: An application of Paulo Freire's epistemology. In I. Shor (Ed.), *Freire for the classroom: A sourcebook for liberatory teaching*. Portsmouth NH: Boynton/Cook.

Frankenstein, M. (1989). *Relearning mathematics*. Free Association Press. London.

Frankenstein, M., & Powell, A. (1989/1992). Empowering non-traditional students: on social ideology and mathematics education. In C. Keitel, P. Damerow, A. Bishop, & P. Gerdes (Eds.) *Mathematics, education and society*. UNESCO.

Freebody, P., & Luke, A. (1990). Literacies' programs: Debates and demands in cultural context. *Prospect, 5*(3), 7–16.

Gee, J. P. (1990). *Social linguistics and literacies: Ideology in discourses*. London: Falmer.

Goddard, R., Marr, B., & Martin, J. (1991). *Strength in numbers*. Melbourne: Division of Further Education and Training.

Harris, M. (1991). *Schools, mathematics and work*. London: Falmer.

Huff, D. (1954). *How to lie with statistics*. London: Gollancz.

Johnston, B. (1994). Critical numeracy? *Fine Print, 16*(4), 32–35.

Johnston, B. (1998a). Adult numeracy. In D. Wagner, R. Venezky, & B. Street (Eds.), *Literacy: An international handbook*. Westview Press, Colorado.

Johnston, B. (1998b). Maths and gender: given or made? In P. Gates (Ed.), *Mathematics education and society—An international conference* (pp. 207–213). Centre for the Study of Mathematics Education, University of Nottingham, 6–11 September.

Johnston, B. (1998c). *Understanding numeracy as practice: Pedagogical implications*. Sydney: University of Technology, Sydney.

Johnston, B., & Tout, D. (1995). *Adult numeracy teaching: Making meaning in mathematics*. Canberra: TAFE National Staff Development Council.

Johnston, B., Baynham, M., Barlow, K., Kelly, S., & Marks, G. (1997). *Effective numeracy pedagogy for young unemployed people*. Sydney: University of Technology, Sydney and Canberra: DEETYA.

Johnston, J., & Dunne, M. (1995). Revealing assumptions: Problematising research on gender and mathematics and science education. In L. Parker, L. Rennie, & B. Fraser (Eds.), *Gender, science and mathematics: Shortening the shadows* (pp. 53–63). Dordrecht: Kluwer.

Joseph, G. G. (1987). Foundations of Eurocentrism in mathematics. *Race and Class, 28*(3), 13–28.

Knijnik, G. (1996). Mathematics education and the struggle for land in Brazil. In *Proceedings of the international Congress on Mathematics Education 8*, Seville.

Kress, G. (1988). Language as social practice. In G. Kress (Ed.), *Communication and culture* (pp. 82–129). Sydney: NSW University Press.

Lave, J. (1988). *Cognition in practice*. Cambridge: Cambridge University Press.

Lee, A., Chapman, A., & Roe, P. (1996). "Pedagogical relationships between adult literacy, numeracy." Research report No. 2, Centre for Language & Literacy, University of Technology, Sydney.

Lévi-Strauss, C. (1974). *Tristes tropiques*. New York: Atheneum.

Marr, B., & Helme, S. (1987). *Maths: A new beginning*. Melbourne: State Training Board of Victoria.

Mellin-Olsen, S. (1987). *The Politics of Mathematics Education*. Dordrecht: D. Reidel.

Mathematics Education Research Group of Australasia. (1991). Conference proceedings. Fourteenth Annual conference of MERGA, Hobart, July 1991. Kingswood, NSW.

Nunes, T., Schliemann, A. D., & Carraher, D.W. (1993). *Street mathematics and school mathematics*. Cambridge: Cambridge University Press.

O'Donoghue, J. (1995). Numeracy and further education: beyond the millennium. *International Journal of Mathematics Education in Science and Technology, 26*(3), 389–405.

Paulos, J. A. (1988). *Innumeracy: Mathematical illiteracy and its consequences*. London: Penguin.

Powell, A. B., & Frankenstein, M. (Eds.). (1997) *Ethnomathematics*. New York: State University of New York Press.

Scribner, S. (1984). Studying working intelligence. In B. Rogoff, & J. Lave (Eds.), *Everyday cognition* (pp. 9–40). Cambridge, MA: Harvard University Press.

Secada, W. (1995). Social and critical dimensions for equity in mathematics education. In W. E. Secada, E. Fennema, & L. B. Adajian (Eds.), *New directions for equity in mathematics education*. Cambridge: Cambridge University Press.

Shan, S.-J., & Bailey, P. (1991) *Multiple factors: Classroom mathematics for equality and justice*. Trentham, Stoke-on-Trent, England.

Skovsmose, O. (1994). *Towards a philosophy of critical mathematics education*. Dordrecht: Kluwer.

Stuckey, J. E. (1991). *The violence of literacy*. Portsmouth, NH: Boynton/Cook.

The Open University (1980). *Mathematics across the curriculum*. London: Open University Press.

Volmink, J. (1992). Non-school alternatives in mathematics education. In C. Keitel, C. P. Damerow, & A. Bishop (Eds.), *Mathematics, education and society* (pp. 59–61). UNESCO Science and Technology Education, Document Series No. 35.

Vygotsky, L. (1986). *Thought and language*. Cambridge, MA: MIT Press.

Wallace, C. (1992). *Reading*. Oxford: Oxford University Press.

Willis, S. (Ed.). (1990). *Being numerate: What counts?* Melbourne: Australian Council for Educational Research.

Willis, S. (1995). Gender justice and the mathematics curriculum: Four perspectives. In L. Parker, L. Rennie, & B. Fisher (Eds.), *Gender, science and mathematics: Shortening the shadows*. Dordrecht: Kluwer.

Yasukawa, K. (1995). Teaching critical mathematics. *Numeracy in focus*, Melbourne Adult Basic Education Resource and Information Service, No. 1, January, 38–42.

Yasukawa, K. (1997). Challenging myths about mathematics learning and teaching. In R. Ballantyne & J. Packer (Eds.), *Reflecting on university teaching: Academics' stories* (pp. 299–309). Canberra: AGPS.

Yasukawa, K. (1998). Looking at mathematics as technology: implications for numeracy. In P. Gates (Ed.), *Mathematics Education and Society—An international conference* (pp. 351–359). Centre for the Study of Mathematics Education, University of Nottingham, 6–11 September.

Yasukawa, K., & B. Johnston (1994). A numeracy manifesto for engineers, primary teachers, historians... A civil society—Can we call it theory? In *Proceedings of the Australian Bridging Mathematics Network Conference* (pp. 191–199). University of Sydney, 10–12 July.

Yasukawa, K., Johnston, B., & Yates, K. W. (1995). Numeracy as a critical constructivist awareness of maths— Case studies from engineering and adult basic education. In *Proceedings of the ICMI Regional Collaboration in Mathematics Education Conference* (pp. 815–826). Monash University, Melbourne 19–23 April.

Zaslavsky, C. (1992). Integrating mathematics with the study of cultural traditions. In C. Keitel, P. Damerow, A. Bishop, & P. Gerdes (Eds.), *Mathematics, education and society* (pp. 14–16). UNESCO Science and Technology Education, Document Series No. 35.

17

Modeling With Purpose: Mathematics as a Critical Tool

Swapna Mukhopadhyay

San Diego State University

Brian Greer

San Diego State University

We take as our starting point that mathematics is a human activity. With obvious simplification, the evolution of this central principle is schematically indicated in Fig. 17.1.

As mathematics education emerged as a field of study in its own right, the main emphasis initially was on experimental studies with an aim of establishing theories of learning and teaching mathematics, the main methodological influences came from psychology, and the main goal of mathematics education was seen as enhancing cognitive development in individual students. This orientation persisted, relatively unchanged, through the first phase of the changes within psychology at the end of the 1950s that came to be known as the "Cognitive Revolution."

However, in reaction to the realization that cognitive science was limited by "deemphasis on affect, context, culture and history" (Gardner, 1985, p. 41) there followed a "second wave" (De Corte, Greer, & Verschaffel, 1996, p. 497) of the Cognitive Revolution in which these aspects of human activity were addressed. Within mathematics education, in particular, this reaction resulted in a change of emphasis whereby the cultural and social contexts are central (e.g., Lerman, 1998). Under the influence of disciplines such as anthropology and sociology, modes of enquiry that are interpretative rather than, in a narrow sense, experimental have been adopted and legitimized. Consistent with this shift of emphasis was a redefinition of the goal of mathematics education as enculturation within a mathematical community.

A further natural and inevitable development has been the recognition that mathematics and mathematics education are, by their very natures, political. Although mathematics educators have been deeply involved for many years in reacting to specific political contexts in many parts of the world (e.g., Fasheh, 1982), the recognition of

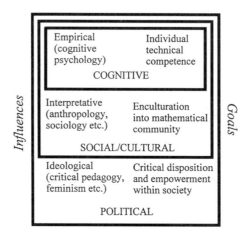

FIG. 17.1. Widening perspectives on mathematics education and associated influences and goals.

mathematics education as *inherently* political is implicit in the view of mathematics as a human activity. Forms of political activism, such as campaigns for equity, and critiques of education, such as Freire's critical pedagogy (Frankenstein, 1983; Freire, 1970), informed this realization, as have historical events. Most pointedly following the creation of nuclear weapons, mathematicians have been forced to realize that what they do is not morally or politically neutral (e.g., D'Ambrosio, 1999).

Conversely, in many parts of the world, governments have increasingly sought to politically shape mathematics education through such control mechanisms as regulation of the initial education and subsequent professional activity of teachers and specification of curricula and assessment. To an unprecedented extent, official and unofficial political groups seek to influence public opinion through the mass media.

By contrast with the goals of mathematics education from the cognitive and sociocultural perspectives, as we have characterized them, we argue in this chapter for a politically defined goal of mathematics education as the empowerment of individuals within society through construction of critical capabilities and the disposition to use them. In order to develop this argument, we begin by suggesting that both the definition of what counts as mathematics and the reasons for teaching mathematics—issues until comparatively recently considered unproblematic, if considered at all—have been problematized. Central to our argument is a view of mathematical modeling as a tool for describing and analyzing aspects of real-world phenomena, social as well as physical.

WHAT COUNTS AS MATHEMATICS?

To ask the question "What is mathematics, really?," as does Hersh (1997), is misguided if the question implies that there exists something unchanging and independent of humanity that mathematics *is* (which is certainly not Hersh's view). On the contrary, accepting mathematics as human activity implies that what counts as mathematics is culturally determined.

As a consequence, the boundaries of what counts as mathematics have been fundamentally challenged. Until relatively recently, for example, accounts of history of mathematics were predominantly Eurocentric. That bias is being undermined by documentation of the contributions of other civilizations (e.g., Joseph, 1992) and more fundamentally by challenges to the belief that it is only academic mathematics (sometimes termed "Western mathematics" but that seems to us to be a misnomer) that really counts as mathematics (e.g., Powell & Frankenstein, 1997). Bishop (1988) argued that all cultures share certain fundamental activities that are inherently mathematical, namely, counting, locating, measuring, designing, playing, and explaining. These activities, across history and across cultures' are not limited to practical issues of survival and problem solving but also include such transcending activities as seeking explanations of our world and pursuing human propensities and endowments for game playing and aesthetic enjoyment (D'Ambrosio, 1999). More generally, there has been increasing recognition of "ethnomathematics," defined as "the mathematics which is practised among identifiable cultural groups, such as national-tribal societies, labor groups, children of a certain age bracket, professional classes, and so on" (D'Ambrosio, 1985, p. 45).

A major inertial force holding back radical reform of mathematics education is the simplistic perception of mathematics prevalent among people in general, including politicians and other policymakers. Mathematics is commonly seen as consisting essentially of computation and formulas, yielding exact and infallible answers, without relevance to everyday life, accessible only to experts, and not open to criticism. Indeed, in many respects mathematics is commonly perceived as the antithesis of human activity—mechanical, detached, emotionless, value-free, morally neutral.

A highly contentious and topical manifestation of divergent perceptions of the nature of mathematics and the goals of mathematics education is ongoing in the United States, in the form of the so-called "Math Wars." Most notably in California, pressure groups seeking to shape the direction of mathematics education are vying for the attention and support of politicians and the general public. Jacob and Akers (1999) charted the remarkable sequence of events in California leading to the domination of the state's policy on mathematics education by groups with a narrow view of mathematics and mathematics education and a clear political agenda. One particular outcome of these developments is that the criteria adopted by the State Board of Education in 1999 require that current and confirmed experimental research should be reflected in any instructional materials adopted.

Table 17.1 shows the interpretation offered by Jacob and Akers (1999) of the views of the psychologists and mathematicians that underpin the approach to mathematics learning supposedly legitimized by experimental research.

To exemplify the evidence on which this interpretation is based, the Preface to Grades 8 through 12 in the Californian mathematics framework states that "Problem solving and symbolic computations are nothing but different manifestations of mathematical proofs" (from the California Department of Education's web site www.cde.ca.gov). By way of example, the solution of

$$x - 1/4(3x - 1) = 2x - 5$$

TABLE 17.1

Views of Psychologists and Mathematicians Influential in Formulating the 1999 California
Mathematics Framework, as Interpreted by Jacob and Akers (1999)

	Psychologists	*Mathematicians*
Skills	Skills are procedures; they must be learned to "automaticity" and may be divorced from meaning; components of a procedure must be mastered before the procedure itself; understanding and problem solving come later and are the result of practicing procedures	Mathematical skills should be learned according to their logical structure; the deductive systems of formal mathematics may provide explicit organization, as in Euclidean geometry or define organization implicitly (say, in lower grades); conceptual understanding is derived from using this logical structure
Problem solving	Problem solving is executing practiced procedures. It may include (a) translation of a question into (b) a known mathematical representation where (c) a previously learned procedure can be applied to justify an answer	Problem solving involves knowing when to apply a general mathematical result (such as a theorem or an established algorithm) to a specific situation to obtain desired information
Conceptual understanding	Conceptual understanding is measured by students knowing when to apply a previously learned procedure; speed and accuracy in procedural performance are essential components and measures of conceptual understanding	Conceptual understanding is measured by students being able to use correct mathematical language and reasoning to support their answers; the deductive structure of formal mathematics, including a clear formulation of hypotheses before drawing conclusions, should provide the basis for this reasoning

is shown as a 16-step two-column formal proof of the "theorem" that "A number satisfies $x - 1/4(3x - 1) = 2x - 5$ when and only when $x = 3$."

The view of how children should be taught mathematics implied by Table 17.1 suggests an underlying metaphor of the child as a computer to be programmed, given the emphasis on flawlessly executing procedures according to rigid formal rules, to the point of automaticity, and the relative unimportance of understanding and contextualization. The emphasis on a child unquestioningly following rules means that this interpretation fits rather well within the thesis put forward by Lakoff (1996) that the fundamental metaphor that underlies conservative philosophy is the "strict father" model of the family.

Within the view characterized in Table 17.1, relationships between formal mathematical structures and aspects of reality that those structures can be used to model are of secondary importance. "What mathematics really is" is confined to the manipulation of formal structures. The links with reality through modeling and the interpretation of derivations from models within a human context lie outside the boundary and are of peripheral importance, at best, in mathematics education. By contrast, we argue that these aspects should be central.

WHY TEACH MATHEMATICS?

In view of the issues just discussed, this question can no longer be answered simply by saying "to pass on a fixed body of mathematical knowledge."

In societal terms, a commonly stated and accepted justification offered is that mathematics education is needed to create a productive and competitive workforce in general as well as a cadre of specialists who will contribute directly to scientific and technological advances and to advances in mathematical theory.

At the level of the individual whose work does not in an obvious way require advanced technical mathematics, the most common answer to the question is "because we need mathematics in our everyday lives." Does this stand up to scrutiny? Beyond basic computation, how much of school mathematics does a person need to function? Not square roots, not solving quadratic equations, not proofs of Euclidean geometry. Moreover, many studies have shown that the methods used by, for example, Liberian tailors (Lave, 1977), young Brazilian street traders (Nunes, Schliemann, & Carraher), and American supermarket shoppers (Lave, Murtaugh, & de la Rocha, 1984)—there are many more examples—are different from the formal methods taught in schools. For a historical example, we may look no further than the fact that people managed to deal with debits and credits for centuries without any formal theory of operations on directed numbers. In short, the appeal to the usefulness for practical life purposes of formal school mathematics as presently constituted is limited (but this conclusion certainly does not imply that mathematics is not important for people's lives).

In terms of the relationship between individual and societal needs, we may ask how well school mathematics prepares people for work and citizenship. D'Ambrosio (1999, p. 138) suggested that "we may be cheating our youth when we say that mathematics, as taught in our schools, opens good perspectives of employment for them." Instead, mathematics too often operates as a filter restricting the choices for individuals. Davis and Hersh (1986) pointedly asked: "Why are so many people studying a subject for which they have, it seems, so little interest, affection, or aptitude? The answer, of course, is simple: "It's required." Yes, but required by what? By whom? For what reason?" (p. 100)

Davis and Hersh discussed this question specifically in relation to the calculus requirements of the University's Business School. Business students report that they never use the calculus they are taught and it is unlikely that many people actually working in business do so either. Why then is calculus a requirement? Davis and Hersh suggested two main reasons. The first is that lack of a mathematics requirement could mean lower prestige for the school. The second is that such a requirement facilitates admission procedures by acting as a screening device.

In contrast to the utilitarian justifications for teaching mathematics, as outlined previously, another argument is that mathematics (the mathematics of all people) should be regarded as part of the cultural heritage of mankind in the same spirit as, say, literature and music. Mathematics is one manifestation of the human propensity to try to make sense of the world that takes its place with others such as science, religion, and philosophy—as D'Ambrosio (1999) pointed out, the separation of mathematics from other ways of interpreting the world and ourselves is a modern phenomenon of Western civilization.

In relation to the theme we are seeking to develop in this chapter, the most important reason for teaching mathematics—both for the empowerment of the individual and for the betterment of society—is to help people become critical thinkers who can use mathematics as a tool for analyzing social and political issues and can reflect on that tool use, including its limitations.

A key aspect of such tool use is the idea of mathematical modeling, as the bridge between mathematics as a means for making sense of aspects of the physical and social world, and mathematics as a set of formal structures. The bare bones of this relationship are typically expressed in the following terms. Aspects of a phenomenon of interest are expressed in mathematical terms by identifying and quantifying variables and relationships between them, forming the basis for a mathematical model. Mathematical procedures are used to work through the implications of that model. Those implications are then interpreted and evaluated in the context of the phenomenon being studied. For a proper description of the modeling process, this minimal schematization needs to be elaborated, of course, to include such aspects as the goals of the modeler, the resources available, the processes of comparing different models, and so on.

In relation to modeling , we may then characterize three nested views of what should be addressed within school mathematics. Broadly consistent with a narrow cognitive perspective is a concentration on the "purely mathematical" aspects, as indicated in Fig. 17.2. Applications are of secondary importance, treated as routine exercises in

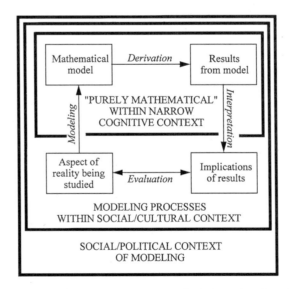

FIG. 17.2. Perspectives on what might be included in school mathematics in terms of modeling.

"executing practiced procedures" and "knowing when to apply a previously learned procedure" (Table 17.1) and as unproblematic in terms of the implicit modeling that underlies them. From the social/cultural perspective, understanding of the context and interpretation of the mathematical results relative to the complexities of that context are part of a broader interpretation of "mathematics." As Romberg (1992) put it: "The point is that discussing and criticizing a mathematical model does not depend simply on technical knowledge about the modeling process. Instead, it also must be based on reflective knowledge about the criteria used in the construction, applications, and evaluations of mathematical models for social problems" (p. 435).

Moreover, models are not necessarily ready made to be taken "off the shelf" but may be dialectically co-constructed in the process of making sense of the phenomenon (e.g., Cobb, 1999).

The social/political perspective shifts to a higher level, in that it is concerned with not simply the analysis of particular models but the nature of the modeling process per se, including understanding that modeling is relative to the goals of the modeler and the resources available and that there are generally alternative models, depending on the assumptions made, that should be subject to criticism.

Most central, from the point of view of the argument we are trying to develop, is the disposition, first, to see social phenomena as open to mathematical modeling as a tool to better understand them and also for polemical purposes and, second, not to accept uncritically a model presented by somebody else without identifying and analyzing its explicit or implicit assumptions (Frankenstein, 1989). The aim, as Apple (1992, p. 439) expressed it, is "creating a citizenry that is not only 'functionally literate,' but *critically literate* as well" (quotes and italics in original).

A CASE IN POINT: WORD PROBLEMS

Word problems provide a telling example of how the purely mathematical can become separated from the experience of children and the sense making that they apply to this experience. As a very young man, Gustave Flaubert wrote a letter to his sister in which he said:

> Since you are now studying geometry and trigonometry, I will give you a problem: A ship sails the ocean. It left Boston with a cargo of wool. It grosses 200 tons. It is bound for Le Havre. The mainmast is broken, the cabin boy is on deck, there are 12 passengers aboard, the wind is blowing East-North-East, the clock points to a quarter past three in the afternoon. It is the month of May. How old is the captain? (cited in Wells, 1997, p. 234).

Inspired by this example, French researchers carried out studies with schoolchildren in which they asked questions such as: "On a ship, there are 26 sheep and 10 goats. How old is the captain?" (Baruk, 1985, p. 23 [translated from French]). A high proportion of the children asked provided numerical answers (mostly 36).

Greer (1993) posed 13- and 14-year-old children in Northern Ireland a number of questions in which realistic considerations make a simplistic calculation problematic.

For example: "An athlete's best time for the mile is 4 minutes and 7 seconds. About how long would it take him to run 3 miles?"

Direct proportionality (i.e., multiplying 4 minutes and 7 seconds by 3) was used without comment by 90% of the children, who thus, apparently, did not make use of their knowledge that a runner cannot maintain speed over longer distances. This initial study was substantially extended by Verschaffel, De Corte, and Lasure (1994) with Belgian children, obtaining very similar results. Subsequent replications in Switzerland, Japan, Venezuela, and Germany yielded highly consistent results, showing that, across a range of questions, children predominantly answered without, apparently, taking realistic considerations into account (Greer & Verschaffel, 1997; Verschaffel, Greer, & De Corte, 2000).

Although the question "How old is the captain?" differs from those used in the later research cited, in that a sensible answer cannot be derived from the information provided, both sets of studies show an apparent "suspension of sense-making" (Schoenfeld, 1991). Two main reasons may be put forward for this widely documented phenomenon. The first is the stereotyped nature of simple word problems as predominantly used in schools (Nesher, 1980; Reusser, 1988), which leads to the expectation that any such word problem contains two numbers, which are to be combined using addition, subtraction, multiplication, or division. Students develop superficial strategies that do not depend on making sense of the situation described in the text, yet serve successfully to identify the required arithmetic operation. Thus, word problems are predominantly used as routine applications of stock procedures—in line with Table 17.1.

A second, more profound, reason lies in the culture of the classroom, specifically the implicit rules that govern interactions between students and teacher, the "didactical contract" analyzed by Brousseau (1997). In these terms, the behavior of the children may be interpreted as sense making of a different sort, "the construction of a set of behaviors that results in praise for good performance, minimal conflict, fitting in socially etc." according to Schoenfeld (1991, p. 340). Likewise, Gravemeijer (1997, p. 392) commented that "it is not a cognitive deficit as such that causes the abstention from sense-making, but rather that the children are acting in accordance with a typical school mathematics classroom culture" and suggested that, in order to change this, one has to change the didactical contract.

One approach to renegotiating the didactical contract in relation to word problems is to reconceptualize them as exercises in mathematical modeling (Greer, 1993, 1997; Verschaffel et al., 2000). By way of example, consider direct proportionality from this perspective. There are situations in which direct proportionality offers a precise model—for example, a petrol pump where the cost is directly proportional to the number of gallons. (Of course, making the cost of something proportional to its quantity is a law neither of nature nor of society, but a convenient human convention—in many cases, discount is given for quantity, for example). In other situations, proportionality offers a reasonable approximation—if it takes about 5 hours to fly from Belfast to New York, about how long would it take to fly from Belfast to Seattle? In other cases, such as the problem about the runner cited previously, proportionality is not such a good model. In yet other cases, proportionality is clearly inappropriate—if the radius of a circle is increased by a factor of 3, for example, the area does not increase by a factor of 3. Then there are absurdities and jokes such as "If Henry the Eighth had six wives, how many did Henry the Fourth have?" The predominant approach in school mathematics is to assume that all problems that at least ostensibly can be modeled by proportionality are of the first type and should be solved by reaching for a standard procedure. The modeling implicit in applying the procedure is not addressed.

The modeling approach offers many advantages. Briefly:

1. It would undermine the achievement of apparent success through superficial strategies that is made possible by the stereotyped nature of word problems (Nesher, 1980; Reusser, 1988), whereby "most text-book problems are nothing more than poorly disguised exercises in one of the four basic exercises" (Gravemeijer, 1997, p. 390).
2. Through such activities as questioning assumptions and debating the relative merits of rival models, students can be helped to become "flexible discourse and problem comprehenders" (Staub & Reusser, 1995, p. 302).
3. The modeling perspective addresses the concerns raised by what Freudenthal (1991, p. 5) called "the poor permeability of the membrane separating classroom and school experience from life experience" (see also Resnick, 1987).
4. The modeling perspective is pervasive throughout mathematics. Introducing students to this perspective early is arguably a key part of the process of nurturing a mathematical disposition.
5. An understanding of the modeling process and how mathematical models of social phenomena are constructed and interpreted, together with a critical stance toward such models, is an essential part of education for responsible citizenship (Koblitz, 1981; Schoenfeld, 1991).

A justification often put forward for word problems is that they provide simple examples of applications of mathematics to aspects of real life. Strong critiques of this claim discussed in Verschaffel et al., 2000, have been made by, among others, Lave (1992) and Gerofsky (1996). Word problems as typically used in school mathematics are often artificial and, as argued previously, are answered by routine solutions with scant regard for sense making. Insofar as they do relate to students' experience, school word problems rarely deal in any depth with important social and political issues—the sort of "real real-life math word problems" discussed by Frankenstein (1989, 1996).

MATHEMATICS AS A TOOL FOR SOCIAL CHANGE AND INDIVIDUAL EMPOWERMENT

Throughout history, mathematicians have often served political and military masters— and continue to do so. Davis and Hersh (1981, p. 95) identified the explosion of the atomic bomb over Japan as a turning point in terms of moral awareness within the mathematical community:

Individual mathematicians asked themselves in what way they, personally, had unleashed monsters on the world, and if they had, how they could reconcile it with what philosophic views of life they held. Mathematics, which had previously been conceived as a remote and Olympian doctrine, emerged suddenly as something capable of doing physical, social, and psychological damage.

D'Ambrosio (1999) passionately argued that mathematicians and mathematics educators must reflect on this history and on their responsibilities for helping to shape the future.

For an example of mathematics being used as a tool for positive social change, consider the case of Florence Nightingale. Unfortunately, what most people know about her is limited to her role in establishing nursing as a profession, together with the image of "The lady with the lamp." What is, regrettably, much less well known, and neglected by her biographers, is that in pursuing her life-long mission of serving humanity through preventing unnecessary suffering, she relied heavily on statistical methods as tools for argumentation (Graham, 1995)—against, in particular, a male military establishment (Cohen, 1985). Indeed, in the course of this campaign, she developed some of the earliest forms of visual representation for communicating key aspects of data. Later, she was heavily involved with mathematicians and social scientists such as Quetelet who were at the center of the development of applications of statistical methods to social phenomena, and she was a century ahead of her time in trying to promote statistical education.

This example illustrates one way in which mathematics can become a tool for social change, namely through the analysis of data, and the use of this analysis in argumentation. Increasingly, data handling is becoming a part of mainstream curricula in many countries (Shaughnessy, Garfield, & Greer, 1996). Application of data analysis to social, moral, and political questions expands the scope of school mathematics beyond a purely intellectual exercise and can demonstrate to students the relevance of mathematics to their lives. D'Ambrosio (1999) argued that in characterizing an appropriate curriculum for the next century, the narrowly utilitarian goal of "numeracy" should be replaced by the broader goal of "matheracy," commenting: "In proposing matheracy, the intention is to give a much broader dimension to mathematical thinking, stressing its value as an instrument for explaining, understanding and coping with reality in its broad sense. Matheracy is the main intellectual instrument for the critical view of the world" (p. 150).

Discussing why statistics should be taught in school, Cobb (1999, p. 37) suggested that two justifications are generally offered. The first refers to developments in the discipline, with an underlying metaphor of students as apprentice research statisticians. The second recognizes the increasing role of statistical reasoning in work-related activities and informed citizenship. He continues:

> In contrast to these two common rationales, we find a third justification to be far more compelling. Briefly, the increasing use of computers, not just within the discipline but in society in general, has placed an increasing premium on quantitative reasoning in general and on statistical reasoning in particular ... It is already apparent that debates about public policy issues tend to involve reasoning with data. In this discourse, policy decisions are justified by presenting arguments based on the analysis of data. In many respects, this discourse is increasingly becoming the language of power in the public

policy area. Inability to participate in this discourse results in de facto disenfranchisement that spawns alienation from, and cynicism about, the political process. (p. 38)

A telling example is discussed by Koblitz (1981). It concerns an appearance on the Johnny Carson show of Paul Ehrlich, who had written a best-seller called "The Population Bomb." At one point, Ehrlich wrote up in large letters:

$$D = N \times I$$

and explained that D stood for damage to the environment, N for the number of people, and I for the impact of each person on the environment. He claimed that he had demonstrated that the more people, the more pollution. Koblitz (p. 111) commented:

Who can argue with an equation? An equation is always exact, indisputable. Challenging someone who can support his claims with an equation is as pointless as arguing with your high school math teacher. How many of Johnny Carson's viewers had the sophistication necessary to question Ehrlich's equation? Is Ehrlich saying that the "I" for the president of [an irresponsible chemical company] is the same as the "I" for you and me? Preposterous, isn't it? But what if the viewer is too intimidated by a mathematical equation to apply some common sense?

Several other examples illustrating the same phenomena are analyzed by Schoenfeld (1991), who refers to:

... the totalitarian power of mathematics. Throw enough formalism or appeal to mathematical authority in front of people, and they'll back down. For some reason ... people don't expect heavily mathematical statements to make sense to them. They assume they make sense to *somebody* (the "experts"), abdicate responsibility for understanding, and (at least sometimes) accept the statements on face value. (p. 315; italics and brackets in original)

This situation is alarming in a society in which, as Davis and Hersh (1986, p. xv) put it: "The social and physical worlds are being mathematized at an increasing rate" and "We'd better watch it, because too much of it may not be good for us."

In 1992, the Conservative Party in the United Kingdom achieved victory in an election that was expected to result in a "hung" parliament, that is, one in which no party had an overall majority. At the time that the newpapers had to be printed on the evening of the election, the computer model being used was still predicting that a hung parliament was almost certain, with the result that the next day's headlines were wrong. Noticeably lacking in media discussion of these events was a clear explanation that the computer prediction came from a model based on certain assumptions relying on human judgment and that some of these assumptions were unfounded. People were thus left holding the perceptions of computers as predicting results by some sort of "magic" and at the same time capable of making stupid errors.

Recently, a National Lottery was introduced in the United Kingdom. A critical analysis of the workings of this would be a valuable exercise in itself, but for present purposes we want to concentrate on the slogan at the center of the propaganda campaign aimed at persuading the public to buy tickets. The slogan was "It could be you," which is literally true but subtly disguises the situation, namely, that the probability of winning the main prize is very small indeed. By contrast, when the problems with British beef later became apparent, in particular the small probability of contracting "mad cow disease" through eating it, the tone of the government's reassurances to the public was essentially "It couldn't be you," although they did not adopt this as a slogan, for obvious reasons. In neither case did the media provide guidance to the public on the interpretation of small probabilities of events with large consequences.

What these examples are intended to illustrate is that, whether through lack of engagement, abdication of responsibility, or intimidation by mathematics, people do not possess a sense of being able to use mathematical tools to critically evaluate aspects of their culture.

A CASE IN POINT: WHEN BARBIE GOES TO MATH CLASS

We argued that most people do not feel competent to judge applications of mathematics as a tool for analyzing aspects of our society and as a result are disempowered. Nor do they feel competent to use mathematics themselves as a critical tool. They are simultaneously alienated from mathematics and awed by its authority. To change this prevalent mind-set, educational activities are needed that help people realize that they do have the right, and indeed the responsibility, not to accept uncritically mathematical arguments designed to persuade. This is not primarily a matter of people knowing a great deal of formal mathematics—for example, the level of technical mathematics that is needed to spot the weakness in the example from Koblitz presented earlier is not high. Indeed, what is required to see through many abuses of mathematics could be described as being close to common sense. Unfortunately, in the face of apparent mathematical authority, people tend to suspend common sense judgment.

As well as developing the disposition to be critical of arguments presented to them, it is important that people should be disposed and competent to turn a critical eye, using mathematics as appropriate, on social and political issues. Here we present an example of an analysis that turns the spotlight on what is perhaps an all-time favourite, the ultimate icon of American popular culture, Barbie.

The Barbie doll, a product of Mattel, Inc., is 11.5 inches tall, with chest 5.5 inches, waist 2.75 inches, and weight 5 ounces, first marketed in 1959. According to Mattel, typically a girl gets her first Barbie at about age 3 and is given six more Barbies by the time she is 12 years old. The statistics on sales of Barbie are staggering (Mukhopadhyay, 1998, p. 154)—on average two Barbies are sold every second (Lord, 1994, p. 7). Barbie is manufactured in factories in China, Malaysia, and Indonesia, and Mattel has a worldwide market in more than 150 nations throughout the world with sales reaching $1.9 billion in 1997 (Mattel, 1999).

Although often viewed as a stereotypical blonde, Mattel's Barbie is cast as a modern career woman and a role model for girls, appearing as an astronaut, running as a Presidential candidate, as a zookeeper, and, in all, holding more than 75 jobs. The Barbie phenomenon has far-reaching ramifications. Although intended to be a doll, a girl's play object, Barbie bears no resemblance to any chubby-faced typical doll. Rather, she has an adult female body that comes with different hair and skin colors. She is notorious for the size of her wardrobe and wears original creations by top fashion designers. She has been dating Ken, another Mattel product, since 1961. Unlike a stuffed toy or baby doll, Barbie invites identification by girls and thereby stimulates complex expressions of the developing female self. Other social (and consumer) manifestations of the Barbie phenomenon include Barbie festivals (Sarasohn-Kahn, 1996), collector clubs, and annual conventions. The U.S. Postal Service has introduced a postage stamp to commemorate Barbie's place in popular culture.

Barbie's career has not been without controversy. TheTeenTalk Barbie of 1992 shocked and irritated many when she appeared with a preprogramed microchip including the utterance "Math class is tough." Not surprisingly, this enraged the American Association of University Women, the National Council of Teachers of Mathematics, and other concerned citizens (NCTM, 1993), who accused Mattel of reinforcing a stereotype that undermines girls' participation in mathematics (Grossman, 1992; National Council of Teachers of Mathematics, 1993; Wall Street Journal, 1992).

Mattel's shrewd corporate behavior pays attention to the realities of Barbie's consumer clientele. Recently, for example, Barbie for the first time showed some signs of maturity and got a remodeled body with smaller breasts and larger waist (Zeidler, 1997). However, this decision was protested by many of her fans, and the 1998 Barbies also included the much favoured "classic look" (Zeidler, 1997). Barbie has been the focus of attention in popular culture and has generated fiction, artwork, and considerable social analysis; for example, it has been suggested that she transmits conflicting messages on female sexuality (Lord, 1994).

Because Barbie is very familiar to almost all people in the United States—Sarasohn-Kahn (1996, p. 1) reported that she resides in 99% of young homes, an investigation that is initiated by the question "What would Barbie look like if she was as big as one of us?" is culturally relevant, intellectually stimulating, and socially provocative for American students. The task invites the students to participate in imagining a "real-life" Barbie based on the dimensions of an average or a typical member of the group. In order to better understand the contrast between the doll that is often idealized as having a "perfect" human body and the individual chosen for comparison, the contour of that individual is sketched. The projected Barbie, using the computed measures of her relevant body parts is then superimposed on the full-size contour drawing.

One of us (SM) carried out this activity several times in classes for pre-service and in-service teachers (although it is equally well suited for children in middle and high schools). The discourse in the course of the activity is rich and far reaching (see Mukhopadhyay, 1998, for details). Because the course that the investigation takes is dependent on the students participating, the outcomes in terms of details and complexities of their discourse are diverse. However, in general terms, the investigation follows a typical course. When the investigation begins with the distribution of dolls and tape measures to groups of students, mixed in terms of race and gender, there are giggles and laughter as personal anecdotes about Barbie are shared. The strategies of constructing the real-life Barbie begin with measuring different body parts and converting those measures to a real-life scale. Although many of these adults have an antipathy toward mathematics, a not-uncommon characteristic of elementary teachers (at least in the U.S.), the mathematics required by the task is not perceived as daunting in terms of particular formulae to remember and apply, but rather the relevant mediating concepts, such as scaling factor, emerge naturally through negotiation within the group.

Apart from the mathematical skills of proportional reasoning, the starting point of this exercise involves other decision making, namely, finding the representative, or "average," person for the group. Although the students were competent with the computation of averages, the concept of choosing an average person is much more complex, particularly bearing in mind the variation in race and gender within the groups.

In the course of constructing a life-size Barbie, the students recognize how strikingly different, indeed unnatural, Barbie's shape is. Comments such as "Her neck is too long," "Her feet are too small to make anyone stand without a prop," "Her waist is too narrow," and "Her pelvic area is too small to bear a child" are common. Invariably, the students reach a consensus that Barbie's shape is unnatural, a conclusion in agreement with the analysis of Norton, Olds, Olive, and Dank (1996) that the probability of such a body shape is unlikely and would occur in less than 1 in 100,000 in a typical Anglo-Australian population. (To make the same point, and promote self-esteem among normally shaped women, Ruby, an icon of Body Shop, a retailer of health care products, makes the statement, "There are 3 million women who don't look like supermodels and only 8 who do".) Consequently, the students, both men and women, acquire a heightened appreciation for the legitimacy of different body types.

Being aware of multiculturalism and internationalism among their potential customers, Mattel marketed Barbie in several "ethnic" variations (and Becky, a Barbie friend and lookalike in a pink wheelchair was recently marketed, too). Their awareness in creating culturally sensitive dolls was evident not only in the styles of their costumes but also in the colors of their skin and hair. However, working with Barbies of different apparent ethnicity, the students were stunned to find that, irrespective of the pigment of their plastic skin, all Barbies, whether Native American, German, or Polynesian, are identically proportioned—in fact, they share the same mold in the factories in Asia where they are made. The subsequent discussions, passionate and involved, lead to debunking the myth of Barbie as a model for "every girl" when issues about body image and body type in relation to self-worth and cultural identity are examined. These discussions lead further to considerations of the idealization of female attractiveness associated with thinness and diet and the alarming incidence of eating disorders—more than five million Americans, progressively younger children, both girls and boys, of age 10 years and above, have succumbed to eating disorders of various degrees (Mukhopadhyay, 1998, p.157).

Although the task begins with measurements of height and various body parts, the act of sketching out a life-size Barbie and the striking implications of the comparison contribute to an overwhelming "aha" experience for the students. The discourse that results is not limited to the acts of measuring, figuring out the mathematics of scaling, and rendering the drawing but also encompasses the interpretation of the task on personal, social, and political levels. Once the impact of mathematical tools in constructing the full-size Barbie is accomplished, the discussions touch upon far deeper social issues such as consumerism and link naturally to fundamental questions such as commodification of women's bodies and the degree of control over everyone as consumers. The market economy of the production of Barbie at various factories overseas also seriously challenges Mattel's underlying labor policies and exploitation of underage workers. Thus, as a modeling exercise, the task generates exceptionally rich activity at the second level indicated in Fig. 17.2 as the students discuss in depth the implications of what they have discovered and also at the third level, as they become aware and confident of their ability to use mathematics as a tool for critical analysis of an aspect of their culture. The activity, therefore, contributes to social consciousness, "learning to perceive social, political, and economic contradictions, and to take action against the oppressive elements of reality" (Freire, 1970, p. 17).

SUMMARY

Mathematics is a human activity. Starting from this basic tenet, we argued that what constitutes mathematics is much broader than institutionalized academic mathematics. The ethnomathetical perspective emphasizes that mathematics is found in all cultures, both for practical problem solving necessary for survival and for activities that transcend mere survival, such as attempting to explain the world we live in, intellectual and other games, and the aesthetic sense. Moreover, ethnomathemics is found not only in exotic cultures but also in the day-to-day practices of groups within our own culture.

What counts as mathematics is enriched by going beyond manipulation of formal systems to include the modeling of social as well as physical phenomena and the human context of such modeling exercises.

A central message of this chapter is that people should control mathematics as a tool rather than be controlled by it. For example, what are we to make of the fact that children are so intimidated by the implicit rules of school mathematics that they cannot challenge questions of the "How old is the captain?" type? And of the fact that adults cannot challenge abuses of mathematics such as those documented by Koblitz (1981) and Schoenfeld (1991) and, in general, abdicate the right and the responsibility to understand, being both alienated by, and in awe of, mathematics?

One reason for this state of affairs is the lack of cultural support for mathematics. Mathematics generally:

> ...has a bad press, with a widespread public image of being difficult, cold, abstract, and in many cultures, largely masculine. It also has the image of being remote and inaccessible to all but a few super-intelligent beings with 'mathematical minds'. This myth is the prevailing public image in Western Anglophone countries, where many persons operating at high levels of competency in numeracy, graphicacy, computeracy in their professional life happily admit to being no good at mathematics. ...In contrast to the shame associated with illiteracy, innumeracy is sometimes almost a matter of pride amongst educated persons in these countries. (Ernest, 1996, p. 803)

The most important goal of mathematics education, in our view, is not advanced technical expertise for the few (essential though that is), with everyone else receiving at best a watered-down version of the same, which in most cases leads to alienation and disempowerment. Rather it should be the development for the majority of people of an ability and a disposition to use mathematics as a critical tool. To this end, school students need learning experiences that explore complex social and political issues, such as the Barbie example described previously and the "real, real-life" examples discussed by Frankenstein (1996).

REFERENCES

Apple, M. W. (1992). Thinking more politically about challenges before us: A response to Romberg. *Journal for Research in Mathematics Education, 23*, 438–440.

Baruk, S. (1985). *L'age du capitaine: De l'erreur en mathematiques*. Paris: Seuil.

Bishop, A. J. (1988). Mathematics education in its cultural context. *Educational Studies in Mathematics, 19*, 179–191.

Brousseau, G. (1997). *Theory of didactical situations in mathematics*. Dordrecht: Kluwer.

Cobb, P. (1999). Individual and collective mathematical development: The case of statistical data analysis. *Mathematical Thinking and Learning, 1*, 5–43.

Cohen, I. B. (1985). Florence Nightingale. *Scientific American, 250*(3), 98–104, 107.

D'Ambrosio, U. (1985). Ethnomathematics and its place in the history and pedagogy of mathematics. *For the Learning of Mathematics, 5*(1), 41–48.

D'Ambrosio, U. (1999). Literacy, Matheracy, Technoracy: A trivium for today. *Mathematical Thinking and Learning, 1*, 131–153.

Davis, P. J., & Hersh, R. (1981). *The mathematical experience*. Boston: Birkhauser.

Davis, P. J., & Hersh, R. (1986). *Descartes' dream: The world according to mathematics*. Brighton, England: Harvester.

De Corte, E., Greer, B., & Verschaffel, L. (1996). Learning and teaching mathematics. In D. Berliner & R. Calfee (Eds.), *Handbook of educational psychology* (pp. 491–549). New York: Macmillan.

Ernest, P. (1996). Popularization: Myths, massmedia, and modernism. In A. J. Bishop, K. Clements, C. Keitel, J. Kilpatrick, & C. Laborde (Eds.), *International handbook of mathematics education* (pp. 785–817). Dordrecht: Kluwer.

Fasheh, M. (1982). Mathematics, culture, and authority. *For the Learning of Mathematics, 3*(2), 2–8.

Frankenstein, M. (1983). Critical mathematics education: An application of Paolo Freire's epistemology. *Journal of Education, 165*, 315–339.

Frankenstein, M. (1989). *Relearning mathematics: A different third R—Radical maths*. London: Free Association Books.

Frankenstein, M. (1996). Critical mathematical literacy: Teaching through real real-life math word problems. In T. Kjaergard, A. Kvamme, & N. Linden (Eds.), *Numeracy, race, gender, and class. Proceedings of 3rd international conference on Political Dimensions of Mathematics Education* (pp. 59–76). Landas, Norway: Casper Vorlag.

Freire, P. (1970). *Pedagogy of the oppressed*. New York: Continuum.

Freudenthal, H. (1991). *Revisiting mathematics education*. Dordrecht: Kluwer.

Gardner, H. (1985). *The mind's new science*. New York: Basic Books.

Gerofsky, S. (1996). A linguistic and narrative view of word problems in mathematics education. *For the Learning of Mathematics, 16*(2), 36–45.

Graham, A. (1995). The perfect heroine. In A. Graham & J. Fauvel (Eds.), *Empowering students through the history of statistics* (pp. 12–17). London: Open University.

Gravemeijer, K. (1997). Solving word problems: A case of modelling ? *Learning and Instruction, 7*, 389–397.

Greer, B. (1993). The modelling perspective on wor(l)d problems. *Journal of Mathematical Behavior, 12*, 239–250.

Greer, B. (1997). Modelling reality in mathematics classrooms: The case of word problems. *Learning and Instruction, 7*, 293–307.

Greer, B., & Verschaffel, L. (Eds.) (1997). Modelling reality in mathematics classrooms. *Learning and Instruction, 7*(4) [Special issue].

Grossman, L. M. (1992). Educators give Barbie a good dressing-down. *Wall Street Journal*, Sept. 25.

Hersh, R. (1997). *What is mathematics, really?* New York: Oxford University Press.

Jacob, B., & Akers, J. (1999, April). *"Research based" mathematics education policy: The case of California 1995–1998*. Paper presented at the Research Presession of the National Council of Teachers of Mathematics Conference, San Francisco.

Joseph, G. G. (1992). *The crest of the peacock: Non-European roots of mathematics*. London: Penguin.

Koblitz, N. (1981). Mathematics as propaganda. In L. A. Steen (Ed.), *Mathematics tomorrow* (pp. 111–120). New York: Springer-Verlag.

Lakoff, G. (1996). *Moral politics: What Conservatives know that Liberals don't*. Chicago: University of Chicago Press.

Lave, J. (1977). Cognitive consequences of traditional apprenticeship training in West Africa. *Anthropology and Education Quarterly, 7*, 177–180.

Lave, J. (1992). Word problems: A microcosm of theories of learning. In P. Light & G. Butterworth (Eds.), *Context and cognition: Ways of learning and knowing* (pp. 74–92). New York: Harvester Wheatsheaf.

Lave, J., Murtaugh, M., & de la Rocha, O. (1984). The dialectic of arithmetic in grocery shopping. In B. Rogoff & J. Lave (Eds.), *Everyday cognition: Its development in social context* (pp. 67–94). Cambridge, MA: Harvard University Press.

Lerman, S. (1998). Research on socio-cultural perspectives of mathematics teaching and learning. In A. Sierpinska & J. Kilpatrick (Eds.), *Mathematics education as a research domain: A search for identity* (pp. 333–350). Dordrecht: Kluwer.

Lord, M. G. (1994). *Forever Barbie: The unauthorized biography of a real doll*. New York: Morrow and Co.

Mattel, Inc. (1999). *Barbie doll gala kicks off year-long celebration*. Company press release, Mattel, Inc., Feb. 7.

Mukhopadhyay, S. (1998). When Barbie goes to classrooms: Mathematics in creating a social discourse. In C. Keitel (Ed.), *Social justice and mathematics education* (pp. 150–161). Berlin: Freie Universitat Berlin.

National Council of Teachers of Mathematics (1993, January). *NCTM takes stand in Barbie controversy*.

Nesher, P. (1980). The stereotyped nature of word problems. *For the Learning of Mathematics, 1*, 41–48.

Norton, K. I., Olds, T. S., Olive, S., & Dank, S. (1996). Ken and Barbie life size. *Sex Roles, 34*, 287–294.

Nunes, T., Schliemann, A. D., & Carraher, D. W. (1993). *Street mathematics and school mathematics*. Cambridge: Cambridge University Press.

Powell, A. B. & Frankenstein, M. (Eds.) (1997). *Ethnomathematics: Challenging Eurocentrism in mathematics education*. Albany, NY: SUNY Press.

Resnick, L. B. (1987). Learning in school and out. *Educational Researcher, 16*(9), 13–20.

Reusser, K. (1988). Problem solving beyond the logic of things: Contextual effects on understanding and solving word problems. *Instructional Science, 17*, 309–338.

Romberg, T. A. (1992). Further thoughts on the Standards: A reaction to Apple. *Journal for Research in Mathematics Education, 23*, 432–437.

Sarasohn-Kahn, J. (1996). *Contemporary Barbie*. Dubuque, IA: Antique Trader Books.

Schoenfeld, A. H. (1991). On mathematics as sense-making: An informal attack on the unfortunate divorce of formal and informal mathematics. In J. F. Voss, D. N. Perkins, & J. W. Segal (Eds.), *Informal reasoning and education* (pp. 311–343). Hillsdale, NJ: Lawrence Erlbaum Associates.

Shaughnessy, M., Garfield, J., & Greer, B. (1996). Data handling. In A. J. Bishop, K. Clements, C. Keitel, J. Kilpatrick, & C. Laborde (Eds.), *International handbook of mathematics education* (pp. 205–237). Dordrecht: Kluwer.

Staub, F. C., & Reusser, K. (1995). The role of presentational structures in understanding and solving mathematical word problems. In C. A. Weaver, S. Mannes, & C. Fletcher (Eds.), *Discourse comprehension: Essays in honour of Walter Kintsch* (pp. 285–305). Hillsdale, NJ: Lawrence Erlbaum Associates.

Verschaffel, L., De Corte, E., & Lasure, S. (1994). Realistic considerations in mathematical modelling of school arithmetic word problems. *Learning and Instruction, 4*, 273–294.

Verschaffel, L., Greer, B., & De Corte, E. (2000). *Making sense of word problems*. Lisse, The Netherlands: Swets & Zeitlinger.

Wall Street Journal (1992). *Mattel subtracts comment on math from Barbie doll*. October 21.

Wells, D. (1997). *The Penguin book of curious and interesting mathematics*. London: Penguin.

Zeidler, S. (1997). *Barbie doll to get face lift, total makeover*. Reuters, November 17.

18

Contribution
of Ethnomathematics
to Mainstream Mathematics
Classroom Practice

Gloria Stillman
Griffith University, GoldCoast

Jo Balatti
James Cook University, Cairns

> *"The research program Ethnomathematics invites us to look into how knowledge was built through-out history in different cultural environments and continues to be built. It is a comparative study of the techniques, modes, arts, and styles of explaining, understanding, learning about, [and] coping with the reality in different natural and cultural environments."*
>
> —D'Ambrosio, 1998

D'Ambrosio (1997) believed that studying mathematics from an ethnomathematical perspective provides the opportunity to clarify the nature of mathematical knowledge. Part of the inquiry is an attempt to answer the question, "Why is mathematics distinct from—and by many regarded as superior to—other forms of knowledge in modern society?" Ethnomathematics places researchers and teachers in an advantageous position to consider this question, but few current approaches do so.

In many circles, including mathematics education, ethnomathematics is treated to a large extent as an exotic curiosity that can easily be dismissed as having nothing to offer teachers of "real" mathematics. Others perceive it as a dangerous form of pedagogical revisionism leading to the teaching of innumeracy or, more insidiously, as the teaching of "something other than mathematics" (Thomas, 1996, p. 12). These three reactions are particularly prevalent in mainstream Western classrooms but are also found in classrooms in developing countries where Western mathematics is taught.

Several students of the first author, Gloria Stillman, a lecturer in mathematics teacher education, are practicing teachers who returned to their university studies after an absence of several years from higher education. All four undertook ethnomathematical research studies that afforded them a unique opportunity to reappraise their teaching practice and to develop an awareness of the social and cultural bases of mathematics. Although three of the studies (Finau Palaki & Stillman, 1995; Meya, 1994; Waqainabete, 1996) follow fairly traditional ethnomathematical research approaches, Balatti's study (1996) is of major interest in this chapter as it constitutes a new application of the ethnomathematical perspective to a mathematics found in modern Western societies. This chapter shows that ethnomathematics does, indeed, have much to offer teachers, particularly those in upper secondary school classrooms.

DIFFERING CONCEPTIONS
OF ETHNOMATHEMATICS AND THEIR
IMPLICATIONS FOR RESEARCH STUDIES

There are many points of confusion and contradiction within the field of ethnomathematics. As pointed out by Barton (1996), these stem mainly from contradictions about the meanings of the term *ethnomathematics*. Three highly influential writers in this area are Paulus Gerdes of Mozambique, Marcia Ascher of the United States of America and Ubiratan D'Ambrosio of Brazil. Their evolving conceptions of *ethnomathematics* are discussed in relation to this issue. These differing conceptions and their implications for ethnomathematical research studies are also illustrated using the four studies mentioned previously.

Ethnomathematics: The Mathematics Implicit in Cultural Practices

In his early work, Gerdes (1988) wrote of a "spontaneous, natural, informal, indigenous, folk, implicit, non-standard, and/or hidden (ethno)mathematics" (p. 138). Gerdes' (1994) aim was "to reconstruct or unfreeze the mathematical thinking that is hidden or frozen in old techniques" (p. 20). Thus, for Gerdes at this time, ethnomathematics was the mathematics implicit within cultural practices. His early examples were traditional practices that were mathematized using Western mathematics. He described mathematical ideas that were hidden in examples of practice such as the Sona (sand drawings) of the Tchokwe of northeastern Angola (Gerdes, 1991). Research studies using this definition of ethnomathematics sought to "uncover the hidden mathematics" (Gerdes, 1994, p. 20) in these practices.

Meya's (1994) study of the fighting shields of his homeland, the Highlands of Papua New Guinea, embraced this definition of ethnomathematics. He explored the mathematical properties of the Regular Shield made by specialist shield makers for warriors to use in tribal fights. According to Meya, "It is extremely difficult for students to understand the mathematics implicit in the construction of the shield or in other cultural contexts unless they are guided and trained to research such cultural practices to identify the mathematics hidden in doing the task" (p. 6). The mathematics he identifies in the shield-making process is still the Western conceptions of symmetry, geometrical shape, and properties. At no time is the basis of that knowledge scrutinized nor is there any suggestion that other non-Western conceptions of mathematical knowledge may be possible. The end results are some interesting illustrations of Western mathematical concepts.

Ethnomathematics: The Study of the Mathematical Ideas of Traditional Peoples

On the surface, Ascher's work appears to be similar to this work of Gerdes. Ascher (1991) defined ethnomathematics as "the study of the mathematical ideas of traditional peoples" (p. 1), which is a revision of the definition used earlier in Ascher and Ascher (1986) where the term "non-literate" was used instead of "traditional." In an author's note, dated 1995, to a reprint of this early article in Powell and Frankenstein (1997), Ascher and Ascher expand on this definition, "To us, mathematical ideas include those involving number, logic, spatial configuration and, more significant, the combination or organization of these into systems and structures" (p. 25). From the beginning of her work, Ascher was interested in the systematic study of cultural practices from a mathematical perspective, whereas Gerdes was at first interested in isolated examples of elaborations of Western mathematical ideas that could be perceived to be embedded in the cultural practices themselves. The greatest drawback of Ascher's definition, however, is that it is rather restrictive of the cultures that can be the subject of this research.

Waqainabete's (1996) study was inspired by Ascher's definition. Waqainabete lamented the lack of achievement of her fellow Fijians in the public examinations in mathematics at the end of secondary schooling. In her opinion, the reason for this underachievement is

> The mathematics curriculum in Form Five and Form Six in the Fijian education system is too abstract and very much geared toward a Westernised culture. Generally, the Fijian student fails or achieves poorly in the Mathematics examination because there is no correlation between the Mathematics learnt in the school and the life lead at village level. (p. 2)

She suggests "a possible way forward for Fiji is to recognize the student's traditional mathematical knowledge embedded in their indigenous culture and incorporate this in the existing Mathematics curriculum to help them to grasp the mathematical concepts" (p. 5). She provides the foundation from which others may do this by conducting an ethnomathematical study into the cultural activities of the indigenous Fijians using Ascher's definition as her basis.

Several cultural activities are identified "which seem to indicate the implementation and application of some mathematical knowledge" (p. 10). These include a dating system, a record system using knotted strings (e.g., for women to record the first 100 nights after a death), conceptions of time based on nature not clocks, counting, measuring, and estimating lengths and weights. They also include patterns in wood carving, weaving, tapa making (imprinting of Tongan bark cloth), cloth dying, pottery, canoes, and decorations of household objects and geometrical shapes in ceremonial objects such as the hemispherical kumete, the vessel for storing yaqona or kava drink during ceremonial occasions, or the semicylindrical vessel used for making vakalolo (a Fijian dessert). In addition, Waqainabete provides a systematic ethnomathematical analysis of the house-building activities of the Nasevauwa clan of Moala, Lau.

In this latter analysis, Waqainabete uses Western mathematical ideas both to describe the house building process and, subsequently, to examine the mathematical conceptions involved. However, there are examples where other-than-Western conceptions of knowledge are apparent, but these are not explored further. The timing of the house building, for example, is based on the time when the doi tree used for house posts is flowering, the time when the reeds used for the walls and thatching are mature, the time after harvesting when there are still plenty of yams available for exchange for building materials with other tribes, and the time when no hurricanes are expected. A second example is the use by the house builder of a young man of good physique as the standard of measurement.

Waqainabete's reason for not pursuing these possible differences in the conception of time is related to her intention in conducting the study. She wanted to demonstrate that Fijian cultural activities are inherently mathematical and believed that "the Fijian students can be taught to be mathematically literate if the education officials recognise the mathematical concepts embedded in the various Fijian cultural activities and introduce teaching strategies that would incorporate these concepts without changing the context" (p. 40).

Ethnomathematics: The Cultural Anthropology of Mathematics and Mathematics Education

In his later work, Gerdes (1994) described ethnomathematics "as the field of research that tries to study mathematics (or mathematical ideas) in its (their) relationship to the whole of cultural and social life" (p. 20). Ethnomathematics is, therefore, seen as being part of the present, not just the study of mathematized practices from the past. As a research perspective it takes on particular sociopolitical aims as it draws "attention to the fact that mathematics (its techniques and truths) is a cultural product" (p. 20). For example, it raises the awareness of formerly colonized peoples to the African and Asian origins of a substantial part of their school mathematics curriculum that is generally accepted as being of Western origins. For Gerdes, then, ethnomathematical research became "the cultural anthropology of mathematics and mathematics education" (p. 20).

In a similar vein, Finau Palaki's ethnomathematical study of Tongan Tapa designs (Finau Palaki & Stillman, 1995) takes on a sociopolitical perspective. She was particularly inspired by Millroy's (1992) notion that "studying the mathematics of cultural groups could generate cultural reaffirmation as well as individual empowerment through the feeling of ownership" (p. 50). By uncovering the mathematical ideas in the design practices of Tongan craft work, she had the opportunity to integrate these mathematical ideas into her mathematics classroom. Not only would her students be drawing on their sociocultural environment for their classroom activities but she would have the opportunity to raise to consciousness the "oppressed mathematics" (Gerdes, 1994, p. 19) embedded in this cultural–economic activity. In doing so, the mathematical nature of this craft work would be acknowledged, and tapa making would cease to be seen as undervalued women's work.

Ethnomathematics: The Mathematics Practiced Among Identifiable Cultural Groups

The studies reviewed so far give the impression that ethnomathematics is limited to the mathematical ideas of non-Western peoples. This is not so. D'Ambrosio (1985), who is acknowledged as the father of the modern ethnomathematical movement, wrote of a much broader conception of the term, saying that ethnomathematics is

> the mathematics which is practised among identifiable cultural groups, such as national-tribal societies, labor groups, children of a certain age bracket, professional classes, and so on. Its identity depends largely on focuses of interest, on motivation, and on certain codes and jargons which do not belong to the realm of academic mathematics. (p. 45)

As Powell and Frankenstein (1997) pointed out,

> Within this conception, cultural groups within Western societies also have an ethnomathematics. . . industrial engineers, children, peasants, computer scientists, for example— have distinct ways of reasoning, of measuring, of coding, of classifying, and so on. Consequently each group has their own ethnomathematics, *including* academic mathematicians" (p. 7).

In an earlier note, D'Ambrosio (1992) also addressed the connection between academic mathematics and the ethnomathematical research program. He said that such a program has at its heart the notion that mathematics is socially and culturally constructed. He describes the research program of ethnomathematics in its most general sense as "the study of the generation, organization, transmission, dissemination and the use of [the] jargons, codes, styles of reasoning, practices, results and methods" used to make mathematical meaning (p. 1184).

Unlike the previous three studies discussed, Balatti's study (1996) is concerned with the mathematics produced by a contemporary vocational group working within a highly technological culture in Western society. Using an ethnomathematical perspective it describes the mathematics that the financial planning industry mass produces in written form for the consumption of clients or potential clients. The major data sources were prospectuses and advertisements as they are the main genres used by the industry in written communication. This ethnomathematics is produced by an industry that in many ways displays the key characteristics of modern Western societies and as such exhibits many of the salient features of other ethnomathematics of advanced capitalist societies that are directly experienced by the consumer. The second aim of the study therefore was to develop an ethnomathematical framework that could be used to describe other mathematics operating in such societies.

The ethnomathematical reading of the data was guided by a list of questions generated from Skovsmose's (1994) notion of mathemacy that he describes as competency in mathematical knowing, technological knowing, and reflective knowing. The questions were:

1. How do the "universal" mathematical activities of "counting, measuring, locating, designing, playing and explaining" (Bishop, 1988, pp. 22–23) present themselves in the context of financial planning?
2. What meanings are conveyed by mathematical language?
3. What are the "implicit" and "explicit" mathematics in the texts?
4. What assumptions are being made about mathematics by the producers and consumers of the texts?
5. How is the discourse of mathematics embedded in other discourses operating in society?
6. What mathematical engagement does the producer of the text expect of the consumer?
7. What does it mean to be mathematically literate in this site?

These questions produced a framework that described the ethnomathematics of financial planning at five different but intersecting levels.

The first level of mathematics, the implicit mathematics, was explored by describing some of the *mathematizations* that underpin the financial planning industry (e.g., the unit trust, time, indices such as the Australian Stock Exchange All Ordinaries Index, and negative gearing). Although sometimes made explicit, these mathematizations are more often than not silently embedded in texts produced by financial planning institutions.

The second level comprised *explicit mathematical content* such as percentages and graphical representations. The more commonly used examples of mathematical language and notation (e.g., $\$5,000 < \$25,000$ to indicate amounts between $\$5,000$ and $\$25,000$ rather than $\$5,000$ is less than $\$25,000$), concepts such as average (e.g., quarterly averages and average monthly return), and mathematical representations, which included tables and a variety of graphs, were identified and described.

The third layer of mathematical meaning was found by exploring *how the mathematics in the texts interacted with the discourses of risk, expertise, and consumption* that are intrinsic to an advanced capitalist society. For example, the expertise of financial planning confronts the discourse of risk in two diametrically opposed ways: on the one hand, engaging with the expertise generates risk, whereas, on the other, it counteracts risk. Mathematical ideas are evident in both processes. The client engages in risk at a number of different levels. With the inevitability of risk comes the need for security and trust. The interplay among risk and trust, expertise, and self-reliance is explicitly demonstrated in company advertisements in the financial planning industry. Clients are told that the individual can only trust himself or herself and then shown how this can only be done with the expertise of the company.

The fourth dimension of the mathematics of financial planning constituted *the system of values* carried within it and how these values were manifested and expressed via the four other dimensions of the mathematics. As this level will be dealt with at some length in the remainder of this chapter, examples will not be given now.

The fifth and final aspect concerned *the nature and degree of mathematical engagement solicited by the texts* from their readers (e.g., the intentional use of mathematical tables and graphs to obfuscate by generating complexity and thereby implying control and knowledge). Most of the explicit mathematical content found in the texts takes one of three forms. The first is mathematical text that may be described as instructional and occurs in some advertisements and, to a greater extent, in prospectuses. One company's prospectus, for example, provides directions on how to calculate the desired amounts for investment. The second kind of explicit mathematical text is expository. It is text that explains a mathematically based concept or process such as how distributions are calculated for a particular investment fund. The third kind of mathematical text contains mathematics that the writer assumes the targeted reader understands. This ranges from the four basic operations to more complex mathematics such as logarithmic scales on graphs. Indices such as inflation and market indicators are examples of mathematical ideas that are often used without explanation.

The degree of mathematical engagement solicited by the texts from the readers is examined using Skovmose's three types of knowing—mathematical, technological, and reflective.

Mathematical knowing refers to the mathematical concepts, skills, and language that are traditionally considered as mathematics. It requires skills in reading the three types of explicit mathematical text described. It also includes the skill of reading mathematical text in conjunction with nonmathematical text. As this reading takes place in the specific context of financial planning, interpreting such items as performance tables for a trust, for example, requires knowledge of the context such as economic cycles and the nature of interest markets in which the trust invests.

Technological knowing refers to applying or understanding the applications of mathematics in the context of financial planning. Sometimes the applications require language specific to this context. Terms and phrases such as real return and indexation, for instance, are necessary in describing the processes in funds management. From the potential client's point of view, the core application of mathematical knowing is understanding the relationship among return, risk, and time. The client then has to match goals and constraints that could be financial, emotional, or situational to the most suitable return/risk/time configuration. Technological knowing is about realizing the limitations built into any mathematizations supposedly supplied to help make this decision in an informed manner. The performance of a fund, for example, is often compared with the performance of an appropriate index such as a share price index or the Consumer Price Index. One amount is placed in the fund and a similar amount is placed in the index. Graphs are then drawn depicting purely hypothetical situations to guide the client's decision making. In reality, it is impossible to invest in these indices. Comparisons illustrated by such graphs are produced by creating a mathematical possibility, not a practical reality.

Although competence in mathematical and technological knowing is a prerequisite to Skovmose's reflective knowing, he would argue that the reader of texts does not need to have the expertise of the economist or the accountant. What are needed are skills that are important to reflective knowing. These include (a) an ability to ascertain the reasonableness of assumptions in scenarios presented in advertisements and prospectuses,

(b) appreciation of the significance of changes in variables such as inflation rate and monthly contributions, (c) discernment of what the mathematics in a situation does not do (e.g., the use of tables to illustrate the performance of a fund does not show the fluctuations that occur during any window of time within the larger time frame), (d) awareness of the value dimensions associated with mathematical text and how it is used to persuade, and (e) an ability to investigate the political dimensions of financial planning.

It is primarily in addressing the fourth of the levels of her analytical framework that Balatti explores D'Ambrosio's question about the superiority of mathematical knowledge cited at the beginning of this chapter. Bishop (1988) attributed the superior position of Western mathematics to its perceived ability to impose control, order, and therefore dominion over humankind's environment. Furthermore, it is seen as providing ways of defining and solving problems that are regarded as rational and objective. It is believed that these combined qualities permit effective harnessing of all kinds of resources, whether they be natural, economic, social, or interpersonal. Its supposed logic and objectivity also imbue mathematics with a sense of neutrality and openness—it hides nothing and favors no one. However, as Bishop points out, for most people, mathematics is opaque rather than transparent.

The values identified by Bishop (1988) in Western mathematics are clearly obvious in the mathematics of financial planning. Marketers in financial planning are very sensitive to the ways in which mathematics, like any system of signs, has the ability to project values that elicit emotional and intellectual responses in potential clients that can be exploited to effect the purchase of their products. Mathematical interpretation of an event or situation projects the idea of *authority and certainty*. For example, statistics are used by insurance companies to argue the need for life insurance, and an added degree of authority comes from the quoting of statistics from scientific health studies.

Mathematics also projects a sense of *conciseness and preciseness*. Tables and graphs, for example, capture large quantities of information in a relatively small amount of space and are used as devices to manufacture authoritative "factual" versions of reality. The past is given definition and so is the future. Tables and graphs project a sense of definitiveness, with no blurry edges.

Although the power and authority of mathematics is always implied, it is often overtly stated. Appeals are often made in financial advertisements to the superiority of mathematics over any other form of knowing in its ability to discern the truth. For example, a particular investment house claims that any time is a good time to enter the stock market, providing, of course, that the investor is prepared to take a long-term viewpoint. This claim is substantiated by presenting the following scenario.

"Let's assume that you put $5,000 into the Australian sharemarket (as represented by the All Ordinaries Accumulation Index) at the worst possible time every year (the month that the sharemarket hit its highest point of the year) since 1983. Many people may imagine that the value of their investment would not grow very much, or may even decline. However, *the figures below tell a different story* [italics added]" (Rothschild Australia Asset Management brochure cited in Balatti, 1996, p. 133).

A table is then produced that provides the indisputable evidence that profit is made even when timing is at its worst. The authority of "the figures" is appealed to as telling the correct story.

It is possible to infer from the discussion so far that authors of prospectuses and advertisements exploit the values in mathematics to attract readers to their company or product. This is not always the case. Sometimes the intent is to attract the interest of a certain type of potential client while actively discouraging the attention of others.

For example, one advertisement consisting of mathematics and wordy text flatters those readers who regard themselves as mathematically astute. The advertisement promotes the need to save consistently, as soon as possible, and preferably through the company's product. About three fourths of the full-page advertisement is devoted to explicating the principle of compound interest, and only three paragraphs are dedicated to the product that provides a suitable vehicle to execute such a plan. The text exploits the authority, objectivity, and absolute neutrality associated with mathematics. This is the reason that most of the advertisement focuses on the mathematics. It is easier for the reader to be convinced by the universality of a mathematical principle than by the company's product.

The visual focus of the advertisement is a table displaying the values of two disciplined savings plans, one from age 21 to 65 and another from 36 to 65. In the first plan the investor starts at age 21 to invest $2,000 indexed at an inflation rate of 4% pa every year for 15 years. The investor then stops contributing to the plan but leaves the money already in the plan to grow for the next 30 years. In the second plan the investor starts at age 36 to invest the equivalent future value of $2,000 (e.g., $3,602 at age 36) indexed at an inflation rate of 4% per annum every year for the next 30 years. The table reveals that at age 65 the first investor has a bigger investment than the second.

The table exudes certainty, consistency, clarity, and control. In actual fact, this mathematical presentation is projecting a grossly distorted picture of reality. The neatly packaged algorithm presented in a neat systematic table does not demonstrate the effects of the many variables that impact on such a plan when implemented. There are years, especially in a 40-year time frame, when returns are negative, zero, very high, and very low, but this is avoided by assuming that there will be an average return of 7.6% per annum. Furthermore, very few people consistently save without interruption, without changing the amount saved, without withdrawing funds, or even without prematurely terminating the plan. It is a rare person indeed who increases savings to keep up with inflation. This advertisement is a typical example of how mathematics is used to construct an idealistic, frozen reality far removed from the vagaries of life.

The advertisement also blatantly capitalizes on the interplay between the openness of mathematics and its mystery. Although appearing to appeal to the mathematically literate, the advertisement exploits the sense of mystique many people feel about mathematics. The concept that one moment is shrouded in mystery and, in another, shines like a beacon light is compound interest. The advertisement states in its second paragraph: " 'It' is 'the magic of compound interest', and it isn't really magic at all— it's simple mathematics. But magic for most is more intriguing than maths, so let's think of it as magic" (Bankers Trust advertisement cited in Balatti, 1996, p. 212).

For the less mathematically inclined, the play between "magic" and "maths" only intensifies the mystery, even if once there had been no mystery. Many readers are likely to stop reading the text at this point, if not earlier. It is likely that this is the intent of the advertisement as it appears to be designed to discriminate. It targets select readers through the use of relatively sophisticated levels of literacy and numeracy, an appeal to a particular set of values, and the availability of disposable income.

The ability of the advertisement to discriminate in this way is clearly portrayed in an interview between the researcher and a 45-year-old woman, Mary. Mary had highly developed literacy skills but she was unable to understand much of the mathematical content when asked to read the advertisement. Because she did not understand the mathematics and because the context was an advertisement, Mary concluded that the advertisement was lying. "This isn't the kind of advert for the likes of me. If I hadn't realised before, when I got to 'really learn and profit from it' I would have realised I'd been tricked" (Balatti, 1996, p. 238).

In fact, government agencies monitor the activities of financial institutions, including literature they produce. The adequacy of Mary's mathematical cultural capital and mathematical literacy skills in making an informed decision are of concern here. It was distrust based on lack of understanding rather than knowledge that prompted Mary to dismiss the advertisement. A healthy scepticism for the advertisement need not be a bad thing, providing it is the result of a critical evaluation of its contents. Mary's evaluation was severely hamstrung by her limited skills in understanding the mathematics in this context.

Although Mary's mathematical knowing (Skovsmose, 1994) may have been limited, she was very aware of the hegemonic characteristics of mathematics as the following excerpts reveal:

> **Mary:** What does it mean (pause). I don't understand (long pause). You save the equivalent of $2000 (pause) but really you're saving $3600? Because there's a hell of a big difference isn't there?
> **Researcher:** What do you think of the table?
> **Mary:** I didn't look at it. I looked at the $3600 and tried to add on another $3600 but it didn't work out. So I didn't bother. (Balatti, 1996, p. 237)

The table made no sense to her, but she knew that at least part of its purpose was to "make it look scientific" and hence lend credibility to the advertisement. She was also aware of the sense of objectivity embedded in mathematics and its perceived capacity to present the truth in its purest form. She commented on the manipulative value of the advertisement when it pretended to assume that the reader would be checking the figures presented. "It says 'as you check these basic calculations'. As if you'd sit and check them. Another manipulation—we haven't got any secrets—it's all here for you to see" (Balatti, 1996, p. 239).

Mary's sense of disempowerment in this arena of mathematical activity was apparent. She was uncertain as to what may constitute legitimate mathematics, and she ignored most of the advertisement as soon as her figures did not match those of the advertisement. She certainly did not accept the challenge to demystify "the magic of compound interest" by using so called "simple mathematics." On the contrary, Mary gave the impression that she would have felt more comfortable and confident if compound interest had stayed in the realm of magic. She said: "They tell me to think in terms of magic but then spend three paragraphs talking maths to me. In fact the whole of the advert except the first two paragraphs is maths" (Balatti, 1996, p. 239).

IMPLICATIONS FOR THE CLASSROOM

Implications of the Ethnomathematics in the Studies for the Mathematics Classroom

In all four studies, the researchers have been working within their own culture, and their intention has been to use the products of their research in their own classrooms. This intention is in line with Nebres' (1988) summation of efforts to link ethnomathematics to classroom mathematics "[D'Ambrosio's] approach and that of others working on ethnomathematics is to change the canonical school mathematics curriculum to one which arises from and is closely related to the experience of mathematics in a given culture" (p. 15).

Research into the role of contexts in the mathematics classroom indicated its importance in learning (Boaler, 1993; Heckman & Weissglass, 1994; Mellin-Olsen, 1987) and assessment (Stillman, 1998a, 1998b). According to Meya (1994), "the main purpose here is to train students to develop the skill of identifying the presence of Mathematics in real life situations" (p. 6). Another purpose, however, is to illustrate the applicability of mathematics to real-life situations in order to motivate students to learn concepts that are abstract and devoid of meaning in their lives. Finau Palaki and Stillman (1995), for example, showed how the patterns made during the imprinting of tapa can be used in teaching more traditional classroom content such as matrices, vectors, and sequences.

The ethnomathematics of financial planning highlights the difficulty of producing authentic contextualized problems in the classroom. The following is an example that represents a typical attempt at making mathematics real for students: "A person invested $6,000 in a fixed deposit for one year at 10.55% per annum interest. The inflation rate was 5%. What was the effective return on the investment as a percentage if their marginal tax rate was 0.38?" (Peard, Mowchanuk, & Shield, 1993, p. 129)

In many respects, this exercise bears only fleeting resemblance to the real situation it is supposed to reflect. Mathematics in a real-life money management experience is heavily integrated with other text, but the exercise strips away all context, leaving the bare bones of the mathematics component. Furthermore, emphasis on this style of exercise in textbooks implies that the authors assume that the mathematical concepts presented constitute the core of the decision-making process in personal financial planning. Balatti's (1996) study shows that any mathematics involved in a financial planning decision is only one consideration that, depending on the context, has more or less significance for the individual.

A final comment concerns the relevance of the mathematics actually presented in the exercise. The exercise requires the student to calculate precisely the effective return on a fixed deposit. In the second author's experience as a financial planner, very few people (if any) precisely calculate an effective rate of return when deciding on a fixed-term deposit. None of the texts analyzed in Balatti's study required the reader to be able to precisely calculate an effective rate of return. The reasons are provided by the real-life context.

Effective rate of return is dependent on three factors—the inflation rate of the country, the taxation threshold rate of the investor, and the rate of return on the investment.

From the viewpoint of the investor, the first two variables are givens, that is, the individual cannot affect them. The investor's decision-making process then can only influence the effective rate of return through the third factor, that is, by ensuring that the highest rate is selected. In other words, if it is assumed that fixed-term investments were the only option and that return is the only criterion used to select an investment, then the investor does not need to calculate the effective rate of return. All that is needed is to choose the fixed-term deposit that pays the highest return.

This example is the result of the writers of the textbooks, who are mathematics educators, subsuming the mathematics of another site into their own ethnomathematics, which is that of the classroom. In so doing, the mathematics of the "real-life" context is reconstructed, redefined and represented in the likeness of the host ethnomathematics, that is, as classroom mathematics (Dowling, 1998).

Perhaps an alternative is to have other mathematics workers, in this case, financial planners or other appropriate people from the financial planning industry, working with mathematics teachers in preparing more appropriate material. Collaborative relationships of this kind could perhaps extend to joint presentations in the classroom. However, even this approach may be fraught with the problem of readability as is obvious from the complexity of the discussion of the texts so far. Masingila (1993) provided further suggestions for reducing the gap between doing mathematics in school and the mathematics practice in out-of-school situations.

The opportunity for ethnomathematics to redefine and transform the relationship among mathematics, the student, and the teacher has been recognized. Owens (1995), for example, argued that "there is an overlap between cultural mathematics and other cultural issues in education because investigating community mathematics will inevitably involve teachers in a relationship with the community that may or may not have existed before. It seems that often it is the relationship of the person with the community that is in fact the crucial aspect in the success of involving the community in mathematics learning (p.1)." In this instance, the ethnomathematics of financial planning offers the opportunity to both teachers and students alike to be learners of mathematics.

There is a caveat that must be applied, however. It is imperative that such a curriculum does not enhance the hegemony of any particular ethnomathematics such as financial planning and its surrounding rhetoric. The emphasis must be on developing students' capacities to critique them. How this may be done is addressed in the next section.

Applications of the Ethnomathematical Approaches Used in the Studies for the Mathematics Classroom

Mathematizing Cultural Practices and Artefacts.   One method of exposing the mathematical aspects in an ethnomathematical study (used by Finau Palaki, Meya and Waqainabete) is to mathematize cultural practices or artefacts by translating these practices or the construction or use of the artefacts into mathematical terminology and to relate this to existing mathematical terminology. Stillman (1995) provided an example of how upper secondary students might do this. The Igbo game Igba-ita from Nigeria is investigated from both an anthropological and mathematical perspective. Although such an approach seeks to promote cultural diversity, to "illustrate the cultural richness of mathematics, and improve the self-esteem of minority students" (Murtadha-Watts & D'Ambrosio, 1997, p. 770), there is a danger. If the mathematization by Western students is not accompanied by an anthropological investigation, the process divorces the cultural practices from their context and trivializes and fragments them from their real meaning in context. Another criticism often leveled at this approach by Western researchers exploring the cultural heritage of other cultures or indigenous researchers working within their own cultural heritage is that ethnomathematics may become "its own form of cultural imperialism, by 'imposing' the academic mathematics curriculum on, for example, African cultural artefacts and practices" (Powell, Knijnik, Gilmer, & Frankenstein, 1998).

Ethnomathematical Readings of Texts Produced by Different Vocational Groups in Capitalist Societies.   The primary sources of data used in Balatti's study were the mathematical artefacts produced by a vocational group. The qualitative analysis of these texts required multiple readings of the texts at a number of levels. One level consisted of identifying the mathematically recognizable concepts and skills required to comprehend the content. At another level, the reading involved discerning the utilitarian, social, and cultural purposes of the mathematics. This was achieved by analyzing the mathematical language used and by exploring how the discourse of mathematics interacts with the other discourses operating in the context of financial planning. Students and teachers together can engage in ethnomathematical readings of texts produced by the mass media. The approach used in this study with appropriate modifications that account for age, interests, and students' abilities can be effectively employed in the classroom. The texts that are the basic resources needed are easily and cheaply accessible.

Deconstructing or decoding mathematical text is a way of understanding the mathematics of contexts other than that of financial planning. Mathematics other than that of money penetrate the life worlds of citizens in equally powerful and pervasive ways. These include the mathematics used to convey information, research, and recommendations in the fields of health and medicine, science, economics, and government.

The benefits of this approach lie especially in their potential for developing a critical mathematical awareness in the learners of mathematics. Ethnomathematical readings of texts provide opportunities for teachers and students to explore how mathematics is construed and used in mass-produced texts. In the case of the financial institutional artefacts discussed, the ultimate purpose is to encourage the consumer to consume.

Although the following observation was made about media messages in general, it is also pertinent to mathematical messages conveyed by the media:

> As long as you are unable to decode the significance of ordinary things, and as long as you take the signs of your culture at face value, you will continue to be mastered by them. But once you see behind the surface of a sign into its hidden cultural significance, you can free yourself from that sign and perhaps find a new way of looking at the world. You

will control the signs of your culture [rather] than having them control you. (Solomon, 1988, p. 8)

Ethnomathematical Readings of Textbooks. If one accepts the notion that school mathematics that has been described, analyzed, and critiqued extensively is also an ethnomathematics, then Balatti's (1996) study provides the opportunity for comparison of two ethnomathematics coexisting in, and produced by, the same capitalist culture. A useful medium of comparison that is consistent with the methodology used in Balatti's study is the written texts produced in the two sites. To a limited extent, mathematics education textbooks have been studied from a sociocultural perspective (Dowling, 1991, 1998; McBride, 1994). A comparison between the texts may be in terms of the language and concepts used, the genres of mathematics utilized, the purposes for which the mathematics is intended, and the contexts in which the mathematics is embedded. In this way, the degree and nature of the engagement required by the reader, how the reader is positioned, and the values embedded in the mathematical texts may also be explored and compared. Such comparisons may afford the opportunity for further exploration of the relevance of the current curriculum in terms of content and delivery.

IMPLICATIONS FOR FURTHER RESEARCH

Using Skovmose's Framework in Other Contemporary Ethnomathematical Studies

Balatti (1996) used Skovmose's framework to identify the skills and knowledge required in order to be mathematically literate in the context of financial planning. This was illustrated previously in the interview with Mary. The use of this framework to identify the skills and knowledge required in order to be mathematically literate in other contexts would be a fruitful area for further research, especially in comparison with other ethnomathematical studies where the focus is contemporary.

Teachers as Ethnomathematical Researchers

In light of the experiences of the four teachers who conducted the studies discussed in this chapter, teachers in Western classrooms and in other classrooms where Western mathematics is valorized have much to gain by becoming ethnomathematical researchers. Ernest (1989) describes teacher beliefs about the teaching of mathematics as encompassing teachers' views or conceptions of the nature of mathematics as well as their models or views of the nature of mathematics teaching and the process of learning mathematics. Furthermore, Lappan et al. (1988) claimed that teacher beliefs seldom change dramatically without significant intervention. Lappan and Theule-Lubienski (1994) suggested that an opportunity for changing their beliefs is essential for teachers' development. From the perspective of the professional development of teachers, engagement in ethnomathematical research studies as reviewed previously has been shown to be a suitable vehicle for providing the opportunity for teachers to reconsider and perhaps reconceptualize their beliefs by reflecting on the nature of mathematical knowledge.

REFERENCES

Ascher, M., & Ascher, R. (1986). Ethnomathematics. *History of Science, 24*, 125–144.

Ascher, M. (1991). *Ethnomathematics: A multicultural view of mathematical ideas*. New York: Brooks/Cole.

Balatti, J. (1996). *An ethnomathematics of financial planning*. Unpublished master's thesis, James Cook University, Townsville, Queensland, Australia.

Barton, B. (1996). Making sense of ethnomathematics: Ethnomathematics is making sense. *Educational Studies in Mathematics, 31*, 201–233.

Boaler, J. (1993). The role of contexts in the mathematics classroom: Do they make mathematics more "real"? *For the Learning of Mathematics, 13*(2), 12–17.

Bishop, A. J. (1988). *Mathematical enculturation: A cultural perspective on mathematics education*. Dordrecht: Kluwer.

D'Ambrosio, U. (1985). Ethnomathematics and its place in the history and pedagogy of mathematics. *For the Learning of Mathematics, 5*(1), 44–48.

D'Ambrosio, U. (1992). Ethnomathematics: A research program on the history and philosophy of mathematics with pedagogical implications. *Notices of the American Mathematical Society, 39*(10), 1183–1185.

D'Ambrosio, U. (1997). Where does Ethnomathematics stand nowadays? *For the Learning of Mathematics, 17*(20), 13–17.

D'Ambrosio, U. (1998). *Ethnomathematics: The art or technique of explaining and knowing* (P. B. Scott, Trans.). Las Cruces, NM: International Study Group on Ethnomathematics (original work published 1990).

Dowling, P. (1991). A touch of class: Ability, social class and intertext in SMP 11-16. In D. Pimm & E. Love (Eds.), *Teaching and learning school mathematics*. London: Hodder & Stoughton.

Dowling, P. (1998). *The sociology of mathematics education: Mathematical myths/pedagogic texts*. London: Falmer.

Ernest, P. (1989). The impact of beliefs on the teaching of mathematics. In P. Ernest (Ed.), *Mathematics teaching:The state of the art* (pp. 249–253). New York: Falmer.

Finau Palaki, K., & Stillman, G. (1995). *Geometrical skill behind the Tongan Tapa designs*. Paper presented at the international History and Pedagogy of Mathematics Conference on Ethnomathematics and the Australasian Region held at Cairns, June 30–July 4.

Gerdes, P. (1988). On culture, geometrical thinking and mathematics education. *Educational Studies in Mathematics, 19*(2), 137–162.

Gerdes, P. (1991). *Lusona: Geometrical recreations of Africa*. Maputo, Mozambique: African Mathematical Union and Higher Pedagogical Institute's Faculty of Sciences.

Gerdes, P. (1994). Reflections on ethnomathematics. *For the Learning of Mathematics, 14*(2), 19–22.

Heckman, P. E., & Weissglass, J. (1994). Contextualized mathematics instruction: Moving beyond recent proposals. *For the Learning of Mathematics, 14*(1), 29–33.

Lappan, G., Fitzgerald, W., Phillips, E., Winter, M. J., Lanier, P., Madsen-Nason, A., Even, R., Lee, B., Smith, J., & Weinberg, D. (1988). *The middle grades mathematics project. The challenge: Good mathematics—taught well* (Final report to the National Science Foundation for grant #MDR8318218). East Lansing: Michigan State University.

Lappan, G., & Theule-Lubienski, S. (1994). Training teachers or educating professionals? What are the issues and how are they being resolved? In D. F. Robitaille, D. H. Wheeler, & C. Kieran (Eds.), *Selected lectures from the 7th international Congress on Mathematical Education* (pp. 249–261). Sainte-Foy, Canada: Les Presses de l'Universitè Laval.

Masingila, J. (1993). Learning from mathematics practice in out-of-school situations. *For the Learning of Mathematics, 13* (2), 18–22.

McBride, M. (1994). The theme of individualism in mathematics education: An examination of mathematics textbooks. *For the Learning of Mathematics, 14*(3), 36–42.

Mellin-Olsen, S. (1987). *The politics of mathematics of education*. Dordrecht: D. Reidel.

Meya, D. K. (1994). *Mathematics in a cultural context: The fighting shield of the Highlands of Papua New Guinea*. Unpublished manuscript, James Cook University, Townsville, Queensland, Australia.

Millroy, W. L. (1992). An ethnomathematical study of the mathematical ideas of a group of carpenters. *Journal for Research in Mathematics Education Monograph No. 5*. Reston, VA: NCTM.

Murtadha-Watts, K., & D'Ambrosio, B. S. (1997). A convergence of transformative multicultural and mathematics instruction? Dilemmas of group deliberations for curriculum change. *Journal of Research in Mathematics Education, 28*(6), 767–782.

Nebres, B. F. (1988). School mathematics in the 1990's: Recent trends and the challenge to developing countries. In A. Hirst & K. Hirst (Eds.), *Proceedings of the sixth international Congress on Mathematics Education* (pp. 11–28) held at Budapest, Hungary, 27 July–3 August.

Owens, K. (1995). *Implementing ethnomathematics in the classroom*. Paper presented at the international History and Pedagogy of Mathematics Conference on Ethnomathematics and the Australasian Region held at Cairns, June 30–July 4.

Peard, R., Mowchanuk, T., & Shield, M. (1993). *Maths A Book 2: Interactive maths*. Milton, Queensland: Jacaranda.

Powell, A. B., & Frankenstein, M. (Eds.). (1997). *Ethnomathematics: Challenging Eurocentrism in mathematics education*. Albany, NY: SUNY.

Powell, A.B., Knijnik, G., Gilmer, G., & Frankenstein, M. (1998). Critical mathematics. In P. Gates (Ed.), *Mathematics education and society, Proceedings of the 1st international Mathematics Education and Society Conference* (p. 45) held at Nottingham University, 6–11 September.

Skovsmose, O. (1994). Towards a critical mathematics education. *Educational Studies in Mathematics, 27*(1), 35–57.

Solomon, I. (1988). *The sign of our times*. Los Angeles, CA: Jeremy Tarcher.

Stillman, G. (1995). Ethnomathematics—A source of investigations in the later years of secondary school. *Teaching Mathematics and Its Applications, 14*(1), 15–18.

Stillman, G.A. (1998a). Engagement with task context in applications tasks: Student performance and teacher beliefs. *Nordic Studies in Mathematics Education, 6* (3/4), 51–70.

Stillman, G.A. (1998b). Task context and applications at the senior secondary level. In C. Kanes, M. Goos, & E. Warren (Eds.), *Teaching in new times, Proceedings of the twenty-first annual Conference of the Mathematics Education Research Group of Australasia Incorporated* (vol. 2, pp. 564–571). Gold Coast, Australia: MERGA.

Thomas, R. (1996). Proto-mathematics and/or real mathematics. *For the Learning of Mathematics, 16*(2), 11–18.

Waqainabete, R. (1996). *Fijian ethnomathematics*. Unpublished manuscript, James Cook University, Townsville, Queensland, Australia.

19

Teaching and Learning School Mathematics by Building on Students' Out-of-School Mathematics Practice

Joanna O. Masingila
Rapti de Silva
Syracuse University

It is generally accepted that learning and doing mathematics is an act of sense making and involves cultural, social, and cognitive phenomena that cannot be separated (Schoenfeld, 1989). In past and current generations, mathematics has developed out of human needs situated in cultures and societies—needs for overcoming obstacles or for explaining phenomena. However, most mathematics taught in schools is divorced from the context in which it developed and from contexts in which the mathematical ideas might arise and be meaningful to learners. This is contrary to recent theories of mathematical learning that view all learning as situated (Crawford, 1996; van Oers, 1996; Voight, 1996).

We agree with this view of learning and see all learning as driven by striving for goals and seeking to overcome obstacles. We do not propose that teachers need to return to the original contexts out of which mathematical ideas developed, although these can be powerful contexts in which to learn mathematics; rather, we contend that there are many contexts out of which mathematics can be learned and that school mathematics should be learned through contexts that are meaningful to the learner, and, as such, this may imply having curricula that are locally specific. We concur with Lave and Wenger (1991) that school mathematics is itself a form of situated learning and, thus, takes place within contexts. However, context itself is insufficient; the context must be meaningful, indeed mathematically meaningful, to the learner.

In this chapter, we discuss some historical examples from social and cultural situations in which people sought to make sense of things from within contexts and developed mathematical ideas out of these contexts. We then tie this in with school mathematics and discuss a four-year, National Science Foundation-funded project entitled, *Connecting In-school and Out-of-school Mathematics Practice*,[1] in which we (a) investigated how middle school students use mathematical ideas in a variety of out-of-school situations and then (b) used ideas from these situations to support the students' classroom learning and examine how they made sense of ideas mathematically. We end the chapter by proposing how a learning theory and an instructional theory might be merged with a team approach to teaching and learning to address the issues we raise in this chapter.

MEANINGFUL MATHEMATICAL CONSTRUCTIONS ARE OFTEN NEED-BASED

Sociocultural Constructions

> The oldest mathematical tablets we have date from 2400 B.C., but there is no reason to suppose that the urge to create and use mathematics is not coextensive with the whole of civilization. In four or five millennia a vast body of practices and concepts known as mathematics has emerged and has been linked in a variety of ways with our day-to-day life. (Davis & Hersh, 1981, p. xi)

Not only has mathematics been linked with our day-to-day lives, but throughout history mathematical ideas have developed out of contexts and situated needs to understand and explain phenomena or accomplish tasks. For example, Joseph (1991) noted that mathematics "initially arose from a need to count and record numbers" (p. 23). There have been many other needs for which mathematical ideas formed at least part of the solution. Herodotus, the Greek historian from the 5th century B.C., wrote that Egyptian geometry originated out of the need to redetermine the boundaries of farmland after the annual flooding of the Nile River.

> Sesostris [Pharaoh Ramses II, c. 1300 B.C.] divided the land into lots and gave a square piece of equal size, from the produce of which he exacted an annual tax. [If] any man's holding was damaged by the encroachment of the river... The King... would send inspectors to measure the extent of the loss, in order that he might pay in future a fair proportion of the tax at which his property had been assessed. Perhaps this was the way in which geometry was invented, and passed afterwards into Greece. (1984, p. 169):

Although there is no documentary evidence that the Egyptians were aware of even a particular case of the Pythagorean theorem, it appears that they constructed some method of determining square corners (Eves, 1983) because of their need to determine land boundaries.

Likewise, the development of numeration systems with groups or bases arose out of the need to count large numbers of objects. Number systems with place value

---

[1] This research was funded by a National Science Foundation-sponsored grant (RED-9550147) awarded to the first author under the Faculty Early CAREER Development Program.

developed out of the need to work efficiently with computing large numbers. It is "not that arithmetic was impossible in non-positional number systems. . . but rather that computations were often cumbersome or relied on a mechanical device such as an abacus or a counting-board, or even cowrie shells. The crucial advantage of. . . [a number system with place value] is that it gave birth to an arithmetic which could be done by people of average ability, not just an elite" (Joseph, 1991, p. 48).

The Babylonian numeration system was a system with place value that developed from the cultural and economical needs to compute large numbers. The Babylonians used two symbols (one representing 1 and one representing 10); these symbols were combined to represent quantities. Quantities greater than 59 were represented using repeated groupings of 60. Spaces were used to separate multiples of powers of 60. This was confusing, though, because until about 300 B.C. the Babylonian system lacked the concept of zero, and so the spaces were sometimes ambiguous.

Although we do not use the same numeration system that the Babylonians developed, there are ideas that were developed through that system that are contained in the Hindu-Arabic numeration system that the majority of the world uses today. The most important idea developed in the Babylonian system is the concept of place value. We might argue that the Hindu-Arabic numeration system is more efficient and flexible than the Babylonian numeration system because not only is the Hindu-Arabic numeration system additive, multiplicative, have a base, and have place value (four features that the Babylonian system also had), but we additionally have the concept of zero and have a unique representation system. However, even though the Babylonian numeration system was later surpassed by other numeration systems, there were valuable things contained in that numeration system, which developed out of sociocultural practices, that were built upon.

Mathematics is often created by persons trying to make sense of particular mathematical problems. Descartes was inspired to bring together algebra and geometry to create analytic geometry, which made use of the tool that we now call Cartesian coordinates, while trying to solve a mathematical problem that baffled the ancient Greeks, in the general case: "If $p_1, \ldots, p_m, p_{m+1}, \ldots, p_{m+n}$ are the lengths of $m + n$ line segments drawn from a point p to $m + n$ given lines, making given angles with these lines, and if $p_1 p_2 \ldots p_m = k p_{m+1} p_{m+2} \ldots p_{m+n}$, where k is a constant, find the locus of P" (Eves, 1983, p. 260). In fact, Descartes was so fascinated with the power of analytic geometry to solve problems previously thought unsolvable that he "resolved to quit only abstract geometry, that is to say, the consideration of questions which *serve only to exercise the mind*, and this, in order to study another kind of geometry, which has for its object the explanation of the phenomena of nature" (Kline, 1972, p. 302, italics in original).

In-School Constructions

Although mathematical ideas have developed from within social and cultural situations as ways to overcome obstacles or to explain phenomena, when these same mathematical ideas are presented to students through school mathematics, the contexts out of which the need for the mathematics arose is usually long forgotten. The original context or need is forgotten or hidden as the idea has become more generalized. Unlike out-of-school mathematics practice where persons may generalize procedures within a context but may not be able to generalize to another context because problems tend to be context specific, in-school mathematics practice has generalization as one of its goals (Masingila, Davidenko, & Prus-Wisniowska, 1996). We recognize the importance in school mathematics for students to be to able to generalize beyond a context, but we question the way that students get to this generalized understanding.

People make sense of things from within contexts that are meaningful to them, and, if students do not have meaningful contexts from which to make sense of mathematics then the mathematical knowledge they construct is isolated from their out-of-school mathematics practice and difficult for them to draw on when appropriate (Masingila, 1993, 1994). To illustrate this point, Gay and Cole (1967) included the following story in their book describing their study of the Kpelle in Liberia. Gay and Cole found that measures of volume were used by the Kpelle in situations where the amount of a given material was important. Buying and selling rice, the staple food of the Kpelle, were two such situations.

> The local trade uses what is called a *sâmo-ko*, "salmon cup," for dealing rice. It is the large size tin can (U.S. #1) in which salmon is normally packed. Since few of the Kpelle are wealthy enough to afford tinned salmon, it is not clear why they used this term.... The cup the trader uses to buy rice has the bottom rounded out by long and careful pounding, but the cup he uses to *sell* rice does not have the rounded bottom. This is the source of his profit. (1967, p. 64)

Kpelle children were exposed to this method of measuring from a very early age when they accompanied their mothers to the market place to buy rice. However, when the children entered school (a Western school), they were taught the English System of Measurement via rote memorization. Gay and Cole found that, although the children had an informal understanding of measurement from their out-of-school experiences, they neither understood, nor properly used, the system of measurement taught in school because this formal way of measuring was not linked with their informal understandings. Barcellos (1981) noted that, for children learning mathematics divorced from their culture's everyday mathematics practice, applying the mathematics is very difficult because they have learned it outside of their culture.

When children's mathematics learning in and out of school are connected, they can support the other, helping the children to become more mathematically powerful. Brenner (1985), in her work in Liberia, studied the traditional arithmetic procedures used by the Vai of Liberia and then examined how elementary children in this area combined or reconciled their traditional arithmetic practice with that taught in school. She found that the "children used a combination of Vai, school, and invented arithmetic algorithms during both individual testing and classroom lessons. ... each method tended to be used with problems that were amenable to that particular approach" (1985, p. 182). Rather than the different arithmetic methods interfering with each other, Brenner observed that the students were "able productively to mix the two systems of doing arithmetic," and the Vai methods actually might have facilitated "acquisition of the school methods" (1985, p. 182). The students were able to reconcile and combine the different arithmetic systems because "the teachers themselves accommodated this process because they acknowledged the legitimacy of traditional Vai arithmetic procedures and structured classroom lessons so that children could display their mastery rather than their mistakes" (1985, p. 185).

Saxe (1979, 1981, 1982, 1991) also found that Oksapmin children in Papua New Guinea were able to accommodate out-of-school mathematics in their in-school learning. He studied the Oksapmin of Papua New Guinea "for the purpose of studying the development of mathematical understandings in a non-Western culture" (1991, p. 1). He found that the Oksapmin use "very different ways of thinking and very different procedures for accomplishing everyday problems" (1991, p. 1). For example, the Oksapmin use a complex system of body counting involving 27 body parts: "A number is expressed by pointing to a particular body part (like the neck) and saying the body-part name" (1991, p. 1). Saxe (1982) found that this complex, indigenous system of body counting is actively used by children in the classroom but is transformed to be useful in doing school mathematics.

Sometimes the differences between mathematics practice in and out of school may be inherent. For example, a mathematical concept may be understood and used differently in everyday situations than the way it is taught in school (e.g., de Abreu & Carraher, 1989). We believe, however, that, although some differences may be inherent, these differences can be narrowed so that, instead of being disjoint activities that do not influence each other, mathematics learning and practice in and out of school can build on and be connected with each other. We now discuss a research project that aimed to connect middle school students' in-school and out-of-school mathematics practice by engaging them in learning mathematics via contexts that were part of their out-of-school experiences.

CONNECTING IN-SCHOOL AND OUT-OF-SCHOOL MATHEMATICS PRACTICE

In a recent National Science Foundation-sponsored project, *Connecting In-school and Out-of-school Mathematics Practice*, we sought to engage students in learning mathematics through the use of contexts that were meaningful to the students. The goals of the 4-year project were to (a) investigate how middle school children use mathematical ideas in a variety of out-of-school situations and (b) use ideas from the children's out-of-school activities to support their classroom learning and examine how they make sense of ideas mathematically. In this chapter, we focus particularly on how students' mathematical understandings developed out of dealing with obstacles that arose during the activities.

The research framework guiding the study is Saxe's (1991) Emergent Goals framework that is based on the coordination of constructivist and sociocultural views of cognition and has as its core construct the shaping and reshaping of individual goals

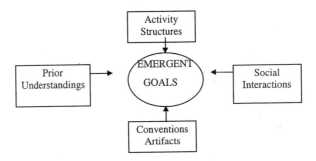

FIG. 19.1.   Four-parameter model. From *Culture and Cognitive Development: Studies in Mathematical Understanding*, by G. B. Saxe, 1991, Hillsdale, NJ: Lawrence Erlbaum Associates.

(emergent goals) as a function of the interplay between the four parameters is outlined in Fig. 19.1.

In particular, the study is based on the belief that "mathematical environments take form as children construct and accomplish goals and subgoals that are grounded in their prior understandings. . . [and] children's construction of mathematical goals and subgoals is interwoven with the socially organized activities in which they are participants" (Saxe & Bermudez, 1996, p. 52).

Adapting the analytic components of Saxe's framework, our specific aims have been to (a) gain insight into the goals that emerge during children's out-of-school activities by examining the activity structure, the social interactions that occur, the conventions and artifacts used during the activities, and the children's prior understandings; (b) explore the kinds of cognitive forms and functions that children construct to accomplish their emerging goals; and (c) examine the interplay among these various cognitive forms by studying how and if students are able to use cognitive forms in a school setting that they have appropriated in an out-of-school setting.

Children's Mathematical Environments

In order to gain insight into the out-of-school mathematical environments of children, we collected data on the mathematics practice of six middle school children during the summer and fall of 1995. We collected data through (a) activity sampling with electronic pagers and logs, (b) observations of each child in a number of out-of-school activities that we thought were potential mathematical environments, (c) interviews with children about logs and observations that focused on their mathematics practice, (d) logs kept by children and parents about the mathematics they used and that they perceived their parent/child use, and (e) interviews with children and parents about these logs and their activities. We transcribed the interviews and analyzed the data over the spring and summer of 1996 using qualitative methods of data analysis.

With the three analytic components guiding our data analysis, we observed that children (a) used a number of mathematical concepts and processes, often within a single activity, (b) made decisions and used strategies that took into account the constraints of a given situation and led to the modification of their goals and the optimization of results, and (c) tried to communicate their ideas by using a limited, and thus often incorrect, mathematical vocabulary that suggested a burgeoning awareness of the complex relationships and ideas that they dealt with in their activities (de Silva, Masingila, Sellmeyer, & King, 1997).

While analyzing the data, we also became aware of the potentially rich contexts for mathematics that many of the children's activities offered. These were the kind of macrocontexts in which we saw the possibility of exploring multiple mathematical concepts, although the children, constrained by their own conceptualizations of what constitutes mathematics, rarely identified more than a few concepts. Some of the contexts we identified and hypothesized might be familiar to the majority of students we would be working with in the classroom research phase were soccer, miniature golf, board games, summer jobs, miniature models, summer camp, crafts, music, and studying foreign cultures.

Children's Mathematical Goals

In many of these contexts, the mathematical goals that we glimpsed children construct were fleeting, interwoven, and constrained by the structure, conventions, and artifacts of the particular activity, the children's prior understandings, and the social interactions that occurred. For example, when we asked what math she saw in soccer, Kristen observed that "there are definitely angles—angles of a shot set-up" (interview 7/95), but did not identify any other mathematical ideas. After we observed her play soccer, it was evident that, although the word "angle" was used in a number of stock phrases relating to the strategy used, the players seemed to learn what constitutes a "good" angle through conditioned exposure and direct stimulus—"your responses [to the coach's instructions] become automatic; you don't have time to think or estimate" (Kristen, interview 7/95). Kristen went to soccer camp because she hoped to be on the team the following year and her experience was limited. As a novice, the construction of the potentially complex goal of why an angle is the "best" for a given situation did not seem required of Kristen as much as experiencing the success that follows the identification of the best angle (Masingila & de Silva, 1997).

On the other hand, Linus, who had played ice-hockey for some years and was the goalie on his team, did not get any help from his coach who did not know much about goal tending. In fact Linus said that he (Linus) "went to goalie camp. . . and. . . learned how to talk to [his] players more and [he] can teach the coach" (interview 10/95). Although he too spoke of reacting without really thinking when faced with a player/puck coming toward him, unlike Kristen, Linus was able to elaborate on why he thinks of angles at that moment and to analyze the merits of different "angles" of attack:

Researcher: So what's the difference between attacks from the side or straight on?
Linus: Straight on's the hardest because they have the whole goal, but if they are over here (points to the left side of the goal—see Fig. 19.2) the angle is easier to cut. If they come straight, they can hit both sides but if they come in here (points to the side) they still have both sides but not as much area. (interview 10/95)

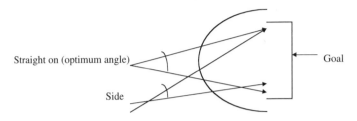

FIG. 19.2. Illustration of Linus' explanation for different attacks on the goal.

Although he used the word area, Linus appeared to be optimizing the angle for attacking the goal as illustrated in Fig. 19.2. (It is not clear what he meant by area—if it is the areas of the "triangles" formed by the rays defining the extremes of the possible attacks, they are the same. However, because he said it was easier to "cut the angle" from the side, it seems likely that, when he said area, he actually meant angle. Elsewhere in the interview he also spoke of moving up close to the attacker and staying near him or her by skating backward and of doing "the butterfly," a blocking maneuver that optimizes the "screen" he places in front of the angle of attack. Although he was not asked to explain how these maneuvers help minimize the angle of attack, his other explanations suggest that he probably would have been able to do so. Linus seems to at times have a role similar to that of Kristen's coach in deciding on the strategy to be adopted by the other players: "all the ice on our half of the rink is mine so I can tell a guy where to skate. . . I might tell our guys who to cover. . ." (interview 10/95). The complexity of the mathematical goals he constructed were probably a result of the greater demands placed on him as well as his greater experience and expertise that gave him more vocabulary and constructs to discuss (de Silva, Masingila, Sellmeyer, & King, 1997).

The Search for a Meaningful Context

Based on such glimpses of the mathematical environments that these students could or did construct, we began to explore other "cultural forms" (Saxe, 1991) in the contexts identified that could provide a basis for students' cognitive development. Our goal was to develop a unit that used students' "spontaneous concepts [to] enrich [mathematical] concepts with meaning and [to decide which mathematical] concepts would offer generality to the students' development of further spontaneous concepts" (Saxe, 1991, p. 12).

Through our negotiations with the classroom teacher we worked with, we settled on a context (a) that was familiar to our six respondents and (b) with which we thought most students in this school would have some experience. The context we chose was miniature golf. For 4 weeks in March and April 1997, students in three Grade 6 classes[2] (comprised of 11- and 12-year old students) participated in a teaching experiment where they investigated mathematical ideas through this context. The entire unit was centered around the "problem" of designing a miniature golf course. Although this is likely not a problem many of the children would face in their

---

[2]The classes were labeled by the school day period. The three classes were called Math 6, Math 7, and Math 9.

out-of-school activities, we found that the idea of what would constitute a good minia-ture golf course arose during our observations with our six respondents and we believed it was a situation that would appeal to the students' familiarity with miniature golf and their experience in designing and building models in other classes and hobbies while providing a fertile context for their own problem posing. Gurtner, Leon, Nunez, and Vitale (1993) expressed the sentiments of many of today's mathematics educators when they concluded that "it is important that the modelling activity, in a class context, be part of a larger project, which includes the choice of a problem which is significant to the pupils" (p. 67).

In keeping with the beliefs guiding our study, we designed the unit to connect with the "cultural forms" of the children's out-of-school experience by having miniature golf holes set up in class periodically and by taking a field trip to a miniature golf course. We designed worksheets to pose problems that arose out of their experience and designed the instruction to assist students in generalizing from their "spontaneous concepts" to generalized mathematical concepts. We envisioned active student partic-ipation in terms of discussion, hands-on exploration, and journal writing on assigned topics.

Need-Based Problem Solving

As the students worked on different phases of the design project, they encountered problems with which they had to deal. One such problem was how to measure and reproduce a curved side of a miniature golf hole. The mathematics involved in mea-suring and reproducing a curve is rarely included in the middle school curriculum; indeed, students do not usually encounter these mathematical ideas until they are in a calculus class. However, this was a problem (an emerging goal) that arose out of the students' involvement in the design project, and the mathematical knowledge the students constructed developed out of their efforts to overcome this problem.

This problem arose when the students visited a miniature golf course and took measurements and made sketches with the eventual goal of making scale drawings of the holes. The students found that many of the miniature golf holes at the course had curved sides, and the students struggled with what measurements to take and how to measure when they encountered these holes in the midst of their activity. We observed that it was during this activity, while working with others and using measuring tools, that the students began to identify, struggle with, and come up with strategies for overcoming this problem.

After analyzing the students' written records of their work at the miniature golf course, we realized that the students had used a variety of strategies that could lead to fairly good approximations of a curve. Often their strategies seemed incomplete; they may have used a potentially valid technique of approximation but perhaps they did not implement it consistently around the curve, rather for only the tightest part of the curve. At other times, the students recorded only some measurements, as if they did not perceive a need to coordinate two measures to locate a point.

Although we had not planned originally to explore approximating a curve, the richness of the students' pictorial, verbal, and written representations encouraged us

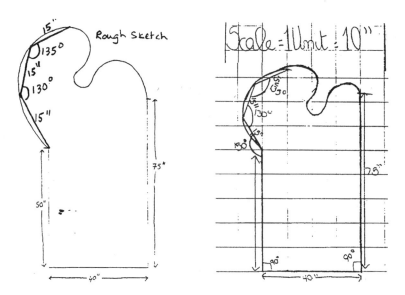

FIG. 19.3.   Example of a student's polygonal approximation of a curved hole.

to have them dig further into the problem. We had already planned a series of activities on scale drawings of polygonal shaped holes and, because one of the student-generated strategies was to approximate the curve through the use of segments, we were able to extend these activities to a polygonal (secant line) approximation of a curve by reminding students of their struggles with and ideas for measuring a curved side. Using an overhead projection of the rough sketch of a hole with a curved side, we asked students where the line segments should be drawn and then what measurements they needed to reproduce the segments. The students asked for the lengths of the line segments and the measures of the angles formed by consecutive segments. We supplied these measurements and then had the students make a scale drawing of the hole using this information. After they completed the scale drawing, they sketched in what they thought would be the outline of the curved side, based on their polygonal approximation (see Fig. 19.3).

We then facilitated a class discussion on how they could achieve a better approximation. Many students suggested shortening the line segments and increasing their number, and we observed that all students came to realize that, the more line segments used, the better the approximation. As more than one student noted, the polygon "becomes the curve."

We followed up this activity with a journal assignment that we hoped would provide (a) stimulation for those students still struggling with the conceptualization of the problem and (b) awaken new problems, such as how good an approximation is and in what ways could an approximation be made better, for other students. The journal assignment (see Fig. 19.4) used strategies that we gleaned from the students' recorded efforts at the miniature golf course.

The students in the three Grade 6 classes had a variety of responses to this journal assignment, with many students revealing quite sophisticated thinking about the

Assignment #3: Five different strategies that students in Math 6, 7 and 9 have come up with for measuring a curved side of a hole are shown below.

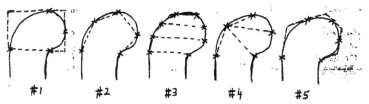

- Pick the one that you think is best.

- Explain what measurements you need to take.

- Explain why you think this is the best way to measure a curved side.

FIG. 19.4.   Journal assignment on reproducing a curved side.

FIG. 19.5.   Student's diagram combining strategies #2 and #5.

problem. About half of the students chose strategy #2, which was the one articulated by several students in class and used in the previously mentioned class activity. However, a large number of students who chose this strategy suggested reasons that indicated that they had thought beyond the class discussion. One student noted that "it measures the inside of the curve. So to make it curved you just curve the straight lines a little bit" (Kate, Math 7).

Another student chose strategy #5 and commented that "some of the other ones aren't accurate and are very hard to do. The one in the middle [strategy #3] isn't accurate at all and looks like it doesn't even work" (Ashley, Math 7). Several students suggested similarities between strategies #2 and #5, saying: "the others don't measure all the parts of the curve or twist" (Mike, Math 6); "these two 'experiments' are almost the same, for one has the dotted outline on the inside and the other one has it on the outside" (Sally, Math 7). One student, although officially choosing strategy #5, wrote that "an even tighter method might be to use #2 and 5, having the stars at the same places" (Erica, Math 9). This student sketched a diagram illustrating her integrated method that showed how the space within which to estimate the curve is made "tighter" by using both the secant line and tangent line approximations (see Fig. 19.5).

Although the majority of the students did not appear to arrive at the same place mathematically as Erica, all of the students demonstrated that they had grappled with what had become a real problem for them and developed shared mathematical understandings about how to reproduce a curve. Students returned to this problem later in the unit, after having explored the path of rebound when a ball hits a straight side, when they posed for themselves the question "how would a ball rebound after hitting a curved side?" Many students pursued this problem to varying degrees, and some concluded that it would behave in a similar fashion if one thought of the curve "being straight for just a tiny bit" at the point of impact (i.e., a tangent line approximation of the curve near the point of impact). Some students even referred to strategy #5 from the journal assignment as the way they were thinking about the curve in trying to determine the path of rebound. Even though many of these students had not chosen strategy #5 as their choice for approximating the curve, their reference to this strategy in this later activity indicates they were continuing to grapple with the relative merits of approximation (de Silva, Masingila, & Sellmeyer, 1999).

BUILDING ON STUDENTS' OUT-OF-SCHOOL
MATHEMATICS PRACTICE

Just as people throughout history have developed mathematical ways of making sense of things and overcoming obstacles, the Grade 6 students in our teaching experiment classes developed mathematical ways of meeting the goal that emerged from their activity to reproduce a curved side of a miniature golf hole. Repeatedly, we have found similar instances, in analyzing the data from these three classrooms, where students have drawn on their prior understandings, social interactions, the activity structure, and artifacts to reason within and beyond the context and to develop mathematics.

Unfortunately, learning mathematics in school through social and cultural contexts—where the contexts are meaningful to the learner and the mathematics develops out of situated needs—is a rare occurrence. We see this type of learning situation as an essential factor in helping students reason their way to mathematical understanding. Having students learn through meaningful contexts may imply that curricula is locally specific; obviously, there are many places in the world where miniature golf would not be a meaningful context for students.

As we have noted previously, context itself is insufficient; the context must be mathematically meaningful to learners. In the example discussed earlier of the Kpelle children learning the English System of Measurement, the classroom teachers did not make use of the mathematically meaningful context of measuring rice as a context from which to help the students make further mathematical constructions about measurement ideas. Thus, the children were not able to build on their out-of-school understandings of measurement. Just as the Babylonian numeration system contained features that were valuable and were incorporated into later numeration systems, the local Kpelle measurement practices have important measurement concepts embedded in them that could help schoolchildren make sense of other measurement systems. Brenner's (1985) and Saxe's (1982) work demonstrate how out-of-school practices can support and enable learning of in-school mathematical practices.

Planning in-school mathematical experiences that build on students' mathematical understandings from out-of-school is a critical, but very difficult, task. Realistic Mathematics Education (RME), developed in The Netherlands, offers an approach that we have found helpful through its key characteristics of reinvention through progressive mathematization, didactical phenomenological analysis, and use of emergent models (Gravemeijer, 1998). In RME, the curriculum developer or teacher develops a set of instructional activities that give students the opportunity to reinvent mathematical ideas. The teacher searches for problem situations in which "situation-specific approaches can be generalized and. . . situations that can evoke paradigmatic solution procedures" (Gravemeijer, 1998, p. 60). These problem situations then can be used to help students develop emerging models that can bridge "the gap between students' informal knowledge and formal mathematics" (p. 62).

We have found both Saxe's framework for analyzing children's learning environments and the instructional theory of RME to be helpful in thinking about teaching and learning mathematics in school by building on students' out-of-school mathematics practice. Furthermore, we find that taken together they offer mathematics educators much more than taken separately. Saxe's theory provides insight into how "mathematical environments take form as children construct and accomplish goals and subgoals that are grounded in their prior understandings" (Saxe & Bermudez, 1996, p. 52). Mathematical environments arise only as individuals structure mathematical goals in the midst of socially organized activities. Their work calls out the importance of a careful examination of the goals that emerge through children's work (both in and out of the classroom) and the realization that, whereas students can be working on the same mathematical activities in the classroom, they can be engaged with different mathematical environments.

Although Saxe's work discusses the formation of mathematical environments, it does not offer much assistance for instructional practices. The instructional theory of RME provides mathematics educators with a theoretical framework to guide curriculum development with a goal of helping students in their mathematizing. What is missing, in our opinion, from RME is the focus of looking at the goals that emerge during the out-of-school and in-school mathematical activities through which the mathematical environments are formed. It is not enough for the teacher to set "out a path of instructional tasks along which the reinvention process can proceed" (Gravemeijer, 1998, p. 57). Rather, the instructional tasks must be designed based on the mathematical environments that the students are forming while considering the mathematical ideas that the larger community has agreed upon as important.

Thus, we find that considering Saxe's framework together with the instructional theory of RME provides mathematics educators with a more comprehensive sociocultural view of how children learn mathematics and how we might best teach them mathematics. We believe that, in thinking pragmatically about how teachers in classrooms might build on students' out-of-school mathematics practice, this can only be accomplished through teams of teachers and researchers.

The National Council of Teachers of Mathematics (NCTM), in their recommendations for the Grades 5 through 8 curriculum, advocates the use of problem situations that:

> establish the need for new ideas and motivate students. . . as the context for mathematics
> . . . Although a specific idea may be forgotten, the context in which it is learned can
> be remembered and the idea re-created. In developing the problem situations, teachers

should emphasize the applications of mathematics to real-world problems as well as to other settings relevant to middle school students. (1989, p. 66)

In order for teachers to meet this challenge, they need to be aware not only of "settings relevant to middle school students" (NCTM, 1989, p. 66) but also of the potential mathematics in such settings and the students' ability to grapple with such mathematics. Thus, teachers also need to make connections between the in-school and out-of-school experiences of their students.

The importance of also making connections within the mathematical curriculum is emphasized in the Mathematical Connections standard for Grades 5 through 8: "The intent of this standard is to help students broaden their perspective, to view mathematics as an integrated whole rather than as an isolated set of topics, and to acknowledge its relevance and usefulness both in and out of school" (NCTM, 1989, p. 84).

Teaching mathematics as an integrated whole would require making explicit the connections among topics often taught in isolated chunks during the school year. One way of achieving this could be through the use of macrocontexts (Bransford, Hasselbring, Barron, Kulewicz, Littlefield, & Goin, 1989) that provide a rich source of mathematical problems whose solutions would require the exploration of multiple mathematical concepts.

We believe that teachers and researchers working together as a team can find and develop macrocontexts that will be mathematically meaningful to the children in a particular classroom/school and through which the students can develop mathematical environments. This will involve careful observations of the children to see the mathematical goals they construct through their activity. This is not an easy task, as we found in our observations of our six respondents, but an essential one if we are to understand how children learn. As Saxe and Bermudez (1996) noted, "Children's learning environments, whether in or out of school, can only be adequately understood insofar as we can document the goals with which children are engaged" (p. 67). Likewise, seeing the potential in contexts for students' progressive mathematization requires the adults planning the instructional sequences to have deep and connected mathematical understandings themselves and the ability to recognize potential emerging models in the students' work.

What we are proposing is quite demanding and that is why we believe that it may only be possible with a partnership approach to classroom teaching and learning. In our case, we had a team comprised of a classroom teacher and two former classroom teachers who had become researchers. Each member of the partnership brought a particular expertise and made unique contributions. Through our observations of the six respondents we were able to observe children's construction of mathematical goals within contexts that were meaningful to them. By analyzing the expectations of the intended curriculum and considering our observations of the children, we were able to develop an instructional sequence through which we thought the students could create mathematical environments and mathematize their activity. The goal was to capitalize on the emerging models the students developed and guide them in generalizing their mathematical understandings of ideas that arose through the miniature golf context to other contexts, including abstract mathematical contexts. Figure 19.6 illustrates how

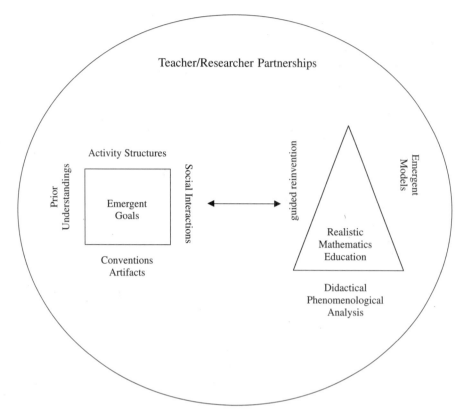

FIG. 19.6.   Teacher–researcher partnerships utilizing the Emergent Goals and RME frameworks.

we envision a partnership of teachers and researchers might utilize the Emergent Goals and RME frameworks in planning for teaching and learning that builds on students' out-of-school mathematics practice.

REFERENCES

Barcellos, A. (1981). Universal primary education. In L. A. Steen & D. J. Albers (Eds.), *Teaching teachers, teaching students: Reflections on mathematics education* (pp. 120–125). Boston: Birkhauser.

Bransford, J., Hasselbring, T., Barron, B., Kulewicz, S., Littlefield, J., & Goin, L. (1989). Uses of macro-contexts to facilitate mathematical thinking. In R. Charles & E. Silver (Eds.), *The teaching and assessing of mathematical problem solving* (pp. 125–147). Reston, VA: National Council of Teachers of Mathematics.

Brenner, M. (1985). The practice of arithmetic in Liberian schools. *Anthropology and Education Quarterly, 16*(3), 177–186.

Crawford, K. (1996). Cultural processes and learning: Expectations, actions and outcomes. In L. P. Steffe, P. Nesher, P. Cobb, G. A. Goldin, & B. Greer (Eds.), *Theories of mathematical learning* (pp. 131–148). Mahwah, NJ: Lawrence Erlbaum Associates.

Davis, P. J., & Hersh, R. (1981). *The mathematical experience*. Boston: Houghton Mifflin.

de Abreu, G. M. C., & Carraher, D. W. (1989). The mathematics of Brazilian sugar cane farmers. In C. Keitel (Ed.), *Mathematics, education and society* (pp. 68–70), (Science and Technology Document Series No. 35), Paris: UNESCO.

de Silva, R., Masingila, J. O., & Sellmeyer, N. (1999). Sixth graders pose and explore the problem of reproducing a curve. *Manuscript submitted for publication to the Committee for the 2001 Yearbook of the National Council of Teachers of Mathematics*. Reston, VA: National Council of Teachers of Mathematics.

de Silva, R., Masingila, J. O., Sellmeyer, N., & King, K. J. (1997). *Exploring multiple mathematical concepts within a single context*. Paper prepared for the Annual Meeting of the National Council of Teachers of Mathematics (Poster Session), Minneapolis, MN.

Eves, H. (1983). *An introduction to the history of mathematics* (5th ed.). Philadelphia: WB Saunders.

Gay, J., & Cole, M. (1967). *The new mathematics and an old culture: A study of learning among the Kpelle of Liberia*. New York: Holt, Rinehart and Winston.

Gravemeijer, K. P. (1998). From a different perspective: Building on students' informal knowledge. In R. Lehrer & D. Chazan (Eds.), *Designing learning environments for developing understanding of geometry and space* (pp. 45–66). Mahwah, NJ: Lawrence Erlbaum Associates.

Gurtner, J. L., Leon, C., Nunez, R., & Vitale, B. The representation, understanding and mastery of experience: Modelling and programming in a school context. In J. de Lange, I. Huntley, C. Keitel & M. Niss (Eds.), *Innovations in maths education by modelling and applications* (pp. 63–68). Chichester, England: Ellis Horwood.

Herodotus (1984). *The histories*. London: Penguin Books.

Joseph, G. G. (1991). *The crest of the peacock: Non-European roots of mathematics*. London: Penguin Books.

Kline, M. (1972). *Mathematical thought from ancient to modern times*. Oxford: Oxford University Press.

Lave, J., & Wenger, E. (1991). *Situated learning: Legitimate peripheral participation*. Cambridge, UK: Cambridge University Press.

Masingila, J. O. (1993). Learning from mathematics practice in out-of-school situations. *For the Learning of Mathematics, 13*(2), 18–22.

Masingila, J. O. (1994). Mathematics practice in carpet laying. *Anthropology and Education Quarterly, 25*(4), 430–462.

Masingila, J. O., Davidenko, S., & Prus-Wisniowska, E. (1996). Mathematics learning and practice in and out of school: A framework for connecting these experiences. *Educational Studies in Mathematics, 31*(1 & 2), 175–200.

Masingila, J. O., & de Silva, R. (1997). *Understanding angle ideas by connecting in-school and out-of-school mathematics practice*. In J. Dossey, J. O. Swafford, M. Parmantie, & A. E. Dossey (Eds.), Proceedings of the 19th annual meeting of the North American Chapter of the International Group for the Psychology of Mathematics Education (vol. 1, pp. 215–221). Columbus, OH: ERIC Clearinghouse for Science, Mathematics, and Environmental Education.

National Council of Teachers of Mathematics (1989). *Curriculum and evaluation standards for school mathematics*. Reston, VA: National Council of Teachers of Mathematics.

Saxe, G. B. (1979). A comparative analysis of the acquisition of enumeration: Studies from Papua New Guinea. *The Quarterly Newsletter of the Laboratory of Comparative Human Cognition, 1*, 37–43.

Saxe, G. B. (1981). Body parts as numerals: A developmental analysis of numeration among remote Oksapmin populations in Papua New Guinea. *Child Development, 52*, 306–316.

Saxe, G. B. (1982). Developing forms of arithmetic operations among the Oksapmin of Papua New Guinea. *Developmental Psychology, 18*(4), 583–594.

Saxe, G. B. (1991). *Culture and cognitive development: Studies in mathematical understanding*. Hillsdale, NJ: Lawrence Erlbaum Associates.

Saxe, G. B., & Bermudez, T. (1996). Emergent mathematical environments in children's games. In L. P. Steffe, P. Nesher, P. Cobb, G. A. Goldin, & B. Greer (Eds.), *Theories of mathematical learning* (pp. 51–68). Mahwah, NJ: Lawrence Erlbaum Associates.

Schoenfeld, A. H. (1989). Problem solving in context(s). In R. I. Charles & E. A. Silver (Eds.), *The teaching and assessing of mathematical problem solving* (pp. 82–92). Hillsdale, NJ: Lawrence Erlbaum Associates.

van Oers, B. (1996). Learning mathematics as a meaningful activity. In L. P. Steffe, P. Nesher, P. Cobb, G. A. Goldin, & B. Greer (Eds.), *Theories of mathematical learning* (pp. 91–114). Mahwah, NJ: Lawrence Erlbaum Associates.

Voight, J. (1996). Negotiation of mathematical meaning in classroom processes: Social interaction and learning mathematics. In L. P. Steffe, P. Nesher, P. Cobb, G. A. Goldin, & B. Greer (Eds.), *Theories of mathematical learning* (pp. 21–50). Mahwah, NJ: Lawrence Erlbaum Associates.

V

RECENT DIRECTIONS IN GENDER AND MATHEMATICS EDUCATION

Perhaps the most established area of research undertaken from a social perspective relates to questions of gender and mathematics education. Historically, the field's genesis was in the psychological paradigm, exemplified by the exploration of *sex differences*. Links were also made to biological differences. The change in terminology to *gender differences* was significant and heralded a clear recognition that observable differences were social, rather than biological, in origin. Because findings indicated that males appeared advantaged over females with respect to mathematics learning outcomes, early studies focused on identifying the factors contributing to females' observed disadvantage. This early research was critiqued in that it seemed to portray that "women were deficit" and that females should strive to attain these "higher" male norms. As feminist voices grew louder and feminist theoretical models became more sophisticated, alternative perspectives were postulated, and these assumptions were questioned and challenged. It was also argued that other social factors including class (socioeconomic status), ethnicity (culture), race, and religion also needed to be considered to untangle and understand the complex interactions that contributed to observable gender differences. Rather than waning in interest and energy, this area of research evolved in response to new questions and theoretical perspectives. The research techniques adopted to explore gender issues have been at the vanguard of the alternatives now used by many mathematics education researchers and are reflected in the chapters included in this section.

Chapter authors have covered a range of contemporary gender-related issues. Despite our concerted efforts to encourage contributions from authors from non-Western and non-English speaking background nations, regrettably their voices are still under-represented here.

Particularly in more affluent English-speaking nations of the world, there has been increasing concern about the educational needs of boys. There are growing signs that boys are also viewed as disadvantaged in fields traditionally regarded as "male domains," including mathematics. If the media are to be believed, this is true in Australia. In their chapter, Helen Forgasz and Gilah Leder re-examine gender equity issues from males' as well as females' perspectives. Findings from four studies involving participants of different ages illustrate changing patterns of beliefs, and differences among ethnic groups. The extent to which boys, rather than girls, are now perceived as educationally disadvantaged is discussed.

Some of the early criticisms of research on single-sex schooling were addressed in the unique setting in which Joanne Rossi Becker reports on the evaluation of a "single-gender academy." Special funds set aside within the Californian state budget had been used to provide a male and a female academy with comparable offerings and physical designs at the same site. The author was invited to evaluate one of these academies. Ethnographic methods were used to determine if the single-gender academy provided an equitable setting for the young women and men. The study examined whether teachers structured curriculum and instruction differently for the two groups and if females played a different classroom role than that exhibited in many studies of coeducational classrooms.

Research on gender issues in mathematics at the tertiary level is fairly limited. Leone Burton reports the results of an interview-based study with 35 male and 35 female practicing research mathematicians. The mathematicians' epistemologies and the impact of them on their professional lives were explored. The study documents the effects the sex of these mathematicians had on their understanding and practice of their discipline, whether the female and male mathematicians were differently distributed among the disciplinary areas of mathematics, and whether the career experiences of the men and women differed. The findings are related to the learning of mathematics in schools where, the author argues, homogeneity reflects a discipline that has been dominated by male styles, choices, and expectations.

Particularly in more affluent nations, the use of technology within education is receiving increased attention. The wide adoption of the technology and its early association with "male" subjects such as mathematics has raised questions related to gender and technology. Nicola Yelland describes findings from a research project in which pairs of children (girls, boys, and boy/girl) interacted with computer-based LOGO learning tasks embedded within a mathematics curriculum. The strategies used by the pairs of children as they solved the problems were examined. Differences evident in the tactics deployed and the interpersonal exchanges among the various dyadic pairs are presented. The author also discusses the use of higher-order thinking skills in problem solving and the ways in which teachers can scaffold children's learning to support the use of these strategies.

Concerns about equity in mathematics classrooms are central to many reform initiatives around the world. Drawing on previous research on gender and mathematics and various feminist perspectives, Joanne Goodell and Lesley Parker develop a detailed operational definition of the essential features of the ideal *connected equitable mathematics classroom* (CEMC). Students, classroom practices, and the curriculum form the three focal elements. Research evidence is presented that highlights factors facilitating or preventing a group of teachers from implementing particular features of the CEMC in their mathematics classrooms.

20

"A+ for Girls, B for Boys": Changing Perspectives on Gender Equity and Mathematics

Helen Forgasz
Deakin University

Gilah Leder
La Trobe University

Education is a basic [human] right and an essential tool for achieving goals of equality, development and peace. Non-discriminatory education benefits both girls and boys.
—United Nations 4th World Conference on Women (1995, p. 1)

SETTING THE SCENE

Achieving gender equity has been a high priority in Australia, as in many other countries. Abundant legislation has been put in place to address discriminatory practices in fields as diverse as education, the law, employment, and welfare. For over two decades, State and Federal government reports on girls' education identified specific school-related factors that perpetuated inequities. More recently, concerns have been expressed about problems experienced by boys. Again, as apparent from English and American publications, this trend is not unique to Australia. Focusing attention on boys' education provoked a range of reactions, often fueled by media debate. Emotive language and spurious assertions based on selective statistical data often misinform the public and disguise the still-significant inequities for girls in postschool options. Anxiety has also been widely expressed that funding for research on boys might occur at the expense of funding for research on girls. At the same time, an important outcome of highlighting boys' educational needs is the challenge to liberal feminism that male behaviors and outcomes are the desirable norm to which women should strive. These assumptions have underpinned previous policy, much research, and many intervention programs aimed at overcoming females' educational disadvantage.

In this chapter, a range of gender equity issues is examined from males' as well as females' perspectives, with a particular focus on mathematics education. The chapter commences with a brief historical overview of gender-equity issues in education in Australia. A review of relevant contemporary research literature is followed by a critique of recent print media reports on the educational attainments of boys and girls. How well the often ambivalent and emotive reports of gender equity issues reflect the opinions, experiences, and challenges faced by students in contemporary society is also explored. We address this issue by drawing on findings from four of our research studies. Collectively, these findings reveal both persisting and changing patterns of beliefs with respect to gender-equity issues of long-standing concern in the field of mathematics education. In the final section of the chapter, we speculate on the consequences of the directions emerging from our explorations of equity considerations in mathematics education.

Gender Equity and Education in Australia: Yesterday and Today

Equity issues have been on the Australian national educational agenda for some time. The seminal report *Girls, Schools and Society* (Commonwealth Schools Commission, 1975) identified areas of girls' educational disadvantage within the broader context of Australian society. A decade later, *The National policy for the education of girls in Australian Schools* (Commonwealth Schools Commission, 1987) required state governments to implement systemic and school-based initiatives to address the issues. That these policies have had an impact can be gauged from statistics that indicate that, across Australia, more females than males now complete Grade 12 studies and participate in higher education. However, gendered patterns of differences in participation rates in some disciplines are still evident, for example, there are more males in science- and technology-related courses and more females in the humanities and social sciences (Forgasz, 1998a). In educational and employment spheres considered high status, males continue to dominate and prosper. Social expectations can contribute to gender divisions in curricular and occupational participation rates. Kelly (1986), for example, found that many parents held gender-stereotyped attitudes to male and female societal roles. Although generally not opposed to their children taking on jobs stereotypically associated with the opposite sex, they did not envisage this happening.

More recently there has been growing acceptance, despite evidence to the contrary, that there is no longer a "problem" for women in society nor for girls in education. The focus switched to boys, both in Australia and elsewhere (e.g., the United Kingdom; see Weiner, Arnot, & David, 1997). Representative of this trend in Australia is the New South Wales inquiry into boys' education (O'Doherty, 1994). This report drew attention to aspects of school life and societal expectations that appear deleterious to boys' learning and their future lifestyles:

- Compared to girls, boys have a lower retention rate to Grade 12; poorer academic outcomes and attitudes to learning; higher representation in remedial programs; greater literacy difficulties; more behavior problems, referrals to welfare counselors, and school suspensions; higher suicide rates; and make more traditional and narrower curriculum choices.

- Boys also display lack of communication and dispute resolution skills, low self-esteem, reluctance to be seen to excel except in sport, lack male role models in primary schools, and display a detrimental overestimation of abilities.

Males' behavior, like that of females, appears to be shaped by societal expectations and clearly warrants further investigation.

Student ethnicity (race/culture) is receiving increasing attention in areas of educational research (e.g., mathematics; see Secada, Fennema, & Adajian, 1995; Trentacosta, 1997). In Australia, Polesel (1997) conducted a study that focused on the experiences of Greek girls in a working class school. These girls were found to have the lowest confidence of all groups measured. Polesel (1997) argued that the interaction of school-based gender stereotypes and aspects of Greek culture that supported boys' education over girls' undermined the Greek girls' confidence and expectations, "particularly in the gender sensitive domain of mathematics" (p. 42). In four schools (2 high and 2 low socioeconomic status) with predominantly non-English-speaking background enrollments, Pearn, Brew, Leder, and Bishop (1996) found that gender differences in attitudes toward mathematics were consistent with earlier findings. School differences were also noted. For example, in one school, students reported far more teacher support than seemed to be available in the other schools. Interactions between gender and cultural background were also found by Bishop and Leder (1999) in a recently completed study involving students from eight co-educational secondary schools in the metropolitan area of Melbourne. There appeared to be greater differences in self-appraisal on a host of variables between boys from Anglo cultural and non-Anglo cultural backgrounds than between girls from these groups. The findings from these studies imply that the interaction of ethnicity and the school attended also seems to contribute to patterns of difference in boys' and girls' mathematics learning outcomes.

Several Australian studies have revealed relationships between school type attended and socioeconomic background and levels of achievement and/or participation rates in school subjects (e.g., Lamb, 1997; Teese, Davies, Charlton, & Polesel, 1995). Ainley and Daly (1997) investigated a wider range of variables influencing participation in advanced mathematics across Australia, including: gender; prior achievement in mathematics; parental education; socioeconomic status; ethnic background; and school type, location, and whether schooling took place in a single sex or co-educational environment. They concluded that:

> In terms of malleable factors . . . , the results suggest that improving levels of prior mathematics achievement, and thereby enhancing students' sense of competence, could be the most effective way to raise levels of participation . . . [S]tructural solutions such as single sex schooling would appear to be unlikely to result in any substantial change. (p. 12)

Space constraints in this chapter do not allow a more-detailed account of the complex of interacting factors with the potential to influence the educational outcomes of males and females in mathematics and other subject areas (e.g., see Leder, Forgasz, & Solar, 1996, for an extensive review). Despite the documented advances for girls, caution is needed in concluding that boys are now the educationally disadvantaged group (e.g., Foster, 1994). This is not to argue that the education system is necessarily meeting boys' needs. On the contrary, there is strong evidence that the system is failing both girls and boys in different ways. Beliefs and attitudes appear to be changing, however. In the next section we examine the role played by the print media in shaping attitudes and beliefs. The focus is on how the Australian print media has reported equity issues in education generally and, in particular, the inferences that can be drawn from reports of high-status (university selection) examination results.

Messages Conveyed in the Media

Messages similar to those raised by O'Doherty (1994) about boys' educational disadvantage in the state of New South Wales have also been conveyed in newspaper reports. Many of the concerns about boys are not new (see Francis, 1977). Yet, in the past, the areas in which girls outperformed boys were not considered particularly important nor did society seriously challenge boys' (or men's) behaviors. Hence, the issues received scant mainstream research (or media) attention.

Leder (1995) argued that media reports can strongly influence public opinion. Despite the now strong participation by women in higher education and all aspects of the workforce, articles describing the balancing act required between their personal and professional lives are still considered newsworthy. Stories about successful men rarely contain such themes. Misleading stories can distort readers' beliefs and attitudes. For example, in some articles that report that boys' achievement levels have fallen behind girls', it is sometimes implied that this is because girls have received preferential treatment at the expense of boys (e.g., Messina, 1997).

Consider the messages conveyed to the public about factors implicated in differing patterns of high-stakes educational achievement in the following quotations from newspaper stories reporting Australian Grade 12 results in 1997: "Private, Jewish and girls schools have continued their remarkable dominance of the state VCE system, according to exclusive school indices" (Schools that top the list, 1997, p. 41) "Students from the leading private schools dominate the 1997 roll call of the nation's smartest— and girls, Jewish and Asian students consistently topped the class" (Jones, 1998, p. 7).

Consider, also, the following extracts (in italics) drawn from articles in the Herald Sun of December 16, 1997. The relevant "success" factors implied are shown in parentheses:

- private schools dominated (school type: government/non-government)
- girls performed better than boys (gender)
- all girls schools made up half of the top 22 colleges *and* only two boys-only schools were in the top 22 (gender; single-sex/co-education)
- Jewish secondary schools again displayed their high academic standards (religion/culture)

- the big surprise was. . . a tiny rural prep-to-VCE school (school size; rural/urban; P-12 continuity of attendance at one school/primary to secondary change of schools)
- the only state school to finish higher than. . . was. . . an exclusive boys' school that selects its students (selectivity: by ability; school type; single-sex/co-education)
- eighteen of the top 22 were private schools in Melbourne's east or south-east (school type; socio-economic factors)
- half of the top 10 state schools were in country Victoria (rural/urban)
- three state schools made it into the top group (school type)
- only one Catholic school [a girls school] . . . made the top ranks (school type: government/ Catholic/independent; socio-economic factors; gender; single-sex/ co-education)

Comments made by Lee Dow (1997, p. 19) further reinforce the impression gained that ethnicity and language background are potential contributors to successful educational outcomes. Arguments used to explain the high performance of certain groups of students included: "the commitment to learning from recent immigrant communities," "the achievement of Asian students bolsters the performance of many schools," and "the achievement of Jewish schools . . . points less to social and financial advantage than to a community . . . recognised for its respect and value of educational excellence." Similar points have been raised in British newspaper reports. For example, in an article reporting the "independent school league tables" results for the 1996–1997 school year, Clare (1997) wrote that "single-sex schools dominated the upper reaches . . . with girls' schools outnumbering boys' by two to one" (p. 12). How do members of the public, including parents, interpret the complexity conveyed by the messages in such newspaper reports?

Zevenbergen (1998) surveyed newspapers in New South Wales and Queensland from November 1995 to March 1996, a period when 1995 Grade 12 examination results were reported. That year girls had outperformed boys in Tertiary Entrance Scores [TES] (based on Grade 12 results). According to Zevenbergen (1998), the "results were reported in ways which did not celebrate the gains [by girls], but rather saw them as problematic for schools, society and in particular, for boys" (p. 61). Attacks on feminist educators were not uncommon. The impression gained from the articles was that girls' now being more successful than boys was inequitable and that "boys have become the victims of feminist agendas" (p. 61). Zevenbergen (1998) noted a number of prevalent themes emerging in explanations for boys' poorer performance:

- the "macho" image of Australian men: being rugged, tough, involved in sport and anti-intellectual
- boys' behaviour and self-esteem—both linked to the need to conform to the "macho" image
- boys need stronger role models in schools—a need for more male primary teachers and more male teachers of arts/humanities at the secondary level
- boys' slower maturity levels compared to girls
- the assessment system favors girls

Zevenbergen concluded that the image portrayed in the media reports:

> is a scenario in which boys are being excluded from success at schools because of the success of feminist reforms . . . [This] has helped to fuel the conservative debate that there is something wrong with our schools and that our boys are now innocent victims of an inequitable system. (p. 67)

An overview of Sydney Morning Herald articles during the same period was reported by Coupland and Wood (1998). They discussed community reactions to the issue of girls' improved performance. The debate was prolonged with academics writing articles and members of the public submitting letters to the editor. Their findings confirmed those of Zevenbergen (1998). Coupland and Wood (1998):

> . . . were shocked to realise that people thought there was something to be concerned about now that girls were doing better than boys, while for years the status quo of boys doing better was simply accepted as the natural order of things . . . Very few reports actually said anything congratulatory about the females' performance! Anecdotes and speculations appeared to speak louder than considered arguments and detailed research. (p. 243)

Media articles such as those cited above capture society's continuing interest in gender issues generally and in mathematics education in particular.

ILLUSTRATIVE RESEARCH FINDINGS

A brief overview of the findings from four of our recent research studies is presented in this section. Each focuses on pertinent gender issues. In the first study we describe some of the daily experiences and feelings of mature-age tertiary students pursuing courses in mathematics—home lives, study habits, motivations, and achievements. The second study involved an intensive investigation of a small group of male and female Grade 7 students observed over an extended period as they worked collaboratively on a mathematics task. We tentatively predicted each student's future involvement with mathematics and we discuss what eventuated when the students completed high school. Students', teachers', and parents' perceptions of gender equity in schooling was the focus of the third study. Findings from one primary school in which extensive data were gathered are discussed. Finally, in the fourth study we present findings from the trial of a new instrument designed to measure the extent to which mathematics is stereotyped as a gendered domain. Although each study involved only a limited sample of Australian (Victorian) students, we believe that together they present a sufficiently comprehensive picture to allow cautious generalizations beyond the limited groups involved.

Study 1. The Lives of Mature-Age Tertiary Mathematics Students

As part of a longitudinal study of mature-age students (at least 21 years of age at the commencement of their studies) enrolled in mainstream tertiary mathematics courses, we gathered data from a variety of sources, including survey questionnaires, interviews, and regular e-mail/snail mail correspondence (see Forgasz, 1998b, for details). These data provided information at varying levels of depth about students' motivations and classroom experiences. We wanted to know more about how their daily lives affected their tertiary studies. To do so, we used a slightly modified form of the Experience Sampling Method (ESM)—a technique adopted by Csikszentmihalyi, Rathunde, and Whalen (1993) to gather data from talented teenagers. We provided participants with pagers and sent out six signals daily for a period of six consecutive days. As each signal was received (or as soon as possible after) participants filled out a fairly detailed Experience Sampling Form [ESF] on which they recorded their actions, thoughts, and feelings (see Fig. 20.1 for sample items from the ESF).

Data were gathered from 21 participants. The response rate of around 80% exceeded our minimum expectation of about 67%. We selected two students, Ann and Howard (pseudonyms), both of whom were in permanent relationships and had children, to highlight the gender-related issues that emerged.

Name _____

Date _____   Time Beeped _____ Time filled out _____

As you were beeped:

(You may have been engaged in an academic, household, employment related or leisure pursuit. Any of these are relevant for the purpose of this study)

Where were you?   _____

Who were you with?   _____

What were you thinking about? _____

Tick the column which best describes your response to each of the following questions

	Not at all	A little	Moderately	Quite a bit	Completely
Were you concentrating?					
Were you living up to your own expectations?					

In the table below you are asked to describe your mood as you were beeped …. Tick the appropriate column which best describes your mood along (the) continuum.

	Very	Quite	Neither	Quite	Very	
happy						sad
lonely						sociable
distracted						focussed

If you had the choice when you were beeped:

What would you prefer to have been doing? _____

Any other comments? _____

FIG. 20.1. Excerpts from the experience sampling form.

About Ann and Howard.   Ann was a full-time student who was studying at the university of her first choice. She was married, with three children, and lived in her own home. Her husband had recently been transferred to take up a responsible, well-paid position in the city in which they now lived. She had decided against going to university when she left school because she was unsure about her career goals, wanted a break from formal studies, and needed to work to support herself. Her family had not discouraged her from taking that break. Marriage and children had precluded her from returning to study until much later in life.

When we interviewed Howard early in the study he was also a full-time student, but not at the university of his first choice. Like Ann, he had attended a coeducational government school in the metropolitan area and was born in Australia. His wish to travel and to have a break from formal study were important reasons for the delay between leaving school and embarking on his current course. Howard was also living with a permanent partner and had one child. His partner had given up her tertiary studies to stay home to look after the child while Howard completed his degree. (See Brew, 1998; Forgasz, 1998b, for more detailed descriptions of these two students.)

A Week in the Life of Ann and Howard.   Ann and Howard participated in the pager component of the study over almost the same period. Howard's 6-day sequence began on a Tuesday; Ann's on the Wednesday of the same week. They responded well to the pager requests. Ann returned 36 ESFs (100%) and Howard completed 33 of the possible 36 sheets (92%). As for the larger group (see Leder, 1998), for both students "study" was the activity most frequently caught at the time of paging: some 33% for Ann and 37% for Howard. Both were caught eating and doing chores with about equal frequency. Ann's high strike rate during her part time job (25%) revealed a major difference in their daily responsibilities—Howard was not engaged in paid work. More often than Ann, Howard was paged while he was studying, with his family (25% for Howard, less than 10% for Ann), in transit to university (5% of the times we paged him, none for Ann), and while sleeping (some 5% of the times we sought information, none for Ann, although she described herself as relaxing about the same number of times). Ann was more likely than Howard to be engaged with others during class time, less likely to be studying alone, more likely to be involved in paid work, more likely to be relaxing alone, less likely to be watching TV, and less likely to be with her children or with other members of the family.

The analyses of the ESFs revealed that Ann was being pulled in many directions: home, family responsibilities, the desire to gain some independence through her part-time earnings, and to do well in her course. The wish for more personal space and time and for uninterrupted periods to study were themes captured by many of her responses. Howard's concern to spend time with his child, his pleasure when he mastered assignments and other hurdles set in the course, and considerable flexibility in organizing daily activities were recurring themes in his ESFs. A comparison of Ann's and Howard's responses about their feelings during study times suggested that Howard was a more-satisfied and less-frustrated student. He apparently found it easier to concentrate, felt better about himself, considered that he was living up to his own expectations as well as those of others, rated his level of success higher than did Ann,

TABLE 20.1

Responses from Ann and Howard While Doing Chores or With Family Members

Ann	Howard
At 7:30 a.m.; Ann is in the kitchen at home cutting sandwiches for her husband and children; in response to the prompt "what were you thinking about?," she writes "I wish my husband would make his own lunch !" [exclamation mark in the original] To the questions "Who would you have preferred to be with?" and "What would you have preferred to be doing?" she answered "by myself" and "asleep," respectively	It is 7:30 a.m.; Howard is in the shower, "washing/ waking up"; he is trying to decide whether or not to go for a swim; he writes that he would have much preferred to be sleeping still and to be with his partner
It is just after 10:00 p.m.; Ann is at home in the laundry doing the washing while she is thinking about "Fathers Day shopping"; she would have preferred to be "by myself" and to be "having a coffee and reading the paper (i.e., swap places with my husband)"	At 4:20 in the afternoon, Howard is by himself, "pulling weeds out of our hedge"; he was working in the garden as part of his study break and was thinking about "what to do next"; he felt that he had earned his break because "I had just gotten a major part of my programming assignment to work, before I had taken a break"; he would have preferred to have been with "some classmates (to brag?!)" [punctuation in the original] and would rather have been "swimming or (in the) spa; I think I'll reward myself with a cup of tea and chocolate treats"
2:35 p.m.; Ann is in a coffee lounge in the country and is having lunch with her mother-in-law to celebrate the latter's birthday; her ESF, completed an hour after she received the signal, reveals quite graphically how much she would have preferred to be studying for her examination and how frustrated she is by the intrusion of her mother-in-law's visit into her daily routine and study time: "my mother-in-law is staying for 3 weeks; I wish she would go home or alternately not talk continuously"	Howard's last signal for the day came at 8:35 p.m.; he indicated that he was at home, with his daughter, and that the two of them were bouncing on the bed; and why was he doing that particular activity? Because his daughter insisted; "What were you thinking about?" "Getting some sleep"

and showed a higher level of satisfaction. Yet, Ann seemed to attach much importance to her study activities and to the importance of her studies in enabling her to reach her ultimate goal. She faced a number of obstacles and competing demands, not apparent for Howard as illustrated by the responses when both were signaled while doing chores or with family members (Table 20.1).

Some of the activities in which Ann and Howard were engaged in a typical week seem to confirm gender stereotypes, others to challenge them. For example, Ann continued to have the major responsibility for household and child-rearing tasks. Her husband, she indicated at various times, tolerated rather than supported her student role. Seemingly afraid of having her return to studies interpreted as frivolous and irresponsible, Ann imposed on herself the additional burden of contributing to the household budget through part-time work. In these circumstances, with little more than grudging support from her husband and mother-in-law, her intrinsic motivation to embark and continue on her studies needed to be high. She, but not Howard, was involved in paid work. Howard's return to study seemed to be more accepted by his partner. He referred to her demands on his time for assistance with child care rather than for economic support.

Ann's and Howard's self-descriptions of study-related issues revealed quite different patterns of interpretation of study events, self-perceptions, and pressures put on themselves or by others. The overall survey of activities in the larger sample revealed much overlap with those depicted by Ann and Howard. Despite the many individual differences captured, there were other implicit and explicit references to the pressures imposed by traditional gender roles. Such themes, we reported in an earlier section, are also highlighted in popular media reports, particularly those that emphasize the social and personal sacrifices that need to be made by achieving women.

Study 2. Predicting Students' Futures From the Past

Five Grade 7 students, three girls and two boys, were observed for eight consecutive mathematics lessons as they worked collaboratively on a realistic mathematics problem—whether the school should build a new canteen. The task included analysis of a survey of the perceived needs and spending patterns of students in the school and an appreciation of the impact of other costs associated with running a canteen. The lessons were videotaped and transcribed. The main aim of our study was to infer students' levels of cognitive and affective engagement with mathematics and to determine whether these behaviors were predictive of future involvement with mathematics.

To corroborate the inferences we drew from the observations, data were gathered from several other sources: field notes, students' perceptions of each lesson recorded on "Today's maths lesson" sheets, interviews, and a range of self-report measures (see Leder & Forgasz, 1997, for more details on the instruments). The teacher was also asked to rate the students' mathematics achievements; all were considered to be very good or excellent at mathematics. Five years after the classroom observations, four of the five students were interviewed and asked to complete forms. The information sought included parents' occupations, subjects studied at school, achievement levels, and involvements in co-curricular activities. On completing their Grade 12 studies, we were able to track their subsequent educational paths.

The affective measures we had gathered from self-report data and from observed classroom behaviors did not always match. There was greater consistency for the boys than for the girls. The videotapes revealed that the boys, Brian and Mark, were very focused on the mathematical demands of the group activity. They successfully shrugged off requests to complete tasks they did not want to do. The girls were more concerned with peripheral tasks, such as the presentation of the group report. One girl, Jenny, showed remarkable leadership skills. She directed the group in what needed to be done, checked on the boys' calculations, but did not directly engage in any mathematical computations. Cheryl did what was asked of her. Carol was marginalized by the group. She was assigned menial tasks, such as sharpening pencils. Her often useful suggestions were ignored by members of the group and by the teacher. From our detailed analyses of the vast amount of data we gathered, we were more confident about the boys persisting with mathematics than we were about the girls. We were least confident of Carol's future involvement, although she was clearly a capable student.

Our predictions, based on information gleaned while the students were in Grade 7, were largely borne out for four of these students (Brian had left the school). Their Grade 12 mathematics choices had followed gender-stereotypic lines. Mark was the only one who had studied the most demanding option offered. He told us that his parents, both mathematics teachers, had supported his subject choices. At interview, he mentioned engineering as his chosen career direction. We subsequently learned that he had received an offer to study for an engineering degree. Carol had studied the middle-level mathematics offering in Grade 12. Mathematics, she told us, was her least favorite subject. She was hoping to study a combined arts/science course at university. She was offered an appropriate tertiary place. Like Carol, Cheryl had studied the middle-level Grade 12 mathematics. She did so because she believed that mathematics was necessary for her preferred career direction—accountancy. Cheryl received an offer to study commerce. Jenny had chosen to study for the International Baccalaureate [IB] rather than the local Grade 12 course of study. This option was available at the school. She studied mathematics, but not the highest level subject, as part of her IB course. Her father, an ambulance paramedic, had been the inspiration for her desire to study medicine. Her results were outstanding, good enough to be offered a place in medical school.

Our research questions were very ambitious, and we recognized the danger in seeking to predict students' long-term involvements with mathematics based on a snapshot of some eight consecutive lessons spread over 2 weeks. We have already noted the need for extreme caution when generalizing beyond a small sample. However, the intensive and extensive observations possible in a small group yielded a great amount of information and illustrated the tacit support shown by the classroom teacher, whose competence is not in question, for the students' chosen tasks: the boys' commitment to mathematical reasoning and calculations and the girls' attention to various aspects of the organizational and presentation requirements. There was no evidence of a challenge by the teacher to these self-selected roles nor records of any attempts to encourage the students to vary or diversify their roles. We found that the multiple data sources we used, including the detailed observations of the students' cognitive and affective behaviors during mathematics lessons, provided data fully consistent with the students' Grade 12 mathematics subject choices and postschool educational pathways, with only Mark selecting the most demanding mathematics course.

Study 3. Perceptions of Gender Equity in a Primary School

Data for this study were gathered at an outer suburban government coeducational primary school. Students' home backgrounds could most aptly be described as "middle class." Our intention was to probe students' attitudes to gender as revealed both inside and outside the classroom and the extent of the influence of members of the school community (parents and teachers) on those attitudes. Because of the integrated nature of curricula in Victorian primary schools, in which timetable distinctions into different subjects such as "history," "English," and "mathematics" are largely irrelevant, our focus was on gender issues more generally rather than on students' attitudes to mathematics and related activities per se.

Eight Grade 4 and seven Grade 6 students, six teachers, and four parents were interviewed. Questions ranged from matters to do with friendship groups and attitudes to particular subjects and to school in general. Specific questions explored the kinds of characteristics that make for popularity, attitudes to girls' and boys' high achievement, whether particular subjects were perceived to be more appropriate for one sex than the other, and what kinds of activities students take part in at lunchtime. On the one hand, our limited sample restricts generalizabilty beyond our study. On the other hand, the detailed, in-depth cross-validation and triangulation of our data by interviewing students, their teachers, and parents reinforces the robustness of our conclusions. The school at which this study took place is like many other primary schools in Victoria. There is no reason to assume that our findings would not be replicated at other schools, with other groups of participants.

Three major themes emerged from the analysis of the interview data: peer relations inside and outside the classroom, attitudes to achievement and to subjects, and the influence of critical others on perceptions of gender equity. A brief overview of the findings is presented under these headings.

Peer Relations and Classroom Behaviors.   Students preferred to work and play with members of their own sex. Equal-opportunity groups was a phrase much in vogue in the school, although it seemed to have acquired a limited meaning when applied to classroom activities, becoming shorthand for "This task will be completed with a member of the opposite sex." for example:

> "Well, Miss S. says "Oh equal opportunity groups," so everyone goes "Oooh." You want to be with all of your friends and you have to go with girls and boys groups. We all complained at the start but after a while you just get used to them" (Year 4 girl).

There was a pervasive sense that girls and boys were not necessarily comfortable working together, not just because they were unsure what to talk about but also because differences of style and approach made collaboration difficult. It was interesting to note how some of the comments pointed toward stereotypical differences between men and women in terms of interests and habits:

> "It's just like if you're working together you, like, talk about sports and that. If girls, you don't know what to talk about" (Year 4 boy).

> "I don't like working with boys. They never listen. They're just stupid, you know. It's just hard because they're always saying stuff, absolutely stupid, and it's got nothing to do with it" (Year 4 girl).

> With projects I tend to work with a girl because we kind of, like, think the same, whereas a boy wouldn't think to do borders and have neat headings and all that kind of stuff, whereas girls would think, Oh, you've got to have a border and a neat heading and everything. Where some boys will just do rubbish headings. (Year 6 girl)

This last observation is fully consistent with the students' choices of activities in the mathematics classes we observed in the project described in Study 2.

Most children felt that teachers told off boys more often and that indeed they were more likely to misbehave. The kinds of offenses were likely to be different.

> I: What would a boy get in trouble for?
> S: Probably flying an aeroplane around the room or something.
> I: What do girls get in trouble for?
> S: Probably chatting. . . . (Year 4 boy)

Attitudes to Achievement and to Subjects.   There was a pervasive sense—from students, teachers and parents—that it was girls who performed better academically. The reason given for this was usually connected with girls' higher motivation, that boys cared less about their results and were less likely to be bothered to make the effort, whereas girls wanted to do well and spent time on detail. These opinions are remarkably similar to the themes promoted in the media and described in an earlier section.

> Boys just want to go, like, and work. They're sick of school, they hate school. And girls just want to get a better education. They think of their education but boys don't. They just want to get out of school (Year 4 boy)

> Because I think girls, they put their heads together and they aim for a high mark. And yet boys kind of, like, don't aim for a high mark. Like they'll study, oh yeah, that's enough, now let's go play, whereas girls can be studying 24 hours a day. . . . Girls aim for an A+, boys only aim for a B, and a B's all right, whereas girls have to get an A+. (Year 6 girl)

A mother of a Grade 6 child thought that, although boys and girls had the same options open to them and girls now did mathematics and science instead of the home economics subjects as she herself had done, boys "choose to miss out a lot of the time—they sit back and listen rather than be outgoing." Another mother said that girls were interested in boys but still put school work ahead, whereas boys "lost their brains somewhere between 14 and 18 years old." She added: "I think the boys' priorities would be sport, football, cricket. You know girls' priorities would be doing homework, coming home, reading, doing things like that. . . ." Motivation was seen to work differently where sport was concerned, however. Boys were perceived to be better at sport, and this was attributed to the fact that they tried harder and cared more about winning. It may well be that some boys would have preferred to behave differently, but peer pressure did not allow it.

When asked to say whether certain things (e.g., football, art, being smart, etc.) were boy things, girl things, or there was no difference, most students labeled mathematics and science as girl things, along with working hard. Being smart was something that could apply to both boys and girls but was more likely to apply to girls.

> "This is pretty mean but I do think (girls are smarter than boys). [They] just seem to catch on a bit quicker" (Year 4 girl).

Influence of Critical Others on Students' Perceptions of Gender Equity. Most of the teachers in the school were women. Students were asked about the proportion of male to female teachers and why this might be so. Several views reflected implicit attitudes to the ways in which gender, careers, and behavior might be related. For example,

I: Most of the teachers at this school are they male or female?
S: Female.
I: Why is that?
S: Boys might enjoy doing other stuff. And girls enjoy teaching.
I: Why do girls enjoy teaching?
S: Because they enjoy children and that.
I: What sort of stuff do boys want to do?
S: Football, racing, rugby.
I: Are they the sort of jobs that boys want to do when they grow up?
S: They might like to be a doctor or something.
I: What else?
S: A dentist. A principal. (Grade 4 girl)

In the view of the mother of a Grade 6 girl, growing up is more difficult for boys than for girls, "because it's still the old attitude of males being brought up to be the main money bring inner sort of thing and the girls are there to be not, career women too, but also be mums ... There's more responsibility for a man than there is for a girl."

The picture created by the participants in this study was that of a world where new images of gender equity wrestle with what was (or was perceived to be) reality. Our data, like those reported by Colling (1992), Ludowyke and Scanlon (1997), and O'Doherty (1994), indicated that boys are perceived to have generally poorer attitudes to schoolwork and lower achievement levels than girls. Students' views generally mirrored those of their teachers and parents. That many students in our sample regarded mathematics and science as girl things differs from findings typically reported in earlier research as well as from societal expectations prevalent in earlier years.

Several parents reflected on the ways in which the roles their children were likely to play in relationships and in the workforce differed from their own. They felt that there were tensions, particularly for boys, in relation to these changes. They also spoke of their own uncertainties as to how best to prepare their children, particularly if their own families did not serve as models for the kinds of roles they hoped their children might adopt. Perpetuation in the media, as documented by Buchbinder (1997), of stories subtly reinforcing gender-stereotyped behaviors possibly at variance with those favored by the home and school may exacerbate these tensions and uncertainties.

Study 4. Tapping Beliefs About the Stereotyping of Mathematics as a Gendered Domain

The stereotyping of mathematics as a male domain is often included in models postulating explanations for the under-representation of women in the mathematics and

TABLE 20.2

Items Included in the *Who and Mathematics* Trial Instrument

Qn	Item	Qn	Item
1	Think mathematics will be important in their adult life	12	Find mathematics easy
2	Think the mathematics test must have been easy if they do well	13	Think they did not work hard enough if they do not do well in mathematics tests
3	Get on with their work in mathematics classes	14	Give up when they find a mathematics problem is too difficult
4	Are not good at mathematics	15	Tease girls if they are good at mathematics
5	Need mathematics to maximize future employment opportunities	16	Care about doing well in mathematics
6	Are thought of as "nerds" if they do well in mathematics	17	Think it is important to understand the work in mathematics classes
7	Worry if they do not do well in mathematics	18	Expect to do well in mathematics
8	Are asked more questions by the mathematics teacher	19	Think it is OK to be excellent at mathematics
9	Get the wrong answers in mathematics	20	Mathematics teachers spend more time with them
10	Mathematics teachers think they will do well	21	Distract other students from their mathematics work
11	Need more help with mathematics	22	Tease boys if they are good at mathematics
		23	Likely to work with computers in future jobs
		24	Consider mathematics to be boring

science fields (see Leder, 1992). The *Fennema-Sherman Mathematics Attitude Scales* [MAS] (Fennema & Sherman, 1976) have been used extensively in research on gender differences in mathematics learning outcomes and are comprised of nine subscales, including the *Mathematics as a male domain* [MD] scale. Forgasz, Leder, and Gardner (1999) recently argued that the MD scale should be revised because the assumptions underpinning the development of some of the items were anachronistic and the interpretations of responses to particular items were no longer valid.

A new instrument, loosely based on the MD subscale and aimed at measuring the extent to which mathematics is now stereotyped as a gendered domain, has recently been trialed (see Forgasz, Leder, & Barkatsas, 1998). The themes explored overlapped those tapped by the original MD scale but the response format differed substantially. The *Who and mathematics* instrument consisted of 24 items (see Table 20.2). For each item, students selected one of the following alternatives:

BD: Boys definitely more likely than girls
BP: Boys probably more likely than girls
ND: No difference between boys and girls
GP: Girls probably more likely than boys
GD: Girls definitely more likely than boys

The participants in the trial were 536 (281M, 255F) Grade 7 to 10 students from eight co-educational schools in Victoria (although findings from only seven schools were reported by Forgasz, Leder, & Barkatsas, 1998). For each item, a chi-square test was conducted to examine for gender differences in response patterns. As has been constantly emphasized in the past, many students were found not to hold gender-stereotyped views about aspects of mathematics learning, that is, ND was the most common response to most items. When we examined the remaining replies, response patterns confirmed earlier research findings for 11 items. Previous results appeared to be challenged for the remaining 13 items, which were grouped as follows: perceptions of ability (6 items: 4, 6, 9, 11, 12, & 18), effort (2 items: 13 & 14), teacher factors (2 items: 8 & 10), and other (3 items: 16, 19, & 24). The findings implied apparent shifts in some key beliefs previously identified as critical to girls' continued participation in mathematics. The patterns of beliefs emerging from the trial data were summarized by Forgasz, Leder, and Barkatsas (1998, p. 19) as follows:

- Beliefs about ability: an apparent shift from boys to girls being perceived as more competent mathematically.
- Beliefs about effort: some apparent changes—girls now seen to be more likely than boys to persist with difficult problems; girls still more worried than boys about mathematics achievement levels; girls now more likely than boys to blame lack of effort if they do not perform well.
- Beliefs about classroom behaviours: no change—boys are the distractors and teasers of others, girls are on-task and help others.
- Beliefs about mathematics-related careers: no change—computers and mathematics-related careers still considered more appropriate for boys.
- Considering Australia's multicultural profile, it was also of interest to know if views would vary among students from different cultural backgrounds. Among the trial schools was one affiliated with the Jewish community (school J) and one associated with the Greek community (school G). Students enrolled in these schools share strong, yet vastly different, ethnic and religious backgrounds. The data from the two schools were compared to those from all other schools combined.

In general, the response patterns to items at the two ethnic schools were similar to those of students in all the other schools. However, chi-square tests revealed statistically significant differences by school attended on nine items, which were categorized as follows: future careers (1 & 23), classroom factors (3, 15, & 20), mathematical ability (6, 11, & 12), and confidence (7). Students at School J were found to hold the most traditionally stereotyped views that future careers involving mathematics were more likely for males than for females (items 1 & 23). At the same time, with the highest proportion of ND responses on 16 items (2, 6, 8, 9, 10, 11, 12, 14, 15, 16, 17, 18, 19, 20, 22, & 24), these students were generally found to hold less stereotyped views than other students. This apparent inconsistency may be attributable to the Jewish community's well-known emphasis on the importance of learning for both boys and girls, highlighted by Lee Dow's comments in the media as reported in an earlier section of this chapter, but with more stereotyped parental expectations of gender-appropriate postschool options. At School G, the image portrayed of mathematics classrooms was more strongly consistent with a "male enclave" than could be inferred from the responses of students at the other schools (items 3 & 15). These students also believed more strongly than the rest that girls were more likely than boys to worry if they did not do well in mathematics (item 7). The findings for School G appear to support Polesel's (1997) observation that, in the Greek culture, boys' education can be more highly valued than girls' and that this, in combination with school-based gender stereotypes, might undermine Greek girls' confidence particularly in gender sensitive domains such as mathematics.

In summary, the findings from this new instrument provide evidence of changing beliefs about mathematics as a gendered domain, strongly imply that gender and cultural backgrounds interact in shaping belief systems, and illustrate the importance of the values and traditions embedded in the social environment in shaping students' beliefs about aspects of mathematics and gender.

WHAT DO THE FINDINGS FROM THE FOUR STUDIES TELL US?

We deliberately selected and reported studies spanning a wide age range—primary-aged students, Grade 7 to 10 students, and mature-age tertiary students—to illustrate contemporary perspectives on gender equity issues in mathematics education. The data presented revealed a co-existing duality—some patterns of gender difference have persisted over time, yet some practices and beliefs appear to be changing. Findings from the study of gender equity in the primary school (Study 3) and from the trial of the *Who and mathematics* instrument (Study 4) are clearly representative of this duality. The primary students' views of men's and women's careers and of classroom realities with respect to gendered patterns of behavior, for example, were consistent with previous research findings. Yet beliefs that mathematics and science were "girl things" and that girls are generally the high achievers were not. Ambivalence and tension in regard to girls' and boys' future roles and educational outcomes were evident among the parents. The secondary students' responses to many items on the *Who and mathematics* instrument also imply changing perspectives on particular aspects of mathematics education and were consistent with the primary students' views. Inappropriate classroom behavior was considered the realm of the boys. Girls were viewed as more able mathematically, for example.

From the results of the longer-term involvement with mathematics of the five students observed when in Grade 7 (Study 2) and of the study of mature-age students (Study 1), there appear to be fewer signs of change. The small sample size in both studies is balanced by the rich, intensive, and extensive sets of data gathered. Despite continuing with mathematical studies in Grade 12, the choice of mathematics subjects was found to be consistent with past, gender-stereotyped patterns. Only Mark had chosen the most challenging option available at that level. Is it a coincidence that 5 years earlier we had observed Mark and Brian grappling persistently with the mathematical tasks of the project, whereas the girls in the same group attended, lesson after lesson, to the presentation of the data and the organization of the various jobs to be done? As mentioned earlier, at no stage during our extended period of observation did we notice any challenge to these self-selected roles. Rather, the group was regarded as working effectively and productively. At no stage did it appear that the longer-term implications of the students' choices were being considered. The lifestyles and affective responses of the two mature-age tertiary mathematics students, Ann and Howard, also reverberated with past societal expectations of men's and women's roles.

Our findings revealed that traditional gender roles and expectations can continue to affect, in subtle ways, how and what mathematics students value and learn. The extent to which mathematics is perceived to be a "male domain" seems to be waning and, particularly among younger students, girls' mathematical potential is no longer regarded as inferior to boys'. However, more males than females continue to study the most demanding mathematics courses offered and are found in mathematically related careers. This state of affairs still appears to be considered appropriate, more so among some groups than others. Boys' classroom behavior and general attitudes toward learning were clearly recognized as deleterious but, as earlier researchers pointed out, the forms in which these are manifest can also affect girls' learning, particularly in traditionally male-dominated fields of endeavor. Similarly, societal expectations of women's roles as primary child carers and homemakers were also shown to persist, as revealed by the lives of the two mature-age students, Ann and Howard.

Yet we should not forget that it was possible for Ann to return to study in what was once regarded as a male domain and that Howard seemed to recognize and accept that he, as well as his partner, was responsible for child care. Among the parents we interviewed there was a clear recognition that the values and customs of their own youth should not be replicated uncritically and that their children were growing up in a world with fewer formal constraints imposed by gender. The increased confidence in their own ability as learners of mathematics shown by many of the girls who completed our questionnaire and the widespread recognition that male norms and expectations should not remain unchallenged (e.g., their often excessive preoccupation with sport and its heroes) are other significant indicators of a changing culture less accepting of invisible barriers imposed by labels such as gender or race and more prepared to consider individual needs.

REFERENCES

Ainley, J., & Daly, P. (1997). *Student participation in mathematics courses in Australian secondary schools*. Paper presented at the annual Conference of the American Educational Research Association, Chicago.

Bishop, A. J., & Leder, G. C. (1999). *Exploiting cultural diversity in the mathematics classroom*. Unpublished raw data.

Brew, C. (1998). *Finding a way through the national enrolment data—light at the end of the tunnel*. Paper presented at the annual Conference of the Australian Association for Research in Education. Adelaide, December.

Buchbinder, D. (1997). *Manners maketh man: Men's health and the cultural representation of masculinity*. Paper presented at the second National Men's Health Conference, Fremantle, Australia, October 29–31.

Clare, J. (1997, Aug. 23). Single-sex colleges dominate with 45 out of top 50 places. *The Daily Telegraph*. p. 12.

Colling, T. (1992). *Beyond mateship: Understanding Australian men.* Sydney: Simon & Schuster.

Commonwealth Schools Commission (1975). *Girls, schools and society.* Canberra, ACT: Author.

Commonwealth Schools Commission (1987). *A National policy for the education of girls in Australian schools.* Canberra: Author.

Coupland, M., & Wood, L. (1998). What happens when the girls beat the boys? Community reactions to the improved performance of girls in final school examinations. In C. Keitel (Ed.), *Social justice and mathematics education. Gender, class, ethnicity and the politics of schooling* (pp. 238–244). Berlin, Germany: Freie Universität Berlin.

Csikszentmihalyi, M., Rathunde, K., & Whalen, S. (1993). *Talented teenagers.* Cambridge: University of Cambridge Press.

Fennema, E., & Sherman, J. A. (1976). Fennema-Sherman Mathematics Attitude Scales. *Catalog of selected documents in psychology, 6,* 31 (Ms. No. 1225).

Forgasz, H. J. (1998a). The typical Australian university mathematics student: Challenging myths and stereotypes? *Higher Education, 36*(1), 87–108.

Forgasz, H. J. (1998b). 'Why study mathematics?' Tertiary mathematics students tell all! Paper presented at the annual conference of the Australian Association for Research in Education. Adelaide, December.

Forgasz, H. J., Leder, G. C., & Barkatsas, T. (1998). Mathematics—For boys? For girls? *Vinculum, 35*(3), 15–19.

Forgasz, H. J., Leder, G. C., & Gardner, P. L. (1999). The Fennema-Sherman "Mathematics as a male domain" scale re-examined. *Journal for Research in Mathematics Education, 30*(3), 342–348.

Foster, V. (1994). *"What about the boys!" Presumptive equality, and the objuscation of concerns about theory, research, policy, resources and curriculum in the education of girls and boys.* Paper presented at the AARE Annual Conference, Newcastle.

Francis, B. (1977). *Committee on equal opportunity in schools: Minority report.* Melbourne: Government printer.

Jones, C. (1998). Dux of 97: Wealthy, private and female. *The Weekend Australian*, p. 7.

Kelly, A. (1986). Gender roles at home and school. In L. Burton (Ed.), *Girls into maths can go* (pp. 90–109). London: Holt, Rinehart & Winston.

Lamb, S. (1997). Gender differences in mathematics participation: An Australian perspective. *Educational Studies, 23*(1), 105–125.

Leder, G. C. (1992). Mathematics and gender: Changing perspectives. In D. A. Grouws (Ed.), *Handbook of Research in Mathematics Education* (pp. 597–622). New York: Macmillian.

Leder, G. C. (1995). Learning mathematics: The importance of (social) context. *The New Zealand Mathematics Magazine, 32*(3), 27–40.

Leder, G. C. (1998). *But what do you do all day?* Paper presented at the annual conference of the Australian Association for Research in Education. Adelaide, December.

Leder, G. C., & Forgasz, H. J. (1997). A case study in mathematics: Looking back towards the future. *The Australian Educational Researcher, 24*(3), 97–113.

Leder, G. C., Forgasz, H. J., & Solar, C. (1996). Research and intervention programs in mathematics education: A gendered issue. In A. Bishop, K. Clements, C. Keitel, J. Kilpatrick, & C. Laborde (Eds.), *International handbook of mathematics education, Part 2* (pp. 945–985). Dordrecht: Kluwer.

Lee Dow, K. (1997). Parents' right to know. *Herald Sun*, p. 19.

Ludowyke, J., & Scanlon, J. (1997). *Improving the school performance of boys.* North Melbourne, Victoria: Victorian Association of Sate Secondary Principals.

Messina, A. (1997). Boys trail further behind in VCE. *The Age*, p. A3.

O'Doherty, S. (1994). *Inquiry into boys' education 1994. Challenges & opportunities: A discussion paper.* NSW: Ministry of Education, Training and Youth Affairs.

Pearn, C., Brew, C., Leder, G., & Bishop, A. (1996). Attitudes towards mathematics: What about NESB students? In P. C. Clarkson (Ed.), *Technology in mathematics education: proceedings of the 19th annual Conference of the Mathematics Education Research Group of Australasia* (pp. 445–452). Melbourne: Mathematics Education Research Group of Australasia Inc.

Polesel, J. (1997). Gender, ethnicity and mathematics: The experience of Greek girls in an Australian High School. *Education and Society, 15*(2), 37–47.

Schools that top the list. (1997, Dec. 17). *Herald Sun.* p. 41.

Secada, W. G., Fennema, L. B., & Adajian, L. B. (Eds.) (1995). *New directions for equity in mathematics education.* Cambridge: Cambridge University Press.

Teese, R., Davies, M., Charlton, M., & Polesel, J. (1995). *Who Wins at School?* Melbourne: Department of Education Policy and Management, The University of Melbourne.

Trentacosta, J. (1997). *Multicultural and gender identity in the mathematics classroom. A gift of diversity. 1997 yearbook.* Reston, VA: National Council of Teachers of Mathematics.

United Nations Fourth World Conference on Women: Draft plan for action (1995). *Unequal access to and inadequate educational opportunities.* Linkages: A multimedia resource for environment and policy makers, available on-line [http://www.iisd.ca/linkages/4wcw/dpa-021.html].

Weiner, G., Arnot, M., & David, M. (1997). Is the future female? Female success, male disadvantage, and changing gender patterns in education. In A. H. Halsey, P. Brown, H. Lauder, & A. Stuart Wells (Eds.), *Education, economy, culture and society.* Oxford: Oxford University Press.

Zevenbergen, R. (1998). Gender, media, and conservative politics. In C. Keitel (Ed.), *Social justice and mathematics education. Gender, class, ethnicity and the politics of schooling* (pp. 59–68). Berlin, Germany: Freie Universität Berlin.

21

Single-Gender Schooling in the Public Sector in California: Promise and Practice

Joanne Rossi Becker

San Jose State University

Researchers and policymakers in the United States continue to be concerned about the achievement and participation of young women in mathematics. Although there has been considerable increase in the numbers of women receiving bachelor's degrees in mathematics, the number continuing on for advanced degrees is still far short of parity. In mathematics-based fields such as engineering and computer science, in addition, the situation is even worse. In 1994, only 16% of engineering and 28% of computer science bachelor's degrees were earned by women (Chronicle of Higher Education, 1996). Mathematics course taking at the high school level is still one variable found related to choice of college major and achievement. A study of the 1990 National Assessment of Educational Progress (Davenport, Davison, Kuang, Ding, Kim, & Kwak, 1998) found that the pattern of gender differences in mathematics course taking paralleled trends in higher education, with males taking more advanced courses and achieving more.

As research on gender and mathematics matured since the 1970s, it evolved from positivist approaches, in many of which deficit models were implicit in the framing of the research, to the use of feminist paradigms (Fennema, 1996). Even our language changed, moving away from discussion of "sex differences" to "gender differences" as a declaration that gender is socially constructed and differences are not biologically determined. Many scholars have come to acknowledge rather than deny gender differences while working to ensure that the Euro-American male model is not regarded as the epitome. Theoretical frameworks such as Women's Ways of Knowing (Belenky, Clinchy, Goldberger, & Tarule, 1986, 1997) have stimulated new scholarship that promises to provide more information on teaching and learning of mathematics than older paradigms (see special issue of Focus on Learning Problems in Mathematics,

1996). This theoretical work raises questions. Do girls and women bring alternative ways of knowing and alternative concerns into the mathematics classroom? If so, what are the implications for the mathematics education of girls and women?

One perspective in the United States propounds that gender separation in mathematics is a way to provide the kind of educational environment conducive to both the achievement of girls and young women and the sustenance of their self-esteem. This approach is somewhat controversial for several reasons. First, it appears to some in the United States to be in violation of federal law in the form of Title IX of the Educational Amendments Act of 1972. That law prohibits sex discrimination in all programs administered by educational institutions receiving federal funds. Second, opponents argue that teachers need to find ways to design classrooms that provide a positive and equitable milieu for both men and women, as these would better reflect real-world social interactions (Mael, 1998).

In 1997 and 1998, the governor of California appropriated special funds in the budget to fund Single Gender Academies[1] at several sites around the state. Districts that received the grants had to provide a male and a female academy, full day, with comparable offerings and physical designs. As internal evaluator for one funded site in the San Francisco Bay Area, I conducted an ethnographic study of the academies at this site; this chapter reports on that research project.

BACKGROUND

Single-gender schooling has a long tradition in the United States, primarily in the private sector. As a result, most of the research conducted in this country focusing on girls' schools has occurred in Catholic schools or private schools (American Association of University Women Educational Foundation, 1998). In recent years there has been considerable interest in single-gender schooling in the public sector as a means to provide more equitable education for both males and females, particularly in sex-typed fields such as mathematics. Unfortunately, the research base in the United States has not kept up with the theoretical assertions in favor of single-gender schooling. Although there is some support for the claim that single-gender schooling in mathematics is positive for females, much of that research has been done in other countries and its generalizability to the United States is problematic (Mael, 1998).

Two recent reviews of single-gender schooling document the difficulties of methodology and generalizability inherent in much of the research (American Association of University Women Educational Foundation, 1998; Mael, 1998). The AAUW Educational Foundation report concluded that:

- There is no evidence that single-gender education is generally better than coeducation.
- Single-gender settings produce positive results for some students in some settings.

---

[1] "Academy" is the term used by the State of California to denote single-gender schools in the public arena.

- The long-term impact of single-gender education on males and females is unknown.
- Single-gender classes and schools can reinforce sex stereotypes as much as coeducational programs.
- Single-gender schooling is so broad as to defy generalization.

Mael (1998) provided an extensive examination of the various theoretical perspectives that argue for single-gender schooling. Reviewing much of the same research as the AAUW Education Foundation, Mael concluded that the research evidence supporting either single-gender or coeducational schooling is mixed. Mael asserted that the predominance of research suggests benefits for single-gender schools, although the effects are more pronounced for females than males, possibly because most of the research focused on female issues. Mael called for much more research into the differing dynamics of all-male and all-female classes.

Forgasz (1995) reported results of a quantitative study of attitudes of students in single-sex and coeducational schools of comparable socioeconomic background in Australia. Her results were inconclusive, that is, for females, neither the single-sex nor coeducational mathematics classes proved more effective in promoting attitudes related to gender differences in learning mathematics. Forgasz recommended qualitative studies to examine subtle classroom processes that may be contributing to gender differences in affective variables. Leder and Forgasz (1998) concluded that new approaches to gender equity should include males as well as females. In this chapter I report on a study that proposed to fill some of the gap in the literature by examining both a male and a female single-gender setting.

METHODS

Because I was interested in providing a rich description of the single-gender academies at this site [hereafter referred to as Amber Heights[2]-Male and Amber Heights-Female], I planned an ethnographic study that combined classroom observations, informal and formal interviews with teachers and the program coordinator, student surveys and interviews, and collection of ancillary materials such as assessments and student work. The main goal of the study was to determine if the single-gender setting provided an equitable educational experience for the young women and men. Some specific questions relative to mathematics included:

- Do teachers structure mathematics curriculum and instruction differently for the two groups?
- Do young women play a different, more active role in the mathematics classroom than that exhibited in studies of coeducational classrooms in the United States?
- What was the nature of the teacher–student interactions in the mathematics classes?

---

[2] All names have been changed to protect confidentiality.

- Did the single-gender settings affect students' achievement levels and attitudes toward mathematics?
- What was the overall culture of the mathematics classes?

The focus of my work was the academies as a whole; therefore, I visited and interviewed in mathematics, science, Spanish, computer fundamentals, and English classes. During the same time, under my direction, a graduate student conducted a more-intensive study of the Amber Heights-Female mathematics class only (Burns, 1998); some of her findings will be incorporated in this chapter. Because of the focus of this volume and my own interests, this report concentrates on findings related to mathematics. However, at times I will integrate findings from the academies as a whole, particularly as they help us understand the mathematics setting better.

The data set for this study included the following: 50 classroom observations, one formal and numerous informal interviews with five teachers and the program director, beginning and ending surveys of students, interviews with nine students, and assessments and student work. Analysis of the ethnographic data followed the domain analysis of patterns across all types of data as outlined in Spradley (1980).

This study took place during the 1997 to 1998 academic year, the first year of operation of the single-gender academies at Amber Heights. Because of lateness of funding and the difficulty getting students to apply, the academies did not actually start operating until the second semester of the academic year, in January 1998.

RESULTS

The Setting

Amber Heights is a large, comprehensive, coeducational high school in a large high school district in an urban area in the vicinity of San Francisco, CA. The district wrote a successful proposal to seek state funding of two single-gender academies the first year monies became available. Because of my prior work with this district and my research on gender, I was asked to help in the writing of the proposal. I endeavored to provide background research, resources for teachers' edification, advisory board suggestions, and other help as best I could. Thus, I had experience with the Amber Heights academies from their inception.

The district decided to house the single-gender academies at Amber Heights for several reasons. First, the state required that both a male and female academy, with comparable offerings and facilities, be developed. Amber Heights had the space for portable classrooms to house the single-gender academies. Second, Amber Heights has a number of other special programs within the district that draw students from around the district. The district administration judged that it would be easier to attract students to these new academies at a physical site that parents already chose for students.

In order to attract both students and teachers, the grant funded an extra planning period for participating teachers to enable them to spend time mentoring students, communicating with parents, and planning together. Thus the teachers taught four rather than the standard five classes a day.

Amber Heights is a large campus with a new science building and separate clusters of classrooms for other disciplines. The student body is "majority minority," that is, most of the students are Latino/Latina, African American, or of Asian descent, with Vietnamese predominating. The district purchased two new temporary buildings in which most of the academy classes were taught. Although new, they were rather barren for most of the semester. The academies also had considerable money for equipment; thus 30 PowerMacs were purchased, but these did not arrive until 2 months into the second semester.

Because the academies were housed on an existing campus, the students had the opportunity to mix with other students of both genders during lunch and brunch, before and after school, and even during changes between classes.

The Participants

The district had difficulty attracting students and teachers to the academies. Although they had originally planned in the proposal for three ninth-grade classes of males and three of females, they only were able to attract one class of each, and both were small. The female class had 21 students; 8 were Latina, 5 African American, 3 Asian American, 3 East-Indian American, and 2 Euro-American. The male class had 14 students; 6 were Asian, 5 African American, 2 Latino, and 1 Euro-American. One East-Indian female studied geometry independently, so she did not attend the algebra 1 class with the rest of the young women. This student, a traditional Muslim, was placed in the program at her father's request because he did not want her attending coeducational classes; thus, he was willing for her to study mathematics on her own to facilitate her placement in the program.

Most of the students, in a short survey early in the program, said that they joined the gender academies because their parents had forced them to do so. Other predominant reasons were to get better grades, to learn more, and to get a new experience. Only one young woman stated that she wanted to be in a school with only girls.

The teachers were all relatively young, and each taught a class in both Amber Heights-Female and Amber Heights-Male. The same teacher, a fairly inexperienced Asian American, taught the algebra 1 class and the computer fundamentals class; that was his whole teaching assignment. The Spanish teacher was a Latina, the integrated science teacher a Euro-American female, and the English teacher also a Euro-American female. The latter three taught the male and the female classes, and two other classes in the regular school. The academies administrator, Mr. Green, was a young Euro-American male who had other administrative duties as well but spent most of his time with the gender academies. He took another administrative position in the district at the end of the academic year; this represented a promotion according to district personnel with whom I checked.

The algebra classes had a change in instructor that occurred in March 1998, that is, there was one teacher (a middle-aged Euro-American male) from the end of January until the beginning of March. Explanations of the change varied according to informants' perceptions. The teacher felt that he had requested the change because the students were too unruly and unmotivated; a student (female) said many of the young women had walked out of class one day, marched en masse to Mr. Green's office, and demanded a new teacher. Mr. Green said that he had students (more female than male) in his office every day complaining about the mathematics/computer teacher. At any rate, the change seemed to be mutually satisfying; the teacher was happy to be back in the regular Amber Heights setting, and the students, both male and female, seemed to like the new teacher better.

The Academic Program

The students of each gender attended every class as a group: mathematics, Spanish, computer fundamentals, English, integrated science, and physical education. Each group, male and female, was assigned to a portable classroom and attended everything except science and physical education in that one room. The room was equipped with individual student desks, a teacher's desk, whiteboards, an overhead projector, and, later in the semester, computers and a printer. As the semester progressed, the classroom became more welcoming and vibrant as student work from English and Spanish decorated the room.

That the students stayed together all day created some personality problems. The intention was to have three classes of each gender and mix them up for each subject; however, the small number of enrollees precluded this approach. The administrator, teachers, and the students disliked having every class with the same group of students. As the administrator commented, if a problem occurs between students in a regular school setting, they have some time in the next class to cool off; in this situation, problems were amplified. Among the males, the problems tended to be competition; among the females, problems arose from gossiping or talking about other students.

> Ming (female) stated that "being in the same class with the same girls really gets on your nerves." Mr. Kim agreed: ". . . having them stay together is really rough on them . . . They tend to get really territorial about their equipment, their materials, their classroom. And I just think seeing each other all day is just not healthy for most of them."

As stated previously, the teachers taught both the male and the female classes. This was done to adhere to state requirements that the programs and curriculum be identical; the administrators felt that that could only be accomplished with the same teacher. When questioned, it was evident that no thought was given to having gender or ethnic role models for each academy.

In fact, I judged that there was no real philosophical reason for having the two gender academies; I came to this conclusion from working on the proposal and trying to ascertain some rationale for the program from administrators. The district saw the funding as a way to get some additional money and to provide a special program that might benefit at-risk students of color. However, there was little or no thought to how one might take advantage of the single-gender nature of the two academies in terms of variation in curriculum and instruction. In fact, administrators stressed the need to have the two academies be as identical as possible.

The administrator of the two academies, Mr. Green, also had no special interest in gender issues. He opined that he applied for the position because it was an opportunity to move into an administrative role in the district and because he viewed it as an opportunity to try to integrate curriculum across the various disciplines. However, Mr. Green admitted in June that such integration had never materialized.

The Amber Heights academies had financial resources for a variety of special field trip activities, which students seemed to enjoy but which were not obviously integrated into the curriculum. For example, one day they canoed on the San Francisco Bay on a naturalist expedition; however, when that occurred, the topic being studied in science did not relate to the experiences on the Bay. On another field trip they saw "The Phantom of the Opera"; again, observations that week did not reveal any discipline connections to the activity.

Mr. Green also had plans for full integration of use of technology in the classes; however, the late start of the academies in January and the further delay in getting the computers he had ordered hindered that intention.

One aspect of the special program that did materialize was the contact among teachers and students and their parents. The extra planning period enabled teachers to spend time to stay in touch with parents and keep them informed of their child's progress. Although I did not interview parents, Mr. Green informed me that this aspect of the program encouraged most parents to enroll their child as much as any other; they felt, accurately, that their child would get special attention. Mr. Green pointed out that he thought at least one student, an African-American female, would have dropped out of school had it not been for the extra attention she received at Amber Heights-Female.

Professional Development

Some attempt was made to inform teachers about issues of gender and how the single-gender setting might be used to foster equity. Before classes began in January, a one-day workshop was conducted by two equity experts whose strength lie in issues of race and class. One of the experts did another one-day workshop during spring break. However, these sessions were not mandatory, and the mathematics teacher did not participate in any of them. There was no indication from class observations or teacher interviews that the teachers gave specific thought to adapting curriculum and instruction to meet the needs of females or males. Teachers had not discussed or considered individually the role curriculum might play in reproducing inequality (Willis, 1996). In fact, teachers made a point of keeping the curriculum (and instruction) the same for both groups of students.

I provided Mr. Green with an extensive bibliography on issues of gender, especially related to single-gender schooling (e.g., American Association of University Women Educational Foundation, 1998; Hollinger & Adamson, 1992a, 1992b). I never saw a special library of materials set up for the teachers, so I do not know if he acted on these suggestions. Teachers were unable to name specific items they had read relative to gender issues in teaching.

Nonmathematical Curriculum and Instruction

Details about the curriculum in each class are beyond the scope of this chapter. Suffice it to say that every effort was made to have an identical curriculum in all classes. However, by observing males and females in separate classes but with the same teacher, one could compare how the two groups reacted to the curriculum and instruction. For example, in English, mandatory reading was the same for the male and the female classes. During one observation, students were discussing the beginning of *Great Expectations*. I observed both the male and female class that day. The questions asked relative to the reading were the same in both classes; however, the discussion differed because the teacher, Ms. Gold, asked questions that pertained to students' own lives.

Ms. Gold asked if the treatment of Pip by his sister reminded them of anything in their own home or a friend's home. The young women stressed how mean Pip's sister was; the discussion strayed into one about battered women. Some students thought Pip's sister might be battered, so she projected her anger onto him. Then they discussed what they thought about Pip, focusing on his manners and that he was smart and brave. In the class of young men, the same questions elicited somewhat different responses. The young men thought Pip's sister was mean and ugly. They felt that Pip was gentle, not raised to fight back. As one African-American male said, "where I come from if you get hit you fight back."

Science provided other examples of nearly identical lessons except for the discussion points brought up by the students. In a discussion of cycles in nature, the young men asked about the big bang and stomach gas (lots of giggles); were these examples of cycles? The young women gave examples of seeds growing to plants, which then produced more seeds, and human reproduction. They discussed the latter with maturity and lack of snickering.

In Spanish class, an excellent example arose of how students of each gender might react differently to the same instructional strategy. At the end of the unit, as review, the teacher, Ms. Perez, used the game "Pictionary." In this game, she divided the class into two groups. Each group sent up to the board one student each; the teacher showed the volunteers a word in Spanish. They then had to draw a picture of it to help their team guess the word. The first team to guess correctly got a point. In the course of a period, the teacher had each student up at the board at least once. However, the male and female classes reacted completely differently to this game format. In the male class (observed first), the young men were very engaged by the game. They acted very competitively, complained if they did not agree with a point decision, and jumped up and down and gave each other high-fives when one team won. In the female class, many of the young women did not pay much attention to the game. Most went to the board when called on reluctantly; very few guessed words for their team. They seemed uninterested in who won and, several times, forgot to record their team's point. There was no reaction when the period ended and one team was declared the winner; they just seemed happy the class was over.

In general, the teachers were observed to use identical curriculum and instructional strategies with the two groups of students. Although Ms. Gold told me she felt she could use less-structured activities with the young women because they were better behaved and more mature, I observed no instances of that type of change in methodology. All of the nonmathematics teachers seemed to make a special effort to engage all of the students in class activities; there was lots of student–teacher interaction and obvious efforts by Ms. Gold, Ms. Kay (science), and Ms. Perez to interact positively with every student at least once each class period. Although no disparities in interaction patterns were discerned in the female classes for these three teachers, the same was not true for the male classes. In those classes, two African-American males were very active, asking lots of questions, volunteering to answer many times, and also getting reprimanded and sent out of the room for misbehavior. One of these two students, Steve, typically interacted with the teachers two to three times as often in one class period as the next most-active student. His behavior in mathematics was very similar.

The Mathematics Classes

The students who attended the Amber Heights gender academies had a wide range of abilities and experiences. The two academies targeted students with high academic potential who had had previous difficulty succeeding academically; thus, many of the students did not identify themselves as high achievers. Several students had taken algebra at the middle school level and were repeating the class. Some students excelled and earned high grades in algebra, whereas others had not passed the first semester of algebra, struggled during the second semester, and had to repeat the course in summer school.

The mathematics teacher, Mr. Kim, volunteered for the program, but, because he was not the initial choice of teacher, he really joined the program to help out when the first teacher changed assignment. In fact, his schedule was the easiest to change within the department. Also, that he was the newest teacher might have stimulated him to try to assist when an urgent need for a teacher arose in March.

Mr. Kim began teaching in the Amber Heights academies with preconceived ideas about the students. He commented about the students: "Well, I had got information about what I was getting, so I kind of knew what to expect. Very low level in the math portion. Discipline problems. Problems outside of the classroom at home. So I—much of what I expected was pretty true."

Perhaps Mr. Kim's expectations affected his curriculum and choice of instructional strategies.

The Curriculum.   The curriculum used was based on a very traditional algebra 1 book, the same being used throughout Amber Heights' regular program, *Merrill Algebra I: Applications and Connections* (Foster, Winters, Gell, Rath, & Gordon, 1995). Mr. Kim occasionally assigned worksheets from *Algebra with Pizzazz!* (Marcy & Marcy, 1984). The content covered in second semester included graphing linear equations; solving systems of equations by graphing, substitution, and linear combination; laws of exponents; simplifying polynomials; scientific notation; operations with polynomials; factoring; and solving equations by factoring. Mr. Kim planned to cover more topics: "I didn't cover everything we were supposed to cover. Coming in, the class was already way, real far behind. . . . What we didn't get to was square roots, rational expressions, and the quadratic formula. So we only covered maybe two-thirds of what we were supposed to."

The content presented to both classes was identical; no curriculum adaptations for either gender were noted.

Instructional Strategies Used.   The instruction in the mathematics classes was primarily teacher directed. Mr. Kim would check students' homework, answer questions from the homework, lecture on new material by presenting examples, and then give 10 minutes for students to work individually or in groups on homework. Most students in both classes socialized during this 10 minutes. The problems demonstrated in class and given as homework were always the easiest available in the book; no graphing calculators or other technology were used during mathematics instruction. New concepts were introduced in an abstract manner, with definitions first, then examples, and most instruction was algorithmic in nature. No discovery lessons were observed nor was any use of real-world examples of algebra noticed. Instruction was identical in both academies; unlike in other disciplines, the content was never related to students' lives, so that there was no opportunity to capitalize on different interests or predilections of students.

Interaction Patterns.   Mr. Kim asked a large number of knowledge-level questions, questions that necessitated only a specific numerical or algebraic answer rather than a process or explanation. No higher-cognitive-level questions were observed in over 30 days of observations. Because he always asked open questions to which students volunteered, rather than calling on specific students, participation in the class was primarily voluntary. Mr. Kim also spent considerable class time, in both classes, disciplining students, often to no avail. At times he seemed to give up trying to reach most of the students; he would lecture to, and interact with, the few who were paying attention and responding and ignore the rest. For example, in one observation, one female African-American student spent the whole period coloring in a coloring book; Mr. Kim never reprimanded her. This student was quite loud and vocal; Mr. Kim seemed happy that she was at least quiet that day.

Consistent with what was found in the other disciplines, in the female mathematics class there was no pattern in which a small number of students dominated the conversation at the expense of the rest of the class. The male class was also consistent with the other disciplines, but in this case a few young men interacted much more with the teacher; two were African American and one was Latino.

Students in both classes who received positive responses from the teacher were more likely to volunteer; however, the converse was not true. The amount of attention received from the teacher, whether positive or negative, seemed most related to how often a student interacted in class.

Classroom Atmosphere. Although the Amber Heights-Male mathematics class conformed to a typical co-educational math class, with a few males dominating the classroom discourse, the Amber Heights-Female class proved to be quite different. Not only did no females dominate the discourse, but the classroom milieu was decidedly cooperative in nature due to students' behavior. The female students shared work and materials readily, they supported their peers through positive reinforcement and encouragement, they were willing to help others, they demonstrated a group identity by speaking as "we," not "I," and they were noncompetitive regarding grades (Burns, 1998).

Student Attitudes About Mathematics. The female students, in contrast to the male, seemed to enjoy learning mathematics in the all-female setting; 10 out of 15 who answered the question stated they enjoyed the single-sex setting. Consistent with other research, the males sex stereotyped mathematics more than the females; 12 males thought math was a subject more for boys than girls; only 1 female expressed that opinion, whereas 13 said math was for both. The female students noticed the more cooperative nature of the mathematics class and seemed to appreciate the all-girl setting. Jennifer stated "I like it better because there are less distractions." Rosa agreed, writing on a survey that "You don't have boys in the classroom distracting you."

CONCLUSIONS

The Amber Heights female and male academies represent to me opportunity squandered. Because of lack of planning, lack of a coherent philosophical mission for the academies, and lack of adequate teacher professional development, an ideal situation in which to experiment with curricular and instructional adaptations that might foster achievement and social development of females and males was wasted. This is perhaps even more true in the case of mathematics than in the other disciplines. By relating content to students' lives, the other teachers were at least able to keep both males and females engaged and motivated; even *Great Expectations* came alive for these diverse students. Although the females had better grades in all subjects than did the males, mathematics represented the only subject in which a majority of the students of both genders failed.

However, despite the obstacles, the females themselves made the mathematics classroom environment different from a typical coeducational setting (Bailey, 1993; Becker, 1981). Behaviors that were *not* observed were perhaps the most telling. The young women did not call each other names, did not compare grades, did not comment about which students were best, were not reluctant to admit confusion or ask questions, and did not compete to finish first (Burns, 1998). They also did not dominate the classroom discourse or make fun of others for being incorrect or not understanding.

These behaviors were not reinforced by the teacher. The young women seemed inclined to cooperative, not competitive, behaviors. This classroom provided an ideal setting in which the teacher could have focused on female learning styles (Belenky et al., 1986, 1997) and equitable treatment. Despite this missed opportunity, the young women still created a unique classroom atmosphere. What more might have been accomplished with a knowledgeable and supportive teacher remains for another study in a setting more conducive to exploring this question. Certainly much more research on single-gender schooling is needed in the United States before policy concerning this important question—single-gender vs. coeducational schooling—can be resolved.

REFERENCES

American Association of University Women Educational Foundation (1998). *Separated by sex: A critical look at single-sex education for girls*. Washington, DC: The Foundation.

Bailey, S. M. (1993). The current status of gender equity research in American schools. *Educational Psychologist, 28*(4), 321–339.

Becker, J. R. (1981). Differential treatment of females and males in mathematics classes. *Journal for Research in Mathematics Education, 12*(1), 40–53.

Belenky, M. F., Clinchy, B. M., Goldberger, N. R., & Tarule, J. M. (1986 and 1997). *Women's Ways of Knowing: The Development of Self, Voice, and Mind*. New York: Basic Books,.

Burns, A. (1998). An examination of the nature of a single-sex mathematics class. Unpublished master's thesis, San Jose State University, San Jose, CA.

Chronicle of Higher Education. (1996). The nation: Students. (September 2).

Davenport, E.C., Davison, M.L., Kuang, H., Ding, S., Kim, S.-K., & Kwak, N. (1998). High school mathematics course-taking by gender and ethnicity. *American Educational Research Journal, 35*(3), 497–514.

Fennema, E. (1996). Mathematics, gender and research. In G. Hanna (Ed.), *Towards Gender Equity in Mathematics Education: An ICMI Study* (pp. 9–26). Dordrecht: Kluwer.

Focus on Learning Problems in Mathematics 18 (Winter, Spring, & Summer 1996).

Forgasz, H. (1995). Girls' attitudes in mixed and single-sex mathematics classrooms. In B. Grevholm and G. Hanna (Eds.), *Gender and mathematics education: an ICMI study* (pp. 167–177). Lund, Sweden: Lund University Press.

Foster, A., Winters, L., Gell, J., Rath, J., & Gordon, B. (1995). *Merrill Algebra 1: Applications and connections*. Lake Forest, IL: Glencoe.

Hollinger, D., & Adamson, R. (Eds.). (1992a). *Single sex schooling: Perspectives from practice and research*. Washington, DC: U.S. Department of Education.

Hollinger, D., and Adamson, R. (Eds.). (1992b). *Single sex schooling: Proponents speak*. Washington, DC: U.S. Department of Education.

Leder, G., & Forgasz, H. (1998). Single-sex groupings for mathematics: An equitable solution? In C. Keitel (Ed.), *Social Justice and Mathematics Education: Gender, class, ethnicity, and the politics of schooling* (pp. 162–179). Berlin: International Organisation of Women and Mathematics Education and Freie Universität Berlin.

Mael, F. A. (1998). Single-sex and coeducational schooling: Relationships to socioemotional and academic development. *Review of Educational Research, 68*(2), 101–129.

Marcy, S., & Marcy, J. (1984). *Algebra with pizzazz: practice exercises for first year algebra*. Palo Alto, CA: Creative Publications, Inc.

Spradley, J.P. (1980). *Participant observation*. New York: Holt, Rinehart and Winston.

Willis, S. (1996). Gender justice and the mathematics curriculum: Four perspectives. In L. H. Parker, L. J. Rennie, & B. J. Fraser (Eds.), *Gender, science and mathematics: Shortening the shadow* (pp. 41–52). Dordrecht: Kluwer.

22

Fables: The Tortoise? The Hare? The Mathematically Underachieving Male?[1]

Leone Burton
The University of Birmingham

I drew arrows in different colours to follow the path of her lover's mathematics, and hers. I used single lines for her, and double lines for his. I used all the colours of the spectrum. Slowly the sad empty room became as bright as a rainbow. It was like drawing two different journeys across a map, her journey and his. It took the rest of my adolescence. And though I joined up many arguments, by the time I'd left school, I could see how different two journeys could be.[2]

For more than 20 years in the United Kingdom, especially since the passing of the Sex Discrimination Act in 1975, and at least 10 more years in the United States, concerns have been expressed about the participation and achievement gap in mathematics studies between females and males. At the outset, the gap that was raising concern was in schools where, despite equal numbers and apparent equal access, considerably more boys than girls were presenting themselves for, and gaining success at, public examinations in mathematics. In the past 5 or so years, growing concern has been publicly expressed about the performance of boys, particularly in the United Kingdom, in relation to the examination taken at 16+, the General Certificate of Secondary Education (GCSE). However, a report in *The Times* in 1992 not only drew attention to the steadily widening gap with girls but pointed out that "male candidates were much more likely to achieve the maximum points score used for university entrance. One in eight boys had the equivalent of three A grades compared with one in 11 girls."

---

[1]A version of this chapter was published in *Gender and Education*, Vol. 11, No. 4, pp. 413–426. Used here by permission from the author.

[2]Woolfe, S. (1996). *Leaning Towards Infinity* (p. 282). Sydney, Australia: Random House.

Furthermore, "studies at Oxford and Cambridge universities suggest that male students widen the lead they acquire at A level" (O'Leary, 1992).

In a recent seminar paper, Jannette Elwood and Chris Comber summed up the current position:

> Media coverage, which has followed the publication of results, especially in the last two years, has made much of this perceived under achievement of boys and has contributed much to the growing backlash against girls' success. One such headline asks: "They're falling behind girls at school. Are boys in terminal decline?" (The Independent, 18th October 1994)... The purpose of the statistical review in this last section has been to show that the patterns of performance, especially at A level, are more complex than is generally assumed and at one of the most important stages of schooling and examining, males are still ahead. (1996, p. 5)

So, little has changed in terms of the grasping of opportunities for a future in the mathematical area. Despite the undoubted evidence overall of the underachievement of some boys at the end of compulsory schooling, a pattern of disparity in favor of males continues as students go forward toward choosing a mathematical career and embarking upon the necessary study at university. Elaine Seymour and Nancy Hewitt reported for the United States on:

> the low ratios of women-to-men among college freshmen indicating an intention to major in science and engineering-five or six men to one woman in engineering, and two or three men to one woman in the sciences... the proportions of women and men who declare an intention to enter mathematics majors are similar... their [women's] persistence rates are significantly lower than those of their male peers... [so] the under-representation of women increases during the undergraduate years. This picture is especially puzzling because there is some evidence that women entering S.M.E. [science, mathematics, engineering] majors have higher average performance scores than their male counterparts. (1997, p. 234)

When it comes to taking up career positions in universities as research mathematicians, Christine Heward and her colleagues have pointed out that "[w]hile women now constitute half of the undergraduate students in higher education in the UK and the representation of members of minority ethnic groups is rising steadily, this is not reflected in the composition of the academic profession, especially its senior echelons" (1995, p. 152).

In this chapter, I report on a recent study that involved the participation of some practicing research mathematicians in the university sector. I wanted to investigate to what degree career differences were reported by female and male mathematicians both from the perspective of their experiences and from the ways in which they understood and practiced their discipline. I was interested in asking how this information compared with pupil experiences in schools and whether I could find evidence of continuities and discontinuities that may be relevant to the issue of achievement and representation in the discipline.

CAREER RESEARCH MATHEMATICIANS

In 1997, I undertook a study of some women and men in career positions as university mathematicians. I wanted to find out how they come to know mathematics, what their feelings are about the nature of knowing mathematics, and what career experiences they have had that might have influenced the positions they take. I approached female mathematicians because one of my interests was in similarities and differences between the sexes, and I knew from previous work (Burton, undated) that female mathematicians were more difficult to find than males. They were invited to be interviewed about their "life history" as mathematicians, especially their feelings about the nature of knowing mathematics for them, and how they come to know. When a female agreed to participate, I asked her to nominate a male in her institution who was equally agreeable to join the study. Although the choice of male, and reasons for choice, were left to the female participant, the majority chose someone at the same level of the hierarchy as themselves. However, I do have three pairs who are marital partners. By this means (snowballing), I gathered 70 participants, 35 women and 35 men. My participants were well spread in terms of their employment status (see Table 22.1).

There were twice as many male as female professors; however, we are looking at very small numbers, and so these can only be observations about the distribution of my participants. The Oxbridge (the universities of Oxford and Cambridge) system is such that I have listed anyone who is not a reader or professor as a lecturer, including some who have senior administrative responsibility and others who are tutorial fellows. I interviewed at 22 institutions, of which 4 were new universities, in England, Scotland, and Ireland, North and South.

I met all except six participants face-to-face in their offices, the remainder being interviewed by telephone. The interviews ran from an hour to the longest, which was $2\frac{1}{2}$ hours. Most were between $1\frac{1}{4}$ and $1\frac{1}{2}$ hours. The telephone interviews were among the shortest, and I attribute that to the lack of personal, nonverbal information to both parties in the conversation. (For a useful discussion on telephone interviewing, see Miller, 1995.) However, it is also fair to say that, overall, the interviews with my female participants were longer than those with the males, and I conjecture that the reverse would have been the case if I had been a male. All the interviews were tape recorded and, additionally, I took notes. Prior to the interview, I sent a list of areas that

TABLE 22.1
Distribution by Status

	Postdoctoral	Lecturer	Senior Lecturer	Reader	Professor	Senior Research Officer	Research Fellow
Females	1	19	7	3	3	1	1
Males	1	17	9	2	6		

I wanted to explore about them and about their coming to know mathematics. I invited them to delete anything that they did not wish to discuss. No one requested any deletion. I also gave them details about the conduct of the study, including my commitment to return to them notes of the interview for agreement/amendment or deletion prior to my undertaking analysis. They were, of course, assured of confidentiality.

In this chapter I report on three conjectures with which I began. First, there is considerable evidence that the career experiences of males and females differ substantially, and so I was interested to see if this was the case for these mathematicians and, if so, in what ways. Second, previous work (Burton, undated) had found that female mathematicians were more likely to be in some areas than in others, so I expected that the distribution across the mathematical specialities would be different for women and men. Third, I believed that the process whereby mathematicians are cultured into their discipline during their period of study would lead to there being no substantial differences between the ways in which females and males understand and practise mathematics, that is, I believed that where I found differences between mathematicians, gender would not be an important variable. I will deal with each of these conjectures in turn. In the final section I relate my findings to the learning of mathematics in schools and point to lessons that I believe must be learned if success in mathematics is to be equally achievable by any pupil who desires, or needs, it. I also address the evidence my study adds to the debate about boys' underachievement.

DO FEMALES AND MALES HAVE DIFFERENT CAREER EXPERIENCES?

Some of my female participants, similarly to those in many other studies, had different career patterns from their male counterparts. Such differences have been extensively reported in the literature (e.g., see Acker & Feuerverger, 1996; Aisenberg & Harrington, 1988; Heward, 1996; Lie & O'Leary, 1990; Marshall, 1984; Morley & Walsh, 1996) and, as Christine Heward has pointed out, "depend[s] on an understanding of 'career'" (1996, p. 11). One frequently explored phenomenon is that of women who "tread water" while in their childbearing years, and this is certainly one difference on which my participants reported. However, additionally they spoke about themselves in distinctive ways, they discussed PhD supervision differently, they reported examples of sexist behavior, and a few spoke of their negative experiences of Oxbridge. I deal with each of these in turn.

Treading Water

None of my male participants experienced the kinds of delays in completing their formal education on which some females reported. Among my participants, in every case such career breaks were to do with marriage and children, whereas a year out between, say, school and university, was seen as an enhancement to education and certainly not as a disadvantage. Four typical examples follow: "I actually went to university 8 years after I left school" (Female pure mathematics Lecturer). "At the end of my undergraduate career, I married and started a family. I had seven years off with the children and then came back to do a PhD" (Female pure mathematics Lecturer).

A third described how she went into teaching straight from graduating. After about 3 years, married, she started a research degree but had to move with her husband when he was posted abroad. Returning 3 years later, with a child, she began again but had to change her area. Again, a posting abroad left her working at her dissertation on her own in a foreign country. She finally submitted it as an MPhil but has maintained her research career despite her lack of a PhD. She said: "It has taken twelve years for me to discover that everyone else doesn't know much more about it than I do" (Female pure mathematics Lecturer).

The fourth went to Oxbridge where she was unsupported and undirected. She dropped out, married, had children, and, while her husband completed his qualifications and began an academic career, she spent 10 years outside mathematics by which time she had lost self-confidence. She reclaimed her academic interests through voluntary work and gaining a language "Ordinary" level GCE after which she applied to start a mathematics degree at the university where her husband was then working. She got her degree and then a PhD: "I do now describe myself as a mathematician but I think for a long time I just said 'I do maths'" (Female Senior Lecturer applied mathematician).

Hearing stories such as these, I felt enormous respect for the ways in which these women persisted, managed complicated lives in a manner that enabled them to continue their studies, and often had to cope with the kinds of social and personal problems and responsibilities from which their male counterparts are frequently protected by their female partners. However, the academic world in which they have chosen to make their careers values only the products of their academic work, neither recognizing nor respecting the contribution that some of these experiences could make to the organization and management of their institutions. Despite starting out on their university lives qualified and motivated equivalently to the males, these females' ambitions now lie in their work and not in expectations of higher status within the academic world. That they were aware of this was demonstrated when they pointed out that, in involving a male colleague at the same level of the hierarchy to join the study as their "pair," they might have to choose someone considerably younger.

Self-Image

Women are frequently described, especially in the gender and mathematics literature, as lacking in confidence. The notion of "confidence" is treated unproblematically (see Clute, 1984), and the idea is now very widespread that females are less confident than males in the mathematics classroom, although it could be that they are just more willing than males to express their lack of certainty. Indeed, so widespread is this assumption of female lack of confidence that one begins to wonder how much of a self-fulfilling prophecy it has become. In schools, confidence is persistently linked to "ability" and achievement, and it is possible that part of learning to be a mathematician is also learning about the kind of behaviors that are deemed appropriate for your sex. Many of my female participants described themselves as lacking in confidence. For example: "I tend to think things I do aren't terribly important which is probably to do with my own lack of confidence" (Female applied mathematics Lecturer). "I am so inclined not to believe myself, I have to be 105% certain that I know something before I believe it" (Female pure mathematics Lecturer).

One woman described by her colleagues as very able and respected said: "Maybe a personal chair would be over-reaching myself" (Female Reader in applied maths).

They were also good at self-labeling and at picking up the labels pinned on them by others: "I don't think I am a very original person" (Female pure mathematics Lecturer). "At 23 or 24 I felt like the thickest PhD student ever. It ceased to matter what I had done. My perception of my work was completely out of kilter. All these men talked. I couldn't talk" (Female pure mathematics Lecturer). "If I am stuck, I try to think if I have been stupid. I have a great tendency to assume that it is me" (Female pure mathematics Lecturer).

However, lest it be imagined that only women spoke in this way: "Mathematics had always been easy but it had never occurred to me that I was good enough to do it" (Male applied mathematics post-doctoral fellow). "Some people can face a problem that is rather ill-defined and we don't know what the answer is and there are others, and I am one of them, who are a bit more uncertain when faced with new challenges" (Male Lecturer in statistics).

One way of expressing your self-image is by describing whether you see yourself as centrally placed in your discipline. If you don't, a way of coping with that is to distance yourself from the behavioral norms that you observe because, once inside, you will be expected to conform to these norms. I asked my participants "Who are the mathematicians?" One of my female participants expressed what was said many times over by females: "I consider myself a mathematician because I lecture and research in mathematics and I suppose that by definition makes me a mathematician. But I have met people whom I consider to be 'real' mathematicians and I am not one of those people" (Female pure mathematics Lecturer).

But there was another variant which was equally widespread:

I suppose I feel that people whose life and soul is entirely within mathematics and they have a high profile on the public front I would consider to be mathematicians. People who are so engrossed in it that they cannot see anything else in life. I don't think it is a particularly admirable state. (Female applied mathematics Senior Lecturer)

And if it isn't an admirable state, then:

I didn't want to be totally obsessed with mathematics. There were too many other things that I enjoyed... there was the maths building which was a really nice environment but you did see people sitting around on their own at blackboards scribbling away. There was an obsessive sense about it. (Female pure mathematics Senior Lecturer)

The culture of the profession, in this case in the USA, may set up personal conflict: "In the States, I worked in an Institute where the work was unsupervised but the atmosphere was highly competitive. I became disillusioned with that, and the sense of self-belief that Americans seem to have but also the fact that everything had to be instantly commercially viable" (Male applied mathematics Lecturer).

Once established, competition operates everywhere. For example, in seminars: There is a particular culture which we are not used to where a seminar is a defence of your result against the audience which interrupts all the time, questions you aggressively, it is highly competitive. I hate that. The seminar is based upon the following structure—here is somebody's results. . . here is why it is wrong, aren't they idiots. Nasty. I can't cope with that. (Female Reader in pure mathematics)

or in the collaborative role: "I think two of us were trying to play the same role and I felt challenged all the time. It was also too competitive and the wrong things were made too important. One of the collaborators was used to a very argumentative style and I hated it" (Female pure mathematics Lecturer).

Male feelings of insecurity with respect to language may lead to cultural constraints on their view of mathematics: "There is a macho view that the verbal is a corruption and a mortal danger. That once you get into words there is an associated lack of rigour" (Female pure Senior Lecturer).

Research Supervision

There is great room for damage as well as advantage within the research supervisory relationship, and it is an area which, in most universities, has not been addressed from the perspective of staff development. For some of my participants, it worked very well indeed, although a few males acknowledged that they were aware that there were colleagues who were less well supervised by the same supervisor. Others suffered. Often, but not always, these were women. "One thing I learnt from my own experience of undergraduate and postgraduate work was the isolating experience of being the only one" (Female pure mathematics Lecturer). "I never got beyond being intimidated by my supervisor and the earlier part of my PhD left me feeling that I wasn't well able to cope and there wasn't much help or support" (Female Senior Lecturer in Statistics).

> I started off with the Head of Department as supervisor. He is a bit intimidating as a person. I couldn't cope with his style. After a while I was adopted by another lecturer so I switched. This was good initially but then I realised that perhaps the second supervisor had a slightly false impression of me and thought that I was needing looking after so we discovered that personality-wise we weren't really suited.. (Female pure mathematics Lecturer)

Not one of my 70 participants had been supervised by a female. However, many of the women were currently supervising, so this is, presumably, a transient phenomenon. However, for one of my male participants: "My supervision was an awful experience because my supervisor was, in my judgment, an emotional bully" (Male applied mathematics Senior Lecturer).

Because so many were reporting unsatisfactory experiences when they were supervisees, I asked if, when they became supervisors, they applied this learning to reflect on how they would supervise. The majority said that they did not. They felt that every student was an individual and must be treated as such. They did not seem to feel that there were things that could be generalized and learned. However, most of the women made statements consistent with one or both of the following: "I do try not to be remote and to be approachable" (Female applied mathematics Lecturer). "I am sure that students can benefit from working on problems together. It is how I learnt. . . As a supervisor, I make myself available, but I think students often find help in other places, from other students" (Female applied mathematics Lecturer).

Many of the women who were supporting students working together explained how they had helped this to happen in their institution. Only at Oxbridge did such staff/student seminars seem to have a long history and those who had experienced them spoke positively of these experiences and their attempts to institutionalize something similar.

Both men and women expressed concerns about the supervisory relationship, often in respect of the practice of supervisors of mathematics research providing supervisees with the problem(s) on which they work for their PhD. This poses a challenge to many prospective supervisors that they find to be very onerous. From the disciplinary perspective, it ensures both continuity and control—practices that can be very different from those that may be found outside of mathematics.

Finally I was told a story of sexual harassment represented in the tip of the iceberg that follows:

> The supervision was good in terms of work but he wanted more than that so there were personal difficulties and I was too young to know what was going on and appreciate that I had to do something about it. So it was difficult and I did have to manage not to be on my own with him. Obviously I was very reliant on him and the working relationship was good but it still makes me feel pretty angry about his behaviour. (Female pure mathematics Senior Lecturer)

The misuse of power, the location of blame and management on the recipient of the behavior, and the expectation that it must be possible to separate the personal from the professional are all present in this story. We see them again in the next section.

Sexist Behavior

> . . . Whilst the head of the group is married to a feminist woman, he is sexist and he couldn't quite believe that a woman could do the kind of stuff that they did. There was a definite prejudice. The second supervisor was very different. Again, pretty sexist but he was keen to have someone working with him so he did give me quite a lot of support. . . I occasionally get in touch, but he never gets in touch with me. (Female Reader in applied mathematics)

"In the first couple of weeks at university, one of my lecturers said 'Now you girls, I want you to be married to maths. I don't want you getting up on top of your wardrobes and saying go away, go away. This is to be a real marriage" (Female pure mathematics Lecturer). "A colleague who was at a conference where someone was discussing my work referred to me as 'she' to which the response was that that work could not have been written by a woman. That happened in the 70s" (Female Reader in pure mathematics).

In looking at applications for a postdoctoral position, a supervisor "made a comment that if it was a choice between someone like me and a man with a family he would give it to the man [and] a younger colleague mentioned to me when I got my PhD when was I going to marry and he asked what else was there for me to do now I had my PhD?" (Female Reader in applied mathematics)

One participant said: "I think there is a body of mathematicians who make the rules up, and I don't understand how they have made them up, therefore they can't be logical so they must just make them up because they are part of the Old Boys' Club" (Female pure mathematics Senior Lecturer).

These quotations describe the ways in which some men construct the mathematics environment so that their female colleagues can be in no doubt about their lack of "proper" fit. There is clearly ambivalence because an able woman can and does contribute, but, although that contribution may be valued, she does not necessarily feel valued unequivocally. Most woman academics can recount experiences of this kind, no matter their seniority or their specialism.

> The inner battle that professional women fight is particularly difficult because its terms are rarely clear. Unpredictably, women will encounter trouble that looks like a knot of circumstance that they seek to pull loose, not recognizing at its center—except possibly in retrospect—a profound conflict concerning their own identities. (Aisenberg & Harrington, 1988, p. 8)

Oxbridge

The culture of mathematics classrooms is not only one that reifies confidence and "ability" but also has a "sink or swim" feel to it. Many of my participants referred to lack of support or nurturing when they were doing their undergraduate or their postgraduate degrees. Whether it is due to the predominance of the role of Oxbridge in the training of future mathematicians or to some imbalance in the distribution of the participants in my study, almost half of my participants had experience of Oxbridge as career mathematicians and/or as learners (see Table 22.2). That this is not an artefact of this study is borne out by Halsey (1992). The teaching and learning style that dominates in Oxbridge, and that clearly suited some, equally failed to meet the needs of others. (I refer to Oxbridge in order to offer my participants some protection.)

TABLE 22.2
Experience of Oxbridge

	Oxbridge Only, Undergraduate	Oxbridge Only, Postgraduate	Oxbridge, Undergraduate and Postgraduate	Graduated elsewhere, Working Oxbridge
Female	6	1	5	1
Male	2	5	5	5

"At Oxbridge I felt that I was being put down all the time and I am still quite angry about it. I could have done so much more with a bit of encouragement" (Female pure mathematics Lecturer).

> I went to Oxbridge but I left after a year and took a year out. I had found that year really hard. I thought the mathematics was beyond me. I think their system is very bad for a certain kind of person. They don't do any nurturing. Your main source of knowledge was the hell of one-to-one tutorials. I used to feel ill every week before seeing my tutor.

A year later, at another university, she

> started really enjoying mathematics. Basic things that I hadn't been able to grasp at Oxbridge I got interested in there. (Female pure mathematics Lecturer)

She went on to complete a master's degree and a PhD. The lack of nurturing was underlined by another female who had gone to Oxbridge as an Exhibitioner and said that "I didn't even find the Library til the third year" (Female Statistics Professor).

ARE FEMALES AND MALES DIFFERENTLY DISTRIBUTED IN THEIR MATHEMATICAL SPECIALITIES?

As the Table 22.3 shows, females and males in my study were well distributed across pure and applied mathematics and statistics. Although these distinctions are neither robust nor prevalent everywhere outside, or even inside, of the United Kingdom, from the perspective of my participants' confidentiality and the small numbers in some specific cells, it seemed more useful to use these three groupings.

My previous work (Burton, undated) led me to expect that I would find more female statisticians and fewer female applied mathematicians. This is not the case among the group that I interviewed, although the pure mathematicians do dominate; I did not choose for specialities or search within particular speciality groups. When a prospective female participant asked me if there were any criteria for choosing a "pair," I said I did not mind as long as I was given information about the grounds for the choice. In no case was I led to feel that the choices caused any problems to the study. However, they were almost always made on level in the hierarchy and frequently on speciality. So a female applied mathematics lecturer was more likely to

TABLE 22.3
Distribution within Mathematics

	Pure Mathematics	Applied Mathematics	Statistics
Females	17	10	8
Males	15	13	7

choose a male-applied mathematics lecturer, and this is one explanation for why the numbers are so close within specialities. However, some women did have difficulties in persuading a male colleague to participate, so it is fair to remark that my males might be less representative of the kinds of men in academic mathematics than my females, not as mathematicians, but as people. In summary, then, females, in my study, were as well distributed as males but, also, were themselves well distributed across pure mathematics (48.5%), applied mathematics (28.6%), and statistics (22.9%).

DO FEMALES AND MALES THINK ABOUT AND PRACTISE MATHEMATICS DIFFERENTLY?

My third conjecture that the sociocultural system that produces mathematicians is far stronger than differences in gender was borne out by my participants. I found, of course, many different ways of "understanding" mathematics, including a small number of mathematicians (12 of the 70) who did not adopt the simple objectivist, positivist stance on the discipline expressed as follows: I think it is there and it is waiting to be discovered.

The existence of wide diversity on the nature of mathematics in a group of 70 mathematicians must lead us to expect that vastly different positions do exist within the discipline on important issues such as its nature, how you work within the discipline, how you come to know something, and how you know when you know. It is clear that this diversity should, but at present does not, affect the wider view on mathematics and especially the view that influences what is done in schools. I will take this up in the conclusion. Where there are patterns, these are more likely to exist within a speciality than across specialities, but even within, say, applied mathematics, I found quite substantial differences in how members of my group of mathematicians understood their discipline. The following quotations give a small sense of this diversity.

I think that math is a creation of our minds that sometimes coincides with reality in a useful way.

There is something too strong in it for mathematics to be considered a cultural artefact.

I realized that the mathematics wasn't out there, you didn't stumble upon it, it is in my head, and that was the biggest shock of my life.

I take a sort of Chomskian view of mathematics. There is some deep structure in it that causes us to do the mathematics we do. It isn't out there in any sense, but it goes against the evidence to say that it is all invented.

Mathematics is a product of people. It does turn out to be extremely useful. However, even utility is a cultural product.

Gender did not feature as relevant to these differences. The range of quotations underlines how heterogeneous are the views of these mathematicians about the nature of mathematics. Despite the assumption widespread in society generally that mathematics is actually mathematic, that "s" at the end of the word is central to the breadth and diversity of positions that these mathematicians are adopting.

CONCLUSION: FABLES AND REALITIES. SCHOOL TO UNIVERSITY? UNDERACHIEVING BOYS?

The impression that I have been given and on which I have reported in this chapter is of two distinct cultures affecting career mathematics, a female and a male. As with all cultural differences, there are individuals who either span both cultures or who lie close to the alternative. However, the overall impression is that their gender affected their careers in important ways that have been addressed in the first section of the chapter. It would appear from my participants that the women's and the men's career paths are certainly not the same as they recounted their own difficulties with the cultural climate—particularly its competitiveness, the use of language, the role of supervision, the privileging of certain kinds of people, and their behaviors. These support the norms that operate in favor of the existing majority and leave the rest stigmatized as unacceptably "other."

> [I]t is time to go beyond simple accusations of a discriminatory climate... it is what the university stands for, and what it rewards and what it ignores, that is at issue. The disadvantage that women encounter is more systemic than it is intentional-though no less problematic for all that. (Acker & Feuerverger, 1996, pp. 417–418)

I believe that the spread of my participants across the mathematical specialities and what I think is best described as their heterogeneity on the nature of mathematics, irrrespective of sex, is both to be expected and a source of strength within the discipline. If mathematics *were* as homogeneous as is sometimes pretended to be, and mathematicians matched that homogeneity, not only would the discipline itself suffer from these constraints but the people within it would be unable, and possibly unwilling, to draw on their differences to influence their work. Of course, some of my participants would deny that their mathematics was a function, in part, of their personal history, seeing it as "objective" and independent of individual influence, but they have colleagues who do not agree with them. So my interviews were a source of great interest, partly because the people I was interviewing were so different, had such varied histories, experienced life in so many different ways. However, here I must introduce a caveat. Although I interviewed equal numbers of men and women, all except one of my participants were white and European. (Some had come to the United Kingdom from the [white] Commonwealth.) Not all, but most, were first-language English speakers. Only by extending the study outside of Europe and outside of the white community would I be in a position to draw stronger conclusions. However, the universality of the mathematics culture is so pervasive and exerts such a hegemony that possibly local culture would be unable to intrude upon mathematical culture. That is a conjecture yet to be tested.

Nonetheless, similarities were also very noticeable. I have used quotes that were representative of the statements of sufficient numbers of participants so that they can be relied on not to be maverick. However, where many fewer men have been quoted, such as in the section on "self-image," this is because there were very few who expressed the kind of self-doubts more frequently heard from the women, and none talked in terms of sexist behavior. My male participants either spoke positively of Oxbridge or, where there was a caveat, this was described in very personal terms. For example: "At school I had been best at lots of things and I was horrified to discover at Oxbridge that I wasn't the brightest mathematician there" (Male pure mathematics Lecturer).

So the fable of the underachieving boy has not yet permeated the lived experiences of the professional mathematician in universities to the degree where a diminution of the masculinist culture is observable. Whether it will, in the future, is an empirical question that it is yet too early to test. Like the hare of the fable, there are small indications that the practices and beliefs of the past, which constitute the pervasive masculinist culture, are at risk of challenge. However, this does not appear to be intruding on the current conviction of many male mathematicians of the rectitude of the positions they adopt with respect to their perceived superiority. Some women are complaining about many of the manifestations of this culture and, indeed, attempting changes, and, like the tortoise, they are making slow and steady progress. Their numbers, however, are still very small. They are more broadly spread across the discipline, but the power is not distributed. To be accepted, some women seem to feel the need to demonstrate the acceptability of those aspects of the culture against which other women react so powerfully. For example, in the content analysis of their published papers that I undertook with a colleague, we have noted that it is more likely to be men who deviate from, or reject, positivist language. (See Burton & Morgan, 2000)

Most distressing is the difference between the richness of mathematics understood by my participants and the narrow, bounded subject encountered at school. One offered a definition of the discipline: "Mathematics is that part of knowledge where structures can be abstracted and axiomatized in a completely systematic way without the recourse to examples" (Male pure mathematics Lecturer).

I would like to draw out the difference between the mathematics of this quotation and the mathematics of the extract that headed this paper, a mathematics that is responsive to the person and can represent or describe very different journeys. The existence of a highly prescriptive mathematics that does not match the discipline experienced by all of those within it should raise questions about who feels included and who is, or feels themself, excluded. In mathematics, the underachieving boy is, in fact, an underachieving person, a person who finds little motivation or interest to pursue mathematics. Numbers entering university mathematics degrees have been falling for some time. Among those who are undertaking mathematical study, males continue to be in the majority, and, among those gaining employment in universities, females are still rare. The further up the hierarchy one goes, the rarer are the females. That they are there at all and in growing numbers demonstrates that being female is not the indicative criterion that is excluding women. That is, women who fail to enter mathematics are not doing so because women's mathematical minds are not quite able to cope. The kinds of descriptions reported upon here are of a culture, not of intellect. Cultures are created by and for people and are changeable by people but only if they want to change them. At the present time, the culture of schooling is in conflict with the disciplinary culture in many different ways. Schools are pushed to demonstrate equal access and opportunity, but the pervasive culture of the discipline is of exclusivity. Schools are expected to teach mathematical content that is narrow and prescriptive and in no way matches what mathematicians describe as their focus. Schools, and universities, choose to teach mathematics in a way that is restrictive, homogeneous, and expert dominated. However, the same people in universities are practicing a mathematics that is rich, heterogeneous, and people created. Finally, many pupils in schools speak of mathematics as boring (see Boaler, 1996; Keys & Cres, 1993). My participants presented a world of excitement, of fun, of challenge, of fascination. Let two of them have the final word: "It is very exciting when you make a connection, put a piece in a jigsaw, see how some ideas that were understood by one group of people were exactly what another group of people needed to make something work" (Female applied mathematics Lecturer). "When I think I know, I feel quite euphoric. So I go out and enjoy the happiness. Without going back and thinking about whether it was right or not, but enjoy the happiness. When I discover something, I just enjoy the feeling" (Male pure mathematics Lecturer).

ACKNOWLEDGMENTS

I thank my participants for the generosity of time and the reviewers of the chapter for their helpful comments.

REFERENCES

Acker, S., & Feuerverger, G. (1996). Doing good and feeling bad: The work of women university teachers, *Cambridge Journal of Education, 26*, 401–422.

Aisenberg, N., & Harrington, M. (1988). *Women of academe: Outsiders in the sacred grove*. Amherst, MA: University of Massachusetts Press.

Boaler, J. (1996). Learning to lose in the mathematics classroom: A critique of traditional schooling practices in the UK. *Qualitative Studies in Education, 9*, 17–33.

Burton, L. (undated). *Directory of women in departments of mathematics, statistics and computer science in universities and polytechnics in the United Kingdom*. London: Thames Polytechnic.

Burton, L., & Morgan, C. (2000). Mathematicians Writing. *Journal for Research in Mathematics Education, 31*, 4, 429–453.

Clute, P. S. (1984). Anxiety, method, and college mathematics achievement. *Journal for Research in Mathematics Education, 2*, 203–220.

Elwood, J., & Comber, C. (1996). *Gender differences in 'A' level examinations: New complexities or old stereotypes?* Seminar paper given at the Associated Examining Board, January 25.

Halsey, A. H. (1992). *Decline of donnish dominion*. Oxford: Clarendon Press.

Heward, C. (1996).Women and careers in higher education: What is the problem? In L. Morley & V. Walsh (Eds.), *Breaking boundaries: Women in higher education*. London: Taylor & Francis.

Heward, C., Taylor, P., & Vickers, R. (1995). What is behind Saturn's Rings?: Methodological problems in the investigation of gender and race in the academic profession. *British Educational Research Journal, 21*, 149–163.

Keys, W., & Cres, F. (1993). *What do students think about school?* Slough: National Foundation for Educational Research.

Lie, S. S., & O'Leary, V. E. (1990). *Storming the tower: Women in the academic world*. London: Kogan Page.

Marshall, J. (1984). *Women managers: Travellers in a male world*. Chichester: John Wiley & Sons.

Miller, C. (1995). In-depth interviewing by telephone: Some practical considerations. *Evaluation and Research in Education, 9*. 29–38.

Morley, L., & Walsh, V. (Eds.). (1996). *Breaking boundaries: Women in higher education*. London: Taylor & Francis.

O'Leary, J. (1992). Boys turn the tables on girls in latest A-level examinations, *The Times*, 10 November.

Seymour, E., & Hewitt, N. M. (1997). *Talking about leaving: Why undergraduates leave the sciences*. Oxford: Westview Press.

23

Girls, Mathematics, and Technology

Nicola Yelland
Queensland University of Technology

This chapter considers the strategies and interactions of young children as they worked on technology-based activities embedded within a mathematics curriculum.[1] The children worked collaboratively in pairs (boy, girl, or boy/girl) on tasks in a curriculum unit that contained both on- and off-computer tasks related to length and space concepts. Data from this study and others (e.g., Yelland, 1994a, 1995a, 1995b) highlighted that the ways in which young children collaborate, and the strategies that they used to solve novel problems were related to the gender composition of the pair and other factors, such as the structure of the task, prior mathematical knowledge, self-efficacy, the role of the teacher or peers, and engagement with the material and ideas. Data are presented here to illustrate the complex nature of performance in computer-based mathematical tasks. They highlight a number of critical teaching and learning issues that should be considered in order to maximize learning opportunities for all children in early mathematical experiences.

GENDER ISSUES IN MATHEMATICS EDUCATION

One of the most enduring problems when considering the performance of students in mathematics has been that, invariably, the established benchmarks of performance are characterized by the "male" performance. This has been eloquently revealed in the work of Gilligan (1982) and Walkerdine (1988). The consequences are far reaching

---

[1] Investigations in Number, Data & Space. Dale Seymour Publications.

because female performances have frequently been described in terms of either their inferiority to males or what they lack in sophistication, rather like the young child in Piaget's theories (Piaget, 1953).

The evidence to support gender differences in mathematical performance has tended to focus on upper primary- and secondary-aged children, and it would seem that opinions amassed over the last two decades have been divided (Leder, 1992). Although some studies reported differences in performance based on gender, these differences have frequently been attributed not only to the mathematical content area but also to the format of questions and the test context. In contrast, evidence of performance and gender differences in mathematics in the early childhood years is scant (Barnes & Horne, 1996) and cannot be used to assist researchers and educators to understand the variations that have been reported in the secondary years of schooling.

Spatial knowledge is central to the research presented here and represents one aspect of mathematics in which male superiority over females has long been accepted as a reality, based on results obtained from various tests. However, the contention that the superior performance of males in this area has been a major factor affecting performance overall in mathematics is not supported by research (Tartre, 1990). A close examination of the literature reveals that the nature of such differences may be more complex than originally thought. For example, as early as 1966, Maccoby stated that, even in the early years, boys were consistently better than girls in spatial tasks. Later, in 1972, Maccoby and Jacklin asserted that spatial knowledge was the main source of gender differences. However, by 1974, they had changed their view to conclude that higher test scores by males were only related to one aspect of spatial knowledge, spatial visualization, with no differences being apparent until adolescence.

Affective aspects of performance have also been important when considering gender differences in mathematics (e.g., Fennema, 1980; Leder, Forgasz, & Solar, 1996). Fennema (1980) concluded that the literature strongly supported the notion that differences in confidence–anxiety level accounted for differences in performance. She maintained that gender differences in performance could be associated with behavior such as anxiety and lack of confidence and that girls often exhibited both in mathematical activity. Affective variables are important because, if girls regard themselves as inferior to boys in mathematics, if they perceive mathematics to be a male-dominated area, it may restrict their participation and performance and ultimately impact on career choices.

GENDER AND COMPUTERS

The introduction of computers in schools has resulted in discussions about their role in teaching and learning, for some time now. Research about gender and computer use is still in its infancy (Hoyles, 1988). However, the use of computers in schools has often been in the context of mathematics and science. To this extent, the use of computers, like mathematics and science, has been viewed as a male-oriented activity except in the case of word processing, which is not only seen as a "soft" option but one that is more attractive to females (Turkle, 1984).

Research that has explored gender as a variable has, in fact, tended to focus on performance in specific tasks and attitudes toward computers and computing. Again, the results have been equivocal.

With respect to attitude differences, Hughes and MacLeod (1986) reported that, when asked if boys would like computers more than girls, more children associated computers with boys. In a study on the effects of computer use on gender differences in attitudes, Siann, MacLeod, Glissov, and Durndell (1990) found substantial differences in attitudes toward computing prior to participation in computer activities. The boys were more confident in their own performance, showed more interest in the area of computing, and were more likely to associate computing with a need for a high level of performance than were the girls, even though Siann et al. reported that "General attitudes to computer use were similarly positive for both sexes" (p. 183). However, after a computer experience (with Logo, for 12 weeks) the gender differences in attitudes to computing diminished, although the girls' anxiety levels relative to the boys' were reported to increase. An interesting finding of this study with 9-year-old children was that in the mixed gender pairs the boys tended to dominate the sessions but that this did not result in significant attitudinal differences between girls who worked with boys and girls who worked with other girls. The authors did note, however, that when girls worked together in pairs they seemed to gain most cognitively.

Siann and MacLeod (1986) previously reported gender differences in a study of children from a low socioeconomic background. They found that "girls on the whole were less interested and motivated than the boys; secondly, the girls were more disposed to turn to and seek help from the boys than the reverse; and finally, although the girls did seek help from the boys, they resented it when the help was given practically (i.e. by pressing the appropriate keys) rather than verbally" (p. 137). It should be noted that the results were reported in a situation in which girls were only paired with boys. It could be that the boys' tendency to dominate the proceedings that was reported in four out of the five pairs, and in the later research (Siann, et al., 1990), contributed in a major way to the results. Yet there is evidence that males are more confident about using computers as a learning device than females (e.g., Ring, 1991).

In terms of performance, Siann and MacLeod (1986) reported that the boys in their study completed the task faster than the girls, but this was not statistically significant. Other researchers (Chadwick, 1986; Gunterman & Tovar, 1987) have not found significant differences in performance based on gender, whereas the work of (Hughes, Brackenridge, Bibby, & Greenhaugh, 1988) reported significant differences in the performances of girls and boys to the detriment of all-girl pairs.

RESEARCH USING LOGO

The research presented here used a programming language called Logo. Logo was designed to engage children in mathematical experiences, in which they could actively construct and explore concepts using a variety of processes. In one aspect of Logo called "turtle graphics" children can direct a two-dimensional screen turtle around the screen. Many Logo studies described performance and programming styles (e.g.,

Hawkins, Homolsky, & Heide, 1984; Noss, 1984) or the cognitive processes deployed in task solution (e.g., Clements & Nastasi, 1985, 1988; Webb, 1982, 1984). Only a limited number of studies considered performance with reference to the gender composition of pairs, small group, or indeed, individuals (e.g., Gunterman & Tovar, 1987; Hoyles & Sutherland, 1989; Hughes et al., 1988; Yelland, 1994a, 1995a).

Hoyles and Sutherland (1989) described differences in the programming styles and the nature of collaboration between boys and girls. However, at the end of a 3-year study they reported no gender differences in related styles of structured programming. They indicated that a girl was "more likely to share her problem with her partner, her representation of the problem, and her ideas for problem solving" (p. 171) with her partner. At the same time they warned of the dangers of coming to quick and superficial conclusions about supposed gender differences on the basis of short-term results and the use of slogans such as "Girls do not plan and boys do not collaborate in their computer work or boys are better than girls in programming" (p. 177). Their work reinforced the notion that task design and context and developments over time were important elements when describing performance.

In a series of studies, Yelland (1993, 1994a, 1995b) reported that, when children worked, in gender pairs, on computer-based tasks, girl pairs made more moves and took more time to complete a maze task than either boy or boy/girl pairs. In contrast, in tasks with a focus on accuracy, girl pairs performed much better than boy pairs. The results of the studies revealed that performance was moderated by factors such as the task structure, the style of interaction in pairs, and personality characteristics that affected the way in which the problem was solved. Results indicated that performance could also be differentiated according to different levels of operation to task solution that were the result of a number of features, such as comprehension of the task requirements, the selection of appropriate strategies for solution, and the application of selected executive processes. The use of such processes ensured a more effective level of task solution that reflected a greater level of sophistication in the application of problem-solving skills. The studies highlighted qualitatively different levels of performance, ranging from naive to knowledgeable, distinguished according to the types of processes that were deployed in the problem-solving context, and the influence and application of prior knowledge relevant to task solution. The data also indicated that performances were differentiated on the basis of gender only when performance was considered in terms of specific criteria and related to certain types of tasks. Experience in the domain and varying task design and presentation resulted in the disappearance of differences. Differences in styles of collaboration varied according to gender with specific tasks in a new domain. Girl pairs frequently sought more information from each other and used verbal strategies to work through their problem solving. In contrast, boy and boy/girl pairs tended to make more independent moves, that is, moves made without consulting their partner, and when they did the converse it frequently centered on disagreements rather than clarification of ideas and strategies. In an interesting development in another study (Yelland, 1994b), the order of tasks was reversed (i.e., accuracy tasks were presented prior to efficiency based tasks) and no differences were found in the performance of the gender pairs on any parameters.

These results, together with findings from the literature, highlighted the notion that, although there may be differences in performance based on gender, they need to be viewed with task design and context, clearly articulated. The present study sought to add to knowledge about the strategies and interactions of young children as they worked on computer-based tasks in gender pairs. Specifically, it sought to address gender issues in performance that would be important both from a theoretical standpoint and also with respect to the practical aspects of organization and use of computers in schools. It also considered performance over time and in a range of activities that were complemented by off-computer tasks and sharing of solutions. In this way it provides rich data that build on the findings of existing research.

THE STUDY

This research sought to examine and describe the ways in which young children collaborated when presented with novel problems, in a technology-based context. The activities were based on a version of Logo called Geo-Logo[2] embedded within a mathematics curriculum designed to enable the children to investigate mathematical ideas actively. Because the studies focused on the strategies and interactions of pairs of children, the Vygotskian perspective of learning based in the social context of the situation was important. Vygotsky (1978) contended that "All the higher functions originate as actual relations between human individuals" (p. 57). Additionally, his work highlighted the crucial role that speech takes in mediating learning.

The Subjects

The children in the study were from three intact Year 3 classes in a state primary school. Their ages ranged from 7 years, 3 months to 8 years, 4 months, with the average age being 7 years, 9 months. The children were allocated to one of three types of pairs: boy, girl, or boy/girl, based on the teachers' advice about pairing children who were of approximately similar ability in terms of literacy and numeracy skills. None of the children had used Logo prior to the study, and all children had access to a computer in the classroom, which they mainly used for educational games and word processing. Thirty pairs of children were included in the data analysis so that there were 10 of each gender type. The children were withdrawn from their classroom to participate in the study. When they worked on the computer-based tasks both the computer screen and the interactions of the pair were recorded on videotape. The data source was rich because it was possible to simultaneously view the (children's) computer screen and their interactions while they were engaged with particular aspects of a task. In this way it was possible to make detailed analyses of their strategies and interactions with reference to specific aspects of the task that they were working on. Each pair was videotaped during all tasks, and transcripts were made after viewing the tapes.

---

[2]Copyright D. H. Clements, 1994.

Tasks

The analyses will focus on two different tasks. The first, Get the Toys, was a maze activity in which the turtle had to be directed to pick up a toy. Although pairs of children could select different routes to achieve the goal, the activity had a defined outcome and restrictions in terms of the amount and type of commands that could be used. The second task was an open-ended project in which the children were required to draw a picture of their choice.

Get the Toys.   There were three levels in this maze activity. Level 1 was used as a demonstration for the whole group, and level 2 was used for familiarization for each pair before they all attempted to solve level 3. When the turtle reached a toy it was transported to a storage area at the bottom of the screen, and the children were instructed to return the turtle to the elevator in the center of the screen. The activity contained only 90-degree turns, and no other input number was accepted. The children were instructed that they had to take the turtle to the toy and get back to the elevator without running out of energy. They were told that every command they gave the turtle would use up energy, so they would have to be very careful about how many moves they made. A meter on the top of the screen indicated how much energy was being consumed with each command.

In order to select the most efficient route to the toy, children had to coordinate a number of elements. They had to consider distance and the number of turns because each command entered used up the turtle's energy. Thus, the shortest distance to the toy was not always the one that used the fewest commands if it contained a lot of turns. At level 3 of Get the Toys there were three potential routes to the toy (as shown in Fig. 23.1).

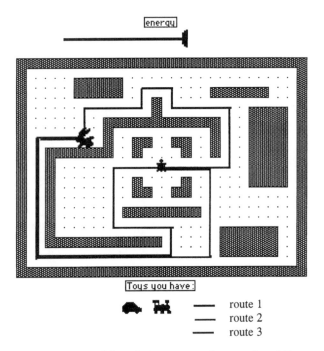

FIG. 23.1. Possible solutions to get the toys (level 3).

The first path (route 1) was "over the top" and although, as previously stated, this appears to be the shortest in terms of distance, it uses more energy because of the number of turns. The second (route 2) was the most efficient in terms of the number of moves, and the third (route 3) could also be used without running out of energy. Additionally, a combination of the routes was also possible as long as the total number of moves did not exceed 31.

FINDINGS

Get the Toys

Table 23.1 shows the number of pairs of each gender type who completed the task, or did not, if the turtle ran out of energy.

The table reveals that the girls were more successful at completing the task requirements than either of the other two gender groupings. A Fisher Exact Probability Test revealed that the only significant difference in performance was between the girl and boy pairs ($p < 0.10$). Stevens (1992) suggested that acceptance of this level of probability in a small sample is reasonable because it affords the opportunity to improve the power of the test. This is an interesting finding and would warrant further investigation with a larger sample of children over time and a range of tasks.

The data indicated that the sources of the differences in performance were complex. They are discussed next in order to elucidate some general trends in problem solving, supported by vignettes from the transcriptions of the videotaped performances.

Choice of Route. First, and most obvious, it was evident that the choice of route had a major impact on success in the task. All the boy pairs took route 1, whereas two boy/girl pairs and one girl pair took a combination of routes 3 and 1, and one boy/girl pair and two girl pairs took route 3. The remaining girl pairs chose route 2, the optimal route for efficiency. An important observation here was that the girl pairs and the boy/girl pairs spent more time articulating which route should be followed. Every girl pair discussed some general features about the hardware, such as the location of the keys that they needed and then talked about the direction of turns (this is my left and my right) and how they would complete the task, before they typed in any moves.

TABLE 23.1
Performance of Gender Pairs in Get the Toys

Groups	Finished	Did not Finish
Girls ($n = 10$)	8	2
Boys ($n = 10$)	4	6
Boy/girl ($n = 10$)	5	5

For example, one girl pair only typed in rt 90 after agreeing on the route by calculating the number of moves it would require:

g1:   Where are the keys that we need?. . . . . . .
g2:   There is the r and the t. . . . and this long one is space . . .
g1:   So we can go across and then down and then across again, up and right and to the bunny . . . 8 moves here and then 5.

Several boy/girl pairs used the same strategy as the girl pairs and talked about the "best way to go." They counted the number of distance moves and turns before deciding which way they should go. Other boy/girl pairs varied in their approach to the start of the task. In some pairs one member immediately took control, made the first move, and then let their partner have a turn. In others, one of the children said "let's go this way" and directed the turtle to follow route 1 by making all the moves, only letting the partner gain control of the keys when they realized they were in trouble, that is, the energy was getting low as indicated by the message that appeared on the computer screen. This style of interaction was not determined by the gender of the child in the pair. In fact, the most interesting observation about the mixed-gender pairs was that they did not seem to follow any predictable pattern of behavior based on gender. In contrast, the girl pairs discussed moves more frequently, and it seemed as if they were not concerned about who actually pressed the keys to effect the move. In contrast, the boy pairs mainly regulated their moves by alternate turn taking.

The boy pairs also moved physically so that they were positioned to type the first move. There was more body contact and raised voices for appeals such as "wait, wait, wait" from the boy pairs. Furthermore, there was no evidence of shared planning regarding the most efficient route. This was despite the fact that some boys obviously differed in opinion about the route to be followed.

After one such incident between two boys, the one without access to the keys said:

b2:   Wait! wait! wait! Count the moves . . . (as the turtle moves) See!! I told you.
         (b1 kept going and typed in fd 20 and fd 10 as b2 said:)
b2:   Right 70
         (Then b1 pushed b2 away so he could not reach the keys.)
b2:   No, no, no, fd 70

The rest of the interaction was characterized by each boy shouting out numbers, with each of them trying to grab each other's hands off the keys.

It should be noted here that, even when route 1 was chosen, as long as the most efficient moves were made in order to reach the toy, there was just enough energy to complete the task and return to the elevator in 31 moves. A combination of route 1 with 2 or 3 was also possible as long as all moves were combined and reduced to the minimum. However, many pairs of children who went on this route ran out of energy because they did not combine moves. The most efficient route in terms of energy (route 2) allowed the children some leeway in terms of optimum moves. They could complete the task with 11 moves to spare, which meant that not every move had to be combined.

Developing Strategies for Problem Solving. The data revealed that the girl pairs who selected the optimal route were also adept in determining the number for the distance that needed to be traveled and, when necessary, could combine moves effectively. They spent time at the start of the task discussing which route should be taken and used the dots on the grid to calculate the exact number needed.

One girl pair also used other effective strategies to meet the task requirements. For example, they figured out that they could just duplicate the moves that had been made in order to get back to their starting position. They were also very effective in using the scaffolding inherent to the task (i.e., the placement of the dots as a guide for distance) and reflected on their situation at every stage of the activity. For example:

g2: OK how much should I put in then for this bit?
g1: (counting the dots) Well this is 4 dots . . . 40, so we need to go fd 40. I will tell you what to press . . . That is it! (g2 typed fd 40.)
   (and later:)
g1: Right, now we have to go forward, how much do you think . . . let's count, you do it G2 counted the dots with her fingers.
g2: It's 1,2,3,4,5,6,7,8,9–90 . . . type in forward 90 (g1 did this.)
g2: Now go rt 90 again
g1: OK (typed rt 90.)
g2: Now this is a big bit! . . . it's 100 because it's more turtle to there! (pointed)
g1: That's not far enough there are more dots.
g2: Well 100 is the biggest, let's try that!

In mixed-gender pairs it was generally observed that the child who had possession of they keyboard made the decision about the command entered, and control of the keyboard was flexible. In one incident, a boy assumed his turn, he said: "I think that 50 will do me" while the girl just watched with no expression, until he indicated that he was going to enter 50 again. She then said: "No it is 60" and, at the same time, she assumed typing as he relinquished his position with no comment. Subsequent moves indicated that they had silently agreed to adopt a strategy of alternate turns for the course of the activity, even though it was apparent from the video that the girl often hesitated and turned to her partner, as if she wanted to ask or receive advice regarding a move.

However, there were also instances in mixed-gender pairs when one member was not sure what to do and sought out the opinion of the partner. As one girl typed in rt 90 her partner seemed confused with the direction of the turtle. He sat next to her, aligning his body in an attempt to determine which direction to turn. She completed the move and said:

g: Great . . look how much energy we have left as she moved away to let him have his go.
b: Which way?
g: Left

He typed left 70. However, she then notified him that this would not work, as only 90 could be used for turns. With this knowledge he deleted 70 and replaced it with 90 and then proceeded to count the dots for the next move, "taking" her turn. He did this independently, without consulting her, typed fd 60, and moved aside for her. They then took alternate turns at the keyboard to direct the turtle to the toy:

g: We need to save some energy (She examined the code). Look here we went fd 40 and then 30 and we should have done 70 . (The boy replied:)
b: Great idea!
g: What now?
b: We go back this way

He outlined the reverse of route 1 with his index finger and, as he did this, the girl nodded in agreement. On the way back they combined moves to save energy on the basis of the girl's suggestion, and the boy generally took on the role of counting the dots whether he was using the keys or not, while he offered praise such as:

b: Good one . . . we got more energy (as she made the moves).

The boy pairs' lack of collaboration was not only apparent on the first move but also by the speed with which they made each move. If one partner disagreed with a move, he would attempt to gain physical control of the keyboard. Verbal reasoning did not appear to be a strategy for consideration, although shouting out a possible move in a loud voice was. In one pair the following scenario was recorded:

b2: 80, 80
b1: No 70
      (b2 typed rt 90 while they argued and b2 still had the keyboard. He counted the dots and typed forward 80.)
b1: That's too far. I told you!
      (b2 typed bk 10 and then deleted it and typed bk 60, and when that did not work for him he deleted it again and entered fd 70, which seemed to be OK for them both. B1 gained control of the keyboard by pushing his partner aside.)
b1: 80
b2: 70
      (b1 typed rt 90 and immediately typed fd 70 – which was his partner's suggestion, although not acknowledged in any way. He typed rt 90 and then paused to count 20, 30, 40, 50. He stopped and counted again "10, 20, 30. . . ." There was more elbowing as b2 took over:)
b1: We're going good!
      (Much of the same type of interaction followed whereby they shouted out numbers that were either ignored by the typist or used without comment. At the toy b1 declared:)
b1: We've won it . . . now we are in trouble (as he pointed to the low energy level).

Using Higher-Order Thinking Skills.   Another possible explanation for the success of the girl pairs could be related to the fact that, in addition to considering each move carefully and asking their partner's opinion, the girl pairs in this study also spent time evaluating each move as it was made and were very effective in determining the success, or otherwise, of the move in terms of reaching the goal. By doing this they often negated the need to go back past their previous move to correct an error, which was a more complex process.

The girl pairs, in this study were effective in determining, combining, and reflecting on their actions. In one interaction, as a pair was trying to position the turtle, the following occurred:

g2: That is good! Now we have to make it go like this. (she positioned her body to demonstrate)

g1: Well that is right (pointed) and it's 90 (meaning forward; G2 typed in the move.)

g2: Now it's your turn to type.

g1: It's not far enough but I'll do it and then we can go more. (They watch as the turtle moved and when it stopped they said:)

g1: It's not far enough! We can do another 100.. no maybe less... how about 80 do you think?

g2: Yes let's try 80. (She typed it in and it was just right.)

g1: Yes that is it!

g2: Now right 90 again. (She made the move while g1 nodded in silent agreement.) Shall we do 100 again up here?

g1: OK. I can type it in.

g2: Yes it is your turn. Type fd space 100. (g1 did this and they watched.)

g1: It's not far enough... we need more.. how many do you think.. it is two dots, um we should do 20 (She typed it in and g2 looked on.)

g2: Yes!!! We are nearly there!... Now we go right 90. (g1 typed it in.)

g2: And now go forward 1, 2, 3, 4, 5–50 and we will be there. (g1 followed the advice.)

g1: We've got it!

g1: We have to go back now. (g1 looked at the commands on the screen. She pointed to the previous move and said.) We need to go Back 50 like here and then it will be a left turn. (g2 looked surprised but did not comment and typed in bk 50. When it worked she typed in lt 90.)

g1: We have to go down so put right 90. (She deleted lt 90 and typed rt 90.)

g2: OK we want to go forwards.

This extract was quite typical of the type of interaction between pairs of girls in the study. They revealed evidence of planning and the interaction that was very much reciprocal in nature with the majority of moves being agreed upon.

However, boy pairs did not demonstrate behavior that indicated that they were evaluating each move as it was made nor did they show that they were thinking ahead and planning. In fact, the boys seemed reluctant to make changes once they had typed in the move. They also made more moves that would have benefited from being combined, which was the main reason that more of them ran out of energy than the girl pairs. This meant that, when they got into problems with energy levels, it was much more difficult to go back and isolate where they went wrong in order to rectify the problem. Consequently, they got themselves deeper into trouble. They demonstrated evidence of their frustration with each other, both verbally and physically, more frequently than either the girl or boy/girl pairs. At one stage near the end of the game two boys engaged in calling each other names like "idiot!" and "dork!" when they realized that they would not make it back. They had no suggestions about how they could regain energy and eventually, as things got more heated, one of them suddenly got up and left his partner to make the final move that would ensure there was no energy left, and thus the game was over.

Affective Interactions. A major feature of the boys' interactions consisted of insulting each other. Although instances of praise were highest between the girls, they were also apparent in some boy/girl pairs. Girls, and boys in boy/girl pairs, would often make positive comments such as "Cool . . . that is what we want" or "Good one! Nice going. I told you it would work!" However, such comments were rare among boys working together, even when a move was made that was useful.

Projects

In the final task, the children were asked to plan and complete a project using the knowledge that they had gained throughout the unit. The planning was first done with a pencil and paper, as a diagram, which contained details of the main features of the picture to be drawn. In most plans this included the use of number labels to indicate the relative size of each element in the picture. When the diagram was completed the researcher talked with the pairs about the plan and how they proposed to start and finish the drawing when on the computer. Each pair then went on the computer to start entering the commands. The ways in which they set out to complete the task requirements were, once again, very different. However, the "final products" all reflected a thorough understanding of the features of Geo Logo and the mathematical concepts inherent to the unit of work.

The Castle. In the example shown in Fig. 23.2, the girl pair meticulously planned their project on paper in great detail, with a lot of discussion about what elements should be included and where they should be located. At every stage consensus was reached before they moved on to consider a new part. All the elements were brought together to create the castle scene. The girls used a form of modular programming that was methodical and systematic and reflected the same care and consensus making that they had exhibited in the early planning of the project. They had already decided what they wanted when they planned their drawing off the computer and once on the computer did not vary their plans at all. Further, although they were typing in the commands, they spontaneously shared the dual roles of keyboard entry and orator of the instructions. Discussions between the girls were always driven by questions about the project, and agreement was usually reached after an initial suggestion. The girls continued the practice, only evident in the girl pairs in this study, of evaluating their progress as they went. In the case of this particular pair their initial planning was so precise that they did not have to modify their plans at all, as previously stated, yet their interactions were characterized by constant references to how well they were going and how it was matching their initial drawing.

The Raft. In contrast the boy pairs did not seem to want to spend a considerable amount of time in the planning phase (off the computer). They produced drawings, as required, but in every boy pair it was apparent that they were longing to get on

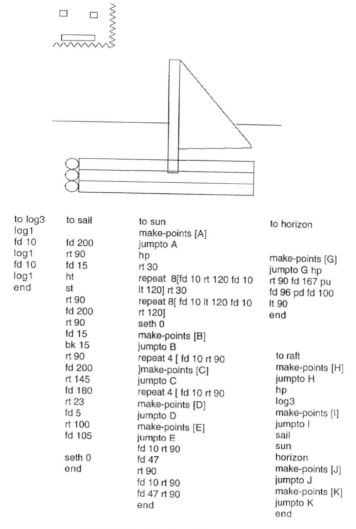

to log3	to sail	to sun	to horizon
log1		make-points [A]	
fd 10	fd 200	jumpto A	
log1	rt 90	hp	make-points [G]
fd 10	fd 15	rt 30	jumpto G hp
log1	ht	repeat 8[fd 10 rt 120 fd 10	rt 90 fd 167 pu
end	st	lt 120] rt 30	fd 96 pd fd 100
	rt 90	repeat 8[fd 10 lt 120 fd 10	lt 90
	fd 200	rt 120]	end
	rt 90	seth 0	
	fd 15	make-points [B]	
	bk 15	jumpto B	
	rt 90	repeat 4 [fd 10 rt 90	to raft
	fd 200	]make-points [C]	make-points [H]
	rt 145	jumpto C	jumpto H
	fd 180	repeat 4 [fd 10 rt 90	hp
	rt 23	make-points [D]	log3
	fd 5	jumpto D	make-points [I]
	rt 100	make-points [E]	jumpto I
	fd 105	jumpto E	sail
		fd 10 rt 90	sun
	seth 0	fd 47	horizon
	end	rt 90	make-points [J]
		fd 10 rt 90	jumpto J
		fd 47 rt 90	make-points [K]
		end	jumpto K
			end

FIG. 23.2.   Year 3 project: The raft.

the computer to enter the commands to complete the picture. In the example shown, (Fig. 23.3) prior to the raft being produced, both boys were clearly eager to rush through the paper-and-pencil phase so they could get on the computer. When on the computer, they produced their product "on the fly" using the same strategy of combining modules to create the whole scene, as the girl pairs had done, but they often made changes that depended on a variety of circumstances. For example, if something was too difficult to draw on the computer, they changed it. They originally planned, and drew, a circular sun. However, when they wanted to use their circle procedure to draw a sun they could not think how to make the circle bigger. So the boy who had control of the keyboard started a "zig zag" line, which obviously looked reasonable to him, because he informed his partner that ". . . it would do" instead of the planned (large) circular sun. The other modifications to the original plan happened when they made a "mistake,"

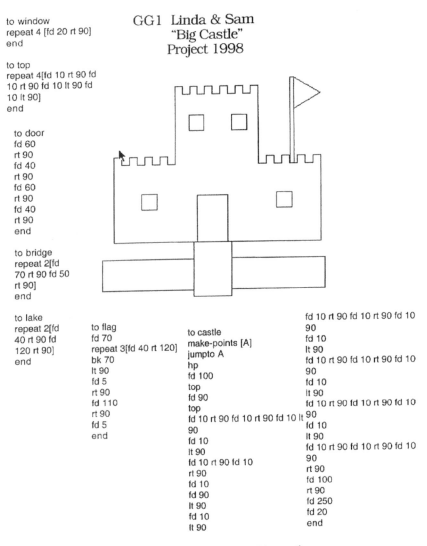

to window
repeat 4 [fd 20 rt 90]
end

to top
repeat 4[fd 10 rt 90 fd
10 rt 90 fd 10 lt 90 fd
10 lt 90]
end

to door
fd 60
rt 90
fd 40
rt 90
fd 60
rt 90
fd 40
rt 90
end

to bridge
repeat 2[fd
70 rt 90 fd 50
rt 90]
end

to lake
repeat 2[fd
40 rt 90 fd
120 rt 90]
end

GG1 Linda & Sam
"Big Castle"
Project 1998

to flag
fd 70
repeat 3[fd 40 rt 120]
bk 70
lt 90
fd 5
rt 90
fd 110
rt 90
fd 5
end

to castle
make-points [A]
jumpto A
hp
fd 100
top
fd 90
top
fd 10 rt 90 fd 10 rt 90 fd 10 lt 90
90
fd 10
lt 90
fd 10 rt 90 fd 10
rt 90
fd 10
fd 90
lt 90
fd 10
lt 90

fd 10 rt 90 fd 10 rt 90 fd 10
90
fd 10
lt 90
fd 10 rt 90 fd 10 rt 90 fd 10
90
fd 10
lt 90
fd 10 rt 90 fd 10 rt 90 fd 10
90
fd 10
lt 90
fd 10 rt 90 fd 10 rt 90 fd 10
90
rt 90
fd 100
rt 90
fd 250
fd 20
end

FIG. 23.3.   Year 3 project: Big castle.

which they incorporated into the computer-based drawing. For example, when they originally planned the raft, the mast was located coming out of the top "log" of the raft. When they started drawing it from the top of the middle log and referred back to their plan, they decided that they would keep it there even though they could have used the slide facility to move it.

Creating Projects with Geo-Logo.   In considering the projects it is neither possible, nor appropriate, to make statements that identify the best or worse, more sophisticated or less, unless we specifically want uniform planning or drawings that reflect specific criteria. The effort and enthusiasm associated with the projects were fairly consistent for all pairs. Furthermore, what would be the point of setting such goals? All the projects by the children reflected an interpretation of the task requirements that is equally valid, but more than that they are testament to the ability of young children to use mathematical concepts in new and vital ways. The task structure facilitated this. It was open ended and gave the children plenty of scope in deciding what the final product should consist of and the means of achieving this.

CONCLUSIONS

Leder (1990) suggested that a goal of research in mathematics education should be to gain information that will promote equity. In order to achieve this we should cease evaluating and comparing female performances in relation to male criteria and become more specific in our work, as Tartre (1990) recommended. Hoyles and Sutherland (1989) also advocated that it is superficial to make conclusions about supposed gender differences on the basis of short-term performance because it can often be misleading. This has been evident in research that has tended to devalue the performance of girls working together (e.g., Hughes et al., 1998) and even suggested that girls need boys in order to perform certain tasks effectively. Data have been presented here to illustrate that this phenomenon may be an artefact of context and task. They revealed that, when young children work with novel problems in computer-based tasks, girl pairs can have greater success than boys, in tasks that involve efficiency and spatial reasoning. In this study it was apparent that girl pairs demonstrated the willingness to use strategies that were effective in the solution of novel problems, characterized by:

- Planning, prior to starting the computer task, and continuing through to task completion.
- Reflecting on the effectiveness of their strategies as they proceeded.
- Predicting the effectiveness of moves that they had made and were about to make.
- Monitoring their progress after each move that they directed the turtle to make.
- Engaging in dialogue about the nature of task solution.
- Working cooperatively to solve the problem.
- Interpreting and understanding the task requirements.

Such behaviors have been characterized by Davidson and Sternberg (1985) as being metastrategic and, as such, represent a higher level of thinking and reasoning than the application of basic strategies such as trial and error.

In a more open-ended task it was also evident that girl pairs did show evidence of different types of collaborations than boy pairs in terms of planning and completion of task requirements. It has been argued here that such comparisons may be redundant because all children met the task requirements while demonstrating commitment and enthusiasm for the task as well as the application of mathematical concepts and skills.

It is now evident that technology is permeating all aspects of our lives and will have a significant impact on the lives of children, both in and out of school contexts. It is hoped that the expertise with technology will not be considered in terms of "hard mastery"

(Turkle, 1984), which may advantage males and put them in a position where they are considered masters of these powerful cultural artefacts. All children irrespective of gender, class, and ethnicity need to be provided with learning opportunities that incorporate the use of various artefacts of technology for effective learning. It is the responsibility of educators to ensure that all children have opportunities to work with a variety of computer applications in both individual and group situations and that every child can access technology so that he or she is able to develop mathematical skills in new and exciting ways.

REFERENCES

Barnes, M., & Horne, M. (1996). Gender and mathematics. In B. Atweh, K. Owens, & P. Sullivan (Eds.), *Research in mathematics education in Australasia*, 1992–1995 (pp. 51–88). Sydney: PRODEC.

Chadwick, C. (1986). *Differential group composition in problem solving using Logo*. Unpublished masters thesis, Concordia University, Montreal.

Clements, D. H., & Nastasi, B. K. (1985). Effects of computer environments on social-emotional development: Logo and computer-assisted instruction. *Logo in the Schools, 2*(2/3), 11–31.

Clements, D. H., & Nastasi, B. L. (1988). Social cognitive interactions in educational computer environments. *American Educational Research Journal, 25*(1), 87–106.

Davidson, J. E., & Sternberg, R. J. (1985). Competence and performance in intellectual development. In E. Niemark, R. Delisi, & J. L. Newman (Eds.), *Moderators of competence* (pp. 43–76). Hillsdale, NJ: Lawrence Erlbaum Associates.

Fennema, E. (1980). Sex related differences in mathematics achievement. In L. H. Fox, L. Brody, & D. Tobin (Eds.), *Women and the mathematical mystique* (pp. 76–93). Baltimore: John Hopkins University Press.

Gilligan, C. (1982). *In a different voice*. Cambridge, MA: Harvard University Press.

Gunterman, E., & Tovar, M. (1987). Collaborative problem solving with Logo: Effects of group size and group composition. *Journal of Educational Computing Research, 3*(3), 313–334.

Hawkins, J., Homolsky, M., & Heide, P. (1984). *Paired problem solving in a computer context*. New York: Bank Street College of Education.

Hoyles, C. (1988). Review of the literature. In C. Hoyles (Ed.), *Girls and computers* (pp. 5–12). London: Institute of Education, University of London.

Hoyles, C., & Sutherland, R. (1989). *Logo mathematics in the classroom*. London: Routledge, Kegan, Paul.

Hughes, M., Brackenridge, A., Bibby, A., & Greenhaugh, P. (1988). Girls, boys and turtles: Gender effects with young children learning with Logo. In C. Hoyles (Ed.), *Girls and computers: General issues and case studies of Logo in the mathematics classroom* (pp. 31–39). London: Institute of Education, University of London.

Hughes, M., & MacLeod, M. (1986). Using Logo with very young children. In R. W. Lawler, M. D. Boulay, M. Hughes, & H. MacLeod (Eds.), *Cognition and computers* (pp. 179–219). Chichester: Ellis Harwood.

Leder, G. (1990). Gender differences in mathematics. In E. Fennema & G. Leder (Eds.), *Mathematics and gender* (pp. 10–26). New York: Teachers College Press.

Leder, G. (1992). Mathematics and gender: Changing perspectives. In D. A. Grouws (Ed.), *Handbook of research on mathematics teaching and learning* (pp. 597–622). New York: Macmillan.

Leder, G., Forgasz, H. J., & Solar, C. (1996). Research and intervention programs in mathematics education: A gendered issue. In A. J. Bishop, K. Clements, C. Keitel, J. Kilpatrick, & C. Laborde (Eds.), *International handbook of mathematics education (Part 2)* (pp. 945–988). Dordrecht: Kluwer.

Maccoby. E. M., & Jacklin, C. N. (1974). *The psychology of sex differences*. Stanford: Stanford University Press.

Noss, R. (1984). *Creating a mathematical environment through programming: A study of young children learning Logo*. London: University of London Institute of Education.

Piaget, J. (1953). The origins of intellect in the child. London: Routledge, Kegan, Paul.

Ring, G. (1991). Student reactions to courseware: Gender differences. *British Journal of Educational Technology, 22*(3), 210–215.

Siann, G., & MacLeod, M. (1986). Computers and children of primary school age: Issues and questions. *British Journal of Educational Technology, 2*(17), 13–144.

Siann, G., MacLeod, H., Glissov, P., & Durndell, A. (1990). The effects of computer use on gender differences in attitudes to computers. *Computers in Education, 14*(2), 183–191.

Stevens, J. (1992). *Applied multivariate statistics for the social sciences.* Hillsdale, NJ: Lawrence Erlbaum Associates.

Tartre, L. A. (1990). Spatial skills, gender and mathematics. In E. Fennema & G. Leder (Eds.), *Mathematics and gender* (pp. 27–59). New York: Teachers College Press.

Turkle, S. (1984). *The second self: Computers and the human spirit.* New York: Simon & Schuster.

Vygotsky, L. S. (1978). *Mind in society: The development of higher psychological processes.* Cambridge, MA: Harvard University Press.

Walkerdine, V. (1988). *The mastery of reason: Cognitive development and the production of rationality.* London: Routledge.

Webb, N. (1982). Student interaction and learning in small groups. *Review of Educational Research, 52*(3), 421–445.

Webb, N. (1984). Microcomputer learning in small groups: Cognitive requirements and group processes. *Journal of Educational Psychology, 76*(6), 1078–1089.

Yelland, N. J. (1993) Learning with Logo: An analysis of strategies and interactions. *Journal of Educational Computing Research, 9*(4), 465–486.

Yelland, N. J. (1994a). A case study of six children learning with Logo. *Gender and Education, 6*(1), 19–33.

Yelland, N. J. (1994b) The strategies and interactions of young children in Logo tasks. *Journal of Computer Assisted Learning, 10*(1), 33–49.

Yelland, N. J. (1995a). Collaboration and learning with Logo: Does gender make a difference? In J. Schnase & E. Cunnius (Eds.), *Computer Support for Collaborative Learning* (pp 397–401). Rahaw, NJ: Lawrence Erlbaum Associates.

Yelland, N. J. (1995b). Logo experiences for young children: Describing performance, problem-solving and the social context of learning. *Early Child Development and Care, 109*, 61–74.

24

Creating a Connected, Equitable Mathematics Classroom: Facilitating Gender Equity

Joanne E. Goodell
Cleveland State University

Lesley H. Parker
Curtin University of Technology

As far back as the early 1900s, studies of educational achievement in the United States were reporting sex differences in achievement in mathematics, in males' favor (Leder, 1992). As noted by Weiner (1994), however, serious research into gender equity in mathematics was not undertaken until the late 1960s, when gender was problematized as an educational issue. Three decades of such research have now resulted in a large body of literature on differential patterns of participation and performance for males and females in mathematics. Comprehensive international comparative studies, meta-analyses, and reviews of this research (e.g., Husen, 1967; Leder, 1992; Linn & Hyde, 1989; Locan, Ford, & Greenwood, 1996; Robitaille & Garden, 1989) reveal that, over time, sex differences in both performance and participation in mathematics have declined to the point where they are now quite small, although males still outnumber females in higher-level mathematics courses in many countries (Dekkers, deLaeter, & Malone, 1991; Hanna, 1996; National Science Board, 1996). Further, as found by Leder (1992), the differences vary across time and content, as well as country, and appear to be explained by a complex interaction of multiple factors rather than by one specific factor.

The last three decades have also seen considerable effort put in to reforms and initiatives aimed at ameliorating gender differences in mathematics. Some previous research (Leder, Forgasz, & Solar, 1996) classified interventions by program type, time, school calendar, targeted population, education focus, strategy, elements of success, creation of new organizations, and teaching and learning strategies and, from this analysis, developed characteristics of exemplary programs and common elements emerging. In this chapter, we focus further on reforms in mathematics education, presenting an analysis that is framed in terms of three broad categories of reform: student related, teacher related, and curriculum related. From a synthesis of recent literature on such reforms, we distill the essential features of an ideal gender-equitable classroom, which we term the Connected, Equitable Mathematics Classroom (CEMC).

In the first section, we examine student-related research that has investigated attitudes, affective variables, and differing ways of knowing, and we critique student-focused initiatives. We then focus on classroom practices, drawing together the literature pertaining to pedagogical and assessment practices, including the well documented differential treatment of males and females in mathematics classrooms and the influence of various modes of assessment. In this section, we discuss recent reforms that have been influenced by National Council of Teachers of Mathematics (NCTM; 1989, 1991, 1995) documents. Finally, we explore literature that attributes gender differences to traditional mathematics curricula and that takes the view that such curricula are disconnected from the real world and are highly masculinist in orientation.

From this analysis, we develop a definition of what, given contemporary evidence from practice and research, appears to be the ideal CEMC. Following this definition, we explore, through data from a large-scale reform project in the United States, the possibilities and limitations of implementation of the CEMC by mathematics teachers. We conclude the chapter with a short discussion of the implications of this work for reformers and equity advocates.

STUDENT-RELATED RESEARCH

Past Explanations and Reforms

Student-related explanations for gender differences in achievement are premised frequently on the view that there is some kind of deficit on the part of females (Willis, 1996). In mathematics, the deficit is seen to reside in personal characteristics influenced by a range of affective variables and spatial abilities. The latter have received a great deal of research attention over a long period, with some studies (e.g., Fennema & Tartre, 1985) demonstrating that poor spatial skills affect females more than males in terms of their overall achievement. Others (e.g., Linn & Hyde, 1989), in considering this evidence, point to the importance of previous experience in relation to spatial abilities and question the validity of the linking of these abilities definitively to sex differences in mathematics achievement.

In relation to affective variables, a recent meta-analysis of 100 studies of gender differences in mathematics performance and 70 studies of gender differences in mathematics-related attitudes and affect (Frost, Hyde, & Fennema, 1994) found small nonsignificant effect sizes favoring males for mathematics performance and small nonsignificant effect sizes for females' negative attitudes and affect. Although differences in affect were small, females were consistently shown to have more negative attitudes toward mathematics than males, and the problem of females' low participation was attributed to consistently negative mathematics-related attitudes and affect. Myer and

Koehler (1990) and Leder (1992) showed that studies about confidence and related variables most often found that low confidence was related to poor performance and was also predictive of gender differences in participation. In a similar vein, Sowder (1998) concluded that mathematics achievement differences could be attributed to girls' preference to use less-risky strategies. Others (e.g., Eccles, 1989) have shown that females see mathematics as less useful to and appropriate to their futures than do males, and fear-of-success studies have shown that females, more so than males, perceive mathematics to be incongruent with their sex role and, as a result, fear success in mathematics (Leder, 1992).

Building on research such as that outlined previously, interventions focused on students have generally endeavored to change females' attitudes and to involve more females in mathematics. Some have tried to make mathematics seem more enjoyable through after-school clubs and other extracurricular activities (Campbell, 1995; Stage, Kreinberg, Eccles, & Becker, 1985), whereas others have tried to increase the confidence and skills of prospective students so that they will have the "courage" to continue with mathematics (Clewell, Anderson, & Thorpe, 1992). Some have also tried to raise females' awareness of the importance of mathematics and, to this end, have involved their community and parents. These programs included conferences such as the "Expanding your Horizons in Math and Science" (Stage et al., 1985) program, visits to nontraditional work places or visits from speakers who are employed in nontraditional jobs, use of media campaigns such as one in Western Australia to convince girls that "maths multiplies your choices" (Willis, 1995), and the use of videotapes highlighting the variety of careers that require mathematical competence (Fennema, Wolleat, Pedro, & Becker, 1981).

As noted by Campbell (1995), such programs appear to have been aimed at changing the girls and little else. The problems of poor participation and performance in mathematics were located with the females, and solutions focused on changing females in various ways. Furthermore, few of these projects re-examined students after they had left the special program and entered traditional mathematics courses. In fact, evidence would suggest (Campbell, 1995) that females typically do not continue with those advanced-level courses to which they gain entry through involvement in special programs. In a similar vein, Willis (1995) pointed out that these types of interventions "may actually reinforce the notion that 'the problems' of girls and mathematics lie outside the classroom and school" (p. 188). Further, she and others contend that encouraging girls to continue to participate in traditionally structured mathematics classes may even lead to negative or destructive experiences.

Focus on Students: The Way Forward?

Research that challenges the deficit view of females provided a basis for approaches to mathematics education that focus not on changing the females themselves but more on the teaching/learning interaction. As shown by Becker's (1995) review of early research on intellectual and moral development, all too often, theories were based on work with only male subjects (e.g., Kohlberg, 1969; Perry, 1970). Becker noted that theories built from research on all-male samples tended to portray women as inferior or lacking. The deficit view of female development was also challenged by Gilligan (1982), when she postulated that women's moral development follows a path different from that of men's and is based on different values.

Belenky, Clinchy, Goldberger, and Tarule (1986) continued the work of Gilligan, Perry, and Kohlberg. They interviewed 135 women, exploring their experiences and problems as learners. They described how these women viewed reality and drew conclusions about truth, knowledge, and authority. Belenky et al. identified five distinct "Ways of Knowing," a progression that was different from those proposed by Perry (1970) and Kohlberg (1969).

Building further on this work, Baxter Magolda (1992) worked with both males and females in her longitudinal study of college-age students' intellectual development. She identified four patterns in students' intellectual development, which she also termed "Ways of Knowing." Within each of the first three patterns, she found two strands that, to some extent, were sex linked. Rather than suggesting how to change the students, she suggested both a number of ways of teaching responsively to students who have different ways of knowing and several teaching strategies that can build connection with students. This pointed to reforms that focused more on pedagogy and on teaching/learning strategies, known as "Connected Teaching" (discussed further in the next section).

Pierce (1998) also reached similar conclusions following her review of the work of a number of researchers investigating differences in the way males and females learn. She concluded that "[w]e need . . . an expanded, more inclusive model of critical thinking that includes relational as well as rational orientations, affective as well as analytical intelligence, subjective as well as objective knowledge (p. 63)." She suggested that educators must vary their methods to account for differences in learning styles, thus making it possible for all students to feel valued, secure and comfortable enough to learn. Similarly, Noddings (1998), from a feminist perspective, questioned why girls were not more interested in mathematics as they progressed through school and suggested that, in order to broaden the appeal of traditional mathematics to women, teaching strategies be changed to involve contexts in which girls are more interested.

PEDAGOGY, ASSESSMENT, AND TEACHER-RELATED RESEARCH

This second major category of explanations and initiatives is concerned with what teachers do in their classrooms. Within this category are explanations that attribute gender differences in performance and participation to pedagogical or assessment practices that are discriminatory toward females.

Explanations

Pedagogy

A large body of research on the pedagogy of mathematics has identified a number of teacher-related factors that are associated with female underparticipation and underachievement in mathematics. Broadly speaking, these relate to the following four areas.

Teacher Attention.   Two important reviews of research about teachers' treatment of students in the classroom (Kelly, 1988; Koehler, 1990) have shown that, especially in science, mathematics, and social studies classrooms, males receive

- More attention from teachers in terms of help, interactions, and informal contacts, particularly from male teachers.
- A higher proportion of criticism for their behavior.
- A greater amount of work-related criticism.

Although the cumulative effects of these patterns are not known because the link between teacher attention and student achievement has not been properly researched, overall, it appears that females may be disadvantaged by the structure and climate of many mathematics classrooms, even those that are taught by caring and highly competent professionals, as they were in Leder's (1989) study. Hyde and Jaffe (1998), for example, have attributed achievement differences to teachers' tendency to treat girls and boys differently and to "allow" boys to use invented algorithms more than girls.

Teacher Expectations and Attributions.   Studies of teachers' attributions and beliefs about male and female students (Fennema, Peterson, Carpenter, & Lubinski, 1990) revealed that teachers tend to overestimate boys' potential in mathematics and underestimate that of girls and that, in addition, teachers tended to attribute causation of boys' successes and failures to ability and girls' successes and failures to effort. Fennema (1990) and Secada (1992) also studied teacher expectations about how well females are likely to achieve in mathematics, a factor that was once thought to affect achievement significantly. They concluded that the link between teacher expectations and student success was not clearly established, particularly as it relates to gender. They suggested that the whole area of teacher expectations and how these were related to teacher behavior and student achievement was complex and under-researched.

Friendly Learning Environments.   Eccles (1989) reviewed a number of studies that examined classrooms in which there were fewer sex differences in mathematics and more positive attitudes by females toward mathematics. She found that these classrooms were characterized by cooperative activities, hands-on learning, extensive career guidance, and low levels of social competition. She concluded that activities that are not conducive to females' learning and motivation in mathematics include competitive activities, public drill and practice, social comparison, and domination of classroom interaction by a few students.

Stereotypes, Language, and Discrimination.   Researchers (e.g., Solar, 1995) have shown that any form of discrimination in mathematics classrooms, such as sexist humor, can have detrimental effects on females' attitudes toward mathematics. Others (e.g., Koehler, 1990) demonstrated that the use of stereotypes that portray mathematics as a male domain and the consistent use of male names and masculine contexts in test questions reinforce an image of mathematics as a male domain.

Assessment

Format. Significant effects associated with the format of assessment have been found by numerous researchers, including Murphy (1982), Bolger and Kellaghan (1990), Linn and Kessel (1995), and Parker and Tims (Goodell) (1995). Although the magnitude of these differences varied across ethnic and racial groups in the different subjects, the pattern of discrepancies remained essentially the same, with males performing better than females on multiple-choice items compared to other items (e.g., extended response) and on external examinations compared to school-based assessments.

Context. Context effects have been established, with males and females performing differently on questions set in different types of contexts (Anand & Ross, 1987; Doolittle & Cleary, 1987; Harding, 1979). The 1981/1982 round of the Assessment of Performance Unit (APU) surveys in the United Kingdom concluded that it would be possible to engineer or remove group differences by manipulating the format or context of items used (Gipps & Murphy, 1994). Generally, research about context seems clear on at least one point: students will do better on a task if it is set in a context with which they can connect or to which they can relate because of their previous life experiences.

Content. Content effects occur when groups of students perform differently on different content set in the same format. A number of researchers (Doolittle & Cleary, 1987; Kim, Plake, Wise, & Novak, 1990) found evidence to support the claim that females perform better than males on routine and computational tasks. Evidence to support the claim that males are better at geometry tasks, problem solving, and questions involving speed, ratio, and proportional reasoning has been provided (Doolittle & Cleary, 1987; Edwards, 1984; Kim et al., 1990; Lane, Wang, & Magone, 1995). In contrast, however, Becker (1990) found, in a study of performance on the SAT in the United States, that algebra items were easier for males. Furthermore, the Assessment of Performance Unit (APU) surveys (1975–1989) demonstrated that males performed better than females on measurement and ratio problems (Gipps & Murphy, 1994).

Reforms Focused on Changing Teaching and Assessment Practices

As intimated earlier, feminist teachers trying to connect women with mathematics have long advocated the use of cooperative groups, the teaching of problem solving, and the use of inquiry methods that employ real-world contexts (Morrow & Morrow, 1995). Similarly, the use of a variety of forms of assessment, to allow for different ways of knowing and of demonstrating knowledge, has also been supported and practiced by feminist educators for some time. Increasingly, over recent years, the use of such strategies has also been advocated by mainstream educators. Many recent reforms have emphasized the importance of changing teaching practices as a way to improve equity outcomes, for example, through the NCTM (1989, 1991, 1995) teaching, curriculum, and assessment standards for school mathematics. These practices have been linked to the concept of "connected teaching," which, as indicated earlier, emphasizes the connections among teacher, student, and the curriculum.

According to Belenky et al. (1986), connected teaching involves both the teacher and the student in the learning process. Teachers are called on to make transparent their modes of thinking, illuminating right and wrong turns in a path toward finding a solution to a problem. The teacher's role is analogous to that of a midwife, helping students to bring out their own ideas. This is in contrast to the typical role of a teacher as more like a banker who deposits knowledge in the learner's head. Becker (1995) applied the Belenky et al. (1986) framework to her research in mathematics education. She outlined how the ideas of connected teaching apply to teaching and learning mathematics, making the point that mathematics needs to be taught as a process, not a universal truth. In connected teaching, teacher and student engage in the process of thinking and discovering mathematics together. Alternate methods of solution are encouraged and groups are created in which members can nurture each other's thoughts to maturity. Diversity of approach is welcomed in discussions. Truth or knowledge is constructed through consensus, not through conflict. Connected teachers are portrayed as trusting their students' thinking and encouraging them to expand upon it. These pedagogical techniques shift the focus of learning from the teacher as provider of knowledge to the student as participant in constructing his or her own knowledge. Jacobs and Becker (1997) outlined four principles that facilitate connected teaching: using students' own experiences, writing, cooperative learning, and developing a community of learners.

Baxter Magolda (1992) stressed the need for connection with students as a way of helping students confirm their way of knowing. She advocated the use of three principles that should ensure that confirmation is balanced by some contradiction, which aids in "adjusting one's way of knowing to account for new experience" (Baxter Magolda, 1992, p. 270). The principles are "validating the students as knower, situating learning in the students' own experience, and defining learning as jointly constructing meaning" (Baxter Magolda, 1992, p. 270). Baxter Magolda also discussed the importance of linking all three concepts. She pointed out that validating the student as knower is largely achieved through developing student voice. By situating the learning in students' own experience, a link is provided so that students can connect with the subject as well as the teacher. The process of jointly constructing meaning in the classroom is marked by attachment and connection and will not occur in a classroom characterized by separation or abstraction.

As discussed in detail by Goodell (1998), several recent studies have shown the effectiveness of connected teaching—Boaler (1997) in two U.K. schools; Silver, Smith, and Nelson (1995) in the QUASAR project in the United States; Knapp, Shields, and Turnbull (1995) in a study of 140 teachers in high-poverty U.S. elementary classrooms; Rogers (1990, 1995) in relation to college-level mathematics; and Tate (1995) in a study of one teacher's success in providing meaning to mathematics through students' exploration of a problem of immediate relevance to them (viz., the close proximity of their school to a number of liquor stores).

CURRICULUM-RELATED RESEARCH

Explanations and Reforms

The most recent body of literature that attempts to explain inequities in mathematics education—low participation and performance of women—centers around the whole curriculum, especially in terms of its design, content, and structure. Oakes (1990), for example, has shown that tracking or streaming to provide a differentiated curriculum for specific groups of students can lead to long-term inequities linked to race and gender. In terms of content, Lustig (1989) challenged the current mainstream curricula in mathematics on the grounds that they do not challenge patriarchy or recognize the importance of female-centered study. She cited Jan Harding's work in the United Kingdom as an example of an inclusive curriculum because it was designed within a social context and included issues relevant to women's lives. Overall, a gender-inclusive curriculum, which encompasses all aspects of the curriculum, not just gender-inclusive teaching strategies, is what is advocated. Damarin (1995), for example, believed that ". . . instructional research and practice related to the improvement of the mathematical conditions of women must at every level honor the individual gendered student . . . [and that at least] some of the answers to 'the problem of women and mathematics' will be found at the level of the global structure of the curriculum" (Damarin, 1995, p. 249).

Frankenstein (1995) was concerned also with the human and social aspects of the mathematics curriculum and with using mathematics to challenge the existing social order. She suggested reforming the curriculum to include problems based on economic, political, and social issues. She argued that the mainstream mathematics curriculum did not empower students, but instead produced a mathematically disempowered person, who avoided numbers, and was not able to deal with the statistical data that are integral to economic, political, and social issues.

Of more concern to Burton (1995) was the repositioning of mathematics in a cultural context. She suggested that the perceived maleness of mathematics is an artifact of its production and its producers. She argued for a social constructivist approach to the curriculum, focused on the interaction among individuals, society, and the knowledge from which knowledge mathematical meaning is created. She advocated challenging the masculine basis from which mathematics has been constructed as a solution to the problem of making the mathematics curriculum more equitable.

As described in detail elsewhere (Goodell, 1998), innovative projects in different parts of the world, representing a variety of curriculum and education systems, provided the kind of gender-inclusive curriculum depicted previously. These include those described by Willis (1989), Barnes (1991, 1993), and Frid and Winnett (1996) in Australia; Frankenstein (1995), Lappan, Fey, Fitzgerald, Friel, and Phillips (1997), and National Center for Research in Mathematical Sciences Education & Freudenthal

Institute (1997) in the United States; and Lange (1987) and Verhage (1990) in The Netherlands.

DEFINING THE CEMC

To this point in the chapter, research into explanations for and reforms to overcome gender differences in mathematics have been presented under three broad categories related to students, teachers, and the curriculum. Each of these three areas of research provided insights into factors that can facilitate the creation of a Connected, Equitable Mathematics Classroom (CEMC). From this analysis and synthesis, the following 12 characteristics of the CEMC have been distilled:

1. *All students have access to academically challenging mathematics curricula.* This is a fundamental principle of equitable education in any area of the curriculum. In relation to the CEMC, as shown by the research reviewed here, if females choose not to enroll in more advanced mathematics courses, then the reasons they have so chosen should be sought and dealt with appropriately. If females are denied access through restrictive scheduling or tracking practices, these should be eliminated.

2. *Students are encouraged to develop confidence in their mathematics ability and positive attitudes toward mathematics.* Characteristics of students that influence motivation, such as lack of self-confidence and not seeing the importance of mathematics, need to be recognized and dealt with. Teachers should help less-confident students become more assured by leading these students toward experiencing success through academic progress.

3. *Basic skills are developed that will enable students to be mathematically literate in the world outside school.* Again, as shown by this research, lack of necessary skills can be a hindrance to students' academic progress; so, for a classroom to become equitable, these factors should be addressed. Teachers in a CEMC emphasize the importance of mathematics to students and the significance of mathematics to their futures and provide activities that are enjoyable and that enhance the basic skills and confidence of all students.

4. *The learning environment encourages students to develop their own voice and construct their own knowledge.* In a CEMC, teachers are no longer merely knowledge providers, standing at the front of the classroom writing notes on the board for students to copy into their notebooks. The teacher must be the facilitator, helping students to construct their own knowledge by establishing learning situations in which this is possible, for example, through the use of hands-on manipulatives, whole-class discussion, group discussion, or presentation of project work. When introducing a new concept, teachers should always strive to find an activity that leads students to discover the concept first, before presenting theory, rules, and examples. A personal characteristic of students that must be developed in the CEMC is student "voice"—the ability to speak up for oneself. This characteristic is essential in enabling students "to evaluate knowledge critically, assess biased perspectives, analyze complex situations and make wise choices" (Baxter Magolda, 1992, p. 391). In the CEMC, students

negotiate meaning within a learning community. Student voice is developed through students actively engaging with mathematics problems that are set in a context that is relevant to students' lived experiences. An atmosphere of trust and mutual respect naturally facilitates students developing their voice. Teachers need to be seen as partners in the learning process, not dominant authority figures to facilitate the development of students' voice. As noted by Pierce (1998), instructional practices and processes are sources of meta-learning, and when leaders share power and responsibility they send a powerful message of equality to participants.

5. *Teachers have high expectations for all of their students.* An aspect of teacher behavior that is crucial to the CEMC is the setting of high standards and having high expectations for all students. In their portrait of a connected teacher, Belenky et al. (1986) described the teacher as "rigorous." Standards of mathematical accuracy and precision should not be sacrificed in the name of "connection."

6. *Teachers connect mathematics with the real world through the use of appropriate contexts for problems, the provision of career information, and a focus on social issues that affect all students (such as ecology and health).* A CEMC must also provide students with access to information about careers involving mathematics so that they are more able to make informed choices about their future directions. A CEMC will demonstrate the importance of mathematics to students and allow them to see where mathematics fits into society and their futures. Introductory activities should be set in real-world contexts that have personal meaning to students. Teachers connect mathematics to students through the use of real-world problems set in personally meaningful contexts. Baxter Magolda's (1992) three principles ". . . validating the students as knower, situating learning in the students' own experience, and defining learning as jointly constructing meaning" (p. 270) are emphasized.

7. *Teachers are able to recognize and act on inequities in their classroom.* Research presented in this chapter has shown that certain pedagogical and assessment techniques have the capacity to introduce bias in the classroom. Teachers must be informed of these possibilities and be empowered to act accordingly. Monitoring the frequency and direction of classroom interactions through audio- or videotaping can be helpful. For teachers, the importance of self-analysis, knowledge of recent research, and application of the findings of that research cannot be overemphasized.

8. *Teachers use a variety of teaching and assessment practices.* Different learning styles are taken into account through the use of a variety of teaching strategies so that all students are taught at least some of the time in a style that suits them. Teachers should use a range of pedagogical techniques in order to cater to a variety of students' learning styles. Individual teachers can ensure that their own assessments are varied in context and format, assess what is taught and valued in the curriculum, and allow all students to demonstrate their knowledge. In terms of the context of assessment problems, the teacher should ensure that contexts that appeal to the interests and background experiences of all students are utilized wherever possible.

9. *The curriculum is designed within a social and cultural context, challenges stereotypes, and values the contributions of women and minority groups.* The curriculum must value the culture and background experiences of all learners through the use of nonstereotypical language in texts and through using contexts for teaching and

assessment that are inclusive of the range of contemporary students' experiences. The contributions of women and minorities to the dominant culture, as well as to minority cultures, must also be included. Mathematics teachers should not consider that history is the sole province of the social studies teacher. It is also appropriate to discuss with students why the contributions of women and minorities have been ignored by the mainstream for so long.

10. *The curriculum includes real-world problems set in a variety of contexts that value and take into account the range of student backgrounds and experiences.* Through the application of mathematics to real-world problems, students should be able to use their mathematical skills to understand world problems such as poverty, health, ecology, population, and the distribution of wealth. A critical aspect of being able to apply mathematics to real-world problems is being able to understand the mathematics that is presented every day in the media. Newspapers and television news reports should be an everyday feature of mathematics classrooms. Having students keep a mathematics journal, in which they are able to write about their daily "mathematical experiences," will help teachers identify appropriate contexts for their students.

11. *The curriculum includes a focus on issues of social justice and world problems that enables students to challenge social conditions. There may be some element of social action by students.* A further aspect of the connected equitable mathematics curriculum is that it should include some form of social action. Tate (1995) cited the example of students in an urban area in the United States researching and acting on the illegal liquor outlets near their school. This example emphasized the importance of the teacher having the freedom to adapt the curriculum sufficiently to allow her students to solve mathematical problems that have personal meaning and relevance to them.

12. *The curriculum explicitly states equity goals.* The curriculum should explicitly empower students to challenge the hegemony of traditional study. The stated objectives of the curriculum should make clear to all students that the learning opportunities are designed within a social and cultural context that includes the experiences of all students, connects mathematics to the real world, and includes aspects of social action. The CEMC must be premised on a "can-do," outcomes-focused curriculum, facilitating, to paraphrase Frankenstein (1995), a mathematically empowered person, who does not avoid numbers, and is able to deal, as an effective citizen, with the kinds of data that are fundamental to a grasp of economic, social, and political issues.

IMPLEMENTING EQUITY AND REFORM IN MATHEMATICS CLASSROOMS

In this section, we examine the facilitators and barriers teachers encountered when trying to implement the CEMC in the context of a large reform project in the United States. Although not focused only on gender equity, this project did espouse many of the features of the CEMC throughout its professional development programs, and equity for all students was a major theme for the whole project.

The project studied was one of several funded by the National Science Foundation as a Statewide Systemic Initiative (SSI) designed to improve science and mathematics education for all students. The SSI described here began by offering professional development opportunities to middle-school mathematics teachers. Content-based, 6-week summer institutes, based on the philosophy of the successful University of Washington Physics by Inquiry courses and on the NCTM standards, had a strong equity focus and incorporated many of the goals of the CEMC (Goodell, 1998). Teachers in these institutes also had to commit to participate in six follow-up workshop days spaced throughout the next academic year, where the focus was on appropriate pedagogy and assessment. A detailed description of the links between the CEMC and the SSI can be found in Goodell (1998).

A comprehensive evaluation of this SSI was begun in 1995 and continued through 1999. Data presented here were obtained in 1995 and 1996. Both quantitative and qualitative data were collected as part of this evaluation. A statewide random sample of approximately 100 schools in which one or more teachers of Grades 6 through 9 had participated in the SSI's professional development activities (henceforth referred to as SSI teachers) was chosen. In 1995, over 100 SSI and 400 non-SSI mathematics teachers in the random-sample schools completed questionnaires. In 1995 and 1996, case studies were conducted at seven carefully chosen sites. At these 3-day site visits, one seventh- or eighth-grade SSI mathematics teacher was observed and interviewed, and students in both the SSI and a matched non-SSI teachers' classes completed questionnaires and achievement tests. Additionally, three students (reflecting a range of abilities) in one of the SSI teacher's classes were interviewed. The focus of the teacher interviews was on facilitators and barriers teachers encountered in implementing the suggested reforms. The focus of the student interviews was on what typically happened in their mathematics classes. A cross-site analysis of these data (Goodell, 1998) pointed to a number of elements that were necessary to facilitate the implementation of the features of the CEMC in classrooms. Barriers faced by these teachers were also identified. Using a framework suggested by Rossman (1993), these elements are grouped in four dimensions as outlined in the following:

Technical: Professional knowledge and skills and the means by which they are acquired.

Cultural: Values, beliefs and school norms—both in terms of a general ethos and competing perspectives that contend with each other.

Political: Matters of authority, power, and influence, including the negotiation and resolution of conflicts.

Moral: Matters of justice and fairness.

The Technical Dimension

The first element in the Technical dimension was the professional development experience itself. Many of the teachers interviewed thought that their experience with the SSI enabled them to change not only their teaching practices but also the way they thought about teaching. The perception of most teachers was that, without that experience, it would have been unlikely that they would have made any changes. This finding supported the findings of the quantitative analysis showing that participation in the SSI was associated with teachers adopting reformed teaching practices consistent with the CEMC.

A second element identified in both quantitative and qualitative data concerned the availability of appropriate classroom teaching resources to support new approaches. Some teachers did not need extensive or specialized resources to connect mathematics to the students' experiences and helped students to develop a voice through constructing their own knowledge. For other teachers, however, lack of such resources made the process of even attempting inquiry lessons a rather arduous task, resulting in a somewhat disjointed approach.

The third element identified was the availability of a network of colleagues, with whom teachers could discuss their successes and failures, both face-to-face in follow-up sessions and through an electronic network provided by the SSI. This was especially valuable for those teachers who were the only ones in their school involved with the SSI. Being able to communicate with a similarly placed colleague who had succeeded with CEMC strategies appeared to be one of the most critical elements in encouraging teachers to take risks in their classrooms with new types of teaching methods.

The fourth element concerned the equity content of the professional development experience. This was illustrated most clearly by one particular teacher who mentioned during her interview that she and others in her institute were annoyed at the way the equity components of the professional development were handled—they felt that there was too much emphasis on issues that were of no concern in the rural areas (where most of them taught) and not enough on gender-equity issues. However, other evidence provided in the interviews suggested that the gender-equity components of the institutes may nevertheless have had some positive impact on teachers' awareness of equity issues, given that most teachers mentioned in their interviews that they were aware of potential gender-equity problems in their classrooms.

The Cultural Dimension

Cultural elements that emerged as important at a number of sites were concerned with the general atmosphere of the school. The culture of some schools seemed to be quite negative, even threatening for some teachers. At Urban Middle (names of all schools and teachers are fictitious) the school population, both staff and students, was very transient. The principal appeared to be aware of the problems this caused but had been unable to do anything about it. The teacher interviewed felt constrained in her teaching by the constant absence from school of many of her students. At another school, Daniel Miller Middle, the teacher interviewed said that, although she wasn't concerned over personal safety, she was aware that some people were. However, she was afraid to take risks in her teaching for fear of her classes becoming uncontrollable, which many at the school appeared to be. These two teachers cited students' poor attitudes as the main problem preventing their students from maximizing their potential, and they blamed parents for transmitting these attitudes toward school to their children. In addition, some teachers tended to hold expectations of their students that were stereotyped in accordance with their perceptions of the students' background. They had low expectations of what their students were capable of and, in association with this, did not attempt many inquiry lessons. Thus, these cultural aspects seemed to affect these teachers adversely and inhibit their efforts at implementing CEMC teaching practices.

There were, however, other examples where teachers were not so greatly influenced by the apparent nature of the school culture. A teacher at J. Adams Middle (which was in the same urban school district as Urban Middle), for example, initiated contact with parents rather than waiting for parents to come to see her. J. Adams Middle also had a homework hotline that students or their parents could call to check what homework had been assigned on any particular day. The atmosphere of those schools in which teachers had made most progress toward the ideal CEMC—Macon and J. Adams Middle— appeared to be more stable, with a more cohesive staff and a supportive principal. This was in contrast to those schools where the teachers appeared to have made least progress toward the ideal CEMC—Urban Middle and Daniel Miller Middle—where a general feeling of unrest, disorder, and a lack of support was felt by visitors and teachers alike. This dimension overlaps with the political dimension discussed later.

The Political Dimension

The first element in the Political dimension identified in both the quantitative and qualitative data analysis was related to the influence of the state-mandated proficiency test in determining not only what content was taught but how it was taught and assessed. In this state, the proficiency test is a statewide multiple-choice test that all students are required to pass in order to graduate high school. Students first take this test in eighth grade and retake it until they pass. Interview data would suggest that many SSI teachers, when doing concentrated proficiency-test preparation, did not use inquiry teaching methods because they considered them too time consuming. They also focused on only multiple-choice assessment formats because they believed that their students needed maximum practice with this format. Although students stated in their interviews that they enjoyed inquiry lessons, and most teachers talked about how their use of a CEMC-based pedagogy seemed to enhance students' long-term retention of concepts, teachers felt pressured by district administrators to resort to drill and practice methods when preparing for proficiency tests.

An important Political element affecting teachers' moving toward an ideal CEMC was the principal's initial and continuing support of the teacher and of the teacher's efforts to implement reform. Having a supportive principal gave some teachers the freedom and the encouragement to take risks with their teaching and use a variety of teaching and assessment practices.

The third important political element was the degree of control that teachers had over the curriculum. Curriculum content was typically tightly controlled by school districts and indirectly by the state through their Model Curriculum on which proficiency tests were based. Teachers were not able to influence curriculum decisions or even decisions about textbook adoption in most cases.

The Moral Dimension

The Moral dimension is concerned with matters of justice and fairness. The first issue identified here was the continued practice, in most schools visited during the site visits, of tracking or streaming by providing a differentiated mathematics curriculum for students grouped on previous achievement or ability. This practice has been shown by previous research (Oakes, 1990) to lead to inequitable education for some students, particularly women and minority students; however, the findings of such research appeared to have had little impact on most of the schools in this study.

Another Moral issue concerned the morality of expecting teachers to incorporate hands-on activities when there was so little money available for them to purchase even basic equipment such as simple calculators. One school in particular appeared to be very poorly funded, with not even enough funds to properly equip classrooms with suitable desks and chairs. The issue of disparity in funding between school districts in this state and across the United States is one that received a great deal of attention recently and is not likely to be resolved in the near future.

Proposed Fifth Dimension: A Personal Philosophy of Caring

One aspect that seemed to enable teachers such as Ms. Arnold at Macon Junior High and Ms. Michaels at J. Adams Middle School to move closest toward achieving the CEMC was a personal philosophy of teaching that was based on an overt care and concern for their students. Both of these teachers were able to overcome many obstacles faced by other teachers who did not appear to have this philosophy. Lack of classroom resources, poor student motivation, lack of parental support, and lack of an accessible network of other SSI teachers were not deterrents for these teachers. Their overriding focus was on the students, and they nearly always seemed to be able to overcome Technical or Cultural obstacles in the way of helping students achieve their potential. Their success in overcoming Political or Moral obstacles was more limited, however, possibly because classroom teachers generally do not have the power to influence such aspects. This suggests that reforms need to move beyond the level of the individual teacher as the focus of change, toward a broader focus on the school and school district, particularly toward those administrators with the power to eliminate Political or Moral obstacles. Implications such as this are discussed in the next section, which focuses on challenges for educational researchers, reformers, equity advocates, and practitioners.

IMPLICATIONS AND CHALLENGES

This study established, from teachers' reports and observational data, that, in comparison to non-SSI teachers, SSI teachers implemented at least some of the reformed, CEMC-based teaching practices advocated by the SSI. Analysis of the student achievement data from the 1995 sample showed that students in SSI teachers' classes achieved significantly higher results than their non-SSI counterparts. Subgroup analysis revealed that most of the gains could be attributed to female students, particularly African-American females (Goodell, 1998). However, there are still many questions about how to achieve gender-equity goals in reforming mathematics classrooms that need research-based answers.

For example, the interaction between gender and race needs further exploration, building on previous research. Culturally relevant teaching, or multicultural education as it is sometimes known (Banks, 1995), also emphasized the concepts of connected teaching. Ladson-Billings (1995) discussed one teacher who was particularly successful with African-American children in her classroom. The teacher employed techniques such as constantly praising students, focusing on mathematics for the entire lesson, helping students to make the transition from what they know to what they don't know, getting to know each student in depth, and extending students past what they already know. Lipman (1995) discussed the attempts of three teachers in reforming schools to make their classrooms relevant for African-American children. Methods they employed included setting high standards, helping students connect their experiences to academic knowledge, challenging students with academic content, respecting students, relating prior knowledge to new content, and impressing upon students their potential to make a difference for themselves, their families, and society as a whole—all strategies that resonate with the CEMC.

Challenges for Reformers

An important finding from this study was that some SSI teachers chose not to use inquiry-based teaching practices to prepare their students for proficiency tests because they thought these practices were too time consuming and would therefore not adequately prepare students for the tests. Given that it appears that females were most advantaged by the inquiry methods, a teacher's decision not to use these methods may be particularly disadvantaging to females. This presents a challenge for reformers— how to convince teachers that the use of inquiry teaching does not disadvantage students but in fact would advantage them if employed over an extended period. Related to this is how to ensure that school- and district-level administrators support and understand the potential of the reforms offered. Teachers indicated in their interviews that it was often pressure from administrators that made them revert to drill and practice methods for preparing students for proficiency tests.

Another related question is how to scale-up the reform to encompass all teachers without actually mandating it. Mandated changes have been shown to have limited long-term impact (Fullan, 1993), and there is rarely the time or money to reach all teachers. Convincing nonparticipating teachers of the efficacy of the CEMC-based teaching and learning, especially for female students, must be a priority for reformers. This makes it very important to continue to collect achievement data over time and to disseminate to teachers and district administrators results such as those found in this study. This SSI has done that with the production of A Pocket Panorama (Kahle & Rogg, 1996, 1997). These brochure-style publications, which outline some of the results of the evaluation in an easy-to-read format, have been widely distributed to every school district across the state and to other educational institutions around the United States.

A final important challenge for reformers is how to help teachers adapt existing curriculum materials to support the goals of gender equity and reform in general and how to evaluate appropriate new curriculum materials. Many of the recent NSF-funded curriculum projects now have a large research base to validate their use and implementation in new situations. Future reformers can easily take advantage of this. Evidence from this study suggests that the progress of reform could be enhanced if teachers were not continually faced with having to adapt resources for every inquiry lesson.

Challenges for Equity Advocates

An important challenge for equity advocates is how to transmit equity goals to participants in a reform without engendering a proactive rejection or backlash. A potential for such backlash was hinted at by one teacher in this study when she described how the group of teachers attending her institute were resentful of the amount of time spent in that institute talking about equity issues, which they thought were not appropriate for their situations. Although only mentioned by one of the seven teachers interviewed, this could have threatened the success of the whole professional-development program. Thus, not only is it important to consider issues of statewide or national concern but local concerns must also be incorporated into discussions about equity conducted during institutes.

Related to this is the need for teachers to be given the skills to monitor their own classroom interactions with students. Interaction patterns once established can be difficult to change. Developing techniques to assist teachers in analyzing their own patterns of interaction in the classroom should be a priority for professional development programs focused on gender equity.

A third challenge for equity advocates is how to ensure that classroom teachers are empowered to question and challenge the scope, sequence, and content of the curriculum so that they may adopt a perspective appropriate to their circumstances. Changing pedagogical practices without the ability to challenge the curriculum will not lead to a CEMC.

CONCLUSIONS

In this chapter, we constructed an operational definition of the CEMC grounded firmly in past research on gender equity in mathematics education. We have drawn from research focused on students, pedagogy, and the curriculum, and we have incorporated research into both explanations for gender differences and, at the same time, reforms based on those explanations. We cited evidence, from a statewide study, of the effectiveness of CEMC strategies in relation to student achievement in mathematics, especially the improvements in the achievement of African-American females. We have hinted that, although we have conceptualized the CEMC predominantly on the basis of research on gender equity in mathematics, the 12 features of the CEMC outlined earlier would apply equally to classrooms in which issues of race and culture are of concern. We are aware that there may need to be some additional considerations made, especially if Ladson-Billings' culturally relevant criteria were of prime importance. Others (e.g., Willis, 1996), however, have also made the suggestion that principles of equity developed from a gender perspective have relevance to issues of race and culture.

Our definition of the CEMC has been framed in ways that aim to make it meaningful for a range of audiences, including researchers, reformers, equity advocates, teacher educators, and teachers. In the sense of the latter group, we recognize that implementing such a definition carries with it many challenges, some of which, in current education systems, are beyond the control of individual teachers. Given the solid grounding of this definition of a CEMC in research and successful practice, we are confident that it provides a framework for progress toward more gender-inclusive and equitable mathematics teaching. The CEMC, with its emphasis on real-world connected problems and students jointly constructing their own meanings, shows great promise as a model for helping students to become seekers of knowledge rather than remaining empty vessels waiting to have knowledge deposited in them.

ACKNOWLEDGMENTS

The preparation of this study was sponsored in part by the National Science Foundation, Grant # OSR-92500 (J. B. Kahle and K. G. Wilson, co-principal investigators). The opinions expressed are those of the authors and do not necessarily reflect the position of the National Science Foundation.

REFERENCES

Anand, P. G., & Ross, S. M. (1987). Using computer-assisted instruction to personalize arithmetic materials for elementary school children. *Journal of Educational Psychology, 79*(1), 72–78.

Banks, J. A. (1995). Multicultural education: Historical development, dimensions, and practice. In J. A. Banks (Ed.), *Handbook of Research on Multicultural Education* (pp. 3–24). New York: Macmillan.

Barnes, M. (1991, 1993). *Investigating change: An introduction to calculus for Australian schools*. Carlton, Victoria: Curriculum Corporation.

Baxter Magolda, M. B. (1992). *Knowing and reasoning in college—Gender related patterns in students' intellectual development*. San Francisco: Jossey-Bass.

Becker, B. J. (1990). Item characteristics and gender differences on the SAT-M for mathematically able youths. *American Educational Research Journal, 27*(1), 65–87.

Becker, J. R. (1995). Women's ways of knowing in mathematics. In P. Rogers & G. Kaiser (Eds.), *Equity in mathematics education: Influences of feminism and culture* (pp. 163–174). London: Falmer.

Belenky, M. F., Clinchy, B. M., Goldberger, N. R., & Tarule, J. M. (1986). *Women's ways of knowing: The development of self, voice and mind*. New York: Basic Books.

Boaler, J. (1997). Equity, empowerment and different ways of knowing. *Mathematics Education Research Journal, 9*(2), 325–342.

Bolger, N., & Kellaghan, T. (1990). Method of measurement and gender differences in scholastic achievement. *Journal of Educational Measurement, 27*(2), 165–174.

Burton, L. (1995). Moving towards a feminist epistemology of mathematics. In P. Rogers & G. Kaiser (Eds.), *Equity in mathematics education: Influences of feminism and culture* (pp. 209–225). London: Falmer.

Campbell, P. B. (1995). Redefining the "girl problem in mathematics". In W. G. Secada, E. Fennema, & L. B. Adajian (Eds.), *New directions for equity in mathematics education* (pp. 225–241). Cambridge: Cambridge University Press.

Clewell, B. C., Anderson, B., & Thorpe, M. E. (1992). *Breaking the barriers: Helping female and minority students succeed in mathematics and science.* San Francisco: Jossey-Bass.

Damarin, S. (1995). Gender and mathematics from a feminist standpoint. In W. G. Secada, E. Fennema, & L. B. Adajian (Eds.), *New directions for equity in mathematics education* (pp. 242–257). Cambridge: Cambridge University Press.

Dekkers, J., deLaeter, J. R., & Malone, J. A. (1991). *Upper secondary school science and mathematics enrolment patterns in Australia, 1970–1989.* Perth, WA: National Key Centre for School Science and Mathematics, Curtin University of Technology.

Doolittle, A. E., & Cleary, T. A. (1987). Gender-based differential item performance in mathematics achievement items. *Journal of Educational Measurement, 24*(2), 157–166.

Eccles, J. S. (1989). Bringing young women to math and science. In M. Crawford & G. Gentry (Eds.), *Gender and thought: Psychological perspectives* (pp. 36–58). New York: Springer-Verlag.

Edwards, J. (1984). Raelene, Marjorie and Betty: Success of girls and boys in the Australian Mathematics Competition. *Australian Mathematics Teacher, 40*(2), 11–13.

Fennema, E. (1990). Teachers' beliefs and gender differences in mathematics. In E. Fennema & G. C. Leder (Eds.), *Mathematics and gender* (pp. 169–187). New York: Teachers College Press.

Fennema, E., Peterson, P. L., Carpenter, T. P., & Lubinski, C. A. (1990). Teachers' attributions and beliefs about girls, boys and mathematics. *Educational Studies in Mathematics, 21,* 55–69.

Fennema, E., & Tartre, L. (1985). The use of spatial visualization in mathematics by boys and girls. *Journal for Research in Mathematics Education, 16*(3), 184–206.

Fennema, E., Wolleat, P. L., Pedro, J. D., & Becker, A. D. (1981). Increasing women's participation in mathematics: An intervention study. *Journal for Research in Mathematics Education, 12*(1), 3–14.

Frankenstein, M. (1995). Equity in the mathematics education: Class in the world outside the class. In W. G. Secada, E. Fennema, & L. B. Adajian (Eds.), *New directions for equity in mathematics education* (pp. 146–164). Cambridge: Cambridge University Press.

Frid, S. D., & Winnett, S. (1996). *The connected classroom: Empowering grades 6–7 students' mathematics learning.* Paper presented at the Annual Meeting of the American Educational Research Association, New York.

Frost, L. A., Hyde, J. S., & Fennema, E. (1994). Gender, mathematics performance and mathematics-related attitudes and affect: A meta-analytic synthesis. *International Journal of Educational Research, 21,* 373–385.

Fullan, M. G. (1993). Innovation, reform, and restructuring strategies. In G. Cawelti (Ed.), *Challenges and achievements of American education* (pp. 116–133). Alexandria, VA: Association for Supervision and Curriculum Development.

Gilligan, C. (1982). *In a different voice.* Cambridge, MA: Harvard University Press.

Gipps, C., & Murphy, P. (1994). *A fair test? Assessment, achievement and equity.* Buckingham: Open University Press.

Goodell, J. E. (1998). *Equity and reform in mathematics education.* Unpublished doctoral thesis. Curtin University, Perth, Western Australia.

Hanna, G. (1996). Introduction—Towards gender equity in mathematics education. In G. Hanna (Ed.), *Towards gender equity in mathematics education* (pp. 1–7). Dordrecht: Kluwer.

Harding, J. (1979). Sex differences in examination performance at 16+. *Physics Education, 14,* 280–284.

Husen, T. (1967). *International study of achievement in mathematics.* New York: John Wiley & Sons.

Hyde, J. S., & Jaffe, S. (1998). Perspectives from social and feminist psychology. *Educational Researcher, 27*(5), 14–16.

Jacobs, J. E., & Becker, J. R. (1997). Creating a gender-equitable multicultural classroom using feminist pedagogy. In J. Trentacosta & M. J. Kenney (Eds.), *Multicultural and gender equity in the mathematics classroom: The gift of diversity. 1997 Yearbook* (pp. 107–114). Reston, VA: National Council of Teachers of Mathematics.

Kahle, J. B., & Rogg, S. R. (1996). *A pocket panorama of the Landscape Study.* Oxford, OH: Miami University.

Kahle, J. B., & Rogg, S. R. (1997). *A pocket panorama of the Landscape Study, 1996.* Oxford, OH: Miami University.

Kelly, A. (1988). Gender differences in teacher-pupil interactions: A meta-analytic review. *Research in Education, 39,* 1–23.

Kim, H., Plake, B. S., Wise, S. L., & Novak, C. D. (1990). A longitudinal study of sex-related item bias in mathematics subtests of the California Achievement Test. *Applied Measurement in Education, 3*(3), 275–284.

Knapp, M. S., Shields, P. M., & Turnbull, B. (1995). Academic challenge in high-poverty classrooms. *Phi Delta Kappan,* (June), 70–76.

Koehler, M. S. (1990). Classrooms, teachers and gender differences in mathematics. In E. Fennema & G. C. Leder (Eds.), *Mathematics and gender* (pp. 128–148). New York: Teachers College Press.

Kohlberg, L. (1969). Stage and sequence: The cognitive-developmental approach to socialization. In D. A. Goslin (Ed.), *Handbook of socialization theory and research* (pp. 347–480). Chicago: Rand-McNally.

Ladson-Billings, G. (1995). Making mathematics meaningful in multicultural contexts. In W. G. Secada, E. Fennema, & L. B. Adajian (Eds.), *New directions for equity in mathematics education* (pp. 126–145). Cambridge: Cambridge University Press.

Lane, S., Wang, N., & Magone, M. (1995). *Gender-related differential item functioning on a middle-school mathematics performance assessment.* Paper presented at the annual meeting of the American Educational Research Association, San Francisco.

Lange, J. d. (1987). *Mathematics, insight and meaning.* Utrecht: OW & OC.

Lappan, G., Fey, J. T., Fitzgerald, W. N., Friel, S. N., & Phillips, E. D. (1997). *The Connected Mathematics Project.* Palo Alto, CA: Dale Seymour.

Leder, G. C. (1989). Do girls count in mathematics? In G. C. Leder & S. N. Sampson (Eds.), *Educating girls: Practice and research* (pp. 84–97). Sydney: Allen and Unwin.

Leder, G. C. (1992). Mathematics and gender: Changing perspectives. In D. A. Grouws (Ed.), *Handbook of research on mathematics teaching and learning* (pp. 597–622). New York: Macmillan.

Leder, G. C., Forgasz, H. J., & Solar, C. (1996). Research and intervention programs in mathematics education: A gendered issue. In A. J. Bishop, K. Clements, C. Keitel, J. Kilpatrick, & C. Laborde (Eds.), *International Handbook of Mathematics Education* (pp. 945–985). Dordrecht: Kluwer.

Linn, M. C., & Hyde, J. S. (1989). Gender, mathematics, and science. *Educational Researcher, 18*(8), 17–27.

Linn, M. C., & Kessel, C. (1995). *Participation in mathematics courses and careers: Climate, grades, and entrance examination scores.* Paper presented at the annual meeting of the American Educational Research Association, San Francisco, CA

Lipman, P. (1995). "Bringing Out the Best in Them": The contribution of culturally relevant teachers to educational reform. *Theory Into Practice, 34*(3), 202–208.

Locan, J., Ford, P., & Greenwood, L. (1996). *Maths & science on the line: Australian junior secondary students' performance in the Third International Mathematics and Science Study.* Melbourne, Victoria: The Australian Council for Educational Research.

Lustig, A. (1989). Non-sexist education and paradigms for change. *Curriculum perspectives, 9*(4), 17–27.

Morrow, C., & Morrow, J. (1995). Connecting women with mathematics. In P. Rogers & G. Kaiser (Eds.), *Equity in mathematics education: Influences of feminism and culture* (pp. 13–26). London: Falmer.

Murphy, R. J. L. (1982). Sex differences in objective test performance. *British Journal of Educational Psychology, 52*, 213–219.

Myer, M. R., & Koehler, M. S. (1990). Internal influences on gender differences in mathematics. In E. Fennema & G. C. Leder (Eds.), *Mathematics and gender* (pp. 60–95). New York: Teachers College Press.

National Center for Research in Mathematical Sciences Education & Freudenthal Institute (Ed.). (1997). *Mathematics in context: A connected curriculum for graders 5–8.* Chicago: Encyclopedia Britannica Educational Corporation.

National Council of Teachers of Mathematics (NCTM) (1989). *Curriculum and evaluation standards for school mathematics.* Reston, VA: National Council of Teachers of Mathematics.

National Council of Teachers of Mathematics (NCTM) (1991). *Professional standards for teaching mathematics.* Reston, VA: National Council of Teachers of Mathematics.

National Council of Teachers of Mathematics (NCTM) (1995). *Assessment standards for school mathematics.* Reston, VA: National Council of Teachers of Mathematics.

National Science Board (1996). *Science and engineering indicators 1996.* Washington, DC: U.S. Government Printing Office.

Noddings, N. (1998). Perspectives from feminist philosophy. *Educational Researcher, 27*(5), 17–18.

Oakes (1990). Opportunities, achievement, and choice: Women and minority students in science and mathematics. *Review of Research in Education, 16*, 153–222.

Parker, L. H., & Tims (Goodell), J. E. (1995). *Different modes of assessment in science and mathematics: A systematic interaction with gender.* Paper presented at the annual meeting of the National Association for Research in Science Teaching, San Francisco.

Perry, W. G. (1970). *Forms of intellectual and ethical development in the college years: A scheme.* Troy, MO: Holt, Rinehart & Winston.

Pierce, G. (1998). An inclusive paradigm for education: Valuing the different voice. *Initiatives, 58*(3), 57–66.

Robitaille, D. F., & Garden, R. A. (1989). *The IEA study of mathematics II: Contexts and outcomes of school mathematics.* Oxford: Pergamon Press.

Rogers, P. (1990). Thoughts on power and pedagogy. In L. Burton (Ed.), *Gender and mathematics: An international perspective* (pp. 38–46). London: Cassell.

Rogers, P. (1995). Putting theory into practice. In P. Rogers & G. Kaiser (Eds.), *Equity in mathematics education: Influences of feminism and culture* (pp. 175–185). London: Falmer.

Rossman, G. (1993). *Building explanations across case studies: A framework for synthesis.* ED 373115. Boulder, CO: Colorado University School of Education.

Secada, W. G. (1992). Race, ethnicity, social class, language and achievement in mathematics. In D. A. Grouws (Ed.), *Handbook of research on mathematics teaching and learning* (pp. 623–660). New York: Macmillan.

Silver, E. A., Smith, M. S., & Nelson, B. S. (1995). The QUASAR project: Equity concerns meet mathematics education reform in the middle school. In W. G. Secada, E. Fennema, & L. B. Adajian (Eds.), *New directions for equity in mathematics education* (pp. 9–56). Cambridge: Cambridge University Press.

Solar, C. (1995). An inclusive pedagogy in mathematics education. *Educational Studies in Mathematics, 28,* 311–333.

Sowder, J. (1998). Perspectives from mathematics education. *Educational Researcher, 27*(5), 12–13.

Stage, E., Kreinberg, N., Eccles, J., & Becker, J. R. (1985). Increasing the participation and achievement of girls and women in mathematics, science, and engineering. In S. S. Klein (Ed.), *Handbook for achieving sex equity through education* (pp. 237–268). Baltimore, MD: John Hopkins University Press.

Tate, W. F. (1995). Returning to the root: A culturally relevant approach to mathematics pedagogy. *Theory Into Practice, 34*(3), 166–173.

Verhage, H. (1990). Curriculum development and gender. In L. Burton (Ed.) *Gender and mathematics: An international perspective* (pp. 60–71). London: Cassell.

Weiner, G. (1994). Equality and quality: Approaches to changes in the management of gender issues. In P. Ribbins & E. Burridge (Eds.), *Improving education: Promoting quality in schools* (pp. 114–125). London: Cassell.

Willis, S. (1989). The education of girls in mathematics and science. *Curriculum Perspectives, 9*(1), 21–26.

Willis, S. (1995). Gender reform through school mathematics. In P. Rogers & G. Kaiser (Eds.), *Equity in mathematics education: Influences of feminism and culture* (pp. 186–199). London: Falmer.

Willis, S. (1996). Gender justice and the mathematics curriculum: Four perspectives. In L. H. Parker, L. J. Rennie, & B. J. Fraser (Eds.), *Gender, science and mathematics: Shortening the shadow* (pp. 41–51). Dordrecht: Kluwer.

Author Index

Abraham, J 152, 162
Acker, S 297, 298, 311, 382, 390, 392
Acland, H 231
Acquarelli, K 246, 250, 251
Adajian, L. B 96, 349, 364
Adamson, R 373, 378
Adler, J x, xxv, 163, 169, 182, 185, 188, 197, 199
Agudelo, C 55
Aichele, D. B 167, 168, 182
Ainley, J 349, 364
Aisenberg, N 382, 390, 392
Alecio, R 154, 162
Alrø, H 50, 53
Altbach, P. G 151, 162
Anand, P. G 416, 428
Anderson, B 413, 430
Anderson, J. G 236, 240, 251
Anderson, S. E 268, 275
Anyon, J 257, 275
Apple, M 1, 4, 15, 42, 53, 105, 107, 110, 162, 187, 199,
    244, 245, 251, 257, 262, 275, 283, 292, 301, 310
Aranador, L. C 125, 132
Arias Ochoa, M 163, 167, 182
Arnol'd, V. I 103, 110
Arnot, M 348, 364
Arnove, R. F 151, 162
Aronowitz, S 47, 53
Artigue, M 41, 53

Ascher, M 113, 118, 132, 136, 148, 282, 292, 314,
    315, 327
Ascher, R 315, 327
Astone, N. M 229, 230
Atkin, J. M 190, 193, 199
Atweh, B ix, xxii, xxiv, 75, 77, 163, 164, 167, 169, 182
Ausubel 77
Aziz, A 131, 132

Back, K 84, 93
Bailey, P 282, 293
Bailey, S. M 375, 377, 378
Baird, J 172, 179
Bakalevu, S 138, 148
Baker, D. A 279, 283, 286, 292
Bakhtin, M. M 23, 35
Balatti, J x, xxvi, 113, 278, 313, 314, 317, 320, 321,
    322, 323, 325, 326, 327
Ball, B 101, 110
Bandura, A 221, 231
Bane, M. J 231
Banks, J. A 262, 275, 426, 428
Banu, H 61, 71
Barcellos, A 332, 343
Barkatsas, T 361, 362, 365
Barlow, K
Barnes, C 246, 253, 394, 408
Barnes, M 418, 428
Barnes, R. H 141, 148

Barrier, E 123, 126
Bartolini Bussi, M. G 5, 10, 15
Barton, B x, xxiv, 76, 135, 148, 327, 314
Baruk, S 301, 310
Baudrillard, J 21, 24, 35
Bauman, Z 29, 35
Baxter Magolda, M. B 414, 417, 418, 420, 428
Beaton, A. E 217, 230
Becker, A. D 429
Becker, B. J 428
Becker, J. R x, xxvi, 346, 367, 377, 378, 413, 417,
     428, 429, 431
Begle, E. G 236, 237, 248, 251
Belenky, M. F 367, 377, 378, 414, 417, 420, 428
Bell, G 122, 123, 132
Benmayor, R 234, 252
Berends, M 252
Bermudez, T 334, 341, 342, 343
Bernal, M. E 252
Bernstein, B 1, 5, 15, 24, 35, 206, 212, 215
Betz, N. E 217, 230
Bibby, A 395, 396, 408
Bibby, N 152, 162
Bishop, A. J xix, 61, 71, 38, 86, 87, 90, 91, 93, 145,
     148, 152, 161, 162, 168, 182, 248, 250, 282, 292,
     295, 310, 318, 320, 327, 349, 365
Black, P 190, 193, 199
Black, S 283, 292
Blase, J 226, 230
Blau, P. M 23, 35
Blum, W 59, 71
Boaler, J 42, 53, 323, 327, 392, 417, 428
Boero, P 5, 15
Bohl, J 49, 53
Bolam, R 173, 182
Bolger, N 416, 428
Borba, M 41, 53
Borko, H 167, 168, 171
Bot, M 186, 198
Bourdieu, P xxv, 1, 19, 21, 22, 24, 28, 35, 53, 201,
     202, 204, 205, 214, 257, 267, 275
Bowles, S 244, 251, 256, 257, 269, 275
Boykin, A. W 258, 259, 275
Brackenridge, A 395, 396, 408
Bradby, D 236, 247, 252
Brennan, M 110
Brenner, M 332, 333, 340, 343
Brew, C 349, 354, 365
Bringhurst, R 140
Brinkworth, P 102, 110
Britton, E. D 123, 126, 133
Brodie, K 10, 15, 37, 53, 199
Brousseau, G 41, 53, 302, 310
Brown, A 14, 15, 33, 35, 90, 93
Brown, A. J 33, 35
Brown, C. A 167, 168, 171, 182
Bruce, R 77, 94
Bryant, P 113, 133

Bryk, A. S 218, 220, 224, 226, 227, 231
Buchbinder, D 360, 364
Buriel, R 236, 240, 251
Burkhardt, H 5959, 71
Burns, A 370, 377, 378
Burton, L xi, xxvi, 50, 53, 379, 381, 382, 388, 392,
     418, 428, 346
Butcher, J 141
Buxton, L 428
Buzan, B 124, 132
Buzan, T 124, 132

Campbell, E. Q 226, 230
Campbell, P. B 255, 275, 429
Canburn, E (See d'Canburn)
Cardoza, D 236, 240, 251
Carnoy, M 151, 162
Carpenter, T. P 415, 429
Carr, W 169, 170, 172, 173, 174, 178, 182
Carraher, D. W 36, 63, 72, 293, 298, 311
Carraher, T. N 63, 72, 333, 334
Castells, M 30, 35, 52, 53
Castro, M 55
Chadwick, C 395, 408
Chapman, B 63, 72, 288, 293
Charlton, M 349, 365
Chen, M 227, 232
Chevallard, Y 64, 72
Christiansen, I. M 49, 53
Christiansen, J. M 66, 72
Clare 351, 364, 365
Clark, J 197, 199
Clarke, D. M 99, 111
Clarkson, P. C xi, xxiv, 75, 77, 90, 93, 122, 132, 233,
     247, 248, 252
Cleary, T. A 416
Clements, D. H 396, 397, 408
Clements, K 88, 90, 93, 96, 110, 168, 182
Clements, M. A 83, 85, 87, 89, 93, 97, 99, 100, 101,
     110, 113, 122, 132
Clewell, B. C 413, 429
Clinchy, B. M 367, 378, 414, 417, 428
Clute, P. S 383, 392
Cobb, P 301, 304, 310
Cockcroft, W 21, 35, 285, 292
Coe, A. S 220, 231
Cogan, L. S 123, 126
Cohen, D 231
Cohen, L 304, 310
Coladarci, T 228, 231
Cole, M 4, 5, 7, 11, 15, 139, 148, 224, 252, 332, 344
Coleman, J. S 226, 230
Colling, T 360, 365
Collins, J 205, 207, 213, 215
Comber, C 380, 392
Confrey, J 12, 15
Connell, R. W 32, 35
Cooley, M 25, 35

Coombs, P. H 151, 162
Cooney, T. J 231
Cooper, B 11, 15
Cota, M. K 252
Cotton, T 43, 53
Couthourd, M 205, 215
Coupland, M 352, 365
Coxford, A. F 167, 168, 182
Crawford, K 10, 15, 169, 182, 229, 329, 343
Crawley, F. E., III 220, 231
Cres, F 392
Croninger, R. G 227, 231
Crosswhite, F. J 231
Crump, T 138, 148
Csikszentmihalyi, M 353, 365
Cummins, J 146, 148

d Canburn, E 236, 252
D' Ambrosio, B. S 151, 161, 162, 248, 253
D'Ambrosio, U 41, 53, 63, 72, 90, 93, 110, 136, 146,
    148, 152, 162, 282, 288, 292, 295, 297, 299, 300,
    304, 310, 313, 314, 317, 320, 323, 325, 327
Damarin, S 418, 429
Damerow, P xix, 62, 72
Damnjanovic, A xix, 62, 72
Dank, S 308, 31
Dapueto, C 15
Darlinghammond, L 226, 231
Davenport, E. C 223, 231, 367, 378
Davidenko, S 332, 344
Davidson, J. E 407, 408
Davies, A 100, 110
Davies, M 348, 349, 365, 366
Davis, D 84, 93, 330, 343
Davis, P. J 65, 72, 284, 292, 299, 303, 305, 311
Davis, R. B 178, 181
Davis, S 89
Davison, M. L 231, 367, 378
Davydov, V. V 8, 13, 15
Dawe, L 247, 252
Day, C 6, 15
De Abreu, G. M. C 33, 343
De Corte, E 295, 302, 303, 310, 311
De la Cruz, Y 241, 252
De la Rocha, O 35, 298, 311
De Lange, J 60, 72, 186, 198
De saint Martin 250, 214
De Silva, R xv, xxvi, 278, 329, 335, 336, 340, 344
De Vore, P. W 61, 72
De Wit 93
Deboer, G. E 228, 231
Deer, E 10, 15
Dehaene, S 128, 132
Dekkers, J 411, 429
DeLaeter, J. R 411, 429
Denny, P 140, 148
Dewdney, A. K 283, 292
Ding, S 231, 367, 378

Doolittle, A. E 416, 429
Dossey, J. A 231, 236, 243, 244, 253
Dowling, P. C xi, xxiii, 1, 14, 15, 19, 20, 22, 23, 24,
    26, 29, 30, 35, 90, 93, 324, 326, 327
Doyle, K 100
Dressman, M 107, 110
Dugoni, B. C 236, 252
Dunne, M 11, 15, 284, 292
Durkheim, É 4, 24, 35
Durndell, A 395, 409

Eccles, J. S 413, 415, 429, 431
Echols, F. H 227, 232
Eco, U 24, 35
Edwards, D 8, 15, 205, 215
Edwards, J 416, 429
Ellerton, N 83, 85, 87, 88, 89, 90, 93, 99, 100, 101,
    106, 110, 113, 122
Elliott, E 169, 173, 182
Ellsworth, E 13, 15
Elwitz, U 62, 72
Elwood, J 380, 392
Erickson, F 206, 215
Ernest, P 69, 72, 283, 292, 309, 310, 326, 328
Evans, J 6, 13, 16
Evans, R 90, 93, 168, 182
Eves, H 330, 331, 344

Fairhall, U 135, 148
Fals-Borda, O 173, 180, 182
Fasheh, M 151, 152, 162, 248, 252, 282, 288, 292,
    295, 310
Fennema, E 96, 168, 170, 182, 349, 365, 378, 394,
    408, 415, 429
Ferrari, P 15
Ferrero, E 15
Feuerverger, G 314, 316, 324, 327, 382, 390, 392
Fey, J. T 418, 430
Finau Palaki, K 314, 316, 324
Finlow-Bates, K 11, 16
Fischbein, E 12, 16
Fitzgerald, W. N 418, 430
Flores, W xi, xxv, 165, 233, 234, 253
Florio, S 206, 215
Fogel, W 235, 252
Foong, P. Y 122, 132
Ford, P 411, 430
Fordham, S 260, 261, 275
Forgasz, H ix, xxvi, 42, 54, 346, 347, 348, 350, 353,
    354, 356, 365, 430
Foster, A 350, 375, 378
Foucault, M 24, 35
Fraivillig, J 122, 123, 132
Francis, B 350, 365
Frank, R xi, xxiv, 76, 135, 137, 148
Franke, M. L 168, 170, 182

Frankenstein, M 42, 49, 54, 55, 62, 63, 66, 72, 90, 93, 148, 243, 244, 252, 282, 288, 292, 296, 297, 301, 303, 310, 314, 317, 325, 327, 418, 421, 429
Freebody, P 288, 292
Freire, P 47, 54, 173, 182, 239, 309, 310
Frid, S. D 418, 429
Friel, S. D 418, 429, 430
Freudenthal, H 60, 72
Frost, L. A 412, 415, 429
Fukuyama, F 46, 54
Fullan, M. G 426, 429
Fuson, K 122, 123, 132

Gaffney, J 227, 231
Galperin, P. Y 6, 16
Gamoran, A 218, 227, 231
Garden, R. A 411, 430
Gardiner, T 101, 107, 110, 127
Gardner, H 295, 310
Gardner, P. L 361, 365
Garfield, J 304, 311
Garuti, R 15
Gates, P 43, 53
Gay, G 262, 275
Gay, J 139, 148, 332, 334
Geary, D. C 122, 123, 128, 132
Gee, J. P 289, 292
Gell, J 375, 378
Gellert, U xii, xxiii, 2, 57, 69, 72
Gerdes, P 19, 20, 21, 35, 62, 64, 72, 113, 132, 136, 148, 151, 152, 161, 162, 186, 199, 314, 315, 316, 327
Gerofsky, S 303, 310
Giddens, A 45, 54, 79
Gill, J 227, 231
Gillett, G 5
Gilligan, C 1, 152, 162, 393, 408, 414, 429
Gilmer, G 325, 328
Ginitis, H 231, 244, 251, 256, 257, 269, 275
Gipps, C 416, 429
Giroux, H 70, 72, 174, 182
Glasersfeld, E. von 4, 17, 41, 54, 77
Glissov, P 395, 409
Goffman, E 70, 72
Goldberger, N. R 367, 378, 414, 417, 428
Gómez, P 55, 172, 183
Gonzalez, R 230, 242, 252
Gonzalo, I 123, 126
Goodell, J. E xii, xxvi, 346, 411, 416, 417, 418, 421, 426, 429
Gordon, B 375, 378
Gordon, P 28, 35
Gordon, S. E 10, 16
Graham, A 304, 310
Gramsci, A 257, 275
Grant, C. A 262, 275
Gravemeijer, K. P 60, 72, 302, 303, 310, 341, 344
Green, P. J 236, 237, 252
Greenfell, M 205, 215

Greenhaugh, P 395, 396, 408
Greenwood, L 411, 430
Greer, B xii, xxvi, 278, 295, 301, 302, 303, 304, 310, 311
Griffin, P 244, 252
Griffiths, H. B 39, 54
Grissmer, D. W 242, 252
Grossman, L. M 307, 310
Grouws, D. A 168, 182
Grundy, S 169, 170, 180, 181, 182
Gunew, S 80, 93
Gunterman, E 395, 396, 408
Guppy, N 89, 93
Gurtner, J. L 337, 344
Guthrie, G 126, 132

Habermas, I 179
Halsey, A. H 388, 392
Hanna, G 414, 429
Hannaford, C 54
Harding, J 416, 418, 429
Hargreaves, A 85, 90, 93, 168, 180, 182
Harker, R. K 202, 215
Harré, R 3, 4, 5, 14, 16
Harrington, M 382, 387, 392
Harris, M 87, 93
Harris, P 139, 148
Hart, L 42
Harvey, F 143, 148
Harvey, W. B 261, 262, 275
Havelock, R 173, 182
Hawkins, J 396, 408
Haywood, H. C 7
Heath, S. B 202, 206, 209, 212, 215
Heckman, P. E 323, 327
Heide, P 245, 252, 396, 408
Held, D 45, 46, 54
Helme, S 285, 293
Henry, M 79, 80, 86, 89, 90, 93, 94
Herbst, P 14
Hersh, R 113, 132, 284, 292, 295, 299, 303, 305, 310, 330, 343
Herodotus 330, 344
Heward, C 380, 382, 392
Hewitt, N. M 380, 392
Heyns, B 231
Hiebert, J 189, 199
Ho Sui-Chu, E 226, 229, 231
Hobson, C. J 226, 230
Hoffer, T. B 220, 231, 243, 252
Holland, P. B 227, 231
Hollinger, D 373, 378
Holzman, L 7, 17
Homolsky, M 396, 408
Hoosain, R 122, 133
Hopkins, D 173, 182, 227, 231
Horne, M 394, 408
Horwood, J 101, 110, 113, 132

Houang, R. T 118, 121, 133
Howson, A. G 39, 54
Hoyles, C 394, 396, 407, 408
Huberman, A. L 173, 182
Huff, D 283, 292
Hughes, M 365, 396, 407, 408
Hunter, I 28, 30, 35
Huntley, I 59, 71
Husen, T 411, 429
Hyde, J. S 411, 412, 415, 429, 430

Ilango, R 128, 133
Ilon, L 80, 93
Ingels, S. J 236, 252
Isackson, N 235, 252

Jablonka, E xii, xxiii, 2, 57, 61, 70, 72
Jacklin, C. N 394, 408
Jacobs, J. E 297, 298, 311, 429
Jacobsen, E 81, 83, 89, 93, 96, 109, 111
Jacucyn, N 245, 253
Jencks, C. S 226, 231
Jenkins, R 202, 215
Jess, K 51, 54
Johnson, D. C 186, 199
Johnson, M. L 137, 148, 239, 252
Johnston, B xii, xxv, 85, 93, 105, 111, 277, 279, 286,
    290, 292, 293, 294
Johnston, J 284, 293
Jonas, S 154, 162
Jones, C 350, 364
Jones, L 227, 231
Jones, P 92, 93
Jorde, D 123, 126, 133
Joseph, G. G 113, 133, 248, 252, 268, 275, 282, 292,
    295, 311
Jump, T. L 245, 252
Jurdak, M 151, 160, 162

Kahle, J. B 151, 160, 162, 426, 429
Kaiser, G 42, 55, 113, 133
Kamler, B 106, 111
Kanes, C 168, 169, 171, 182
Karpov, Y. V 7, 15
Kaur, B 124, 133
Kawanaka, T 189, 199
Keitel, C xiii, xix, xxiii, 2, 57, 59, 62, 63, 66, 70, 71,
    72, 86, 93, 96, 11, 168, 182
Kellaghan, 416, 428
Kelly, A 348, 365, 429
Kelly, D. L 230
Kelly, G. P 151, 162
Kemmis, S 99, 111, 169, 170, 172, 173, 174, 178, 179,
    180, 182
Kepner, H. S. Jr 245, 253
Kerckhoff, A. C 218, 231, 227
Kessel 416
Keys, W 392

Khuzwayo, H 42, 54
Kifer, E 231
Kilpatrick, J 55, 83, 85, 86, 89, 93, 94, 168, 183
Kim, H 416, 429
Kim, S 231
Kim, S-K 367, 378
King, K. J 335, 336, 344
Kirby, S. N 252
Kirshner, D 197, 199
Kitchen, R. S xiii, xxiv, 76, 151, 152, 162
Klein, M 10, 15
Kline, M 102, 111
Knapp, M. S 417, 429
Knight, G. P 250, 252
Knight, J 93
Knijnik, G 49, 54, 282, 293, 325, 328
Koay, P. L 122, 130, 133
Koblitz, N 303, 305, 306, 309, 311
Koehler, M. S 413, 429, 430
Kohlberg, L 413, 414, 415, 430
Kotzmann, E 70, 72
Kreinberg, N 413, 431
Kress, G 93, 289, 293
Kuang, H 231, 367, 378
Kuhn, T. S 14, 15, 77
Kuku, A 87, 93
Kwak, N 231, 367, 378

Laborde, C 168, 182
Lacan, J 10, 16
Laclau, E 24, 35
Ladson-Billings, G 262, 275, 426, 428, 430
Lakoff, G 136, 137, 148, 298, 311
Lamb, S 226, 231, 349, 365
Lane, S 245, 253, 416, 430
Lange, J. D 418, 430
Lankshear, C 178, 182
Lappan, G 326, 327, 418, 430
Lasalle, J 302, 311
Lave, J 5, 6, 7, 16, 20, 25, 26, 35, 46, 54, 90, 94, 115,
    133, 188, 199, 285, 293, 299, 303, 311, 329, 344
Lawton, D 28, 35
Lean, G. A 138, 148
Lear, J. M 152, 162
Le Compte, M. D 263, 276
Leder, G. C xiii, xxvi, 42, 54, 218, 231, 346, 347, 349,
    350, 356, 365, 413, 415, 430
Lee Dow, K 351, 365
Lee, A 283, 293
Lee, K. P 122, 130, 134
Lee, P 135, 144, 148
Lee, V. E 218, 226, 227, 231
Lelliott, A 199
Lemke, J. L 205, 206, 208, 212, 215
Lemut, E 15
Leon, C 337, 344
Leong, Y. P 122, 130, 132, 134
Leont'ev, A. N 5, 10, 16

Lerman, S xiii, xxviii, 1, 3, 5, 7, 8, 9, 10, 11, 12, 13, 14, 16, 43, 54, 96, 105, 111, 295, 311
Levin, S. L 98, 105, 111
Levinson, S 137, 143, 144, 148
Lévi-Strauss, C 283, 284, 293
Lewis, R 104, 111
Licón-Khisty, L 42, 54
Lie, S. S 382, 392
Lim, T. K 128
Lim, H. B. G 122, 130, 133, 134
Lim-Foo, V 126
Lincoln, Y. S 152, 162
Lingard, B 79, 80, 89, 90, 94
Linn, M. C 411, 416, 430
Lipka, J 138, 141, 146, 148
Lipman, P 426, 430
Liss, S 153, 162
Lo Bianco, J 104, 111
Locan, J 411, 430
Lopez-Real, F 130, 134
Lord, M. G 306, 307, 311
Love, E 191, 192, 199
Lovitt, C. J 99, 111
Lua, S 130, 133
Lubinski, C. A 415, 429
Lucy, J 136, 143, 148
Ludowyke, J 360, 365
Luke, A 288, 292
Luria, A. R 7, 12, 16, 24, 35
Lustig, A 148, 418, 430
Lyons, J 144, 148

Ma, X xiii, xxv, 164, 217, 222, 223, 224, 225, 226, 227, 228, 229, 231
Mac Lane, S 136, 137, 148
Maccoby, E. M 394, 408
MacGregor, M 248, 252
MacKenzie, D. A 30, 35, 72
Mackey, K 127, 133
MacLeod, H 395, 408, 409
MacLeod, M 395, 408
Mael, F. A 368, 369, 378
Magone, M 416, 430
Maher, C. A 178, 182
Malone, J. A xxii, 59, 71, 411, 429
Mandela, N 47, 54
Marcos xxiv
Marcy, J 375, 378
Marcy, S 375, 378
Marion, S. F 228, 231
Marlowe, B. A 126, 133
Marr, B 285, 293
Marshall, J 382, 392
Martin, B 43, 54, 285
Martin, M. O 230
Martinez, A 169
Marx 4, 6, 10, 11, 32

Masingila, J. O xiv, xxiv, 278, 324, 328, 329, 332, 335, 336, 340, 344
Mason, J 60, 72
Mastan 130
Matos, J. F 10, 16
Matos, J. M 49, 54
Matte-Blanco, I 24, 36
Mattel, Inc. 306, 311
Matthews, J 245, 252
Mazzo, J 244, 253
McBride, M 326, 328
McGinn, N 79, 80, 94
McIntyre, D 79, 80, 94
McKnight, C. C 118, 121, 123, 1226, 133
McLanahan, S. S 229, 230
McLeod, D. B 69, 218, 231
McLuhan, M 77, 94
McNamara, D. R 77, 94
McPartland, J 226, 239
Mehan, H 205, 206, 215, 226, 230
Mehrtens, H 42, 54, 205, 206, 215
Meira, L 8, 16
Mellin-Olsen, S 38, 54, 62, 66, 72, 95, 111, 152, 161, 162, 288, 293, 323, 328
Menninger, K 138, 148
Mercer, N 8, 15, 205, 215
Messina, A 350, 365
Meya, D. K 314, 323, 324, 327
Meyer, M. R 23, 35, 412
Michelson, S 231
Middleton, J. A 250, 252
Miller, C 381, 392
Miller, J 220, 232
Miller, K. E 244, 253
Millet, A 189, 199
Millroy, W. C 316, 327
Minick, N 5, 16
Mitchelmore, M xxii
Miura, I 122, 133, 226, 230
Moody, V xiv, xxv, 165, 255
Moore, W 243, 252
Mora, D 38, 54
Moreira, D 49, 54
Morgan, C 51, 54
Morley, L 382, 392
Morrow, C 416, 430
Morrow, J 416, 430
Moschkovich, J. N 248, 252
Moser, U 123, 126, 133
Mouffe, C 24, 35, 45, 54, 123
Mousely, J 168, 171, 183
Mowchanuk, T 323, 328
Mukhopadhyay, S xiv, xxvi, 278, 295, 306, 307, 308, 311
Mulligann xxii
Muller, C 229, 232
Mullis, I. V. S 230, 236, 243, 252
Mumme, J 246, 251

Mura, R 69, 72
Murphy, P 429
Murphy, R. J. L 416, 430
Murtadha-Watts, K 325, 328
Murtaugh, M 35, 299, 311
Myer, M. R 430

Naidoo, A 38, 54
Nastasi, B. K 396, 408
Nebres, S. J x, 81, 90, 94, 323, 328
Nelkin, D 63, 73
Nelson, B. S 239, 245, 253
Nelson, D 113, 133
Nesher, P 302, 303, 311
Newman, F 7, 17
Nicholls, J 103, 111
Nielsen, L 50, 55, 105
Nisbet, S 168, 169, 171, 182
Niss, M 39, 55, 59, 71, 98, 111
Noddings, N 178, 179, 182, 414, 430
Northfield, J xxii, 171, 179, 182
Norton, K. I 308, 311
Noss, R 396, 408
Novak, C. D 416, 429
Nunes, T 26, 36, 90, 94, 113, 133, 285, 293, 295, 311
Núñez, R 136, 137, 148, 337, 344

Oakes, J 148, 229, 232, 243, 244, 253, 254, 272, 275, 418, 425, 430
Ochoa, D. A xiv, 163, 167, 182
O'Doherty, S 348, 350, 365
O'Donoghue, J 285, 293
Ogbu, J. U 257, 258, 259, 260, 261, 266, 272, 273, 274, 275
Olds, T. S 308, 311
O'Leary, J 380, 392
Olive, S 308, 311
Olsen, A 84, 93
Olszewski-Kubilius, P 227, 232
Ormell, C 61, 73
Ortiz-Franco, L xiv, xxv, 165, 233, 248, 253
Owen, E. H 236, 243, 253
Owens, K xxii, 324, 328

Padilla, A 252
Page, M. L 126, 133
Parenti, L 15
Parke, L 411, 430
Parker, L. H xv, xxvi, 346, 416, 429, 430
Parkyn, L. K 153, 162
Passeron, J. C 22, 35, 205, 214, 257, 267, 275
Patronis, T 50, 55
Paulos, J. A 283, 293
Payne, J. J 228, 232
Peard, R 323, 328
Pearn, C 349, 365
Pedro, J. D 413, 429
Perry, P 51, 55, 172, 183

Perry, W. G 413, 414, 430
Petersen, A. C 246, 253
Peterson, P 415, 429
Phillips, E. D 418, 430
Phillips, G. W 236, 243, 253
Piaget, J 6, 10, 17, 24, 35, 77, 394, 408
Pierce, G 414, 420, 430
Pimm, D 191, 192, 199
Pinxten, R 143, 148, 149
Plake, B. S 416, 429
Polesel, J 349, 365
Povey, H 98, 111
Powell, A. B 49, 55, 62, 72, 282, 292, 297, 311, 315, 317, 325, 328
Prager, J 259, 260, 276
Prawat, R. S 132, 136, 133
Preissle, J 263, 275
Price, E 248, 252
Print, M 94
Prus-Wisniowska, E 332, 344

Rahman, M. A 173, 182
Raizen, S. A 123, 126, 133
Rasidah Junaidi 122
Rath, J 243, 252, 375, 378
Rathunde, K 353, 365
Raudenbush, S. W 220, 224, 226, 232
Redmond, S. W 11, 13, 17
Reese, C. M 244, 253
Reich, M 244, 253
Reid, J-A 106
Reiman, A. J 168, 169, 183
Resnick, L. B 303, 311
Restivo, S 113, 133
Reusser, K 302, 303, 311
Reyes, L. H 256, 276
Riessman, C. K 154, 162
Ring, G 395, 408
Rizvi, R 79, 80, 89, 90, 94
Roberts, J 21, 35, 226, 231
Robinson, H. A 174, 183
Robitaille, D. F 78, 85, 86, 94, 411, 430
Roe, P 288, 293
Rogers, L 86, 94
Rogers, P 42, 55, 113, 133, 417, 430, 431
Rogg, S. R 426, 429
Rogoff 4
Romberg, T. A 178, 182, 301, 311
Rose Dalilah Ramlee 126, 133
Rosenholtz, S 226, 229, 232
Ross, S. M 416, 428
Rossman, G 421, 431
Rotman, B 138, 149
Rumberger, R. G 227, 232

Sachs, J 29, 30, 36, 172, 183
Sagan 21
Saegusa, A 95, 111

Sakdiah Ladi 13, 134
Sánchez, F. L 176, 183
Santoro, N 106
Santos, M 10, 17
Sarasohn-Kahn, J 307, 311
Saussure, F. de 24, 36
Sawada, T 123, 126, 133
Sawiran, M 87, 94
Saxe, G. B 333, 334, 336, 340, 341, 342, 344
Scali, E 15
Scanlon, J 360, 365
Schliemann, A. D 35, 63, 72, 293, 298, 311
Schmidt, W. H 118, 121, 123, 126, 133
Schoenfeld, A. H 302, 303, 305, 309, 311, 329, 344
Schultz, J. J 206, 215
Schumpeter, J 45, 55
Scribner, S 285, 293
Secada, W. G 96, 111, 187, 199, 218, 231, 236, 253,
    274, 276, 283, 293, 349, 365, 415, 431
See, K. H 129, 133
Seligman, M. E. D 129, 133
Sellmeyer, N 335, 336, 340, 344
Sells, L. W 217, 231
Seymour, E 168, 380
Shan, S. J 282, 293
Shaughnessy, M 304, 311
Sherman, J. A 361, 365
Shield, M 323, 328
Shield, P. M 417, 429
Shimizu, K 123
Shor, I 173, 182
Siann, G 395, 408, 409
Sierpinska, A 55, 94
Silver, E. A 83, 85, 86, 94, 239, 245, 253, 417, 431
Sim, W. K 131, 133
Simon, J. M 153, 155, 162
Sinclair, J. McH 205, 215
Singer, J. D 218, 232
Skovsmose, O xv, xxiii, 2, 37, 41, 50, 53, 55, 64, 66,
    70, 72, 73, 88, 90, 94, 105, 111, 186, 198, 288,
    293, 317, 319, 322, 326, 328
Slavin, R. E 227, 232, 272, 276
Slonimsky, L 199
Smart, T 227, 231
Smith, J. B 226, 227, 230
Smith, L 4, 17
Smith, M. S 231, 239, 245, 253, 417, 431
Smith, R 29, 30, 36
Smith, T. A 230
Smyth, J 70, 73
Soberon, E 143, 149
Soh, K. C 125, 133
Sohn-Rethel, A 62, 73
Solar, C 42, 54, 350, 365, 415, 430, 431
Solomon, I 326, 328
Solomon, R. P 257, 273, 275
Sowder, J 413, 431
Souviney, R 81, 94

Spania, P 250, 252
Spradley, J. P 370, 378
Sprinthall, N. A 168, 169, 183
Stage, E 413, 431
Stanic, G. M. A 42, 55, 256, 276
Staub, F. C 303, 311
Steen, L. A 303, 311
Steffe, L. P 10, 14, 17
Sternberg, R. J 407, 408
Stevens, J 399, 409
Stiff, L. V 261, 262, 275
Stigler, J. W 125, 133, 189, 199
Stillman, G xv, xxvi, 113, 278, 313, 314, 316,
    323, 324, 328
Stone, M. H 39
Strauss, A. L 263, 276
Street, B 283, 292
Struik, D. J 139, 149
Stuckey, J. E 283, 284, 293
Sullivan xxii
Susperregi, M 137, 148
Sutherland, R 396, 407
Swafford, J. O 231

Talyzina, N. F 6, 17
Tan, A. G 126, 134
Tartre, L. A 407, 429
Tarule, J. M 367, 378, 428
Tate, W. F 243, 248, 253, 417, 421, 431
Taylor, R 154, 162
Taylor, S 79, 80, 86, 90, 93, 94
Teese, R 349, 365
Teh, K. C 121, 134
Tesch, R 263, 276
Theule-Lubienski, S 326, 327
Thies-Sprinthall, L 168, 169, 183
Thom, R 136, 149
Thomas, J xv, xxiv, 75, 95, 96, 97, 102, 109, 111
Thomas, R 313, 328
Thompson, A 168, 183
Thompson, D. R 245, 253
Thorpe, M. E 413, 429
Tienda, M 237, 253
Tims (Goodell), J. E 416, 430
Tomlinson, J 104, 112
Tout, D 286, 293
Travers, K. J 78, 85, 86, 94, 231, 395, 396, 408
Trentacosta, J 96, 112, 349, 365
Trinick, T 135, 139, 140, 148, 149
Troyna, B 178, 182
Truran, J 102, 110
Turkle, S 394, 408, 412
Turnbull, B 147, 429

Ursiskin, Z 85, 86, 94

Valencia, I. N 125, 132
Valero, P xvi, xxiii, 2, 37, 44, 46, 51, 54, 55, 172, 183

Valsiner 7
Valverde, G. A 118, 121, 123, 126, 133
Van der Veer 7, 17
van Dooren, I 143, 148, 149
van Oers, B 329, 343
Veloo, P. K xvi, xxiv, 76, 113, 122, 126, 130, 134
Verhage, H 418, 431
Verschaffel, L 295, 302, 303, 310, 311
Vile, A 9, 11, 17
Villaseñor, A. Jr 245, 253
Vitale, B 337, 344
Vithal, R 43, 50, 55, 88, 94
Voight, J 212, 215, 329, 344
Volmink, J 41, 55, 283, 294
Vui, T 125, 132
Vygotsky, L. S 1, 5, 6, 7, 8, 10, 12, 17, 24, 36, 285, 295, 397, 409

Wacquant, L. D 204, 215
Walcott, R 13, 17
Walkerdine, V 10, 13, 17, 393, 409
Wallace, C 289, 293
Walsh, V 382, 392
Wang, N 416, 430
Waqainabete, R 314, 315, 316, 324, 328
Waters, M 78, 79, 80, 94
Watson, A xii, 5, 7, 10, 17
Watson, H xii, 142, 143, 144, 149
Webb, N 396, 409
Weber, M 23, 24, 36
Weiler, K 256, 276, 288
Weiner, G 348, 367, 431
Weissglass, J 288, 323
Wells, D 310, 311
Wenger, E 5, 188, 189, 329, 344
Wertsch, J. V 5, 7, 11, 17
Whalen, S 353, 365
White, K. R 236, 253
Whitson, J. A 197, 199
Whorf, B 135, 136, 142, 147, 149
Wiegel, H. G 10, 14, 17
Wienfield, F. D 226, 230
Wilder, R. L 136, 149

Wiley, D. E 118, 121, 123, 126, 133
Wilkins, R 100, 112
Wilkinson, M 172, 179, 180, 183
Willett, J. B 218, 232
Williams, J 113, 133
Williamson, S 252
Willis, P. E 31, 36, 206, 212, 215, 257, 273, 275
Willis, S 106, 112, 283, 293, 378, 412, 413, 418, 428, 431
Willms, J. D 221, 224, 225, 226, 227, 228, 229, 232
Winbourne, P 6, 7, 11, 17
Winnett, S 148, 418, 429
Winters, L 375, 378
Wise, S. L 416, 429
Wit, H de 93
Wittgenstein, L 4, 6, 12, 17
Wolfe, R. G 123, 126
Wolleat, P. L 413, 429
Wong, K. Y xvi, 76, 113, 120, 122, 123, 126, 129, 131, 133, 134
Woo, J. H 123, 132
Woolfe, S 379
Wood, L 352, 365

Yamaguchi, K 220, 232
Yap, S. F 122
Yasukawa, K xvi, xxv, 277, 279, 280, 286, 290, 293, 294
Yasumoto, J 227, 232
Yates, K. W 279, 286, 294
Yeatman, A 174, 183
Yelland, N. J xvi, xxvi, 346, 393, 396, 409
Yong, B. C. S 120, 122, 134

Zaitun Binti Hj Mohd Taha xvi, xxiv, 76, 124, 127, 129, 134
Zaslavsky, C 236, 245, 253, 282, 294
Zeidler, S 307, 311
Zemelman, H 45, 55
Zevenbergen, R xvi, xxvii, xxv, 42, 55, 62, 97, 112, 164, 201, 215, 351, 352, 366
Zimmer, J 72
Zuber-Zkerrit, O 178, 182

Subject Index

Abacus 127, 128
Ability (*see also* Competence) 7, 9, 26, 40, 48, 51, 52,
    59–61, 63, 67, 68, 117, 131, 145, 219, 223, 227,
    228, 265, 269, 271, 285, 289, 309, 331, 351, 326,
    349, 351, 362, 364, 357, 383, 387, 397, 497, 412,
    415, 419, 425
Aboriginal 10, 104, 139
Achievement 6, 57, 67, 68, 86, 90, 104, 126, 129,
    130, 136, 145, 146, 217–220, 223, 224, 227,
    228, 235–251, 283, 303, 315, 349, 350–352,
    356, 358, 359, 362, 363, 367, 368, 370, 375,
    377, 379, 380, 382, 383, 390, 391, 411, 412,
    415, 425–427
Action research 89, 169, 173, 174, 179–181
Africa/African 82, 316, 325
African Mathematics Union 82, 87
African Americans/Blacks xxv, 165, 223, 225, 233,
    235, 242, 245, 255–275, 371, 373–376, 426, 427
North American 107
American Association of University Women 307, 368
American Indian/Natives 236, 258, 308
Anglo–American 115
Anglo–European 81, 83, 85, 105
Anglo–Saxon/Anglo xix, 368
Anthropology xxiv, xix, 76, 205, 325
Argentina 234
ASEAN xxiv, 76, 113, 114
Asia/Asian 81, 87, 103, 113–134, 223, 233, 236, 247,
    316, 371

Australia/Australian 81–2, 84, 86, 88, 95, 97–99,
    101–104, 106, 167, 171, 172, 233, 286,
    347–350, 354
Australian Association of Mathematics Teachers 104
Autonomy 80, 104, 170, 179

Babylonian 331, 340
Barbie doll 306–309
Basque 142
Bilingual/multilingual 121, 136, 233, 247, 248
Bolivia 234
Boys/males xxvi, 13, 156, 220, 345, 346, 347–364,
    367–378, 379, 391, 393–408, 411, 412, 415
    disadvantage 347–350, 379, 380, 390–392
Brazil 77, 151, 234
British 76, 81, 114, 118
British Colombia 140
Brunei Darussalam 76, 113–132

Calculators 127–129, 376
Central America 76, 234
Class (*see* Socioeconomic)
Chile 234
CLAME 82
Cambridge examination 119, 132
Canada 77, 105
Catholic 351
China/Chinese 115, 117, 122–3, 127, 258, 277, 306
Chreods 82

Cockroft Report 115, 127
Collaboration/collaborative xxiii, 79, 80, 84, 86, 89,
    91, 162, 171, 174, 176, 178, 180, 197, 324, 352,
    356, 393, 402, 407
Colombia 37, 44, 77, 234
Colonial/colonialism 81, 114, 117, 151, 152 (see also
    cultural imperialism)
Competency 11, 39, 48, 49, 66, 70, 90, 103, 248, 284,
    285, 317, 319, 362, 413 (see also ability)
Computer 115, 128, 129, 372, 371, 393–407
Connected Equitable Mathematics Classroom xxvi,
    346, 411–428
Connected In-School and Out-Of-School Mathematics
    Practice xxvi, 228, 330, 333
Constructivism/constructivist xxi, 6, 10, 201, 79, 115,
    178, 201, 280, 286–289, 333
    Critical constructivism 287–290
Critical mathematics 48, 49, 50, 90, 186, 286–290,
    325
Critical theory xx, 255, 256
Cuba/Cuban 158, 234, 251
Cultural capital 28, 29, 32, 201, 257, 267
Cultural imperialism (see also
    Colonial/colonialism) 110, 325

Democracy/democratic xx, xxiii, 2, 4, 37–53, 75, 115,
    117, 153, 185, 187
Democratic competence 59, 64
Denmark 44
Developing nations/countries xvii, 46, 76, 78, 81,
    83–85, 87, 98, 105, 152, 161, 162
Didactique des Mathematique (journal) 82
Discursive 4, 6, 10, 12–14, 204–206
    Discursive saturation 24–26, 28
Domains of practice
    esoteric 21, 22, 23, 26, 28
    public 20, 22, 23, 26, 32
Dominican republic 234

Educational Studies in Mathematics 82, 83
Egypt/Egyptian 330
El Salvador 77, 237, 351
Empowerment/disempowerment 37, 40, 47, 62, 89, 90,
    168, 169, 170, 178, 181, 191, 203, 210, 248, 283,
    296, 300, 303, 306, 310, 316, 322
English (language) 121–123, 136, 139, 142–144, 235,
    241, 345, 370, 372
Epistemology xxvi, 61, 176, 346
Equity/equitable xxv, 51, 52, 90, 91, 96, 187, 185, 262,
    348, 351, 360, 407, 411, 412, 418, 421, 423,
    425–428
Ethnic/ethnicity xx, 10, 67, 104, 113, 115, 116, 165,
    222, 233, 243, 255, 258, 345, 346, 349, 408, 416
Ethnography/ethnographic 207, 356, 369, 370
Ethnomathematics xx, xxi, xxiv–xxvi, 48, 49, 50, 59,
    63, 64, 79, 87, 88, 90, 92, 96, 113, 121, 136, 147,
    152, 185, 186203, 248, 277, 278, 282, 288, 297,
    309, 313–327

Everyday /realistic/real world/out of school
    mathematics xxv, xxvi, 1, 2, 11, 20, 57, 58, 62,
    68, 69, 158, 195, 277, 278, 285, 291, 299, 310,
    323, 324, 329–343, 356, 376, 416, 419, 420
Euro-American 367, 371
Europe/European 97, 136, 138, 139, 278, 390
Euskara 142, 143

Feminism/feminist xx, xxiii, xxvi, 1, 80, 345–347, 352,
    367, 414, 416
Filed 201–203
Fiji 138, 315, 316
Financial planning 317–327
For the Learning of Mathematics 82
France/French 81, 126, 136, 139, 142, 233

Gay rights 80
Gaze 22
Gender 113xx, xxii, xxvi, 10, 32, 42, 43, 51, 67, 218,
    219, 222, 243, 249, 283, 345, 348–364, 367–378,
    379, 392, 393–408, 411–428
Gender and computers 354–360
Gender/sex stereotypes 349, 349, 363, 369, 377, 415,
    420
Germany/German 42, 44, 69, 124, 189, 308
Girls/females 13, 68, 219, 202, 225, 345, 246–364,
    367–378, 393–409, 379, 411–415
Global/globalization xx–xxiv, 46, 48, 5275, 78–93,
    95–110, 115, 233
    global curriculum 88–87, 98, 103, 109
Greek 330, 331, 349, 362, 363
Government xxiv, 45, 75, 115, 155, 167, 322, 325,
    346
Guatemala xxiv, 76, 151–162, 234, 251

Habitus 201–207, 209, 212–214
Haida 145
Hispanic (see Latinos)
Homogenous/homogeneity 80, 90, 390
Honduras 234
Hong Kong 81
Human rights 80

ICMI/ICME xix, xxi, 81, 82, 84, 86, 92, 95, 105, 109
Ideology/ideological 39, 41, 42, 51, 98, 115–117,
    161, 257–259, 266, 267, 273, 274, 283, 284,
    287, 289
India/Indian 277
Indigenous 76, 97, 118, 135–148, 154, 156, 259
Indo-European 76, 142, 144
Indonesia 103, 141, 306
Intra American Commission on Human Rights 153
Internationalization xxiv, 75, 78–93, 97, 98
International Journal on Proof 82
Interent 77, 115
International Organization of Women in Mathematics
    Education 82
Islam/Muslims 121, 371

Japan/Japanese 95, 103, 124, 189, 258, 277, 303
Jew/Jewish 350, 362
Journal for Research in Mathematics Education 82, 83
Justice (*see* Social justice)

Kedang 141
Kpelle 139
Korea/n 258

Latin America 77, 79, 81, 82, 235
Latinos/as xxv, 152, 153, 156, 165, 223, 225, 233–251, 371, 376
Language/linguistic xxiv, xix, 42, 76, 90, 113, 121, 122, 135–148, 164, 158, 159, 189, 201, 204–206, 240, 243, 247, 248, 351, 325, 390
Liberia 332
Linguistic capital/habitas 204, 205, 207, 214
Local xxiii, xxiv, 46, 115, 152, 175
Logo xxvi, 346, 395, 397
London Mathematics Society 101
Longitudinal 218, 202, 222, 225, 227, 229, 230, 241, 352

Malay language 122, 123
Malaysia 76, 81, 87, 103, 113–132, 306
Male domain/dominated 158, 161, 219, 360, 361, 364, 416
Maori 135, 138, 139, 140
Mathematical literacy/mathemacy xxiii, 2, 37, 38, 58, 59, 61, 67, 69, 70, 316, 317, 322, 326, 419 (*see also* Numeracy)
Mathematical register 202
Mathematics Education Research Group of Australasia xxii, 82, 186, 287
Mathematics Teacher (journal) 101
Mexico/Mexican xxv, 167–181, 258, 234, 236, 248
Mimesis 21
Mozambique 19, 314
Multicultural 104, 115, 121
Multi Modal Teaching Strategy 126
Myth/mythological 1, 7, 20–22, 26, 28, 32, 34
  certainty 21, 22
  emancipation 20
  participation 20, 26, 28, 32, 34
  reference 21, 22, 26, 28, 34

Narrative 50, 153, 154
National/nation state 3, 46, 67, 89, 90, 98–100, 115, 117, 151, 152
National curriculum 2, 88, 105, 115, 156, 168
National Assessment of Educational Progress 240, 244, 367
National Center for Educational Statistics 233, 237–242
National Council for Teachers of Mathematics 38, 39, 115, 120, 167, 168, 307, 412, 417
National Research Council 63

Netherlands 340, 419
New Zealand 135, 139
Nicaragua 38
Nigeria 325
Non-English speaking 83
Numeracy xxiii, xxv, 104, 105, 277, 279–292, 304, 322, 397 (*see also* Mathematical literacy)

OECD 95, 218
Out-of-school mathematics (*see* Everyday mathematics)

Papua New Guinea 233
Participation/representation 164, 197, 217–230, 348, 349, 379, 380, 412–414, 418
Pedagogy xxv, 22, 23, 26–28, 30, 31, 34, 98, 115, 159–161, 178, 185, 188, 195, 197, 201, 202, 205, 213, 279, 414, 417, 420, 422, 424,
Peru 234
Phenomenology 263, 341
Philippines/Filipinos 81, 258
Philosophy of Mathematics Education (journal) 82
Politics/political xxiv, 1, 38–40, 45–47, 67, 95–110, 113, 115, 187, 198, 234, 295, 296, 283, 284, 418, 424, 425
Postmodern xx, xxiii, 1, 11, 78, 178
Professionalization/professional 89, 99, 109, 164, 187, 173, 181
Professional development xxiv, 75, 160, 163, 164, 167–181, 178, 179, 189, 192, 289, 326, 421, 422, 427
Psycholinguistics 247, 248
Psychology/psychological xix, xx, xxiii, 1, 3, 4, 7, 11, 13, 14, 44, 58, 60, 161, 176, 218, 219, 295, 287, 298, 345
Psychology of Mathematics Education xx, 82
Puerto Rico/ Puerto Rican 234, 251
Public examinations 129, 130

Realistic Mathematics Education 186, 340, 341, 343
Real-world/life (*see* Everyday mathematics)
Research in Mathematics Education xix, xx, xxii, 38, 40, 44, 82, 83, 86, 105–106
  agenda/further 48–53, 246–250, 326, 327
Resources xxv, 151, 164, 170, 171, 185–198, 224, 244, 373, 423, 425, 145
Rukunegara 117

Singapore 76, 81, 113–132
  Singapore Pledge 117
Single-sex schools 346, 349, 351, 367–378
Situated Socio-Cultural Model xxiv, 76, 113–132
Social class (*see* socioeconomic)
Social context 4, 41, 49, 95, 96, 98, 103, 201, 255, 262, 280, 295
Social justice/justice 51, 52, 103, 176, 185, 186, 278, 421, 425
Sociocultural xxv, 1, 4, 5, 7, 10, 12, 76, 113, 115, 165, 196, 220, 255, 278, 283, 296, 333, 341, 389

Socioeconomic xx, 27, 39, 42, 43, 51, 67, 104, 164, 165, 186, 201–214, 218, 222, 223, 225, 227, 233, 235–237, 240, 243, 256, 257, 345, 349, 351, 369, 395, 408
Sociolinguistics 7, 10, 205
Sociological/sociology xix, xx, 4, 11, 13, 45, 49, 113, 218
socio-political 151–62
Soviet Union/Russia 81, 103, 108, 139
South Africa xxv, 37, 38, 42, 44, 52, 185–198
South East Asia 79, 81, 82
    South East Asia Mathematics Society 82
Spain/Spanish (country) 81, 140, 142
Spanish (language) 154, 159, 172, 174, 175, 370, 372, 374
Standard Average European 136, 144
Strategic Social action 24
    articulating 24, 25
    generalizing 24
    localizing 24–26, 28, 30, 33
    specializing 24–26, 28, 30, 33
Student Teams Achievement Divisions 125, 126
Sweden 233
Switzerland 126

Taiwan 241
TEBES xxv, 136, 172–178
Technology/technological (*see also* gender and computers) 39–40, 57, 58, 61, 65, 66, 346, 373, 376, 393–408

Third World 3, 151, 152, 161
TIMSS 57, 124, 125, 130, 189, 217
Tracking 243, 271, 272, 425
Triadic dialogue 206, 208, 209, 211–214

United Kingdom/England/British/English xxiii, 1, 77, 81, 82, 85, 88, 101, 233, 280, 305, 306, 348, 347, 351, 378, 380, 388, 416
United States of America/North America/American xxv, 38, 44, 77, 81, 82, 85, 88, 124, 125, 151, 158, 163, 165, 167, 168186, 189, 217, 228, 233, 234, 237, 240, 249, 258, 297, 314, 367, 368, 347, 379, 380, 384, 390, 411, 412, 416, 417, 421, 425
UNESCO xix, xxi, 78, 81, 96

Venezuela 38
Vietnam/Vietnamese 81
Voice 12, 13, 22, 419

Western 2, 3, 63, 297, 313–317, 320, 332
White (race) 234, 236–243, 246, 250, 258–260, 262, 270, 272
Wisconsin Model 218
World Bank 81, 98
World Mathematics Year xxi

Yoruba 143
Yucatec 143, 144
Yup'ik 138, 139, 141, 146

Zone of Proximal development 7, 8, 10–13